Readings in African American Church Music and Worship

G-5655

Readings in African American Church Music and Worship

Compiled and edited
by James Abbington

GIA Publications, Inc.
Chicago • www.giamusic.com

G-5655
Copyright © 2001
GIA Publications, Inc.
7404 S. Mason Ave., Chicago, IL 60638
www.giamusic.com
ISBN: 1-57999-163-7
Book layout and design: Robert Sacha
Printed in the United States of America

Dedicated
in
Loving Memory
of
Dr. Wendell P. Whalum, Sr.
(1932-1987)
and
in Honor of
Dr. Eileen Southern

Table of Contents

Foreword by James Abbington xiii

Acknowledgements xvi

I. Historical Perspectives

CHAPTER 1   "Of the Faith of the Fathers" by William Edward
               Burghardt DuBois from *The Souls of Black Folk* 3

CHAPTER 2   "The Negro Spiritual" by John W. Work III from *The
               Papers of the Hymn Society*, XXIV 15

CHAPTER 3   "Introducing the African American Churches" by William
               D. Watley from *Singing the Lord's Song in a Strange Land:
               The African American Churches and Ecumenism* 27

CHAPTER 4   "The Performed Word: Music and the Black Church" by
               C. Eric Lincoln and Lawrence H. Mamiya from *The Black
               Church in the African American Experience* 39

CHAPTER 5   "The Use and Performance of Hymnody, Spirituals, and
               Gospels in the Black Church" by Portia K. Maultsby from
               The Papers of The Hymn Society 77

CHAPTER 6   Introduction: "In the World, but Not of It" by Cheryl J.
               Sanders from *Saints in Exile: The Holiness-Pentecostal
               Experience in African American Religion and Culture* 99

II. Surveys of Hymnals and Hymnody

CHAPTER 7   "African American Song in the Nineteenth Century: A
               Neglected Source" by Irene V. Jackson-Brown from *The
               Black Perspective in Music* 117

CHAPTER 8   "Hymnals of the Black Church" by Eileen Southern
from *The Black Christian Worship Experience:*
A Consultation 137

CHAPTER 9   "Published Hymnals in the African American Tradition"
by Melva Wilson Costen from *The Hymn* 153

CHAPTER 10   "Black Hymnody" by Wendell P. Whalum from *Review*
and Expositor, Vol. LXX, No. 3 167

CHAPTER 11   "Hymnody of the African American Church"
by Don Lee White, from the 2000 Hampton University
Ministers' and Musicians' Conference, previously
unpublished 185

III. Liturgical Hymnody

CHAPTER 12   "The Liturgy of the Roman Rite and African American
Worship" by J-Glenn Murray, S.J., from *Lead Me,*
Guide Me 201

CHAPTER 13   "The Gift of African American Sacred Song"
by Sister Thea Bowman, F.S.P.A.
from *Lead Me, Guide Me* 209

CHAPTER 14   "Music Among Blacks in the Episcopal Church: Some
Preliminary Considerations" by Irene V. Jackson-Brown
from *Lift Every Voice and Sing* 217

CHAPTER 15   "Introduction: Why an African American Hymnal?"
by Harold T. Lewis from
Lift Every Voice and Sing II .235

CHAPTER 16   "Hymns and Songs: Performance Notes" by Horace
Clarence Boyer from *Lift Every Voice and Sing II* 239

CHAPTER 17   "Service Music: Performance Notes" by Carl Haywood
from *Lift Every Voice and Sing II* 247

CHAPTER 18   "Worship and Culture: An African American Lutheran
Perspective" by Joseph A. Donnella II, John Nunes, and
Karen M. Ward from *This Far by Faith* 249

CHAPTER 19   "Leading African American Song" by Mellonee V. Burnim
from *This Far by Faith* 257

IV. Worship

CHAPTER 20   "Worship Activities" by Benjamin Elijah Mays and Joseph
William Nicholson from *The Negro's Church* 267

CHAPTER 21   "The Tradition of Worship" by William D. Watley from
*Singing the Lord's Song in a Strange Land: The African
American Churches and Ecumenism* 281

CHAPTER 22   "Some Aspects of Black Worship" by Charles G. Adams
from *The Andover-Newton Journal*, No. 3, Vol. 11 297

CHAPTER 23   "The Liturgy of Zion: The Soul of Black Worship"
by William B. McClain from *Come Sunday: The Liturgy of
Zion* 315

CHAPTER 24   "Encountering Jesus in Worship" by Zan W. Holmes, Jr.,
from *Encountering Jesus* 327

CHAPTER 25   "The Dynamics of Black Worship: A Psychosocial
Exploration of the Impulses That Lie at the Roots of Black
Worship" by Edward P. Wimberly from *The Black Christian
Worship Experience: A Consultation*, Vol. XIV 339

CHAPTER 26   "Definitions of Praising and a Look at Black Worship"
by Brenda Eatman Aghahowa from *Praising in Black and
White: Unity and Diversity in Christian Worship* 353

CHAPTER 27   "Indicted" by V. Michael McKay
from *Gospel Industry Today* 379

V. Composers

CHAPTER 28   "Church Music by Black Composers: A Bibliography of
Choral Music" by William Burres Garcia from *The Black
Perspective in Music*, Vol. 2, No. 2 385

CHAPTER 29   "Introduction" by Evelyn Davidson White from *Choral
Music by African American Composers: A Selected, Annotated
Bibliography* 409

CHAPTER 30   "Black Composers and Religious Music"
by Geneva Southall from *The Black Perspective in Music*,
Vol. 2, No. 1 419

VI. The Organ

CHAPTER 31   "A History of the Pipe Organ in the Black Church"
by Wayne A. Barr from *The History of the Pipe Organ in
Black Churches in the United States of America*, from a
University of Michigan School of Music Dissertation,
previously unpublished 429

CHAPTER 32   "The Church Organist, African American Organ Music,
and the Worship Service: A Useful Guide"
by Mickey Thomas Terry, from the 2000 Hampton
University Ministers' and Musicians' Conference,
previously unpublished 433

CHAPTER 33   "Service Playing for Organists"
by James Abbington, from the 1999 Hampton University
Ministers' and Musicians' Conference,
previously unpublished 445

VII. Contemporary Perspectives

CHAPTER 34   "What Lies Ahead?" by Wyatt Tee Walker from
*Somebody's Calling My Name: Black Sacred Music and Social
Change* 459

CHAPTER 35   "Conflict and Controversy in Black Religious Music"
by Mellonee V. Burnim from *African American Religion:
Research Problems and Resources for the 1990s* 481

CHAPTER 36   "Church Music: A Position Paper" (with special
              consideration of music in the Black Church)
              by Wendell Phillips Whalum 499

CHAPTER 37   "Music and Worship in the Black Church"
              by J. Wendell Mapson, Jr., previously unpublished 519

CHAPTER 38   "Black Sacred Music: Problems and Possibilities"
              by Jeremiah A. Wright, Jr., from a United Theological
              Seminary Dissertation, previously unpublished 525

CHAPTER 39   "Christ Against Culture: Anticulturalism in the Gospel of
              Gospel" by Jon Michael Spencer from *Protest and Praise:
              Sacred Music of Black Religion* 531

CHAPTER 40   "I Am the Holy Dope Dealer: The Problem
              with Gospel Music Today" by Obery M. Hendricks, Jr.,
              written in 2000 553

Contributors 591

Foreword

by James Abbington

As a student at Morehouse College in Atlanta between the years 1980 and 1983, I was privileged to take two courses—Readings in Music History and Introduction to Church Music—with my teacher, mentor, and musical idol, the late Dr. Wendell P. Whalum. I was so fascinated and captivated by his ability to accurately recall sources right off the top of his head. He could tell you the title of the book, author, chapter, place of publication, publisher, and year it was published. It was in that course that I was introduced to two books that have influenced my musical studies until this very day as a professor of Western Music History, Introduction to Church Music, and African American Music History.

The first book was *Source Readings in Music History*, compiled and edited by Oliver Strunk. This compilation made available for the first time in its history a representative selection from all of the great writings on music from the times of ancient Greece through the Romantic era. The reader can acquire a comprehensive knowledge of the history of musical thought and of the changing ideas and interpretations of music throughout the ages.

It was in this single work that I read the philosophical theories of Plato and Aristotle that embody the Greek view of music, the writings of the Church Fathers from Clement of Alexandria to St. Augustine, the elaborate theories of the medieval scholars, the first stirrings of modern concepts among Renaissance musicians, and the psychological attitudes of the Baroque writers. The eighteenth and nineteenth centuries are represented by significant selections from Jean Paul, E. T. A. Hoffman, Weber, Schumann, Berlioz, Liszt, and Wagner. This book opened up a whole world of musical insight and permitted me to discover the intellectual and aesthetic foundations of western musical development.

The second book was entitled *Readings in Black American Music*, edited by Eileen Southern. She is also the author of *The Music of Black Americans*, now in its third edition, published by W. W. Norton & Company (New York). Eileen Southern is not only one of the finest musicologists to be found anywhere in the world (who happens to be African American), but she has consistently pioneered the most critical and scholarly research in African American music. Her years at Harvard University were fruitful, productive, and bountiful. There she founded and edited the journal, *The Black Perspective in Music*, from 1973–1990.

The purpose of her collection was to make available to persons interested in the history of Black Americans a representative number of authentic, contemporary documents illustrating that history from the seventeenth century to the present time. The main criterion used in selecting the readings was their relevance to the history of music, and although the readings follow in chronological order, they are grouped under topics that derive from the history. To my knowledge, *Readings in Black American Music* represents the first publication of a documentary history of African American music that not only covers the full three and a half centuries of the sojourn of African Americans, but their African heritage as well.

It was in this volume that I read the statements of Black music makers to the accounts of eyewitnesses to musical events, and to the writings of persons deeply involved with the music of Black folk in one way or another. Thus, I was acquainted with the writings of Frederick Douglass, W. E. B. DuBois, Richard Allen, Daniel A. Payne, William C. Handy, Will Marion Cook, "Dizzy" Gillespie, Hall Johnson, John W. Work, Mahalia Jackson, William Grant Still, and T. J. Anderson, to name a few.

I recall in the Introduction to Church Music class Dr. Whalum's frustration and impatience with not having a source that contained significant writings about music in the African American church. He would place articles on reserve in the library from his personal collection and assign readings from journals, books, and periodicals to complement the textbook. What a journey we encountered!

Several years ago, I was privileged to meet a lifelong friend and colleague of Dr. Whalum's, Professor Evelyn Davidson White, a retired professor of music and director of the Howard University Choir in Washington, DC. She told me the story of her book, *Choral Music by Afro-American Composers: A Selected, Annotated Bibliography*, published by The Scarecow Press (Metuchen, NJ). An assignment to a class at Catholic University in Washington, DC yielded insufficient sources for her students. A nun replied to a correction on her assignment, "Professor White, how would I know that Blacks did not write some of these spirituals?" She could not refer her to a source, and that question became the impetus to her book.

Much like Professor White, I have discovered that I cannot refer students, scholars, and colleagues to a source that appropriately covers the topic of music and worship in the African American church without sending them on the same journey that I encountered at Morehouse.

I have compiled chapters, essays, articles, and unpublished papers on music and worship in the African American church during the twentieth century by pastors, scholars, theologians, historians, ethnomusicologists, organists, professors, and conductors. I feel that their writings represent some of the greatest writings, musical comment and discourse, histories, perspectives, and concepts on the subjects. I have not sought to give this book a spurious unity by imposing upon it a particular point of view. At the same time, the book has of itself a natural unity and continuity of another sort. I have divided the readings into seven categories: (1) Historical Perspectives; (2) Surveys of Hymnals and Hymnody; (3) Liturgical Hymnody; (4) Worship; (5) Composers; (6) The Organ; and (7) Contemporary Perspectives, with a selected bibliography.

Of the items included in this volume, only eight essays (as notated in the Acknowledgements) have not been previously published. In determining what and how to annotate, I have simply given the title of the article, the author's name, and the book or journal in which it appeared. The writings speak for themselves!

When I shared my vision and desire with Edward J. Harris, President, and Robert J. Batastini, Vice President and Senior Editor of GIA Publications in Chicago, they were enthusiastic, supportive, and offered me a contract. I am eternally grateful and indebted to GIA for their commitment to music in the African American church. In 1987, GIA published *Lead Me, Guide Me: An African American Catholic Hymnal*, and in 2001, they published the *African American Heritage Hymnal*, the first non-denominational African American Protestant hymnal. The African American Church Music Series by GIA is another component of that commitment to the music of the African American church worship experience by African American composers.

The debt that I have incurred from the giant contributors to this volume is beyond verbal and monetary gratitude. A biographical statement for each contributor is provided in the back of this book. I am most appreciative of the quiet, meticulous competence of Vicki Krstansky, who typeset the entire book, and for my editor, Linda Vickers, with her painstaking efficiency and patience, Denise Wheatley, editorial assistant, Robert Sacha, graphic designer, Yolanda Durán, graphic designer for the cover illustration, and the entire GIA family for making this book a reality.

There are those whose telephone calls, e-mails, prayers, and constant encouragement I must acknowledge with deep gratitude and affection: Daisy Ann Barlow, my mother; Wilbur J. Abbington, Sr., my father; Walter Barlow, my stepfather; William and Christine Anderson, my godparents; Pam and Ted Jones, my adopted sister and brother; Reverend Dwight M. Jackson, Pastor of the Amity Baptist Church; my godsent brother and eternal friend; Dr. Calvin B. Grimes, my former professor and Dean of the Division of Humanities and Social Sciences at Morehouse College; Dr. Gale Isaacs and Dr. Charles Tita, my colleagues at Shaw University; Mrs. Mildred Hooker, my secretary; Antwan Lofton, my student assistant and choir business manager; my students at Shaw University, and so many that space will not permit me to list.

Acknowledgements

1. "Of the Faith of the Fathers" by William Edward Burghardt DuBois from *The Souls of Black Folk*, 1903.

2. "The Negro Spiritual" by John W. Work III from *The Papers of The Hymn Society*, XXIV, Copyright © September 10–11, 1961, International Hymnological Conference, New York City.

3. "Introducing the African American Churches" by William D. Watley from *Singing the Lord's Song in a Strange Land: The African American Churches and Ecumenism*, Copyright © 1993, WWC Publications, World Council of Churches, 150 route de Ferney, P.O. Box 2100, 1211 Geneva 1, Switzerland; Wm. B. Eerdmans Publishing Co., 255 Jefferson Avenue, S.E., Grand Rapids, MI 49503; and Africa World Press, Inc., 15 Industry Court, Trenton, NJ 08638.

4. "The Performed Word: Music and the Black Church" by C. Eric Lincoln and Lawrence H. Mamiya from *The Black Church in the African American Experience*, Copyright © 1990, Duke University Press, 905 West Main Street, Suite 18B, Durham, NC 27701.

5. "The Use and Performance of Hymnody, Spirituals, and Gospels in the Black Church" by Portia K. Maultsby from *The Papers of The Hymn Society*, Copyright © 1983, I.T.C. Journal, c/o Interdemoninational Theological Center, 700 Martin Luther King Drive, SW, Atlanta, GA 30314.

6. Introduction: "In the World, but Not of It" by Cheryl J. Sanders from *Saints in Exile: The Holiness-Pentecostal Experience in African American Religion and Culture*, Copyright © 1996, Oxford University Press, 198 Madison Avenue, New York, NY 10016.

7. "African American Song in the Nineteenth Century: A Neglected Source" by Irene V. Jackson-Brown from *The Black Perspective in Music*, Copyright © 1976, Foundation for Research in the Afro-American Creative Arts, Inc., 4187 Surfside Court, Port Charles, FL 33948.

8. "Hymnals of the Black Church" by Eileen Southern from *The Black Christian Worship Experience: A Consultation*, Copyright © 1986, Foundation for Research in the Afro-American Creative Arts, Inc., 4187 Surfside Court, Port Charles, FL 33948.

9. "Published Hymnals in the African American Tradition" by Melva Wilson Costen from *The Hymn*, Copyright © 1989, The Hymn Society, c/o Boston University School of Theology, 745 Commonwealth Avenue, Boston, MA 02215.

10. "Black Hymnody" by Wendell P. Whalum from *Review and Expositor*, Vol. LXX, No. 3, Copyright © 1973, Review and Expositor, 2625 Lexington Road, Louisville, KY 40206.

11. "Hymnody of the African American Church" by Don Lee White, from the 2000 Hampton University Ministers' and Musicians' Conference, previously unpublished.

12. "The Liturgy of the Roman Rite and African American Worship" by J-Glenn Murray, S.J., from *Lead Me, Guide Me*, Copyright © 1987, GIA Publications, Inc., 7404 S. Mason Avenue, Chicago, IL 60638.

13. "The Gift of African American Sacred Song" by Sister Thea Bowman, F.S.P.A., from *Lead Me, Guide Me*, Copyright © 1987, GIA Publications, Inc., 7404 S. Mason Avenue, Chicago, IL 60638.

14. "Music Among Blacks in the Episcopal Church: Some Preliminary Considerations" by Irene V. Jackson-Brown from *Lift Every Voice and Sing*, Copyright © 1981, The Church Hymnal Corporation, 800 Second Avenue, New York, NY 10017.

15. "Introduction: Why an African American Hymnal?" by Harold T. Lewis, from *Lift Every Voice and Sing II*, Copyright © 1993, The Church Hymnal Corporation, 800 Second Avenue, New York, NY 10017.

16. "Hymns and Songs: Performance Notes" by Horace Clarence Boyer from *Lift Every Voice and Sing II*, Copyright © 1993, The Church Hymnal Corporation, 800 Second Avenue, New York, NY 10017.

17. "Service Music: Performance Notes" by Carl Haywood from *Lift Every Voice and Sing II*, Copyright © 1993, The Church Hymnal Corporation, 800 Second Avenue, New York, NY 10017.

18. "Worship and Culture: An African American Lutheran Perspective" by Joseph A. Donnella II, John Nunes, and Karen M. Ward from *This Far by Faith*, Copyright © 1999, Augsburg Fortress, 100 S. Fifth Street, Suite 700, Minneapolis, MN 55402.

19. "Leading African American Song" by Mellonee V. Burnim from *This Far by Faith*, Copyright © 1999, Augsburg Fortress, 100 S. Fifth Street, Suite 700, Minneapolis, MN 55402.

20. "Worship Activities" by Benjamin Elijah Mays and Joseph William Nicholson from *The Negro's Church*, Copyright © 1933, Institute of Social and Religious Research.

21. "The Tradition of Worship" by William D. Watley from *Singing the Lord's Song in a Strange Land: The African American Churches and Ecumenism*, Copyright © 1993, WWC Publications, World Council of Churches, 150 route de Ferney, P.O. Box 2100, 1211 Geneva 1, Switzerland, Wm. B. Eerdmans Publishing Co., 255 Jefferson Avenue, S.E., Grand Rapids, MI 49503; and Africa World Press, Inc., 15 Industry Court, Trenton, NJ 08638.

22. "Some Aspects of Black Worship" by Charles G. Adams from *The Andover Newton Journal*, No. 3, Vol. 11, Copyright © 1971, Andover Newton Journal, c/o Andover Newton Theological School, 210 Herrick Road, Newton Centre, MA 02459.

23. "The Liturgy of Zion: The Soul of Black Worship" by William B. McClain from *Come Sunday: The Liturgy of Zion*, Copyright © 1990, Abingdon Press, 201 Eighth Avenue South, Nashville, TN 37202.

24. "Encountering Jesus in Worship" by Zan W. Holmes, Jr., from *Encountering Jesus*, Copyright © 1992, Abingdon Press, 201 Eighth Avenue South, Nashville, TN 37202.

25. "The Dynamics of Black Worship: A Psychosocial Exploration of the Impulses That Lie at the Roots of Black Worship" by Edward P. Wimberly from *The Black Christian Worship Experience: A Consultation*, Vol. XIV, Copyright © 1986, I.T.C. Journal, c/o Interdenominational Theological Center, 700 S. Martin Luther King Drive, SW, Atlanta, GA 30314.

26. "Definitions of Praising and a Look at Black Worship" by Brenda Eatman Aghahowa from *Praising in Black and White: Unity and Diversity in Christian Worship*, Copyright © 1996, Pilgrim Press, 700 Prospect Avenue East, Cleveland, OH 44115.

27. "Indicted" by V. Michael McKay from *Gospel Industry Today*, Copyright © 2001.

28. "Church Music by Black Composers: A Bibliography of Choral Music" by William Burres Garcia from *The Black Perspective in Music*, Vol. 2, No. 2, Copyright © 1974, Foundation for Research in the Afro-American Creative Arts, Inc., 4187 Surfside Court, Port Charles, FL 33948.

29. "Introduction" by Evelyn Davidson White from *Choral Music by African American Composers: A Selected, Annotated Bibliography*, Copyright © 1996, The Scarecrow Press, c/o Rowman & Littlefield Publishing, 4720 Boston Way, Lanham, MD 20706.

30. "Black Composers and Religious Music" by Geneva Southall from *The Black Perspective in Music*, Vol. 2, No. 1, Copyright © 1974, Foundation for Research in the Afro-American Creative Arts, Inc., 4187 Surfside Court, Port Charles, FL 33948.

31. "A History of the Pipe Organ in the Black Church" by Wayne A. Barr from *The History of the Pipe Organ in Black Churches in the United States of America*, Doctor of Musical Arts Degree—The University of Michigan School of Music Dissertation, previously unpublished.

32. "The Church Organist, African American Organ Music, and the Worship Service: A Useful Guide" by Mickey Thomas Terry, from the 2000 Hampton University Ministers' and Musicians' Conference, previously unpublished.

33. "Service Playing for Organists" by James Abbington, from the 1999 Hampton University Ministers' and Musicians' Conference, previously unpublished.

34. "What Lies Ahead?" by Wyatt Tee Walker from *Somebody's Calling My Name: Black Sacred Music and Social Change*, Copyright © 1979, Judson Press, P.O. Box 851, Valley Forge, PA 19428.

35. "Conflict and Controversy in Black Religious Music" by Mellonee V. Burnim from *African American Religion: Research Problems and Resources for the 1990s*, Copyright © 1992, The New York Public Library—The Schomburg Center for Research in Black Culture.

36. "Church Music: A Position Paper" (with special consideration of music in the Black Church) by Wendell Phillips Whalum, Morehouse College, Atlanta, Georgia. Previously unpublished.

37. "Music and Worship in the Black Church" by J. Wendell Mapson, Jr., previously unpublished.

38. "Black Sacred Music: Problems and Possibilities" by Jeremiah A. Wright, Jr., from United Theological Seminary Dissertation, previously unpublished.

39. "Christ Against Culture: Anticulturalism in the Gospel of Gospel" by Jon Michael Spencer from *Protest and Praise: Sacred Music of Black Religion*, Copyright © 1990, Augsburg Fortress, 426 S. Fifth Street, Minneapolis, MN 55440.

40. "I Am the Holy Dope Dealer: The Problem with Gospel Music Today" by Obery M. Hendricks, Jr., written in 2000.

I.
Historical
Perspectives

Of the Faith
of the Fathers

by William Edward Burghardt DuBois
from *The Souls of Black Folk*, published in 1994

Dim face of Beauty haunting all the world,
    Fair face of Beauty all too fair to see,
Where the lost stars adown the heavens are hurled,—
        There, there alone for thee
        May white peace be.

Beauty, sad face of Beauty, Mystery, Wonder,
    What are these dreams to foolish babbling men
Who cry with little noises 'neath the thunder
        Of Ages ground to sand,
        To a little sand.

                  Fiona Macleod

It was out in the country, far from home, far from my foster home, on a dark Sunday night. The road wandered from our rambling log house up the stony bed of a creek, past wheat and corn, until we could hear dimly across the fields a rhythmic cadence of song—soft, thrilling, powerful—that swelled and died sorrowfully in our ears. I was a country schoolteacher then, fresh from the East, and had never seen a southern Negro revival. To be sure, we in Berkshire were not perhaps as stiff and formal as they in Suffolk of olden time; yet we were very quiet and subdued, and I know not what would have happened those clear Sabbath mornings had someone punctuated the sermon with a wild scream, or interrupted the long prayer with a loud Amen! And so most striking to me, as I approached the village and the little plain church perched aloft, was the air of intense excitement that possessed that mass of Black folk. A sort of suppressed terror hung in the air and seemed to seize us—a pythian madness, a demoniac possession that lent terrible reality to song and word. The Black and massive form of the preacher swayed and quivered as the words crowded to his lips and flew at us in singular eloquence. The people moaned and fluttered, and then the gaunt-cheeked brown woman beside me suddenly leaped straight into the air and shrieked like a lost soul, while round about came wail and groan and outcry, and a scene of human passion such as I had never conceived before.

Those who have not thus witnessed the frenzy of a Negro revival in the untouched backwoods of the South can but dimly realize the religious feeling of the slave; as described, such scenes appear grotesque and funny, but as seen, they are awful. Three things characterized this religion of the slave—the Preacher, the Music, and the Frenzy. The Preacher is the most unique personality developed by the Negro on American soil. A leader, a politician, an orator, a "boss," an intriguer, an idealist—all these he is, and ever, too, the center of a group of men, now twenty, now a thousand in number. The combination of a certain adroitness with deep-seated earnestness, of tact with consummate ability, gave him his preeminence, and helps him maintain it. The type, of course, varies according to time and place, from the West Indies in the sixteenth century to New England in the nineteenth, and from the Mississippi bottoms to cities like New Orleans or New York.

The music of Negro religion is that plaintive, rhythmic melody with its touching minor cadences which, despite caricature and defilement, still remains the most original and beautiful expression of human life and longing yet born on American soil. Sprung from the African forests, where its counterpart can still be heard, it was adapted, changed, and intensified by the tragic soul-life of the slave until, under the stress of law and whip, it became the one true expression of a people's sorrow, despair, and hope.

Finally the frenzy or "shouting" when the Spirit of the Lord passed by, and seizing the devotee, made him mad with supernatural joy, was the last essential of Negro religion and the one more devoutly believed in than all the rest. It varied in expression from the silent rapt countenance or the low murmur and moan to the mad abandon of physical fervor—the stamping, shrieking, and shouting, the rushing to and fro and wild waving of arms, the weeping and laughing, the vision and the trance. All this is nothing new in the world, but old as religion, as Delphi and Endor. And so firm a hold did it have on the Negro that many generations firmly believed that without this visible manifestation of the God there could be no true communion with the Invisible.

These were the characteristics of Negro religious life as developed up to the time of Emancipation. Since under the peculiar circumstances of the Black man's environment they were the one expression of his higher life, they are of deep interest to the student of his development, both socially and psychologically. Numerous are the attractive lines of inquiry that here group themselves. What did slavery mean to the African savage? What was his attitude toward the World and Life? What seemed to him good and evil—God and Devil? Whither went his longings and strivings, and wherefore were his heart-burnings and disappointments? Answers to such questions can come only from a study of Negro religion as a development, through its gradual changes from the heathenism of the Gold Coast to the institutional Negro Church of Chicago.

Moreover, the religious growth of millions of men, even though they be slaves, cannot be without potent influence upon their contemporaries. The Methodists and Baptists of America owe much of their condition to the silent but potent influence of their millions of Negro converts. Especially is this noticeable in the South, where theology and religious philosophy are on this account a long way behind the North, and where the religion of the poor Whites is a plain copy of Negro thought and methods. The mass of "gospel" hymns which has swept through American churches and well nigh ruined our sense of song consists largely of debased imitations of Negro melodies made by ears that caught the jingle but not the music, the body but not the soul, of the Jubilee songs. It is thus clear that the study of Negro religion is not only a vital part of the history of the Negro in America, but no uninteresting part of American history.

The Negro church of today is the social center of Negro life in the United States, and the most characteristic expression of African character. Take a typical church in a small Virginian town: it is the "First Baptist"—a roomy brick edifice seating five hundred or more persons, tastefully finished in Georgia pine, with a carpet, a small organ, and stained-glass windows. Underneath is a large assembly room with benches. This building is the central clubhouse of a community of a thousand or more Negroes. Various organizations meet here—the church proper, the Sunday school, two or three insurance societies, women's societies, secret societies, and mass meetings of various kinds. Entertainments, suppers, and lectures are held beside the five or six regular weekly religious services. Considerable sums of money are collected and expended here, employment is found for the idle, strangers are introduced, news is disseminated and charity distributed. At the same time, this social, intellectual and economic center is a religious center of great power. Depravity, sin, redemption, heaven, hell, and damnation are preached twice a Sunday with much fervor, and revivals take place every year after the crops are laid by; and few indeed of the community have the hardihood to withstand conversion. Back of this more formal religion, the Church often stands as a real conserver of morals, a strengthener of family life, and the final authority on what is good and right.

Thus, one can see in the Negro church today, reproduced in microcosm, all that great world from which the Negro is cut off by color prejudice and social condition. In the great city churches, the same tendency is noticeable and, in many respects, emphasized. A great church like the Bethel of Philadelphia has over eleven hundred members, an edifice seating fifteen hundred persons and valued at one hundred thousand dollars, an annual budget of five thousand dollars, and a government consisting of a pastor with several assisting local preachers, an executive and a legislative board, financial boards, and tax collectors; general church meetings for making laws; subdivided groups led by class leaders, a company of militia, and twenty-four auxiliary societies. The activity of a church like this is immense and far-reaching, and the bishops who preside over these organizations throughout the land are among the most powerful Negro rulers in the world.

Such churches are really governments of men, and consequently a little investigation reveals the curious fact that, in the South at least, practically every American Negro is a church member. Some, to be sure, are not regularly enrolled, and a few do not habitually attend services; but, practically, a proscribed people must have a social center, and that center for this people is the Negro church. The census of 1890 showed nearly twenty-four thousand Negro churches in the country, with a total enrolled membership of over two and a half million, or ten actual church members to every twenty-eight persons, and in some southern states, one in every two persons. Besides these, there is the large number who, while not enrolled as members, attend and take part in many of the activities of the church. There is an organized Negro church for every sixty Black families in the nations, and in some states for every forty families, owning on an average a thousand dollars worth of property each, or nearly twenty-six million dollars in all.

Such, then, is the large development of the Negro Church since

Emancipation. The question now is, what have been the successive steps of this social history and what are the present tendencies? First, we must realize that no such institution as the Negro church could rear itself without definite historical foundations. These foundations we can find if we remember that the social history of the Negro did not start in America. He was brought from a definite social environment—the polygamous clan life under the headship of the chief and the potent influence of the priest. His religion was nature worship, with profound belief in invisible surrounding influences, good and bad, and his worship was through incantation and sacrifice. The first rude change in this life was the slave ship and the West Indian sugar fields. The plantation organization replaced the clan and tribe, and the White master replaced the chief with far greater and more despotic powers. Forced and long-continued toil became the rule of life, the old ties of blood relationship and kinship disappeared, and instead of the family appeared a new polygamy and polyandry which, in some cases, almost reached promiscuity. It was a terrific social revolution, and yet some traces were retained of the former group life, and the chief remaining institution was the priest or medicine-man. He early appeared on the plantation and found his function as the healer of the sick, the interpreter of the unknown, the comforter of the sorrowing, the supernatural avenger of wrong, and the one who rudely but picturesquely expressed the longing, disappointment, and resentment of a stolen and oppressed people. Thus, as bard, physician, judge, and priest, within the narrow limits allowed by the slave system rose the Negro preacher, and under him the first African American institution, the Negro Church. This church was not at first by any means Christian nor definitely organized; rather, it was an adaptation and mingling of heathen rites among the members of each plantation and roughly designated as voodooism. Association with the masters, missionary effort, and motives of expediency gave these rites an early veneer of Christianity, and after the lapse of many generations the Negro Church became Christian.

Two characteristic things must be noticed in regard to this Church. First, it became almost entirely Baptist and Methodist in faith; secondly, as a social institution, it antedated by many decades the monogamy Negro home. From the very circumstances of its beginning, the church was confined to the plantation and consisted primarily of a series of disconnected units, although later on some freedom of movement was allowed; still, this geographical limitation was always important and was one cause of the spread of the decentralized and democratic Baptist faith among the slaves. At the same time, the visible rite of baptism appealed strongly to their mystic temperament. Today, the Baptist

Church is still the largest in membership among Negroes and has a million and a half communicants. Next in popularity came the churches organized in connection with the White neighboring churches, chiefly Baptist and Methodist, with a few Episcopalian and others. The Methodists still form the second greatest denomination, with nearly a million members. The faith of these two leading denominations was more suited to the slave church from the prominence they gave to religious feeling and fervor. The Negro membership in other denominations has always been small and relatively unimportant, although the Episcopalians and Presbyterians are gaining among the more intelligent classes today, and the Catholic Church is making headway in certain sections. After Emancipation, and still earlier in the North, the Negro churches largely severed such affiliations as they had had with the White churches, either by choice or by compulsion. The Baptist churches became independent, but the Methodists were compelled early to unite for purposes of Episcopal government. This gave rise to the great African Methodist Church, the greatest Negro organization in the world, to the Zion Church and the Colored Methodist, and to the Black conferences and churches in this and other denominations.

The second fact noted, namely that the Negro Church antedates the Negro home, leads to an explanation of much that is paradoxical in this communistic institution and in the morals of its members. But especially, it leads us to regard this institution as peculiarly the expression of the inner ethical life of a people in a sense seldom true elsewhere. Let us turn, then, from the outer physical development of the Church to the more important inner ethical life of the people who compose it. The Negro has already been pointed out many times as a religious animal—a being of that deep, emotional nature which turns instinctively toward the supernatural. Endowed with a rich, tropical imagination and a keen, delicate appreciation of nature, the transplanted African lived in a world animate with gods and devils, elves and witches; full of strange influences—of good to be implored, of evil to be propitiated. Slavery, then, was to him the dark triumph of evil over him. All the hateful powers of the underworld were striving against him, and a spirit of revolt and revenge filled his heart. He called up all the resources of heathenism to aid—exorcism and witchcraft, the mysterious Obi worship with its barbarous rites, spells, and blood sacrifice even, now and then, of human victims. Weird midnight orgies and mystic conjurations were invoked, the witch-woman and the voodoo-priest became the center of Negro group life, and that vein of vague superstition which characterizes the unlettered Negro even today was deepened and strengthened.

In spite, however, of such success as that of the fierce Maroons, the Danish Blacks, and others, the spirit of revolt gradually died away under the untiring energy and superior strength of the slave masters. By the middle of the eighteenth century, the Black slave had sunk, with hushed murmurs, to his place at the bottom of a new economic system and was unconsciously ripe for a new philosophy of life. Nothing suited his condition then better than the doctrines of passive submission embodied in the newly learned Christianity. Slavemasters early realized this and cheerfully aided religious propaganda within certain bounds. The long system of repression and degradation of the Negro tended to emphasize the elements in his character which made him a valuable chattel: courtesy became humility, moral strength degenerated into submission, and the exquisite native appreciation of the beautiful became an infinite capacity for dumb suffering. The Negro, losing the joy of this world, eagerly seized upon the offered conceptions of the next; the avenging Spirit of the Lord enjoining patience in this world, under sorrow and tribulation until the Great Day when He should lead His dark children home—this became his comforting dream. His preacher repeated the prophecy, and his bards sang—

"Children, we all shall be free
When the Lord shall appear!"

This deep religious fatalism, painted so beautifully in "Uncle Tom," came soon to breed, as all fatalistic faiths will, the sensualist side by side with the martyr. Under the lax moral life of the plantation, where marriage was a farce, laziness a virtue, and property a theft, a religion of resignation and submission degenerated easily in less strenuous minds into a philosophy of indulgence and crime. Many of the worst characteristics of the Negro masses of today had their seed in this period of the slave's ethical growth. Here it was that the home was ruined under the very shadow of the church, White and Black; here, habits of shiftlessness took root, and sullen hopelessness replaced hopeful strife.

With the beginning of the abolition movement and the gradual growth of a class of free Negroes came a change. We often neglect the influence of the freedman before the war because of the paucity of his numbers and the small weight he had in the history of the nation. But we must not forget that his chief influence was internal—was exerted on the Black world; and that there he was the ethical and social leader. Huddled as he was in a few centers like Philadelphia, New York, and New Orleans, the masses of the freedmen sank into poverty and listlessness—but not all of them. The free Negro leader early arose, and his chief characteristic was intense earnestness and deep feeling on the slavery question. Freedom became to him a real thing and not a dream. His religion became darker and more intense, and into his ethics crept a note of revenge, into his songs a day of reckoning close at hand. The "coming of the Lord" swept this side of death, and came to be a thing to be hoped for in this day. Through fugitive slaves and irrepressible discussion, this desire for freedom seized the Black millions still in bondage and became their one ideal of life. The Black bards caught new notes, and sometimes even dared to sing—

"O Freedom, O Freedom, O Freedom over me!
Before I'll be a slave
I'll be buried in my grave,
And go home to my Lord
And be free."

For fifty years, Negro religion thus transformed itself and identified itself with the dream of abolition, until that which was a radical fad in the White North and an anarchistic plot in the White South had become a religion to the Black world. This, when Emancipation finally came, it seemed to the freedman a literal coming of the Lord. His fervid imagination was stirred as never before, by the tramp of armies, the blood and dust of battle, and the wail and whirl of social upheaval. He stood dumb and motionless before the whirlwind: What had he to do with it? Was it not the Lord's doing, and marvelous in his eyes? Joyed and bewildered with what came, he stood awaiting new wonders till the inevitable Age of Reaction swept over the nation and brought the crisis of today.

It is difficult to explain clearly the present critical stage of Negro religion. First, we must remember that living as the Blacks do in close contact with a great modern nation and sharing, although imperfectly, the soul-life of that nation, they must necessarily be affected more or less directly by all the religious and ethical forces that are today moving the United States. These questions and movements are, however, overshadowed and dwarfed by the (to them) all-important question of their civil, political, and economic status. They must perpetually discuss the "Negro Problem"—must live, move, and have their being in it, and interpret all else in its light or darkness. With this come, too, peculiar problems of their inner life—of the status of women, the maintenance of home, the training of children, the accumulation of wealth, and the prevention of crime. All this must mean a time of intense ethical ferment, of religious heart-searching and intellectual unrest. From the double life every American Negro must live, as a Negro and as an American, as swept on by the current of the nineteenth while yet struggling in the eddies of the fifteenth century—from this must arise a painful self-consciousness, an almost morbid sense of personality and a moral hesitancy which is fatal to self-confidence. The worlds within and without the Veil of Color are changing, and changing rapidly, but not at the same rate, not in the same way; and this must produce a peculiar wrenching of the soul, a peculiar sense of doubt and bewilderment. Such a double life, with double thoughts, double duties, and double social classes, must give rise to double words and double ideals, and tempt the mind to pretense or to revolt, to hypocrisy or to radicalism.

In some such doubtful words and phrases can one perhaps most clearly picture the peculiar ethical paradox that faces the Negro of today and is tingeing and changing his religious life. Feeling that his rights and his dearest ideals are being trampled upon, that the public conscience is ever more deaf to his righteous appeal, and that all the reactionary forces of prejudice, greed, and revenge are daily gaining new strength and fresh allies, the Negro faces no enviable dilemma. Conscious of his impotence and pessimistic, he often becomes bitter and vindictive; and his religion, instead of a worship, is a complaint and a curse, a wail rather than a hope, a sneer rather than a faith. On the other hand, another type of mind, shrewder and keener and more tortuous too, sees in the very strength of the anti-Negro movement its patent weaknesses, and with Jesuitic casuistry is deterred by no ethical considerations in the endeavor to turn this weakness to the Black man's strength. Thus, we have two great and hardly reconcilable streams of thought and ethical strivings; the danger of the one lies in anarchy, that of the other in hypocrisy. The one type of Negro stands almost ready to curse God and die, and the other is too often found a traitor to right and a coward before force; the one is wedded to ideals remote, whimsical, perhaps impossible of realization; the other forgets that life is more than meat and the body more than raiment. But, after all, is not this simply the writhing of the age translated into Black—the triumph of the lie which today, with its false culture, faces the hideousness of the anarchist assassin?

Today, the two groups of Negroes—the one in the North, the other in the South—represent these divergent ethical tendencies, the first tending toward radicalism, the other toward hypocritical compromise. It is no idle regret with which the White South mourns the loss of the old-time Negro—the frank, honest, simple old servant who stood for the earlier religious age of submission and humility. With all his laziness and lack of many elements of true manhood, he was at least open-hearted, faithful, and sincere. Today he is gone, but who is to blame for his going? Is it not those very persons who mourn for him? Is it not the tendency, born of reconstruction and reaction, to found a society of lawlessness and deception, to tamper with the moral fiber of a naturally honest and straightforward people until the Whites threaten to become ungovernable tyrants and the Blacks criminals and hypocrites? Deception is the natural defense of the weak against the strong, and the South used it for many years against its conquerors; today, it must be prepared to see its Black proletariat turn that same two-edged weapon against itself. And how natural this is! The death of Denmark Vesey and Nat Turner proved long since to the Negro the present hopelessness of physical defense. Political defense is becoming less and less available, and economic defense is still only partially effective. But there is a patent defense at hand—the defense of deception and flattery, of cajoling and lying. It is the same defense which the Jews of the Middle Age used and which left its stamp on their character for centuries. Today, the young Negro of the South who would succeed cannot be frank and outspoken, honest and self-assertive, but rather he is daily tempted to be silent and wary, politic and sly; he must flatter and be pleasant, endure petty insults with a smile, shut his eyes to wrong; in too many cases he sees positive personal advantage in deception and lying. His real thoughts, his real aspirations, must be guarded in whispers; he must not criticize, he must not complain. Patience, humility, and adroitness must in these growing Black youth replace impulse, manliness, and courage. With this sacrifice there is an economic opening, and perhaps peace and some prosperity. Without this there is riot, migration, or crime. Nor is this situation peculiar to the southern United States—is it not rather the only method by which undeveloped races have gained the right to share modern culture? The price of culture is a lie.

On the other hand, in the North the tendency is to emphasize the radicalism of the Negro. Driven from his birthright in the South by a situation at which every fiber of his more outspoken and assertive nature revolts, he finds himself in a land where he can scarcely earn a decent living amid the harsh competition and the color discrimination. At the same time, through schools and periodicals, discussions and lectures, he is intellectually quickened and awakened. The soul, long pent up and dwarfed, suddenly expands in newfound freedom. What wonder that every tendency is to excess—radical complaint, radical remedies, bitter denunciation, or angry silence. Some sink, some rise. The criminal and the sensualist leave the church for the gambling-hell and the brothel, and fill the slums of Chicago and Baltimore; the better classes segregate themselves from the group-life of both White and Black, and form an aristocracy, cultured but pessimistic, whose bitter criticism stings while it points out no way of escape. They despise the submission and subserviency of the southern Negroes, but offer no other means by which a poor and oppressed minority can exist side by side with its masters. Feeling deeply and keenly the tendencies and opportunities of the age in which they live, their souls are bitter at the fate which drops the Veil between; and the very fact that this bitterness is natural and justifiable only serves to intensify it and make it more maddening.

Between the two extreme types of ethical attitude which I have thus sought to make clear wavers the mass of the millions of Negroes, North and South; and their religious life and activity partake of this social conflict within their ranks. Their churches are differentiating—now into groups of cold, fashionable devotees, in no way distinguishable from similar White groups save in color of skin; now into large social and business institutions catering to the desire for information and amusement of their members, warily avoiding unpleasant questions both within and without the Black world, and preaching in effect if not in word: *Dum vivimus, vivamus*.[1]

But back of this still broods silently the deep religious feeling of the real Negro heart, the stirring, unguided might of powerful human souls who have lost the guiding star of the past and are seeking in the great night a new religious ideal. Some day the Awakening will come, when the pent-up vigor of ten million souls shall sweep irresistibly toward the goal, out of the valley of the shadow of death, where all that makes life worth living—liberty, justice, and right—is marked "For White People Only."

---

1 "While we live, let us live."

The Negro Spiritual

by John W. Work III
from *Hymn Society Papers*, XXIV
International Hymnological Conference
New York, published on September 10–11, 1961

Almost a hundred years ago, 1867, William Allen published what is generally accepted as being the first collection of American Negro folk songs, *Slave Songs of the United States*.[1] In 1873, Fisk University published its first collection of spirituals,[2] which was followed shortly by other volumes collected by various persons. Prior to the publication of these collections, several journals had published interesting articles calling attention to this extensive body of song.

However, the attention of the United States and Europe was dramatically drawn to the spirituals by the Fisk Jubilee Singers with their history-making concert tours extending from 1871 to 1878. The unprecedented achievements and spectacular incidents which attended these concerts and tours have been described and noted well, though probably inadequately estimated, in book and magazines—some fairly recent.

People heard in these songs many new, stirring musical elements. Let us list a few of these:

1. New rhythms and use of syncopation.
2. Melodic phrases which were a combination of segments and repetitions.
3. Melodies with new tonal combinations and new cadences. (You will observe that I am using the term "new" rather than "strange" because enjoyment of these songs did not have to grow on the listeners. It was immediate and spontaneous.)

What person in the European tradition had heard such melodies as these?

Walk Together, Children
Roll, Jordan, Roll
I, John, Saw the Number (a minor melody beginning with the
    subdominant)
Hammering
Calvary
Run, Mourner, Run
My Soul's Been Anchored in the Lord
Going Home in the Chariot in the Morning

Following the tours of the Fisk Jubilee Singers, further favorable attention was drawn to the spirituals by Anton Dvorák's estimation of Negro folk song as worthy thematic material in creating serious American music and his own employment of "Swing Low, Sweet Chariot" as the opening theme of his *New World Symphony.*

In 1905, the Oliver Ditson Company commissioned the Afro-Anglican composer Samuel Coleridge-Taylor to transcribe twenty-four Negro melodies for piano and invited the famous educator, Booker T. Washington, to write a preface to the volume.[3] The preface has been frequently quoted, and the transcriptions have been widely performed.

Up to this time, publishers of spirituals were mostly concerned with collections and arranging them for performance—and, I might add, with good commercial results. In 1914, the eminent music critic Henry F. Krehbiel published his now-famous treatise, *Afro-American Folk Songs.* In this work, which went into many editions, the objective was the analysis and study of the music of these songs. This volume brought the spiritual to the attention of the non-music scholar. Sociologists, anthropologists, English scholars, and theologians began to write treatises and articles analyzing the spiritual in the areas of their specific interests.

In 1893, Richard Wallaschek, European anthropologist, wrote that the spiritual was not a Negro original but was imitative of the White hymns, gospel songs, and folk songs with which the Negro was surrounded.[4] This question of the originality of the Negro spiritual occupied the attention of the scholars in the 1920s and 1930s.

Dr. George Pullen Jackson, at the time Professor of German at Vanderbilt University, wrote a sizable book in 1933 entitled *White Spirituals of the Southern Uplands.*[5] In this book, Dr. Jackson claimed that the Negro spiritual was a derivative of White spirituals and gospel songs. He cited numerous examples of Negro spirituals which were strikingly similar to White songs. He proved undeniably that some of the Negro spirituals were imitations. But there were many more that he did not so classify. He could not! The invalidity of his contention lay in the author's reliance upon the verse of the songs rather than upon the music, and upon ignoring the most highly determining factor in the question—the musical form of the spirituals. By far the largest number of the spirituals embrace the African "call and response" chant form, first noticed by Krehbiel but frequently overlooked by the later non-music scholars.

Several years ago an internationally renowned anthropologist came to Fisk University as a guest lecturer. He delivered a speech on one occasion to a closed society "across town" in which he stated unequivocally that Negro spirituals were imitations of Scotch, Irish, and English folk songs. Apparently, he was unaware that there was a newspaper reporter in attendance and was as chagrined as we on the campus were to see in the paper the next morning an important headline describing the professor's statement about the spirituals. Ironically, the article made no mention of the subject of the professor's speech or his treatment of it. The eminent professor was bombarded with questions by persons on the campus which he could not answer satisfactorily. Finally, the harassed professor admitted that he knew nothing about spirituals—nor music—but in his speech had echoed the point of view held by Dr. Wallaschek.

It is not the plan of this paper to dwell on the point of the originality of the spiritual or the amount of African survival to be found in it, but merely to list it as one of the problems considered by scholars in their study of spirituals. It would be safe to accept the opinion expressed by Dr. Newman White in his very excellent book *American Negro Folk Songs:* "The songs of the Negro today are beyond question the Negro's songs—They have become thoroughly naturalized as vehicles of the Negro's imagination."[6]

A second problem which has engaged the attention of scholars in the study of the spirituals is the meaning of their words. Probably no one today knows what the first Africans in America thought and sang about. When Negro song evolved into the spiritual in the eighteenth century as the Negro embraced Christianity and flowered in the early nineteenth century, we were given a mass of study material. To whom was the spiritual singer singing—to himself—to God—or to a neighbor? When the Negro slave sang "My Lord's Goin' to Move This Wicked Race," to whom was he referring? Was this "wicked race" generic or was it the group of plantation owners? What was the intended meaning of the line "Nobody knows who I am," or the line "Hold the wind, don't let it blow"? What did the singer mean when he sang, "I'm going to stand on a sea of glass"?

Dr. White contends that the lines and various expressions to be found in the spirituals are entirely biblical and worshipful. He singles out none that he can label as protest or warning, free of its biblical association.

On the other hand, Dr. Miles Mark Fisher, a theologian, surprises us in his recently published dissertation with the theory that these songs served as signals to convene secret meetings. He proposes that the favorite spiritual "Steal Away to Jesus" was authored by Nat Turner who used the song to convene his followers and who led the slave insurrection at Southampton, Virginia, in 1831.[7] Fisher's claim for this origin of "Steal Away" seems to confute the formerly accepted story which places the origin of "Steal Away" in the Red River area in Arkansas and defines its function as the signal to gather for forbidden religious meetings.[8]

The "wilderness" used in so many spirituals, according to Dr. Fisher, was something more than some "woods." The "wilderness" was the secret meeting place of the Negroes, and in the song it was the signal alerting them to a pending meeting. Dr. Fisher cites many similar double meanings of words and phrases usually regarded as commonplace. Whatever the meaning of these poetic lines in 1840, post-Civil War use of the same lines has eliminated hidden meanings—or so we presume.

The classical spirituals, these songs whose forms evolved among the unlettered Negro folk of the nineteenth century, were conceived as linear music, without the aid of the keyboard. Other musical instruments—fiddles, guitars, etc.—were forbidden by Church policy. The song creators conceived the spirituals without the use of keyboard, and the congregation sang them without keyboard support or the experience of listening to a keyboard. These songs had no preconceived harmony, and in the rural churches they were sung without harmony. Such harmony as one might have heard was an incidental alto or a tenor supplied by individuals who might have had keyboard experience. Occasionally, one heard a bass singing the melody two octaves below the soprano, but never is a real bass part encountered. But in spite of the spiritual's incubation in a purely linear style, the melodies of the spirituals lend themselves readily to four-part harmonization.

There was in the congregational singing the phenomenon of frequent variation of the phrase and improvisation on it. In the city churches, among literate worshipers where hymns are sung from hymnals, there is almost a uniform reliance upon a single melody. But among the rural folk, where the transmitting of songs is entirely oral, not only does the melody undergo some change with each performance but there are frequent changes in the words also. When a collector transcribes a folk melody from an individual folk singer, he knows that he is writing the melody as that particular singer sang it *that time*. The next singer interviewed will surely sing it differently. This variation principle found in individual performance is multiplied a hundred times in congregational singing in a folk performance.

Please indulge me in the unscholarly, overly enthusiastic statement I am about to make. I probably should not include it in such a paper and should keep it associated informally only.

In my opinion, the most beautiful ritual in American worship is the service of the Negro Primitive Baptist Church. This church is primarily a rural folk church found principally in the mid-South. Prior to twenty-five years ago, no musical instrument was used in the service nor was any printed material used except the Bible. The music in the worship service consisted occasionally of spirituals and the wonderful hymns of Dr. Watts never heard outside of worship. These latter hymns begin with a verse intoned by a leader and repeated by the congregation in a long, drawn-out melismatic melody, the original of which might or might not have been taken from the New England hymnody.

However, the original melodies had a definite beat and measure division. As they are sung in this Primitive Baptist style, there is no meter and to me the original melody is not distinguishable. Each singer derives his personal melody from this nebulous original and adds to it his own melismas, interpolations and, in many instances, his own principles. When a hundred aroused singers so intone, the resultant sound is indescribable and impossible to transcribe. Any chording instrument would be totally out of place in such a performance and harmony unthinkable.

Now, to an extent, this variant melodic style of the Dr. Watts singing of the Negro Primitive Baptists is a factor in the singing of the spirituals in the folk church.

To return to the spirituals and the question of harmony, it is important to repeat that in the folk congregational singing, harmony is rare and, where it does occur, it is only incidental. But an important purveyor and creator of spirituals, the folk quartet or folk ensemble does use harmony and a style of free counterpoint to a remarkable degree. The tonic, dominant, and subdominant chords with various added notes are their chief stock in trade. The IV with the third raised which featured the quartet singing of fifty years ago has almost disappeared from use. Minor triads are used infrequently. In fact, these ensembles rarely sing in the minor key. The congregations, however, sing in the minor key frequently.

About thirty years ago, in the new kind of gospel song which emerged, the piano was added to the music of the folk church. Not only did the piano bring dance rhythms to the music, but it also brought a harmonic texture out of which the new melodies and a new type of melody—an inferior type of melody—grew. I choose to call the new gospel songs the *new spirituals*. They are created by the same folk who created the older spirituals. They serve the same folk worship function. But now harmony becomes an important factor in the folk church, although it is subordinate to the new dance rhythms.

In another folk church, the Holiness Church, other instruments—the tambourine, guitar, and some woodwind instruments—have been added to the musical accompaniment. Time does not permit further development of this point. I am not sure but that any discussion of spirituals should be labeled: Spirituals BI (spirituals before instruments) and Spirituals AI (spirituals after instruments).

Except for this reference to the present-day gospel song, this discussion is concerned entirely with the nineteenth century spiritual, which I term the "classical spiritual."

A few spirituals appearing in collections are written in 3/4 and 6/8 meter. These are rare and atypical—and probably non-Negro. The meters of the spiritual are 4/4 and 2/4. These may be in a slow swing with two beats to the measure or in a rapid, fiery four beats to the measure stimulated by foot beats and hand claps, actual or implied. These rhythms are unrelenting and dictate the limits of the melody. The melody must conform to the demands of the rhythm. In some collections, 5/4 and 6/4 measures do appear. The accuracy of these is challenged. Any individual informant might have sung the song with these unusual measures, but it is doubtful whether a congregation would sing the song with such an interrupted rhythm. Slowly sung triplets do occur in spiritual melodies, and 12/8 rhythms do feature the dance music of the secular Negro folk song, particularly the blues.

The rhythm and melody take precedence over words in the spirituals. So strong is the dominance of music over words that deleting word syllables may occur which alter the intended meaning of the singer. In the spiritual "I've Found Free Grace an' Dying Love," note that the phrase is obviously the opposite of the intended meaning. In the rhythmic pattern, allowance was made for one syllable on the fourth beat when originally there were two in the word phrase "an' undying Love." One of these must be omitted. Unfortunately as a result, the important qualifying syllable "un" was sacrificed in favor of the unimportant "an'."

Because of these essential rhythmic patterns which evolved, the words were frequently compressed into one thought often repeated and nonsensical, or trivial words were inserted to fill the demands of the patterns. For instance:

Little David, play on your harp, Hallelu, Hallelu
Little David, play on your harp, Hallelu.

The word "hallelu" is not necessarily a dialect term. It was compressed into "hallelu" by the demands of the rhythmic patterns. The complete "hallelujah" is commonly encountered in the songs.

Or consider this example:

My troubles is hard, Oh yes
My troubles is hard, Oh yes
My troubles is hard, Oh yes
Yes indeed my troubles is hard.

In fact, the dominance of this rhythmic pattern was surely a factor in the creation of dialect—not the only one, but an important one. In one instance, the verses to a well-known song say "I wonder where Brother Moses' gone" or "I wonder where Sister Mary's gone." But never, "I wonder where Brother Elijah's gone." Here the pattern is destroyed. This verse is heard, "I wonder where Brother 'Elijah's gone." This is not illiterate speech. Rather it is a line dictated by the dominance of the rhythmic patterns.

A word pattern inspired the musical pattern, as is true of all good vocal music, but in the case of the Negro folk song, the musical pattern once established dominates the words for the remainder of the song. It must be observed that some of these patterns, used repeatedly because of their appeal, became idioms and were added to the racial repertory. These idioms and their countless variants were the common property of the song creator and the group alike. Such idioms are melodically distinctive and immediately recognized by the folk group, and freely reproduced by it. Sometimes the idiom is distinguished by certain notes, such as the flatted seventh and flatted third.

The following is a common but distinctive melodic pattern. If one of you should visit a rural folk church service during a prayer or the sermon, you surely would hear a member, usually a woman, hum this musical phrase:

She would just as likely interpolate "Well, Well, Well." A charming little pattern in the minor mode—*re do la*. It is not only a charming pattern, but it is an important and frequently used one. Practically every one of the true Negro spirituals has in it a characteristic pattern.

Most of the spirituals are in the major mode. But there are many in the minor or at least in the Aeolian mode. Occasionally, one is encountered which is neither. The spiritual "I Ain't A-Goin' to Die No More" is such a song.

There is a wide variety of features in the melodies of the spirituals—some are fast, others slow, some phrases are sustained, as contrasted with fragmentary melodies; melodies which ascent by leap, melodies which descend by leap, some melodies with a wide compass, and melodies with a narrow compass. One such song, "Keep A-inching Along," consists of only three notes and has a compass of a major third. Its interest is found in the distribution of the notes and the rhythmic patterns. Two other songs, "Hammering" and "T'was on One Sunday Morning," have a range which exceeds an octave.

Musically, spirituals may be classified into three large groups or types: the "call and response" chant; the slow, sustained, long-phrase melody; the syncopated, segmented melody.

The first of these, the "call and response" chant, may be identified by the alternation of a solo verse line with a choral response of a short phrase or word. The leader's call changes from line to line but the choral response rarely changes, though it may be in two parts and on occasion may have an ending phase which serves as a release. These songs usually are characterized by a rapid tempo and a pounding rhythm, although the best-loved and best-known of all spirituals, and one which illustrates the form well, "Swing Low, Sweet Chariot," is sung in the opposite manner. Answering the leader who sings many lines beginning with "Swing Low, Sweet Chariot," the chorus responds with the line "Coming for to carry me home." The well-known song "Go Down, Moses" uses the choral response "Let my people go" to answer the leader's varying call line. Another striking example of this type of song is "Walk Together, Children."

"Deep River," "Lord, I Want to Be a Christian," "O the Rocks and the Mountains Shall All Flee Away," "My Lord, What a Morning," and "There Is a Balm in Gilead to Heal the Sin-sick Soul" are good examples of the second type of spiritual, having slow, sustained, long-phrase melodies.

In general, the best-liked of the spirituals are those with the episodic segmented melodies and the syncopated rhythms. These are the third type of spirituals. Such songs as "Little David, Play on Your Harp," "O Give Me Your Hand," "Got Religion All Around the World." "Oh Bye and Bye I'm A-going to Lay Down My Heavy Load," "Ain't Goin' to Study War No More," and "Ain't I Glad I Got Out of the Wilderness" are good examples.

In the folk community, the church sponsored and controlled certain semireligious activities. Important among these were musical programs. Featured performers on these occasions were the folk quartets who, in addition to the traditional spirituals, created and performed another type of spiritual—the ballad spiritual. Certain singers had the inimitable ability to create chain verses commemorating the feats of prominent biblical characters. Most of you are familiar with the spiritual extolling the exploits of Joshua at the battle of Jericho. David and Daniel have come into their share of honor. Perhaps the man who captured the fancy of these song creators more than any other was Samson. There are several songs and many verses devoted to the exploits of this strong man. But not only did the folk singers single him out for attention. Did not two opera composers do the same? This ballad type of spiritual pays homage mostly to Old Testament heroes. But the most beautiful of all these songs goes to the New Testament for its subject, Mary, in "Mary Was the Queen of Galilee."

I have described for you how spirituals were performed in folk churches—without harmony, with no varying dynamics, and with freely sung melodies. Now let us return to the Fisk Jubilee Singers in 1871. Their director wrote the melodies down, thereby making each written version permanent. His next step was to supply these melodies with academic harmony. The best possible voices were carefully trained and blended to give these songs an artistic interpretation. The result of this treatment, an epochal result, was the successful translation of the spiritual from the rural church to the formal concert hall.

The Coleridge-Taylor transcription of the Negro melodies for the concert piano have been mentioned. A few years later, Harry T. Burleigh began his important series of arrangements of spirituals for solo voice and piano. Some of America's finest singers added these to their recital repertory. Through this series, America learned to love "Deep River," "Go Down, Moses," and "Nobody Knows the Trouble I've Seen."

But the spirituals remained largely a body of music to which America listened with great pleasure. In 1914, R. Nathaniel Dett published a spiritual arranged for chorus.[9] To this spiritual he added an easy-flowing counterpoint. He also created a three-part song form, adding a middle section using original music in a new key. The result was the anthem "Listen to the Lambs," which became one of the most widely used church anthems as well as a concert piece. Another translation! The spiritual was no longer a folk song in library archives, or the plaintive melody sung to guitar or piano accompaniment, or the subject of a paper. In its arranged form it became music which was alive and an active addition to the American choral repertory, enjoying fast-growing appreciation.

The inevitable happened, of course! Every uninspired, unskilled music writer in the country began to arrange spirituals. His rarely varied equipment was a syncopated melody, a pungent verse line, a diminished seventh chord, and a very loud tone to end on. All sorts of banalities crept in. Hardly before the arranged spiritual became recognized as a form, it fell into disrepute, and the composer who made these arrangements, whether excellent or poor, became stigmatized.

However, the lesser composer pointed the way. Writing in the Bulletin of the American Choral Foundation for May 5, 1959, Harvard University's G. Wallace Woodworth gives a place to the arranged spiritual in the American choral repertory. When the better composer is moved to write choral music with the Negro spiritual as his thematic material, particularly if he gives his attention more to the folk idioms and patterns than to the entire melody, I predict that a new era will unfold. Last year I heard just such a work by the eminent composer, Gail Kubik. A most effective piece of music.

Most of this paper has been devoted to the musical aspect of the spiritual, in which the thesis has been advanced that the words of the spirituals are subordinate to the music. There is no intention here to minimize the great beauty and tremendous religious appeal of the verse of the spiritual.

In the intensive search today for new music to enrich the church service, new hymns and hymn sources are being studied and evaluated. It is gratifying to persons from Fisk, where such a thing is traditional, to observe the growing use of spirituals in church activities throughout America. Today, though the worship service has not found a place for the spiritual, spirituals are now sung generally at vespers and other special services.

In the past, there have been three deterrents to the use of spirituals in the church worship service. The first of these has been the failure of some serious worshipers to differentiate between the spiritual of worship and consecration and the highly rhythmical spiritual.

As a matter of fact, this recreational type of spiritual was rarely used in the worship service of the folk church, where reverence and dignity were demanded. The folk church created songs unsurpassed in these qualities. Some of these songs are appropriate for the most reverent worship service and could contribute to the highest kind of religious experience. Examples of such songs are "The Religion That My Lord Gave Me Shines Like a Morning Star," "I Know the Lord Has Laid His Hands on Me," "All I Want Is a Little More Faith in Jesus," "Were You There When They Crucified My Lord?" and "Lord, Make Me More Holy."

The second deterrent to the use of the spirituals in worship has been their unfortunate association with the banalities of the entertainment stage, where they are performed and sometimes featured. Too often in the entertainment area, the religious significance of the spirituals is distorted and abused.

Another deterrent to the use of the spiritual in our present-day church service is the problem of performance. To sing spirituals effective in the traditional, unaccompanied style demands either experience in the tradition or some training in this performance. To surmount the difficulties of performance in the church service, a subdued and carefully selected organ accompaniment is recommended, and at the present time the use of the sustained, long-phrase melody is urged.

Congregational singing of the spiritual is not practicable at present even though informal group singing at vespers and similar meetings is becoming a popular activity. Composers have not given their attention to the preparation of these songs for congregational use. In planning for hymnals for the future, some editorial board may commission a sensitive writer to make appropriate settings of spirituals for congregational use in the worship service. If this is properly done, a new inspirational resource will have been added to church worship—and the third translation of the spiritual will have been effected.[10]

---

1 William Allen, *Slave Songs of the United States* (New York, 1867).

2 G. D. Pike, *The Jubilee Singers* (Boston, 1873).

3 Samuel Coleridge-Taylor, *Twenty-four Negro Melodies, Transcribed for the Piano,* Op. 59 (Boston, 1905).

4 Richard Wallaschek, *Primitive Music* (London, 1893).

5 George Pullen Jackson, *White Spirituals of the Southern Uplands* (Chapel Hill: The University of North Carolina Press, 1933).

6 Newman White, *American Negro Folk Songs* (Cambridge, Harvard University Press, 1928), p. 25.

7 Miles Mark Fisher, *Negro Slave Songs in the United States* (Ithaca: Cornell University Press, 1953), p. 66.

8 John W. Work (Sr.), *Folk Song of American Negro* (Nashville: Fisk University Press, 1915), p. 77.

9 R. Nathaniel Dett, "Listen to the Lambs" (New York: G. Schirmer, Inc., 1914).

10 In this paper, I have given credit to the scholars who have written treatises on the spirituals and to the composers who have translated them for our use. No paper would be complete which did not give high credit to the folk song collectors without whose work all I have been talking about would be impossible—men like George L. White, John and Alan Lomax, Emmet Kennedy, George Ballanta-Taylor. And I hope you will not regard me as immodest in adding the names of my father and uncle, John W. and Frederick J. Work, to this list.

Introducing the African American Churches

by William D. Watley
from *Singing the Lord's Song in a Strange Land:*
The African American Churches and Ecumenism, published in 1993

When one is an oppressed minority on soil where one is made to feel like an eternal foreigner or intruder, one is in an extremely precarious position. The legitimate rallying cry "one person, one vote" does not guarantee that one's community will receive justice, for a resented minority can always be outvoted by a racist majority. When one has been kidnapped from one's native land and then made a slave on strange soil, one cannot tell one's oppressor to "go home" or to "give us back our land." When one is a minority and racism is inherent to the majority culture, which attempts to blend every color but Black—or that unique blend of Blackness known as African American; when that majority culture has a tradition of racial misunderstanding and mythology and a history of exclusion that predates the founding of the republic, one must forge one's identity and affirm one's being in the face of overwhelming odds and a constant barrage of negative reinforcements.

In 1903, the great scholar W. E. B. DuBois wrestled with the dilemma of being African American:

> It is a peculiar sensation, this double-consciousness, the sense of always looking at one's self through the eyes of others, of measuring one's soul by the tape of a world that looks on in amused contempt and pity. One ever feels his twoness—an American, a Negro; two souls, two thoughts, two unreconciled strivings; two working ideals in one dark body, whose dogged strength alone keeps it from being torn asunder.

> The history of the American Negro is the history of this strife—this longing to attain self-conscious manhood, to merge his double self into a better and truer self. In this merging he

wishes neither of the older selves to be lost. He would not Africanize America, for America has too much to teach the world and Africa. He would not bleach his Negro soul in a flood of White Americanism, for he knows that Negro blood has a message for the world. He simply wishes to make it possible for a man to be both a Negro and an American without being cursed and spit upon by his fellows, without having the doors of opportunity closed roughly in his face.[1]

One is awed to realize that this struggle described by DuBois at the dawn of the twentieth century still portrays the existential search for meaning of many African Americans at the threshold of the twenty-first century.

In the long night of struggle and search for meaning, what has kept African Americans from nihilism or capitulation to the assaults of "outrageous fortune"? What has fueled the energies of African Americans to keep toiling on through a night more desolate and dreary than "a thousand midnights," looking for a star of hope? Whence comes such a firmly fixed faith that refuses to die, but continues to proclaim that "there's a bright side somewhere" and a "new day's a'coming"? What gave African Americans a sense of belonging when they felt like "a motherless child...a long ways from home"? What anchored their souls in trouble, stabilized their psyche, kept their hearts from drinking the bile of hatred, and put a heaven in their view even as they labored in the midst of hellish realities? What institution or enterprise has empowered a community and given hope to an oppressed people struggling for self-realization in a hostile majority situation? For African Americans there can be but one answer—the African American religious enterprise and its major institutional embodiment, the African American Church.

What is this often misunderstood, caricatured, mystical experience and institution which has emboldened the spirits, made glad the hearts, and stabilized a community of people? What is this galvanizing force that is loved and believed in and ardently followed by so many, while remaining an enigma to others?

African American religion is the matrix of African American life and the institutional fulcrum of the African American community. It is the crucible in which African American culture, music, art, literature, and philosophy were formed and the anvil on which African American economics, politics, and survival skills were forged. Although Islam, Judaism, and various African and West Indian traditions are represented in the religious landscape of African Americans, the vast majority of African American believers are Christian.

And the vast majority of these belong to the historic and independent African American churches.

There are significant numbers of African American believers and congregations in predominantly White denominations—the "majority churches" in the U.S. context. These believers and congregations are authentically and unashamedly African American in their life, witness, ministry, work, and worship. Belonging to a "majority denomination" does not shield these believers and congregations from the barbarous onslaught of culturally systematic and ecclesially systemic racism. These believers and congregations, like their brothers and sisters in the independent and historic African American denominations, bear on their bodies the marks of the Lord Jesus Christ which represent both crucifixion and resurrection. However, in this work the term African American Church will be used to refer primarily to the mainline independent historic denominations in the African American community.

The African American Church

Who then are the African American churches? What distinguishes them from other ethnic churches throughout the world?

The historic Black or African American churches are more than the regional branch of a broader worldwide communion whose constituency and leadership is of a particular ethnic identity. Although the churches on which we shall focus are primarily African and American, their boundaries extend beyond the borders of a particular country. They are international in their organization and inter-racial and intercultural in their membership.

The African American churches are primarily the independent indigenous institutions of a "third-world" people in a "first-world" context. They are the creations of a domestically colonized people of primarily African descent whose social location is the White West but whose mission is international. While ecumenical cooperation and joint ventures in some specific projects have been part of their history, these churches are completely autonomous, answerable to no other ecclesiastical body beyond themselves for their actions, and dependent on no other sources for their financial support. These are the churches that African Americans have built from the bricks they have made, even as they gathered their own straw.

Primarily Baptist and Methodist in theology and liturgy, these churches came into existence because of the racism of institutionalized White religion in the United States. From the perspective of many African Americans, racism has been and continues to be the greatest heresy and the major church-dividing issue since Christianity was first preached to the enslaved sons and daughters of Africa. These churches came into being because even illiterate slaves saw the glaring discrepancies between what was preached to them and what was practiced towards them. White Christians would not countenance relating to Blacks as equal members and participants in the household of faith; but powerless slaves would not abide segregated pews, segregated altars and communion tables, or a gospel that taught submission to the yoke of slavery as consistent with the will of God. Although racism was not the direct cause of each of the African American churches, racism is the reason for the existence of the African American religious enterprise.

Of the numerous independent African American churches, this chapter focuses on seven historic independent communions which have a broad national following, an international focus, and an expanding ecumenical consciousness.

Black Methodist Communions

The African Methodist Episcopal Church (A.M.E.)

The African Methodist Episcopal Church dates from a walkout at St. George's Methodist Church in Philadelphia, Pennsylvania, in 1787. The incident that led to the founding of African Methodism was related by Richard Allen, founder and first consecrated bishop of the A.M.E. Church:

> A number of us usually attended St. George's Church on Fourth Street; and when the Colored people began to get numerous in attending the church, they moved us from the seats we usually sat on, and placed us around the walls, and on Sabbath morning we went to church and the sexton stood at the door and told us to go in the gallery. He told us to go, and we would see where to sit. We expected to take the seats over the ones we formerly occupied below, not knowing any better. We took those seats. Meeting had begun, and they were nearly done singing, and just as we got to our seats, the elder said, "Let us pray." We had not been long on our knees before I heard considerable scuffling and low talking. I raised my head up and saw one of the trustees, H. M., having hold of the Reverend Absolom Jones, pulling him up off of his knees, and saying, "You must get up—you must not kneel here." Mr. Jones replied, "Wait until prayer is over." Mr. H. M. said, "No, you

must get up now, or I will call for aid and force you away." Mr. Jones said, "Wait until prayer is over, and I will get up and trouble you no more." With that he beckoned to one of the other trustees, Mr. L. S., to come to his assistance. He came, and went to William White to pull him up. By this time prayer was over, and we all went out of the church in a body, and they were no more plagued with us in the church.[2]

From these beginnings the African Methodist Episcopal Church has grown to become the largest of the Black Methodist communions. Its membership in the U.S. is in the 3.7 million range. It also claims over 1 million members in Africa and the Caribbean.[3]

The African Methodist Episcopal Zion Church (A.M.E. Zion)

The African Methodist Episcopal Zion Church also had its origins in the late eighteenth century when a group of African Americans broke away from the John Street Methodist Episcopal Church in New York City. The English-based Methodist societies had early taken a stance against slavery and welcomed African Americans into their membership. But growing numbers of African Americans (40 percent by 1793) created tension and resentment among Whites who could not control the work of the Holy Spirit among Blacks who were evidently taking too seriously the gospel message of the efficacy of Jesus Christ's redeeming blood for all humanity. Discrimination in worship and liturgy, and refusal to fully ordain African American preachers and allow them equal status with White clergy in the annual conferences hastened the move towards separation.

Voluntary separation and the need to devote a disproportionate amount of their resources to supporting their own communions have been the price African Americans have been willing to pay to enjoy the independence of being full and equal members of the household of faith. The scandal of a divided witness has been the price the White Christian Church has been willing to pay to maintain ecclesiastical and social racism.

The A.M.E. Zion Church has been long known as the "Freedom Church." It claims such famous abolitionists as Sojourner Truth, Harriet Tubman, Jermain Lougen, and Frederick Douglass, who was licensed as a local A.M.E. Zion preacher. It was the first Methodist denomination to extend the vote and clerical ordination to women. As in all the other African American denominations, Whites have long been admitted to membership and permitted to hold any office in the church. If their numbers have remained small, it has not been due to hesitancy or refusal on the part of African American Christians to receive them as full and equal members of the community of faith. With a membership of 1.5 million (of which 100,000 are in Africa and the Caribbean), the A.M.E. Zion Church is the second largest of the Black Methodist denominations.

The Christian Methodist Episcopal Church (C.M.E.)

The fact that one cannot understand the history of Christianity in the U.S. without taking racism and slavery into account applies not only to the African American churches but also to the White majority churches. Several of these agonized and eventually split over slavery along the same North and South political lines of demarcation that identified the anti- and pro-slavery sides in the U.S. Civil War.

The Methodist Episcopal Church was one such denomination. After the Civil War, the Methodist Episcopal Church South, like the rest of the region in which it was located, was faced with the question of what to do about the African American former slaves who had remained in the bosom of the church during the war. How were these newly freed slaves to fit within a church of former slaveholders which faced massive reorganization problems? As the Methodist Episcopal Church South wrestled with the issue of the Black presence in its midst, the freed slaves were contemplating their own ecclesiastical destiny. They wanted to test their newfound wings of freedom ecclesiologically and theologically as well as economically, politically, and socially; and they had the wisdom to recognize that a church of former slave-holders would grant only limited independence to a group of former slaves in its midst.

In December 1870, a group of former slaves met in Jackson, Tennessee, "to organize a separate and independent church for Colored persons who had been members of that church while they were slaves and who chose to remain in it in order to get their own independent church upon the authority and goodwill of the White church."[4]

The tension and legal wrangling involved in the breakaway of the A.M.E. Church and the A.M.E. Zion Church were absent at the formation of the Christian Methodist Episcopal Church. Separation was mutually acceptable to Blacks, who wanted independence, and Whites, who were prepared to consent to it, considering the uncertain future of race relations in the South in the aftermath of the Civil War. Because of the amicable terms of this separation, the C.M.E. describes itself as "the only independent Black Methodist body organized with the full cooperation along with the ecclesiastical and legal authority of the White denominations out of which it had come."[5]

The original name of the C.M.E. Church—Colored Methodist Episcopal Church—was changed in 1954 to *Christian* Methodist Episcopal Church. The smallest of the three African American Methodist communions, the C.M.E. Church has a membership of approximately 900,000 in the United States and 75,000 overseas.

African American Baptists

Although Methodists constitute the oldest denominations among African Americans, the oldest congregations are Baptist. The first historically acknowledged Baptist churches of African American ancestry were the African Baptist or "Bluestone" Church of Mecklenberg, Virginia, established in 1758, and the Silver Bluff Baptist Church of Silver Bluff, South Carolina. Official records indicate that the Silver Bluff Church was established between 1753 and 1755, though the cornerstone of the present edifice claims a date of 1750.[6]

It was founded by a slave named George Liele who, like a number of other early African Americans, was converted in that period of revivalism in U.S. colonial history known as the Great Awakening. Before emigrating to Jamaica in 1782 or 1783, Liele also lived and preached in Savannah, Georgia, where one of his converts, a slave named Andrew Bryan, organized the First African Baptist Church around 1788.

These early churches indicate the long tenure of the African American religious enterprise within U.S. religious history, a reality that has too often been ignored in literature on the subject. The exclusionary nature of racist White American scholarship has meant that African American religious history is either not mentioned at all or treated as if the African American churches were some historically late sect or corrupt deviations from the "legitimate" mainstream churches. As a result, American churches are often viewed as poorly grafted shoots onto the "true vine" of U.S. religious life, or as undisciplined vines growing all over the ground among the stately oaks of the mainstream churches, or as the illegitimate and inferior offspring of a noble heritage.

However, these early beginnings of African American churches indicate that organized Christianity among African Americans predates the war that separated the colonies from Britain and established the United States as a distinct political entity. (This war, commonly known as the Revolutionary War or the War of Independence, is looked upon as neither by many African Americans, who question how a war that left enslaved so many people, many of whom shed their blood on the side of the victors, can be considered revolutionary. The war was fought for White, not Black independence, and when it ended the status of Blacks had not changed.)

Although there were doctrinal differences between the Methodists and Baptists, who had the greatest success in evangelizing the slaves, their treatment and perception of their Black constituency was the same. Black Baptists faced the same ecclesiological, liturgical, and theological racism as Black Methodists—segregated pews, segregated communion, hesitation or refusal to grant licenses to preach to Black candidates for ministry, and a perverted gospel whose main theme was "slaves, obey your masters."

An illuminating aspect of U.S. religious history is that during the revivals of the "Great Awakening" Blacks and Whites were often converted in the same worship services. It was as if the Holy Spirit in one magic moment was able to break through the racist ethos and social climate surrounding the worship context. The tragedy of U.S. religious history is that the equality of the conversion experience was not strong or lasting or far-reaching enough to withstand the mores of the times, which pressured the church and the individual White believer to conform to racist social norms rather than to transform them.

An integrated ecclesial life could not exist in a slave culture that espoused Black inferiority. Thus, Baptist associations that allowed full Black participation stopped working when African Americans began to swell the membership rolls. Black Baptists, like their Methodist sisters and brothers, soon discovered that they would have to establish their own associations if they were to worship God in complete and total freedom.

Although the drive for freedom was equally intense among African American Baptists and Methodists, Black Baptists had greater difficulty in establishing formal denominations. Before the Civil War, the Methodists were headquartered in the North, where the restrictions on access and movement were not as onerous as in the antebellum South, where the Baptists were predominant. Slave revolts like the Nat Turner rebellion in Virginia (1831) and planned insurrections such as those by David Prosser (1800) and Denmark Vesey (1822) in South Carolina further restricted independent religious activities among southern slaves. In fact, the first organization of African American Baptists beyond the local church level was not in the South but in the West—the Providence Association in Ohio in 1834. This was followed by Union Association in Ohio (1836), the Wood River Association in Illinois (1839), and the Amherstberg Association in Canada and Michigan (1841).[7] After the post-Civil War reconstruction and in the latter part of the nineteenth century, there were several attempts by Black Baptists to organize a national body or denomination.[8]

The National Baptist Convention, USA (NBC, USA)

The persistent vision of a national Black Baptist communion led in 1895 to the founding of the National Baptist Convention, USA, in Atlanta, Georgia. With a membership of 7.5 million communicants, the NBC, USA is the largest African American denomination and is considered by some to be the largest African American organization in existence. Its membership encompasses nearly one-fourth of the entire Black population of the U.S. and at least a third of the estimated number of Black members of Christian churches. Affiliated with it are more than 29,000 clergy, 30,000 local churches, 4,700 associations, and 59 state conventions.[9] The National Baptist Convention, USA also has missions in Africa, Nicaragua, Japan, and the Bahamas.[10]

The National Baptist Convention of America (NBCA)

The National Baptist Convention of America evolved as an identifiable entity in 1915. With an estimated membership of 3.5 million, it is the second largest of the African American Baptist conventions. It has about 7,800 local congregations with an average membership of 280, and about 2,500 to 3,000 clergy. A substantial number of NBCA churches are small, rural congregations. Some 400 associations and thirty-five state conventions in twenty-seven states are affiliated with the convention.[11] It has missions in Africa, Jamaica, Panama, the West Indies, and the Bahamas.

With the National Baptist Convention of America, the National Baptist Convention, USA, and the Progressive National Baptist Convention (PNBC), dual membership is not only possible but often practiced. Because a congregation or a minister can be a member of more than one convention, the total of the conventions cannot be the only index for determining the number of African American Baptists.

The Progressive National Baptist Convention (PNBC)

The Progressive National Baptist Convention (PNBC) came into existence in 1961 and involved such prominent names among African

American Baptists and in ecumenical circles as Gardner C. Taylor, Martin Luther King, Sr., Martin Luther King, Jr., and Benjamin Mays. As its name implies, the Progressive National Baptist Convention was envisioned as a reformist movement within traditional African American Baptist circles.

The smallest of the three National Baptist conventions, the PNBC has a constituency of 1.2 million members and 1,000 clergy in 1,000 churches. The average congregational size of 1,000 is due to the fact that large urban churches constitute the bulk of the membership of the Convention. Divided into four regions (Southern, Southwestern, Midwestern, and Eastern), the PNBC has thirty-five state conventions.

African American Pentecostalism

Any thorough study of current African American religion and church life must take into account the rise of Pentecostalism as a vibrant, vital, growing, and radicalizing liturgical force in Black American church life.

Since the days of the New Testament, the Church at various times and in various places has experienced the charismatic eruptions (glossolalia, healings, miracles, prophesy) currently labeled as Pentecostalism. But modern Pentecostalism owes much of its life and character to the African American quest for in-depth spirituality. First- and second-generation African American slaves adapted the free-style Baptist and Methodist worship to their needs in contradistinction to the formal Anglican tradition.

> Pentecostalism was a religious revolt against churches, White and Black, that refused to hold on to a spirituality that was characterized as ignorant and overly emotional. The social context of this period was one of rampant racism by Whites, who were taking back all of the advances made by African Americans during reconstruction. This new era of Pentecostal leadership was growing while an accommodating philosophy of gradualism was being pushed by Booker T. Washington and his associates. Spiritually, the combination of rampant racism in the White community and the philosophy of political conservatism in the American community led to a Christianity that was racist, politically conservative, and spiritually imperialistic. It was in this social and spiritual context that modern Pentecostalism was born.[12]

In April 1906, a Pentecost experience like that described in Acts 2 occurred in a prayer meeting of African Americans assembled in a private home in Los Angeles, California. As the holiness preacher William Seymour began to expound Acts 2:4, an episode of tongues-speaking (glossolalia) enraptured those present. This Pentecost experience lasted for three days. As word of it spread, such crowds gathered that larger accommodations had to be sought. A facility was found, and the spiritual awakening that began in a private home on Bonnie Brae Street continued in a mission on Azusa Street.

The Azusa Street Revival, as it is now called, lasted from 1906–1909, and marked the beginning of the modern Pentecostal expansion. Whites as well as Blacks were drawn to Seymour's ministry on Azusa Street. Thus, Pentecostalism, though Black in origin, was inter-racial in character at the beginning. However, so demonic is the influence of racism that as Pentecostalism developed institutionally, it separated along social as well as doctrinal lines. Lincoln and Mamiya have observed the irony that "Black Pentecostals, who founded the movement, have historically been excluded from ecumenical Pentecostal bodies such as the Pentecostal Fellowship of North America, as well as the National Association of Evangelicals."[13]

The Church of God in Christ (COGIC)

The Church of God in Christ (COGIC) largest branch of the Pentecostal Diaspora among African Americans. In 1893 its founder, Bishop Charles Mason, had a personal experience of sanctification which he began to expound as doctrine. Personal hardship and ostracism by some established churches were the results of his evangelical moralizing sanctity. However, in 1906, after steady growth despite the hardships that he encountered, the St. Paul Church of God in Christ was erected, and the denomination was incorporated in Memphis, Tennessee.

After receiving the baptism of the Holy Spirit and experiencing glossolalia at the Azusa Street mission in 1907, Bishop Mason affirmed the practice of speaking in tongues and encouraged the congregations of the COGIC to do the same. The general assembly was divided on the question of whether the baptism of the Holy Spirit and glossolalia were normative. Representatives of the twelve churches who agreed with Bishop Mason's view met in the first Pentecostal General Assembly in Memphis in November 1907, which has come to be regarded as the official founding date of the Church.

From representatives of twelve churches in 1907, the Church of God in Christ has grown to a membership of 3.5 million constituents with an overseas membership of over half a million. An interesting aspect of the Church is its peace witness. Members of the Church serve in the military only in non-combatant roles. Mason himself was a pacifist and, despite his support of the law and of the war bond drive, was jailed a number of times during World War I because of his views.

The COGIC's eightfold increase in membership from 50,000 constituents in the 1920s to 400,000 in the 1960s and again to 3.5 million by the beginning of the 1990s gives it the distinction of being the fastest-growing communion among the historic African American churches.[14] Although the Church of God in Christ is not a member of the World Council of Churches (WCC), it has been a significant participant in the ecumenical activities of the WCC's Black Church Liaison Committee.

---

1 *The Souls of Black Folk,* p. 45f.

2 *The Life Experiences and Gospel Labors of the Rt. Rev. Richard Allen,* p. 25.

3 Lincoln and Mamiya, *The Black Church in the African American Experience,* p. 54.

4 Othal Lakey, *The History of the CME Church,* p. 24.

5 Ibid., p. 15.

6 Lincoln and Mamiya, *op. cit.,* p. 24.

7 Ibid., p. 26.

8 Limitations of space do not permit a more detailed account of the founding and emergence of African American Baptist communions. Those interested in a more thorough study are referred to James Washington, *Frustrated Fellowship: The Black Baptist Quest for Social Power,* and Leroy Fitts, *A History of the Black Baptists.* Peggy Shriver's summaries in *Having Gifts that Differ* are also helpful.

9 Lincoln and Mamiya, *op. cit.,* p. 31.

10 Shriver, *op. cit.,* p. 115.

11 Lincoln and Mamiya, *op. cit.,* p. 35.

12 Frank M. Reid III, *A Black Church's Understanding of the Holy Spirit* (unpublished D.Min. dissertation, United Theological Seminary, 1990), p. 38f.

13 Lincoln and Mamiya, *op. cit.,* p. 79.

14 Ibid., pp. 80–85.

The Performed Word: Music and the Black Church

by C. Eric Lincoln and Lawrence H. Mamiya
from *The Black Church in the African American Experience*,
published in 1990

Make a joyful noise unto the Lord, all ye lands
Come before his presence with singing.
—Psalm 100

I got a song, you got a song
All God's children got a song
When I get to heaven gwine to sing-a-my song
I'm gwine to sing all over God's heaven!
—Traditional African American Spiritual

The sermon, or more accurately the *preaching*, is the focal point of worship in the Black Church, and all other activities find their place in some subsidiary relationship. In most Black churches, music, or more precisely *singing*, is second only to preaching as the magnet of attraction and the primary vehicle of spiritual transport for the worshiping congregation. In some of the more traditional churches, even the sermon (and often the prayers of the ministers or deacons) are still "sung" in a kind of ritualistic cadence peculiar to the Black Church.[1] The preacher who is particularly skilled at this kind of musical eloquence is usually highly regarded as adept in his profession, and his church is almost certain to be blessed with a large and faithful membership.

In the Black Church, good preaching and good singing are almost invariably the minimum conditions of a successful ministry. Both activities trace their roots back to Africa where music and religion and life itself were all one holistic enterprise. There was no disjunction between the sacred and the secular, and music, whether vocal or instrumental, was an integral aspect of the celebration of life, as indeed was the dance which the music inspired in consequence of its evocation of the human spirit. So it was that music initially assumed a major role in the Black experience in religion as the West African Diaspora sought to adapt to the new forms of spiritual intercourse to which they were eventually introduced in the United States. First of all, music served the important function of convoking the cultus, that is, assembling the faithful to a common place and a common experience of worship. Once this was accomplished, it functioned to transcend or to reduce to insignificance those social, cultural, or economic barriers which separate individuals in their secular interests in order that genuine corporate worship might take place.

Congregational singing is a well-known device for the temporary reduction of social alienation and for the accomplishment of an ad interim sense of community. In the Black Church, singing together is not so much an effort to find, or to establish, a transitory community as it is the reaffirmation of a common bond that, while inviolate, has suffered the pain of separation since the last occasion of physical togetherness. In the words of James Cone: "Black music is unity music. It united the joy and sorrow, the love and the hate, the hope and the despair of Black people.... It shapes and defines Black being and creates cultural structures for Black expression. Black music is unifying because it...affirms that Black being is possible only in a communal context."[2] Undoubtedly this was a significant factor in the failure of Blacks to find meaningful participation in the White churches of the slave era where they could not express themselves or celebrate their sense of community through the communal songs born of a common experience.

Since there was no substantial involvement of the transplanted Africans in American Christianity until the early eighteenth century, there was an interspace of almost one hundred years during which there was no significant, identifiable cult of African spirituality capable of sustaining the body of religious traditions they are presumed to have brought with them. This problem was exacerbated by the deliberate dispersion of Africans speaking the same language and sharing common tribal affiliations as a hedge against conspiracy or insurrection. For the same reasons, the practice of heathen rites, that is, African religion, was generally forbidden in any case, as was the use or possession of drums upon which the celebration of traditional African rituals depended. In spite of such obvious obstacles to the retention and the transmission of the African's cultural heritage in the new context of the

American experience, the evidence that critical elements of that heritage managed to survive and their adaptation in the New World is substantial, especially in religion.[3]

Black singing and the performance practices associated with it is perhaps the most characteristic logo of the African heritage retentive in the Black Church, whether it is the singing of songs or the "singing" of sermons and prayers. A study of Black singing, then, is in essence a study of how Black people "Africanized" Christianity in America as they sought to find meaning in the turn of events that made them involuntary residents in a strange and hostile land.

The first Black church of record was established at Silver Bluff, South Carolina, sometime between 1750 and 1777. However, because of the universal proscription against Black churches and the inconvenience associated with permitting African Americans to attend White churches, the Christian experience was hardly available to Black interest before the revival movement known as the Second Great Awakening, which swept the American frontier between 1780 and 1830. While African Americans gained some introduction to Christian life through the efforts of the Anglican-sponsored Society for the Propagation in Foreign Parts after 1701, the plantation-based services of the S.P.G. missionaries and their successors made only a modest impact upon the captive slave population, which if it heard them at all, heard them without zeal. But it was the spiritual romance of the camp meetings of the Awakening that first stirred the religious imagination of the Black Diaspora, and brought thousands of displaced African Americans and their descendants into meaningful Christian communion for the first time.

The Black Spirituals:
Spontaneous Creation in Preaching and Prayer

In the early days of the Black Church, the spontaneous creation of spirituals during the preaching event was a common feature of Black worship. These spirituals undoubtedly grew out of the preacher's chanted declamation and the intervening congregational responses. Little by little this musical call and response became a song. Having witnessed such an event at a religious meeting of slaves on a Georgia plantation, Ella Clark shared this reminiscence:

> So many wonder about the origin of spirituals.... A large
> number had their origin in the camp meetings and other

41

religious services where emotions were stirred and excitement was at a high pitch. The words and music were spontaneous and extemporaneous, and were in a large measure their own, suggested by some strong sentences in the sermon, or some scripture emphasized and repeated. More often than not the preacher was interrupted in his sermon by a song leader who was moved to answer him in song.[4]

Some spirituals generated from the extemporaneous preaching event may have lasted only for the heightened moment, while others were perpetuated through the oral tradition. Oral transmission meant that spirituals were constantly recomposed and rearranged, so that a single spiritual might eventually have numerous musical and textual variations. This process was complicated by the fact that true to their African counterparts the spirituals were a principal means of transmission of oral history. Hence, they were subject to constant embellishment as the Black experience unfolded against a backdrop of divine succor and leadership.

Like the sermon, prayer was also delivered in a kind of sing-song declamation which evoked musical response from the worshipers. Natalie Curtis Burlin describes in detail a spiritual emanating from an extemporaneous prayer event:

> Minutes passed, long minutes of strange intensity. The mutterings, the ejaculations, grew louder, more dramatic, till suddenly I felt the creative thrill dart through the people like an electric vibration, that same half-audible hum arose—emotion was gathering...then, up from the depths of some "sinner's" remorse and imploring came a pitiful plea...sobbed in musical cadence. From somewhere in the bowed gathering another voice improvised a response...then other voices joined the answer, shaping it into a musical phrase, and so, before our ears, as one might say, from this molten metal of music a new song was smithed out, composed then and there by no one in particular and by everyone in general.[5]

Calculated Composition

There is little documentation regarding the notion that spirituals were the formal compositions of individuals, but the most likely candidate for this recognition is once again the creative Black preacher. Scarcely literate, he did not notate his compositions of course, but probably kept tempering a catchy tune and text until a spiritual song was fashioned. Many ex-slaves confirmed this procedure when recalling that the songs they sang during slavery were taught to them by their preachers. Such evidence has led contemporary researchers to conclude that a substantial number of spirituals were composed by Black preachers specifically for liturgical use.

Eileen Southern located the first general recognition of the spiritual as a distinctive form of Black worship in the camp meetings of the revival movement called the Second Awakening:

> They were singing songs of their own composing, which was even worse in the eyes of the officials. The texts of the composed songs were not lyric poems in the hallowed tradition of Watts, but a stringing together of isolated lines from prayers, the Scriptures, and orthodox hymns [with] the addition of choruses and…refrains between verses.… Nevertheless from such practices emerged a new kind of religious song that became the distinctive badge of the camp meeting movement.…
>
> Song leaders added choruses and refrains to the official hymns.… They introduced new songs with repetitive and catchy tunes. Spontaneous songs were composed on the spot.… The new songs were called "spiritual songs" as distinguished from the hymns and psalms.[6]

Whatever its origin, it seems clear that it was the "Negro Spiritual" which first developed as the signature of serious Black involvement in American Christianity. William B. McClain describes the spirituals as "songs which speak of life and death, suffering and sorrow, love and judgment, grace and love, justice and mercy, redemption and conciliation."[7] The spiritual was the expression of the full range of life experiences garnered by the slave. At Fisk University where the Negro spiritual first gained international acclaim through the performances of the famous Fisk Jubilee Singers in the late nineteenth century, they were described by Professor John Wesley Work as the slave's "sweet consolation and his messages to Heaven, bearing sorrow, pain, joy, prayer and adoration." Comments Work, "The man though a slave, produced the song, and the song in turn produced a better man.… How could a man be base who looked ever to the hills?… The creator of those songs had now become his own creation."[8]

Textual Sources of the Spiritual

Howard Thurman explains that "it was dangerous to let the slave understand that the life and teachings of Jesus meant freedom for the captive and release for those held in economic, social, and political bondage."[9] In consequence, the slaves fashioned most of their spirituals from the Old Testament narratives, which were appealing because of their simplicity and because of God's direct intervention in human affairs in the interest of the oppressed. But in spite of the strongest restrictions against Black literacy, some slave preachers learned to read and introduced themselves and their congregations to the New Testament. A spiritual recorded at a mid-nineteenth century North Carolina revival is evidence:

> A local preacher among them started some well-known hymn
> of which they would sing a line, and then Joe [the preacher]
> would improvise a chorus to which they all kept admirable
> tune and time. A favorite chorus was
> > I want to die in the field of battle
> > > Good Lord when I die;
> > I want to die in the field of de battle
> > > Fighting for the Lord.
> This would [be followed by] a line of "I want to die like Moses
> died," and [then] with Elijah, Daniel, David, and all the Old
> Testament saints, and then Peter and John, Martha and Mary
> would be taken [up], until they were exhausted.[10]

Among the few spirituals which mention Jesus specifically are "Ride on King Jesus," "A Little Talk with Jesus Makes It Right," and "Steal Away to Jesus." These depict Jesus as protector, comforter, friend, redeemer, and refuge rather than as liberator.

Not all spirituals were biblically derived. Several evolved from private moments of "instant religion." This is particularly evident in the sorrow songs, such as "I've Been 'Buked and I've Been Scorned," "Sometimes I Feel Like a Motherless Child," and "Nobody Knows the Trouble I've Seen."

Eschatology in the Spiritual

It is understandable that spirituals were typically other-worldly in theology, for there was nothing in the present world which offered much consolation to the slaves. "When all hope for release in this world seems unrealistic and groundless," explains Howard Thurman, "the heart turns to a way of escape beyond the present order."[11] Paradoxically, though many of the spirituals spoke of "heaven," this eschatological realm was actually anchored firmly in this world, first in their coded meaning, and second in their therapeutic value as survival tools. Regarding the former, James Cone offers this insight:

> Although the Black spirituals had been interpreted as being exclusively other-worldly and compensatory, our research into the testimonies of Black slave narratives and other Black sayings revealed that the theme of heaven in the spirituals and in Black religion generally contained double meanings. "Steal away" referred not only to an eschatological realm, but it was also used by Harriet Tubman as a signal of freedom for slaves who intended to run away with her to the north, or to Canada.[12]

It is likely, then, that to the slave heaven meant both that eschatological realm, *and the North*—whichever happened to have come first; or the latter first and the former later.

On the other hand, through the singing of spirituals the enslaved were able to release their repressed emotions and anxieties and simultaneously experience the exhilaration of being creative under circumstances of unbelievable stress. They sang, hummed, clapped, moaned, stomped, and swayed themselves into a remarkable transcendence over their oppressive condition, and so dredged up the spiritual inspiration needed to endure until God would move to change their circumstances for the better.

The Shout

A stubborn retention of African religious ritual firmly fixed in the transition to Christian forms in America is the "ring shout" or simply "shout." After the regular religious services were over, or on special "praise nights," the benches in the early Black churches or "praise houses" would be pushed back against the wall so that the dancing could begin. The dancers or "shouters," as they were called, would form a circle, and to the cadence of a favorite shout song or "running spiritual" would begin a slow, syncopated shuffling, jerking movement "bumped" by the hand clapping or body slapping of those waiting on the sidelines. The tempo gradually quickened, and during the course of the dance (which might last for seven or eight hours), shouters who became possessed, or who dropped from sheer exhaustion, were immediately replaced by others waiting to take their places. An 1862 account of a shout observed on

St. Helena Island, South Carolina, gives a detailed description of this very popular ritual:

> [W]e went to the "shout," a savage, heathenish dance out in Rina's house. Three men stood and sang, clapping and gesticulating. The others shuffled along on their heels following one another in a circle and occasionally bending the knees in a kind of curtsey. They began slowly, a few going around a[nd] more gradually joining in, the song getting faster and faster til[l] at last only the most marked part of the refrain is sung and the shuffling, stamping and clapping gets furious.[13]

While some firsthand observers went so far as to describe the shouters as "getting the power," or being "filled with the Spirit," others considered the shout to be a remnant of savage idol worship or to be mere "frolic."

Eileen Southern writes with insight about the true meaning of the shout and about the cultural perspectives that obscure its significance:

> While White observers admitted the strange attraction of the shout, they generally disapproved of it, regarding the holy dance as barbaric and even lascivious. Knowing nothing of African traditions, the observers failed to appreciate the two most important elements of the shout: (1) Shouters used dance as a means of communication with God in the same way that song and prayer are used, and (2) shouters reached the highest level of worship when the Holy Spirit entered their bodies and took possession of their souls. *Nowhere in the history of the Black experience in the United States was the clash of cultures—the African versus the European more obvious than in the differing attitudes taken towards ritual dancing and spirit possession.* [Italics supplied.][14]

In traditional African religions, music included dancing; no distinction is made. All forms of music involved bodily movement. For the Africans who converted to evangelical Christianity, the prohibition against dancing had to be respected. Black Christians justified their ring shout by saying that dancing involved crossing one's feet; in shouting the feet did not cross but it involved a slow shuffle step and a swaying bodily movement.[15]

Such cultural differences die hard and they transcend racial boundaries. In the early days of the developing Black Church, A.M.E. Bishop Daniel

Alexander Payne, founder of Wilberforce University, was unrelenting in his denunciation of spirituals, which he called "cornfield ditties," and the ring dance, which he described as "ridiculous and heathenish." Even James Weldon Johnson concluded that shouts were "neither true spirituals nor truly religious." Instead, he considered them "semi-barbaric remnants of primitive African dances" which were at best "quasi-religious."[16] But if these Black critics seemed overly sensitive in their denunciations, perhaps John Work's review of the reasons will be helpful in at least giving perspective to their annoyance. Professor Work writes (whose life's work with the Fisk Jubilee Singers was devoted to the performance of the spirituals): "Naturally enough when the Negro found himself free, he literally put his past behind him. It was his determination that as far as within him lay, not one single reminder of that Black past should mar his future. So away went all those reminders into the abyss of oblivion."[17] Consigned to the "abyss" with the spiritual, the ring dance or the shout has been largely abandoned, except in Black Holiness and Pentecostal sects where forms of the "holy dance" are still continued.[18] The spirituals live on in other forms.

Hymn-Lining Tradition

The tradition of lined hymn singing in the Black Church commenced in the early nineteenth century. Its precursor was the psalm-lining of the Calvinists, which was perpetuated in the American colonies by the Puritans. *The Bay Psalm Book* (1640), the first church music published in America, was their source of texts. In the singing of the psalms, a deacon or preacher intoned a line or couplet which was then sung by the congregation. This responsorial delivery was the answer to the dilemma of pervasive illiteracy among the Puritans, no less than to the lack of hymnbooks.

The publications of Dr. Isaac Watts's *Hymns and Spiritual Songs,* in 1707, initiated the interest in hymnody. Watts's hymns, with their vivid imagery, gradually displaced the pallid, metricized psalmody. Eventually, those slaves permitted to attend church with their masters would acquire the lining technique, and that style of singing gradually became commonplace in their own Baptist and Methodist churches. But as the late Wendell Whalum observed, "The Black Methodists and Baptists endorsed Watts's hymns, but the Baptists 'blackened' them."[19] What Whalum meant was that since Watts's hymns were texts only, the borrowed tunes from Euro-American hymns and folk songs were Africanized by the distinctive mode of Black singing. Some of the tunes may also have been of African origin or, like some spirituals, may have been spontaneous creations of an individual or a congregation of Black worshipers. But regardless of origin, because of the tradition of improvisation during performance, every melody executed in the Black idiom was a new creation each time it was sung.

Although it was most frequently Watts's hymns which were sung in the lined style, an 1862 account of a religious meeting of slaves proves that some original textual creations did evolve extemporaneously: "The prayer over, they all rise and sing, the leader 'deacon' [gives] out one line at a time in his sing-song and at the top of his voice, and the whole congregation sings in the most intensified hard-shell twang they can possibly attain. Frequently, the leader makes up his hymn as he goes along."[20] Since the hymn-liner composed as he proceeded, the lined style was probably responsible for the creation of certain of the hymns we now identify as spirituals.

Meter Music

The lined style of unaccompanied singing is called "meter music" because the hymn texts are constructed in poetic meter. The most frequently used meters in hymnody are *short, common,* and *long.* In the Watts style of singing, the particular meter determines how a hymn is to be lined and what tunes can be used.

Short meter (SM) is a four-line stanza with six syllables in lines one, two, and four, and eight syllables in line three (6.6.8.6.). The deacon or preacher, in this instance, intones a couplet which the congregation echoes in a slow, drawn-out intonation (for example, "Come, Ye That Love the Lord").

Common meter (CM) is literally the most common. It is a four-line stanza with eight syllables in lines one and three, and six syllables in lines two and four (8.6.8.6). Here, also, the leader intones couplets (for example, "Amazing Grace, How Sweet the Sound").

Long meter (LM) should not be confused with the term "long-metered singing," which Blacks use to describe the elongated lined singing style. Long meter is a four-line stanza with eight syllables per line (8.8.8.8.). Here, the leader intones only one line before the congregation takes it up (for example, "Go Preach My Gospel, Saith the Lord").

Post-Bellum Period to the Present

In the post-Emancipation era, the lined singing style of Dr. Watts's hymns became even more prominent in the Black Church. First of all, the educated or progressive class of Blacks disdained the spirituals because they were reminiscent of slavery. And secondly, the spirituals of the "invisible" slave church were antistructural, while worship in the institutional church was very structured. Wyatt Tee Walker provides further explanation regarding the appeal of Watts's hymnody:

> Since the lyrics were from the dominant White culture and slaves were now free, the impulse for imitation was natural and understandable, religiously and otherwise. Given the association that the spirituals had with the slave experience and the quest for expanding the Black people's religious life and expression, the meter music found fertile ground for development and use immediately following the freeing of the slaves.[21]

But this style was also appealing because the metrical quatrains with rhymed line endings made the texts lyrical and easy to remember. And of course, the responsorial pattern of singing was traditional.

Hymn-lining, long discontinued in the White church and in most Black churches as well, is still to be found occasionally in a few Black congregations in the South, particularly in rural areas, and sometimes in storefronts of the lower economic strata in the cities of the North. In some churches of predominately middle-income Baptists, it is practiced in prayer meetings and informal devotional services carried on by the senior adults. In Baptist churches with a preponderance of lower-income members, it is even more prominent and may be the principal mode of congregational singing.

Social Salvation Hymns in the Black Church

Social gospel hymnody reflects the emphasis on the social concerns of the church which evolved during the historic "social gospel movement," which challenged American Christianity from about 1880 to 1930. In contrast to evangelical hymnody, which addresses the redemption and salvation of the individual, this social hymnody stressed the collective life, rebuked the sins of society, and predicated the establishment of the kingdom of God on earth as the fulfillment of God's plan for perfect brotherhood: "The new hymns have been increasingly songs of human brotherhood; of the redemptive social order rather than the salvation of the individual soul; and of the higher patriotism which looks beyond the nation to mankind."[22] These hymns, therefore, were particularly important to Black Christians who were the principal victims of adverse social conditions.

Much of this hymnody, first published in journals of social science, was eventually compiled in special editions. Among them were Mabel Mussey's *Social Hymns of Brotherhood and Aspiration* (1914), and Henry Sloane Coffin and Ambrose W. Vernon's *Hymns of the Kingdom of God* (1926). The poems in these and similar collections gradually penetrated the hymnals of virtually every Protestant denomination, including the mainline Black denominations. The four most recent A.M.E. Church hymnals (1892, 1941, 1954, 1984), for example, symbolize its acceptance in the Black Church in that they show increased emphasis on social themes from one edition to the next. The 1892 volume, *The African Methodist Episcopal Church Hymn and Tune Book*, contains (out of 760 pieces) seven social gospel hymns.

The 1941 *A.M.E. Hymnal,* also known as the *Richard Allen A.M.E. Hymnal,* contains (out of 461 pieces) eighteen social gospel hymns. The 1954 *A.M.E.C. Hymnal* contains (out of 673 pieces) twenty-six social gospel hymns. And the 1984 *A.M.E.C. Bicentennial Hymnal* contains (out of 670 pieces) twenty-five social gospel hymns.[23] While these figures represent only one of the major Black churches, (and one which from its inception has held a strong emphasis on social issues), other Black churches have similar histories of social gospel involvement. The choice of such hymns for congregational singing was vocal and spiritual affirmation of the nascent social theology struggling for expression in the Black Church.

Because there was no social gospel hymnody written by Blacks to accost their specific social circumstances (and there would not be any until the Civil Rights movement), the social hymns of White writers had to suffice. But only some of their hymns were directly relevant to African American social concerns, while most were not.

One social gospel hymn by John Oxenham that became popular among Black Christians was "In Christ There Is No East or West." Set to the melody of a Black spiritual, this hymn opens with a celebration of human fraternity:

> In Christ there is no east or west
> > In Him no south or north,
> But one great fellowship of love
> > Throughout the whole wide earth.

> In Him shall true hearts everywhere
> > Their high communion find;
> His service is the golden cord
> > Close binding all mankind.

These two stanzas anticipate the third which offers a dictum the oppressed needs to have reaffirmed as often as possible: There is not only east or west and no south or north, but of critical importance, there is also no Black or White in the family of God:

> Join hands, then, brothers of the faith,
>   Whate'er your race may be;
> Who serves my Father as a son
>   Is surely kin to me.

In addressing the idea of human oneness in the body of Christ, the hymnist also suggests that there is an equality in Him which ignores the accidents of race:

> In Christ now meet both east and west,
>   In Him meet south and north:
> All Christly souls are one in Him
>   Throughout the whole wide earth.

"America the Beautiful," "My Country 'Tis of Thee," and "The Star Spangled Banner" are nationalistic social gospel hymns frequently sung in Black churches on ceremonial occasions. Heard less often is "God Save America," by William G. Ballantine, even though it speaks of "higher patriotism" which transcends national affinity in a more universal interest.[24]

> God save America! Here may all races
>   Mingle together as children of God,
> Founding an empire on brotherly kindness,
>   Equality in liberty, made of one blood!

This hymnody looks beyond denominationalism to ecumenism, beyond nationalism to universality, and focuses the attention of the worshipers, not only on the salvation of their individual souls, but also on the salvation of their larger collectivity beyond the bounds of race. Hence, it is a development of significance often overlooked in the assessment of the moral maturity of the Black Church.

Gospel Music

According to Eileen Southern, just as the spiritual was a development of the camp meeting phenomenon of the Second Awakening, so did the Protestant City Revival Movement create gospel hymnody, a new song genre

51

"more relevant to the needs of the common people in the rapidly growing cities.... The gospel song evolved in urban settings, in huge temporary tents erected for revival meetings by touring evangelists in football stadiums and mammoth tabernacles."[25] Black gospel quickly distinguished itself from its White counterpart by the body rhythms, the call-and-response patterns, and the improvisations characteristic of African music. Perhaps for these same reasons, gospel music became anathema for more traditionally oriented churches and their leaders and spokesmen. Sociologist Joseph R. Washington, whose strong misgivings about Black folk religion in general were voiced in his well-known book, *Black Religion,* is caustic in his assessment of Black gospel:

> The joy expressed in meetings [ghetto religious services] was sealed within, giving birth to the most degenerate form of Negro religion—gospel music.
>
> Gospel music is the creation of a disengaged people. Shorn from the roots of the folk religion, gospel music has turned the freedom theme in Negro spirituals into licentiousness. Ministers who urge their people to seek their amusement in gospel music and the hoards of singers who profit from it lead the masses down the road of religious frenzy and escapism.[26]

In a later work, *Black Sects and Cults,* Washington comments that gospel music is basically blues and jazz disguised in "spiritual garb," and that "jackleg preachers" go from "rags to riches" by bringing these masqueraded secularisms into sacred worship.[27] Sociologist E. Franklin Frazier is considerably more benign in his assessment. "Gospel songs," Frazier avers, "express the deep religious feelings of the Negro masses who are increasingly exposed to life in the American community."[28] These negative assessments aside, Black gospel music has undergone several developmental phases and it has a pervasive appeal in most Black worship settings.

The Transitional Period of Gospel Music

There is common agreement among students of the phenomenon that distinctive Black gospel music is rooted in the ghetto experiences of African Americans in the large cities of America, and that its development transcends at least three identifiable stages. The first stage has been called the transitional period, or the pre-gospel era. This epoch commenced around 1900 with the gospel hymns of Rev. Charles Albert Tindley, a Black Methodist minister born in Maryland around the beginning of the Civil War. In the Methodist tradition of itinerancy, Tindley preached throughout the area and gained some prominence as a camp meeting preacher and singer. By the turn of the century, he had settled in Philadelphia where he founded the church which now bears the name Tindley Temple United Methodist Church. Tindley's church became famous for its concerts and new music, much of which was written by himself. In 1916, he published *New Songs of Paradise,* a collection intended for informal worship. This early collection included the song that would fifty years later be known around the world as the signature of the Civil Rights movement, "I'll Overcome Someday." These were the first Black gospel songs ever to be published, and they eventually found a place in the music of the Black Church, regardless of denomination. By the beginning of World War II, the collection had gone through seven editions.

Tindley wrote songs incorporating the Black folk imagery which attempted to interpret the oppression African Americans faced as they settled in the cities of the North, an experience not essentially different from that which produced the spirituals. Unlike the spirituals, however, the Tindley gospel songs have few references to the Old Testament characters and events. The Tindley hymns (which are congregational songs), admonish those who suffer the storms of life to stand fast in Christ. They are songs of dependency ("I Will Go if My Father Holds My Hand"), songs of ascendancy ("A Better Home"), songs of hope ("Some Day"), and songs of faith ("I'll Overcome Someday"). But the Tindley songs are not simply other-worldly. They are also addressed to helping the oppressed to survive *this* world.

Nevertheless, Tindley's hymns still tend to have a heavenward polarity. Like the spirituals, they depict heaven as the ultimate triumph over earthly oppression, a utopian realm of relaxation and family reunion. It is not the descendance of the Kingdom of God to earth preached by such social gospelers as A.M.E. Bishop Reverdy Ransom but the ultimate harvest to be reaped once the storms of the life have been successfully weathered.

The Traditional Period: The Golden Age of Gospel

The traditional period, also called the "golden age of gospel," commenced around 1930 with the compositions of Thomas A. Dorsey. Admittedly influenced by Tindley's songs, Dorsey earned the title "The Father of Gospel" due to his tireless promotion of the idiom. An ex-blues musician who first learned his music in the church and later played piano for Ma Rainey, "Georgia Tom" (as he was then known) brought elements of the blues into gospel. His blues-like gospel songs reflect the same eschatology as the Tindley hymns in their quest for the glorious hereafter that lies just beyond our present travail:

> Precious Lord, take my hand,
> Lead me on, Let me stand,
> I am tired, I am weak, I am worn;
> Through the storm, through the night
> Lead me on to the light,
> Take my hand, precious Lord,
> Lead me home.

Other gospel composers and arrangers who helped spread the gospel of "gospel" are Kenneth Morris, Sallie Martin, Roberta Martin, Theodore Frye, Lucie Campbell, and J. H. Brewster. These writers, along with Dorsey, transformed the congregational gospel hymns of Tindley into songs for church choirs, soloists (for example, Mahalia Jackson), and ensembles—sextets (for example, the Dixie Hummingbirds), quintets (for example, the Five Blind Boys of Mississippi), and quartets (for example, the Sensational Nightingales). But it was Dorsey who first called the church songs "gospel songs."

The transition from congregational hymns to songs for specialized soloists and ensembles had important sociological consequences. While the former united worshipers through the collective activity of singing and declaring theological and doctrinal commonalities, the new style required the congregation to assume the role of audience. In essence, worshipers became bystanders who witnessed the preaching and personal testimonies of singers. At best the congregation was to share in those attestations by affirmative "amens," nodding, humming, clapping, swaying, or occasionally by singing along on choruses and vamps. One unexpected consequence was that Black worshipers and concertgoers often became the audience to a new homiletical gospel experience.

The emergence of a gospel circuit of specialized ensembles and talented soloists performing what seemed to some to be blues disguised in spiritual dress inevitably drew fire from some elements of the Black Church. The comments of E. Franklin Frazier are illustrative: "Some of the so-called advanced Negro churches resented these gospel singers and refused to permit them to sing within their churches. They have gradually become more tolerant and let down the bars as the Gospel singers have acquired status and acceptance within the White world."[29] Although this new music was not readily accepted when it first appeared, in retrospect it sounds almost traditional in comparison with contemporary gospel.

Contemporary Gospel Music

The contemporary period in gospel music dates from the late 1960s and early 1970s when the transition from the typical gospel chorus accompanied by a piano and hand clapping performing in a church had been superseded by ensembles featuring strings, brasses, synthesizers, and electronic instruments performing in a concert hall. The other thrust of the contemporary gospel expression is provided by a new generation of performers or presenters who use the gospel medium as a new homiletical instrument. Some representatives of this new genre are Edwin Hawkins, Andre Crouch, Tremaine Hawkins, and such clergypersons as Rev. James Cleveland, Rev. Al Green, and evangelist Shirley Caesar, who literally preach their compositions to their concert hall congregations. This calling to the "gospel ministry" broadens considerably the penetration and the acceptability of gospel as a legitimate and powerful expression of Black religion. Contemporary gospel has also made greater use of communications media like radio, television, records, and film.

Just as the spirituals were taken outside the formal worship context by the Jubilee Singers of Fisk University to be performed throughout the nation and the world, so it was with gospel brought by performers into the concert halls and recording studios of America. The first instance necessitated the concerted arrangements of spirituals which made them more aesthetic than cathartic. The second inevitably required some musical and textual secularization of gospel. In consequence, the musical development of gospel began to sound more like pop music and jazz, and it seemed to be the catchy rhetorical metaphors and phrases, in what was otherwise a sincere, sacred song, which caught the imagination of the audience. This, in essence, was the secularism which Joseph Washington so adamantly denounced, and it is the principal dilemma which continues to disturb conservative clergy and laity in the contemporary Black church.

In spite of the controversy surrounding it, during this period gospel has not only found a place beside concerted spirituals in the otherwise classical repertoire of Black college choirs, but separate gospel choirs also developed and eventually found wide acceptance, although official administrative approval (and funding) were usually delayed and always apprehensive. Today the Black college that does not have a Black mass choir or some other form of gospel enterprise is the exception rather than the rule. Even Black college students who attend White colleges and universities have often established gospel choirs as an affirmation and continuation of their heritage.

Because gospel has been popularized by college ensembles, students are

55

attracted to those churches in the surrounding community which have contemporary gospel choirs, and usually attend services on the Sundays when those choirs perform. As a result, gospel music groupies of part-time college-age churchgoers have evolved. In lieu of a full commitment to the churches they attend is a fervent subscription to the contemporary gospel they have come to identify as belonging to them and to their generation. In our field research, we found that the Black churches that were most successful in attracting young adults also sponsored gospel music programs.

Gospel in Pentecostalism

Gospel music has played a critical role in the development of Pentecostalism, and reciprocally, Pentecostalism has performed an indispensable service in the development and acceptance of contemporary gospel. It is hardly incidental that the Pentecostal bodies are by far the fastest-growing denominations in the Black Church.

> The gospel tradition was influenced by the older styles of the Negro religious music, and here the split of Holiness groups from the orthodox Negro church was an important event, for it was among the Holiness groups that the free expression of religious and musical behavior common to the rural Southern Negro began to assert itself and undergo further development in an urban setting.
>
> While the use of instruments was forbidden in the orthodox Negro church, their introduction by Holiness groups gave the music a "different sound than just hand clapping."[30]

The Church of God in Christ, more than any other single denomination, has pioneered in the creation of contemporary gospel. It produced such performers as the Hawkins Singers, Andre Crouch, and the Clark Sisters, and their influence has been such that every contemporary gospel choir of whatever church is almost inevitably brushed with elements of Pentecostalism through its music and its performance practices. Only in the Holiness-Pentecostal churches is gospel the customary denominational music.

The style of gospel which prevails at any given Pentecostal church depends partly on the age of the singers. The senior adults tend to prefer the transitional and traditional gospel songs of the Tindley and Dorsey eras, and they sing these when they gather for prayer meetings and pre-worship devotional services which are not usually attractive to youth. On the other hand, the young adults prefer contemporary gospel, and it may predominate the main worship service itself. But whatever the period, the singing is almost sure to be rendered in the form of gospel. "The standard hymns that are used are done much differently than they are written in the hymnals, especially in matters of accent, rhythm, and key. Hymnals are used primarily for the words and melodic line. For the most part, hymns are transliterated into a Gospel mode."[31] The development of gospel music illustrates the dynamic and dialectical interaction between religious and secular forms of Black music. Many Black musicians and artists received their initial musical training in Black churches, developed their talent further in concert halls, nightclubs, and juke joints, and their musical style was combined with the words from hymns or newly created sacred songs in the churches.

Shout

The rhythmically accentuated gospel songs performed by the young adult choirs in the Holiness-Pentecostal churches frequently prompt a "shout" (or holy dance), which E. Franklin Frazier identifies as the "chief religious activity of the members of the Holiness cults."[32] The shout is to gospel and its cult what the ringshout was to the spiritual and the slaves, and what spirit possession was to African sacred song. In all of its forms, the basic religious phenomenon is a spiritual possession experience in which the worshiper "gets happy" or is "anointed by the spirit" and praises God in paroxysmal dance. Frazier believed it to be the "maximum of free religious expression on the part of the participants."[33] In shouting, as in the ringshout and the African trance-like dance, there is a kind of culturally restricted choreography which distinguishes it from secular dance. There is also a method of determining whether the shouter is "dancing in the spirit" or "dancing in the flesh." By suddenly halting the gospel shout music, one is able to check for authenticity. If the dancing continues without the music, it is assumed that it is genuine and induced by the Holy Spirit. But if it ceases, apparently it was not so holy after all and was merely rhythmically induced.[34]

Whether shouting is intense religious expression or simply the opiate of an oppressed people, or both, is not to be determined here, for there are logical arguments supporting both the spiritual and scientific premises. What is indisputable, however, is that the shout serves as a testimony to the shouter's felt sense of Spirit Baptism or sanctification. The shouter is, therefore, someone special in the congregation, a "somebody" who possesses that much-approved "good old-time religion." The result, whether intentional or not, is status, respect, and attention in the church, an achievement which may be difficult to attain in society at large.

Concerted Spirituals

Following emancipation, some members of the African American elite refused to sing spirituals in their churches because they reminded people of the degradation of slavery and they were considered too crude for the formal worship exemplified by the White churches that Blacks often sought to emulate. This attitude is best summarized by A.M.E. Bishop Daniel Payne's famous putdown of the spirituals as "cornfield ditties."[35] Acceptance of these songs came only after they were embellished and rendered in the sophisticated idiom of the European anthem. These anthemized spirituals were a novel development in the Black Church, for they constituted the first substantial body of composed Black sacred music not categorized as folk song. They were neither perpetuated through the oral tradition like spirituals, nor were they simply musical sketches of what was to be filled in with improvisation like the early gospel songs. What the arranger notated in the musical language of the European school was that which was to be sung by trained voices.

The creators of spirituals were untrained, of course, and the writers of gospel were generally self-taught. But the composers of the concerted spirituals were generally among Black America's best-trained musicians, educated at the nation's, even the world's, most prestigious universities and conservatories of music. Among this elite coterie was R. Nathaniel Dett (1882–1943). Dett studied at the Oliver Willis Halstead Conservatory of Music in Lockport, New York (1901–1903). He received his Bachelor of Music degree from the Eastman School of Music in 1930. He continued his education intermittently at the American Conservatory of Music, Columbia University, the University of Pennsylvania, Harvard University, the Fontainebleau School in Paris, and in Munich. Like most of his contemporaries, Dett earned a living as a music educator, having taught and directed choirs at Lane College, Lincoln University (Missouri), Bennett College, and Hampton Institute. And like the Fisk Jubilee Singers, Dett's Hampton Choir performed throughout the United States and Europe, bringing worldwide acclaim not only to Hampton and to himself, but to the spiritual. A portion of each concert program was devoted to his musical arrangements, of which "Don't Be Weary, Traveler," "Listen to the Lambs," "Let Us Cheer the Weary Traveler," and "Don't You Weep No More, Mary" were the most familiar.

Dett's credentials and career are representative of numerous Black composers who arranged spirituals for concert performance. Among them are H. T. Burleigh, John Wesley Work, Hall Johnson, Clarence Cameron White, Samuel Coleridge-Taylor, J. Rosamond Johnson, William Dawson, and William Grant Still. Their works were sung by concert soloists like Roland Hayes and Paul Robeson, and by Black college choirs like the Fisk Jubilee Singers and the Hampton Singers. Today, choir directors, perhaps at every Black college and university in the nation, maintain this tradition of arranging and performing spirituals. Among them are Roland Carter at Hampton Institute, Nathan Carter at Morgan State University, Charles Gilchrist at North Carolina Central University, and Robert Leigh Morris at Jackson State University.

The traditional method of arrangement in the anthem style has been to cast the familiar text and tune of a spiritual into a homophonic (occasionally contrapuntal) setting for choir, with or without a featured soloist and piano accompaniment. For Dett this modernization process did not necessarily improve the spiritual,[36] but it did solve the problem of assimilating it into the sophisticated worship services of the elite Black churches:

> It occurred to this writer that if a form of song were evolved which contained all the acceptable characteristics of Negro folk music and yet would compare favorably in poetic senti-ment and musical expression with the best class of church music, it would be a means of solving the peculiar problem, for being created out of native material, it would save to the Negro and his music all the peculiar and precious idioms, and as a work of art would summon to its interpretation the best of his intellectual and emotional efforts.[37]

On the one hand, the African American religious tradition is maintained through the modernization of spirituals; while, on the other, the arranged spiritual ceases to be authentic and actually becomes an anthem. It ceases to be the congregational folk song that the worshipers sing, or to which they can clap, sway, and respond verbally. It becomes a concert piece to be appreciated artistically. Anthemization, then, has replaced one of the remaining African remnants of religious antistructure with even more structure. It has taken much of the spirit out of the spiritual and has replaced the cathartic with the aesthetic. Critics complain that it has made the Black church more like the White church and less like itself.

Spirituals Arranged as Hymns

The most recent hymnals of mainline Black denominations include a selection of spirituals arranged in four-part harmony as standard hymns. Some hymnologists choose to distinguish these from traditional Euro-American hymns by terming them folk hymns. The 1984 *A.M.E.C. Bicentennial Hymnal*, for instance, contains twenty-five folk hymns arranged by such historic Black composers as H. T. Burleigh and John Wesley Work, and such contemporary arrangers as the late Wendell Whalum. Included are old favorites like "Go Tell It on the Mountain," "We Are Climbing Jacob's Ladder," "There Is a Balm in Gilead," and "Swing Low, Sweet Chariot."

While concerted spirituals are performed by skilled senior choirs, hymnic versions are sung congregationally as were the original spirituals. There is a significant variance, however. The original spirituals were executed improvisatorily and had sufficient space for emotional antistructure. Conversely, hymnic arrangements are generally sung in unison and are highly structured. The more restricted structure allows very little spiritual freedom for church members spontaneously getting happy or crying out in a passion of sorrow. Yet, since hymnody is so important in Methodist and Baptist churches of the higher socioeconomic strata, hymnic arrangements are a means of preserving the spiritual in a musical form to complement their more sophisticated taste, while also perpetuating the important element of congregational singing. Furthermore, hymnized spirituals sung congregationally are more cathartic and less aesthetic than the anthemized spirituals performed chorally. Although the formal structure of the hymn tends to preclude emotional antistructure, congregational singing can nevertheless be cathartically therapeutic. In fact, in the elite Black churches where impassioned expression is considered eccentric, singing is the principal mode of emotional release.

Civil Rights Hymnody: Protest Songs of the Civil Rights Era

During the abolitionist movement in America, protest songs evolved at the hands of such White abolitionists as John Greenleaf Whittier, Elizabeth Margaret Chandler, and William Lloyd Garrison. At the request of the American Anti-Slavery Society, Edwin F. Hatfield, a Presbyterian minister, compiled this hymnody into a volume titled *Freedom's Lyre: Or, Psalms, Hymns, and Sacred Songs, for the Slave and His Friends* (1840). In this collection were both authentic abolitionist hymns and adaptations of extant evangelical hymns. Of the latter, key words and phrases were altered in order to superimpose meaning relative to abolition.

It was this liberative theme of abolitionist hymnody synthesized with the language of social gospel hymnody and the dialectical imagery of the Black spirituals which can be summed up as the major constituents of the songs of the new abolitionist or Civil Rights movement. Although all of these were requisite ingredients, it was the abolitionist element of unconditional liberation that supplied the radical edge which rounded out the character of the freedom songs.

Adaptations of Spirituals and Gospels in the Civil Rights Movement

Like the abolitionist hymnody, some freedom songs were composed specifically for the Civil Rights movement, while most were adaptations of extant songs—in this instance, spirituals and gospels. These genre, which typified a heavenward polarity much like Watts's hymns, also required textual modifications in order to assimilate them into the freedom movement. The gospel song, "If You Miss Me from Praying Down Here," for example, was changed to "If You Miss Me from the Back of the Bus." The spiritual "This Little Light of Mine" became "This Little Light of Freedom." And the spiritual "Woke Up This Morning with My Mind on Jesus" became "Woke Up This Morning with My Mind Stayed on Freedom."

The singing of a particular song during a sit-in, protest march, freedom ride, mass meeting, or other protest activities, typically lasted twenty to twenty-five minutes. This necessitated the composition of new verses for the sake of textual variety during these lengthy involvements. Sometimes verses were prepared for a specific protest occasion; other times they evolved extemporaneously from the emotion generated by the occasion.

The anthem of the Civil Rights movement, "We Shall Overcome," is a synthesis of the spiritual "I'll Be Alright" and the C. A. Tindley hymn "I'll Overcome Someday." The melody is that of the spiritual, and the lyric a variation on Tindley's text. A side-by-side comparison of the two stanzas is instructive:

I'll overcome some day	We shall overcome
I'll overcome some day	We shall overcome
I'll overcome some day	We shall overcome someday.
If in my heart I do not yield	If in our hearts we do believe
I'll overcome some day.	We shall overcome someday.

Even though the first person singular personal pronoun "I" was traditionally considered "communal" in Black culture, the creators of civil rights songs always used the first person plural pronouns—"we" and "our." This was a feature of abolitionist hymnody and social gospel hymnody as well, and in each case the collective language of these protest songs was intended to foster a sense of community as the protesters sought to act as one consolidated body.

Not all extant church songs required textual alteration to meet the needs of the protesters. The spiritual "Wade in Water," for instance, was sometimes sung in wade-in demonstrations which aimed to integrate public swimming pools.[38] Spirituals like "Over My Head I See Freedom in the Air" and "Free at Last" could also be interpreted with relevant intent without textual modification. Although freedom from life and freedom from slavery often had synonymous meaning to the enslaved,[39] their original intent became tangential in the new context in which these songs were sung. What is important is that for the freedom fighters the messages had functional meaning related to their quest for civil rights. The songs of the movement also functioned to sustain the emotional intensity of involvement and commitment among its members. So it is that during this era of protest African Americans "returned to the spirituals, not as songs of faith but as sources of spirited support."[40] Without the enormous contributions of civil rights hymnody, the movement would have been rendered drab and lifeless.

Original Freedom Songs

Like abolitionist hymns, not all freedom songs were adapted from extant material. Some were composed by individuals specifically for events at hand. Each community typically had its own talented songwriters and thus its own freedom songs, the verses of which varied according to the mode of protest in that particular community. Atlanta lauded Bayard Rustin, "an old Lion of the Movement," who was closely associated with Martin Luther King, Jr.[41] Stated Rustin, "I was a singer and I wrote songs and they were topical about what was happening, and Abernathy would usually introduce them."[42] Greenwood, Mississippi, had Sam Block whose song, "Freedom Is a Constant Dying," is a personal reflection of the suffering endured during the struggle:

> They say freedom is a constant dying (repeat 3 times)
> O Lord, we died so long
> We must be free.
> We must be free.

In Sam Block's reminder: "O Lord, we died so long/We must be free" is evidence that these militant protest songs veiled in lamentation have much in common with the "sorrow songs." In a sense, they are the neospirituals of the new abolitionists who sought a second emancipation for their people.

Professional Freedom Singers

Given the African American penchant for making and for being entertained by music, it was inevitable that the freedom songs, or some of them, would find professional expression. One very distinctive retention of African Americans from the African experience is the celebration of every phase of life with music, and the thin, wavy line that separates the religious enterprise from any other. For the African, all life was religious, and religion was all of life. And life without music was no life to speak of. In consequence, the disjunctions between the sacred and the secular in music are not always apparent, especially to those who perform it. In the course of the freedom movement, many new songs were composed to address specifically the goals and the interests of the struggle. Other familiar songs were adapted. These original and adapted freedom songs were not only sung congregationally at mass meetings and demonstrations, they were also performed professionally by ensembles like the Nashville Quartet, Guy Carawan and the Freedom Singers, Carlton Reese's Gospel Freedom Choir of the Alabama Christian Movement for Civil Rights, and the Freedom Singers.

Of these groups, the Freedom Singers, an affiliate of the Student Non-violent Coordinating Committee, gained a national reputation:

> The Freedom Singers were the major group responsible for spreading freedom songs over the nation. Their main body of songs came from the Nashville sit-ins, the Albany movement and the songs of the jailed CORE and SNCC freedom riders at Parchman penitentiary, Mississippi....
>
> The group was formed with the aim of raising money and spreading the ideas of SNCC. All the singers were SNCC field secretaries. They did not sing with instruments. They used the same basic equipment—hands, feet, and strong voices—that they used while leading mass meetings in the South.[43]

And

...there has never been a singing movement like this one. Perhaps it is because most of them were brought up on the gospel songs and hymns of the Negro church in the South; perhaps also because they are young; probably most of all because what they are doing inspires song. They have created a new gospel music out of the old, made up of songs adapted or written in jail or on the picket line. Every battle station in the Deep South now has its Freedom Chorus, and the mass meetings there end with everyone standing, led by the youngsters of SNCC, linking arms, and singing.[44]

The Music of the Freedom Movement

The lyric religion of the freedom songs was a principal stimulus in the sustained efforts of the Civil Rights movement to achieve social change through nonviolent protest. As one student of the movement observed: "When police clubs, snarling dogs and hoses start to attack the line of march, praying to one's self gives some courage, but when hundreds sing their hopes together the songs provide the shield and identification necessary to withstand even the fury of the hostile mob."[45] Having been at the forefront of countless freedom marches and mass meetings, Martin Luther King, Jr., confirmed the power and the indispensability of music in the struggle:

An important part of the mass meetings was the freedom songs. In a sense the freedom songs are the soul of the movement. They are more than just incantations of clever phrases designed to invigorate a campaign; they are as old as the history of the Negro in America. They are adaptations of the songs the slaves sang—the sorrow songs, the shouts for joy, the battle hymns, and the anthems of our movement. I have heard people talk of the beat and rhythm. "Woke Up This Morning with My Mind Stayed on Freedom" is a sentence that needs no music to make its points. We sing these freedom songs today for the same reason the slaves sang them, because we too are in bondage and the songs add hope to our determination that "we shall overcome."[46]

While King's statement emphasizes the importance of the texts of the freedom songs, psychologist Carl Seashore offers an instructive comment on the critical part that rhythm played in the protest songs: "Rhythm gives us a feeling of power; it carries…. The pattern once grasped, there is an assurance of ability to cope with the future. This results in…a motor attitude, or a projection of the self in action; for rhythm is never rhythm unless one feels that he himself is acting it, or, what may seem contradictory, that he is even carried by his own action."[47] Hence, when King says, "These songs bind us together, give us courage together, help us to march together," he is perhaps unconsciously including in his assessment a tribute to Seashore's dictum that rhythm "carries."

The songs of the Civil Rights era were the first openly armigerous or militant music to come out of the Black Church. The spirituals, while based upon freedom themes, were not extrinsically militant; they were "songs of protest, in acceptable and thinly veiled form against the conditions of life."[48] Abolitionist hymnody, though composed under the aegis of religion on behalf of the slaves, was basically the work of White abolitionists; and social gospel hymnody, a White Protestant entity, decried the sins of society but remained only tangential to the critical issues of African American social concern. The blues lamented the social, political, and economic oppression common to the Black experience, but they were outside the legitimate periphery of the Black Church. And of all these genre, it is paradoxical that gospel is the most Christocentric and yet the least radical.

The freedom songs did not passively lament the Black condition; they made God active in human history day by day with social agitation. African Americans were not just singing about freedom, they were systematically seeking it, and their songs were deliberate instruments tactically utilized in the effort. Freedom songs chronicle the historic events of the various forms of protest, personal reflections, testimonials, and religious responses to the oppressive forces opposing the struggle for freedom. As the spirituals provide an authentic window for religion in the life of the slave, so do the freedom songs offer a documentary on what the lives of Black people were like in America one hundred years after slavery had ended.

Types of Music in the Contemporary Black Church

Charles Wesley wrote more than seven thousand hymns, setting the musical tone for the Protestant Church in America for generations. Today, fewer than one hundred are used in the Black Church. James Cone explains that a major reason for the decline of Wesleyan hymnody is that in European hymnody in general the textual focus is seldom on liberation. Freedom has always been an intimate concern of the Black Church, and in its pilgrimage toward that goal, the much-used songs of Charles Wesley seemed increasingly inexpressive of the urgencies felt by Black people. "White Christianity may refer to liberation in limited times and places, as shown by abolitionists, the social gospel preachers, and the recent appearance of liberation theologians in Europe and North America, but liberation is not and never has been the dominant theme in White church songs, prayers, and sermons."[49] In the chronology of A.M.E. Church hymnals of 1892, 1941, 1954, and 1984, there is a steady decrease in the number of Wesley hymns, from 210 (out of 760 hymns) in the 1892 volume to forty-six (out of 670) in the 1984 volume. Of the forty-six Wesley hymns in the 1984 A.M.E. Church *Bicentennial Hymnal,* only two, "Come, Thou Long-Expected Jesus" and Try Us, O God," could be considered thematically significant to Black worshippers. And in *Songs of Zion,* a 1981 "songbook from the Black religious tradition" sponsored by the United Methodist Church, of 285 offerings only two were from Charles Wesley, and one of those, "Father, I Stretch My Hands to Thee," was in the special category of "response." By contrast, *Songs of Zion* lists ninety-eight songs as "Negro Spirituals and African American liberation songs."[50]

It has been said of Wesley that "one of the most characteristic features of his hymns is the way in which, no matter with what earthly subject they begin, they end in heaven."[51] And even those based on social themes are never in danger of becoming earthbound."[52] However, despite the elements of lethargy that linger from the early days of its development when the open appreciation for freedom was tantamount to insurrection, on the whole the Black Church has both revered Charles Wesley and transcended him. Certainly the theology implicit in his hymns does not express the full range of Black Church interests for today, nor do they address with sufficient candor and specificity the critical issues of African American existence in a world where God is expected to identify himself with the oppressors of the earth *in this world.* "Singing," says W.B. McClain in *Songs of Zion,* "is as close to worship as breathing is to life" and life in the contemporary Black church is earth-oriented though heaven-bound.

Wattsian Hymnody

On the whole, Isaac Watts's hymns have been more successful in the Black Church than Charles Wesley's. Again using the chronology of A.M.E. hymnals of 1892, 1941, 1954, and 1984 as a barometer, while the 1892 hymnal has (out of 461 hymns) forty-six by Watts, the 1984 hymnal retains thirty-six (out of 670).

The imagery in Watts's hymns has always found favor with the African American worshiper. They were the principal hymns sung in the lined tradition during the antebellum and post-bellum eras, such that lined singing was commonly known as the "Dr. Watts style." During the "golden age of gospel," ensembles like the Clara Ward Singers performed the Watts hymns in a gospel idiom alongside the gospel songs of Thomas Dorsey and J. H. Brewster. Currently many of the Watts hymns are traditional in the Black Church:

> O God, our help in ages past,
> Our hope for years to come,
> Our shelter from the stormy blast,
> And our eternal home.

Compared to the hymns of Wesley and other evangelicals, Watts's hymns more often seem to have particular signification for contemporary African American worshipers, but like the former, they also tend to have a heavenward bent which is generally pronounced in the closing stanza. Often commencing with a social theme, Watts's hymns almost predictably take a Calvinistic excursus toward heaven (much like the sermon climaxes of the Black folk preacher). Consequently, the Old Testament theology of God as liberator of the oppressed is severely dampened by the centrality of praise for the Sovereign Lord.

Social Gospel Hymnody

Although social gospel hymnody is a White Protestant entity, social hymns like "Onward Christian Soldiers" and "In Christ There Is No East or West" are more relevant to African American liberation than evangelical hymnody. In spite of their empiricism, however, social gospel hymns have failed to displace, not only the Watts and Wesley hymns, but also the old favorites of James Montgomery ("Angels from the Realms of Glory"), John Newton ("Amazing Grace"), William Cowper ("There Is a Fountain Filled with Blood"), and Fanny J. Crosby ("Jesus Is Tenderly Calling You Home").

This preference for the evangelical is not necessarily a reaffirmation of the other-worldly focus that has been considered traditional to the Black Church. It is in part attributable to the deep cisterns of spirituality with which the Black Diaspora have been endowed by African traditional religions. Second, it is a result of attachment to the favorite old tunes and texts whose familiarity gives consolation to those who must constantly endure disconsolation. Again, change does not come readily to religion in any case, for religion is the prime custodian of what tradition has sanctified. The newer hymns of the social gospel have not prevailed against these odds, however unseemingly the paradox, for they come closer to the liberation theology of the freedom songs than any other music in the Black Church.

The Hymn-Lining Tradition

The lined tradition has been partially maintained in the contemporary Black Methodist churches. In the A.M.E. Church, for example, the congregational chanting of the Lord's Prayer (immediately following the sermon) is lined-out by the minister, but usually in a spoken rather than sing-song declamation. Further, when introducing the morning hymn, the A.M.E. minister reads a stanza or two, and then advises the congregation that they are to stand and sing with the choir. By the initial lining, deference is paid to tradition when that feature was a necessary modus vivendi because of the generalized illiteracy among church members and the lack of hymnals.

In the early Black Baptist and Methodist "word hymnals," the meter indications (SM, CM, LM) enabled the song leader to select short, common, and long meter tunes (maintained by the oral tradition) to match the meter of the poetry. Although modern hymnals have texts and tunes already suited, the meters are provided to allow their interchanging. Some of the more sophisticated hymnals go so far as to include a metric index which facilitates commutation. This would enable a pastor to introduce to a congregation a new or more theologically suitable common meter hymn paired with a well-known common meter tune. While this technique is rarely used in the Black Church, by maintaining the familiar the minister is likely to be more successful in introducing the unfamiliar. The Black Methodists have transformed the lined tradition into something creative and functional in the methodic mode of worship, but, history is indebted to the Baptist churches for keeping alive this authentic tradition which is nearly two centuries old in the Black Church.

Gospel Music

While gospel music has been generally accepted by most Black churches, there are still some prominent segments within elite Black Baptist and Methodist churches and among some traditionalists who customarily express annoyance with, or outright rejection of gospel music, both in terms of its often problematic theology and because of its alleged secularity. The problem begins with the fact that gospel choirs often select their repertoires based on what is popular on the radio or television, despite the fact that not all gospel packaged commercially is ideal for worship. Because commercialization presupposes secularization, it is inevitable that many metaphors and musical embellishments acceptable for secular performance are considered unacceptable in a worship setting. Another problem is that gospel songwriters compose their songs based on their personal theology, or without consideration of theological implications rather than with any official theological canon in mind. Generally speaking, the theology of contemporary gospel may be loosely classified as continuing in the evangelical tradition of Tindley and Dorsey; hence, there can be a musical retreat from what is happening in the Black community rather than a response to it. Finally, there is probably a denominational bias against gospel in some churches because of its strong Pentecostal identification. This is a problem of increasing significance for both the Black Church and American Christianity in general, Catholic as well as Protestant, as the contemporary charismatic movement presses hard against conventional concepts in the characterization of religion in America. We turn next to some sociological data on the Black Church and music.

Sociological Data on the Black Church and Music

In our survey of 2,150 Black churches nationwide, we found that the vast majority of churches had at least two or more choirs. Table 38 indicates that only 436 (20.3 percent) churches had only one choir.

Table 38
Church Music: Number of Choirs in Black Churches

Number	Total	Urban	Rural
One	436 (20.3%)	265 (17.4%)	171 (27.7%)
Two	514 (23.9%)	319 (20.8%)	195 (31.5%)
Three	428 (19.9%)	312 (20.4%)	116 (18.7%)
Four	291 (13.5%)	245 (16.0%)	46 (7.4%)
Five	209 (9.7%)	167 (10.9%)	42 (6.8%)
More than 5	132 (6.2%)	111 (7.2%)	21 (3.4%)
No response	140 (6.5%)	112 (7.3%)	28 (4.5%)
Total N =	2,150		
Urban N =		1,531	
Rural N =			619

Average number of choirs per church = 2.89 or 3 choirs

The average number of choirs for the total sample was 2.89 (or three) choirs per church. This average number gives an indication of how important music and singing are in Black churches. Even poor Black churches with very few material resources invested what little they had in their musical program. In our previous findings regarding paid church staff members in Black churches, musicians (choir directors, pianists, and organists) ranked first, ahead of church secretaries and custodians. The results in table 38 also point to a slight urban-rural difference in the number of choirs supported by the churches. The majority of the rural churches, 366 (59.2 percent), had only one or two choirs, while the majority of the urban churches, 835 (54.5 percent), had three or more choirs. Obviously, Black urban churches have a larger population base to draw on.

In attempting to assess the changing scene of music in the Black church, the survey also asked pastors what types of music are approved for use in the church. Table 39 shows that the vast majority of Black churches 2,084 (96.9 percent) approved of the use of some form of gospel music (the survey did not distinguish between the types of gospel music given in the historical overview above), and only 33 (1.5 percent) did not approve. Spirituals were also approved by the majority of respondents, 2,002 (93.1 percent), with a slight urban-rural difference: 1,486 (97.1 percent) urban churches approved of spirituals, while only 516 (83.4 percent) of rural churches did so.

Table 39
Church Music: Type of Music Approved for Use in Worship Services

Number	Total	Urban	Rural
I. Gospel Music?			
Yes	2,084 (96.9%)	1,489 (97.3%)	595 (96.2%)
No	33 (1.5%)	21 (1.4%)	12 (1.9%)
No response	33 (1.5%)	21 (1.4%)	12 (1.9%)
II. Spirituals?			
Yes	2,002 (93.1%)	1,486 (97.1%)	516 (83.4%)
No	114 (5.3%)	24 (1.6%)	90 (14.5%)
No response	34 (1.6%)	21 (1.4%)	13 (2.1%)

Number	Total	Urban	Rural
III. Other Black Music (e.g., jazz, blues, etc.)?			
Yes	448 (20.8%)	408 (26.6%)	40 (6.5%)
No	1,595 (74.2%)	1,030 (67.3%)	565 (91.2%)
No response	107 (5.0%)	93 (6.1%)	14 (2.3%)
Total N =	2,150		
Urban N =		1,531	
Rural N =			619

The greatest ambivalence was shown toward other types of Black music like jazz and blues, for use in Black churches. Only 448 (20.8 percent) said they approved of the use of jazz and blues in church settings, while 1,595 (74.2 percent) said no, they disapproved. There is a significant urban-rural difference in the attitudes of pastors toward the use of other Black music in church: 408 (26.6 percent) of the urban pastors said that they approved of using other Black music and only forty (6.5 percent) of the rural pastors approved. The Black clergy of urban churches were far more willing to experiment with other types of Black music for use in worship than the rural clergy. In some of the non-Pentecostal urban churches we visited, the pastors were willing to allow the use of musical instruments other than the piano and organ, like drums, trumpets, saxophones, and clarinets. For example, a Baptist pastor in Newport News, Virginia, who was a trained professional musician, taught youngsters in his church how to use different musical instruments during the week; a full set of drums was placed next to the piano in his church's sanctuary.

The whole musical scene in the Black church is a fluid, dynamic, and constantly changing one. Before he died, Duke Ellington composed many pieces of jazz-based sacred music that could be played in worship settings. Just as the introduction of a blues rhythm and style in the synthetic product called gospel music caused enormous controversy among Black church members, the introduction of more jazz into worship settings will also stir the pot. For example, W. C. Handy's father, an A.M.E. pastor, once viewed his son's work as the "devil's music." However, with the passage of time gospel music has received near universal acceptance in most quarters of the Black Church, as our data above has indicated. Among those who are on the cutting edge of musical experimentation in the Black Church is Rev. Wyatt Tee Walker of the Canaan Baptist Church in Harlem. With his keen sense for dramatic presentation, Walker's congregation meets in a converted theater. The gospel choirs at Canaan are accompanied by instrumental groups and sometimes appropriate modern dance segments are incorporated into the worship setting. Walker has also written a book that relates Black church music to social change.[53] The Word is performed not only in his sermons, but in the musical program of the church.

Conclusion

As some commentators have observed, the contributions of African Americans to the musical heritage of the United States have been enormous, often constituting the original and primary innovations in music from spirituals and gospel to blues, ragtime, jazz, rock and roll, soul, and rap; the core of American music has derived from Black culture.[54] Walker has extended that insight by arguing that Black religious music has been "the primary root of all music born in the United States."[55] However, in spite of the importance of the topic of music in the life of the Black church, very little attention has been paid to it by the scholars of religion and there have been even fewer empirical studies.[56] We have attempted to fill the gap by providing a broad survey of the development of music in the Black Church and by examining some of the new trends in musical experimentation. As we pointed out at the beginning of this chapter, the music performed in Black Churches is a major way of attracting members and sustaining their spiritual growth. Just as we can speak about the charisma of the preacher, that ineffable quality or gift that draws and attracts people, there can also be the charisma of music in the form of a choir, choir director, soloist, or musical program. Our field research has shown that among Black young people, teenagers, and young adults, gospel music programs constitute the major drawing card.

Music in the Black Church is a dynamic phenomenon, always subject to the tension between religious traditions and customs and the musical styles of the day. However, the boundary line between sacred and secular Black music is often a thin one. We have pointed out that one of the trends of music in Black churches is to find appropriate ways of incorporating musical styles like jazz and blues and even modern dance into worship settings. In our last chapter, we turn to other trends that will probably affect Black churches in the twenty-first century.

1 For an analysis and examples of the sung sermon, see the fine study by Gerald L. Davis, *I Got the Word in me and I can sing it, you know: A Study of the Performed African-American Sermon*. The title of our chapter, "The Performed Word," borrows from Davis's view of performance in the sermon and extends it to the musical ministry of the Black Church. The Word is performed and made alive not only in the preaching but also in the music.

2 James H. Cone, *The Spirituals and the Blues*, p. 5.

3 Of. Miles Mark Fisher, *Negro Slave Songs in the United States;* Mitchell, *Black Preaching;* and Southern, *The Music of Black Americans.*

4 Ella Anderson Clark, "The Reminiscences of Ella Anderson Clark," MS, pp. 41–42, James Osgood Andrew Clark Papers.

5 Natalie Curtis-Burlin, "Negro Music at Birth," *The Musical Quarterly 5* (October 1919): 88.

6 Southern, *The Music of Black Americans* (second edition), p. 85.

7 William B. McClain, "The Liturgy of Zion" (Unpublished manuscript).

8 John Wesley Work, *Folk Songs of the American Negro*, pp. 110–120.

9. Howard Thurman, *Deep River and the Negro Spiritual Speaks of Life and Death*, p. 21.

10 William Grove Matton, "Memoirs 1859–1887," MS, chapter 6, p. 2.

11 Thurman, *Deep River*, p. 29.

12 James H. Cone, *For My People: Black Theology and the Black Church*, p. 63.

13 Laura M. Townes, Diary, MS, April 28, 1862 entry, Penn School Papers.

14 Southern, *The Music of Black Americans*, pp. 170–171.

15 See LeRoi Jones's explanation of this shout phenomenon among converted slaves in *Blues People*.

16 James Weldon Johnson and J. Rosamond Johnson, editors, *The Book of American Negro Spirituals*, p. cc.

17 Work, *Folk Songs*.

18 One example of a modified "ringshout" is found in the offertory ritual of Daddy Grace's United House of Prayer for All Peoples. With Bishop Daddy Grace William McCullough sitting on his elevated throne, the congregation formed a large circle, and to the accompaniment of a brass band, members shuffled forward swaying from side to side and dropped their offering in collection plates at the front. As a form of offertory musical chairs, people who ran out of money sat down, while others continued. Unpublished field study of Daddy Grace's United House of Prayer for All People by Lawrence H. Mamiya (Union Theological Seminary, 1967).

19 Wendell P. Whalum, "Black Hymnody," *Review and Expositor 70*, no. 3 (Summer 1973): 347.

20 Simeon A. Evans to Mother, MS, August 21, 1862.

21 Wyatt Tee Walker, *"Somebody's Calling My Name": Black Sacred Music and Social Change*, p. 84.

22 Henry Wilder Foote, *Three Centuries of American Hymnody,* p. 307.

23 Compiled by Jon Spencer, editor, *Journal of Black Sacred Music* (1988).

24 Foote, *Three Centuries,* p. 307.

25 Southern, *The Music of Black Americans,* p. 402.

26 Joseph R. Washington, Jr., *Black Religion,* pp. 51–52.

27 Joseph R. Washington, Jr., *Black Sects and Cults,* p. 78.

28 Frazier, *The Negro Church in America,* p. 89.

29 Ibid., p. 78.

30 George Robinson Ricks, *Some Aspects of the Religious Music of the United States Negro,* pp. 131, 132.

31 Paris, *Black Pentacostalism,* p. 57.

32 Frazier, *The Negro Church in America,* p. 61.

33 Ibid., p. 59.

34 William T. Dargan, "Congregational Gospel Songs in a Black Holiness Church: A Musical and Textual Analysis," p. 63.

35 Walker, *A Rock in a Weary Land,* pp. 22–24.

36 R. Nathaniel Dett, "Negro Idioms in Motets and Anthems," Program Notes.

37 R. Nathaniel Dett, "Development of Negro Religious Music," in *Negro Music,* p. 5.

38 Mancel Warrick, et al., *The Progress of Gospel Music: From Spirituals to Contemporary Gospel,* p. 56.

39 Thurman, *Deep River,* p. 32.

40 Washington, *Black Religion,* p. 207.

41 Howell Raines, *My Soul Is Rested: Movement Days in the Deep South Remembered,* p. 52.

42 John Dunson, *Freedom in the Air: Movement of Songs of the Sixties,* pp. 66–67.

43 Ibid., p. 64.

44 Howard Zinn, *SNCC: The New Abolitionists,* p. 4.

45 Dunson, *Freedom in the Air,* pp. 66–67.

46 Martin Luther King, Jr., *Why We Can't Wait,* p. 61.

47 Carl E. Seashore, *Psychology of Music,* p. 162.

48 Washington, *Black Religion,* p. 207.

49. James H. Cone, "Black History: The Black Church's Role, Theology, and Worship seen in an Historical and Theological Interpretation," visiting lecture, Duke University (January 11, 1981).

50 J. Jefferson, Cleveland and Verolza Nix, editors, *Songs of Zion.*

51 Frank Baker, *Charles Wesley's Verse,* pp. 15–16.

52 J. Ellsworth Kalas, *Our First Song: Evangelism in the Hymns of Charles Wesley,* p. 33.

53 Walker, *"Somebody's Calling My Name": Black Sacred Music and Social Change.*

54 Ibid., p. 15. Also see the following: Levine, *Black Culture and Black Consciousness;* and Southern, *The Music of Black Americans.*

55 Walker, *"Somebody's Calling My Name": Black Sacred Music and Social Change.*

56 To his credit, James Cone saw the importance of black music as a major resource for Black liberation theology in his book, *The Spirituals and the Blues.* However, many of the classic historical and sociological studies of Black churches by G. Carter Woodson, Benjamin Mays, and Joseph Nicholson, St. Clair Drake and Horace Cayton, E. Franklin Frazier, and Gayraud Wilmore have neglected this vital area.

The Use and Performance of Hymnody, Spirituals, and Gospels in the Black Church

by Portia K. Maultsby[1]
from *The Papers of The Hymn Society,* published in 1983

Introduction

Since the seventeenth century, Black Americans have participated in two culturally distinct religious traditions. The first tradition represents that associated with White Protestant denominations. The second was independently developed by Blacks, utilizing the concepts and practices retained from their West African heritage. These two traditions are easily distinguished by ideology, worship style, and musical practices. The musical repertoire of Black congregations that adhered to White Protestant doctrines is derived from official hymnals which include psalms, hymns, and spiritual songs. Conversely, the repertoire of churches, whose religious ideology is uniquely Black, consists of Black folk spirituals and gospels. Songs of these two idioms are derived from several sources: 1) West African musical traditions; 2) Black secular idioms; 3) original Black compositions; and 4) White Protestant psalms, hymns, and spiritual songs.[2]

The music, which characterizes autonomous Black congregations, differs in function and performance style from that of Black congregations that adhere to the doctrines of the White Protestant church. Music performed by the former group constitutes an integral and intrinsic part of the liturgy. The manner in which this music is performed is based on the aesthetic principles and social norms that have evolved from West African cultures. Whereas spirituals and gospels are the dominant musical forms found in autonomous Black churches, White Protestant hymns, especially those of Isaac Watts and the Wesley brothers, continue to be mainstays of the repertoire even today. When performed, however, these songs either conform to the dictates of Western European traditions or congregations may choose to modify them in accordance with African American aesthetic principles.

The use and performance of music in the Black church will be explored in this discussion through an examination of 1) the events that led to the conversion of Blacks to Christianity, 2) the formation of independent Black religious groups, and 3) the social and cultural milieu which fostered the development of a unique Black religious music.

The Conversion of Slaves to Christianity During the Seventeenth and Eighteenth Centuries

During the seventeenth century, before slavery became a dominant institution in the United States, northern Blacks were exposed to most aspects of White culture. They generally lived in the homes of their masters and worked beside them in farms, in stores, and in the kitchen. The exposure of these slaves to Christianity was the moral responsibility of the families with whom they lived. For this reason, the clergy expressed constant concern about the recreational activities of slaves.[3] They interpreted these African-derived activities as contrary to the teachings of Christianity. The Reverend Morgan Godwin in 1680 expressed his disapproval:

> …nothing is more barbarous, and contrary to Christianity, than their…*Idolatrous Dances,* and *Revels;* in which they usually spend the *Sunday.*… And here, that I may not be thought too rashly to impute *Idolatry* to their *Dances,* my Conjecture is raised upon this ground…for that they use their Dances *as means to procure Rain:* Some of them having been known to beg this Liberty upon the Week Days, in order thereunto.[4]

Puritans and clergymen of the New England colonies believed that a knowledge of Christian concepts would encourage slaves to reject these so-called "sinful" activities and instead participate in religious activities. In an attempt to create satisfactory alternatives, slaveholders were encouraged or required by law to provide servants and slaves with religious instruction.[5]

Conversion to Christianity required a familiarity with the music repertoire sung during religious activities. Therefore, psalm and hymn singing was included in the religious instruction given to Blacks. The English practice of "lining-out, where…each line was read or intoned by the minister or some other person before it was sung by the congregation," was used to teach these songs to Blacks.[6] With a knowledge of psalms and hymns, Blacks were able to become active participants in a variety of religious activities at church and in the home of their masters.[7] The singing of psalms and/or hymns was included in exclusively Black religious assemblies. In one instance, a group of slaves living in Boston in 1693 agreed to always sing a psalm between two prayers during their Sunday worship.[8] By the end of the eighteenth century, many Blacks were widely respected for their knowledge of psalm and hymn singing, and some could be found serving as singing-school masters for all White participants in northern colonies.[9]

Whether attending White churches or conducting their own services, Blacks were expected to sing songs from the established repertoire of Protestant hymnody according to the prescribed musical norm. For this reason, northern Blacks were unable to develop a distinct body of religious music prior to the founding of independent Black churches.

In contrast to the system of slavery in the North, many slaves in southern colonies lived on large farms and plantations that were located some distance from the master's house. The master and his family, therefore, had little if any influence on the religious education of these slaves.[10] The first surveys of religious conditions among slaves in the United States was initiated by the Bishop of London in 1724. The responses from southern missionaries indicated that cultural differences, misunderstandings, language barriers, and resistance of slaveholders interfered with proselytizing efforts.[11] During the latter part of the eighteenth century, these efforts were intensified by Presbyterian and Methodist evangelists of the Great Awakening Movement. Camp meetings, stemming from this Movement, attracted a sizeable number of Blacks including slaves and freedmen. The emotional nature and informal structure of these meetings allowed Blacks to respond in a manner that was less restrictive than that tolerated by missionaries of the Anglican clergy. Furthermore, these services bore some resemblance to practices Blacks had retained from West African cultures. In spite of the appeal of these camp meetings among Blacks, the numbers converted to Christianity in the eighteenth century were very small in proportion to the thousands who were totally unaffected.[12]

The system of slavery in southern colonies prevented slaveholders and other Whites from defining the cultural frame of reference for slaves. Because slaves were isolated from mainstream society and had limited contact with Whites, they were able to establish their own values, customs, and musical tradition. Missionaries constantly complained about the "barbaric" cultural practices of slaves and sought to impose their own values by converting them to Christianity. Evangelists of the eighteenth century emphasized the importance of music in their proselytizing efforts upon discovering that "slaves preferred the musical activities of the religious experience above all else."[13] The Reverend Samuel Davies, who recognized the value of music to potential Black converts, commented:

> I cannot but observe that the *Negroes,* above all the Human
> Species, that I ever knew, have an Ear for Musick, and a kind
> of extatic [sic] Delight in *Psalmody;* and there are no books
> they learn so soon or take so much Pleasure in, as those used
> in that heavenly Part of divine Worship.[14]

The success of Davies, a Presbyterian, in attracting slaves to his services, encourage the Anglican clergy to place a greater emphasis on music. In 1768, William Knox observed: "The Negroes in general have an ear for musick [sic], and might without much trouble be taught to sing hymns, which would be the pleasantest way of instructing them, and bringing them speedily to offer praise of God."[15]

Toward the end of the eighteenth century, missionaries conceded that slaves were not willing to abandon their African world-view and musical practices for Christianity. They then were forced to modify their strict interpretation of religious doctrines and incorporate musical practices of slaves when providing religious instruction or conducting services. Bishop Porteus of London, in 1784, even recommended that the clergy compose new songs in the musical tradition of slaves:

> Many of the Negroes have a natural turn for music, and are
> frequently heard to sing in their rude and artless way at their
> work. This propensity might be improved to the purpose of
> devotion...by composing short hymns...set to plain, easy,
> solemn psalm tunes, as nearly resembling their own simple
> melody as possible.... These might be used not only in church,
> but when their task was finished in the field, and on other joy-
> ous occasions. This would make them see Christianity in a
> much more pleasing light than they generally do...and would
> be found probably a much more effectual way of fixing their
> attention...than any other that can be devised.[16]

The Bishop also encouraged the insertion of religious elements in the recreational activities of slaves by providing "the help of a little sacred melody adapted to the peculiar taste and turn of the Africans." Bishop Porteus and other members of the clergy adopted the philosophy that religious songs with an African flavor would increase the church attendance of slaves, prevent them from participating in "heathenish Sunday recreations," and provide them with an "instrument of moral and religious improvement" in the home.[17]

Despite this philosophy, slaves continued to define their priorities according to their *own* sense of values and customs. Charles Ball, a slave, summed up the response of slaves to Christianity:

> There is, in general, very little sense of religious obligation, or duty, amongst the slaves on the cotton plantations; and Christianity cannot be, with propriety, called the religion of these people.
>
> On Sunday afternoon we had a meeting...sang and prayed; but a great many of the people went...in search of fruits.[18]

Even though slaves were taught the psalms and hymns of Isaac Watts and other composers, missionaries eventually came to realize that slaves would not give up their own musical repertoire for that of Christian churches. The musical compromises made by missionaries paved the path for the evolution of a distinct African American religious musical tradition beginning in the latter part of the eighteenth century.

The Nineteenth Century Revival Movement and the Musical Tradition of Slaves

The nineteenth century Revival Movement proved effective in converting slaves as well as southern Whites to Christianity. By the 1830s, the majority of southern Whites had become Christians themselves. As a result, the earlier resistance and indifference slaveholders expressed toward providing religious instruction for slaves also diminished.[19] With the widespread approval of slaveholders, evangelists intensified their efforts to convert slaves by attracting them to camp meeting revivals.[20]

Descriptions of these meetings reveal practices similar to those of African rituals. Observers noted that loud emotional cries and groans could be heard throughout the service. In addition, men and women were known to leap out of their seats, scream, jerk, shout, fall into convulsions, speak in tongues, and engage in a holy dance.[21] Music played an important role in creating an emotional atmosphere during camp meetings. The hymns and spiritual songs, which were an integral part of services, were sung in a manner that resembled the musical practices of slaves. Many songs were performed in a call-response format, while others adhered to the verse-chorus structure. These practices enabled the congregation to join in on a familiar chorus or repetitive lines.[22]

Slaves responded to these familiar performance trends by participating with "exhubrance [sic] and excitement." Many nineteenth century accounts of singing at camp meetings give special attention to the singing that came from the Black side of the tent. As two observers noted:

> Their shouts and singing were so very boisterous that the singing of the White congregation was often completely drowned in the echoes and reverberations of the Colored people's tumultuous strains.[23]

> At every service, the Negroes were present in large numbers in a special section reserved for them, and many of them made professions of religion. Their singing was inspiring and was encouraged and enjoyed by the White congregation, who would sometimes remain silent and listen.[24]

At the end of a camp meeting service, Blacks continued to sing throughout the night after returning to their segregated tents. One witness noticed that Blacks seldom went to sleep when services lasted past midnight; instead they would sing hymns until half-past five in the morning.[25]

John Watson, a Methodist minister, criticized these unsupervised activities. He was particularly critical of the original songs Blacks sang:

> Here ought to be considered too, a most exceptional error, which has the tolerance at least of the rulers of our camp meetings. In the *Blacks'* quarter, the Colored people get together, and sing for hours together, short scraps of disjoined affirmations, pledges, lengthened out with repetition *choruses.*

> We have too, a growing evil, in the practice of singing in our places of public and society worship, merry airs, adapted from old *songs,* to hymns of our composing: often miserable as poetry, and senseless as matter, and most frequently composed and first sung by the illiterate *Blacks* of the society.[26]

Watson also expressed his disapproval of the negative influence that Blacks had on the musical practices of Whites:

> …the example has already visibly affected the religious manners of some Whites. From this cause, I have known in some camp meetings, from 50 to 60 people crowd into one tent, after the public devotions had closed, and there continue the whole night, singing tune after tune, scarce one of which were in our hymnbooks.[27]

The comments of Watson and the observations of his contemporaries provided evidence for the existence of a unique Black religious music tradition in the nineteenth century. It appears that Blacks, when under the supervision of Whites, generally adopted those customs that met the expectations of those in charge. However, away from Whites, and in their own quarters, Blacks adhered to familiar customs of African cultures. The spontaneous singing and other unpredictable practices that characterized camp meeting services served to reinforce traditional customs of slaves. These newly developed practices were merged with those of West African traditions to provide the foundation for the establishment of a Black religion and a corresponding Black religious musical tradition.

The Establishment of a Black Church and a Black Musical Tradition

The Revival meetings held by nineteenth century evangelists produced a steady increase of Blacks who became Christians. Their numbers grew in such proportions that existing religious facilities and clergy could no longer adequately service the Black community. In towns, Blacks generally would attend services with Whites, but their increased membership made it necessary for the clergy to conduct special afternoon or evening services. Churches in rural areas often were too small to accommodate large groups of slaves. Some slaveholders provided for their religious worship by building special "praise houses" on the plantation. The insufficient number of clergy to conduct weekly services for slaves led to the systematic training of Black preachers beginning in the late eighteenth century.[28]

Black spirituals evolved in southern plantation "praise houses" and in northern independent Black churches, where religious meetings were conducted by slaves and freedmen. "The foundation for its style was established by slave preachers, whose chanted sermons and improvised songs motivated sung responses from the congregation."[29] These preachers, when unsupervised by Whites, established musical trends, structured their services, and interpreted Biblical passages from the cultural perspective of their Black congregations. Practices associated with African rituals were fused with those of Christian origin to represent the world-view of Blacks in the United States.[30] This fusion led to the development of a Black style of preaching which emphasized congregational participation. Elements that characterize this dramatic and intense style of Black preachers include: 1) the use of vocal inflections, which produced a type of musical tone or chant, and facilitated the dramatic and climactic style of preaching; 2) the use of repetition for highlighting phrases of text; 3) the use of rhythmic devices for stress and pacing; and 4) the use of call-response structures to stimulate "spontaneous" congregational responses.[31]

The chanted prayers and sermons of Black preachers together with spontaneous verbal, physical, and musical responses from the congregation did not meet the approval of missionaries.[32] The Reverend Robert Mallard, son-in-law of missionary Charles Colcock Jones, expressed his displeasure after witnessing a service conducted by Blacks in Chattanooga in 1859:

> I stood at the door and looked in—and such confusion of sights and sounds!... Some were standing, others sitting, others moving from one seat to another, several exhorting along the aisles. The whole congregation kept up one loud monotonous strain, interrupted by various sounds: groans and screams and clapping of hands. One woman specially under the influence of the excitement went across the church in a quick succession of leaps: now down on her knees...then up again; now with her arms about some brother or sister, and again tossing them wildly in the air and clapping her hands together and accompanying the whole by a series of short, sharp shrieks.... Considering the mere excitement manifested in these disorderly ways, I could but ask: What religion is there in this?[33]

The organized, yet flexible structure of Black religious services accommodated a variety of individual and group forms of religious expression. Freedom of religious expression has always been a cultural value that is not merely tolerated but highly respected among Blacks. Those who criticized this practice failed to understand that Black religious trends, including the use of music, were rooted in an African cultural tradition, and therefore differed both philosophically and ideologically from religious practices associated with Protestantism, Judaism, and Catholicism. These differences were observed by a visitor from the British Isles, who stated that:

> ...the Negro of our southern States prefers going to a church or meeting composed of peoples of his own color, and where no Whites appear. Slaves, also, sometimes prefer places of worship where greater latitude is allowed for noisy excitement...than would be tolerated in the religious assemblies of White people.[34]

These cultural and philosophical differences, together with discriminatory practices, were major factors in the establishment of independent Black churches in the North.

In 1787, in response to direct acts of discrimination in Philadelphia's St. George's Methodist Episcopal Church, Blacks withdrew their membership. They later founded two Black churches in 1794. One of these churches, Bethel African Methodist Episcopal Church, became the model for other independent Black churches founded in the nineteenth century. Bethel's founder and minister, Richard Allen, was successful in gaining full control of his church in 1816 when he won a legal battle that severed all ties with the affiliate White church, St. George's. This victory influenced similar developments in other cities and contributed to the formalization of a Black religious ideology in the North.[35]

Richard Allen chose to establish a form of worship based on the aesthetic and cultural reference of his Black congregation. Allen modified the Methodist worship style to accommodate his congregation and, in doing so, his services took on the character of those conducted by slave preachers on southern farms and plantations. Allen also reshaped the musical tradition of the Methodists. In addressing his congregation on the inadequacy of Methodist and other denominational hymnbooks, he stated: "Having become a distinct and separate body of people, there is no collection of hymns we could with propriety adopt."[36] Allen solved this problem by publishing a hymnal. *A Collection of Spiritual Songs and Hymns Selected from Various Authors by Richard Allen, African Minister,* "for the exclusive use of his congregation" in 1801.[37]

This hymnal contains fifty-four hymn texts, including those of Isaac Watts, the Wesleys, and other hymns popular among the Methodists and Baptists. In the second edition, also printed in 1801, Allen added ten hymns including some of his own compositions. This edition differed from the standard hymnal in that Allen made textual changes in some of the original fifty-four hymns. He replaced complex words and phrases with simpler ones so that the songs "would have more meaning for the illiterate worshippers" in his congregation.[38] He also added repetitive refrain lines and choruses to the orthodox hymns. This new text, easily memorized by members who could not read, was sung after each verse. By making these textual changes, Allen insured the complete participation of all church members in the worship.[39]

Further evidence that the singing in Allen's church was governed by the aesthetic principles and musical norms of the Black musical tradition is provided in the following description by Paul Svinin, a Russian visitor, who visited Allen's congregation in 1811:

> ...at the end of every psalm, the entire congregation, men and women alike, sang verses in a loud, shrill monotone. This lasted about an hour. When the preacher ceased reading, all turned toward the door, fell on their knees, bowed their heads to the ground and set up an agonizing, heartrending moaning. Afterwards, the minister resumed the reading of the Psalter and when he had finished, sat down on a chair; then all rose and began chanting psalms in chorus, the men and women alternating, a procedure which lasted some twenty minutes.[40]

These musical practices observed by Svinin were condemned by the White Methodist clergy, who objected to the changes made in orthodox hymns, as well as to the use of original songs and the unique singing style, none of which conformed to the Euro-American aesthetic of reverence and refinement. Allen's innovations set a precedent for musical practices that became commonplace in other Black Methodist churches.

Whereas some northern Black ministers modified the structure of traditional Protestant services to meet the special cultural and religious needs of their congregations, others elected to structure their worship around the doctrines, literature, and musical practices of White denominations. One of the first major conflicts that divided the membership of independent Black churches was musical practices. Daniel A. Payne, who later became a bishop in the African Methodist Episcopal Church, campaigned to change the style of worship that characterized this church. Influenced by his training at a Lutheran seminary and his tenure as pastor in a Presbyterian church, Payne addressed the problem of the A.M.E. Church in the following manner:

> The time is at hand when the minister of the A.M.E. Church
> must drive out this heathenish mode of worship or drive out
> all the intelligence, refinement, and practical Christians....[41]

Payne opposed the singing of spirituals, which he referred to as "cornfield ditties." He also objected to the hand clapping, foot stomping, and "voodoo dances" that generally accompanied the spirituals. Payne was committed to teaching and preaching "the right, fit, and proper way of serving God."[42]

Bishop Payne made his first "improvement" in the service of Black Methodists by replacing the practice of "lining-out"—a holdover from the seventeenth century English music tradition—with choral singing and instrumental music. These changes were instituted in Philadelphia (1841–1842) and in Baltimore (1848–1849). Many members responded to these so-called "improvements" by complaining: "You have brought the devil into the Church, and therefore we will go out." According to Payne, "when choirs were introduced in the church, many went out of Bethel, and never returned."[43]

The adoption of choral singing in many northern Methodist churches resulted in withdrawals and splits throughout the United States. In spite of controversy regarding his innovations, Payne approved of the sweeping changes he had made:

> The moral and religious effects of choral singing have been
> good, especially when the whole or a majority of the choir
> were earnest Christians. I have witnessed spiritual effects
> produced by Bethel choir in Philadelphia, and by Bethel choir
> in Baltimore, equal to the most unctuous sermons from the
> lips of the most eloquent and earnest preachers, so that
> Christians did rejoice as though they were listening to the
> heavenly choir which the shepherds heard on the plains of
> Bethlehem announcing the advent of the Savior.
>
> In a musical direction, what progress has been made
> within the last forty years! There is not a church of ours in any
> of the great cities of the republic that can afford to buy an
> instrument which is without one; and there are but few towns
> or villages where our Connection exists that are without an
> instrument to accompany the choir....[44]

Bishop Payne's ideology regarding the "proper way of serving God" was shared by Black ministers of independent Presbyterian and Episcopal churches. These churches exercised strict control over the order of worship, and over the actual training of ministers as well. Black ministers in these denominations:

> ...were not permitted to expound the Scriptures, or to exhort, in words of their own; to use extemporary prayer, and to utter at such times, whatever nonsense and profanity might happen to come into their minds....
>
> When the Colored class leaders in the Protestant Episcopal Church were allowed to meet for religious exercises, they were accustomed to use *no other worship than* the regular course prescribed in the Book of Common Prayer for the day. Hymns or psalms out of the same book were sung, and a printed sermon read.... No extemporary address, exhortation, or prayer, was permitted, or used....[45]

The first African Episcopal Church of St. Thomas, founded in Philadelphia in 1794 by Absalom Jones, adhered to the established doctrines of the Episcopal Church. It was Jones's decision to "abide by traditional practices even if it meant some personal sacrifice, for the sake of psychological equanimity and denominational support."[46] Unlike the church founded by Richard Allen, St. Thomas did not permit spontaneous verbal, physical, or musical responses. Absalom Jones along with Bishop Payne rejected the notion of a Black religious ideology and aligned their churches with the White denominational counterpart.

Although Jones and Payne established a precedent for musical practices in northern independent Black churches, some congregations refused to accept their ideology. In 1850, for example, Fredrika Bremer visited an African Methodist church in Cincinnati and gave this account of the musical practices she witnessed:

> I found in the African Church African ardor and African life. The church was full to overflowing, and the congregation sang their own hymns. The singing ascended and poured forth like a melodious torrent, and the heads, feet, and elbows of the congregation moved all in unison with it, amid evident enchantment and delight in the singing, which was in itself exquisitely pure and full of melodious life.[47]

This description of Black singing styles provides evidence of cultural practices that were retained in many African Methodist churches even after Payne had instituted his radical changes. The ideology espoused by Richard Allen and southern Black slave preachers had a greater impact on the musical tradition of pre-twentieth century Black religious groups than did those of Bishop Payne and Absalom Jones. In fact, only a small percentage of Blacks were committed to the philosophy of Payne and Jones. The majority of Blacks attended churches where services reflected *their* religious practices, *their* daily experiences, and *their* musical traditions.

The spiritual tradition[48] that evolved in autonomous Black churches has been described by various missionaries, European visitors, and American observers as "wild hymns," "barbaric songs," and "nonsensical chants." These accounts support the theory that the Black spiritual tradition differed radically from that of White Protestant hymnody. Descriptions of Black singing practices also expose the use of a different aesthetic criteria for musical performances. Many observers interpreted Black spirituals as "strange" and "weird" strains of disjointed and meaningless texts which were not sung but "yelled," "hooted," and "screamed."[49]

These inaccurate and biased descriptions demonstrate the need for extreme caution when imposing western European musical forms and aesthetics upon musical traditions having a non-European cultural base. Black spirituals are grounded in a West African aesthetic which defies characterization and qualitative assessment from a purely European frame of reference. The use and performance style of Black spirituals, therefore, can be described accurately and only from an African American cultural and musical perspective. The musical norms and aesthetics that govern the singing of Black Americans are representative of a cultural value that places emphasis on free expression and group participation. In view of this perspective, Black spirituals were almost always accompanied by gestures, dance, and verbal interjections, and represented an intrinsic part of the religious service.

Primary features which distinguish the Black spiritual tradition are: 1) the call-response structure; 2) extensive melodic ornamentation (slides, slurs, bends, moans, shouts, wails, grunts, etc.); 3) complex rhythmic structures; and 4) the integration of song and dance. Each of these elements is rooted in the principle of improvisation. The prevalence of the call-response structure facilitates both individual expression and congregational participation. The soloist, who presents the call, is free to improvise at will, while the congregation provides a stable repetitive response.

The use of melodic ornamentation in the Black spiritual enables singers to employ a number of vocal techniques that add variety and intensity to performances. This intensity is increased by the layering of rhythmic hand clapping and foot stomping patterns which results in complex rhythmic structures. These rhythmic structures provide the basis for gestures and religious dance movement.

Spontaneous gestures and dance movements, which accompany singing, dictate other rules for performance. Often the length and tempo of a spiritual, for example, is determined by the degree to which a congregation becomes emotionally and physically involved in the singing. The integration of song and dance was recorded by both Black and White observers. The following description was provided by a former slave, who preached for Black congregations during the 1830s:

> The singing was accompanied by a certain ecstasy of motion, clapping of hands, tossing of heads, which would continue without cessation about half an hour; one would lead off in a kind of recitative style, others joining in the chorus.[50]

The use of improvisation in Black song and dance accommodates the personal, spontaneous, and creative approach to musical performance.

The norms and aesthetics established by Blacks for musical performances were also applied to songs from White Protestant traditions. Frequently, these songs were transformed beyond recognition into a Black spiritual. An English musician, who toured the United States from 1833 to 1841, witnessed this transformation process while visiting a Black church in Vicksburg, Virginia:

> When the minister gave out his own version of the Psalm, the choir commenced singing so rapidly that the original tune absolutely ceased to exist—in fact, the fine old psalm tune became thoroughly transformed into a kind of Negro melody; and so sudden was the transformation, by accelerating the time, that, for a moment, I fancied that not only the choir but the little congregation intended to get up a dance as part of the service.[51]

A similar situation was observed by Frederick Law Olmsted in 1853 who heard a hymn changed into a "confused wild kind of chant."[52] Elizabeth Kilham, a school teacher in the South, expressed the widely held viewpoint that "Watts and Newton would never recognize their productions through the transformations they have undergone at the hands of their Colored admirers."[53]

The musical norms and aesthetic principles that govern the use and performance of Black spirituals are fundamental to worship in autonomous Black congregations. The establishment of a Black worship style and a Black musical tradition demonstrates that Black Americans historically resisted the concepts, norms, and aesthetic principles of religious and musical traditions that conflicted with their own cultural viewpoints. Independent Black congregations had the freedom to engage in a form of worship that reflected their own cultural perspectives and musical tradition which emerged out of an African rather than an Euro-American heritage. The worship style and corresponding musical tradition established by Black congregations in the eighteenth century were retained and expanded upon in the twentieth century Black church.

Music in the Twentieth Century Black Church

Following the emancipation of slaves in 1865, the plantation system was replaced by segregated communities throughout the United States. This new social environment continued to keep Blacks isolated from mainstream society. Within the confines of the segregated community, Blacks relied on their own established cultural norms as a basis for self-identification, social interaction, and group solidarity.[54] Because these cultural values were most freely expressed in the Black church, this institution soon became the focal point of the Black community. The religious traditions practiced by Blacks in earlier centuries provided the foundation for worship styles and musical practices used in the twentieth century Black church.

The music found in the earliest autonomous Black church at the turn of the century consisted of spirituals and lined-out hymns. The addition of tambourines, drums, piano, horns, and later guitar and Hammond organ to the traditional accompaniment of hand clapping and foot stomping led to the emergence of an original body of Black religious music known as gospel. Even though the first gospel songs were derived from spirituals, the use of instruments as an integral part of gospel singing distinguishes the two religious musical traditions.[55]

Gospel music, in its developing stages, was performed only in the Black "folk church." This church, associated with Holiness, Pentecostal, and Sanctified sects, is distinguished from independent and mainline denominations such as Methodist, Baptists,[56] Presbyterian, Episcopalian, and Lutheran churches by its ideology and worship style. Whereas Black mainline churches evolved from their White Protestant counterparts, Black "folk churches" were created when dissatisfied members of these and other churches sought their independence. The official doctrine of the Black "folk church" encouraged free expression which unveiled itself in spontaneous testimonies, prayers, and musical expression. In evaluating the distinctiveness of the musical tradition in this church, Pearl Williams-Jones, gospel music scholar and performer, draws these conclusions:

> The traditional liturgical forms of plainchant, chorales, and anthems do not fulfill the needs of traditional Black folk religious worship and ritual. They are unrelated and inappropriate as vehicles for folk-style religious worship services because liturgical musical forms do not represent the dominant cultural values of the Black community. These values encompass the whole gamut of Black expressiveness— which is relevant to the ritual of Black folk-style worship— singing and preaching, linguistics, testifying and praying. They are unique, personal, and highly valued within the community for their aesthetic values.[57]

Members of holiness groups were not allowed to interact with those belonging to non-holiness churches due to theological differences. Therefore, gospel, the music which characterized these groups, was not heard by the majority of Black Americans until Black Methodist and Baptist songwriters introduced gospel compositions in their individual churches.[58] The first attempt to capture the urban Black experience through religious song was made by Methodist minister, Charles Albert Tindley, who wrote his first songs between 1900 and 1906. These hymn-styled songs incorporated melodic and rhythmic principles of gospel singing from the Black "folk church." Under Tindley's influence, Thomas Dorsey, a Baptist, developed an original gospel style that was distinctively different from the tradition of hymnody. Dorsey's blues-based melodies and harmonies, combined with his ragtime, boogie-woogie piano style, captured an urban religious spirit that gave rise to a tradition of composed Black gospel songs.[59]

Because gospel music expressed the essence of contemporary Black culture, it has moved beyond the boundaries of the Holiness-Pentecostal churches into many mainline Black churches, ranging from Baptist to Catholic parishes. Mellonee Burnim sums up the importance of gospel music in present day Black religion by stating, "In the same way that the Negro spiritual was fundamental to the religion of the Black slave, so is gospel music the backbone of contemporary Black religion."[60]

The use and performance of gospel varies within the Black church. In Holiness-Pentecostal churches, gospel is an intrinsic part of the worship and is sung by both the choir and congregation. Pre-1950s gospel styles, known as traditional gospel, dominate congregational singing, while choirs more frequently incorporate stylistic trends from commercial or contemporary repertoire. In independent and mainline churches, gospel is sung in conjunction with songs from the official hymnbook. Gospel selections are sung by a gospel choir at prescribed places in the worship. Hymns, which frequently are accompanied by gospel harmonies and rhythms on the piano and organ, form the basic repertoire for congregational singing in these churches.[61]

In all Black churches, gospel music is sung according to the musical norms and aesthetics that defined the spiritual tradition. Just as improvisation is fundamental to the performance of Black spirituals, it serves as the basis for interpreting the skeletal outline of melodies, harmonies, rhythms, texts, and accompaniment found in the printed score of Black gospel music. Renditions of gospel songs, therefore, may vary considerably from the music notation, and the performers rarely sing a song the same way twice. Even though gospel songs are interpreted differently by various performers, the musical vocabulary, technical devices, and performance practices that represent a Black musical aesthetic dictate the fundamental style that characterizes gospel singing. Research recently conducted by Burnim[62] on the gospel tradition reveals that there are three primary areas of significance in gospel music performance: 1) quality of sound; 2) style of delivery; and 3) mechanics of delivery. Quality of sound is determined by the manipulation of elements of timbre, range, and shading which contribute to the overall tonal "complexity sought for and desired in this tradition." Such manipulations result in 1) sudden changes in timbre which extend from lyrical to raspy and percussive; 2) extreme and often sudden dynamic and tonal contrast; 3) the use of the falsetto voice; and 4) the juxtaposition of different vocal and instrumental textures.[63]

The style of delivery in gospel music greatly mirrors Black cultural customs and behavior. The performer is expected to communicate through both musical and physical means. This prescribed mode of presentation demands that performers demonstrate their total involvement by utilizing the entire body—head, hands, and feet. The importance of song and movement in Black culture is further seen in the synchronized movements displayed by gospel choirs when they "march" into the church during a processional and when they "step," clap, and "shout" to the music performed during the worship.[64]

The quality of sound and style of delivery contribute to the intensity of a gospel performance. This intensity, however, is controlled by the mechanics used for delivery. Through the use of a variety of technical and improvisatory devices, performers are able to manipulate time, text, and pitch. Time, according to Burnim, includes rhythmic aspects as well as structural elements of the performance. Rhythmic structures often are expanded from the simple to the complex by "gradually adding layers of hand claps, instrumental accompaniment, and/or solo voices." Likewise, the length of gospel song can be expanded by repeating phrases and entire sections of a song and by adding a vocal or instrumental cadenza at the end of a song. In such cases, the intensity builds because each repetition brings more rhythmic activity as well as textual and melodic variations.[65]

The manipulation of pitch results from melodic improvisation. Performers of gospel music employ a variety of technical devices to change or expand the melody including: repetition and the extensive use of melismas, shouts, slides, slurs, moans, grunts, etc.[66] A successful performance of gospel music is dependent on a performer's ability to manipulate time, text, and pitch while adhering to cultural concepts that identify a Black musical tradition. These three basic components, operating in conjunction with one another, are

> ...subject to constant interpretation and reinterpretation by individual performers. Through cultural immersion, one learns how to determine which structural, rhythmic, textual, and melodic units are potentially expandable, then demonstrates the knowledge in his or her own personal way during performance.[67]

The use and performance of gospel and spirituals in the Black church were determined by the cultural values established and adhered to by Black Americans. These values, derived from West African cultures, serve to dictate the musical norms and aesthetic principles that characterize the Black musical tradition. This tradition differs from non-Black musical traditions because the conceptual framework that governs musical performances emphasizes freedom of expression and group participation. The use and performance of Black music, therefore, are determined by these two factors.

Conclusion

Although performances of gospel and spirituals employ musical styles and other features found in non-Black musical traditions, they are used in a way that reflects the musical criteria and meets the cultural expectations of Black Americans. Musical performance in the Black church incorporates a variety of techniques that mirror Black cultural values and accommodate Black cultural customs and behavior. This conceptual approach to music-making gave rise to a body of religious music that differed in style and presentation from other religious musical traditions. Black spirituals and gospel music are unique components of the African American religious tradition; their incorporation into the Black worship service represents one of the overriding features which distinguish the Black church from all others.

---

1 Dr. Maultsby is Associate Professor of African American Studies and staff member of the African American Arts Institute at Indiana University, Bloomington. An earlier version of this article appeared in *Jahrbuch Für Liturgik und Hymnologie* (1983). This present version appeared in *The Western Journal of Black Studies* (Vol. 7, No. 3, 1983) and is reprinted with permission of the editors.

2 Eileen Southern, ed., *Readings in Black American Music* (New York: W. W. Norton, 1971), p. 110; Dena Epstein, *Sinful Tunes and Spirituals* (Urbana, IL: University Illinois Press, 1977), pp. 217–237, 276–278; Jeanette R. Murphy, "The Survival of African Music in America" in *The Negro and His Folklore,* ed. Bruce Jackson (Austin, TX: University of Texas Press, 1967), pp. 327–329; Elizabeth Kilham. "Sketches in Color: IV," in *Jackson,* pp. 120–133; and Pavel P. Svinin, *Picturesque United States of America!* 1811, 1812, 1813, ed. Avrahm Yarmolinsky (New York: William Edwin Rudge Inc., 1930), p. 30.

3 Winthrop Jordan, *White Over Black* (Chapel Hill: The University of North Carolina Press, 1968), p. 66; Leon F. Litwack, *North of Slavery* (Chicago: The University of Chicago Press, 1961), pp. 4–6; and Epstein, *Sinful Tunes,* p. 101.

4 Morgan Godwin, *The Negro's & Indians Advocate, Suing for Their Admission into the Church: or a Persuasive to the Instructing and Baptizing of the Negro's [sic] and Indians in our Plantations...*(London: Printed by F.C., 1680), p. 33.

5 Eileen Southern, *The Music of Black Americans* (New York: W. W. Norton, 1971), pp. 35–37, 60.

6 Epstein, *Sinful Tunes,* p. 202.

7 Southern, *The Music of Black Americans,* pp. 33–42.

8 Robert Stevenson, *Protestant Church Music in America* (New York: W. W. Norton, 1970), p. 93.

9 Stevenson; and Southern, *The Music of Black Americans*, pp. 79–81.

10 Eugene D. Genovese, *Roll, Jordan, Roll: The World the Slaves Made* (New York: Pantheon Books, 1974), pp. 7–25; Kenneth Stampp, *The Peculiar Institution* (New York: A. A. Knopf, 1956), pp. 30–41; and John Blassingame, *The Slave Community* (New York: Oxford University Press, 1972), pp. 154, 172–177.

11 William Stevens Perry, ed., *Historical Collections Relating to the American Colonial Church*, Vol. 1 (Virginia: n.p., 1870), pp. 267, 278, 283.

12 Epstein, *Sinful Tunes*, pp. 104–109.

13 Southern, *The Music of Black Americans*, p. 58.

14 Quoted in Benjamin Fawcett, *A Compassionate Address to the Christian Negroes in Virginia, and Other British Colonies in North America, with an Appendix Containing Some Accounts of the Rise and Progress of Christianity Among the Poor People*, 2nd ed. (London: Slop., 1755), p. 37.

15 William Know, *Three Tracts Respecting the Conversation and Instruction of the Free Indians and Negro Slaves in the Colonies. Addressed to the Venerable Society for Propagation of the Gospel in Foreign Parts* (London: n.p., 1768), p. 39.

16 Quoted in Epstein, *Sinful Tunes*, p. 108.

17 Epstein, pp. 108, 109.

18 Charles Ball, *Slavery in the United States: A Narrative of the Life and Adventures of Charles Ball, a Black Man, Who Lived Forty Years in Maryland, South Carolina and Georgia, as a Slave...*(New York: J. S. Taylor, 1837), pp. 201–203.

19 Epstein, *Sinful Tunes*, pp. 111, 195.

20 Southern, ed., *Readings in Black American Music*, p. 104; William Henry Foote, *Sketches of North Carolina, Historical and Biographical...*(New York: R. Carter, 1846), pp. 391–392, 402–404.

21 Stampp, *The Peculiar Institution*, p. 376; and Southern, *Readings*, pp. 113–115.

22 Gilbert Chase, *America's Music from the Pilgrims to the Present*, 2nd ed., rev (New York: McGraw-Hill, 1966), pp. 208–231.

23 Southern, *The Music of Black Americans*, p. 95.

24 John Dixon Long, *Pictures of Slavery in Church and State*, 3rd ed. (Philadelphia: Author, 1857), pp. 159–160.

25 Southern, *Readings*, p. 106.

26 Ibid., pp. 62–63.

27 Ibid., p. 64.

28 Epstein, *Sinful Tunes*, pp. 196–197, 200–201, 229–230.

29 Portia K. Maultsby, "Afro-American Religious Music: A Study in Musical Diversity," *The Papers of The Hymn Society of America* XXXV: 8.

30 Southern, *Readings in Black American Music*, pp. 113–115; Long, *Pictures of Slavery*, p. 383; and Mary Boykin Chesnut, *A Diary from Dixie*, ed. Ben Ames Williams (Boston, MA: Houghton Mifflin, 1949), pp. 148–149.

31 Maultsby, "Afro-American Religious Music," p. 7.

32 Long, *Pictures of Slavery*, pp. 383–384; and Epstein, *Sinful Tunes*, pp. 202–207.

33 Robert Manson Myers, ed., *The Children of Pride; A True Story of Georgia and the Civil War* (New Haven, CT: Yale University Press. 1972), pp. 482–483.

34 Robert Baird, *Religion in the United States of America. Or an Account of the Evangelical Churches in the United States* (Glasgow: Blackie and Son, 1844), p. 77.

35 Portia K. Maultsby, "Music of Northern Independent Black Churches During Antebellum Period," *Ethnomusicology* XIX: 407–411.

36 Allen, quoted in Charles Wesley, *Richard Allen Apostle of Freedom* (Washington, DC: The Associated Publishers, Inc., 1939), p. 167.

37 Southern, *The Music of Black Americans*, p. 85.

38 Southern, Ibid., p. 89.

39 Southern, *Readings*, pp. 52–61.

40 Svinin, *Picturesque United States*, p. 20.

41 Quoted in Miles Fisher, *Negro Slave Songs in the United States* (Ithaca, NY: Cornell University Press, 1953), p. 190.

42 Southern, *Readings*, pp. 69–70.

43 Ibid., p. 65.

44 Ibid., pp. 68, 66.

45 *Practical Considerations Founded on the Scriptures, Relative to the Slave Population of South Carolina...By a South-Carolinian* (Charleston, SC: Printed by A. E. Miller, 1823), pp. 33–36.

46 Wesley, *Richard Allen*, pp. 73–79; and Cf. Carol George, *Segregated Sabbaths* (New York: Oxford University Press, 1973), pp. 62–63.

47 Southern, *Readings*, pp. 112–113.

48 Black spirituals exist in many forms and styles. Those that evolved in autonomous Black churches are known as folk spirituals. This spiritual form was later transformed into Europeanized choral songs by college choirs of southern Black institutions beginning in the 1870s.

49 Epstein, *Sinful Tunes*, pp. 130, 220, 228, 230; and Charles Colcock Jones, *The Religious Instruction of the Negroes in the United States* (Savannah, GA: T. Purse, 1842), p. 266.

50 James L. Smith, *Autobiography...including, also, Reminiscences of Slave Life, Recollections of the War, Education of Freedmen, Causes of the Exodus, etc.* (Norwich: Press of the Bulletin, 1881), pp. 163–164.

51 Henry Russell, *Cheer! Boys, Cheer!: Memories of Men and Music* (London: J. Macqueen, 1895), pp. 84–85.

52 Frederick Law Olmsted, *A Journey in the Seaboard Slave States in the Years 1853–1854, with Remarks on Their Economy...*(New York: G. P. Putnam's, 1904. Originally published in 1856), pp. 26–29.

53 Kilham, "Sketches in Color…," pp. 123–130.

54 For historical information about the status of Blacks after the Civil War, see Franklin E. Frazier, *The Negro in the United States* (New York: The Macmillan Co., 1949), pp. 171–272; Lawrence Levine, *Black Culture and Black Consciousness* (New York: Oxford University Press, 1977); and C. Vann Woodard, *The Strange Career of Jim Crow,* 2nd rev. ed. (New York: Oxford University Press, 1966), pp. 11–65.

55 Pearl Williams-Jones, "Afro-American Gospel Music: A Crystallization of the Black Aesthetic," *Ethnomusicology* XIX: 374, 381, 383; and Mellonee Burnim, "The Black Gospel Music Tradition: Symbol of Ethnicity," thesis, Indiana University, 1980, pp. 3–4.

56 The worship style of the Primitive Baptist Church resembles that of Pentecostal congregations.

57 Pearl William-Jones, "The Musical Quality of Black Religious Folk Ritual," Spirit I: 21.

58 Horace Boyer, "Gospel Music," *Music Educators Journal* XIV: 37.

59 Arna Bontemps, "Rock, Church, Rock!", *Common Ground* III: 76–77; and Boyer, pp. 36–38.

60 Burnim, "The Black Gospel Music Tradition," p. 125.

61 Maultsby, "Afro-American Religious Music," p. 15.

62 Burnim, "The Black Gospel Music Tradition," pp. 136–178.

63 Ibid., pp. 139–146.

64 Ibid., pp. 146–157.

65 Ibid., pp. 157–167.

66 Ibid., pp. 167–169.

67 Ibid., p. 178.

Introduction: "In the World, but Not of It"

by Cheryl J. Sanders

from *Saints in Exile: The Holiness-Pentecostal Experience in African American Religion and Culture*, published in 1996

One of the earliest uses of the term "Sanctified church" occurs in the anthropological writings of Zora Neale Hurston. Her book, *The Sanctified Church*, is mainly an anthology of assorted primary source materials compiled and published posthumously in 1981 that features only one brief essay bearing the same title. In that essay, she defines the Sanctified church as a revitalizing phenomenon that had arisen among various groups of "saints" in America. It is not a new religion and "is in fact the older forms of Negro religious expression asserting themselves against the new." Moreover, the Sanctified church is a "protest against the high-brow tendency in Negro Protestant congregations as the Negroes gain more education and wealth."[1] She identifies two branches of the Sanctified church: the Church of God in Christ and the Saints of God in Christ. The Sanctified church is closely related to three distinct Old and New World religious traditions: African religion, White "protest Protestantism" and Haitian vaudou. In this regard, Hurston sees "shouting" as nothing more than a continuation of the African possession by the gods, acknowledges the existence of "strong sympathy" between the White and Negro "saints," and notes the similarities between the dance of the saints and the steps seen in Haiti when a man or a woman is "mounted" by a *loa*, or spirit.[2] Sociologist Cheryl Townsend Gilkes has defined the Sanctified church as a segment of the Black Church that arose in the late nineteenth and early twentieth centuries, beginning the end of Reconstruction, in response to and largely in conflict with postbellum changes in worship traditions within the Black community. Its distinguishing mark is adherence to the traditions of oral music and ecstatic praise associated with slave religion. The label "Sanctified church" emerged within the Black community to distinguish congregations of "the saints" from those of other Black Christians, especially the Black Baptists and Methodists who assimilated and imitated the cultural and organizational models of European-American patriarchy. This label acknowledges the sense of ethnic kinship and consciousness underlying the Black religious experience and "designates the part of the Black religious experience to which a saint belongs without having to go through a dizzying maze of organizational histories involving at least twenty-five denominations."[3]

The picture is even more complex than Gilkes indicates; more than one hundred church bodies listed in the *Directory of African American Religious Bodies* can be identified with the Sanctified church tradition, and a few of these actually include the word *Sanctified in* their official names, for example, Christ Holy Sanctified Church of America, Inc., Christ's Sanctified Holy Church, Church of God (Sanctified Church), and Original Church of God (or Sanctified Church).[4] However, the Directory does not use the term "Sanctified" as a general category and, instead, employs the more cumbersome and perhaps more technically accurate designation "Pentecostal/Apostolic, Holiness, and Deliverance." The article presented as a historical overview of this category of churches in the Directory was written by theologian William C. Turner, Jr., who emphasizes the reform aspects of the Holiness/Pentecostal/Apostolic churches as a "segment of the Black church that desperately sought restoration and revival through a recovery of latent spirituality."[5] These churches were led by Black Christians around the turn of the century who "came out" of the mainline Black denominational churches and sought "the deeper life of entire sanctification" and Spirit baptism: "Their initial concern was not so much to start a new denomination as to call the existing ones back to the wells of their spirituality."[6]

Turner cites Leonard Lovett's list of the five original groups in Black Holiness-Pentecostalism, shown here in order of date founded: (1) United Holy Church of America (1886); (2) Fire Baptized Holiness Church of God in the Americas (1889); (3) Church of Christ Holiness, U.S.A. (1894–1896); (4) Church of God in Christ (1895–1897); and (5) Pentecostal Assemblies of the World (1914–1924).[7] Turner clearly delineates the similarities and differences of the various groups within the Holiness/Pentecostal/Apostolic movement. A historical chronology is implicit in the categories. Four of the five churches—the United Holy Church of America; the Church of Christ Holiness, U.S.A.; the Church of God in Christ; and the Fire Baptized Holiness Church of God in the Americas—were originally Holiness bodies formed before the turn of the century around the doctrine of sanctification.

Three of these—the United Holy Church of America, the Church of God in Christ, and the Fire Baptized Holiness Church of God—embraced Pentecostal teachings and practices after the 1906 Azusa Street Revival in Los Angeles, following the lead of William J. Seymour. The Church of Christ Holiness, U.S.A. remained a Holiness group under the leadership of Charles Price Jones after he parted company with Charles Harrison Mason, founder of the Church of God in Christ. The Pentecostal Assemblies of the World had its beginnings as a product of the Azusa Street Revival—which is to say, as a Pentecostal body—but took on the Apostolic doctrine and identity in 1914 after the rebaptism of G. T. Haywood of Indianapolis and his followers "in Jesus' name."

What the Holiness, Pentecostal, and Apostolic Churches all have in common is an emphasis on the experience of Spirit baptism. A crucial point of disagreement is whether a person must speak in tongues (glossolalia) to validate his or her Spirit baptism; "the tongues doctrine unites Pentecostals and Apostolics, and divides Holiness believers from the former two."[8] Some Holiness believers reject glossolalia altogether; others appreciate and/or practice speaking in tongues without insisting on the doctrine of tongues. The Holiness emphasis is on sanctification, or personal holiness, whereas the Pentecostals and Apostolics emphasize spiritual power. Apostolics differ from the other two groups primarily on theological grounds. They reject the doctrine of the Trinity, adhering instead to belief in the "oneness of God" as revealed in Jesus Christ. They do not use the trinitarian formula (i.e., "in the name of the Father, the Son, and the Holy Ghost") for baptism as is characteristic of other Christian churches: they baptize in Jesus' name. Hence, the Apostolics are occasionally referred to as "Jesus only" or "Jesus' name" churches. Although some of these churches practice speaking in tongues and some baptize only in Jesus' name, all adhere to some form of doctrine and practice of sanctification; thus, the term "Sanctified church" is inclusive of them all. Historically. these churches have been known to preach and promote an ascetic ethic forbidding the use of alcohol tobacco and other addictive substances, gambling, secular dancing, and the wearing of immodest apparel.

In view of this understanding of the Holiness, Pentecostal, and Apostolic Churches as components of a historical movement among African American Christians to promote sanctification and Spirit baptism in some distinct form, it is now possible to formulate a comprehensive definition of the Sanctified church that builds on the thought of Turner, Hurston, and Gilkes but adds a needed ethical dimension: The *Sanctified church is an African American*

Christian reform movement that seeks to bring its standards of worship, personal morality, and social concern into conformity, with a biblical hermeneutic of holiness and spiritual empowerment. This ethical emphasis is a critical element in the definition because the Sanctified churches are congregations of "saints," an ethical designation members apply to themselves as an indication of their collective response to the biblical call to holiness. The saints follow the holiness mandate in worship, in personal morality, and in society, based on a dialectical identity characteristic of the tradition: "in the world, but not of it." This dialectical identity reflects the social aspect of exilic consciousness, as manifested in the saints' awareness of alienation or separation from the dominant culture, based on racial differences and religious practices.

African Religious Traditions in the Sanctified Church

As Hurston observed, the practices of shouting and spirit possession in the Sanctified church movement are readily associated with African traditional religious and diasporic worship practices. Afrocentric philosopher Molefi Asante, for whom Pentecostal worship was a formative influence, stated in his book *Afrocentricity* that "the music and dance of the church may be the essence of our Africanity."[9] Without specifically naming the Pentecostal or Sanctified tradition, Asante describes the "general experience of those traditional Black churches which have emerged out of the roots of our past" as "truly an African expression":

> The panorama of Africa is not merely unfolded but expanded and amplified in the religious drama. More than this, the church services become a collective outpouring of the soul with some people getting more possessed than others but no one really escaping the influence of possession even if it is no more than the slight tapping of the foot. Syncopated pianos and organs and hand clapping often drive the faithful into ecstasy. The rhythms run to be free, individuals shout and moan, the preacher directs this "mass madness," which is really not madness, by the call and response, and suddenly the whole congregation is praising the Lord.[10]

He claims that the African slaves, whose manner of "getting religion" was imitated by White evangelicals, were actually replicating in America the same ecstatic religious behavior practiced in Africa. What the Africans were "getting" was the same "ecstatic combinations produced by the polymeters of

African music. In the place of drums the African-American substituted hand-clapping, foot-stomping, head-shaking, body-moving rhythm—all in an attempt to drive the self into further possession, by the Lord."[11] Asante offers this portrayal of the distinctive worship practices of the Sanctified church tradition as his best evidence to support an essentialist argument for the unique nature of the African people, at home or in diasporic communities. He seems less interested in the ethical meaning of these worship practices in the American context, except to note that they were imitated and not initiated by Whites.

In his 1978 doctoral dissertation comparing Black political and religious movements, Pentecostal political scientist James S. Tinney identifies three dominant Africanist themes with Black Pentecostalism: spirits, magic, and eschatology. In this cosmology, the functions of good spirits, or angels, are absorbed by one divine Spirit, the Holy Ghost. The functions of the supremely evil spirit known as "the Devil" or "Satan" are assumed by legions of evil spirits called "demons." Thus, an eternal conflict is presupposed between demons and the Holy Ghost:

Worship services may often begin with an exorcism ("cast out the demons of fear, cast out the demons of despair, cast out the demons of unbelief"). Illnesses, physical or psychological compulsions, and "besetting sins" are also subject to exorcisms. But so is the environment, the social and political order. Politics is not evil, but it is subject to control by the Holy Ghost or demons. The same goes for political communities. The kingdom of God is nothing more or less than the world in which the Holy Ghost reigns.[12]

Although Tinney acknowledges that the term "magic" is not used in these churches, he nevertheless argues that Pentecostal rituals for supernatural healing directly repeat African practices in an effort to "tap and harness spiritual power" in order to make it serve the believer in a beneficial way. It should be noted that most of the healing practices Tinney designates as African and magical—such as prayer, anointing the sick with oil, laying on of hands, and the commission of special cloths or handkerchiefs—are also found in the New Testament.[13] The African eschatology Tinney ascribes to Black Pentecostals is a realized eschatology that claims in this life those things that religions generally hold as rewards for the faithful in the afterlife.

One does not wait to die in order to attain perfection; he can attain it in this life. One does not wait for death to bring relief from illness and disease; healing and miracles are offered now. One does not wait to receive spirit energy in another world; it, too, is available in the Holy Ghost experience now.[14]

103

In a separate monograph, Tinney offers further corroboration of the relationship between Black Pentecostalism and traditional African religions by describing the receptivity of Africans to the Pentecostal revival: "When news of the [Pentecostal] revival reached Africa, it was not regarded as an entirely 'new' phenomenon. For the very practices of Azusa Street had long been known in the Motherland even before any Azusa-inspired messenger arrived."[15] He has in mind here several African independent Christian groups of the "Pentecostal variety," such as the movement led by Prophet Harris, which had already emerged without White supervision in West Africa prior to the Pentecostal revival. He estimates that the majority of the more than 6,000 independent church organizations in Africa are Pentecostal. Ethically, these churches bear similarity to the Sanctified church tradition in America with respect to their cultural and political resistance to White imperialists and missionaries.

John Philips has commented that few historians, ethnographers, or sociologists of religion have explored the African origins of White religious belief and behavior. He is of the opinion that it is no easy matter to distinguish the uniquely African elements of Pentecostal and Holiness worship practices because much that is often considered peculiarly Black about Black Pentecostal and Holiness churches is often equally characteristic of White churches. The characteristic features of Pentecostal churches that are demonstrably African in origin include possession trances, ritual dancing, drumming, and ecstatic speech (thought to be the language of angels or spirits).[16] Philips asserts that, in order to write the definitive statement about African cultural survivals in the United States, one must acquire a triple expertise—as an Americanist, an Africanist, and a Europeanist.[17] His conclusion that "as much African culture survives now among Whites as among Blacks" pushes him to endorse anthropologist Melville Herskovits's view that much African culture survives in the United States and at the same time to assent to sociologist E. Franklin Frazier's argument that African culture is not the distinguishing characteristic of African American society.[18]

Adopting a "hemispheric perspective," historian of religion Joseph Murphy sees Black religion in the United States as a special articulation of an African-derived spirituality that has kindred expressions throughout the Americas.[19] Murphy compares five traditions—Haitian *vaudou*, Brazilian *candomblé*, Cuban *santería*, Revival Zion in Jamaica, and the Black church in the United States—in somewhat ahistorical broad strokes. He uses a Church of God in Christ congregation in Washington, DC as his primary source of data representing the Black church, a choice based on the impression that the Pentecostals alone have preserved the shout and spirit possession in the United States. Murphy makes the important assumption that what might seem to outsiders to be mere "motor behaviors" remembered from Africa are actually expressions of a dynamic, incarnated spirituality found throughout the Diaspora.[20] He is aware of the relative weakness of surviving African religious customs in the United States compared with those in the Caribbean and South America, a distinction that also rests at the root of the classic debate between Herskovits and Frazier.

The emphasis on spirituality rather than theology in the comparative study of diasporic religious traditions enables Murphy to make an interesting point concerning differences in denotation of racial terms as applied to the church: "The Black Church is both 'Black' in its independent wisdom arising from its exclusion from White America, and it is 'African American' in its development of a spirituality born in Africa."[21] This line of thought encourages reflection on the ethical meaning of the Sanctified church tradition. Murphy believes that the religious traditions of the African Diaspora are alike in that each shares a social history of enslavement and racial discrimination, and each became the focus for an extraordinary struggle for survival against and triumph over brutal systems of exploitation. Moreover, they share an elevated sense of solidarity against injustice and a commitment to the protection and advancement of their communities, understood as the "work" of the "spirit."[22] Importantly, he proffers this ethical evaluation of the roles these traditions have played in fostering cultural and political change without relinquishing the belief that "the spirit is a real and irreducible force uplifting communities throughout the African Diaspora."[23]

Christianity and Social Ethics among the Slaves

It seems that the religion of the African Americans in bondage should not be designated as slave religion any more than Judaism should be called slave religion because of the formative role a slave community played in its early history. The religion of the enslaved Christians was an amalgam of Christian and African practices and beliefs, with the slaves' distinctive African practices noted more frequently in the sources than their generic Christian beliefs. However, the slaves who were Christian were very forthright about identifying themselves as Christians, as can be readily observed in published collections and analyses of ex-slave narratives and oral histories, such as *Cut Loose Your Stammering Tongue, Deep Like the Rivers, God Struck Me Dead,* and

105

Weevils in the Wheat.[24] The Christian Community in bondage produced a significant social and ethical critique of the hypocrisy of White Christianity, insofar as it promoted and justified slaveholding. This critique was thoroughly documented by the painful scars of their own flesh and by the stories and memories of collective suffering at the hands of people who called themselves Christians. It is important to appreciate that there were Christians within the slave community who saw themselves as having a special social-ethical imperative: to seek freedom by resisting, in the name of Christ, the social, cultural, ecclesial, and philosophical structures Whites had erected, in the name of Christ, to keep them in bondage.

One noteworthy example of the tradition of resistance among enslaved Christians is that of Harriet Tubman. The fact that she led hundreds of slaves in the escape from bondage to freedom is widely known. What is hardly ever addressed in the many references to her heroism is the depth of her Christian faith and conviction. In a fit of rage, Tubman's slave master had thrown a heavy weight at her, breaking her skull and inflicting severe brain damage that plagued her from childhood to old age with a sleeping disorder. At one point she became bedridden for several months, and in this condition she prayed unceasingly for her master to be converted to Christianity. Her prayers of intercession took an interesting turn when she learned of her master's plans to sell her:

> Den I heard dat as soon as I was able to move I was to be sent
> with my brudders, in the chain-gang to de far South. Then I
> changed my prayer, and I said, "Lord, if you ain't never going
> to change dat man's heart, kill him, Lord, and take him out of
> de way, so he won't do no more mischief." Next ting I heard
> ole master was dead; and he died just as he had lived, a wicked,
> bad man.[25]

She regretted that her prayers were responsible for her master's death, but at that point she began to recover and to seek sanctification:

> 'Pears like, I prayed all de time, about my work, eberywhere I
> was always talking to de Lord....When I took up de broom
> and began to sweep, I groaned, "Oh, Lord, whatsoebber sin
> dere be in my heart, sweep it out, Lord, clar and clean, but I
> can't pray no more for pore old master.[26]

Her prayers for purification from sin thus superseded her prayers of intercession for her master.

Tubman began to see visions of horsemen and shrieking women and children being torn from each other and "a line dividing the land of slavery from the land of freedom, and on the other side of that line she saw lovely White ladies waiting to welcome her, and to care for her."[27] Guided only by the North Star, she set out to find liberty. Her ethical rationale for seeking freedom and for using violence, if necessary, to secure it was clearly reasoned out and articulated in terms of doing the will of God:

> I had reasoned dis out in my mind; there was one of two things I had a right to, liberty or death; if I could not have one, I would have de oder; for no man should take me alive; I should fight for my liberty as long as my strength lasted, and when de time came for me to go, de Lord would let dem take me.[28]

When Tubman succeeded in making her escape, she crossed the line in fulfillment of one aspect of her vision of freedom, but there were no "lovely White ladies" to welcome her. She used the language of exile to describe her initial experience and impressions of freedom, again with prayer as her principal context for both thought and action:

> I had crossed de line of which I had so long been dreaming. I was free; but dere was no one to welcome me to de land of freedom. I was a stranger in a strange land, and my home after all was down in de old cabin quarter, wid de ole folks, and my brudders and sisters. But to dis solemn resolution I came; I was free, and dey should be free also; I would make a home for dem in de North, and de Lord helping me, I would bring dem all dere. Oh, how I prayed den, lying all alone on de cold, damp ground: "Oh, dear Lord," I said, "I haint got no friend but you. Come to my help, Lord, for I'm in trouble."[29]

The task of liberating others from bondage can be seen as Tubman's constructive response to the experience of exile. She solicited God's help in her efforts to create a community of exiles who could welcome each other to the land of freedom. There is a clear correlation between Tubman's stages of spiritual development and her stages of preparation for the work of liberation through escape and escort, between the intensification of her life of prayer and her deepening resolve to liberate her people. Her work was carried out with a keen sense of utter dependency on God, and the testimony of sanctification emerged as a significant element of her spiritual and political formation.

The single best account of the Christian faith and collective spiritual experiences of the slave community in the United States remains Albert J. Raboteau's *Slave Religion* (1978). Although Raboteau does not mention the Sanctified tradition, he is aware of the ethical dilemma faced by slaves who wanted to dance their religion in conflict with the mores of White and Black evangelicals:

> Despite the prohibition of dancing as heathenish and sinful, the slaves were able to reinterpret and "sanctify" their African traditional dance in the "shout." While the North American slaves danced under the impulse of the Spirit of a "new" God, they danced in ways their fathers in Africa would have recognized.[30]

Raboteau directs his attention to the shout through the critical eye of African Methodist Episcopal Bishop Daniel Payne, author of what has become the classic statement of the Black evangelical rejection of Black folk religion and worship styles:

> About this time [1878] I attended a "bush meeting.".…After the sermon they formed a ring, and with coats off sung, clapped their hands, and stamped their feet in a most ridiculous and heathenish way. I requested the pastor to go and stop their dancing. At his request they stopped their dancing and clapping of hands, but remained singing and rocking their bodies to and fro. This they did for about fifteen minutes. I then went, and taking their leader by the arm requested him to desist and to sit down and sing in a rational manner. I told him also that it was a heathenish way to worship and disgraceful to themselves, the race, and the Christian name.[31]

Raboteau suggests that the holy dance of the shout may have been a "two-way bridge connecting the core of West African religions—possession by the gods—to the core of evangelical Protestantism—the experience of conversion." In the book he divides his attention between these two "core" elements in slave religion and describes with care the impact of both the African religious heritage and American evangelization efforts by using a host of primary and secondary sources representing the vantage point of the slave. Yet, he concludes that, notwithstanding, continuities in performance styles from Africa to America among the slaves, "in the United States the gods of Africa died."[32]

In Raboteau's view, the influence of African religion on the Protestant revivalist tradition is more a matter of style than content. He draws a similar conclusion concerning the development of the Negro spirituals: "African style and European hymnody met and became in the spiritual a new, Afro-American song to express the joys and sorrows of the religion which the slaves had made their own."[33] After presenting a strong case for the distinctive nature of slave religion, with an emphasis on the slaves' ethical sensitivity to White Christian inhumanity, brutality, and hypocrisy, Raboteau somewhat forces the conclusion that there was a genuine religious mutuality between Black and White Christians during slavery. His description of this religious mutuality reflects the practices and character of the holiness tradition:

> Religion, especially the revivalistic, inward, experientially orient-ed religion to which many slaves and masters adhered had an egalitarian tendency which occasionally led to moments of genuine religious mutuality, whereby Blacks and Whites preached to, prayed for, and converted each other in situations where the status of master and slave was, at least for the moment, suspended. In the fervor of religious worship, master and slave, White and Black, could be found sharing a common event, professing a common faith and experiencing a common ecstasy. [34]

Curiously absent from this discussion of mutuality is evidence of White Christian repentance for sins perpetrated against the slave.

Writing against the view that slave religion was merely compensatory otherworldliness, Raboteau evaluates the distinctive moral ideas of the slave community and the attitude of moral superiority some of them had in relation to Whites. Fundamental to the slave community's ethics is the rejection of the master's religion as hypocritical, which becomes a basis for some of them to refuse to obey moral precepts held up to them by Whites and to justify stealing, lying, extramarital sexual relations, and other violations of "White" Christian mores. Raboteau contrasts the moral behavior of the sinners and saints among the slaves with some ambivalence. Although some slaves rejected the moral system preached by the master and his preachers, others devoted themselves to a life of virtue in which they developed both a sense of personal dignity and an attitude of moral superiority to their masters, a morally suspect attitude that could simultaneously support compliance to the system of slavery and buttress the slave's own self-esteem.[35] Raboteau describes the actions and attitude of a pious Christian slave who forgave his master for wrongly punishing him for something he had not done, thereby acquiring "the leverage of moral virtue by which to elevate his own self-worth," and who subsequently escaped slavery with a somewhat guilty conscience.[36] Some pious slaves drew a distinction between sacred and secular dancing but would be forced to dance against their will to please their masters during the Christmas holiday celebrations.[37] Moreover, prayer became an important symbol of resistance for a people forbidden to pray. There are instances in which slaves were whipped and punished for praying. During the Civil War, some Whites even attempted to coerce their slaves into praying for the success of the Confederacy.[38]

Sterling Stuckey's *Slave Culture* lifts up one specific aspect of slave religion—the ritual of the shout—in a general discussion of nascent Black nationalism. He attempts to make a connection between the African nationalism of the slave community, consisting of values that bound slaves together and sustained them under brutal conditions of oppression, and the nationalist theory developed by David Walker, Henry Highland Garnet, W. E. B. DuBois, and Paul Robeson. Stuckey sees the ring shout as a ritual of Black unity that not only enabled the slaves to overcome barriers of language and ethnic difference but also in the twentieth century "continued to form the principal context in which Black creativity occurred."[39] He celebrates the importance of the ring shout for jazz musicians like Milt Jackson and Thelonious Monk, who were familiar with it because they lived near one of the Sanctified churches during childhood. Yet, his only example of its importance in contemporary sacred culture is taken from James Baldwin's novel *Go Tell It on the Mountain*. Stuckey says of the Black nationalist theorists, "Most were exposed to main currents of African culture without understanding how those currents might contribute to the surge toward liberation they wanted to initiate."[40] It seems that the key to understanding these currents and their liberating potential is to recognize, first of all, the religious and ethical meanings that cultural practices like the ring shout have for the people who are engaged in them. Moreover, that shouting is praise may be totally incomprehensible to people who never practice it, and this simple fact must be kept in mind. Stuckey takes great care to show how much exposure Walker, Garnet, and the others had to ring shouts during their childhood or at some other time. However, he does not seem to appreciate the necessity of maintaining a sacred interpretation of this ritual in addition to observing its secular implications and effects.

Harriet Tubman provides an illuminating example of the discrepancy between the religious sensibilities of the cultural nationalist and the religious "folk."

> She rose singing, "My people are free!" "My people are free!" She came down to breakfast singing the words in a sort of ecstasy. She could not eat. The dream or vision filled her whole soul, and physical needs were forgotten. Mr. Garnet said to her: "Oh, Harriet! Harriet! You've come to torment us before the time; do cease this noise! My grandchildren may see the day of the emancipation of our people, but you and I will never see it." "I tell you, sir, you'll see it, and you'll see it soon. My people are free! My people are free."[41]

Obviously, Garnet did not appreciate Tubman's ecstatic, exuberant display of emotion at the breakfast table, he did not comprehend the reason why she rejoiced, and he was not convinced that her vision of freedom had any authority or veracity. From her perspective, however, the manner, rationale, and content of her praise were entirely in order because she was overwhelmed by the belief God had given her a revelation of the emancipation of her people. Nationalist theorists and historians alike will continue to underestimate the depths of African culture in America, as Stuckey claims they have done, as long as they persist in writing off the religious meaning that shouting and other Black folk rituals have in the minds of the believers, while basing their theories solely on the grounds of the social, cultural, and political significance these practices have in the minds of unbelieving intellectuals.

Emergence of the Sanctified Church as a Christian Renewal Movement

David Daniels, a church historian who is an ordained minister in the Church of God in Christ, has written a doctoral dissertation on the Holiness movement in Mississippi as a renewal movement among African American Baptists from 1895 to 1905. He is concerned to show how the Holiness movement negotiated the deconstruction of the theological world of slave religion and the reconstruction of a new theological world, making it a third force in African American Christianity.[42] Daniels posits his "third force" argument over against Gayraud Wilmore, James Tinney, and Cheryl Townsend Gilkes, who, in his view, fail to see the Holiness movement as a reform movement because they have adopted Carter G. Woodson's "twoforce" scheme and identify the movement with the conservatives or traditionalists (bound by ignorance, dogmatism, otherworldliness, and emotionalism) and not with the progressives (committed to education, innovation, and this-worldliness): "It is more than the perpetuation of slave religion as Wilmore notes, or a mere expression of slave religion as Tinney and Lovett argue, or a reaction to the progressive reforms being undertaken in African American Christianity as Townsend-Gilkes contends."[43] Daniels argues that the Holiness movement in Mississippi, under the leadership of Charles Price Jones and Charles Harrison Mason, was able to reject the negative attitude toward slave religion that the progressives held and advocate the moral, ecclesial, liturgical, and pastoral reforms that the progressives embraced. One of Jones's principal contributions to the movement was linking salvation to the formation of character, which he envisioned as a more important foundation of society than family, politics, economics, or even the church.[44] Bishop Mason, founder of the Church of God in Christ, defended a continued utilization of the liturgical practices of slave religion, in particular, "the elements of the rituals associated with the ring shout, supplemented by moral reforms and the experience of sanctification.[45]

A similar argument is made with respect to the Azusa Street Revival: It was a product of former slave William J. Seymour's restructuring of slave religion and not just a product of slave religion generally defined. This restructuring argument is significant because it goes beyond the observations made by Raboteau, Stuckey, and others that African worship styles and practices were reserved in slave religion and in subsequent developments in Black culture. Daniels gives important attention to the substance and content of Black folk religion and acknowledges critical changes and transformations Black Christians effected in their religion as they made the transition from slavery to freedom. Unlike most other scholars, who have analyzed the ring shout in terms of emotional release or African-derived spirit possession, he gives priority to the religious meaning of this practice and to the ways in which it has been adapted into contemporary Sanctified church rituals, such as tarrying (a ritual invocation of the manifestations of the Holy Spirit) and the holy dance.

At the turn of the century, the ecclesiastical courts in the local Baptist associations and state convention of Mississippi, upheld by the state Supreme Court, disfellowshipped Jones and Mason because their teachings concerning the nature of the Church were no longer palatable to their Baptist clergy brethren. By this process, the Holiness movement was expelled from the Baptist denomination and, in effect, became marginalized in African American Christianity.[46] Once Jones, Mason, and their followers were expelled by the

Baptist denominational authorities, they gained new authority and insight to engage in the reformation of American Christianity and the advancement of African American people. In other words, they were able to make themselves at home in the Sanctified church, a sacred space "in the world, but not of the world," where meaningful worship traditions could be preserved, practiced, and produced unencumbered by charges of heathenism or heresy.

---

1 Zora Neale Hurston, *The Sanctified Church* (Berkley: Turtle Island, 1981), p. 103.

2 Ibid., 104–107.

3 Cheryl Townsend Gilkes, "The Role of Women in the Sanctified Church," *Journal of Religious Thought* 43, no. 1 (Spring–Summer 1986), p. 25; and Gilkes "Together and in Harness: Women's Traditions in the Sanctified Church," *Signs: Journal of Women in Culture and Society* 10, no. 4 (Summer 1985), pp. 679-680.

4 Wardell Payne, ed., *Directory of African American Religious Bodies* (Washington, DC: Howard University Press, 1991), pp. 82–116.

5 William C. Turner, Jr., "Movement in the Spirit: A Review of African American Holiness/Pentecostal/Apostolics," in Payne, *Directory*, p. 248.

6 Ibid.

7 Leonard Lovett, "Black Holiness-Pentecostalism: Implications for Ethics and Social Transformation" (Ph.D. dissertation, Emry University, 1978), p. 13.

8 Turner, "Movement in the Spirit," p. 253.

9 Molefi Kete Asante, *Afrocentricity* (Trenton, NJ: Africa World Press, 1988), p. 74.

10 Ibid.

11 Ibid.

12 James S. Tinney, "A Theoretical and Historical Comparison of Black Political and Religious Movements" (Ph.D. dissertation, Howard University, 1978), pp. 232–233.

13 Ibid., p. 234.

14 Ibid., pp. 236–237.

15 James S. Tinney, "The Blackness of Pentecostalism," *Spirit 3*, no. 2 (1979), p. 29.

16 John Edward Philips, "The African Heritage of White America," in *Africanisms in American Culture*, Joseph E. Holloway, ed. (Bloomington: Indiana University Press, 1990), p. 231.

17 Ibid., p. 237.

18 Ibid., p. 227.

19 Joseph M. Murphy, *Working the Spirit: Ceremonies of the African Diaspora* (Boston: Beacon Press, 1994), p. 4.

20 Ibid., p. 146.

21 Ibid.

22 Ibid., p. 2.

23 Ibid., pp. 2–3.

24 See Dwight Hopkins and George Cummings, eds., *Cut Loose Your Stammering Tongue: Black Theology in the Slave Narratives* (Maryknoll, NY: Orbis, 1990); Thomas L. Webber, *Deep Like the Rivers: Education in the Slave Quarter Community, 1831–1865* (New York: W. W. Norton, 1978); Clifton Johnson, ed., *God Struck Me Dead* (1969; reprint, Cleveland: Pilgrim Press, 1993); Charles L. Perdue, Jr., et. al., eds., *Weevils in the Whear* (Bloomington: Indiana University Press, 1976); and Cheryl J, Sanders, "Slavery and Conversion: An Analysis of Ex-Slave Testimony" (Ph.D. dissertation, Harvard University, 1985).

25 Sarah Bradford, *Harriet Tubman: The Moses of Her People* (New York: Corinth Books, 1961), pp. 23, 24.

26 Ibid., p. 25.

27 Ibid., p. 26.

28 Ibid., p. 29.

29 Ibid., p. 31-32.

30 Albert J. Raboteau, *Slave Religion* (New York: Oxford University Press, 1978), p. 72.

31 Daniel Alexander Payne, *Recollections of Seventy Years,* quoted in Ibid., p. 68. 1st publ. 1886 (New York: Arno Press and the New York Times, 1969), pp. 253–255.

32 Raboteau, *Slave Religion*, p. 86.

33 Ibid., p. 74.

34 Ibid., p. 314.

35 Ibid., p. 301.

36 Ibid., p. 302.

37 Ibid., p. 224.

38 Ibid., pp. 307–309.

39 Sterling Stuckey, *Slave Culture: Nationalist Theory and the Foundations of Black America* (New York: Oxford University Press, 1987), p. 95.

40 Ibid., p. ix.

41 Bradford, *Harriet Tubman, pp.* 92–93.

42 David Douglas Daniels III, "The Cultural Renewal of Slave Religion: Charles Price Jones and the Emergence of the Holiness Movement in Mississippi" (Ph.D. dissertation, Union Theological Seminary, 1992), p. 89.

43 Ibid., p. 16.

44 Ibid., p. 234.

45 Ibid., p. 185.

46 Ibid., p. 268.

II.
Surveys of Hymnals and Hymnody

African American Song in the Nineteenth Century: A Neglected Source

by Irene V. Jackson-Brown
from *The Black Perspective in Music,* published in 1976

An important, yet neglected nineteenth century anthology of African American religious songs is Marshall W. Taylor's hymnal, *A Collection of Revival Hymns and Plantation Melodies,* which was published in 1883.[1] Perusal of the literature on African American music reveals only two sources which refer to Taylor's collection. One source, John Lovell's *The Black Song: The Forge and the Flame* (1972), merely states that Taylor published the hymnal. While Lovell indicates the title and date of publication, he gives no indication that the publisher is a Black minister.[2] A second source, Alain Locke's *The New Negro* (1925), includes Taylor's hymnal in a bibliography of African American music. Locke's citation suggests that Taylor published two collections: one, *A Collection of Revival Hymns,* in 1882 and a second collection, *Plantation Melodies,* in 1883.[3] However, research to date does not support the idea that Taylor published the hymnal in two separate collections.

Taylor's hymnal is cited in the extensive bibliography of Black ministers compiled by Ethel L. Williams, entitled *Afro-American Religious Studies: A Compiled Bibliography with Locations in American Libraries* (1972). One entry there, *The Greatest Bicycle Rider,* has been incorrectly listed by Ethel L. Williams as Marshall W. Taylor's biography.[4] Actually, the book is a biography of Marshal M. ("Major") Taylor, who was the first Black to participate in cycle racing in the United States in the nineteenth century, and not a biography of Marshall W. Taylor, whose hymnal is the focus of this present study.

Taylor's work continues a tradition established by Richard Allen, who compiled and published a denominational hymnal for the A.M.E. (African

Methodist Episcopal) Church in 1801. It is this writer's hypothesis that Taylor's hymnal is the second landmark in the history of African American denominational hymnals and, thus, is of great significance. It appears that Taylor's collection was the first hymnal designed for use by African Americans whose membership was in the predominantly White M.E. (Methodist Episcopal) Church.

Marshall W. Taylor was born July 1, 1846, in Lexington, Kentucky, the son of former slaves.[5] Little else is known about Taylor's parents, Samuel and Nancy Ann Boyd. His mother was anxious about the education of her children (all boys) and insisted that they receive a "city" education.[6] Apparently Taylor's mother bore the responsibility for bringing up the Taylor boys, their father having died sometime in the 1850s. Nancy Ann Boyd Taylor taught her son, Marshall, some of the songs that were later to be collected in his hymnal. In the Introduction to the collection we are informed that:

> The hymns were obtained from his [Taylor's] mother, a most
> devout Christian woman who was set free, with many others,
> just before the time of her son's birth.[7]

In 1866, at the age of twenty, Marshall Taylor began teaching in Kentucky and two years later was elected president of one of the educational conventions in Kentucky.[8] He was licensed to preach in 1868 and was ordained in 1872. During the 1870s, Taylor held pastorates in Texas, Missouri, Kentucky, and Indiana in addition to holding several offices in the Lexington Conference of the Methodist Episcopal Church. William J. Simmons mentions in his book, *Men of Mark: Eminent, Progressive and Rising* (1887), that Taylor was sent to Union Chapel in Cincinnati from 1877–1878.[9] No minister is listed for Union Chapel, however, in the Cincinnati directory for 1877.[10] In the Cincinnati directory for 1878, a listing appears for a Rev. Marshall Taylor at 92 Everett Street, but Taylor's name is not included in the directory listing for the church that Simmons claims was pastored by Taylor from 1877–1878.[11] The church listing for 1878 appears as: "Union Chapel (Colored) services morning and evening."[12] It was the practice to list the minister's name with the church listing.

During the 1880s, Taylor became prominent in the M.E. Church as a result of his activities within the Lexington Conference. In 1880, he was a member of the delegation that represented the M.E. Church at the General Conference of the A.M.E. Church. He made the following report of this delegation to the Eighteenth General Conference of the M.E. Church:

We reached St. Louis, Missouri, and presented our credentials.... The day following was appointed for our reception. As
soon as we entered the General Conference rooms, we were
escorted by the committee to the platform...[and] we were
most warmly received. We then presented the greeting of your
body and made an address expressive of your brotherly
affection for them, and of your deep interest in their welfare,
concluding with the hope of a growing fraternity and a closer
alliance between these children of a common parent....[13]

Taylor resided in Cincinnati through the early 1800s and held an important post in the Lexington Conference. The Cincinnati directory listing for
Taylor in 1881 reads, "Taylor, Marshall W., D.D., presiding elder, Ohio
District, Lexington Conference, M.E. Church, 19 Noble Court."[14] It appears
that Taylor moved to New Orleans probably in 1886, three years after the
hymnal was published.[15]

In the Preface to his collection, Taylor has written:

The melodies and songs have been gathered from every direction, and the music prepared by Miss Josephine Robinson and
Miss Amelia C. Taylor. The arrangement and supervision of
the work was largely done by Mrs. Kate Taylor, my wife, and
the copying by Miss Hettie G. Taylor.[16]

In the effort to identify those who helped in the preparation of the
hymnal, I have attempted to reconstruct a history of the Taylor family. The
most useful source for reconstructing the history of the Taylor family was
Wendell P. Dabney's book, *Cincinnati's Colored Citizens*, which was published
in 1926, although the only explicit reference to the Taylors in the Dabney
study is a brief biographical sketch of Mary E. Beckley Taylor, who was the
wife of Marshall's brother, James Taylor. But from this sketch, it can be
deducted that Amelia and Hettie were nieces of Marshall Taylor, daughters of
his brother James. No date is given for the marriage of James Taylor and Mary
Beckley. It is of interest to note, however, that a Mary E. Taylor was listed in
both the 1873 and 1874 Cincinnati directories as a teacher, but that James
Taylor's name did not appear in the directory until 1876. His occupation at
that time was listed as "huckster," which here is to mean a "seller of produce."[17]
Another revelation in the Dabney study of Blacks in Cincinnati is that Mary
E. Beckley Taylor was a member of the M.E. Church and was an active

member of Union Chapel until her death.[18] Union Chapel was Marshall Taylor's pastorate from 1877–1878, according to Simmons.[19]

The James A. Taylor family was prominent in Cincinnati, and this middle-class security continued through the 1920s. "Many market stands were owned by families of note, among them the Taylors."[20] Amelia C. and Hettie G. Taylor taught at the Douglas School in Cincinnati until 1925, the year of their retirement. Apparently they did not marry and were among the property owners in Cincinnati's west end. Less is known about Marshall Taylor's wife, Kate, who was also involved in the preparation of Taylor's song collection. We know only that Taylor's wife had been a slave.[21]

The music for the collection was prepared by Josephine Robinson, who is referred to as the "composer." In the Introduction, we are informed:

> The tunes accompanying these songs were caught by the musical composer as they were sung in her hearing. This composer was once a slave, and is well acquainted with all the characteristics of the music and the sons prevalent in the religious meetings of the Colored people.

Little else has been disclosed about Josephine Robinson; her name does not appear in any of the Cincinnati city directories dating from 1873 to 1881. And her musical activities are not mentioned by James Monroe Trotter in his book, *Music and Some Highly Musical People* (1878), which offers extensive coverage of the musical activities of Blacks in Cincinnati, Louisville, and New Orleans. These three cities, as has been pointed out, were focal points in Taylor's ministry.

A Collection of Revival Hymns and Plantation Melodies

The collection was published in 1883 by Marshall Taylor and W. C. Echols of Springfield, Ohio. The hymnal was successful, and within a month after the first issue all copies of the first edition were sold.[22] A second edition was published and was distributed by several publishers in addition to Taylor and Echols: Walden and Stowe (Cincinnati, Chicago, St. Louis) and Phillips and Hunt (New Orleans). Echols, Walden and Stowe, and Phillips and Hunt generally published M.E. literature in the late nineteenth century.

It is curious that Taylor's hymnal was not indexed in *The American Catalogue*, 1876–1884 or *The American Catalogue*, 1884–1890, which supposedly lists all American publications for the years 1876 through 1890. Another of Taylor's books, *The Life, Travels, Labors and Helpers of Mrs. Amanda Smith*,

The Famous Negro Missionary Evangelist, published in 1886 by Cranston, was indexed in *The American Catalogue,* 1884–1890.[23] The fact that the hymnal was not indexed obviously is no indication of its lack of popularity, acceptance, or use. It is clear, moreover, that though Taylor designed the hymnal for use by a particular audience, it was widely accepted by both White and Black clergy and laymen. The following excerpts from some of the testimonials that were appended to the Collection give evidence of its wide appeal:

> The book very happily supplies a need long felt....
> There should be a copy in every household because it contains
> the original spiritual songs of our slave parents....
> It is a valuable contribution to the history of the Colored race
> in America.[24]

In addition to receiving support from individuals, Taylor's hymnal received the endorsement of the Louisville District Conference, the Ohio District Conference, and the Bowling Green District Conference of the M.E. Church.

Marshall Taylor's intentions in compiling the collection are explicitly stated in the Preface:

> I propose to preserve the history.... My work is to rescue
> them, lest after all these good fruits they themselves perish
> from the minds of men.... This collection is no competitor
> with other books of songs; it fills a place and supplies a want
> wholly its own....

And Taylor also advised that "almost any Colored person can sing the pieces."[25]

The songs contained in the hymnal are of two classes. One class is comprised of songs to which the author refers as "revival hymns." The second class is identified as "plantation melodies." The revival hymns were songs developed by Blacks as a result of their participation in the camp meetings of Whites, a phenomenon that began in Kentucky in 1801. The songs of the second class, the plantation melodies, are "the stuff of the slave experience."

Taylor writes that there was respect for tradition in terms of the use of certain melodies with certain texts, yet some melodies were "originally prepared for use only in this book." With respect to the song texts Taylor writes:

> Verses apparently meaningless have been given an interpreta-
> tion which render them no less beautiful, but far more useful.
> The syntax has occasionally been corrected, but the dialect is

left unchanged, as it was desired to preserve in their original grandeur the forms of speech.[26]

Of the 170 songs contained in Taylor's hymnal, 150 include both text and music, while twenty of the hymns include text only. In addition to indicating in some instances an author's or composer's name under the title of each song, Taylor has provided the scriptural text on which the song text is based.

The songs, for the most part, have been notated in quadruple meter except for occasional instances of compound triple meter. The following keys are represented (the number following the key designation refers to the number of songs in the collection that are notated in that particular key): G (68); F (29); D (18); C (13); E-flat (8); B-flat (7); A (6); and E (1). All melodies are written in major keys. The hymns are arranged primarily for two voices, soprano and bass. The bass line usually consists of a I–IV–V–1 root progression. There is occasional four-part writing and "European harmonic canons have been observed."[27]

Because many of the melodies were apparently notated during actual performance, variants were inevitable. In terms of actual performance, adjustments (i.e., fitting syllables or text to music) must have been difficult, for the text is not indicated on the score. Consider, for example, the relationship between the words and melody for song No. 86, "Go Down Moses."

The first phrase of the text contains eight syllables and set syllabically would accommodate the first two measures. Since the second textual phrase of the text contains five syllables, presumably the word "go" is to be sung to the two quarter notes E F (m. 4). Some confusion arises in the text setting for the first phrase of the chorus. Apparently the second line of text in the chorus is to be sung to the notes beginning on the third beat of the third measure of the chorus.

We can only make educated guesses about performance practice in relationship to Taylor's hymnal. More than likely the melodies were not sung as written, and probably the practice of lining-out was employed.

Taylor's introduction gives just a glimpse of African American folk song tradition in the mid-1880s:

> The songs and melodies, as we now have them, are obviously the growth of many years and of a great variety of circumstances. At first...spontaneous, unpremediated [sic] expression of aroused sensibilities...they were...repeated and rehearsed by multitudes of sympathetic souls.... That period of growth...has closed. For now a period of change, of schools

and book-learning…has not only begun, but made considerable progress among the Colored people of the South, which
will probably work as great a transformation in their musical
tastes as in other matters.

The importance of Taylor's hymnal is such that it must be brought to the
attention of scholars. The present discussion suggests some of the merits of the
collection and, hopefully, will provoke further investigation of African
American sacred song in the nineteenth century.

Example 1
86. Go Down, Moses

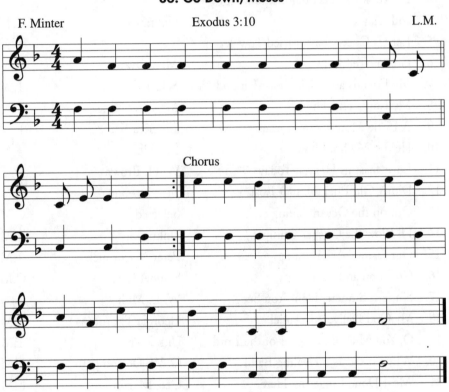

Verse: When Israel was in Egypt land,
              Let my people go,
            Oppressed so hard, they could not stand,
              Let my people go, etc.

Chorus: Go down, Moses, 'way down in
              Egypt land,
            Tell King Pharoah, to let my
              people go.

Appendix

Contents of *A Collection of Revival Hymns and Plantation Melodies* by Marshall W. Taylor, D.D. (Musical compositions by Miss Josephine Robinson; copied by Miss Amelia C. and Hettie G. Taylor)[28]

	TITLE	AUTHOR AND/OR COMPOSER	METER[29]
1.	Don't You Hear Jerusalem Mourn?	W. L. Muir	C.M.
2.	I Want to Be a Soldier	Unknown	C.M.
3.	I Have a Little Time, 't ain't Very Long	Kate Taylor	P.M.
4.	He Took My Feet out of the Mire and Clay	Unknown	L.M.
5.	Let Us Cheer the Wearied Traveler		L.M.
6.	Go and Tell Jesus	Matt Owens	P.M.
7.	My Friends and Neighbors, Far and Near	Selected	L.M.
8.	My Lord, This Union	Margaret Hines	L.M.
9.	A Little More Faith in Jesus	America Bell	L.M.
10.	He Set My Soul Free	H. Tolbert	P.M.
11.	Love-feast in Heaven Today	W. H. Brown	
12.	Didn't Old Pharaoh Get Lost?	M. Macoomer	L.M.
13.	Out on the Ocean Sailing	Selected	C.M.
14.	I'll Blow the Gospel Trumpet	Unknown	L.M.
15.	Our Lamps Are Burning	Peter Macormick	P.M.
16.	Go Thou and Prophesy	Samuel Kays	C.M.
17.	Sinners, Sinners, Don't You See	W. L. Muir	
18.	My God Delivered Daniel	Georgia Thornton	C.M.
19.	O, You Must Be a Lover of the Lord	Unknown	P.M.
20.	Why Gilead Is a Healing Balm	G. W. Downing	P.M.
21.	'Most Done Lingering Here	Geo. Martin	L.M.
22.	Come Now, My Dear Brethern	Selected	L.M.
23.	Little Children, You'd Better Believe	Chas. Coates	C.M.
24.	Don't You Grieve After Me	Scott Ward	P.M.
25.	Resurrection of Christ	W. L. Muir	P.M.
26.	Christian Warfare		P.M.
27.	Golden City	A. Kemp	P.M.
28.	The Martyr's Deliverance		P.M.
29.	The Old Ark	Kate Taylor	L.M.
30.	The Tree of Life	Margaret Hines	P.M.

	TITLE	AUTHOR AND/OR COMPOSER	METER
31.	Perfect in Jesus	Selected	C.M.
32.	Coming of the Savior	W. H. Vaughn	P.M.
33.	Trust in the Promise	Selected	P.M.
34.	Brethern, We Have Met to Worship	Selected	L.M.
35.	Lis'ning All the Night	Grandfather	P.M.
36.	The Lonesome Graveyard	J. H. Parker	L.M.
37.	Sing It Out with a Shout	Selected	P.M.
38.	Will You Open Your Hearts and Let the Master In?	Unknown	C.M.
39.	The Holy War	A. Kemp	L.M.
40.	Make Ready	Hattie Hill	P.M.
41.	Let Thy Kingdom, Blessed Savior	Selected	P.M.
42.	What Is It to Be a Christian?	Josie Robinson	L.M.
43.	The Life-boat	J. Courtney	P.M.
44.	We Are Toiling Up the Way	Selected	P.M.
45.	Shout, Shout, You Are Free	Sallie Washington	L.M.
46.	Missionary's Departure	J. L. Soward	
47.	Christian Prospect	Prof. Draper	P.M.
48.	The Dying Christian	Selected	L.M.
49.	Beautiful Zion	W. L. Muir	P.M.
50.	How Happy Are They		P.M.
51.	Blessed Be the Name of the Lord	J. J. W. Bowman	C.M.
52.	Silence in Heaven	W. H. Vaughn	P.M.
53.	The Happy Man	Selected	C.M.
54.	When the Tempest Passes Over	D. Tucker	P.M.
55.	I'm Just a-Going Over Home	Parker Brown	P.M.
56.	Go Bear Your Burden in the Heat of the Day	A. A. Whitman	L.M.
57.	The Rock that Is Higher than I		
58.	Come, Great Deliverer	Selected	L.M.
59.	From Every Graveyard	Abe Booker	P.M.
60.	Heaven Bells	L. Facing	P.M.
61.	Hunting My Redeemer	M. Macoomer	L.M.
62.	God Is Always Near Me	Wm. Polley	P.M.
63.	Exile from Eden	A. J. Warner	P.M.
64.	Washed in the Blood of the Lamb	J. Battees	L.M.

	TITLE	AUTHOR AND/OR COMPOSER	METER
65.	The Old Church Yard	Mother	P.M.
66.	Proud Babylon's Fall	Hattie Hill	L.M.
67.	Slavery Is Dead	B. J. Carter	
68.	A Little Talk with Jesus	Hattie Steward	P.M.
69.	Come Ye that Love the Lord	C. J. Nicols	P.M.
70.	Walk Jerusalem Just Like Job	Edw'd Nathan	L.M.
71.	Gideon's Battle	W. J. Brown	L.M.
72.	Christ Is All the World to Me	S.P.M.	
73.	The Book of Revelation	Geo. Martin	P.M.
74.	Drooping Souls	Selected	P.M.
75.	The Venturing Ground	W. H. Vaughn	L.M.
76.	Song of the Hill	D. N. Mason	
77.	Who Is He?	Aaron Jones	
78.	Will You Meet Me at the Gathering?	D. Tucker	P.M.
79.	Get Ready, There's a Meeting Here Tonight	Chas. T. Jones	L.M.
80.	The Resurrection of Christ	L. Facing	
81.	The Prodigal Son	Selected	P.M.
82.	I'm on My Journey Home	Geo. W. Leach	C.M.
83.	The Wandering Sheep Restored	Selected	S.M.
84.	My Redeemer	D. Tucker	P.M.
85.	The Heavenly Railroad	Nancy Taylor	P.M.
86.	Go Down, Moses	F. Minter	L.M.
87.	They Say There's a Land O'er the Ocean	D. Tucker	P.M.
88.	The Mourner's Race	D. Tucker	P.M.
89.	Rise and Shine	D. Tucker	P.M.
90.	Going to Wake Up the Dead	Sallie Washington	P.M.
91.	The Gospel Train	A. Jamieson	P.M.
92.	Look Away to Bethlehem	A. A. Price	
93.	The War, Christians, Is 'Most Over	R. J. Coleman	
94.	Jesus Loves Even Me	Hatton	P.M.
95.	Mercy's Free	Lester	P.M.
96.	The Young Christian	Chas. Munday	
97.	Joseph Made Known to His Brethern	Selected	
98.	The Children of God	J. J. W. Bowman	P.M.

	TITLE	AUTHOR AND/OR COMPOSER	METER
99.	The Dying Christian	J. H. Parker	L.M.
100.	He Saves to the Uttermost	Prof. Draper	P.M.
101.	What's the News?	J. L. H. Sweres	P.M.
102.	Mixture of Joy and Sorrow	Selected	P.M.
103.	It Is I	Selected	P.M.
104.	When We've Nothing Else to Do	D. Tucker	
105.	The Cross and Crown	Selected	C.M.
106.	Christian Liberty	D. Tucker	
107.	We'll Sing All Along the Way	Jerry Washington	
108.	Dialogue Between a Believer and His Soul	Selected	P.M.
109.	Come, Brethern and Sisters	Selected	
110.	Jesus Knows My Heart	Edw'd Freeman	
111.	What the Pilgrim Says	J. L. H. Sweres	P.M.
112.	Waiting Tonight	M. Macoomer	C.M.
113.	Going to Rise A-shouting	Alex MacDade	
114.	Methodism and Methodist Doctrine	Hatton	
115.	Steal Away Home to Jesus	Margaret Hines	P.M.
116.	The Heavy Cross	Geo. F. Carr	P.M.
117.	Keep Me from Sinking Down	M. Gooseland	
118.	Sweet Heaven	Geo. W. Hatton	L.M.
119.	Been in the Grave and Arose Again	H. C. Miller	P.M.
120.	Sweet Chariot	Jessie Munday	L.M.
121.	Come Down, Angel, Trouble the Water	W. H. Bowman	
122.	Jesus Is a Rock in a Wearied Land	Margaret Nicols	
123.	Suffer Little Children	Mrs. Kate Taylor	
124.	Wondrous Love	Selected	
125.	Over Me	Julius Roberts	P.M.
126.	Keep A-praying	Maria Coward	P.M.
127.	Roll, Jordan, Roll	Uncle Jordan	P.M.
128.	When the Bridegroom Came	Margaret Lapsley	P.M.
129.	The White Pilgrim's Grave	Selected	
130.	The Church of God	H. W. Tate	L.M.
131.	No One Like Jesus	Original by W. H. Vaughn	
132.	That Great Day	J. H. Parker	
133.	Took the Lord Away	W. H. Vaughn	

TITLE	AUTHOR AND/OR COMPOSER	METER
134. Out on the Ocean	W. M. Johnson	
135. Waiting on the Lord	W. H. Evans	C.M.
136. Remember Your Creator	Walker Robinson	
137. Jesus, Set Me Free	Jerry Washington	
138. Honor the Lamb	Patsey Nathan	
139. Going Home	Wm. Warrington	
140. Feeble Man	J. W. Penelton	
141. Let Me Die Like Simeon Died	W. H. J. Macdade	
142. The Lamps All Lit Up on the Shore	Jacob Hart	P.M.
143. Give Me More Religion	Mrs. E. J. Penelton	P.M.
144. Gone Up Through Great Tribulations	D. Tucker	
145. The Home Just Beyond		
146. The Hammers Ring	Chas. Macpheters	
147. Done Took the Children Out of Pharaoh's Hand	Josephine Robinson	
148. Shouting on the Other Shore	America Bell	
149. The Heavenly Choir		
150. Gim'me de Wings		
151. Death Stole My Mother Away[30]	J. H. Parker	
152. Southern Home	E. W. S. Hammond	
153. Christian Warfare	E. W. S. Hammond	
154. Do You Think I'll Make a Soldier?		
155. Ring Dem Charming Bells	E. W. S. Hammond	
156. Will You Go, Sinners, Go?		
157. Consecration Hymn	A. Kemp	
158. Over the River	Hatton	
159. The Traveler's Farewell		
160. Death, the Monster		
161. Traveling through the Wilderness		
162. The Prodigal Son		
163. The Lord Will Provide		
164. Save Me, Lord, Save Me		
165. March On		
166. Wrestling with God		
167. The Judgment		
168. The Final Day		

TITLE	AUTHOR AND/OR COMPOSER	METER
169. Arise, O Zion		
170. Longing for Rest		

Example 2
3. I Have a Little Time, 't ain't Very Long

Kate Taylor   2 Tim. 4:2   P.M.

1. Preaching soon in the morning,
   Preaching soon in the morning,
   Preaching soon in the morning,
       I hope I'll join the band.

   Chorus:
   I have a little time, 't ain't very long;
   I have a little time, 't ain't very long;
   I have a little time, 't ain't very long;
       And I hope I'll join the band.

2. Praying soon in the morning, etc.
3. Seeking soon in the morning, etc.
4. Rising soon in the morning, etc.
5. Shouting soon in the morning, etc.

Example 3
4. He Took My Feet out of the Mire and Clay

Unknown   Psalm 40:2   L.M.

Chorus

1. I'm sometimes up and sometimes down,
    He took my feet out of the mire and clay.
   Sometimes I feel I'm Heaven bound,
    He took my feet out of the mire and clay.

   Chorus:
   I'm so glad, I'm so glad, yes, I'm so glad
   He took my feet out the mire and clay.

2. I wish these mourners would believe
   That Christ is waiting to receive.

3. Let every Christian trim his lamp.
   Jesus is marching through the camp.

4. I have my breast-plate sword and shield,
   Boldly I'll march through Satan's field.

5. O come, young converts, can't you tell
    How Jesus saved your soul from hell?

Example 4
29. The Old Ark

Kate Taylor
Gen. 7:18
L.M.

1. Noah built an Ark, he built it on the ground;
    My Lord sent rain, to move the ark along.

    Chorus:
    The old ark's a-moving, moving, children,
    The old ark's a-moving right along.

2. Daniel in the lion's den
    Sung and prayed in spite of men.

3. Hear me, brethren; hear me, Lord;
    Hear me, brethren, serve the Lord.

4. When I was a mourner, just like you,
    I mourned and prayed till I got through.

5. I come here tonight to sing and pray,
    I hope it may last till break of day.

Example 5
35. Lis'ning All the Night

Grandfather   John 1:29   P.M.

1. Go read the third of Matthew,
        And read the chapter through;
    It is a guide to Christians,
        To tell them what to do.

    Chorus:
    I've been listening all the night long,
        I've been listening all day;
    I've been listening all the night long,
        To hear some sinner pray.

2. In those days came John, the Baptist,
        Into the wilderness,
    A preaching of the gospel,
        Of Jesus' righteousness.

3. Then came to him the Pharisees,
       For to baptized be,
   But John forbade them, saying,
       Repentance bring with thee.

4. Then I'll baptize you freely,
       When you confess your sin,
   And own your Lord and Master,
       And tell you how vile you've been.

5 When John was preaching Jesus,
       The all-atoning Lamb,
   He saw the blessed Savior,
       And said: "Behold the man."

6. Appointed of the Father,
       To take away your sin,
   When you believe in Jesus
       And own him for your king.

Example 6
45. Shout, Shout, You Are Free

Sallie Washington   Zech. 9:9   L.M.

1. Shout, shout, for you are free,
    I heard a mighty rumbling, I couldn't tell where;
   Christ has brought you liberty,
    I heard a mighty rumbling, etc.

   Chorus:
   I'm in a strange land,
    And a great ways from home;
   I'm in a strange land, my Lord;
    Don't talk about suffering here.

2. Brother, don't you think it best,
    I heard a mighty rumbling, etc.
   To carry the witness in your breast?
    I heard a mighty rumbling, etc.

3. I'll tell you what I mean to do,
    I heard a mighty rumbling, etc.
   I mean to go to heaven too,
    I heard a mighty rumbling, etc.

4. Rocks and mountains skip like lambs,
    I heard a mighty rumbling, etc.
   All must come at God's command,
    I heard a mighty rumbling, etc.

1 Copies of Marshall W. Taylor's hymnal, *A Collection of Revival Hymns and Plantation Melodies,* have been located thus far at the following libraries: Howard University (Moorland-Spingarn Collection); Schomberg Collection of the New York Public Library; and Yale University (Sterling Library).

2 Alain Locke, ed., *The New Negro* (New York: Atheneum Press, 1968, ©1925), p. 435.

3 John Lovell, Jr., *Black Song: The Forge and the Flame* (New York: Macmillan Company, 1972), p. 425.

4 Ethel L. Williams and Clifton L. Brown, comps., *Afro-American Religious Studies: A Compiled Bibliography with Location in American Libraries* (Metuchen, NJ: Scarecrow Press, 1972), pp. 165, 250.

5 William J. Simmons, *Men of Mark: Eminent, Progressive and Rising* (New York: Arno Press, 1968, ©1887), p. 733.

6 Ibid.

7 F. S. Hoyt, Introduction to *A Collection of Revival Hymns and Plantation Melodies,* p. ii.

8 Simmons, p. 934.

9 Ibid.

10 *U.S. City Directories: Cincinnati, OH.,* 1877 (New Haven Research Publications, Inc.).

11 Ibid., 1878, p. 929.

12 Ibid., p. 32.

13 *Journal of the General Conference (18th) of The Methodist Episcopal Church,* 1–28 May 1880, p. 505.

14 Taylor received an honorary Doctor of Divinity Degree in 1879 from Central Tennessee College (Nashville), which is now Meharry Medical College; see Simmons, p. 934; *Cincinnati City Directory,* 1881, p. 1076.

15 See Simmons, p. 935. Simmons published his study in 1887, and it is likely that he prepared the manuscript at least one year before its publication. This would suggest that Taylor moved to New Orleans between 1884 and 1886.

16 Taylor, p. 5.

17 *Cincinnati City Directory,* 1873, p. 819; *Cincinnati City Directory,* 1874, p. 880; *Cincinnati City Directory,* 1876, p. 934.

18 Wendell P. Dabney, *Cincinnati's Colored Citizens* (Cincinnati, OH: The Dabney Publishing Co., 1926), p. 281.

19 Simmons, p. 934.

20 Dabney, p. 201.

21 F. S. Hoyt, Introduction to *A Collection of Revival Hymns,* p. ii.

22 From advertisement in the second edition of Taylor's hymnal.

23 A. I. Appleton, comp., *American Catalogue* 1884–1890 (New York: Office of the Publishers' Weekly, 1891), p. 510.

24 Rev. Daniel Jones to Dr. Marshall W. Taylor, August 16, 1882, *A Collection of Revival Hymns*, p. 270; H. W. Tate to Marshall W. Taylor, n.d., p. 271; Prof. S. W. Williams to Taylor, *Collection*, p. 268.

25 From advertisement in second edition.

26 Taylor, p. 7.

27 Taylor, p. v.

28 Quoted from title page.

29 C.M.: common meter; L.M.: long meter; P.M.: particular meter.

30 Nos. 151–170 have texts only.

Hymnals of
the Black Church

by Eileen Southern[1]
from *The Black Christian Worship Experience: A Consultation,*
published in 1986

The first hymnal compiled expressly for the use of a Black congregation was published in 1801. Entitled *A Collection of Spiritual Songs and Hymns, Selected from Various Authors,* it was printed for Richard Allen, who is identified on the title page as "African Minister." Now Richard Allen is justly celebrated as the founder of the world's first Black Christian denomination, the African Methodist Episcopal Church, which he served as the first bishop, and for his civil rights activities in Philadelphia, but little attention has been given to his pioneering role in laying the foundation for Black American hymnody.

The story of the origin of Bethel A.M.E. Church of Philadelphia, which moved into its own building in July 1794, is so well known that it does not require retelling here. Without any doubt, Bethel was a singing congregation from the beginning, and by 1801 would have developed a basic repertory of its favorite hymns. Allen himself would have introduced many hymns to his fledgling flock, hymns that he had picked up during his several years as an itinerant Methodist exhorter before settling in Philadelphia. On the road he came into contact not only with Methodist preachers but also those belonging to Baptist and other sects, and he tucked away in his memory things that later would prove to be useful to him as an "African minister."

We know from contemporary sources that the Black Methodists were noted for their singing and exuberance in worship.[2] The novelty of the 1801 publication arises from the fact of the enterprising young minister's publishing his own hymnal instead of using the official Methodist hymnal. After all, Bethel was still under the governance of the Society in 1801. Allen's hymnal must have been well received, for within the same year a second edition appeared, entitled *A Collection of Hymns and Spiritual Songs, from Various Authors,* this time identifying the compiler as "The Rev. Richard Allen, Minister of the African Methodist Episcopal Church." The title page indicates that the hymnal could be purchased either at the printer's or at 150 Spruce Street, Allen's home address. Fortunately, there is extant a copy of each edition, thus making it possible for scholars to examine this landmark in the history of American hymnody and to assess its value.[3]

The fact that the hymnal ran into two editions within a year suggests not only its popularity among Allen's people but also that more copies might have been published to accommodate the needs of Zoar, the other Black Methodist congregation in Philadelphia at that time. It is certain that some White clergymen knew the hymnal, for the extant copy of the first edition belonged to Ezekiel Cooper, book steward of the Philadelphia Methodist Church with authority for approving all books published by members of the Society. We do not know whether Allen consulted Cooper before publishing his hymnal; it is doubtful that he did so. Cooper may have attempted to exert his authority, however, before the second edition was published, for in his copy, some words in the first hymn, "The Voice of Free Grace," have been scratched out and replaced with other, presumably correct, words. But none of the other hymns presents such emendations, so it appears that Cooper's authority carried little weight with Allen.

The first edition of Allen's hymnal contains fifty-four hymns; the second adds ten more texts, making a total of sixty-four. Some of the hymns most certainly were written by Allen himself, judging from their similarity to hymns he published in other places; others that have all the earmarks of folk hymns may have been penned by Allen's church associates.[4]

Like many other hymnals of the time, Allen's hymnal belongs to the genre of the "pocket hymnal," measuring slightly larger than 5x3 inches in size. Also like other contemporaneous hymnals, Allen's collection contains only texts, without author attributions or references to melodies that would be appropriate for use in singing the hymns. (Later editions of the A.M.E. hymnal would include such references.) I have traced twenty-six hymns to authors by locating concordances in eighteenth century sources.[5] The following Table of Contents taken from Allen's *A Collection of Hymns and Spiritual Songs (1801),* indicates these authors.

Am I a Soldier of the Cross [Isaac Watts]	18
Awake My Heart, Arise My Tongue [Watts]	45
A Solemn March We Make	50

Almighty Love Inspire	59
And Are We Yet Alive [Charles Wesley]	72
As Near to Calvary I Pass'd	82
Behold That Great and Awful Day	11
Behold the Awful Trumpet Sounds	16
Brethren Farewell, I Do You Tell	26
Burst Ye Em'rald Gates and Bring [Kempenfelt]*	60
Come and Taste, Along with Me	10
Come, Christian Friends, and Hear Me Tell	32
Come Let Us Lift Our Voices High [Watts]	35
Come Ye That Know the Lord Indeed	37
Curst Be the Man, Forever Curst [Watts]	38
Come All Ye Weary Travellers	86
Come All Ye Poor Sinners	46
Drest Uniform the Soldiers Are	51
Dear Friends Farewell, I Now Must Go	85
Earth Has Detain'd Me Pris'ner Long [Watts]	27
Early My God, Without Delay [Watts]*	64
From Regions of Love	66
How Lost Was My Condition [John Newton]*	6
How Long Shall Death the Tyrant Reign [Watts]	40
How Happy Every Child of Grace [Wesley]	73
Hail the Gospel Jubilee	75
In Thee We Now Together Come	18
In Evil, Long I Took Delight [Newton]	83
Jerusalem My Happy Home	13
Jesus at Thy Command [Lady Huntingdon]	80
Lord! When Together Here We Meet [Samuel Occom]	30
Lifted into the Cause of Sin	57
Lord What a Wretched Land Is This [Watts]	69
Lo! We See the Sign Appearing	71
My Thoughts on Awful Subjects Roll [Watts]	63
Now Begins the Heav'nly Theme [Martin Madan]	39
Now the Savior Stands A-pleading	61
O Jesus my Savior, to thee I submit	4
O God My Heart with Love Inflame	7
O That I Had a Bosom Friend	14
O Give Me, Lord, My Sins to Mourn	22

O Blessed Estate of the Dead	31
O How I Have Long'd for the Coming of God	48
O When Shall I See Jesus [John Leland]	52
O Don't You Hear the Alarm	34
O, If My Soul Were Form'd for Woe [Watts]*	62
Savior, I Do Feel Thy Merit	21
See the Eternal Judge Descending	34
See! How the Nations Rage Together [Richard Allen]*	78
The Voice of Free Grace [Thursby?]*	3
The Glorious Day Is Drawing Nigh	8
The Time Draws Nigh When You and I	22
Think Worldling, Think, Alas! How Vain!	28
The Trumpet of God Is Sounding Abroad	30
There Is a Land of Pure Delight [Watts]	34
The Great Tremendous Day's Approaching	42
Vital Spark of Heavenly Flame [Alexander Pope]	84
What Poor Despised Company	17
We've Found the Rock, the Trav'ler Cries	20
When I Can Read My Title Clear [Watts]	33
Wake Up My Muse, Condole the Loss	56
Why Should We Start and Fear to Die? [Watts]	65
Ye Virgin Souls Arise [Wesley]*	67
Zaccheus Climb'd the Tree [Newton]	77

While we may assume that Allen's congregation used the same tunes as did other congregations in singing the well-known hymns—such as those written by Isaac Watts, for example, or Charles Wesley—it seems obvious that in some instances the Bethelites must have composed their own melodies or adapted popular street tunes for their purposes.

This landmark hymnal is of historic importance for reasons other than its primacy among Black church hymnals, which in itself is enough to insure the hymnbook a secure place in history. In the first place, it serves as a folk-selected anthology, indicating the hymns that were popular among Black Christians at the beginning of the nineteenth century, for Allen selected hymns freely from the hymnbooks of Baptists and other denominations for his hymnal. His main criterion apparently was whether or not the hymns had appeal for his congregation. In his writings, he expresses concern about the "emotional natures" of his people, many of them ex-slaves, being swallowed up in cold, intellectual rituals. Certainly the hymns in his collection have vivid imagery and highly personalized texts—the kind that would have attraction for the newly converted ex-slaves who comprised his congregation.

Another reason for the historic importance of Allen's hymnal is that it seems to have been the earliest one to include hymns to which "wandering" refrains and choruses are attached; that is, refrains freely used with any hymn rather than affixed permanently to specific hymns. Thus, Allen's hymnal is a primary source for the worship song later to be called the "camp-meeting hymn" and the progenitor of the nineteenth century gospel hymn. While the first decade of the century is notable for its publications of camp-meeting hymn collections, none is dated earlier than 1803—two years after Allen's hymnal was published. Whether or not Black Methodists should be credited with inventing this form, as some contemporary sources imply, certainly Allen must be credited with being the first to publish examples of the form.[6]

It should be observed that the term "spiritual song" in the titles of Allen's collections does not have the meaning it would later have as applying to the folk-composed Negro spiritual. Fine distinctions cannot be drawn between the hymn and the spiritual song in this period. Hymn compilers commonly used such titles as Allen used, as far back as 1651 with the edition of the Bay Psalm Book entitled *The Psalms, Hymns and Spiritual Songs of the Old and New Testaments,* and Isaac Watts uses the term in the title of his landmark publication of 1707, *Hymns and Spiritual Songs,* which was given an American edition in 1739. The three terms, of course, point back to the Scriptures, Col. 3:16, wherein Christians are instructed to teach and admonish one another in "Psalms and Hymns and Spiritual Songs."

Although Allen's collection contains no Negro spirituals, it does indicate the kinds of source materials used by Black Christians in composing Negro spirituals, and thus throws light on the origin of the spiritual. Obviously the Black folk composers culled lines and phrases from their favorite hymns and scriptural passages, and adapted motifs, images, and themes from such sources to compose the texts of their spirituals, to which they then added verses of their own invention. Such a process is revealed by analysis of the text structures and documented in contemporary reports. One disapproving church father complained: "The Colored people get together, and sing for hours together, short scraps of disjointed affirmations, pledges, or prayers, lengthened with long repetition choruses."[7]

A hymn beloved by a Black congregation—say, for example, "Behold the Awful Trumpet Sounds" (No. 10 in Allen's hymnal)—might furnish the poetic tinder for any number of spirituals with its theme of Christians preparing for Judgment Day and its vividly drawn motifs: of the trumpet sounding to raise "the sleeping dead" and call "the nations underground"; of the "world in flames," "the burning mountains," and rocks running "down in streams"; of the "falling stars" and "moon turn'd into blood"; and of the wicked turn'd "unto hell," while the Saints sit "at God's right hand." A list of spirituals using this material would be long indeed, beginning with the ancient "In Dat Day" and including such well-known examples as "My Lord, What a Morning," "Steal Away," and "Rocks and Mountains, Don't Fall on Me," among many others.

Now for a word about the tunes used for singing the hymns in the Allen hymnal. Clearly, it would have been necessary to invent tunes for singing the unorthodox items—that is, the hymns written by Allen and the camp-meeting hymns—since newly invented texts were involved. In addition there is ample evidence that the Black Christians were not averse to drawing upon "merry airs, adapted from old songs" for their specially composed hymns.[8]

Finally, a few statistics: twenty-six Allen hymns have concordances in hymnals published by White compilers before 1801; thirty in collections published after 1801; and eight hymns apparently are unique. Allen's collection undoubtedly includes songs that circulated in oral tradition, which he would have picked up while preaching on circuit. Was he the first to publish these songs, which did not begin to appear in other collections until 1803? What contacts did he have with the Great Revival movement that swept over the nation, particularly in Kentucky, beginning in 1800? Was he the first to publish the Revival movement's camp-meeting songs? These are intriguing questions, for which the present stage of research will not permit immediate answers. But certainly when answers are forthcoming, light will be thrown on the extent to which Black hymnody practices influenced the development of White folk hymnody at the beginning of the nineteenth century.

By the time the A.M.E. Church had won its independence in 1816, its membership numbered in the thousands, and it is highly probable that the Allen hymnal repertory had been adopted by Black Methodist congregations both North and South. Thus, the hymns would have been disseminated throughout the nation, with Blacks sharing in a common oral tradition of hymnody, whether enslaved or free.

In 1818, the Church published a new hymnal, "designed to supersede those heretofore used among us," which had been compiled by a committee consisting of Daniel Coker, James Champion, and Richard Allen (chairman). It is an impressive collection! Consisting of 314 hymns, it is beautifully organized into appropriate sections according to the "various states of Christian experience," and shares some 244 concordances with the official Methodist hymnal of the period.

Richard Allen obviously was concerned about meeting the high standards of the Methodist hymnal in this new publication, although he had no intention of abandoning his independent stance. In the hymnal's preface he notes, "Having become a distinct and separate body of people, there is no collection of hymns we could with propriety adopt," but at the same time, he was careful to select hymns that were held in high "estimation" by others. He concludes, "We flatter ourselves, the present edition will not suffer by a comparison with any collection of equal magnitude."[9]

Gone are many of the vibrant and personalized hymns of the 1801 corpus; only fifteen hymns were carried over into this new edition. Were the other hymns too humble for the proud, new A.M.E. denomination, which was determined to "exhibit to the Christian world [that its] rules of government and articles of faith" would measure up to the highest standards? The discarded hymns were not forgotten, however, by Black worshippers; some lived on in oral tradition, and others were absorbed into the Negro spiritual, if not wholly, then in selected phrases and motifs.

A.M.E. hymnals were published periodically thereafter. In the 1837 edition, each hymn refers to a relevant scriptural verse, identifies its meter (that is, as short, long, common, etc.), and indicates a melody appropriate for use in singing the hymn. In 1898, the A.M.E. hymnal included music for the hymns for the first time. In modern editions, hymnals have included didactic materials along with the hymns, responsive readings, etc. The 1954 edition, for example, carries a lengthy article on the history of Methodist hymnody. Ever so often the Church appointed a committee to update its hymnal and improve the quality of its music—most recently in 1972 when the General Conference appointed a Committee on Worship and Liturgy to carry out its directives in preparation for the edition of 1985.

Through all the years, A.M.E. hymn compilers included, along with the standard Protestant hymns, a small number of hymns written by Black hymnists and composers as well as a few spirituals, but they were careful to weed out songs they regarded as trashy. Again and again, congregations were warned not to sing "hymns of their own composing."[10] In 1883, for example, Minister H. M. Turner (later Bishop) wrote in the preface of the A.M.E. hymnal, which he had compiled, "We have a widespread custom of singing on revival occasions, especially, what is commonly called spiritual songs, most of which are devoid of both sense and reason; and some are absolutely false and vulgar." Despite the fine work of the Fisk Jubilee Singers, the Hampton Singers, and other similar groups, it would be a long time before Negro spirituals were admitted to the ranks of acceptable church music. The battles fought in the nineteenth century over the "respectability" of the spiritual foreshadow similar confrontations today between those who approve of contemporary gospel music and those who regard it as unacceptable in the formal worship service.

Predictably, other Black denominations followed the lead of the A.M.E. Church in publishing their own hymnals. In 1822, Peter Spence published the *Union African Hymnbook* for his Union African Church in Delaware, Maryland, and in 1838, the A.M.E. Zion Church began publishing its own hymnals, entitled *Hymns for the Use of the African Methodist Episcopal Zion Church.* The "Improved Edition" of 1869 consists of 582 hymns compiled under the direction of Christopher Rush, Samuel M. Giles, and Joseph P. Thompson. Each hymn carries an indication of its meter and the name of an appropriate tune for singing it.

To my knowledge, only the three Black denominations discussed above published their own hymnals during the antebellum period. Presumably, other Black churches used hymnals published by the White mother churches. Except for Allen's landmark hymnal of 1801, the hymnals published by the Black church were hardly distinguishable from those of the White church in regard to repertory items, except for their inclusion of a relatively small number of Black-authored hymns. Over the years, they increased markedly in size: an A.M.E.Z. hymnal of 1872, for example, contained 1,129 hymns, while an A.M.E. hymnal of 1880 had 1,089 hymns. Such huge volumes of course proved to be too unwieldy, and later editions appeared in more convenient sizes.

After Emancipation, hymnbooks began to appear that obviously were not intended for use in the formal worship service, but rather for revival meetings, Sunday Schools, and informal gatherings. In 1883, the minister Marshall W. Taylor published a collection, *A Collection of Revival Hymns and Plantation Melodies,* intended primarily for use by Black congregations of the White Methodist Episcopal Church. Consisting of 170 songs, of which twenty have only texts, the collection includes traditional hymns, camp-meeting hymns, spirituals, and religious songs apparently written especially for publication in the hymnal. Some of the hymns were turned into gospel hymns through the addition of choruses to time-honored texts of Watts, Wesley, and others. Few of the songs seem appropriate for use in the formal worship services.[11]

Charles A. Tindley, celebrated for his pioneering Black gospel hymns, undoubtedly originally intended his music for performance in the Bainbridge Street Methodist Episcopal Church of Philadelphia, where he was pastor from 1902 until his death in 1933. But his music proved to have universal appeal, and in 1905 he began to publish collections of his songs. The first, entitled *Soul Echoes,* appeared in two editions (1905, 1909); the second, *New Songs of Paradise,* appeared in six editions during the years 1916–1941. Tindley clearly states his songs were intended for singing in "Sunday Schools, Prayer Meetings, Epworth League Meetings, and Social Gatherings."[12]

A Baptist publication of the early twentieth century, entitled *National Jubilee Melodies* (ca. 1916), also belongs to the informal category of Black church music. The copy I examined carried no date, but the title page identifies the book as the "twenty-third" edition. Now that's evidence of genuine popularity! Published by the National Baptist Publishing Board, the collection consists of old plantation songs which, the preface informs us, have been kept alive by tradition and should be preserved in "book form." K. D. Reddick of Americus, Georgia, and Phil V. S. Lindsley of Nashville, Tennessee, are credited with having collected the songs "from the various rice, cane, and cotton plantations of the South."

The collection of 142 songs includes a wide variety of types—mostly spirituals, both arranged and traditional, but also standard Protestant hymns and gospel hymns. None of the hymns carries the name of author or composer, and some have new titles, but the well-known hymns, such as those of Watts or Wesley, can be identified. As in the Taylor collection, some of the gospel hymns were "made" simply by adding choruses to standard hymns.

Although the Baptists and Methodists pioneered in publishing hymnals for their congregations after Emancipation, it was the Holiness (or Pentecostal) Church that was the direct heir of the plantation-church spirituals, jubilees, and shouts. Charles Price Jones, founder of the Church of Christ (Holiness) in 1895, gave music high priority in the Church and was himself a prolific hymnwriter, having written over a thousand sacred songs during his long life. His first songs date from his pre-Holiness days, when he was still a Baptist minister. He is credited with having published two songbooks, *His Fullness* and *Sweet Selections,* and two editions of the official hymnal of the Church, *Jesus Only Standard Hymnal.*[13] None of these publications was available to me, but I did examine the ten hymns published in the Church's *History,* which indicate Jones's style to be similar to that of other gospel hymnwriters of his time.

The year 1921 brought a milestone in the history of Black church hymnody. In my opinion, *Gospel Pearls,* published that year by the Sunday School Publishing Board of The National Baptist Convention, USA, ranks with Richard Allen's hymnal of 1801 in terms of its historic importance. Like the Allen hymnal, it is an anthology of the most popular Black church music of its time. The Music Committee that compiled the hymnal, under the direction of Willa Townsend, included some of the nation's outstanding composers and performers of religious music—among them, John W. Work, Frederick J. Work, Lucie Campbell, and W. M. Nix—and the resulting product was truly a "soul-stirring, message-bearing songbook."

The publisher notes that the hymnal was born "out of an urgent demand for real inspiring and adaptable music in all of our Sunday Schools, Churches, Conventions, and other religious gatherings." Were Black church people becoming increasingly bored with the staid, standard Protestant hymns that filled their denominational hymnals? At any rate, the diminutive hymnal—it contains only 164 songs—found a welcome place in the sanctuaries of many churches other than those of the Baptists.

Despite its size, *Gospel Pearls* was capable of meeting the needs of the Black church of its time. It contains the old, revered Protestant hymns including those associated by tradition with lining-out practice; the gospel hymns of such White writers as Moody and Sankey, Charles Gabriel, Philip P. Bliss, and Homer Rodeheaver, among others; the gospel hymns of the Black writers Charles Tindley, Lucie Campbell, Thomas Dorsey, and others; jubilee songs and arranged spirituals; and the essential service music. The popularity of the "Pearls" took them into "every phase of public worship," as the compilers had hoped for, and as well into thousands of private homes. It would be more than fifty years before the Black church would produce a hymnal of equal power, musical worth, and emotional appeal to Black Christians.

Although the hymnals used by Four-Shape Note Singers have had negligible impact upon the development of mainstream, Black church music, their existence should be noted. The basic book is W. M. Cooper's *The Sacred Harp,* but often Black communities have their own hymnals, generally entitled *The Colored Sacred Harp.* A copy in my possession was compiled and published by J. Jackson (Ozark, Alabama, 1934), under the auspices of the Dale County Colored Musical Institute and the Alabama and Florida Union State Convention on Composition.[14] It contains the old, familiar, Protestant hymn texts (but set to unfamiliar melodies) and hymns written by laymen of the community. Conspicuously absent are spirituals and gospel songs. It should be observed that seven-note shape singing belongs to the gospel song tradition, and thus differs from four-note shape singing.

Beginning in the late 1970s, the largely Black denominations seem to have awakened to the necessity for publishing hymnals that would confront the demands of the radically changing lifestyles of Black Christians in the last quarter of the twentieth century. The Baptists were the first, in 1977, with their denominational hymnal, *The New National Baptist Hymnal.* Then followed in 1981 the *Songs of Zion,* published by the United Methodist Church, and *Lift Every Voice and Sing,* by the Episcopal Church. In 1982 came *Yes, Lord!,* the first hymnal ever to be published by the Church of God in Christ, and in 1985 there appeared a new edition of the A.M.E. hymnal, *The African Methodist Episcopal Church Bicentennial Hymnal.*

In my opinion, *Songs of Zion,* along with the Richard Allen hymnal of 1801 and *Gospel Pearls* of 1921, must be counted among the great monuments of Black church music. Like its two predecessors, it is an anthology of church music popular among Black Christians of its time, but even more, it is a history of Black church music presented through the music itself. Published under the auspices of the National Advisory Task Force on the Hymnbook Project of the United Methodist Church, the hymnal's genesis was in a conference held at Atlanta, Georgia, in 1973, when it was discovered that the official Methodist Hymnal included only one hymn by a Black composer and only five Negro spirituals.

The thirteen-member committee, chaired by William B. McClain with J. Jefferson Cleveland and Verolga Nix as editors, affirming that the Black religious experience in the United States is unique and, moreover, has made a great impact on the development of the Christian church in general, aimed "to offer the whole church [i.e., not only Black congregations] a volume of songs that can enrich the worship of the whole church." The hymnal is successful even beyond the compilers' lofty ambitions, particularly in making available to the public a repertory of gospel music that hitherto has been generally accessible only through oral dissemination—that is, the live performance or recordings.

Divided into three main sections, each of which begins with a historical introduction, the hymnbook deals with, respectively, hymns, spirituals, and gospel songs. In addition, there is an extremely useful introduction that offers suggestions on how to perform the music to the director, accompanist, and congregation. A fourth section gathers together thirty-three liturgical pieces, most of them written by contemporary Black composers, but also including some standard texts, such as the Doxology and hymns of Watts and Wesley, fitted with new melodies and arranged to serve as offertories, responsories, and the like.

Few of the standard hymns are included among the seventy-two hymns in the first section; most are gospel hymns. The tradition of adding choruses to standard hymns to produce gospel hymns is well observed, and there are also contemporary hymns, which employ the standard four-line form but have gospel-style texts. A novel inclusion is a lined version of the Charles Wesley hymn (using the Martyrdom tune) "Father, I Stretch My Hands to Thee." This may well be the first time anyone has attempted to present a notated lined hymn in a hymnbook, and the fact of its inclusion reflects the importance given by the compilers to the validity of oral traditions.

The second section of the hymnal, which comprises ninety-six songs, is given over to spirituals. Here are all the old favorites of the nineteenth and twentieth centuries, most with simple accompaniments that do not overpower the melodies, and some consisting solely of melodies.

It is the third section of the hymnal that is unique: it contains fifty-one gospel songs of every conceivable variety. Included along with well-known contemporary gospel songs are other types arranged as gospel—for example, "The Battle Hymn of the Republic," "Amazing Grace," "My Faith Looks Up to Thee," among others. The accompaniments are not elaborate, but enough of the style is caught so that a good church pianist with some knowledge of the gospel tradition can perform acceptably from the music.

All the major gospel composers are represented, from Charles Tindley to the young Andrae Crouch and Walter Hawkins, and all the classics of the genre are included, from Tindley's "I'll Overcome Some Day" and Dorsey's "Precious Lord, Take My Hand" to the Walter Hawkins perennially popular "Goin' Up Yonder." Finally, the collection is distinctive because songwriters of the Holiness churches are represented along with the Baptist and Methodist songwriters, and this gives proper recognition to one of the important sources of the gospel tradition.

For scholars of Black church music, perhaps the biggest event of the 1980s was the publication, for the first time, of an official COGIC hymnal. According to a brief introductory note, the title of the hymnal, *Yes, Lord!*, reflects a practice of Charles H. Mason, founder of the Church of God in Christ, Inc., in 1896: when Bishop Mason wanted "to pull the congregation together in commitment and spiritual communion," he would begin the singing of a dynamic, tuneful chant, the text of which repeated the phrase "Yes, Lord" a number of times.[15]

Before discussing this amazing musical document, I should like to take a brief detour to comment on the congregational song. Traditionally, it has had simple melodies and uncomplicated rhythms, and was sung in unison, often without instrumental accompaniment. The unobtrusive four-part harmonizations given the songs in hymnals are for the benefit of the keyboard accompanist and are intended to support, not compete with, congregational singing. Texts may be dramatic or highly personalized, but they are memorable. If hymnals are not available, "lining out" helps the congregation recall the texts, as does also the inclusion of refrains and choruses in the texts.

Yes, Lord! makes a sharp break with the past. In its collection of 506 songs, the handling of the accompaniment, in particular, reflects the importance given to instruments and polyphonic textures in the pentecostal tradition. Except for the old standard hymns (which retain their conventional, four-part harmonizations) the accompaniments are lively and imaginative, promising an extra dimension of richness and excitement to the performance of the songs.

The major gospel composers of three generations are represented, from Tindley to the generation of Roberta Martin, Kenneth Morris, Dorsey, and others, to the generation of Andrae Crouch. In addition there are numerous songs written by pentecostal composers whose names are not familiar outside the Church, such as Mattie Moss Clark and Iris Stevenson, among others.

The collection includes a wide variety of texts: standard hymns are interspersed with gospel hymns, spirituals, patriotic songs, gospel songs, and religious songs in the classical European tradition—for example, St. Francis of Assisi's "All Creatures of Our God and King" and songs of Beethoven, Mozart, and Handel. Turning the pages, one comes across delightful surprises, such as a charming three-part round written by Terrye Coelho, and occasionally a shocker—such as the full, four-part arrangement of the "Hallelujah Chorus" from Handel's *Messiah* (covering six pages).

I became aware several years ago that the Black folk church had adopted this work, that members of the congregation sang along with the choir when it was performed as naturally as if they were singing a hymn or spiritual, taking whichever voice-part they preferred and missing not a single note. The inclusion of the "Hallelujah Chorus" in a hymnal legitimizes the establishing of yet another Black church music tradition.

Finally, I call attention to the closing section, which consists of fifteen traditional pentecostal chants, each in the form of a call-and-response, and four "Amens." Three keyboard "Call-and-Response Accompaniments" are included, with instructions given for choosing the appropriate accompaniment for each chant.

It is significant, as the Black church hymnal approaches its 200th anniversary, that its publishers include White, mainstream denominations as well as Black denominations, and that sects formerly regarded as outside the mainstream—particularly the Pentecostal sects—have begun to publish hymnals, thereby making their congregational songs available to a wide public. The future of congregational singing in the Black church looks bright, indeed, if the hymnals published in the last few years are predictors of things to come.

---

1 Dr. Southern is Retired Professor of Music and of African American Studies at Harvard University and the editor of the Journal, *The Black Perspective in Music*.

2 See, for example, quotations from William Colbert, John Fanning Watson, and William Faux, published in Eileen Southern, *The Music of Black Americans: A History*, 2d. ed. (New York: W. W. Norton, 1983), pp. 77–79.

3 The extant copy of the first edition is deposited in the Garrett Seabury Theological Seminary in Evanston, Illinois; the copy of the second edition is at the American Antiquarian Society in Worcester, Massachusetts. Microprint copies are available in the Shaw-Shoemaker *Early American Imprints*, Series No. 2 [1801–1820], Nos. 38 and 39.

4 Allen's autobiography, *The Life Experience and Gospel Labours of the Right Reverend Richard Allen, Written by Himself and Published by His Request*, includes two hymns—"The God of Bethel Heard Her Cries" and "Ye Ministers That Are Called to Preaching"—and a third, entitled "Spiritual Song," is published in Dorothy Porter, *Early Negro Writing, 1760–1837* (Boston: Beacon Press, 1971), p. 559.

5 See Table 1. My author identifications are bracketed; those marked by an asterisk were kindly communicated to me by Roland J. Braithwaite, professor of music at Talladega College, who presently is engaged in an intensive investigation of the Allen hymnals.

6 See, for example, the excerpt from John Fanning Watson, *Methodist Error (1819)* reprinted in Eileen Southern, *Readings in Black American Music*, 2d ed. (New York: W. W. Norton, 1983), p. 63.

7 Ibid.

8 Southern, *Music of Black Americans*, pp. 77–78.

9 The preface of the 1818 hymnal is reprinted in Southern, *Music of Black Americans*, p. 86.

10 See, for example, Daniel Payne, *The Semi-Centenary and the Retrospection of the A.M.E. Church in the United States of America* (Baltimore: Published by the Author, ca. 1866) and the excerpt from Payne, *Recollections of Seventy Years* (1888) reprinted in Southern, *Readings*, pp. 65–70.

11 See further in Irene Jackson-Brown, "Afro-American Song in the Nineteenth Century: A Neglected Source," *The Black Perspective in Music* 4 (Spring 1976): pp. 22–38.

12 See further in Horace C. Boyer, "Charles Albert Tindley: Progenitor of Black-American Gospel Music," *The Black Perspective in Music* 11 (Fall 1983): pp. 103–132.

13 I am deeply indebted to gospel scholar Horace Boyer, professor of music at the University of Massachusetts at Amherst and currently at the Smithsonian Institution, for making available to me a copy of the *Holiness Church history, History of [the] Church of Christ (Holiness) U. S. A., 1895–1965*, ed. by Otho B. Cobbins (New York: Vantage Press, 1966). I also am grateful to D. Antoinette Handy, at the National Endowment for the Arts, for sharing information with me about the hymnals. Her grandfather, the Rev. Walter S. Pleasants, was one of the founders of the Church of Christ (Holiness) USA.

14 Here I express appreciation to Jack Ralston, professor at the University of Missouri–Kansas City, for presenting me with a copy of the Jackson *Colored Sacred Harp*.

15 Again I acknowledge my indebtedness to Horace Boyer, who kindly lent me his copy of *Yes, Lord!*

Published Hymnals in the African American Tradition

by Melva Wilson Costen[1]
from *The Hymn*, published in 1989

The new explosion of hymnody and hymnal publications in the last few years is replete with reminders of the need for the Church to be inclusive. While the term "inclusivity" brings to mind first and foremost language concerns, there is yet another awareness that is equally significant: inclusivity of the whole Body of Christ. This means all of God's people, especially those who, for whatever reason, have been relegated to the margins of society.

Significant in the latter category are the racial ethnics who are frequently neglected when music of the Church is being considered. While there has been an occasional inclusion of songs from racial ethnic traditions, rarely has there been a desire to include Native Americans, Hispanics, Asians, and African Americans in decision-making positions in the choice of the Church's hymnody. The procedure has been to select songs, then reharmonize and re-textualize them in keeping with the European understandings. Only at the end of this process have persons who created the songs appropriate for worship been made aware of what has been included. All too often the musical and textual re-settings are distortions of the reality of the environment and existential situations in which the songs were forged and spread.

The last ten years have been a time of newness for inclusivity. Not only are hymnal revision committees including a larger number of women, but few denominational hymnal committees are without racial ethnics. In one instance, the Presbyterian Church (USA) has appointed an African American woman to serve as chair of the committee. The United Methodist Church also took this process so seriously that racial ethnics worked diligently to compile a book of hymns and songs, supplementary to the major hymnal. Through this process, songs were selected by the particular community out of their own life experiences. While this new hymnody was shared with particular communities, the entire Church was provided an opportunity to sing *new* songs. This method of appropriating the faith through songs of marginal people allowed the full committee to appreciate and respect other ways of understanding the acts of God in history. Many of these songs are now a part of the whole United Methodist Church. Those whose particular histories these songs reflect were part of the decision-making process which allowed the songs to be included in the United Methodist Hymnal.

While the Vatican II pronouncements are often credited as the source of the plethora of revisions and publications of major denominational hymnody, the African American community identifies another movement in history as its source of origin. While this matter is not a major discussion among African and African American Protestants, this writer concludes that the Civil Rights movement, led by Martin Luther King, is the locus of the affirmation of liturgical life. The fervor of the singing, praying, and preaching was stimulated by the words of Scripture. Jesus came that we all may have life and have it more abundantly. The passage most familiar to an oppressed people was the words read by Jesus from the prophet Isaiah, 61:1–2: "The Spirit of the Lord is upon me, because he has anointed me to preach the Gospel to the poor. He has sent me to proclaim release to the captives and recovery of sight to the blind, to free those who are downtrodden, to proclaim the favorable year of the Lord."

In the ecumenical gatherings of African Americans, we recognized the common roots of the faith and the common shaping of liturgy. Few among those gathered and those who participated in individual churches had not heard the songs, prayers, and styles of preaching engendered by the Civil Rights movement. There was a new surge of ownership of all of the elements of worship created in "invisible institutions" (in brush arbors) and in subsequently built "frame churches" of rural and urban oppressed African Americans. Out of these gatherings had emerged a freedom in an understanding of how God works to free God's people in any age. Thus, a history which continued into the twentieth century evoked an affirmation of biblical and cultural histories.

The Interdenominational Theological Center in Atlanta, Georgia, has taken seriously its responsibility to collect and share the liturgical history of African Americans. This institution, founded in 1959, is a deliberately organized ecumenical and international center for theological education. In 1985, funds were made available to emphasize the liturgical (worship) dimension of the African, African American heritage. In three Consultations on Black Worship, theological leaders, pastors, and musicians gathered across denominational lines to discuss historical facts and current trends among African American congregations. Needless to say, the settings of these consultations, while basically academic, were filled with singing as well as other art forms.

The historical account of hymnals published by African Americans is basic to all church music classes at the Interdenominational Theological Center. While basic hymnody which continues to emerge through the Euro-American tradition is taught as a part of the curriculum, few Master of Divinity and Church Music degree graduates leave without the African American tradition firmly engrained.

The following hymnals stand in the African American tradition. They are listed with historical information.

1801 — Richard Allen, *A Collection of Spiritual Songs and Hymns, Selected from Various Authors*, by Richard Allen, African Minister (printed by Ormond)

> This is the first hymnal compiled expressly for the use of an African American congregation. The compiler, Richard Allen, is the celebrated founder of the African Methodist Episcopal Church (A.M.E.), Philadelphia, Pennsylvania. The importance of this hymnal arises from the fact that Allen and a small group of African Americans pulled away from the White Methodist Episcopal Church when improperly treated. It is of interest that Allen chose to publish his own hymnal rather than use the official Methodist hymnal.
>
> The first edition included fifty-four hymns with text only. It was a pocket hymnal (slightly larger than 5x3) and, like other hymnals of the day, did not list authors of texts, nor references to melodies that might be appropriate.

1801 — *A Collection of Hymns and Spiritual Songs from Various Authors*, by Richard Allen, Minister of the African Methodist Episcopal Church (printed by T. I. Plowman)

> The second edition of Allen's hymnal includes an additional ten texts (totaling sixty-four hymns). The historical importance of these hymnals is that they provide folk-selected anthologies, indicating songs that were probably popular

among African American Christians, across denominational lines, at the beginning of the nineteenth century. A copy of the first edition is available at the Garrett Theological Seminary, Evanston, Illinois. A copy of the second edition is at the American Antiquated Society of Worchester, Massachusetts.

Although the title includes "spiritual songs," it does not include African American spirituals. Twenty-six of the hymns are included in hymnals published by Euro-Americans. Included among the list are hymns by Isaac Watts, Charles Wesley, John Leland, John Newton, and a few by Richard Allen.

Allen's hymnals are apparently among the earliest sources in history that include hymns to which choruses or refrains are attached. Eileen Southern contends that Allen was first to employ the so-called "wandering refrains" (any refrain to any hymn). This improvisatory technique allowed for informality in the worship service.[2]

1818 — *African Methodist Episcopal Hymnal* (?)

This new A.M.E. hymnal included 314 hymns designated, according to the compilers, to "supersede those heretofore used among us." This hymnal was compiled by a committee which included Daniel Coker, James Chapman, Jacob Tapisco, and Richard Allen, chairman.[3] The hymnal was organized into sections according to various states of Christian experience. Hymns were carefully chosen to enhance the Church in doctrine and spiritual food.

It should be noted here that the A.M.E. Church was officially organized in 1816 with a membership in the thousands. A.M.E. hymnals were published periodically after the 1818 publication, but with few substantive changes.

1822 — *The Union African Hymnbook* (published by Peter Spence)

This hymnbook was published by Peter Spence for his newly organized Ezion Union African Church in Wilmington, Delaware.

1837 — *African Methodist Episcopal Hymnal* (revised edition)

In the 1837 edition of the A.M.E. hymnal, several features were added to facilitate usage: a scriptural text was provided for each hymn, along with the meter (common, long, short, and mixed meter) and an appropriate tune for use in singing the hymn.

1838 — *Hymns for the Use of the African Methodist Episcopal Zion Church in America* (A.M.E.Z.)

1869 — *Hymns for the Use of the African Methodist Episcopal Zion Church in America* (A.M.E.Z.) (improved edition)

This "improved edition" included 582 hymns compiled under the direction of Christopher Rush, Samuel M. Giles, and Joseph P. Thompson. Each hymn provided an indication of its meter as well as the tune name appropriate for singing it.

The repertoire of hymnals published by African American churches was similar to those published by White churches, with the exception of a relatively small number of hymns authored by African Americans.

1872 — *African Methodist Episcopal Zion Hymnal*

This hymnal contained 1,129 hymns, a size which must have been quite unwieldy and awkward for general use.

1876 — *The African Methodist Episcopal Church Hymnbook*

Work on this revised edition began in 1868 under the leadership of The Reverend Henry McNeil Turner. When it was completed eight years later, the bishops reported that the hew hymnbook was "a larger, more varied, comprehensive and useful compilation than ever before."[4] It contained 588 pages, 1,115 hymns, chants, and doxologies. This edition became the authorized hymnbook from 1876 to 1892.

1883 — Marshall W. Taylor, *A Collection of Revival Hymns and Plantation Melodies* (published by Marshall Taylor and W. C. Echols)

This collection of 170 songs was apparently the first hymnal designed for use by African Americans who were members of the predominantly White Methodist Episcopal Church. Marshall W. Taylor, the son of former slaves, was a preacher, licensed and ordained in the Methodist Episcopal Church.

Songs are included in this hymnal in two categories as the title indicates: "Revival Hymns" and "Plantation Melodies." The revival hymns are songs developed by African Americans as a result of their participation in (White) camp meetings. "Plantation Melodies" are the religious folk songs shaped out of the American slave experience. One hundred fifty of the songs include both music and text. The remaining twenty songs include text only. Authors' and composers' names are included under the titles of some of the songs. The scriptural bases for texts are also included.

1897 — *African Methodist Episcopal Hymnal*
The General Conference of the A.M.E. Church in 1888 affirmed the need for updating the Church's hymnody. A committee was appointed and was given the mandate to "revise the hymnbook and to compile a new hymnal." It was made clear that the hymnal was to be separate and apart from the hymnbook.[5] The work of the Hymnal Committee was not started until 1892, and the hymnal was published in 1897. This hymnal was used until the publication of a revised edition in 1941.

1908 — Charles A. Tindley, *Soul Echoes* (published by Charles A. Tindley)
This collection of songs by Tindley was perhaps intended as a Black gospel hymn source for his congregation, the Bainbridge Street Methodist Episcopal Church of Philadelphia, where he was pastor from 1902 until 1933. His gospel style is known to have influenced Thomas A. Dorsey (father of Black gospel music) and to have had universal appeal.

1909 — Charles A. Tindley, *New Songs of Paradise* (published by Tindley)
This collection, celebrated as the second edition of Tindley's *Soul Echoes*, appeared actually in six editions from 1916–1941. Tindley indicated that his songs were intended for singing in Sunday School, prayer meetings, Epworth League meetings, and social gatherings.

c. 1916 — *National Jubilee Melodies* (Nashville: National Baptist Publishing Board)

> The actual date of publication of this collection is not clear. This writer has not been able to examine an extant copy of the first edition. The edition examined (listed as the twenty-third edition) includes a handwritten date, 1916.
>
> This collection includes 142 old plantation songs from the "oral tradition, now kept alive in book form." The songs are spirituals (arranged and traditional), some Protestant hymns, and gospel songs. While the hymns do not carry the names of authors or composers and some have new titles, well-known tunes by Watts and Wesley are identifiable. Some of the gospel hymns include simple choruses.

1921 — *Gospel Pearls* (Nashville: National Baptist Convention Sunday School Publishing Board)

> This collection is an anthology of African American church music popular during the early twentieth century. The committee that compiled this hymnal included well-known African American musicians: Willa Townsend, Lucie Campbell, John W. Work, Frederick J. Work, and W. M. Nix. The popularity and emotional appeal of this collection caused it to be used in worship, the home, Sunday Schools, "Singing Conventions," and other religious gatherings. It was continually reprinted, both in standard and shaped-note editions.

1924 — *The Baptist Standard Hymnal* (Nashville: Sunday School Publishing Board, National Baptist Convention, U.S.A.)

> This publication, like the *Gospel Pearls*, became a favorite among congregations, soloists, choirs, and African Americans in general. The 745 musical entries include traditional hymns, spirituals, and gospel songs arranged for mixed choirs and treble voices.
>
> The Music Committee of sixteen included six women! The committee's music director was the highly acclaimed Mrs. A. M. Townsend. Excerpts of the statement of endorsement, signed by leaders in the denomination, provide some indication of the serious attention given this publication: "We the

undersigned have been requested to examine the Baptist Standard Hymnal carefully, give our endorsement to it and...say further that the content is such as cannot fail to provide spirituality and prove a valuable addition to the song service of every church,"[6]

1934 — J. Jackson, *The Colored Sacred Harp* (Ozark, AL: J. Jackson)
This book was compiled and published under the auspices of the Dale County Colored Musical Institute and the Alabama and Florida Union State. Old, familiar Protestant hymn texts are set to new, unfamiliar melodies, composed by the African American Sacred Harp Community.[7]

1941 — *Allen African Methodist Episcopal Hymnal* (Nashville: The African Methodist Episcopal Church)
The committee appointed to prepare this hymnal included familiar A.M.E. personalities: Bishops A. A. Fountain and D. Ward Nichols, Dr. W. K. Hopes, Dr. C. E. Stewart, Dr. W. H. Peck, Professors E. C. Deas, E. A. Clark, and Frederick Hall. This hymnal, which remained in use until the 1954 edition, included traditional Methodist hymnody with a very few songs from the African American tradition.

1954 — *African Methodist Episcopal Hymnal* (Nashville: African Methodist Episcopal Church)

1954 — *African Methodist Episcopal Hymnal* (Nashville: African Methodist Episcopal Church)
In 1953, the bishops of the A.M.E. Church voted to eliminate the name Allen from the hymnal and appointed a committee to revise and update it. The Senior Bishop, D. Ward Nichols, served as chairman with the following members: Bishops S. L. Greene, George W. Baber, L. H. Hemingway, Frederick D. Jordan, The Rev. Wallace M. Wright, Professor A. L. Haskell, Mrs. Harriet B. Wright, and Dr. E. A. Selby.
The inclusion of African American hymnody was again minimal, with a preference for traditional Methodist

hymnody. This edition contained a long and shorter setting of the A.M.E. Holy Communion and Baptism liturgies.

1961 — *The Baptist Standard Hymnal with Responsive Readings* (Nashville: Sunday School Publishing Board, National Baptist Convention, USA)

This is an updated edition of the hymnal of 1924 containing music intrinsic to Black Baptist traditions. This edition includes the subtitle: "A New Book for All Services." Many Black congregations used this compilation regularly until the 1977 publication of *The New National Baptist Hymnal.*

1977 — *The New National Baptist Hymnal* (Nashville: National Baptist Publishing Board)

According to the preface, the *"New National Baptist Hymnal* was conceived and published to serve a two-fold purpose: that of enhancing all aspects of our worship services, and for the preservation of our great religious heritage and musical taste for generations to come." Not only was the chairperson a woman, Mrs. Ruth Lomax Davis, but three additional women served on the six-member committee.

The popularity of the hymnal is attested to by the number of volumes sold and its usage by individuals, congregations, and in homes across denominational lines. Few African Americans are unfamiliar with its contents.

1977 — *His Fullness Songs* (Jackson, MS: National Publishing Board of the Church of Christ [Holiness] USA)

With the publication of this hymnal by the Church of Christ [Holiness] USA, the African American community was made aware of previous publications in this tradition. Since copies of these books are not available for analysis, dates and titles of publications will be noted here: (1) 1899 – *Jesus Only,* No. I; (2) 1901 – *Jesus Only,* No. I and No. II; (3) 1906 – His Fullness.

A larger number of the 512 songs in *His Fullness Songs* were composed by the founder and bishop of this church, Charles P. Jones. Many titles are traditional Protestant hymns and gospel songs which focus on Jesus the Christ. Scriptural texts and category of use are given for all songs. Indexes included are Alphabetical Index of Scripture Readings, Topical Index, and General Alphabetical Index of Songs and Hymns.

1981 — *Songs of Zion* (Nashville: Abingdon Press)
The Supplemental Worship Resource Number 12 was published as a result of a recommendation from the Consultation on the Black Church (Atlanta, 1973), sponsored by the United Methodist Board of Discipleship. The recommendation was that a song book from the Black religious tradition be made available to United Methodist churches. *Songs of Zion* is an anthology of church music important to African American traditions. It is literally a history of African American church music presented through music.

The book is divided into three major sections, each beginning with a historical introduction: Hymns, Spirituals, and Gospel Songs. The final section contains service music composed largely by African Americans. There is also one West Indian folk song, adaptation of spirituals, and a few songs composed by Euro-Americans.

This document is considered by scholars to be the major church musical resource published in recent years.

1981 — *Lift Every Voice and Sing: A Collection of African American Spirituals and Other Songs* (New York: The Church Hymnal Corporation)
This hymnal is the first of its kind for the Episcopal Church. The collection of spirituals provided a needed addition to the traditional spiritual repertoire. The service music, while designed for the Episcopal liturgy, can have...ecumenical usage. The brief history of African American Episcopal music by Dr. Irene V. Jackson-Brown is quite helpful in expanding an understanding of and appreciation for African American Episcopalians.

1982 — *Yes, Lord!* (Memphis: The Church of God in Christ Publishing Board in association with the Benson Company)
This, the first official hymnal of the Church of God in Christ, carries the title of a praise chant composed by Bishop Charles

H. Mason, founder of the church in 1896. Bishop Mason sang this dynamic praise in order to gather the congregation in spiritual communion and commitment.

This is a collection of 506 songs including a wide variety of music and texts from varied traditions. Scriptural texts are provided for each song. Indexes include a Topical Index of Scripture Readings, a Scriptural Index of Readings, an Alphabetical Index of Hymn Titles and First Lines, and a Topical Index of Hymns.

While the Hymnal Task Force is nearly balanced between bishops and laity, only three members are women. Women figured prominently in the work of the Task Force, however, with Ms. Iris Stevenson and Dr. Mattie Moss Clark providing dynamic leadership.

1984 — *A.M.E.C. Bicentennial Hymnal* (Nashville: The African Methodist Episcopal Church)

This is a completely revised edition of the 1954 hymnal, including for the first time a large body of African American spirituals as well as songs from the A.M.E. Church in Africa. This edition represents a significant publication in the observance of the two hundredth anniversary of the A.M.E. Church.

The Commission on Worship and Liturgy of the church emerged as a task force to carry out the directive to "enlarge the content of hymns and liturgical materials, re-editing the entire hymnal."

Consideration was given to a number of concerns, including questions of sexist language, ethnic identity, theological relevance, international inclusiveness, contemporary style, and personal favorites.

There are 670 musical entries, Psalters, Prayers, Three-Year Cycle Lectionary, and the A.M.E. Ritual. The Indexes are extensive, including a Metrical Index of Tunes and an Index of Authors, Composers, and Source Hymns.

1987 — *Lead Me, Guide Me: The African American Catholic Hymnal*
(Chicago: GIA Publications, Inc.)

> This hymnal was "born of the needs and aspirations of Black
> Catholics for music that reflects both an African American
> heritage and our Catholic faith." These are the words of the
> Most Reverend James P. Lyke, O.F.M., Ph.D., Auxiliary
> Bishop of Cleveland and Coordinator of the Hymnal Project,
> and the Reverend William Norvel, S.S.J., President of
> National Black Clergy Caucus.
>
> The 323 songs and very extensive service music are indica-
> tive of serious deliberations and excellent choices! The book is
> carefully structured as follows: Season and Feasts, Solemnities
> of the Lord, and Rites of the Church. Song styles range from
> the simplistic reflection in the spirituals to "hard gospel" with
> intricate accompaniments.
>
> Traditional hymns, contemporary gospels, and composed
> songs, especially by African American Catholics, set this book
> apart as a classic anthology which will certainly find a place
> among Protestants.
>
> The words of dedication deserve full quote here. The book
> was dedicated to Father Clarence Joseph Rivers, Ph.D.,
> "Renowned Liturgist and Musician…who paved the way for
> liturgical inculturation and inspired Black Catholics to bring
> their artistic genius to Catholic worship." (Quoted materials
> are from the Preface of the Hymnal).

1987 — *The Hymnal of the Christian Methodist Episcopal Church* (Memphis:
The CME Publishing House)

> The Christian Methodist Episcopal Church (C.M.E.) found-
> ed in 1870, published its first hymnal in 1890. It was based
> primarily on the hymnal of the Methodist Episcopal Church
> South with a preface by the bishops of the Church and the rit-
> ual of the C.M.E. Church added. Their history of hymnody
> has basically included hymnbooks from other traditions,
> including the *Gospel Pearls*.
>
> The present hymnal, selected by the Commission on
> Hymnal for the church, is in fact *The New National Baptist
> Hymnal* with an additional song by Lucious H. Holsey, one of

the early bishops of the church. Additionally, a C.M.E. Order of Worship, the Rituals of the C.M.E. Church, and a select number of Aids to Worship are included. A new cover was provided with the name and symbol of the Church clearly visible.

---

1 Melva Wilson Costen is professor of Worship and Music at the Interdenominational Theological Center in Atlanta, Georgia. A graduate of Johnson C. Smith University and the University of North Carolina, with a doctorate from Georgia State University, she chairs the Presbyterian Church (USA) Hymnal Committee and has held numerous posts in the Presbyterian Church. She has taught music in the Atlanta public school system, has lectured at numerous schools around the world, and has written and edited many articles related to worship. She and her husband James Costen have three children and five grandchildren.

2 For more detailed information, see Eileen Southern's *Music of Black Americans,* 2d ed. (New York: W. W. Norton, 1983), pp. 75–81. The historical significance of these early hymnals necessitated the extended information provided.

3 *A.M.E.C. Bicentennial Hymnal* (Nashville: The African Methodist Episcopal Church), p. xi.

4 *A.M.E.C. Bicentennial Hymnal,* p. xi.

5 Ibid., pp. xi–xii.

6 I am greatly indebted to Addie N. Peterson, ITC student, and her aunt, Mrs. Neanette Harvey, Mount Bayou, Mississippi, for providing the information from the 1924 edition of *The Baptist Standard Hymnal.*

7 The copy that I own was given to me in 1979 by a Sacred Harp Singer, Mrs. Cleona Berry, at a Hymn Society Meeting in Berea, Kentucky.

Black Hymnody

by Wendell P. Whalum
from *Review and Expositor*, Vol. LXX, No. 3, published in 1973

The most important singular contribution of Black people to the making of American culture is their music. Rooted as it is in every fiber of a certain Black lifestyle, it may reflect, at its depths, a deep sense of longing amidst poor social conditions which the system imposes, or it may, at its height, elevate to a plane of great hope. Of the former, there is never the acceptance on the part of Blacks of their plight or even the slightest intention of being satisfied with it, but there is always the connection with the latter in which moments of deep thinking, joy, happiness, and expectation help to dispel gloom. Hope is always the outcome. This statement refers to the period of the "oral tradition," which begins to end around 1867, with the presence of schools and the strong institutional churches and their new role of educating Black people.

The oral tradition is that period in which the manner of dealing with American life as realized by Blacks themselves is hewn, by them, or with little outside help, from a few sources. The Bible is the best known of these and is the primary source for the thought process. But White family structure, class consciousness, church organization, and the like, were also strong influences on what we find in traditional Black life. The Bible, more than any other one source, provided the textual material for the religious music which is at the very base of a consideration of Black hymnody. The accounts of Moses, Jeremiah, Elijah, Ezekiel, Daniel, John, Matthew, Mark, Luke, and others, take on more significance when interpreted against the backdrop of eighteenth and nineteenth century human bondage. They, and their philosophies, live again in the spiritual music. Through such vivid imagination as the spiritual affords, a boldness in spirit is girded by a faith which becomes an unfailing anchor.

Several writers have raised doubts as to the authenticity of the spiritual as well as all other oral literature of Black people. Since notable responses have been made to these, we will not deal with the subject here. Harold

Courlander[1] has written a valid response to their charges.

Spirituals have their roots in the eighteenth century when need among slaves for expression in a common language was strongest. It is, therefore, not music for the sake of music, but music which is reflective of the experiences of slaves and "freedmen" and music which is, in its most positive sense, communicative—one with the other as well as with the group. It is music that embraces, in varying degrees, the quest for life, love, identity, acceptance, sometimes death, and always freedom. The quest is always there.

Accounts of religious music of the early years of the eighteenth century are scant and must be dealt with on planes of generalities. But Dena J. Epstein[2] has provided an excellent article on the best of the very early sources.

Black hymnody, categorically speaking, must include all serious music that is sacred to the Black experience. This should suggest all the serious music that falls within the boundaries of Christianity as it seized the Black experience as well as that serious music which was sacred to the experience, but not necessarily Christian in nature. (I have noted elsewhere that it is a point of wonder that, as far as we know, the music of Blacks of pre-Christian days could be contained, intact, after the introduction of Christianity.)

The serious sacred music of the oral tradition is primarily individual to group music. It begins with the individual but is made into final composition, finished, and polished by the group.

Those groups who made the music, before and since the Civil War, assembled to work at further definition of their faith and reviving their hope in a delivering God. They also took great pains to "count their blessing." In these meetings where music was sung, there were no observers. An individual contributed a musical "thought," and the group worked it over and over, reshaping phrases, adding and subtracting notes, filling in melodic gaps, adjusting harmony and rhythm. Many spirituals have died when they failed to do what the group intended them to do.

If a member of the group could not sing, he could pat his foot; if he could not pat, he could sway his head; and if he could not do this, he could witness. Everyone was expected to participate.

Another important factor here is that the Black folk church never needed or had a choir. The choir was the entire congregation who, as James Weldon Johnson pointed out,[3] had able and talented musical leaders on whom the body of singers depended for musical guidance.

With the spiritual at the root level, let us attempt, before further discussion, a chart of the growth of Black sacred music:

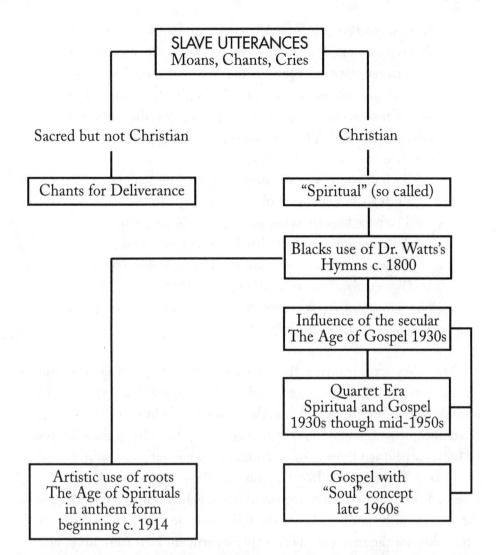

One important point that must not escape the introductory lines of this paper has to do further with the particular group of Blacks who prepared and preserved this music. It is this group that insisted, without full endorsement of the clergy, on taking the music from the slave quarter to the institutional church. It is they who, when warned against using this music in the church, found a place for it in prayer meetings, ring shouts, and services as well as in daily personal and community devotions. It is, therefore, to them that we must give the credit for the preservation of the older music types of which we have only a few examples. And today, isolated in storefront churches, rural towns, and sea islands, they continue to sing the music.

Expressed feelings against the use of spirituals, especially shouting ones, are evident from early church fathers. The activities of the Reverend Richard Allen (1760–1831) are described as follows:

From about 1800, Richard Allen published books of every sort for his parishioners, including hymnbooks. Some of the hymns he personally wrote. Some of his "spiritual songs" are quite conventional, in the tradition of the White spiritual. Others devote themselves to admonitions to improve the flock. For example, Richard Allen did not like shouting Methodists; he thus had his congregations sing,

> Such groaning and shouting, it sets me to doubting,
> I fear such religion is only a dream;
> The preachers are stamping, the people were jumping,
> And screaming so loud that I neither could hear,
> Either praying or preaching, such horrible screeching
> 'Twas truly offensive to all that were there.

The significant factor is that the hymn is directed toward the personal and group behavior of the people.[4]

The years accompanying the establishment of the institutional church are the years that began the cessation of the spiritual. The strongest blow, however, came from Bishop Daniel Payne, who thought that the imitation of established denominations was the best approach. In order to make his point, he honestly belittled those who practiced folklore in religious services.

Bishop Payne (1811–1893) in his excellent document, *Recollections of Seventy Years* (Nashville, 1888), gives us much helpful information along with the account of his attitude about the folk music, to which we have referred. That aside, for the moment, consider these pertinent facts from his book:

1. The first introduction of choral singing into the A.M.E. Church took place in Bethel (Church), Philadelphia, PA, between 1841–1842. It gave great offense to the older members, especially those who had professed personal sanctification. Said they: "You have brought the devil into the Church, and therefore we will go out."

2. So great was the excitement and irritation produced by the introduction of the choir into Bethel Church, that I, then a local preacher and school-master, was requested by the leader of the choir and other prominent members in it to preach a special sermon on sacred music. This I did the best I could. In my researches, I used a small monograph on music written by Mr. Wesley.... The immediate effect of that discourse was to

check the excitement, soothe the irritation, and set the most intelligent to reading as they had never done before.

3. Instrumental music was introduced into our denomination in the year 1848–1849. It commenced at Bethel, in Baltimore....[5]

Now let us return to the tongue-lashing that Bishop Payne gave the group that sang the folk music:

> I have mentioned the "Praying and Singing Bands" elsewhere. The strange delusions that many ignorant but well-meaning people labor under leads me to speak particularly of them. About this time, I attended a "bush meeting," where I went to please the pastor whose circuit I was visiting. After the sermon they formed a ring, and with coats off sung, clapped their hands, and stamped their feet in a most ridiculous and heathenish way. I requested the pastor to go and stop their dancing. At his request, they stopped their dancing and clapping of hands, but remained singing and rocking their bodies to and fro. This they did for about fifteen minutes. I then went, and taking their leader by the arm requested him to desist and to sit down and sing in a rational manner. I told him also that it was a heathenish way to worship and disgraceful to themselves, the race, and the Christian name. In that instance, they broke up their ring but would not sit down, and walked sullenly away. After the sermon in the afternoon, having another opportunity of speaking alone to this young leader of the singing and clapping ring, he said: "Sinners won't get converted unless there is a ring." Said I: "You might sing until you fell down dead and you would fail to convert a single sinner, because nothing but the Spirit of God and the word of God can convert sinners." He replied: "The Spirit of God works upon people in different ways. At camp-meeting, there must be a ring here, a ring there, a ring over yonder, or sinners will not get converted." This was his idea, and it is also that of many others. These "Bands" I have had to encounter in many places, and as I have stated in regard to my early labors in Baltimore, I have been strongly censured because of my efforts

to change the mode of worship or modify the extravagances indulged in by the people. In some cases, all that I could do was to teach and preach the right, fit, and proper way of serving God. To the most thoughtful and intelligent I usually succeeded in making the "Band" disgusting; but by the ignorant masses, as in the case mentioned, it was regarded as the essence of religion. So much so was this the case that, like this man, they believe no conversion could occur without their agency, nor outside of their own ring could any be a genuine one. Among some of the songs of these "Rings," or "Fist and Heel Worshipers" as they have been called, I find a note or two in my journal, which were used in the instance mentioned. As will be seen, they consisted chiefly of what are known as "cornfield ditties:"

Ashes to ashes, dust to dust;
If God won't have us, the devil must.
I was way over there where the coffin fell;
I heard that sinner as he screamed in hell.[6]

Fredrika Bremer (1801–1865), a native of Sweden, wrote the following about the A.M.E. Church in Cincinnati in *Homes of the New World* (1853):

Diary entry Columbia, South Carolina, May 25, 1850—
When at home with Mr. B., I heard the Negroes singing, it having been so arranged by Hannah L. I wished rather to have heard their own native songs, but was told that they "dwelt with the Lord" and sang only hymns. I am sorry for this exclusiveness; nevertheless, their hymns sung in quartette were glorious....

Cincinnati, Ohio, November 27, 1850—
I had in the forenoon visited a Negro Baptist church belonging to the Episcopal Creed. There were but few present, and they of the Negro aristocracy of the city...the hymns were beautifully and exquisitely sung....

In the afternoon I went to the African Methodist Church in Cincinnati, which is situated in the African Quarter.... The singing ascended and poured forth like a melodious torrent, and the heads, feet, and elbows of the congregation moved all in unison with it, amid evident enchantment and delight in the singing, which was in itself exquisitely pure and full of melodious life.

The hymns and psalms which the Negroes have themselves composed have a peculiar naive character, childlike, full of imagery and life. Here is a specimen of one of their popular church hymns:

What ship is this that's landed at the shore?
 Oh, glory, halleluia!
It's the old ship of Zion, halleluiah;
It's the old ship of Zion, halleluiah.
Is the mast all sure, and the timber all sound?
 Oh, glory halleluia!
She's built of gospel timber, halleluiah;
 etc., etc.

After the singing of the hymns, which was not led by any organ or musical instrument whatever, but which arose like burning melodious sighs from the breasts of the congregation, the preacher mounted the pulpit.[7]

These accounts illumine the reasons why the religious folk music of slaves and former slaves faded into the background during the first sixty-five or so years of the nineteenth century. Perhaps it was time for this music to be halted and perhaps it was true that if Blacks were to worship in a nation that recognized hymnbooks, choirs, and organs as necessary entities of the worship service, they should fully understand these aids. But the development progressed, obstinately, to another rather interesting state. While the Methodists were, more or less according to the presiding Bishop, attempting to get in step with England's gift to the religious practices of the New World, the Baptists in no real uniformity were, in the words of Joseph Washington, "slower in developing a structure due to the local autonomy of each congregation."[8] The truth is that Baptists allowed for more individual participation and address to church affairs than the Methodists. The Baptists, therefore, are responsible for developing a "new" kind of Negro singing that utilized the "new" hymntexts in a manner unique to most Black Baptist congregations.

The following account is invaluable in understanding why the spiritual was gradually replaced by hymns in the sacred service. Eileen Southern gives the account of the era as follows:

During the 1730s, a new religious movement swept the (New England and Middle) colonies, the so-called "Great Awakening," bringing with it a demand for the use of livelier music in the worship service. The "new" songs of the movement were hymns; for text they employed religious poems instead of the scriptural psalms. In 1707, Dr. Isaac Watts, an English minister and physician, published a book, *Hymns and Spiritual Songs,* that became immensely popular in the colonies, especially among the Black folk, because of the freshness and vitality of the words. In 1717, he published another collection of his attractive hymns, entitled *The Psalms of David, Imitated in the Language of the New Testament and Apply'd to the Christian State and Worship.* Before long, people began to neglect the psalms, preferring to sing hymns instead, especially since the latter were fitted to lively tunes. Slowly, the various Protestant denominations in the colonies, one after the other, adopted the hymns of Watts. The "Era of Watts" in the history of American religious music had begun....[9]

The Black Methodists and Baptists endorsed Watts's hymns, but the Baptists "blackened" them. They virtually threw out the meter signature and rhythm and before 1875 had begun a new system which, though based on the style of singing coming from England to America in the eighteenth century, was drastically different from it. It was congregational singing much like the spiritual had been in which the text was retained. The melody sung in parallel intervals, fourths and fifths, sometimes thirds and sixths at cadence points, took a rather crudely shaped line which floated melismatically along, being held together primarily by the deacon who raised and lined it. It was this kind of singing that White minister Charles A. Raymond wrote about in *Harper's New Monthly Magazine* in 1863. He entitled his account, "The Religious Life of the Negro Slave." In it he wrote about a service of worship as follows:

In the churches of the cotton-growing states, the Negro deacon is no unimportant personage. He is a pastor without being a preacher; and is also the connecting official link between his Colored brethren in the church and their White associates. What the White pastor can never know, concerning the moral and social characters of the Colored flock, the Negro deacon can know.... Nothing was more suggestive than a meeting for

> the election of a deacon…. In meetings where business is to be transacted, the pastor is necessarily present…. He…calls upon the singers for a hymn, and the meeting is regularly organized. The usual devotional exercises, prayer, and singing occupy about half an hour. These are generally conducted by the Negroes—the pastor being a quiet participator in the worship.

What the gentleman did not make clear, but is nevertheless the practice, is that the devotional exercises which he described are conducted by the deacons. One need only to visit some Baptist churches today, that are a bit more primitive than those on the beaten path, to discover the method outlined herein. In the service, i.e., after the devotions, hymns are sung faithful to the score. In lining, the deacon gives out two lines of the hymn at a time and then leads the congregation in singing. Though the congregation is used to the method and the text, they enjoy and follow this practice as it has been done in the past. When the deacon motions for the congregation to stand, it is understood that the current stanza will be the concluding one. Most of the hymns sung in this manner are hymns of Dr. Watts. A substantial number of Black Baptist churches have "Dr. Watts Choirs" as a regular part of their musical offering in divine worship services.

The "Dr. Watts's" gave way in the late nineteenth century to a still more varied and interesting type. It is known in several Holiness churches as shaped-note singing. In this type is employed a "professor" who teaches to "singing classes" the method of singing note shapes with their names, do, re, mi, etc. This use of syllables, attractive as it is, has led singing choirs into using the syllables for the first portion of their musical offering in services of worship. A few bodies of worshippers, especially The Church of Christ, Holiness, will use the notes for teaching purposes only and will not sing the notes by syllables in the services. They do maintain the strict square rhythm that they took over from the great White gospel singers of the turn of the century, but the boldness of their voices almost makes one believe that the music, though it is not, is the work of Black composers. Blacks, though, never assumed the authorship of them. They have been accused of such. Truth is that the soft-back books that contain this music are delightful ownership of those who sing from them and not, usually, the property of the church in which they are heard.

When Christianity seized the Black experience, the worshippers took hold of whatever was shared with them and made it into a music of their own. This was not plagiarism. It was an honest effort to give God their best. Many spirituals of this period became a part of many hymns. Two immediately come to mind:

1. Spiritual Refrain:
    He didn't have to wake me, but He did.
    He didn't have to wake me, but He did.
    Woke me up this morning, and started me on my way.
    He didn't have to wake me, but He did.

Verse: (from a hymn)
    Amazin' grace, How sweet the sound,
    That saved a wretch like me,
    I once was lost, but now I'm found,
    Was blind, but now I see.

2. Spiritual Refrain:
    I got to lie down,
    How shall I rise?
    I got to lie down,
    How shall I rise?
    'Got to lie down,
    How shall I rise?
    'Pear fore the judgment bar.

Verse: (from a hymn)
    Dark was the night and
    Cold the ground
    On which my Lord was laid,
    Great drops of blood
    Like sweat rolled down
    In agony He prayed.

Following the second half of the nineteenth century, this method of singing, plus the already mentioned deaconed ones, took hold, and the Baptists and probably only a few Methodists made it into what is still today one of the most beautiful and moving congregational musical offerings to be witnessed. In it there are no musical instruments and usually no hand clapping, though there is always the necessary steady pat of the foot on the carpetless floor of the church. It is also sometimes extremely difficult to understand what words are being sung since many singers slide over the words, saving the vowel sounds for use with the notes. One interested in this aspect of Negro singing should certainly read John Work's article, "Plantation Meistersinger," in *The Musical Quarterly*.[10] Though the texts are from hymnbooks, the music is unquestionably Black.

One thing that must be said is that the music of the oral tradition was a utilitarian music, that is, it aimed at usefulness rather than beauty. It served the needs of the makers. It also reveals, in a peculiar period beginning about 1800, that the minds of the makers of the music were extremely clever and keen in perceiving an increased manner of communication with their fellows.

The insurrections that are well-known occurred during the period when Negroes from the North and Black preachers in the South spoke a rebellious gospel, rooted in the scriptures, to slaves. They were quite successful before being caught. They had a music to accompany it. It was religious music, honest and useful. It braved their hearts and minds and assured their souls that their efforts were at least right in the sight of God. Invoking God's blessing is an inseparable part of much of these "protest" songs. One is:

> Guide my feet, while I run this race (repeated 3 times)
> For I don't want to run this race in vain.

The late Dr. Miles Mark Fisher and the late Dr. John W. Work differed as to place of origin, but agreed that "Steal Away to Jesus" was a signal song for preparation meetings. A very telling one is:

> Get you ready, there's a meeting here tonight
> Come along, there's a meetin' here tonight,
> I know you by your daily walk
> There's a meetin' here tonight.

Another famous one is:

> Walk together children, don't you get weary
> There's a great camp meetin' in the Promised Land.

Another one, less famous, from South Georgia, around Cordele:

> Don't say nothing
> Can't you hear?
> Don't do nothing
> Can't you hear?
> Standin' there behind you
> Lookin' this way,

Don't say nothing
Can't you hear?

Verse:
One man in the wilderness
One man gone to pray
One man gon' go on home
An' run till judgment day.
Hallelujah!

And, of course, there were many more. But again, the marvel is that these, too, could be taken as they were for use in religious meetings with a real Christian motive behind them. That they had double meanings all the more underscores the clever mind of the slave. He knew that the master thought that "When they' singing, they' working."

Miles Mark Fisher[11] attempted a glossary of the meanings of some of the words frequently used in these spirituals. "Satan," says Fisher, is anyone who mistreated the slave. "King Jesus" was the slave's benefactor, "Babylon" and "winter" were slavery, "hell" was being sold farther South, and "Jordan" was the first step toward freedom. Fisher quotes V. F. Calverton, from an article entitled "The Negro and American Culture,"[12] who writes that "there is more, far more, than the ordinary Christian zeal embedded in Negro spirituals. They are not mere religious hymns written or recited to sweeten the service or improve the ritual, they are aching, poignant cry of an entire people."

Of form and style of the spirituals we have said little. John W. Work, in an address to the Hymn Society of America,[13] covers this subject completely.

Musical activity in Black communities around the turn of the century was more secular than sacred in nature. Church music was now fairly well established in the singing of hymns with organ accompaniment as well as anthems. Traditional music, as we have stated, had its place assigned to devotional services which took place before Sunday morning services, in prayer meetings, and in weekly community devotions. The ministers frequently led a meter hymn or a spiritual before or during the sermon, a practice which continues until today. A few churches with outstanding choirs completely threw out the meter hymns and traditional music and engaged in singing cantatas and taking part in music festivals. The greater musical activity, though, by far, transpired in the musical theaters of New York and Chicago and in hotels and auditoriums in other cities where Black composers were busy working out their scores for performances. Scott Joplin, Will

Marion Cook, Eubie Blake, James Reese Europe, and W. C. Handy were among the most active.

Looking backward to 1866, one of the most important events was the organization of the National Baptist Convention. The organization allowed for more association among the clergy and members of that denomination and offered the opportunity for increased activity among the musicians of the churches.

By 1930, a new approach to religious life had been firmly established in the Holiness churches. Music in these churches was, for the most part, sung in the manner of the oral tradition. Efforts to define their reason for being led some of the bodies to use instruments, encourage rhythmic clapping, holy dancing, and speaking in tongues. Instrumental improvisation, in dance-band fashion, for use during the long periods of dancing, was also encouraged. Other Holiness churches, especially The Church of God, Holiness, had a musical hodgepodge in which old spirituals, shape-note hymns, a total of about five bravura anthems, shouting, but no dancing, provided the fare.

In a sense, we must give credit to the Holiness churches for extending the life of the music of the oral tradition. For during their long and important devotional periods, sometimes several per week, many old and, sometimes unfamiliar, spirituals may be heard. Another part of this life extension is the contribution of the Fisk Jubilee Singers who, as pace setters in 1871, revealed to the world the effectiveness of spiritual arrangements.[14]

Many of the Black college and university choirs, glee clubs, and quartets followed the Fisk lead and found audiences, both Black and White, increasingly eager to hear their renditions of sacred and secular Negro music. The quartet feature was effective and many quartets were formed. Quartet singing flourished until the 1950s in a very popular fashion. They sang spiritual arrangements but specialized in those spirituals that contained unusually long narratives. The "Samson" story in the spiritual "Witness for My Lord," the drama in "John Saw the Number," "Daniel in the Lion's Den," "Hebrew Children in the Fiery Furnace," "David and Goliath," and others were, in special church programs, shouting numbers. In theaters and auditoriums, they were "show stoppers." Some of the quartets were of the "hip slapper" type, while others were not only artistic but made up of men with trained voices.

In 1914, R. Nathaniel Dett accomplished a major task. He wrote an anthem, the first, based on a spiritual. After publication, this anthem became part of the repertory of almost every average-to-exceptional choir in the country. Based on the spiritual "Listen to the Lambs," it was very effective.[15]

Dett employed the usual anthem quality but retained the spiritual flavor. He inspired other composers, many of whom were Black, to write spiritual-based anthems which became the pride of collegiate and church choirs.

In 1916, Harry T. Burleigh made a similar contribution when he published a spiritual for solo voice, artistically arranged. Later, many composers followed their lead. James Weldon and J. Rosamond Johnson produced a collection in two different books of spirituals for the solo voice.[16] Hall Johnson began and fully developed his choir, which sang his arrangements primarily. Activities in other places, such as Tuskegee, Fisk, Atlanta, and the like, gave the arrangements wide and numerous performances.

There were, of course, other arrangers and/or composers, such as John W. Work, Willis Laurence James, Clarence Cameron White, Frederick Hall, William L. Dawson, and Kemper Harrold, who seriously worked at reclaiming as much of this music as possible. As it is to be expected, many White arrangers and a few Black ones, too, issued the music without fully understanding the roots and, consequently, gave out many scores that misrepresent the purposes of certain numbers. It has often been surprising to audiences to learn that every folk song of the Negro, with religious words, was not intended or used for worship services. In fact, many of these contain a bit of humor which would never have been permitted in the services of worship. "Little David, play on your harp, hallelu," is a case in point.

The style of the spiritual is simple. The rhythm is most important and that, according to research of John W. Work, "may be slow and pounding" or "hard and driving." Of meter, Dr. Work states, "True spirituals are in either 2/4 or 4/4."[17] They are dignified gems and, of the serious ones, humor is not intended or expected. They lay claim to an interpretation rendered only as a result of a belief and a faith.

The spiritual, therefore, is the root and trunk of Black music. Its influences are felt today in much that we hear.

In the 1930s following the beginning of the Great Depression, another music came to the fore. Called by several scholars the twentieth century spiritual, gospel music was introduced and began its long, winding development. As a result of the impact of this period of want, Pearl William-Jones in her study of African American gospel music has labeled 1900-30: Pre-Gospel Era. She has this to say:

> The rise of gospel music around 1930 is attributable to several
> sociological changes within the Black community, foremost
> among which was the steady increase in migration from the

South by Blacks in search of greater economic opportunities and freedom. With these migrants came their religious traditions which found an outlet for expression in the various humble storefronts and small church buildings which some congregations could afford. E. Franklin Frazier, eminent sociologist of Howard University, has given a very vivid and detailed account of these Black churches in his book, *Black Bourgeoisie*. The musical traditions of these various denominations were maintained in the more fundamentalist-type churches, providing the greatest opportunity for the seeds of gospel music to come into full bloom. This came about in those churches which were not geared to traditional liturgy and formality of religious worship—some Baptist, a few Methodist, and a majority of the Pentecostal or Holiness churches. There was, and has been, an unquenchable thirst among these people for their own music which could express their innermost feelings about God, and their emotional involvement which was a part of this expression. The music at hand was an idiom with which they were all familiar, and it could be created spontaneously. The preacher, the song leader, and congregation all shared equally in those creative moments.[18]

The first three decades of the century also saw the shift, in the world of secular music, from ragtime to blues, to the recording of the blues, and the introduction of jazz. In no small measure did these expressions have their effect on gospel music. In fact, one of the leaders in the gospel music movement, Thomas A. Dorsey (b. 1899), was active as a blues pianist and, before 1919, had been one of the successful pianists in the South, especially in Atlanta.

Dorsey acknowledges that his greatest influence was from Dr. C. A. Tindley, a writer of a number of "soul-stirring" songs.[19] Tindley was in the group that included Dr. and Mrs. Townsend, E. W. D. Isaac, Lucie E. Campbell, and others. Their songs, not known as hymns, were issued in National Baptist Convention publications: *Carols of Glory, Gospel Pearls, Awakening Echoes,* and *The Baptist Standard Hymnal,* and then became the possession of scores of soloists and choirs. A few of them, notably "He'll Understand and Say Well Done," by Campbell, are still sung today.

This group of songwriters inspired Dorsey, who rhythmically stepped up the music by bringing to it more of the idioms that he had used as a blues pianist. (This writer, on more than one occasion, has heard Baptist choruses of five hundred or more led by Miss Campbell, Dorsey, and others, sing this music.) Dorsey was joined by Theodore Frye, Kenneth Morris, Lillian Bowles, Sallie Martin, and Roberta Martin in bringing to the fore gospel music that was, in its early days, rejected by many serious Black musicians. It caused protests in several Baptist churches and split several choirs. Ministers eager to attract the young and the unchurched organized new choirs, not to replace older ones, but to help in "firing" up the services.

In time, robes, stoles, and hoods of many and varied colors and fabrics began to be part of the dress of these new choirs, and demonstrative actions often accompanied their renditions. And the emotional pitch must not be slighted. Without it the numbers fall, sometimes painfully. With it they rise to unbelievable heights. These songs have taken on length according to the way they are received. If an audience is really moved, one song might last fifteen minutes or more.

Compared to spirituals, the texts of "gospels" are weak and audiences will not be able to join in readily since the performers are singing special arrangements. The accompaniments, which are essential, frequently call for piano, Hammond organ, guitar, bass. But, we repeat, emotion is the core.

The sources of the texts are not very different from spiritual textual sources. An early "gospel" which begins, "I was young, but I recall singing songs was mother's joy," moves on to couple with the hymn, "Amazin' Grace." A recent recording by the Hawkins's singers borrows a snatch from the old White gospel hymn, "O Happy Day," and "I Heard the Voice." Others are original in text, but not in music. In fact, Dorsey's famous "Precious Lord" is warmed over "Must Jesus Bear the Cross Alone." The text is new, but the music is not. But let us hasten to explain that this is not intended to steal the compositions of others. As was the case in the era of the oral tradition, one was free to borrow as long as he made the borrowed music better than he found it. Everyone knows that written gospels are mere indications of what the composer intends; the performer is to make it better. If one ever heard Mahalia Jackson sing Dorsey's "Precious Lord," he knows that he certainly did not hear "Must Jesus Bear." He really heard "Precious Lord."

Today, gospel singers have taken the music into nightclub theaters, into jazz festivals, and into formerly conservative Methodist and Congregational churches. Too, beginning at Howard University in 1970, gospel "goes to college."

As stated earlier, the music from the Black church is a music that takes as its license the right to pick and choose that which serves its needs, and if it cannot be found, it may be created. The fact that it begins as outright creation makes creativity part and parcel of all Black music, sacred as well as secular. The offerings are honest and they are intended to serve the human needs of the people, individual and group. As an honest music that, without doubt, has had many positive effects on those who use it, it should have been, at least at the level of the music of the oral tradition, accepted into the larger body of church music of the Christian world. It is the hope of this writer that church musicians will begin to integrate some of it into their music portions of the worship service.

---

1 Harold Courlander, *Negro Folk Music, U.S.A.* (New York: Columbia University, 1963), p. 39:

> Any notion that Negro oral religious literature is primitive or naive…an impression conveyed by numerous literary treatments…certainly does not survive careful reading or hearing. The song "All God's Children Got Wings," far from being quaint or childlike, is an expression of faith couched in symbols that were apparent to most pre-literate slaves and, later, liberated Negroes. While some people must have taken the inherent promises of this song literally, for most Negroes the wings, harps, and shoes must have conveyed simply the idea of relief from a hard and unrewarding life, either in this world or another. If Negro religious imagery is truly "naive," then the burden of responsibility must be borned by the Bible, out of which the imagery is primarily extracted.

> Negro religious literature, like the secular, is marked by an economy of statement, rich and fresh scenes, and the capacity to evoke recognition and response. The entire story of Jonah is presented in a song of fourteen lines, every one of which is visual and dramatic. Many of the songs do not describe events so much as allude to them. Some telescope a variety of allusions into a few tight phrases.

2 See Dena J. Epstein. "Slave Music in the United States before 1860: A Survey of Sources," in *Notes of the Music Library Association.* 20: 195–212, 377–380 (Spring and Summer 1963).

3 James Weldon Johnson and J. Rosamond Johnson, *The Books of American Negro Spirituals* (New York: Viking, 1942), Preface, pp. 21–23.

4 Richard Allen, quoted in John Lovell, Jr., *Black Song: The Forge and the Flame* (New York: Macmillan, 1972), pp. 105–106.

5 Daniel Alexander Payne, quoted in Eileen Southern, *Readings in Black American Music* (New York: W. W. Norton, 1971), pp. 65–70.

6 Quoted in Ibid., pp. 68–69.

7 Fredrika Bremer, quoted in Eileen Southern, *op. cit.,* pp. 107–108 and 112–113.

8 Joseph R. Washington, Jr., *Black Religion* (Boston: Beacon, 1964), p. 200.

9 Eileen Southern, *The Music of Black Americans* (New York: W. W. Norton, 1971), pp. 39–40.

10 John W. Work, "Plantation Meistersinger," *The Musical Quarterly*, 27: 97–106, (January 1941).

11 Miles Mark Fisher, *Negro Slave Songs in the United States* (Ithaca, NY: Cornell, 1953), p. 25.

12 *Saturday Review of Literature.* 22: 17f. September 21, 1940.

13 John W. Work, "The Negro Spiritual." Paper No. XXIV (New York: Hymn Society of America. 1961), pp. 17–27.

14 See J. B. T. Marsh. *The Story of the Jubilee Singers: With Their Songs* (London: Hodder and Stoughton, 1875).

15 R. Nathaniel Dett. "Listen to the Lambs" (New York: G. Schirmer Inc., 1914).

16 James Weldon Johnson and J. Rosamond Johnson, *op. cit.*

17 Work, *op. cit.*, p. 22.

18 Pearl Williams-Jones. "Afro-American Gospel Music (1930–1970)" in the Howard University College of Fine Arts Project in African Music (Washington, DC). See also E. Franklin Frazier, *The Negro Church in America* (New York: Schockern, 1961).

19 See William J. Reynolds. *Songs of Our Faith* (Nashville: Broadman Press, 1964), pp. 423–424, for information on Tindley and a listing of familiar gospel songs by him.

Hymnody of the African American Church

by Don Lee White, previously unpublished

Persons who are involved in research are finding vast materials which shed new light into the mystery of the Black man and his contribution(s) to a great number of the art forms found in the development of the Black Church in America. Hymnody is comparatively one of the new areas of research. This research is not the "gospel song" nor the "traditional spiritual," even though it was interesting to note that R. Nathaniel Dett, in the "Religious Folk Songs of the Negro" indicates that these songs included are hymns.

This compilation is only a selected listing of names of hymn composers and their hymns by Black composers. This list or research is not to be considered in any way complete or exhaustive. This is just a broad spectrum of representative Black composers, historically and including a few currently known composer friends.

There are accounts of Negro congregations singing psalm tunes, and accounts of slave singing-school masters as early as 1693.[1] It is also interesting to note that the "first of eight articles agreed upon by the group of slaves in Boston, who early in October of 1693 started assembling themselves for Sunday evening worship, reads in part: Rules for the Society of Negroes, 1693, printed at Boston in broadside, ca. 1706—between the two prayers, a psalm shall be sung.[2]

Many of the early writers that mentioned the manner and style of singing of the slaves seemed to classify everything they heard into one category, calling it either the "slave song" or the "Negro spiritual." This was probably because of the "shrill unison wail," as described by the Russian traveler visiting Mother Bethel AME in 1815.[3] What was heard could well have been traditional tunes heard by the slaves while attending the White Methodist church,[4] before the split. The slaves were now in a position to sing in their unique way, possibly adding or detracting as they desired to the tunes most popular to them.

In 1801, two collections of hymns were compiled by Richard Allen for the "exclusive use of his congregation." These two early collections contained only the text, no tunes. The Allen hymnbook included two compositions by Allen: "The God of Bethel Heard Her Cries" and "Ye Ministers That Are Called to Preaching"; and a third, entitled "Spiritual Song," is published in Dorothy Porter, *Early Negro Writing,* 1760–1837.[5] Only the texts are found in his autobiography. There is no indication of a tune to use.

> Ye ministers that are called to preaching,
> Teachers and exhorters, too,
> Awake! Behold your harvest wasting;
> Arise! There is no rest for you.
>
> To think upon that strict commandment
> That God has on his teachers laid,
> The sinners' blood, who die unwarned,
> Shall fall upon their shepherd's head.
>
> But, O dear brethren, let's be doing
> Behold the nations in distress;
> The Lord of Hosts forbid their ruin
> Behold the day of grace is past.
>
> We read of wars and great commotions,
> Before the great and dreadful day;
> O, sinner turn your sinful courses
> And trifle not your time away."[6]

A copy of the table of contents from the Richard Allen hymnbook of 1801 can be viewed in *Readings in Black American Music,* Eileen Southern (W. W. Norton & Co., Inc., 1971). A few of the titles of hymns are still included in subsequent revisions of the A.M.E. hymnbook, for example:

> Am I a Soldier of the Cross
> And Are We Yet Alive
> Awake My Heart, Arise My Tongue
> Behold That Great and Awful Day
> Behold the Awful Trumpet Sounds
> Come Let Us Lift Our Voices High
> How Happy Every Child of Grace

Jerusalem My Happy Home
Lo! We See the Sign Appearing
There Is a Land of Pure Delight
When I Can Read My Title Clear

Eileen Southern has identified the authorship of several of the hymns. Eleven of the texts belong to Isaac Watts; two are associated with Charles Wesley; two are associated with John Newton; then one text each for Lady Huntingdon, Samuel Occom, Martin Madan, John Leland, Alexander Pope, and Augustus Toplady.

Hymns and Tune Makers
(African American)

It is interesting to note that several tunes in the A.M.E. hymnals have been given names for the ministers and bishops of the denomination. A few that should be familiar are:

NAZREY (Bishop Willis Nazrey, 1808–1874)
WAYMAN (Bishop Allazander W. Wayman, 1821–1895)
SHORTER (Bishop James Alexander Shorter, 1817–1887)
ARNETT (Bishop Benjamin W. Arnett, 1838–1906)
GRANT (Bishop Abraham Grant, 1848–1911)
ARMSTRONG (Bishop Josiah H. Armstrong, 1842–1898)
EMBRY (Bishop James C. Embry, 1834–1897)

Other favorite metrical tunes are:

METROPOLITAN (C.M.)	"O God We Lift Our Hearts to Thee"
STEWART (L.M.)	"Go Messenger of Christ"
LAYTON (8. 7.)	"O God We Lift Our Hearts to Thee"
AMO TE (11s)	"My Jesus I Love Thee"
EMBRY (11. 10.)	"Hither Ye Faithful"
	"I Give Immortal Praise to God"
ARMSTRONG	"Shout, Shout We're Coming"
ARNETT	"We Launch Today on the Voyage of Life"
GRANT	"Onward, Onward Christian Soldiers"
NAZREY	"We'll Praise the Lord for He Is Great"
SHORTER	"My Infant Lord to Thee I Gladly Bring"

| TURNER | "O, Let Me Go, I Cannot Stay" |
| WAYMAN | "The Friends of Christian Education Call" |

The preface to the hymnbook of 1892 indicates that "...original compositions by our own clergy are Bishops Payne, Turner, Handy, Tanner, and the Revs. H. T. Johnson, J. R. Scott, and J. C. Embry."

Daniel Payne (1811–1893) was the sixth bishop of the A.M.E. Church. During his lifetime, he was well known for his many beautiful hymntexts. A very popular hymntext is "Father, Above the Conclave Sky," with a tune by Bishop John Albert Johnson. This tune is called "Oakville" to commemorate the city in Ontario, Canada, where he was born.

The hymnal of 1897 lists "The work of arranging the hymns and music was done by the Bishop J. C. Embry and Prof. J. T. Layton." The hymnal not only included the compositions of the bishops who made the music arrangements for the hymnal but also the following persons: Benj. William Arnett, Benj. Tucker Tanner, Wesley John Gaines, and T. Wellington Henderson. New names appear in the 1941 revised hymnal with tunes or words by Bishops Gregg and Fountain, Sr.; D. Ward Nichols; plus Dr. C. E. Stewart, Dr. W. H. Peak, Prof. Edward C. Deas, Prof. Frank A. Clark, and Frod. Frederick Hall.

The 1892 edition of the A.M.E. hymnal finds a compilation of the best tunes from past hymnals and the popular hymnist of the Church. Tunes that have lasted for a long time include: METROPOLITAN C.M., OAKVILLE C.M., STEWARD L.M., NAZREY, AMO TE, YE SAINTS OF GOD AWAKE, OUR FATHER'S CHURCH, SHORTER, GRANT, WAYMAN, and ARNETT.

1954 and 1984 Hymnals
(bicentennial hymnal of 1984 and second printing 1986)

Between these two hymnals we now find a large collection of hymns by Black composers. Also found are tunes and words that have become favorites of the A.M.E. Church and also the African American Church in general.

"Tho' the Clouds May Hover O'er Us" (Antonio L. Haskell)
"We'll Praise the Lord" (John T. Layton)
"Praise Jehovah" (E. C. Deas)
"Hark the Voice of Jesus Crying" (C. A. Tindley)
"O the Great Joy That I Find" (Della A. Carter)

Other names of importance, but possibly not A.M.E.:

> Doris Akers
> Vivienne Anderson
> Lucie Campbell
> Andrea Crouch
> Evelyn DeLoache
> Noel Dexter
> Nina B. Jackson
> C. P. Jones
> Edith W. Ming
> J. T. Nickens
> Wendell Whalum

Other Denominational Hymns
(A.M.E. Zion)

All of the African American denominational hymnals indicate in their introductions, prefaces, acknowledgements, or a list of Black composers the hymns included by people of color.

The A.M.E .Zion Church was organized around 1796 and grew out of the John Street Methodist Church of New York. The word "Zion" was not added to the denominational title by a vote of the General Conference of 1848.

The earliest hymnal of the Zion Church dates from around 1838. There were two other hymnals compiled by Christopher Rush, Samuel M. Giles, and Joseph P. Tompson—1869 and 1872. Early hymnists of this denomination are W. J. Walls ("To Judah's Rugged Lofty Land"), Stephen Gill Spottwood ("Jesus My Prayer to Thee Today"), Bettye Lee Roberts Alleyne ("Work of Our Founders We Extol"), and C. C. Alleyne ("Thy Thoughts Concerning Me, O God").

The A.M.E. Church and the A.M.E. Zion Church authorized a joint publication of a hymnal in 1940. It is recorded that progress developed far enough to have a completed manuscript submitted by a joint committee to the General Conference in 1944. Six thousand dollars was set aside to be used for the first payment of the hymnal, but the two commissions could not agree on matters of incorporation. This manuscript is still intact, somewhere in the files of one of the two churches or a committee member.

Other writers include W. E. Carrington, R. W. Shrrill, I. L. Boyd. And from their current hymnal: Mrs. Anne Cheek Scott, Mrs. Delma M. & Rev. Monica Marshall, Rev. Jimmy Allen Thomas, Mr. Samuel Kofo Enninful,

Mrs. Dorothy Sharpe Johnson, and Mrs. Willie B. Heath Boboo.

The African Union Church
(Wilmington, Delaware)

Rev. Peter Spence and forty-two members of the Asbury M.E. Church withdrew from the church and organized the U.A.M.E. Church, September 18, 1813. Rev. Spence was born in Kent County, Maryland, around 1779. Only one hymn by Spence has been submitted by Dr. Dorothy E. Wilmore, district superintendent, with a promise of more information of the church and its music to be submitted. The first hymnbook was published in 1839 and indicated "Collected from different authors."

> Let Zion and her sons rejoice,
> Behold the promised hour.
> Her God both heard her mourning voice,
> And comes to exalt His power.
> It shall be known when I am dead,
> And left on long record.
> That ages yet unborn may read and trust,
> And praise the Lord.

Colored Methodist Episcopal Church
(changed to Colored Methodist Episcopal Church in 1954)

The compiler of the first hymnbook for the C.M.E. Church was Lucius H. Holsey (third Bishop) around 1891. In 1904, compiled by F. M. Hamilton, the book was titled *Songs of Love and Mercy*, with several songs composed by Bishop Holsey and a great number by Hamilton.

> *O Rapturous Scenes*
> O rapturous scenes that wait the day.
> When Thou shall call me home.
> When I shall here no longer stay,
> No longer get weep and moan.

—F. M. Hamilton
words and music to "A Prayer" and
"The Parting Hour Has Come"[7]

To find the music or words to the fifty-four hymns composed by Rev. Hamilton, with additional research to be uncovered, the old hymnals must be found. Unfortunately, the music committee of the C.M.E. Church has duplicated the New National Baptist Hymnal for their 1987 hymnal publication.

The Hymnal of 1899
(Church of Christ – Holiness)

When a person talks about Black hymnwriters, you will always come up with the name Charles Price Jones (1865–1949). His vast output of music for the church includes hymns, anthems, and jubilees. "Charles Price Jones…gave music high priority in the church and was himself a prolific hymnwriter…first songs date from his pre-Holiness days."[8]

C. P. Jones in a typewritten "The History of My Songs" (n.d.) writes, "All of my greatest songs were written before I was fifty years of age, most of them before I was forty."[9] The first song written by Jones was "Jesus Has Made It All Right." It is still carried in the present hymnal, #99.

> I once was a self-banished soul from the Lord,
> And wandered to death in my flight,
> Till Jesus o'ertook me,
> All sinsick and sore,
> And ventured to make it all right.
> (Refrain)
> All right, All right,
> Jesus has made it all right;
> The Father accepts me,
> Salvation is sure;
> For Jesus has made it all right.

The *Jesus Only* hymnal had two publications. The first in 1899 and again in 1901 along with the *Jesus Only* No. I and No. II. There seemed to be another publication called *Selected Songs* (n.d.), then the first issue of *His Fullness Songs* in 1906.

Many songs are sung by Bishop Jones, but people don't realize that the songs they were singing was composed by him.

> "When Judgment Day Is Drawing Nigh, Where Shall I Be?"
> "Jesus Only Is My Motto"
> "Deeper, Deeper"
> "The March of Zion's King"
> "Holiness Thy House Becomes"

"Glorify His Name"
"Bless the Day"
"Hold Us, Savior, to Thy Will"
"I Will Hide"
"Working on the Building"
"Hallelujah! Jesus Saves Me"

Other composers for this denomination included in the hymnal include:

(Mrs.) M. F. Wilson	"Why Do You Stand?"
	"Holy, Holy!"
Sallie Rather	"Sing, Sing, Sing"
	"Holy Spirit, Dwell Within"
(Mrs.) Prentice E. Frazier	"It Was at the Cross"
J. T. Benson (?)	"He Loves Me So"

Also look for the following composers' names: Amilia G. Anderson, D. G. Spearman, Catharin Jane Bonar, J. W. Washington, D. Andre White, J. B. Hunter, Elder Daniel G. Spearnan.

"YES, Lord!"
(1982 – first hymnal of the Church of God in Christ)

Bishop Charles Harrison Mason is recognized as the official founder of the Church of God in Christ. "The earliest collection of hymnody produced for the COGIC is the work of Elder H. C. Jackson, *The Jackson Bible Universal Selected Gospel Songs* (ca. 1940).[10]

This songbook was assembled and published to raise money for the school bearing his name, The Jackson Bible Universal, Inc. He was the founding president and dean of the school.

Names and titles of songs (hymns) to know in the *Yes, Lord!* hymnal are:

Iris Stevenson	"O Give Thanks Unto the Lord"
	"For He Is Good"
	"He Satisfies"
Mattie Moss Clark	"For God So Loved the World"
	"The Beatitudes"
H. J. Ford	"In My Home Over There"
Wallace M. Cryor	"Women of the Church of God in Christ"
Elbernita Clark	"A Praying Spirit"

The Baptist Songbooks and Hymnals

"As early as 1898, the National Baptist Publishing Board began the selection and publication of songbooks suited to the peculiar needs of the (Black) churches."[11] The Publishing Board before 1906 had published more than fifteen songbooks, by various authors, for example:

Celestial Showers #1 and #2 – Prof. William Rosborough

Lasting Hymns (n.d.) – H. A. Boyd, Secretary

Carols of Glory (n.d.) – Music Committee: Mrs. M. M. Isaac, Miss
L. E. Campbell, E. W. D. Isaac, Jr.

Golden Gems (n.d.) – included compositions by: J. B. Parsons, Mrs.
W. Petty, James E. Gayle, Loise King, W. H. Nix, Lucie
Campbell, Thomas Phillips (Rev.), M. C. Durham (Rev.)

Awakening Echoes (n.d.) – Music Committee: Rev. E. W. D. Isaac,
Miss L. E. Campbell, E. W. D. Isaac, Jr.

Gospel Pearls (1921) – by the Music Committee of the Sunday
School Publishing Board: Mrs. Willa A. Townsend, Director

The Baptist Standard Hymnal (1924) – Mrs. A. M. Townsend, editor

I list here the names of these historical persons because the Publisher's Note indicates that they are "our best-known songwriters and song evangelists."

Dr. J. D. Bushell (New York City)

Prof. W. A. Adams (Washington, DC)

Mrs. Carrie Booker Person (Tulsa, Oklahoma)

Mrs. Jeannette Taylor Nickens (Washington, DC)

Mrs. Geneva Bender Williams (Cleveland, Ohio)

Rev. F. Rivers Barnwell (Austin, Texas)

Prof. T. P. Bryant (Chicago, Illinois)

Mrs. Emma J. Hynes (Nashville, Tennessee)

Prof. R. Alwyn Austin (St. Louis, Missouri)

Rev. W. H. Skipwith (Baltimore, Maryland)

Mrs. Katie C. Dickson (Monmouth, Illinois)

Prof. H. B. Britt (Louisville, Kentucky)

Prof. John H. Smiley (Louisville, Kentucky)

Prof. W. M. Nix (St. Louis, Missouri)

Rev. T. W. J. Tobias (New Orleans, Louisiana)

The New National Baptist Hymnal (1977)

Chairperson – Ruth Lomax Davis

Committee members – W. Elmo Mercer, Jaunita Gaffey Hines,
    Virgie C. Dewitty, Rev. A. Charles Bowie, Marena Belle Williams

Special contributors – Anderson T. Dailey, Margaret Douroux,
    Mamie E. Taylor, and Odessa Jackson

This hymnal has included the names of many persons from various denominations: A.M.E., C.M.E., Methodist, COGIC, Church of Christ, Holiness, and Church of Deliverance.

New composers included are:

Magnolis Lewis-Butts	"Let It Breathe on Me"
Ralph Goodpasteur	"God Answers Prayer"
Antonio L. Haskell	"God Shall Wipe All Tears Away"
R. Rosamond Johnson	"Lift Every Voice and Sing"
Geneser Smith	"Only God"
E. C. Deas	"Thy Way, O Lord"
Rev. Clarence H. Cobbs	"How I Got Over"
C. Albert Tindley	"Nothing Between"
	"Some Day"
C. P. Jones	"I'm Happy with Jesus Alone"
Lucie Campbell	"Something Within"
	"Is He Yours?"

Not to Be Forgotten

There are several composers who have probably composed only one song, which was called a hymn. There are others who compiled a book of selected compositions and called it a hymnbook, and others who published a collection of their own writings.

Professor Edward Charles Deas graduated from Edward Waters College in 1891. He studied voice and piano with Miss Helen D. Handy, the daughter of Bishop James A. Handy of the A.M.E. Church. He was born in Florence, South Carolina. To his credit are the following publications: eight gospel song books, six anthems, five services for Easter, and *Gates of Praise* songbook, published in 1916. He conducted choirs in Chicago for several years and died June 1944.

Tunes:
"Hush! Hush My Soul Be Calm and Still"

"Big Business in Glory"
"Praise Jehovah"
"Thy Way, O Lord Not Mine"
"Now As Evening Shadows Falling"
    Compiled and Edited – *Psalms of Victory* (n.d.)
    Pub. E. C. Deas, 5718 Wabash Ave., Chicago, IL

Charles Albert Tindley (1851–1933)

For a complete bio, see Southern, Vol. 2, No. 2, *Perspectives in Black Music,* Fall 1983. Also, Horace Clarence Boyer, "Charles Albert Tindley: Progenitor of Black-American Gospel Music."

Some arrangers for the Tindley hymns are: Francis A. Clark, William D. Smith, Charles Albert Tindley, Jr., Elbert T. Tindley, and his wife, Hazel P. Tindley.

Publications:

Soul Echoes – 1905

New Songs of Paradise Nos. 1–6 (copyright 1941 by Prof. E. T. Tindley) – The index indicates fifty-five songs, including lesser-known hymns, for example:

"A Better Day Is Coming By and By"
"After a While"
"Pilgrim Stranger"
"Christ Is the Way"
"Go Wash in the Beautiful Stream"
"I'm Going There"
"I'll Overcome Some Day"
"Joyous Anticipation"
"Our Suffering Jesus"
"The Heavenly Union"
"Will You Be There"
"I Believe It"
"In Me"

Professor John Turner Layton (1849–1916)

Marshall Taylor (1846–19?)

Randolph Smith

Hiram Simmons (1874–1938)

Had his own publishing company, The Church Music Publishing House in Berkley, Virginia. There is a foundation for his name in Norfolk, Virginia, where most of his music can be found.

> Hymns:
> "Around the Great White Throne"
> "The Lord Will Provide"

Edmond Dede (1827–1848)

John Howardton Smith (1889–1977)

Rev. Silas W. Brister

Marry L. Tate (d. 1930)

Names of Contemporary Composers

Eugene Hancock
Donald Swift
David Hurd
William Farley Smith
J. Jefferson Cleveland
William D. Smith, Jr.
Carl Haywood
Kenneth W. Louis
Morris C. Queen
Roland Carter
Robert Fryson
Doris Akers
Odell Hobbs
J. Edward Hoy
Valerie Clayton
Richard Smallwood
Hezekiah Brinson, Jr.
Iris Stevenson
Anne Cheek Scott
Samuel Kojo Enninful

Rev. Jimmy Allen Thomas
Colbert Croft
Joyce Croft
Rev. Isaiah Jones

---

1 Richard Allen, *The Life Experience and Gospel Labors* (Nashville: Abingdon, 1960), pp. 15–16.

2 Talbot, Fredrick, *God's Fearless Prophet: The Story of Richard Allen* (a pamphlet, n.d.).

3 The edifice of Mother Bethel A.M.E. Church was dedicated on July 29, 1794. The African Methodist Episcopal Church is the first independent Negro (Black) denomination in the United States. Richard Allen (1760–1831) was elected the first bishop of the denomination at the General Conference held in 1816.

4 Sunday morning, 1787, all of the Black members of St George's Methodist Church walked out because a trustee pulled Rev. Absalom Jones from his knees during the prayer hour.

5 See footnote to Hymnal of the Black Church, Eileen Southern – *The Black Perspective in Music*.

6 The Life, Experiences and Gospel Labors of the Rt. Rev. Richard Allen, (Philadelphia, 1833), pp. 73–74.

7 Spencer, Jon Michael, a special issue of *Black Sacred Music*, Vol. 4, No. 1 (Spring 1990), A Journal of Theomusicology.

8 Ibid., E. Southern, p. 135.

9 I have in my possession this history written by Bishop C. P. Jones, given to me by the mother of Mrs. Ernestine Woodard, who accompanied Jones many times as he preached at Christ Church, Los Angeles. It is divided into seven chapters about his beginnings and his music.

10 Jon Michael Spencer, "Unsung Hymns" (a special issue of *Black Sacred Music*), Vol. 4, No. 1, Spring 1990 (Duke University Press).

11 Publisher's note from the National Baptist Publishing Board (Nashville, TN), R. H. Boyd, Secretary, printed on an Anthem Series, 1906.

III.
Liturgical
Hymnody

The Liturgy of the Roman Rite and African American Worship

by J-Glenn Murray, S.J.
from *Lead Me, Guide Me,* published in 1987

What marvels have already been wrought; what challenges we are still called to meet because of the Second Vatican Council! During this Council, our Church leaders called us to reach out to serve and renew our world, to renew our Christian life and worship, a renewal to plumb the very depths of our hearts and spirits. Toward meeting this challenge in life and worship, there has been the ongoing reform of the Roman Liturgy and the recovery of the principle of "full, conscious, and active participation in liturgical celebrations."[1] In addition, the Council urged us to wed the Liturgy and our varied cultures.[2] This marriage, which presupposes and demands in-depth knowledge of both a culture and the Roman Liturgy, is called "acculturation" (the process whereby cultural elements which are compatible with Roman Liturgy are incorporated into it either as substitutes for or illustrations of ritual elements of the Roman rite) and "inculturation" (the process whereby a pre-Christian rite is permanently given a Christian meaning).[3] This marriage is yet a further task to which we must continue to bring our intelligence, genius, artistry, and muscle.

This hymnal, prepared by Black Catholics in the United States of America, attempts both to meet the challenges of our faith and to incorporate the achievements of our centuries of vibrant life in the Spirit. What follows then in this introduction is several points of consideration for the development of Black Catholic worship and music's place in that unique celebration of God's love.

First, let us consider the Liturgy. "The celebration of the Sacred Mysteries is that moment when the Church is most fully actualized."[4] Its purpose is "to make people holy, to build up the Body of Christ, and finally, to give worship to God."[5] It is the "summit toward which the activity of the Church is directed; it is also the fount from which all her powers flow."[6] It is "like a parable [that] takes us by the hair of our heads, lifts us momentarily out of the cesspool of injustice we call home, puts us in the challenging reign of God, where we are treated like we have never been treated anywhere else…, where we are bowed to and sprinkled and censed and kissed and touched and where we share equally among all a holy food and drink."[7] It is and has been for us disenfranchised African Americans a sacred time which is both profound and central; a time of celebration and of wholeness; a time to "sing a new song unto the Lord." (Psalm 98:1)

Second, our celebration is Catholic. What makes our worship truly Catholic is that we all remember, give thanks, and carry out the mandate of Christ Jesus by eating and drinking together, and agree to join the Lord in being broken and poured out for the world as a *sacrificium laudis*—a living "sacrifice of praise." What makes our worship genuinely Catholic is that the community of believers gathers at the table of the Lord, which is both the table of God's Word (the Liturgy of the Word) and the table of Christ's Body and Blood (the Liturgy of the Eucharist), a table at which God's people are nourished by Holy Word and Sacred Meal.[8] What makes our worship uniquely Catholic is that everything that is done in our worship clearly serves (and does not interrupt) this ritual action of Word and Sacrament which has its own rhythm and movement, all built on the direction, rites, and forms of the Roman Catholic Liturgy as they are approved and promulgated. And, what makes our celebration fundamentally "catholic" (universal) is that it is open to welcome the spiritual contributions of all peoples which are consistent with our biblical faith and our historical continuity.

Third, our celebration is Black. While "a rose is a rose is a rose is a rose,"[9] a Louisiana Black Catholic is not a West Baltimore Black Catholic; neither is a New York Haitian Catholic a Los Angeles Black Catholic or a Chicago Black Catholic. What does reveal our worship as authentically Black is the interplay of some or all of the following: our indigenous music, dialogic preaching, effective and spontaneous prayer; a spirit of "fellowship"; hospitality; suspension of time; freedom of expression; body movement; conversion; the use of visual symbols; numerous poetic names for God; silence; clapping; personal testimony; vibrant color, and rich cloth.[10] What makes our worship fundamentally Black is our Black life which arises from and shares in a common history, a common experience, a common struggle, a common culture, and a common soul. What makes our worship uniquely Black is our indomitable and uncanny ability to "sing the Lord's song in a strange land!" (Psalm 137:4)

Fourth, music is integral to our worship. It is integral in that "from ancient times to the present, music has filled in the gaps made by humanity's attempt to express the inexpressible";[11] integral in that "among the many signs and symbols used by the Church to celebrate its faith, music is of preeminent importance";[12] integral in that "among Afro-Americans, just as in African culture, religion permeates the whole of life, and so does music."[13]

Though integral, music is not an end in itself. It must serve the ritual action; it must assist and minister to the community of believers in our celebration of the mighty acts of God and in the renewal of our total commitment of faith. To that end, the value of any musical component must be judged by the following criteria as set forth by

1. our Catholic teaching:[14]
   a. musical — Is there an aesthetic and technical quality in its rhythm, harmony, and melody? Besides the quality of the rhythmic, harmonic, and melodic elements, is there a concern with the wedding of text to music?

   b. liturgical — Is the music appropriate to the nature and importance of the liturgy? Is its theological content sound? Does it take into consideration what parts of the Mass should be sung and the relative festivity of the day (principle of progressive solemnity)?[15] Is there a proper concern for the different roles of the assembly, cantor, choir, instrumentalists? Are the soloists and choir effectively leading and supporting the assembly in its worship of the Lord or are they merely displaying their virtuosity and unduly delaying the particular rite (e.g., Preparation of the Altar-Table and the Gifts, the Sign of Peace)?

   c. pastoral — Is the music appropriate to the ability of the assembly? Does the music in the celebration enable the assembly to express the faith of the Church, in this place, in this age, in our culture, aware that the "United States of America is a nation of nations, a country in which people speak many tongues, live their lives in diverse ways, celebrate events in song and music in the folkways of their cultural, ethnic and racial roots"?[16] and

2. our Black heritage:[17]

    a. It (the musical component) must express the communal nature of the Black experience—we are not alone in our struggle for freedom;

    b. It must hold in tension the emphasis on this world and the expectations of the "new age";

    c. It must balance a freedom of spirit and liturgical restriction, i.e., spontaneity must be tempered with a sense of order and meaningful content;

    d. It must be celebratory.

At this juncture, we would be wise to examine our need to express the complete variety of our Black Catholic musical heritage. In order to express adequately this heritage, we need to be attentive not only to our Euro-American legacy (Latin chants, motets, polyphony, and hymns), but to the musical variety of our African American culture as well. Modern gospel music with its distinct sound, with its freedom of improvisation and its use of percussion: drums, piano, tambourines, and brass-winds, has already added a rich dimension to our liturgical celebrations (e.g., Margaret Douroux's "Give Me a Clean Heart," Andre Crouch's "Soon and Very Soon," and Robert Fryson's "God Is"), and yet gospel music is not the only style of music our heritage has to offer. To be utterly faithful to our heritage, we must use:

    a. spirituals — our forebears' Christocentric commentaries on the past (e.g., "Balm in Gilead") and wellsprings of hope for the future (e.g., "We Shall Overcome");[18]

    b. hymns — those hymns and psalms which used the process of "lining-out," i.e., the process wherein the worship leader spoke a line or so, which the congregation sang thereafter (a very effective tool in a time when illiteracy was widespread and the use of hymnals virtually non-existent: e.g., Charles Gabriel's "His Eye Is on the Sparrow" and William Bradbury's "Jesus Loves Me");[19]

    c. contemporary compositions — music which has its feet firmly planted in the past and yet is attuned to the needs of the faith community today (Clarence Rivers' "God Is Love," Grayson Brown's "Jesus Died Upon the Cross," and Leon Roberts's "Responsorial Psalm: Let Us Go Rejoicing").

Fifth, in order to utilize the rich resources of our past, invite the composition of new music, and use this present volume to its best advantage, let us take the time to sketch the present structure of the Eucharistic Liturgy, "the source and summit" of our liturgical life. We do this because "the first place to look for guidance in the *use* and *choice* of music is the rite itself."[20] Other liturgical celebrations are well examined in the "rites" section of this present volume.

An outline of the Eucharistic Liturgy:[21]

I. Introductory Rites
   Entrance
   Greeting
   The Blessing and Sprinkling of Holy Water
   Penitential Rite
   Lord, Have Mercy
   Glory to God
   Opening Prayer

The purpose of these rites is to help the assembly come to an awareness of itself as a community in celebration. It should be noted that when the Third Form of the Penitential Rite is used, it should function as a "general confession made by the entire assembly and praise of Christ's compassionate love and mercy."[22]

II. Liturgy of the Word
   Reading I
       Responsorial Psalm
   Reading II
       Gospel Acclamation
   Gospel
   Homily
   Profession of Faith
   General Intercessions

The primary focus here is that the assembly *hear* God's message; *digest* it with the aid of psalms, silence (particularly after each of the readings) and the homily; and *respond*, by involving themselves in the great covenant of love and redemption which immediately follows.

II. Liturgy of the Eucharist

A. Preparation of the Altar-Table and the Gifts

The purpose of this rite is to prepare the Table of the Eucharist for the sacrifice. Assembly singing is not always necessary or desirable at this time. Instrumental interludes or the skillful use of a choral repertoire can effectively accompany the procession and preparation of the Gifts and Table, and thus keep this part of the Mass in proper perspective relative to the Eucharistic Prayer which follows.

B. Eucharistic Prayer

This prayer of thanksgiving and blessing is the center of the entire celebration. This prayer is affirmed and ratified by all through acclamations of faith: the Holy, the Memorial Acclamation, and the Great Amen. Since this prayer is central, all these acclamations should be sung by all present. It is further recommended that, for these acclamations, one musical style be employed for greater musical integrity and unity.[23]

C. Communion Rite

The eating and drinking of the Body and Blood of the Lord in the paschal meal is the climax of our eucharistic celebration. The Lord's Prayer, when it is sung, should be in a musical setting that allows all to participate; the Sign of Peace, a time to share Christ's peace, should not interrupt and delay the Communion Rite; the Lamb of God is a litany-song to accompany completely the breaking of the Eucharistic Bread and pouring of the Eucharistic Wine; the distribution of Communion should be done with dignity and warmth; the Communion Song should express and foster a sense of unity. The Prayer after Communion closes this rite.

IV. Concluding Rite
Greeting
Blessing
Dismissal

These send forth each member of the assembly to live what we have celebrated, praising God and blessing the Lord. The

Recessional Song has never been an official part of the rite; hence, musicians are free to plan music which provides an appropriate closing to the Liturgy.

V. In addition
A selection from our diverse Black musical repertory may well be used as a prelude to the Liturgy or as the assembly's preparation to hear the Homily.

Sixth, if our celebration of the Eucharistic Liturgy (and by extension, all the other liturgical rites) is to be both Catholic and Black, then those whose responsibility it is to plan and execute worship must continue to study the Roman Liturgy in order to understand its inner dynamics, come to *appreciate* the significance and integrity of each of its parts, *learn* those places where improvisation may legitimately occur, *keep the assembly central*, *read* voraciously about inculturation, and *remain open* to the Spirit. It can and must be done!

These spirituals, hymns, anthems, songs, and contemporary compositions, many drawn from the rich heritage of sacred music of the Black community, are chosen with the aforementioned challenges in mind. It is our hope that, used with wisdom, sensitivity, and faith, they may prove appropriate, beautiful, and edifying, for the fitting praise of God and the enrichment of us, God's people.

---

1 Second Vatican Council, *Constitution on the Sacred Liturgy*, "Sacrosanctum Concilium" (= "SC") (December 4, 1963), #14.

2 SC, #37. Also, National Conference of Catholic Bishops, "The Church at Prayer—A Holy Temple of the Lord" (December 4, 1983), p. 23, #45.

3 Anscar Chupungo, *Cultural Adaptation of the Liturgy* (New York: Paulist Press, 1982), pp. 81–86.

4 Black Catholic Bishops of the United States, "What We Have Seen and Heard" (September 1984), p. 30.

5 SC, #59.

6 SC, #10.

7 Robert W. Hovda, "The Vesting of Liturgical Ministers," *Worship*, Vol. 54, No. 2 (March 1980), p. 105.

8 Bishops' Committee on the Liturgy, "Music in Catholic Worship" (= "MCW"), revised edition (1983), #43.

9   Gertrude Stein, "Sacred Emily," *Geography and Plays* (New York: Something Else Press, 1922).

10 James P. Lyke, O.F.M., "Liturgical Expression in the Black Community," *Worship*, Vol. 57, No. 1 (January 1983), p. 17.

11 J. Wendell Mapson, Jr., *The Ministry of Music in the Black Church* (Valley Forge: Judson Press, 1984), p. 9.

12 MCW, #23.

13 Mapson, p. 16.

14 MCW, #s 26–41.

15 Bishops' Committee on the Liturgy, "Liturgical Music Today" (= "LMT") (September 28, 1982), #13.

16 LMT, #54.

17 Mapson, pp. 21–22.

18 Ibid., p. 45.

19 Ibid., p. 37.

20 LMT, #8.

21 MCW, #s 44–49, 61, 62, 65, 67, 68, 71, 73.

22 LMT, #21.

23 LMT, #s 14, 17.

The Gift of African American Sacred Song[1]

By Sister Thea Bowman, F.S.P.A.
from *Lead Me, Guide Me*, published in 1987

From the African Mother Continent, African men and women, through the Middle Passage, throughout the Diaspora, to the Americas, carried the African gift and treasure of sacred song. To the Americas, African men and women brought sacred songs and chants that reminded them of their homelands and that sustained them in separation and in captivity, songs to respond to all life situations, and the ability to create new songs to answer new needs.

African Americans in sacred song preserved the memory of African religious rites and symbols, of a holistic African spirituality, of rhythms and tones and harmonies that communicated their deepest feelings across barriers of region and language.

African Americans in fields and quarters, at work, in secret meetings,[2] in slave festivals,[3] in churches, camp meets and revivals, wherever they met or congregated, consoled and strengthened themselves and one another with sacred song—moans, chants, shouts, psalms, hymns, and jubilees, first African songs, then African American songs. In the crucible of separation and suffering, African American sacred song was formed.

In *My Bondage and My Freedom*, Frederick Douglass wrote:

> Slaves are generally expected to sing as well as to work. A silent slave is not liked by masters or overseers. "Make a noise," "make a noise," and "bear a hand," are words usually addressed to the slaves when there is silence amongst them. This may account for the almost constant singing heard in the southern states. There was, generally, more or less singing among the teamsters, as it was one means of letting the overseer know where they were, and that they were moving on with the work.

But, on allowance day, those who visited the great house farm were peculiarly excited and noisy. While on their way, they would make the dense old woods, for miles around, reverberate with their wild notes. These were not always merry because they were wild. On the contrary, they were mostly of a plaintive cast and told a tale of grief and sorrow. In the most boisterous outbursts of rapturous sentiment, there was ever a tinge of deep melancholy.[4]

As early as 1691, slaves in colonial homes, slave galleries, or separate pews participated in worship services with White slave holders. They learned to sing the traditional European psalms and hymns from the *Cambridge Short Tune,* the *Dutch Tune,* or the *Hymns and Psalms* of Dr. Watts, which they loved and adapted to their own style and use.[5] In 1755, Reverend Samuel Davies wrote:

The Negroes…have an Ear for Musick [sic], and a kind of ecstatic Delight in Psalmody and there are no Books they learn so soon or take so much pleasure in, as those used in that heavenly Part of divine Worship.[6]

Slave records dating back as far as 1723 show there were proficient slave musicians—singers and instrumentalists who played fiddle, violin, trumpet, drums, guitar, French horn or flute, slave musicians highly valued for their musicianship, slave musicians, some who were able to read and write.[7]

In 1801, Richard Allen, founder of the African Methodist Episcopal Church, published *A Collection of Hymns and Spiritual Songs, from Various Authors,*[8] hymns and songs which were used by slaves and fugitive slaves in worship. In 1871, the Fisk Jubilee Singers began concert tours of America and Europe, which for the first time brought the original sacred song of Black America to White audiences and to the concert stage. Harry Burleigh, John Wesley Work, James Weldon, and J. Rosamond Johnson scored and arranged Black American sacred songs for soloists and ensembles in concert performance. In 1921, Thomas A. Dorsey, the Father of Gospel Music, composed "If I Don't Get There," and initiated a new rhythm, a new harmony, and a new style. Gospel singers like Kenneth Morris, Roberta Martin, Mahalia Jackson, James Cleveland, and Edwin Hawkins enriched Black sacred song.

In the sixties, Father Clarence Joseph Rivers revitalized Catholic worship, inaugurated a revolution in liturgical music, stirred international interest in the indigenization of Catholic liturgy, and brought new hope, joy, and spirit to millions of Black Americans when he introduced the melodies, rhythms, harmonies, symbols, and rituals of African American sacred song into Roman Catholic worship. His *American Mass Program* and subsequent compositions and recordings popularized Black music for Catholic worship. His *Soulfull Worship* and *The Spirit in Worship*[9] analyzed the history, theology, theory, and practice of Black sacred song and its appropriateness and effectiveness in Catholic liturgy and worship.[10] Rawn Harbor, Grayson Brown, Eddie Bonnemere, Leon Roberts, and others began to compose for Catholic worship.

Black sacred song is soulful song—

1. *holistic:* challenging the full engagement of mind, imagination, memory, feeling, emotion, voice, and body;
2. *participatory:* inviting the worshipping community to join in contemplation, in celebration, and in prayer;
3. *real:* celebrating the immediate concrete reality of the worshipping community—grief or separation, struggle or oppression, determination or joy—bringing that reality to prayer within the community of believers;
4. *spirit-filled:* energetic, engrossing, intense;
5. *life-giving:* refreshing, encouraging, consoling, invigorating, sustaining.

Influenced by Africa, the Middle Passages, the Islands, Europe, and the Americas; created, shaped, treasured, and shared by Black American Christians across time, geographic, socioeconomic, and denominational lines, our heritage of sacred song encompasses a vast variety of kinds, styles, and forms.

Wyatt Tee Walker charts the development of five distinctive kinds of Black sacred music on the following page.

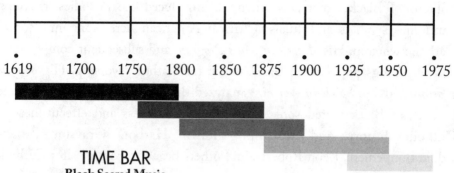

TIME BAR
Black Sacred Music
Period of Development & Dominance

SLAVE UTTERANCES: Moans, Chants, Cries for Deliverance
SPIRITUALS: Faith-Songs, Sorrow Songs, Plantation Hymns, etc.
METER MUSIC: Watts, Wesley, Sankey, et al.
HYMNS OF IMPROVISATION: Euro-American hymns with "beat"
GOSPEL MUSIC: Music of Hard Times (Cross fertilization with secular)

Wendell Whalum shows how the various kinds of Black sacred song are related on the following page.

Black sacred song celebrates our God, His goodness, His promise, our faith and hope, our journey toward the promise. Black sacred song carries melodies and tonalities, rhythms and harmonies; metaphors, symbols, and stories of faith that speak to our hearts; words, phrases, and images that touch and move us.[11]

Stephen Henderson says of Black speech:

> Certain words and construction seem to carry an inordinate charge of emotional and psychological weight, so whenever they are used they set all kinds of bells ringing, all kinds of synapses snapping, on all kinds of levels…I am speaking of words…which have levels of meaning that seem to go back to our earliest grappling with the English language in a strange and hostile land. These words, of course, are used in complex associations, and thus form meaningful wholes in ways which defy understanding by outsiders. I call such words "mascon" words, borrowing from (of all places!) the National Aeronautics and Space Administration. NASA invented the acronym to mean a "massive concentration" of matter below the lunar surface after it was observed that the gravitational pull on a satellite was stronger in some places than in others.

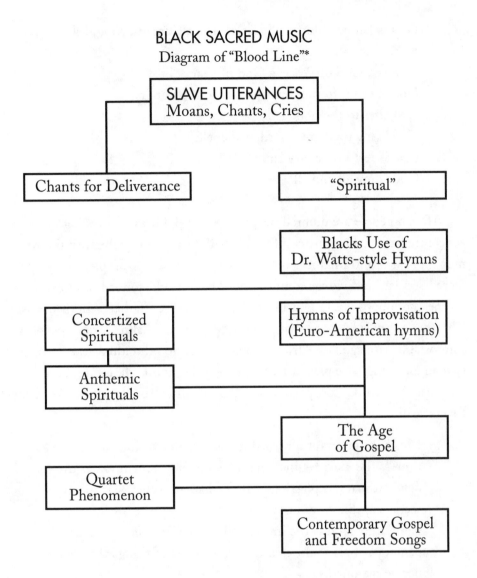

BLACK SACRED MUSIC
Diagram of "Blood Line"*

SLAVE UTTERANCES
Moans, Chants, Cries

Chants for Deliverance

"Spiritual"

Blacks Use of
Dr. Watts-style Hymns

Concertized
Spirituals

Hymns of Improvisation
(Euro-American hymns)

Anthemic
Spirituals

The Age
of Gospel

Quartet
Phenomenon

Contemporary Gospel
and Freedom Songs

* Adapted from Wendel Whalum's diagram appearing in *Review and Expositor*
(Spring 1972), p. 581.

I use it to mean a massive concentration of Black experimental energy which powerfully affects the meaning of Black speech, Black song, and Black poetry—if one, indeed, has to make distinctions.[12]

Black sacred music lifts up biblical symbols which bear the accumulated meanings of four hundred years of experience of the Black community in America:

> God is Father, Mother, Sister, Brother, Captain, King, Liberator,
>   Friend;
> God is a God of Peace, a God of War;
> God is water to the thirsty, bread to the hungry,
>   shelter to the homeless;
> God is my rock, my sword, my shield;
> God is rest in a weary land;
> God is my all and all.

African people are diunital people, seeking richness of meaning in *apparent* contradiction. They are comfortable with bringing together realities which may appear contradictory or in opposition: for example, body/spirit, sacred/secular, individual/community. They reach toward unification or synthesis of opposites. God is like father and mother (father – mother – sister – brother symbols are not sexist). God is like fire and balm. African people are comfortable with symbol. African Americans for four hundred years have used symbol and song to express a faith and yearning too high, too low, too wide, too deep for words, too passionate to be confined by concepts. As Father Rivers writes:

> Music is important for worship because in worship we have to express the inexpressible, the transcendent, human values that defy ordinary expression. Music, like its other self, poetry, seems capable of doing what plain rational words cannot do: namely, to express the inexpressible, to touch men's hearts, to penetrate their souls, create an experience of things that cannot be reasoned.[13]

Black sacred song—old or new, folk or composed, rural or urban, traditional or contemporary—is in a very real sense, the song *of the people.*

- The music comes from a people who share and claim a common history, common experience, common oppression, common values, hopes, dreams, and visions.

- The singer, the singers, the instrumentalists voice the experience and faith of the community.

- The leader (some would say soloist) leads the community in worship. The leader revives and inspirits.

- The worshipping community is active, not passive. People participate—sing, pray, clap, sway, raise their hands, nod their heads. Eye contact, voiced response, the silent testimony of tears, a smile of relief or contemplation or ecstasy says, "This is my story; this is my song."

- The singer is chosen from the people by the people to suit their immediate need.

"Sometimes *I* feel like a motherless child."
"*I* just came from the fountain."
"*I* love the Lord."
"*My* Heavenly Father watches over *me*."

- The first person pronoun, the "I" reference, is communal. The individual sings the soul of the community. In heart and voice and gesture the Church, the community responds.

- The singer lifts the Church, the people, to a higher level of understanding, feeling, motivation, and participation.

Among African peoples, most art is designed for use, that is to express a feeling or insight, to have an impact in the real world.[14] Song is not an object to be admired so much as an instrument to teach, comfort, inspire, persuade, convince, and motivate. Music is chosen precisely for its effect upon the worshipping community. The aim is *effective* worship. Black sacred song is designed to move. It moves because depth of feeling gives it "spiritual power." Father Clarence Rivers explains:

> A singer who performs without feeling lacks soul. As in original biblical concept of the spiritual, the spirit or the soul is the life principal, the source of life and liveliness, of dynamism and movement, of motion and emotion. That which is unmoved and unmoving is not spiritual, it is dead! To be spiritual is to be alive, to be capable of moving and responding to movement.... Since the Spirit moves, that which does not move would seem to lack the presence of the Spirit.[15]

Black sacred song has been at once a source and an expression of Black faith, spirituality, and devotion. By song, our people have called the Spirit into our hearts, homes, churches, and communities. Seeking to enrich our liturgies and lives with the gift of sacred song, we pray:

"Spirit, Sweet Holy Spirit, fall afresh on me.
Every time I hear the Spirit
Moving in my heart
I will pray."

---

1 Confer Pope Paul IV, "To the Heart of African," *The Pope Speaks 14*, (no. 3, 1969): pp. 218–219. This citation concerning cultural pluralism within the Church gives the theological foundation for this essay. Similarly, Pope John Paul II has written numerous commentaries on the place of cultural expression in the Catholic Church.

2 See Miles Mark Fisher *Negro Slave Songs in the United States* (New York: Citadel Press, 1969), pp. 32–33, 66–79.

3 Festivals in which slaves in large numbers sang in their own African languages survived in the English colonies. Africans gathered to share stories, dances, songs, and customs of various nations in Africa. See Miles Fisher *Negro Slave Songs in the United States* (New York Citadel Press, 1969), pp. 66–79.

4 Frederick Douglass, *My Bondage and My Freedom* (New York: 1855), 96, 97.

5 See Eileen Southern, *The Music of Black Americans* (New York: Norton & Company, 1971), pp. 30–45.

6 Quoted in Southern, *The Music of Black Americans*, p. 59.

7 See in Southern, *The Music of Black Americans*, pp. 27–29.

8 Early American Imprints, Nos. 38, 39, Series No. 2 (1801–1820).

9 *Soulfull Worship* (Washington, DC: National Office for Black Catholics, 1974); *Spirit in Worship* (Cincinnati: Stimuli, Inc., 1978).

10 Confer "The Church at Prayer, A Holy Temple of the Lord," December 4, 1983, the National Conference of Catholic Bishops, p. 23, #45; and Second Vatican Council, *Constitution on the Sacred Liturgy*, "Sacrosanctum Concilium," December 4, 1983, pp. 37–40.

11 The Bishops' Committee on Liturgy, "Music in Catholic Worship," revised edition (1983), pp. 3, 41.

12 *Understanding the New Black Poetry: Black Speech and Black Music as Poetic References* (New York: William Morrow & Co., 1973), p. 44.

13 Father Clarence Joseph Rivers, *Soulfull Worship*, p. 39; see also, *The Spirit in Worship*, pp. 14, 15.

14 "The Church at Prayer, A Holy Temple of the Lord," pp. 14, 15.

15 *The Spirit in Worship*, p. 22.

Music Among Blacks in the Episcopal Church: Some Preliminary Considerations[1]

by Irene V. Jackson-Brown
from *Lift Every Voice and Sing*, published in 1981

This essay examines historically the musical activities of Blacks in the Episcopal Church.

To date, scholarly attention has been given primarily to the religious experience of Blacks who were outside mainline denominations. One is hard-pressed to find adequate discussion of Black *religious* activities within the principal churches of America. The situation becomes even more critical when the subject is the *musical* activities of Black people in the larger religious bodies. It is not the intent of this essay to offer an explanation of the paucity of material on Black musical practices in mainline denominations. Rather, the attention of this study is given to the musical activities of Blacks in the Episcopal Church. An analysis of the social forces which gave rise to Black musical attitudes is an important subject. However, a socio-historical examination of the musical activities of Black Episcopalians will be left for another time.

The larger issue that will be addressed in the course of this essay is the religious musical tradition of African Americans.

Scholarly interest in the religious music of African Americans has been almost exclusively devoted to the study of one genre—the spiritual—and of musical activities among Black independent denominations where worship modes are covertly or overtly linked to West African modes.

The account of the English musician Henry Russell who visited the United States from 1833 to 1841 is representative of accounts of Black worship patterns. Russell writes:

> I had long taken a deep interest in Negro life, and I wondered
> whether it was possible that Negroes could originate melody. I
> was desirous of testing this, and I made up my mind to visit
> many Negro meetings throughout several of the states. On my
> entering the chapel at Vicksburg [then a slave town], there was
> a restlessness about the little congregation—whether it
> emanated from one or two White people being present I
> cannot say. There was one peculiarity that struck me forcible.
> When the minister gave out his own version of the Psalm, the
> choir commenced singing so rapidly that the original tune
> absolutely ceased to exist—in fact, the fine old psalm tune
> became thoroughly transformed. For a moment, I fancied that
> not only the choir but the little congregation intended to get
> up a dance as part of the service."[2]

The above description is but one example of the many recorded accounts of
Black worship patterns. However, these accounts focus primarily on
situations that involve the more demonstrative forms of religious behavior
such as shouting, dancing, or glossolalia.

The religious music of African Americans must be thoroughly investigat-
ed and perceptively conceptualized. Therefore, a discussion of religious music
of African Americans—as this essay intends to show—must take into account
not only music in Black independent churches but also the musical practices
of Blacks in mainline denominations.

It will be demonstrated that Blacks in the Episcopal Church have
historically regarded music as central to their Christian lives.

Music and the Antebellum Church

The history of musical practices among Black Episcopalians in a formal
way begins in the latter part of the eighteenth century in Philadelphia with
Absalom Jones and Richard Allen, who together formed "The Free African
Society." Jones went on to found the first Black Episcopal parish in the United
States—St. Thomas African Episcopal Church—which was established in
1794 in Philadelphia. The minutes of the January 18, 1793, meeting of the
"Free African Society," which was attended by Absalom Jones, give the first
glimpse of attitudes about music within the "Society." Since Jones was present
at the meeting and presumably voted on the "recommended rules" of the
"Society," we have some idea about his attitudes regarding music in worship.

From the minutes of this meeting, "it was recommended that at the time of singing, the *congregation* shall stand or keep seated as *they* find freedom, and that the *congregation* should supply such books as are necessary to read, *sing*, and praise the Lord in harmony."[3] We know then that music was an integral part of worship and that *congregational* singing was encouraged. We know also from the minutes that singing should be entered into as a *corporate* act of worship.

In a somewhat less formal sense, the history of music among Black Episcopalians begins in the early eighteenth century with the work of the Society for the Propagation of the Gospel in Foreign Parts which consisted of English missionaries who were sent to the Colonies to Christianize Blacks and Indians.

The early work of the S.P.G. took place in Goose Creek, South Carolina, where slaves were reported to have been converted in 1695 under the Rev. Samuel Thomas. From 1712, the work of the S.P.G. was spearheaded by the Rev. George Ross who, as a missionary, put forth an effort to provide slaves with instruction in church Catechism. His efforts were largely concentrated in Delaware. Ross, in a letter to the S.P.G., indicated that the Quakers gave little attention to instructing slaves and that the few slaves who were baptized belonged to Churchmen, that is Anglicans. Probably the most important and well-known name in connection with the S.P.G. was the Rev. Thomas Bray. An early eighteenth century letter to the S.P.G. from a clergyman, a missionary who served in St. James parish in South Carolina, reported that the work among the Blacks was successful because the Lord's Day was no longer profaned by dancing. One of the conditions of baptism as set down by the White clergymen was that slaves were required to promise that they would not spend the Lord's Day in feasts, dances, and merry meetings.[4]

In addition to being instructed in the church Catechism, Blacks were introduced to the music of the Anglican Church in the way of singing the psalms, as reported by a New York clergyman to the Society in a letter dated December 3, 1726.[5] Missionary activity was moving along full-tilt in Savannah, Georgia, and Charleston, South Carolina, by the 1730s and missionaries requested that the S.P.G. send "Bibles, primers, spelling books, horn books, testaments and *Psalters*."[6] Blacks were taught to sing psalms using a practice referred to as "lining-out." The song leader or precentor would sing one or two lines of the psalm and the congregation followed, repeating the lines with some melodic ornamentation. The practice of "lining-out" was a device used to teach slaves to read and sing from notes.

Contrary to the popularly held notion that Blacks were not attracted to the formality of Anglican worship style, we learn from letters dated September 30, 1745, and March 28, 1751, and sent to the S.P.G. from missionaries in New York that "the singing of a psalm had produced a good effect: it had engaged many of the Negroes to a closer applications in learning to read," and "that Blacks often meet in the evenings on a regular basis for instruction in the singing of the psalm tunes."[7] It seems reasonable to assume from the aforementioned quotes that music was used by Blacks non-liturgically, as a means of providing group solidarity and identity.

Where Blacks worshipped along with Whites, although most often restricted to a special area, or where Blacks worshipped in a separate building under White leadership, Blacks were, by the founding of Black independent churches in the late eighteenth century, beginning to experience musical syncretism within the colonial Church of England. That is, Blacks were fusing certain African and African American musical practices with Anglo-American musical practices.

In a history of Black Episcopalians, Robert Bennett suggests how this musical syncretism manifested itself. Bennett writes:

> In the South, where the majority of Black Episcopalians were to be found and where prior to the Civil War the Bishop of South Carolina claimed more Black communicants than White and where Black churchmen worshipped in separate galleries or chapels, it was this body which described their plantation Holy Communion services in the spiritual, "Let Us Break Bread Together on Our Knees."[8]

Bennett presents us with an intriguing conjecture with his passing comment that suggests Blacks within the Episcopal Church contributed to the growing body of African American religious folk song, to be known later as spirituals. Bennett seems to imply that the spiritual "Let Us Break Bread Together" originated among Black Episcopalians possibly since the kneeling stance is assumed in communion and probably because the administering of the Holy Sacraments is central to Episcopal liturgy. Perhaps what is most intriguing about Bennett's hypothesis is that Blacks other than those who were under the influence of the Methodists and Baptists were not to be excluded from certain musical practices that were popular among the masses of Blacks. These musical practices included the singing of religious folk songs. Before the introduction of the organ in Black Episcopal churches, which occurred in the

1820s, congregational singing made use of the performance practice known as "lining-out."

Most congregations, both Black and White, developed what church authorities called "undesirable" practices in terms of congregational singing before the organ became the standard instrument for accompanying congregational singing. These "undesirable" practices consisted of the use of a highly embellished vocal line. The concerns of the clergy for improved congregational singing gave rise to singing schools, which were intended to promote the "regular" or "correct" way of singing as it was called, or "singing by note." The movement toward the establishment of singing schools began in New England in the eighteenth century, and by the second half of the century had become a regular institution in New England. St. Philip's (New York) established a church music school (to teach "singing by note") which held classes twice a week in the evenings, according to *Freedom's Journal*, October 26, 1827. There seemed to be no opposition to "singing by note" among Black Episcopalians, at least not in New York City or Philadelphia; such was not the case in Philadelphia's Bethel A.M.E. Church where the older people resisted vehemently to "singing by note." Among more enlightened Black Episcopalians and Black independents, the introduction of the choir and organ into the church service, as well as musical literacy, were viewed as *progressive* whereas the older communicants in the A.M.E. denomination regarded the *new practice* of music reading as having brought the devil into the church."[9]

An important musical activity to be noted among Black Episcopalians during the early nineteenth century was church-sponsored concerts. St. Philips (New York) was not only instrumental in establishing church music schools, but also led the way in sponsoring sacred concerts, usually consisting of large choral works often with orchestral accompaniment. Most often, the concerts featured the works of European composers, and occasionally the works of Black composers were presented.[10]

There was a high performance standard placed on music in Black congregations of the Church. Very often on the occasion of institutions and consecrations, clergy commented on the quality of singing. For example, Bishop Kemp, who consecrated St. James (Baltimore), made the following comments in recording the events of that day: "...the congregation was large and devout,...the responses were well made and the chanting and singing quite delightful."[11]

By the 1830s, the organ had become such a tradition at St. Thomas that when the Rev. J. M. Douglas accepted the call to St. Thomas, he described the church in the following way:

> She stood alone in favor of education of ministry and peo-
> ple...and once spoken of in disparaging terms on account of
> care for cleanliness, decency in worship house, her carpeted
> aisles, her pews and *organ,* now closely imitated in all respects.[12]

Among southern Black communicants, it is not known whether communicants were actually able to read music. It is probable that they learned the chants and hymns by rote. However, in instances where singing was done without instrumental accompaniment, the singing was still commented upon as being "acceptable" and "well rendered." Probably, then, careful instruction was given in singing; probably, instruction was given in reading music as well as its performance.

It seems that music within Black Episcopal churches maintained its high quality during the 1840s. Most often, the quality of the music in Black congregations was the subject of comment by clergy who visited these congregations. Such was the case at Christ Church, Providence, Rhode Island, which was admitted as a parish in June of 1843 and was originally led by Alexander Crummell. One of the White clergy who had charge of the parish submitted the following in his annual report:

> This is the only Colored church in New England, though
> there are several meeting houses of different sects in the city of
> Providence. The services, the church, and the worshippers
> present an appearance of order, neatness, and regularity which
> are seldom equated, and can hardly be surpassed. The organist
> is a Colored girl under twenty years of age and the music is
> excellent.[13]

During the 1850s, church music among Black Episcopalians continued to be given careful attention and thus was well performed, particularly since trained Black musicians and composers were often Episcopalians. For example, at St. Philip's Church, Newark, which was instituted circa 1856, Peter P. O'Fake, a notable musician of Newark and a baritone, served as choir director beginning in 1856. Under O'Fake's leadership, the choir received favorable comments from the press.[14]

While Peter O'Fake was active in Newark, William Brady and Thomas J.

Bowers, both Black musicians, concertized in New York and Philadelphia during the 1850s. Little is known about William Brady, who died in 1854, except that he was a composer who James M. Trotter describes as a "composer of a musical service for the Episcopal Church." In addition to his musical activities in New York, Brady performed in Philadelphia from the 1820s through the early fifties. It has not been disclosed whether Brady was a musician in one of the Black Episcopal churches in New York City. However, it is likely that he was a musician at St. Philip's (New York) or at least an Episcopalian, as evidenced by his composing music for the Episcopal service.

Thomas J. Bowers, his brother John C. Bowers, and his sister Sarah Sedgewick Bowers were prominent musicians in Philadelphia beginning in the 1850s and were members of St. Thomas, where their father was senior warden. St. Thomas has a distinctive history of musical activity beginning in the nineteenth century. Maude Cuney-Hare in *Negro Musicians and Their Music* (1936) mentions that much of the sacred music written about 1800 was composed for services at St. Thomas. Both Thomas Bowers and his brother, John served as organists at St. Thomas. The music historian James M. Trotter provides some informative insights into the Bowers family and sheds light on the quality of music in Philadelphia among the "elite," and by extension gives some idea of the quality of music at St. Thomas—at least during the period from the 1840s through the eighties:

> The parents of the subject of this sketch [Thomas J. Bowers] although highly pleased with the natural musical qualities and with the accomplishments displayed by their children, were such strict church people as not to wish them to become public performers. Recognizing the pleasing, refining influence of music, they desired its practice by their children in the home-circle, for the most part; but were not adverse, however, to hearing its sweet and sacred strains issue from choir and organ in church service, not to having their children take part in the same.[15]

By the late 1850s, the use of the organ in worship among Black Episcopalians had influenced Black independent denominations to introduce instrumental music into their worship services as well. The following is an account of the influence that St. James (Baltimore) had on other Black churches in that city, in terms of the introduction of the organ into the worship service:

This was a real novelty and invited strong denunciations from the Colored churches of the city. Reproachful and sneering terms were applied to the church because of this introduction into the public services of the church the "devil's music box." Thus, the Church was an early witness for musical accessories in divine service, as well as for order and decorum in public worship. The indirect influence of St. James has been very great in this city, as the marvelous changes in the conduct of services in Colored churches witnesseth.[16]

By the middle of the nineteenth century, Black Episcopal churches in the North had thriving music programs. In the South on the plantations, musical practices among Black Episcopalians tended to be within the folk tradition, that is, songs were sung unaccompanied.

The account of musical activities on a North Carolina plantation belonging to Ebenezer Pettigrew and Josiah Collins, which reported one hundred Black communicants, is probably representative of performance practices among southern Black communicants. Bishop Ives, who worked among Blacks on this North Carolina plantation, commented on "being struck by the beauty of the singing which is done without instrumental accompaniment."[17] Singing without instrumental accompaniment was also the case at Calvary Church in Charleston, South Carolina, where it was reported that "a choir of Negroes sang the chants and hymns without accompaniment"; this was on the occasion of the consecration of the building in 1849.[18]

Less wealthy parishes were not always able to purchase organs and thus sang without accompaniment. The oral tradition prevailed in parishes such as St. Paul's in Wilmington, North Carolina, which was organized in 1858; in North Carolina it was unlawful to teach reading to Blacks, music was provided by "a choir of Colored persons who were *orally* taught the catechism and to sing the psalms and hymns."[19]

Even when Blacks were taught the hymns and psalms by note or by oral tradition, "undesirable performance practices"—as they were called by educated White and Black clergy—did not seem to develop in Black Episcopal churches as these "undesirable practices" developed in Black independent churches.

The mode of worship among Black Episcopalians became a distinctive feature of worship, so much so that a Swedish visitor to Cincinnati, Ohio, Frederika Bremer, made the following comments in a letter she sent to Sweden from Cincinnati, dated November 27, 1850:

> I had in the forenoon visited a Negro *Baptist church* belonging
> to the *Episcopal Creed.* There were but few present, and they
> were of the Negro [sic] aristocracy of the city. The mode of
> conducting the divine service was quiet, very proper, and a lit-
> tle tedious. The hymns were beautifully and exquisitely sung.[20]

With regard to the "undesirable practices" that developed in Black independent churches, some Black clergy such as Daniel Alexander Payne warned his A.M.E. congregation against "clapping and stamping feet in a ridiculous and heathenish way."[21] Such clergy as Payne seemed to associate demonstrative forms of religious expression with the "unenlightened."

Having been influenced by St. James (Baltimore) in introducing the organ into the church service, Payne mentions that the choir and organ were introduced in the Boston A.M.E. Church in 1867. This event met with no opposition because, Payne says:

> The membership of our church in the enlightened city of
> Boston was so intelligent that they regarded the introduction
> of the choir and the organ as an advanced step in their reli-
> gious public worship.[22]

By the close of the Civil War, a foundation had been laid in Black Episcopal churches for church music that was rich and performed according to high standards. St. Thomas had led the way in this regard. By the mid-1860s, St. Thomas only owed a small balance on her organ, which was a significant achievement. And in the South, by the close of the War, school children were regularly drilled and given instruction in music and singing the chants.[23]

The Post-Bellum Period

Music in Black Episcopal churches had become, by the post-bellum period, a "cultivated" or "genteel" tradition, as distinct from a "folk" or "vernacular" tradition.

Black Episcopal churches persisted in providing quality music in the worship service. The Rev. Calbraith B. Perry, a White cleric, worked in Black congregations in Baltimore from the late 1860s through the late seventies. Having visited St. Philip's mission, established as a Black congregation in 1868, Perry informs us that "it was a small structure but when the service began the small size of the mission was forgotten because of the sweet music."

Perry goes on to add that "despite infrequent clergy leadership, the Colored folks had loyalty and persistently maintained services."[24]

Even in small congregations, Black Episcopalians apparently viewed the organ as a vital component of worship, so much so that at St. Philip's-St. Luke's (New Orleans), organized in 1878, a pipe organ was purchased in 1880 for a congregation of three men and ten women.[25]

Black Episcopal churches were most often noted in accounts of the musical activities of Blacks in urban areas. St. Thomas (Chicago) is notable in this regard. The first rector of St. Thomas, the Rev. James E. Thompson, was apparently critical of the music there and likely guided its direction. St. Thomas (Chicago) was probably one of the churches to which the music historian James M. Trotter refers in discussing the music situation in Black churches in Chicago in the 1870s:

> Besides several fine church-choirs, there is a large organization
> of well-trained vocalists, the performance of which have been
> highly spoken of by journals of Chicago....[26]

It is also interesting to note that all three of Thompson's children were musicians. (One son, J. DeKoven Thompson, composed a song, which was sung at the funeral of President William McKinley.)[27]

While Black Episcopalians primarily sang hymns from the Anglican tradition, in at least one instance sources indicate that Methodist hymns were sung by Black Episcopalians. This was an interesting development. And perhaps the most illuminating discussion in this regard is offered by Calbraith B. Perry in his book, *Twelve Years Among the Colored People* (1884), in which we are provided with a glimpse of the musical activities at St. Mary's Chapel (Baltimore) established in 1878. Perry writes that "a choral service was regularly held on Friday nights and also at 4 p.m. on Sundays after the close of the Sunday School session when people gathered for short musical services."[28]

Perry's descriptions about musical life at St. Mary's indicate that at least one Black Episcopal church had been influenced by Methodist hymnody. The hymns that are mentioned were, as Perry indicates, "familiar hymns" to the congregation of Black Episcopalians. In describing the evening service held at eight o'clock—a shortened form of evening prayer—Perry says that "the chants were sung" and "the hymns were set to inspiriting tunes which were interspersed with familiar Methodist hymns: 'Coronation,' 'There Is a Fountain,' and 'Nearer My God to Thee.'"[29]

These comments of Perry's are revealing for two reasons: it is likely that the musical practices among Black Methodists, at least in the city of Baltimore, had affected Episcopalians; and it is not too farfetched to conclude that the hymn tradition among Blacks was interdenominational, as it continues to be.

Musical people in Baltimore during the 1880s "worthy of mention," include certain choir members of St. Mary's Episcopal Church:

> Mr. H. C. Bishop, general director; Mr. W. H. Bishop, precentor; J. Hopkins Johns, who has a very pleasing voice; Mr. J. Taylor, a fine basso, who has been a member of a meritorious concert-troupe; Mr. C. A. Johnson, organist; and Mr. George Barrett, tenor.[30]

The music historian Trotter goes on to add that C. A. Johnson, the organist, has on "several occasions been the director of excellent public concerts in Baltimore and its vicinity, and is deserving of much praise for his activity in promoting the music-loving spirit. The same may be said of Mr. George Barrett, another member of St. Mary's Choir."[31] C. A. Johnson was also the leader of an association of musicians called "The Monumental Cornet Band," which furnished instrumental music for festive occasions at St. Mary's and in the city of Baltimore.[32] It should be noted that St. Mary's choir members, the organist at the Bethel Methodist Church, and members of the Sharp-Street Church choir were apparently the most musical African Americans in Baltimore at that time. The point is that during the 1880s, music at St. Mary's was more noteworthy than the music at St. James if Trotter's comments are an actual account of the musical situation in Baltimore at that time.

The musical legacy of St. Mary's (Baltimore) was maintained by the Rev. Hutchens C. Bishop, who was the fourth rector of St. Philips (New York) and whose older brothers and sisters were among the pioneers of St. James (Baltimore). Bishop established the second congregation in Baltimore, St. Mary's. Bishop was confirmed at St. Mary's and sang in the choir there. Upon his coming to St. Philip's (New York), Bishop was attentive to the music performed, given his nurturing and the musical activities in which he engaged as a youth."[33] The men and boys choir at St. Philip's became a recognized concert group under Bishop's rectorship.

Bishop's interest in music extended beyond the church. He was a member of the board of directors of the Negro Music School Settlement (New York City).

It was not unusual for Black Episcopal churches to spawn musicians of note and most often these musicians were formally trained. For example, there was Mrs. Arianna Cooley Sparrow who was a member of the Handel and Haydn Society in Boston during the 1880s, and who because of "excellent training retained the natural sweetness of her voice and purity of tone that enabled her to sing acceptably in St. Augustine Episcopal Church (Boston) when over eighty years of age."[34]

By the 1890s, we know for certain that women had been admitted to church choirs. At St. Matthew's (Detroit), where women were admitted to the choir in 1892, they were not allowed in the choir stalls but had to occupy the front pews.[35] (Women, however, had historically served as organists in Black Episcopal churches.)

By the turn of the century, Black Episcopal churches were still recognized for their music. Writing in 1897 about Black life in Philadelphia, W. E. B. DuBois discusses various Black Episcopal churches in that city and goes on to add that the Church of the Crucifixion (which was over fifty years old in 1897) was "perhaps the most effective church in the city for its benevolent and rescue work and it makes especial feature of good music with its vested choir."[36]

In a history of St. Philip's by the Rev. B. F. DeCosta, published in 1889, we are informed that "for the benefit of those who never enjoyed literary privileges, it was the custom, as in many churches *long before,* and *even afterwards,* to line off the psalms and hymns, in order that all might join in the praise of the Almighty God."[37]

The aforementioned quote by the Rev. DeCosta is important for several reasons. Although DeCosta's comments are about a specific Black congregation, by extension we perhaps are provided with some idea about the extent of musical practices in Black Episcopal congregations during the late nineteenth and early twentieth centuries. Contrary to the commonly held notion that all Black Episcopalians were literate, we know from DeCosta's comments that this was not entirely the case, at least not by the beginning of this century. From DeCosta's insights, we can conclude that an oral musical tradition persisted to a degree in Black Episcopal churches into the twentieth century.

From the turn of the century through the early twenties, several events are worth mentioning that directly or indirectly influenced music in Black Episcopal churches. For instance, by 1910, St. Athanasius School, an Episcopal church school for Blacks, was founded which started as a mission in 1884 and developed into a high and training school; among its "efficient department" were domestic science, manual training, and *music.*[38]

Sources disclose that it was not uncommon for priests to be trained musicians in the early twentieth century. For instance, at St. Augustine's (Atlantic City), which was spawned by St. James (Baltimore), there was the Rev. James Nelson Denver, the vicar whom Bragg describes as "having a fair high school education," and "a musician and a general 'hustler'."[39] The Rev. Maximo Duty, vicar of St. Philip's (Richmond) from 1901 to 1903, was also a musician, while the Rev. Isaac A. McDonald, rector of St. Philip's from 1938 to 1942, served also as the choir director.[40]

A "cultivated" musical tradition characterized Black Episcopal churches in urban areas by the early twentieth century—except in some instances where the psalms and hymns were still "lined-out." It has been reported that at a mission in Burroughs, Georgia, communicants employed the practice of "lining-out" during the early twentieth century.[41]

The Contemporary Scene

Church-sponsored concerts that began in the 1820s and continued full swing into the twentieth century in Black Episcopal churches had always provided performance outlets for Black musicians. Marian Anderson gave her first Detroit concert on November 1, 1926, at St. Matthew's Church to raise funds for the rectory.[42]

In the twentieth century, Black congregations of the Church also produced musicians of note. This continued a tradition that had been set in motion during the nineteenth century. For instance Carl R. Diton (1886–1969), composer and teacher, served as organist at St. Thomas (Philadelphia) during the 1920s. Diton is famous for his organ fantasy, based on the spiritual, "Swing Low, Sweet Chariot." He is also well known for his choral arrangements of African American spirituals. Melville Charlton, who was born in New York in 1883, was perhaps the leading organist of the Black race at that time and was the first Black to become a member of the prestigious American Guild of Organists. He was organist at St. Philip's Episcopal Church (New York).[43]

An interesting musical activity developed during the 1930s at St. Ambrose (New York), under the rectorship of the Rev. E. E. Durant. Durant, a West Indian, was concerned that services were "bright and that people entered heartily into singing," and held contests to promote congregational singing. One such contest involved the singing of six hymns; the competition occurred between the men and the women and between the congregation and the choir. Durant was so concerned about the quality of music at St. Ambrose that he always attended all choir rehearsals when he was in the city. About Episcopal churches, he says: "Some people complain about the dullness of some churches, all people like a bright spirited service. I love it myself."[44]

St. Ambrose, under Durant's leadership, spawned at least one musician, an organist of note. Clarence E. Whiteman, presently professor of organ and theory at Virginia State College, served as an acolyte at St. Ambrose and credits this exposure and experience as having influenced his becoming an organist. Whiteman's formal musical education includes degrees from Manhattan School of Music, Guilmant Organ School and the School of Sacred Music, formerly at the Union Theological Seminary (presently at Yale Divinity School), and from Trinity College in London. He served as organist and choir master at St. Philip's (New York) where in 1973, for regular worship, he featured music composed by Blacks.[45]

By the 1960s, the state of congregational singing in many Black Episcopal churches was critical. It is likely that the comments given in the parish profile of St. Philip's (Richmond) are representative of the state of music within Black Episcopal parishes: "The congregation is passive in participating in the service, both in singing and in prayer response."

Presently, there is real effort underway to revitalize and rejuvenate the worship experience among Black Episcopalians. Much of this effort involves the appropriation of traditional materials from the African American experience to the Episcopal liturgy. Perhaps the Rev. Arthur Myron Cochran led the way in his arrangements of music (largely based on African American spirituals) for the Communion Service which were published in 1925 and revived by the St. Augustine's College Choir in a recording of the Cochran Mass, produced by the Rev. Robert B. Hunter (presently rector of Church of the Atonement, Washington, DC).

Making the liturgy relevant to contemporary society and to the African American experience was largely undertaken in the ministry of the late Rev. Lee Benefe and continues in the ministry of the Rev. Kwasi (Anthony) Thornhill, formerly director of the Alexander Crummell Center for Worship and Learning in Detroit, among many others.

The Rev. Thornhill is concerned about the relationship of Word, music, and Mass, and maintains that "the key to bringing Episcopalians together is to break down the separateness between the choir, the congregation, and the minister. The Word, the music, and the Mass must move toward wholeness.... This is achieved in several ways: by altering the Mass into contemporary language, and by experimenting with spatial relationships in terms of the choir, congregation, and the minister, and passing from a strictly hymnbook tradition to one which is oral in the sense that the music and text become so familiar that people are able to enter into the worship experience without being bound to the printed page."[46] The oral tradition about which Thornhill speaks characterizes the religious song tradition of African Americans. And African Americans have historically employed the oral tradition, even in singing hymns written and composed by non-Blacks.

Mainline denominations have begun to recognize the power of Black song and Black worship style and are finding ways of utilizing this music, i.e., African American music, within the framework of their liturgies. Such a movement is underway in the Episcopal Church. For example, the Rev. Wm. James Walker, a Black priest, commissioned Lena McLin, an African American who is a music director and a composer, to compose a Mass for the Episcopal liturgy in which one cannot help but note the African Americanisms in the compositional style. Also at the 1974 meeting of the Union of Black Episcopalians, the music used for the Mass was in the contemporary African American religious music idiom referred to as "gospel." More recently the Office of Black Ministries of the Episcopal Church has undertaken a project of which this essay is a part. This project, a hymnal, calls attention to African American religious songs and other hymns that have been popular among African Americans.

Summary

The activities—music being one—of Blacks in the Episcopal Church need further documentation. This, of course, is a challenge to scholars.

This essay will hopefully provoke more study and research of the musical activities of Black Episcopalians. In the course of this essay, attention was given to highlighting these activities, and in an indirect way topics for future research were illuminated. What are some of the questions that have been raised from this discussion? For this writer, several. For instance, what are the possibilities of an Episcopal source for the African American spiritual, "Let Us Break Bread Together on Our Knees"? Or to what extent were the religious folk songs of African Americans used in Black parishes with Black or White leadership? How were these songs performed? Another question that comes to mind is: what are the cultural and social factors that gave rise to music making among Black Episcopalians? These examples must suffice.

I hope this essay demonstrates the validity of the study of the music of

Blacks in the Episcopal Church and demonstrates that further study of this area is imperative to the history of church music.

---

1 Reprinted with permission of the Historical Society of the Episcopal Church.

2 Gilbert Chase, *America's Music* (New York: McGraw-Hill, 1966), pp. 236–237, quoting Henry Russell, *Cheer Boys Cheer* (n.p., n.d.), pp. 84–85.

3 William Douglas, *Annals of the First African Church* (Philadelphia: Kerg and Baird, 1862), p. 54, (my italics).

4. Edgar E. Pennington, *Thomas Bray's Associates and Their Work Among the Negroes* (Worchester, MA: American Antiquarian Society, 1939), 25 quoting *S.P.G. Series A*, Volume 49 (October 20, 1709); see also Denzie T. Clifton, "Anglicanism and Negro Slavery in Colonial America," *Historical Magazine of the Protestant Episcopal Church* XXXIX (March 1970), pp. 63–64.

5 Pennington, *Thomas Bray's...*, p. 78.

6 Ibid., 17 quoting the "Minutes of the Meetings of the S.P.G. (1729–1735)," pp. 62–65; (my italics).

7 Ibid., 82 quoting *S.P.G. Series B*, XIII, #219 and *S.P.G. Series B*, XIX #68.

8 Robert A. Bennett, "Black Episcopalians: A History from the Colonial Period to the Present Day," *Historical Magazine of the Protestant Episcopal Church*, XLIII (September 1974), p. 239.

9 Daniel Alexander Payne, *History of the A.M.E. Church* (Nashville, TN: Publishing House of the A.M.E. Sunday School Union, 1891), pp. 452–453; D. A. Payne, *Recollections of Seventy Years* (Nashville, TN: 1888), p. 234.

10 Eileen Southern, "Musical Practices in Black Churches...," *Journal of American Musicological Society* XXX (Summer 1977), p. 306, quoting from the concert program as it appeared in *Freedom's Journal*, September 23, 1827.

11 George F. Bragg, *First Negro Priest on Southern Soil* (Baltimore: Church Advocate Press, 1909), p. 13.

12 Douglas, *Annals*, p. 130 (my italics).

13 George D. Bragg, *History of the Afro-American Group of the Episcopal Church* (Baltimore: Church Advocate Press, 1922), pp. 102–103, quoting the *A.M.E. Magazine*, 1845.

14 Eileen Southern, *Music of Black Americans* (New York: W. W. Norton & Co., 1971), p. 122; James M. Trotter, *Music and Some Highly Musical People* (Boston: Lee and Shepherd, 1880; (reprint Chicago: Afro-American Press, 1969), p. 306; O'Fake also had the distinction of being the first Black to conduct the Newark Theatre Orchestra.

15 Trotter, p. 132.

16 Bragg, *First Priest...*, p. 30.

17 John Hope Franklin, "Negro Episcopalians in Antebellum North Carolina," *Historical Magazine of the Protestant Episcopal Church,* XIII/3 (September 1944), p. 221, quoting the *Journal of the North Carolina Convention* (1843), p. 13.

18 Robert F. Durden, "The Establishment of Cavalry Church" (Charleston: Dalcho Historical Society, 1965), p. 82, quoting *The Charleston Gospel Messenger and The Protestant Episcopal Register,* XIX (1852), pp. 215–216.

19 Allen J. Jackson, *100th Anniversary Bulletin of St. Marks Wilmington 1975,* quoting *The Church Messenger* (Winston, NC) July 21, 1881. St. Paul's was a mission of St. Marks which was consecrated on June 18, 1975 (my italics).

20 Quoted in Eileen Southern, *Readings in Black American Music* (New York: W. W. Norton & Co., 1971), pp. 112–113 (my italics).

21 Ibid., pp. 26–64, 68–70.

22 Payne, *History of the A.M.E. Church,* p. 458.

23 George F. Bragg, *The Story of Old St. Stephens* (Petersburg, VA, Baltimore: Church Advocate Print, nd.); Allen E. Jackson, *100th Anniversary Bulletin St. Marks* (Wilmington, NC).

24 Calbraith B. Perry, *Twelve Years Among the Colored People* (New York: James Patt and Co., 1884), p. 22.

25 Rev. Herman Cope Duncan, *History of the Diocese of Louisiana* (New Orleans: A. W. Hyatt, 1883), pp. 227–228.

26 Trotter, *Music and Some Highly Musical People,* p. 321.

27 *The Thirty-Sixth Anniversary Tea Program Bulletin* (St. Thomas, Chicago) Sunday, June 18, 1884; Maude Cuney-Hare, *Negro Musicians and Their Music* (Washington, DC: Associated Publisher, 1936), p. 227.

28 Perry, *Twelve Years...,* p. 75.

29 Ibid., p. 78.

30 Trotter, p. 329.

31 Ibid.

32 Perry, p. 78.

33 Bragg, *Afro-American Group...,* p. 88; Shelton Bishop, "A History of St. Philip's Church," *Historical Magazine of the Protestant Episcopal Church* XII (March 1946), pp. 298–317.

34 Maude Cuney-Hare, *Negro Musicians and Their Music,* p. 221.

35 From *Centennial Celebration Bulletin* 1846–1946, St. Matthew's Episcopal Church, Detroit.

36 W. E. B. DuBois, *The Philadelphia Negro* (New York: Schocken Books, 1899), p. 217.

37 The Rev. B. F. DeCosta, *Three Score and Ten: the Story of the St. Philip's Church New York City* (New York: printed for the parish, 1889), p. 15 (my italics).

38 Bragg, *Afro-American Group,* p. 222.

39 Ibid., p. 174.

40 "Parish Profile," St. Philip's Episcopal Church, Richmond, VA (October 1975) unpublished MS.

41 Personal interview, Dr. Tollie Caution, New York City (April 1978).

42 *Centennial Celebration Bulletin,* 1846–1946, St. Matthew's Episcopal Church.

43 Maude Cuney-Hare, pp. 340–341.

44 Rev. E. Ellio Durant, *The Romance of an Ecclesiastical Adventure* (n.p., n.d. 1946?).

45 Eileen Southern, "Conversation with…Clarence E. Whiteman, Organ-Music Collector," *Black Perspective in Music* (Fall 1978), pp. 168–187.

46 Personal interview, Rev. Kwasi Thornhill, New York City (March 1978).

Introduction:
Why an African American Hymnal?

by Harold T. Lewis
from *Lift Every Voice and Sing II*
published in 1993

The ways in which a people expresses itself musically and liturgically provide us, perhaps, with the most significant insights into its culture. Believing this, and in an attempt to share some of the gifts that Black people bring to the whole church, the Episcopal Commission for Black Ministries, under the aegis of the Church Hymnal Corporation, published *Lift Every Voice and Sing: A Collection of Afro-American Spirituals and Other Songs (LEVAS I)* in 1981. Today, a little more than a decade later, in collaboration with the Standing Commission on Church Music, and again under the aegis of the Church Hymnal Corporation, the Episcopal Commission for Black Ministries now offers *Lift Every Voice and Sing II: An African American Hymnal (LEVAS II)*.

While it is not within the scope of this introduction to give a comprehensive overview of church music among Black Episcopalians, a few observations might enable us to better understand the place of *LEVAS II* in that historical evolution. There is an old French proverb:

"Plus ça change, plus la même chose."
("The more things change, the more they remain the same.")

This adage seems applicable to the development of church music among Black Episcopalians. In an article entitled "Music Among Blacks in the Episcopal Church: Some Preliminary Considerations," which appeared in the *Historical Magazine of the Episcopal Church,* Dr. Irene Jackson-Brown, general editor of *LEVAS I*, writes that in the late eighteenth century, "Blacks were…beginning to experience musical syncretism within the colonial Church of England. That is, Blacks were fusing certain African and African American musical practices with Anglo-American musical practices." She also notes that these "musical practices included the singing of religious folk songs," later to be called "spirituals."

The Reverend Professor Robert Bennett of the Episcopal Divinity School, in an article entitled "Black Episcopalians: A History from the Colonial Period to the Present Day," also in the *Historical Magazine,* suggests that at least one spiritual actually originated among Black Episcopalians:

> In the south, where the majority of Black Episcopalians were to be found and where prior to the Civil War the Bishop of South Carolina claimed more Black communicants than White and where Black churchmen worshipped in separate galleries or chapels, it was this body which described their plantation Holy Communion services in the spiritual, "Let us break bread together on our knees."

After the introduction of the organ, many Black congregations enjoyed reputations for excellence in church music. From the choir stalls of such places as St. Thomas', Philadelphia (founded by Absalom Jones); St. Philip's, New York City; St. James', Baltimore; and Calvary Church, Charleston emanated the sacred strains of Psalter and hymnal. It was not uncommon for such congregations, in addition to liturgical music, to offer afternoon and evening concerts featuring anthems and other choral works of great composers. But the works chosen were almost always European in origin. A Swedish visitor who attended a service in a Black congregation in 1850 included the following comments in a letter home (and I would add parenthetically that the same observations could have been made in 1950):

> I had in the forenoon visited a Negro…church belonging to the Episcopal Creed. There were but few present, and they were of the Negro aristocracy of the city. The mode of conducting the divine service was quiet, very proper, and a little tedious. The hymns were beautifully and exquisitely sung.

We must keep in mind that prior to the Civil Rights movement of the last generation, "Black" was often considered not beautiful at all. Celebrating Black heritage was not always understood as the way to success in a society in which the dominant culture established the standards to be equaled or excelled. If this were true in society in general, it was no less operative in the church, and in the Episcopal Church in particular. Thus, Bishop Turner, in his Introduction to *LEVAS I,* could write:

> Unfortunately, African Americans, particularly those in predominantly White churches, have not felt comfortable using their own music in formal church services, but instead relegated this music to use at civil and social gatherings. Although Black Episcopalians could not or would not use spirituals in their formal worship, they constantly hummed and sang these songs in private.

The Civil Rights movement, it can be argued, gave Black Episcopalians the license to reclaim the outward and visible signs of their Black heritage; and once again, like their forbears of the colonial era, they began to syncretise the clipped cadences of English church music and the syncopations, improvisations, and coloratura of the Black musical medium. The Venerable Hartshorn Murphy, Archdeacon of Los Angeles, in his keynote address entitled "Expanding our Horizons through Evangelism," delivered at the national conference of the Union of Black Episcopalians in 1989, put it this way:

> As a result of the Civil Rights and Black consciousness movements, something remarkable happened…. We as a people rediscovered the validity of "emotionalism" as a religious expression. Where previously, [Black] church ladies in the Episcopal Church would go home on Sunday, remove their veils and gloves, and sing and listen to spirituals and gospel music, today, they want to do that in church, at least occasionally.

To be sure, this conversion experience was not a universal phenomenon among Black Episcopalians. Black Episcopal congregations, like the Church at large, number among their members several converts, who often associated the hymns contained in *LEVAS* with music in their former denominational affiliations. But more and more, spirituals, gospel music, and mass settings reflective of the Black religious experience are enjoying increased prominence, even in those parishes which in a former age, would have limited its mass settings to Willan and Oldroyd, and whose concerts would have featured Vivaldi's "Gloria" or Stainer's "Crucifixion." More correctly, what is happening now is that these parishes are discovering that they can have their liturgical cake and eat it; they can skillfully blend these various elements into a tasteful and artistic whole; like Blacks in the colonial era, they have learned to "syncretise." *"Plus ça change, plus la même chose."*

But clearly, *LEVAS II* is not being published solely to enable previously stuffy Black Episcopalians to become "sanctified" ones. It is intended to be a resource for the whole Church. For as Archdeacon Murphy observes:

> White people, too, want to rejoice and sing "Blessed Assurance" with abandon. This is especially true of young White children who can't get with the program on Sunday mornings after rocking out to Michael Jackson or Whitney Houston all week.

Faithful to the Episcopal Church's new appreciation of multiculturalism, *The Hymnal 1982,* for which *LEVAS II* will serve as a supplement, is a far more inclusive and representative resource than its predecessor. African, Caribbean, Native American, Hispanic, African American, and other sources have been used, to remind worshippers of the rich diversity of all the people of God. We are pleased that the Church's official hymnal includes music, both old and new, reflective of the African American experience, and it is in the spirit of providing additional resources from the Black musical experience that *LEVAS II* is offered to the Episcopal Church at large as well as to our brothers and sisters in the broader ecumenical community. In so doing, we echo the wish of Bishop Burgess, in the Preface to *LEVAS I:*

> It is the hope of the editors and the Commission for Black Ministries that there will be acceptance far beyond those parishes composed largely of Black people. This music will serve the whole Church well, if, in making it its own, it will come to understand something more of the mission of all people in today's world.

The history and theology of the Black Church are embodied in its music. The music of the Black Church, then, is the expression of the struggle, the pilgrimage, and the joy of a people. In an age in which all members of the Church are searching for a renewed sense of spirituality, it seems altogether fitting and proper to look to the music of a people whose religious folk songs are for good reason called spirituals. I commend to you the riches of the Black musical experience, and express the hope that together we may LIFT EVERY VOICE AND SING!

Hymns and Songs: Performance Notes

by Horace Clarence Boyer
from *Lift Every Voice and Sing II*
published in 1993

The African American religious singing tradition is derived principally from musical practices in Africa, the United States, and the Caribbean, and therefore incorporates many and diverse songs and styles. The revised *Lift Every Voice and Sing* reflects this musical diversity through the inclusion of several types of songs. While many of these songs, such as standard Protestant hymns, African and Caribbean songs, "Lift Every Voice and Sing," and "Prayer for Africa" are usually performed as written, others, such as gospel songs and Negro spirituals, are performed in the traditional African American improvised singing style, and therefore warrant some notes on performance practices.

Since the formation of the Fisk Jubilee Singers in 1871, there have been two styles of singing Negro spirituals. The older style is taken directly from the singing of the slaves, and celebrates the nuances of African American folk music, while the newer style is based on European art music practices. Either style is acceptable, but the styles should not be mixed.

To ensure the most meaningful worship experiences with the music of *Lift Every Voice and Sing*, a discussion of pertinent performance practices is herewith provided for consideration.

Voice

A full, free, and sonorous tone is the hallmark of African American singing; therefore, the singer is encouraged to sing with a fully opened throat. A timid or muted sacred singing style does not necessarily connote piety in the traditional African American service. To be sure, there is a cherished tolerance in the African American community for unusual voices, and a *good* singer, one who sings with sincerity and conviction, is preferable to the singer who possesses a *beautiful* voice, but who sings without conviction.

Congregational singing is the means by which diverse individuals and groups worship the Savior as one committed union, and can provide expression for the deepest yearnings. Much of the congregational singing is executed in the responsorial ("call-and-response") manner between a soloist and congregation. The soloist is usually an experienced singer and will deliver the "call" with firmness and conviction. The congregation should be just as firm in delivering the "response," as each part is of equal importance.

Text

Negro spirituals and gospel songs are, in part, characterized by very few words in the text and, therefore, depend upon repetition to convey their message. Originally necessitated by the inability to read and the casual circumstances under which they were created, spirituals contained only a few words so that they could be learned and performed easily. It is not unusual for a spiritual to have only two different lines of text:

> Oh, bye and bye, bye and bye
> I'm gonna lay down my heavy load.

In addition to the text contained in the printed score, additional words and phrases are often interjected during performance. There is, in African American sacred music, a catalogue of *wandering* couplets and quatrains which are employed when extending the performance of a song or when variety of text is desired. In many cases, the selected couplet or quatrain will further the message of the song, though this is not necessarily a qualification for selection. The *spirit* and performance will determine the added texts. Among popular couplets and quatrains are:

> My Lord's done just what He said,
> He heated the sick and raised the dead.

> If you cannot sing like angels,
> If you cannot preach like Paul,
> You can tell the love of Jesus
> And say He died for all.

The tradition is so strong that the text in the printed score will often be discarded in favor of a popular couplet or quatrain. This practice has found its way into gospel music, and often only the refrain of the original composition is retained. Standard textual interpolations such as "Oh, Lord," "Yes, Lord," and "Hallelujah" may often precede a line of printed text but will not interfere with the rhythmic pulse of the song.

Dialect has been retained in many of the spirituals included in the hymnal, which necessitates a word of caution. Dialect should never be emphasized nor delivered with more force than other words in the text. "De" (the) is pronounced as written before words beginning with vowels, while it is pronounced as "duh" when used before words beginning with consonants. Sometimes words are shortened to accommodate rhythmic pulses and at other times extended to lengthen the value of a note. In no case should the singer attempt to correct the language.

While most Negro spirituals refer to "we" and "us," many gospel songs use "I" and "me." The use of the first person pronoun does not exclude the community, but speaks for the community from the vantage of individual piety.

Melody

Melodies in many Negro spirituals and gospel songs are set to five tones (pentatonic) or fewer. Others employ the diatonic (seven-tone) scale, but with the flatted third, sixth, or seventh. These melodies should not be corrected to conform to the diatonic scale, but should be celebrated for their economy and variety. The novice singer may experience some concern when a flatted seventh is accompanied by a diatonic seventh. This soft dissonance is part of the musical fabric of African Americans and can be accommodated with a little practice.

When the spirit of a worship service is especially intense, singers will often embellish (improvise) the melody with additional tones, resulting in an expanded melodic line (see Improvisation on page 243).

Harmony

When accompanied by a chordal instrument, African American folk music employs standard Western European tertian (in thirds) harmony. In *a cappella* singing, however, two additional types of harmony are prominent. The first is *parallel* harmony in which the melody is harmonized by a tone at the interval of a third or sixth, with this intervalic relationship remaining constant throughout the performance of the song. This method of harmonizing does not include contrary and oblique motion, so prominent in western music. The second type of additional harmony is reminiscent of Western European organum of the ninth century, in that intervals of the fourth and fifth are in abundance, while thirds and sixths, the basis of modern music, are rare. Such harmony is usually employed when songs are performed at very slow tempos.

There are very few instances when Negro spirituals and gospel songs are not sung in harmony, and singers are encouraged to create their own harmony when that printed in the score is not easily singable.

Rhythm

The most distinguishing characteristic of African American music is rhythm, and is no less so in sacred singing. Each beat should be clearly articulated and attacked with authority, accenting the principal pulse in a unit stronger than the others. In other instances, the weak beats should be given a stronger accent than the primary and secondary pulses:

$$_1\,2\,_3\,4$$

This is especially necessary when singing in a moderately fast tempo, as foot patting (see below) usually takes place on strong beats, leaving weak beats without accents.

Placing the accent on weak rather than strong beats is a feature of syncopation, in which the accent is removed from strong to weak beats, or any portion of a beat except the beginning. Syncopation should never be rushed, but executed solidly within the pulse, and with heavy accentuation. Rushing or anticipating syncopation will cause an increase in the tempo. It is therefore necessary to maintain a clear sense of where the pulse lies so that the combination of the two will create the cross rhythm desired.

Experienced singers often employ symmetrical and asymmetrical divisions of the beat as rhythmic counterpoint to the established pulse. The inexperienced singer should maintain the basic rhythm in such situations, as the resultant rhythm will be one of intricacy and complexity, characteristic of African rhythm.

Meter and Tempo

Standard meters, such as 4/4, 2/4, and 3/4, have been employed for most of the songs in the hymnal, and should be performed in the standard manner. Gospel songs, on the other hand, very often employ a meter involving multiples of three. Therefore, regardless of the meter signature assigned, moderately slow and slow gospel songs should be performed in 6/8, 9/8, or

12/8. This means, for example, a song assigned a meter signature of 4/4 should be performed in 12/8 by allotting three pulses to each quarter note. "Come, Ye Disconsolate" is assigned a meter signature of 4/4:

When performed as a gospel song, it should be executed as:

Tempo markings have not been indicated in the hymnal, though time and tradition have dictated the tempos at which most of the songs are to be performed. Many of the songs in the hymnal are classified according to tempo, and were assigned tempos when they were created. Negro spirituals are divided into basically two tempos. The *sorrow* song (e.g., "Steal Away") is performed in a slow, languorous manner, while the *jubilee* song (e.g., "Certainly, Lord") should be performed in a brisk, walking tempo. Moderately slow gospel songs (e.g., "Praise Him") should never be performed sluggishly, but in the tempo of a *gospel* waltz, while the *shout* song (e.g., "I'm So Glad Jesus Lifted Me") should be performed at a fast tempo. Occasionally a congregation will elect the Baptist lining hymn style for a song, in which case the song should be performed without a pulse, instead assigning each syllable an amount of time equal to its importance in the text.

While most Negro spirituals and gospel songs are sung in a tempo long associated with the song, the location of a song within the service may dictate a different tempo. If a jubilee song is used as a response to a prayer, the tempo may be much slower than that employed as an independent song, while a slow song may be given a faster tempo during such an activity as the "Peace." Regardless of the tempo assigned, maintain that tempo, always realizing that beneath the foreground tempo, there is a background tempo to which the singer must pay close attention to ensure the lilt and forward motion required.

Improvisation

Altering, rearranging, and spontaneously composing a melodic line to a given harmony are some of the ways in which African Americans personalize music making, both vocally and instrumentally. The process can involve occasionally changing a single tone, substituting different tones for many of the prescribed tones, or completely paraphrasing a melody. In most cases this is not done as a result of knowing other tones of the chord, but by what sounds and feels "right." The experienced singer has a number of stock motives, fragments, or "runs" that can be used in almost any song, and in cases where this is not possible, the singer may simply repeat words or phrases for a number of times. Improvisation is not only applied to the melody, but rhythm, text, and harmony. Adding extra beats during rests, dividing pulses into two accents, or lengthening or shortening a note, adding to or subtracting from words in the original text, and interpolating passing and auxiliary chords to the original harmonies are all features of African American sacred singing.

Along with altering, rearranging, adding, and omitting tones in a given melody, there are timbre variations associated with the African American singing tradition. Among these are the bending of tones, slides, slurs, grunts, wails, runs, turns, chromaticisms, vocables (non-verbal outbursts), screams, and the use of falsetto. Since improvisation is spontaneous, often the singer has no knowledge of what will come forth. Despite this freedom, the singer must always strive to improvise in the style and in the context of the service. Above all, spontaneity is the ruling performance practice in all African American folk singing.

Instruments

While many of the songs in the hymnal might best be accompanied by organ or piano, others may be accompanied by a variety of instruments. There is no prescribed orchestration for gospel songs, but music directors are encouraged to be creative in assigning instruments for such songs. Since most gospel songs are improvised, they are open to accompaniment by any and all instruments. The basic instrument for gospel is the piano. Improvisation in gospel is relatively easy when it is understood that rhythm is much more important than tones. Unless the song is completely unfamiliar to a congregation, the keyboardist need not play the melody, but can provide an improvised accompaniment by dividing quarter notes into eighth notes, employing triplet figures, or playing arpeggios. Since there are very few moments of silence in gospel, rests should be filled in with scales or scalar passages, runs, passing tones, turns, upper and lower neighbor tones, single note or octave interpolations, or glissandi. Balance and taste must dictate when and the amount of improvisation that can support a song. In general, if the singers are vocally active, the accompaniment should be subdued. Where there are open spaces in the singing, the keyboardists should fill in those sections. These devices may also be employed on organ. The Hammond organ, with Leslie B-3 speakers, has long been a favorite gospel music instrument. When organ and piano are used simultaneously, a decision regarding the leader and follower should be clearly understood.

The bass guitar is often used to accompany gospel. When a bass is used, it should supply the root of the chord, with occasional uses of inversion, and should provide a strong accent on the primary beat of a rhythmic unit. The trap drummer should not only supply a strong primary and secondary beat, but the customary "back beat" as well. Horns may double the melody, but are much more effective playing riffs, countermelodies, descants, or obbligatos, always being careful to play during the "response" and not the "call," which is assigned to the leader. Guitars may also double the melody but can be more effective strumming chords. Other percussion instruments, such as cymbals, tambourines, triangles, conga drums, bongos, and maracas, are not intended to keep the beat, but are best used to provide variety within the rhythm. Gospel music bases its use of instruments on Psalm 150, where "everything that hath breath," including instruments, should be used to praise the Lord.

Body Rhythm

All African American folk sacred singing is accompanied by a rhythmic movement of the body. Not only does such movement provide greater rhythmic accentuation in the singing, but frees the body from tension and other "weights" that would interfere with worshipping. Hand clapping, patting the feet, swaying, nodding the head, raising the arms upward, and shouting ("holy" dancing) are all common activities during traditional worship services. These activities should not be affected but should flow from the body as the singer releases unnecessary inhibitions and becomes more involved in the singing and worship.

African Americans firmly believe that the Lord is pleased when His children come before His presence with a song. For the greatest enjoyment of the songs in this hymnal, singers should follow the proclamation of the prophet: "Lift up thy voice like a trumpet."

Service Music: Performance Notes

by Carl Haywood
from *Lift Every Voice and Sing II*, published in 1993

The service music section offers a diverse sampling of musical settings for use during the Holy Eucharist. Every effort has been made to include settings which embrace the African American musical tradition—spirituals, gospels, blues, jazz. We have also included some music indigenous to Africa, the Caribbean, and the broader Anglican Communion. Though this melange of musical expression offers many possibilities for creative worship, it is our fervent hope that priests, deacons, church musicians, and parish liturgical committees will select music for the Eucharist which:

1. affords free expression;
2. promotes congregational participation and a sense of community;
3. captures the essence of the liturgy;
4. enhances spiritual growth and understanding; and
5. develops the parish's musical productivity and potential.

Because the "celebration" involves the entire congregation, the choir, though given some opportunity for individual expression, should maximize its chief function as the congregation's music leader. Therefore, service planners should choose settings that are within the congregation's grasp while occasionally encouraging the choir to introduce new or more difficult settings.

The editorial committee encourages within a single eucharistic celebration the use of parts of the Mass from a variety of musical styles and genres. Such a practice, we believe, will serve to revitalize the service from Sunday to Sunday.

Following the settings of the *Gloria in Excelsis,* three alternate songs of praise appear which may be substituted freely for the standard *Gloria.* Likewise, additional musical responses follow the *Prayers of the People* and may be used before, during, or after the prayers from the *Book of Common Prayer* or prayers from other sources. In the *Book of Common Prayer,* that which is spoken may also be sung. To this end, we have also included settings for the "Memorial Acclamation" and the "Great Amen."

Psalms

The singing of the Psalms is a tradition born of the early Christian church which, in modern times, has been developed for practical application through Anglican and Simplified Anglican Chants. Of course, their performance in the more solemn and traditional "plainsong" is always an option. Care should be taken not to rush their performance but to govern their singing by the demands of natural flow and the rhythm of the words.

The refrains and Psalms at the end of the service music section are arranged for use at the Holy Eucharist. They may also be used at Morning and Evening Prayer, adding the *Gloria Patri* at the end of the Psalm, if desired (the *Gloria Patri is* omitted at the Eucharist). The Psalm texts and chants are only suggestions, for many of the refrains may be used with other Psalm texts, chants, or tones, transposing where necessary. By varying the Psalm texts in this way, certain refrains may be used for several Sundays to foster congregational familiarity.

Simplified Anglican Chants

Simplified Anglican chants are easily performed and mastered by the average congregation. Though written in four-part harmony, they should be performed in unison by the congregation; however, the choir may sing in parts. Each half verse of the Psalm is sung on the reciting note up to the last accented syllable. The word or syllable in bold print (last accented syllable) should be sung to the corresponding darkened whole note chord in the chant. When the Psalm text contains an odd number of verses, the second half of the chant is repeated for one of the verses.

We commend to you the riches of African American music—past and present—as we worshipfully challenge all to "make a joyful noise unto the Lord."

Worship and Culture: An African American Lutheran Perspective

by Joseph A. Donnella II, John Nunes, and Karen M. Ward
from *This Far by Faith*, published in 1999

The dialog between culture and the Christian faith expressed in worship is as old as the faith itself. The Church's basic pattern of liturgy itself has antecedents both in the synagogue service and the festive meal practices of the Jewish people. The service of word and eucharistic meal was further shaped by the cultures in which the first Christians lived.

A recent Lutheran study presents helpful categories for framing and understanding this dialog:

> The reality that Christian worship is always celebrated in a given local cultural setting draws our attention to the dynamics between worship and the world's many local cultures. Christian worship relates dynamically to culture in four ways. First, it is *transcultural*, the same substance for everyone everywhere, beyond culture. Second, it is *contextual*, varying according to the local situation (both nature and culture). Third, it is *counter-cultural*, challenging what is contrary to the gospel in a given culture. Fourth, it is *cross-cultural*, making possible sharing between different local cultures.... *(Nairobi Statement on Worship and Culture*, Lutheran World Federation, 1996).

A Common Heritage

"They devoted themselves to the apostles' teaching and fellowship, to the breaking of bread and the prayers" (Acts 2:42). This is the *transcultural* pattern of weekly Christian worship that is the heritage of all Christians, regardless of culture. Word and sacraments are means of grace through which the gospel of Jesus Christ is communicated to all.

The baptized do not just "get together": they are called and gathered by the Spirit into the very presence of God. God's people do not hear just any word, but the Word of eternal life, Jesus Christ, who changes the heart and enlightens the mind. They do not share just any food, but the very body and blood of Christ. Those who have been gathered, enlightened, and fed do not just "leave," but as disciples of Christ, they are sent forth in mission to speak the word of God and do the work of God in the world. These things are the evangelical content of worship, a common "culture of the gospel" that unites and grounds the whole Christian community.

Worship in the Vernacular

This common heritage of Christian worship inevitably takes on a *contextual* dimension as it makes a home within a wide variety of situations. It reflects the astonishing particularity of the incarnation: the eternal Word, through whom all things came into being (John 1:3), becomes contextual in a human body, a Jewish home, a first century Greco-Roman culture.

Scripture and the Lutheran confessions contain no specific word for culture. However, the Bible does refer to those elements that are understood today as components of culture: world, nation, generation, tribe, people, religion, form, language, custom. The teachings of Jesus in the gospels and the sermons of Paul in the Acts of the Apostles offer many examples of making connections to the cultural context of the hearers.

The confessional writings contain discussions on matters such as ceremonies and adiaphora (matters neither forbidden nor commanded). Furthermore, Martin Luther and other reformers were strong advocates for worship in the vernacular, worship that engaged the people in their own language and made connections to their daily lives. This emphasis on the vernacular is parallel to the contemporary attention given to the cultural contexts in which the people of God worship.

Components of Culture

Additional insight in understanding culture comes from twentieth century liturgical scholar Anscar Chupungco, who proposes that culture includes three components: *values, patterns,* and *institutions. Values* are principles that shape the life and activities of a community and its members.

Examples of values shared widely among cultures are hospitality, leadership, and community. *Patterns* include a group's thought, spoken language, body language, concept of personal space, concepts of time, modes of dress, literature, music, architecture, and all forms of the fine arts. *Institutions* include the rites by which cultural groups celebrate or mark the cycles of life from birth to death.

African Americans within North American Lutheranism

North American Lutherans in the first centuries of immigration were people of Northern European ancestry, focused on nurturing and transmitting the faith primarily among their immigrant groups. It is true that Africans became Lutheran in the Americas beginning in the 1600s (records document that an African man named Emmanuel was baptized in a New York Lutheran congregation in 1669), and that especially in the last century, Lutheran domestic missions both in urban areas and the rural South have carried out ministries among African Americans.

Yet the challenge of transmitting the gospel to people of African descent in the Americas has been exacerbated by the "peculiar institution" of slavery and the seemingly intractable legacy of racism. In succeeding decades, as they continued to be baptized and catechized under Lutheran auspices, African Americans frequently found that their vernacular expressions of worship and song were not recognized by the wider Lutheran community.

A Common Contextual Heritage

While the African American community is not monolithic or uniform, there are many cultural commonalities among African Americans representing a rich cultural vernacular. Some of these similarities have been carried from the African continent, especially West Africa. These are shared with many who live in the "African Diaspora" from Canada to the Caribbean. Most of the shared cultural features probably derive from a common experience of slavery (or cultural subjugation experienced by some Africans who were not enslaved), racism, and the ongoing struggle for full recognition in the Americas. The following are examples of frequently shared cultural features present in African American worship.

Language and Imagery

Not only were slaves discouraged from reading the Bible, but it was actually illegal for slaves to read. This enforced a-literacy compelled many slaves and their progeny to rely on memory for biblical stories. Spirituals and hymns were an important aid to memory, and they often conflated or blended biblical narratives. The value of oral tradition among the people, however, helped to carry on the living voice of the gospel.

In the midst of struggle, Africans in the Americas developed rich and highly textured images to speak of God and of the relationship between God and humankind. This use of symbolic language is far more than a literary technique. The faith of an oppressed people served as a source of empowerment towards physical in addition to spiritual freedom. Many spirituals deliberately used coded language, language useful both in worship and in communicating signals to enable the flight to freedom. At times this language contrasts with more verbally precise hymnological and theological traditions. One is more poetic and expressive, the other more concrete and propositional.

The Future Present

Born out of the legacy of slavery, segregation, and social ostracism, African American prayer and song often speak of God's comfort in time of struggle, God's deliverance from oppression. Another common feature is a proleptic outlook towards heaven. God's future (heaven, kingdom, just reign) is anticipated, not as a means of escape from life, but as a source of sustenance for communal life which has often been difficult.

WORSHIP as a VERB

Worship among African Americans is more verb than noun, a holistic engagement of head, heart, and body touched by the sacred. Telling the story, testifying, preaching, and prayer are communal acts, set in the context of music, movement, and dance. All are infused with a deep awareness of the activity of the Holy Spirit within worship and a readiness for spontaneous response. Liturgy among African Americans often bears a similarity to jazz: improvisation and variation built upon the fundamental shape of the rite.

The Communal "I"

The songs and prayers of African Americans often use first person language: "I want Jesus to walk with me" or "I've just come from the fountain." Observing this practice from outside the culture, some may conclude that this emphasis is individualistic. From within the culture, the opposite is true. There is a profound communal or tribal dimension among Africans and African Americans. In most African cultures, the base unit is the tribe or clan, rather than the individual or the nuclear family. Combine this African tribal antecedent with the African American history of group identity as slaves and the continuing reality of racial oppression, and one discovers a potent cultural undercurrent of collectivism.

In the popular aphorism of West Africa, "I am because we are, and because we are, I am." The use of the first person in worship is a communal "I," understood as "we" by worshipers who share a common history of struggle and striving for justice. Biblical precedents abound, especially in the psalms and in the letters of Paul.

God of Our Ancestors

An additional dimension of this communal sensibility is a profound awareness of the ties that bind living saints to the saints who dwell in light eternal. The African heritage of connectedness to one's ancestors is transformed in the context of Christian faith into a vivid appreciation for the communion of saints, the cloud of witnesses that accompany God's people on the journey of faith. Prayers that call upon the "God of our ancestors" have their lineage in the Old Testament invocation of the God of Abraham, Isaac, and Jacob, and in the frequent uses of this term in the letter to the Hebrews.

This Far by Faith

The interplay between worship and culture is often a messy enterprise. Practices that seem right and salutary in one era or within one culture may be judged odd or quaint in another. Fortunately, the Lutheran heritage welcomes this dialog, calling for unity in the common, evangelical core of worship and at the same time allowing for flexibility and freedom in the ways this essential core is communicated and celebrated.

As the first African American worship supplement prepared for use among Lutherans, *This Far by Faith* joyfully joins this conversation in progress. It is a proposal for addressing issues of worship from a perspective of particular culture and at the same time being faithful to the worship patterns of the Church through the ages. To that end, this volume provides an important contribution to the global discussion on worship and culture by making available to African American Lutherans and to the wider Church some of the riches of African American liturgy and song.

On these pages, witness a living chronicle of a faith journey begun on African soil. This is the pilgrimage of a people leaning on the Lord and trusting in God's holy word. Empowered by the Holy Spirit not to lay their religion down, African American Christians by the grace of God have overcome. They have overcome cultural marginality by finding family in the church. They have overcome dehumanization and oppression by knowing themselves to be God's children. They have overcome trials and tribulations, storms and tempests, to find joy and peace in believing. Hear them as they worship and sing the triumph of trust in God, having come *This Far by Faith*.

Contextual Worship Practices

Symbolic actions and gestures used in worship are drawn from a variety of religious origins and the traditions of particular peoples. Christians have incorporated such cultural expressions within worship by interpreting the gesture in the light of Christian faith, in connection with biblical images, and in association with existing traditions of worship. Some examples include the use of the Advent wreath, candles, processions, and incense; the giving of rings in the marriage rite; or the pouring of earth in the funeral service.

The following practices and expressions, while not universal or exclusive, have been associated with the worship of Africans and African Americans at various times and places.

Space for Worship

Some African traditions value the symbol of the circle or semicircle. Moveable chairs or pews in the place of worship may be rearranged into such configurations.

Processional Music and Dance

Processions at the gathering or sending of the assembly may be accompanied by African drums and dance. Traditional African music forms such as the *lamba* and dances such as the *domba* may be used, and are especially fitting at the celebration of marriage.

Call to Worship

This term is in widespread usage among African American churches, referring to the musical or spoken materials that gather the community for worship, or to a specific dialog, frequently scriptural, that articulates this invitation. Although not African in origin, the call to worship reflects the spirit of the African call-and-response pattern.

Acclamation

In many contexts, joyous, vigorous, and physical response from worshipers is naturally expressed. Such acclamation can include hand clapping and shouts of thanksgiving and jubilation. Ululation is one form of elevated vocal expression of African origin used to sound praise. At other times, the moan or lament is heard. Spontaneous dancing is a form of acclamation appropriate for certain festive contexts.

Posture and Gesture for Prayer

A bowed head, kneeling, and the folding of hands are common prayer postures. In addition, some may use the more ancient practice of extending open arms in prayer and praise, recalling the Psalm, "Let my prayer rise before you as incense, and the lifting up of my hands as an evening sacrifice" (Psalm 141:2).

Libation

Libation is a practice primarily used to accompany a call to worship or gathering prayer. The gesture of libation involves the pouring of a liquid such as water or a fermented drink into the earth or a container of soil. The leader pours from a pitcher or glass during a brief silence that follows each petition or response.

The Bible makes use of the image of pouring or libation in a number of places. These references help to supply meaning to the Christian use of this symbolic act. St. Paul says to the Philippians, "But even if I am being poured out as a libation over the sacrifice and the offering of your faith, I am glad and rejoice with all of you" (Phil. 2:17), and again in the letter to Timothy, "I am already being poured out as a libation…. I have finished the race, I have kept the faith" (2 Tim. 4:6-7). Thus, the image of libation is a metaphor for the dedication of one's self in service for God's sake. The image of pouring is also used as an image for the outpouring of the gifts of the Spirit (Acts 2:33, 10:45).

Communities of faith might consider the use of the libation gesture as a symbolic action of thanksgiving for the creation of humankind from the dust of this earthly home, and thanksgiving for those who have gone before, the mothers and fathers in faith whose mortal remains rest in the earth until the day of resurrection. The gesture may also be a sign of dedication to be poured out for the sake of the world in the same way Christ "poured out himself to death" (Isa. 53:12), even as the church is empowered by the Holy Spirit who has been "poured out on us richly" (Titus 3:6).

Leading
African American Song

by Mellonee V. Burnim
from *This Far by Faith*, published in 1999

The variety of song that finds a home in African American worship presents a similar variety of challenges to those who lead the song of God's people. While many music leaders in communities that use this music have long-standing familiarity with these musical forms, others are seeking help in meeting these challenges, or desire to learn more about a specific genre. What follows is an introduction to the task of inspiring and enabling communities of faith to sing the liturgies and hymns in *This Far by Faith*. It may be a helpful summary and review for the experienced leader, or an overview for the novice with the goal of encouragement to pursue further study and practice.

Knowing and understanding the principles that undergird the performance of African American religious music is one thing, an important first step. Putting these principles into practice is quite another. Performances that look easy when executed by an experienced practitioner of spirituals and gospel music can be quite deceptive. The seemingly effortless melismatic passage or the brilliant display of polyrhythmic clapping comes not from mere spontaneous inspiration, but from years of persistent honing of skills through careful listening, observation, and practice.

For many church musicians, especially those with predominantly classical training, developing proficiency in African American music may pose a great challenge; after all, many of the principles of African American music performance are polar opposites of standard European American musical practices. The first and perhaps biggest challenge is coming to terms with the role of the musical score in African American music. In western music, the score reigns supreme; for the most part, performers are expected to adhere to tempo and dynamic markings. Beyond that, tampering with the melodic line, the rhythm, or the meter is often considered questionable. In contrast, the significance of the score in African American music is determined by the genre or type of music that it represents.

An example from the choral gospel music tradition may be illustrative. As a music whose foundation rests in the oral rather than the written tradition, African American gospel choirs typically learn new repertoire by rote, having heard the chosen selection sung by another group, or having heard the recording on CD, radio, or television. Frequently, no transcription of the selection exists or at least the choir does not have scores. It is the choir director's responsibility to know and demonstrate every vocal line and ensure that the parts blend harmonically.

Even though gospel music is often referred to as a "composed" music (distinguishing it from the spiritual created during slavery whose specific composers are unknown), writers of gospel songs both expect and accept deviation from the score. This improvisational dimension of gospel music performance does not mean that "anything goes." On the contrary, there are boundaries and principles and broadly accepted musical values to guide performers in deciding when, what, and how to do what they do. Only through the discipline of constant practice, generated by a sincere willingness and desire to learn, will the expression of African American music grow to assume personal and collective meaning in worship.

Performance Practice

Three primary areas of significance are identifiable in the performance of African American worship music regardless of genre: quality of sound (timbre), mechanics of delivery (manipulation of musical variables), and style of delivery (physical and visual dimensions of performance). Principles that govern this worship music leadership must not be viewed as inflexible rules that must be applied in the same way in every situation, for the underlying premise of this music is fluidity, constant change. The intent of sharing these fundamental, practical applications is to spark interest and confidence in creating a wider and stronger embrace of African American music, African American culture and, with God's help, African American people.

Quality of Sound

Singing in traditional African American worship is an expression of jubilation, power, and praise. Even when the text of a spiritual communicates lament, the vocal quality of the singer remains strong. Vocalists are expected to convey their total sincerity and complete absorption in communicating both outward, to others present at the event, and upward to God. The vocal timbre in gospel solos may vary constantly, alternately utilizing moans, groans, shouts, wails, and growls. Similarly, in congregational singing the concluding verse or refrain may be hummed, allowing the assembly to experience the song's meaning through another timbral dimension. Whereas in the singing of spirituals the vocal timbre is more closely aligned with that of western music, maximizing the use of the head voice, in gospel music the commanding power of the chest voice is highly valued in women's singing, and male soloists frequently utilize falsetto.

Much congregational song takes the African-influenced form of call/response. The soloist, a strong and experienced singer, will issue the "call" in a firm manner that elicits an equally bold, full-voiced response from the congregation. It may take time and consistent use to develop the trust necessary for this assured back-and-forth song, but it is integral to African American worship.

A highly valued dimension of timbre, representing a continuing African tradition, is percussive delivery both in vocal and instrumental performance. Particularly in highly syncopated songs with faster tempos, short phrases are strongly punctuated to accent the rhythm. For example, in the opening line of "What a fellowship," breaks will commonly occur after "what" and "a." The line is not sung as a single continuing legato melodic phrase, but is instead chopped up into short, percussive fragments. The phrase is deliberately broken after the first word, adding rhythmic and timbral (percussive) interest.

Mechanics of Delivery

This broad category of performance describes the way time (rhythm, meter, tempo, duration), text, pitch, and harmony are conceived in African American sacred music expression, as well as the role of accompaniment and improvisation.

Rhythm

More than by any other factor, African American music is driven by its rhythm. Rhythm is preeminent in both vocal lines and instrumental accompaniment; rhythm establishes the character of the piece. Each beat must be clearly sensed and heard. The principal pulse, of course, is given a strong accent. However, frequently the weak beats (such as 2 and 4 in 4/4) are given an even stronger accent than the primary and secondary ones. To illustrate, look at the spiritual "I'm so glad Jesus lifted me" (#191). It has four quarter note beats per measure and it is played with the accents not only on beats 2 and 4, but on the eighth note offbeats (1 and 2 and 3 and 4 and).

This sort of syncopation pervades all forms of African American worship music. It should never be rushed, always a temptation when you are anticipating the accent. Keep a firm sense of the tactus so that the syncopation can play off of it. As singers become more experienced in this style of music, they will often add layers of symmetrical and asymmetrical beat divisions over the basic pulse, contributing to the characteristic rhythmic complexity. Those less accustomed to the style, however, will be better off maintaining the basic rhythm. Above all, avoid smoothing out the rhythms; to do so will rob the music of its vitality and energy.

While rhythmic precision is critical to the performance of spirituals and gospel music, at the same time, rhythm must never be mechanical. Precision is one thing; rigidity is another. Notes may be held longer or shorter than written, and notes may even be anticipated—coming slightly earlier than indicated in the score. Even in congregational singing, each member of the congregation is free to personalize the singing experience—to make it one's own.

Meter

Meter is another area in which oral tradition frequently takes precedence over what is written. Especially in the case of material borrowed from the classic or revival hymn traditions, a piece written in 4/4 routinely will be sung in 12/8, with a swing. So, for instance, "What a Fellowship" (#220) is often written in 4/4 but played in 12/8. Even songs that keep their 4/4 feel will often have a flexibility in the meter that shows a triple-meter influence.

Tempo

Tradition has come to dictate the tempos at which most African American songs are sung. Spirituals fall, for the most part, into either of two tempos. The sorrow song—such as "Go Down, Moses" (#87)—is sung at a slow tempo, while the jubilee song—such as "Great Day" (#164)—is taken at a brisk walking tempo. Within the arena of the gospel song, the gospel waltz is often employed for slower songs like "What a Fellowship," while shout songs like "I'm So Glad Jesus Lifted Me" would be sung at a quick tempo.

Duration

In traditional African American worship, neither the length of service in general nor the length of the songs in particular is dictated by the clock. Depending upon the quality of the interaction between the performer (preacher or singer) and the working of the Holy Spirit, extemporaneous elements of the worship may be extended or shortened. In congregational singing, it is common for the final chorus of such well-loved hymns as "What a Fellowship" to be repeated as directed by the song leader. Similarly, soloists frequently interject such textual phrases as "I believe I'll say that one more time" to signal repetition of a particular phrase or stanza. In neither of these instances is repetition viewed as boring or grandstanding; instead, repetition serves as an essential tool for generating and sustaining the spiritual fervor that has historically distinguished the worship of African Americans in the United States.

Text

Most spirituals and many gospel songs have very short texts, a feature which was helpful in committing them to memory. These brief texts are, however, repeated many times with improvised variations, the repetition helping to convey their message. Another way in which these texts are extended is through the interjection of "wandering," independent couplets and quatrains such as

> If you cannot sing like angels, if you cannot preach like Paul,
> You can tell the love of Jesus and say he died for all.

Sometimes these insertions are closely related to the text of the song, sometimes not. They are selected according to the spirit of the moment.

Although rhythm is unquestionably preeminent in African American religious music performance, text—the message—must not be minimized. Spirituals and gospel songs are filled with rich biblical imagery and intense devotion. The text, regardless of its relative simplicity or profundity, must be given its due.

Pitch

The concepts of pitch that characterize African American religious music are distinguished in some rather marked ways. First of all, melodic lines in both spirituals and gospel music include a preponderance of blues notes—lowered third, sixth, and seventh degrees in the major scale. Just as rhythms should not be smoothed out, neither should pitches. Even if a flatted seventh in the melody conflicts with a diatonic seventh in the accompaniment, this is considered an acceptable dissonance. Slides, scoops, and bends are all so fundamental to gospel music performance that soloists and congregations alike employ these vocal techniques intuitively. They have learned to value how pitch is conceived in their tradition through the process of years of exposure and practice.

HARMONY

Two styles of harmonization coexist with standard western harmony in unaccompanied singing. The first uses parallel thirds or sixths throughout the song, a constant parallel motion. In the second style, used especially with very slow-moving pieces, a parallel interval of a fourth or fifth predominates, creating an effect similar to organum.

Accompaniment

When not sung unaccompanied, spirituals are often accompanied by acoustic piano alone. In gospel music, as well as gospel interpretations of hymns, piano is still the basis, but instrumentation is unlimited. African American churches often use some combination of piano, electric organ, drums, tambourine, and bass guitar. Accompaniment may also include instruments such as synthesizer, vibraphone, trumpet, saxophone, or flute. In virtually all forms of African American music, instrumental accompaniment functions to complement the voice; its role is not a secondary one, but rather one of equal importance to the voice. At the same time, instruments playing riffs or obbligatos should be careful to play on the "response" sections and not on the "calls" that are reserved for the leader.

Improvisation

In orally based music like African American sacred song, improvisation plays an important role. At least some basic filling in beyond the written notation is essential to accompanying or leading this music. In singing the solo part, the leader will freely add runs, riffs, or motives to make the line more expressive. The melody line itself may be altered; rubato or rhythmic alteration may be employed.

A basic principle for accompanists is that open spaces in the gospel style are almost always filled in by the keyboard. At the very least, this would require repeating chords during longer, held notes. Even more effective would be adding an arpeggiated figure; for instance, leading from one phrase to the next. It requires listening and practice, but such fills can add immeasurably to the song. A next step could be to add a moving bass line.

Few "upper limits" exist for the amount of improvising open to the keyboard player. Once the assembly is familiar with the hymn, even the melody is optional for the pianist. Arpeggios, scale passages, passing tones, upper and lower neighbor tones, even the occasional glissando are all possibilities within the style. Harmonic alterations that support the singing are also welcome. The player must sense when to "let loose" and when, especially as the vocalists become more active, to back off.

Style of Delivery

The style of delivery, or physical mode of presentation of much African American music includes variables which, in the European American tradition, may be considered extraneous. In the African American tradition, however, the visual and kinetic dimensions—the expressive behavior that characterizes performance—are of equal significance to the sonic dimension. In other words, it is not just what is sung, but how it is sung that counts.

The most striking aspect of delivery in African American music is the incorporation of dance. Although "flat-footed" singers have also been a part of African American song tradition, movement in synchrony to the rhythm of the song is very common in worship. However important these kinetic dimensions are to the African American worship experience, they never assume dominance over the singing itself.

Conclusion

These principles of African American musical performance are intended to serve as general guides toward developing musical facility and growth in these styles. Commitment and determination are necessary to internalize these principles, but the end result can be a richly rewarding experience. See the chart on the following page.

A Musical Timeline

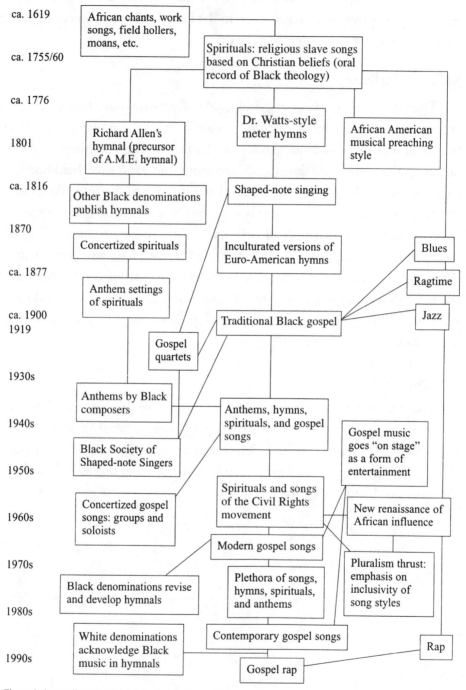

ca. 1619	African chants, work songs, field hollers, moans, etc.
ca. 1755/60	Spirituals: religious slave songs based on Christian beliefs (oral record of Black theology)
ca. 1776	
1801	Richard Allen's hymnal (precursor of A.M.E. hymnal) — Dr. Watts-style meter hymns — African American musical preaching style
ca. 1816	Other Black denominations publish hymnals — Shaped-note singing
1870	Concertized spirituals — Inculturated versions of Euro-American hymns — Blues
ca. 1877	Anthem settings of spirituals — Ragtime
ca. 1900 / 1919	Traditional Black gospel — Jazz — Gospel quartets
1930s	Anthems by Black composers
1940s	Anthems, hymns, spirituals, and gospel songs — Gospel music goes "on stage" as a form of entertainment
1950s	Black Society of Shaped-note Singers
1960s	Concertized gospel songs: groups and soloists — Spirituals and songs of the Civil Rights movement — New renaissance of African influence
1970s	Modern gospel songs — Pluralism thrust: emphasis on inclusivity of song styles
1980s	Black denominations revise and develop hymnals — Plethora of songs, hymns, spirituals, and anthems
1990s	White denominations acknowledge Black music in hymnals — Contemporary gospel songs — Rap — Gospel rap

The vertical center line represents the use of music for worship.
All musical styles overlap, continually influencing and nurturing each other.

© Melva Wilson Costen

IV.
Worship

Worship Activities

by Benjamin Elijah Mays and Joseph William Nicholson
from *The Negro's Church,* published in 1933

The activities of worship are probably the ones most emphasized in the church. Worship in the form of spirituals and hymns, which have always been prominent in the Negro services, preceded the use of the formal service. But a brief review of the history of the churches of this study will show that, since the early days, changes in the manner and spirit of worship have been influenced by changes in the social conditions of the Negro.

During the days of slavery, and in the early days of the organized Negro church, worship was largely begun as an unconscious imitation of the White church; but it soon developed characteristics of its own. The spirituals, which gave free expression to the ravaged feelings and aspirations of the Negro in bondage, expressed his fear, his hope of deliverance, and less often his joy.

Like the minstrel in medieval Europe, the Negro transmitted history, group contributions, and feelings in song. Because of his illiteracy, he depended upon memory. While the spirituals were almost entirely original with him, he readily adopted many of the songs used in the White revival meeting which he attended.

Changes in Manner of Worship

The form and manner of worship has gradually changed in the church. The growing intelligence of the people has encouraged efforts to improve the services of worship. Illiteracy has gradually decreased among Negroes from 70 percent in 1880 to 22.9 percent in 1920, and to 16.3 percent in 1930. This gradual extension of the ability to read and write has permitted the churches to make their services appeal to the intellect as well as to the emotions. More sermons attempt to be thought provoking. The spirituals, along with other published songs and hymns, are still widely used; but no longer is there absolute dependence upon memory. The music in most urban churches is now led by choirs and accompanied by instruments, including organs and orchestral pieces.

The services of the urban churches studied consist of the Sunday church school, the junior church service, and the regular public worship services. Following is an account of each of these activities.

Worship in the Sunday Church School

The worship services of the Sunday church schools are separated into distinct types. Those of the first type include in a single service persons of all ages and experience. These schools usually have an opening and a closing exercise at each Sunday session.

Services of this type are used by about 90 percent of the 608 Sunday church schools. The distribution of time in these schools usually gives thirty minutes each for the opening exercises, the class work, and the closing exercises.

Services of the second type are improved by an attempt to adapt them to differences in age and experience by grading instead of resting upon the assumption that a common service is suitable for all persons regardless of age. About a tenth of the 608 churches follow this form of worship. In these schools, the services are usually held by departments; and the distribution of time is fifty minutes for class work, fifteen minutes for reports and preparation for worship, and twenty-five minutes for actual worship.

One very good reason for grading worship is shown in the schools studied. The content of the worship in which all age groups are included shows that the younger people suffer because, although they outnumber the adults, the services are planned mainly in terms of adult desires and experiences.

The Songs Used in the Schools

The purposeful use of songs as a means of bringing the worshipper to a realization of the church's wealth of history and belief, and of giving him at the same time an appreciation of religious music, is gradually overshadowing other uses suggested by custom or the necessity to "pep up" the service.

The schools in the 608 churches, either by choice or through a lack of knowledge and appreciation, make a wide use of hymns that express, almost wholly, adult ideas of religion and life, which the children have had little or no opportunity to experience and are, therefore, unlikely to understand.

The schools use such songs as "Sweet Hour of Prayer," "Nearer My God to Thee," "Stand Up, Stand Up, for Jesus," "What a Friend We Have in Jesus," "I Came to the Garden Alone," "I Need Thee Every Hour," "Nothing

Between," and others that are distinctly based upon adult experience. It is unlikely that the experiences of persons even fifteen or seventeen years of age would enable them to understand fully the religious significance in such songs. Songs like "All Nature's Works His Praise Declare," "Praise to God and Thanks We Bring," and "Little Voices Through the Temple Stealing," are probably more suitable for younger folk. It is, therefore, pleasant to report that several churches were found using songs of this type.

The Prayers

There are many interpretations of the value of prayer as an element of public worship, among which at least these two may prove generally acceptable. (1) That the public prayer should be social rather than individualistic in its tone and conception, and should assist the worshippers to include others beside themselves in their hopes for higher life. (2) That the prayer should be intelligible to the worshippers.

The prayers used in the schools are in many instances almost entirely addressed to the minds of adults rather than those of children. Two prayers are presented here. These come from a group of stenographic reports of school services in the churches studied.

> Prayer by a Superintendent:
> We thank Thee, Heavenly Father, for this great and grand opportunity; that You have spared us to turn out to the House of worship and hear Thy word once more. Have mercy upon us; bless the Sabbath school this morning; bless the teachers who are trying to instruct the little ones in Thy way as You have said: "Suffer the little children to come unto me, and forbid them not, for of such is the Kingdom of Heaven." Have mercy upon us. We are thankful that we are able to stand together and testify that we have seen another bright morning, while thousands have gone upward and onward. Bless all, Our Heavenly Father, that we are duty bound to pray for. Then, our Heavenly Father, when we have finished our work on earth; when there is no more space between the living and the dead, raise us up to Thy Kingdom. In Jesus' name. Amen.
>
> Prayer by a Superintendent:
> O, Gracious Father, we again assemble in Thy house of worship, asking Thee to have mercy upon us. Lead us in the path

that we should go. Teach us by Thy precepts those things worthy of knowing and worthy of a place in Thy Kingdom. Lead us in the path where righteousness is. Guide us away from those things which beset worries not only in this life, but in the life hereafter. Bless the children who have come and their parents at home working, striving, slaving in order that the lives of these children may be more worthy. Bless those without shelter, clothing, and food. May we ask Thee to take care of the sick; get into the hearts of those people in the world who know Thee not. May they see Thee in their doings and do unto others as they would have others do unto them. Get into their hearts. Teach them Thy way. May the coming of these children here be a coming worthy of the life they have spent. These blessings we ask in the name of Thee, who has taught us when we pray to say: (recital of Lord's Prayer in concert).

General Lesson Reviews and Talks

A large part of the time of the closing exercise in virtually 90 percent of the 608 schools is devoted to lesson reviews. This procedure naturally, and often rightly, is based upon the assumption that everyone has studied the same biblical lesson texts. The reviews seem to be regarded as necessities, although observations reveal that the reviewers seldom present the material even as interestingly as it has already been presented in the classes. Evidently it is hoped that the persons present will all have the same idea of the lesson, and that the conduct of all will be similarly changed. It is doubtful, however, that such an objective can be achieved in a service in which ages vary as widely as from six to seventy. If, however, the work of the classes were accepted as well done, the need of reviews would disappear.

A number of schools, probably a tenth, do not have general lesson reviews, and devote the time to planned services of worship. General observations of these two methods in the churches studied indicate that the latter method seems to produce more satisfactory results. There is usually less noise and moving about. The service proceeds with a greater sense of its achieving its purpose. The pupil participation appears to arise out of interest rather than coercion.

Pupil Participation

The services of worship of the schools are dominated by adult leadership. Duties such as passing and collecting song books and lesson materials, and the running of errands are given over to younger pupils. In many schools in which the services are not well planned, the pupils are permitted to select the songs as they are needed; but very rarely indeed are the younger pupils members of the worship committee or other subordinate activity groups in which they may learn by doing.

The Junior Church

The junior church, an adaptation to the church program during the last one and a half decades, has not become a common activity in the Negro church. Junior church work follows no generally accepted pattern. Each church promoted its junior work according to its own ideas. The thirteen junior churches studied are services or organizations for boys and girls and young people which attempt to serve the religious life of the young folk as the regular church service serves the adult people. The memberships of these churches range between fifty and seventy-five children.

Term "Junior" Not Clearly Defined

If the term "junior" were used in a technical sense, it would cause the junior church to serve those individuals between the ages of nine and eleven as distinguished from those of the primary, intermediate, or other age group. In practice, however, these services include all persons who come. In fact, it includes all those who do not join naturally in the adult service. For this reason, it would probably be better if it were called the "Junior Worship Service of the Church," and the adult service called the "Senior Worship Service of the Church."

When Churches for the Juniors Meet

The junior churches of this study meet on days or nights during the week and on Sunday mornings. Two of the thirteen are known to meet during the week. The remaining eleven of the organizations meet on Sunday morning. In a few of these, the juniors join with the adults in the opening of the adult service. They join in the singing and the prayers; and just before the sermon they go to their own room for a story or talk from their leader. In other instances, the pastor talks to the juniors before they are excused from the adult service.

The most acceptable arrangement appears to be for the juniors to meet in their own room for the entire service. In this case, they have their own pastor, a choir, a governing board of officers, a secretary, a treasury, ushers, and other duplicates of the adult service. As to the time limit for these churches, there seems to be agreement in practice that they should not be more than an hour long.

These worship services are conducted by the minister of the church or his assistant. Most of these leaders have had no formal preparation for this work.

The Regular Public Worship Services

The bearing of the historical development of the church and of the race upon Negro church worship has already been indicated in this chapter. In presenting a discussion of the regular public worship services, it is therefore necessary only to point out some more immediate facts.

Public worship is generally deemed by the church to be of major importance. Hence the buildings are all primarily meeting houses; the largest and best equipped room is the auditorium for public worship. The minister is very often judged upon his ability as a preacher in these services. The services draw the largest regular attendance, between a quarter and a half of the membership, of any activity in the church. And the time allotted to them is the best at the disposal of the church.

Consideration of the elements of the service of worship may serve to illuminate this work of the church.

Songs, Choirs, Instruments

In urban churches, the services of worship usually include a number of musical selections. Among them are the old and new hymns of the church and the spirituals. Singing, in many of the churches, is lead by vested choirs, with the assistance of pipe organs and, in few instances, of brass, reed, or string instruments. In some services, older people occasionally break into song, especially following the sermons. However, in the very formal type of service, this seldom if ever happens.

In all of the services, hymns expressing strength arising from dependence upon God are apparently very acceptable. Usually all of the people in the congregation join with the choir in singing those hymns that are familiar to them. Hymnals are used by most churches. However, in a few churches the worshippers depend largely upon memory.

The choirs use a variety of anthems in addition to leading the congregations in the singing of spirituals and hymns. Of the 609 urban churches, about 85 percent have choirs.

Prayers

The prayers in the services of worship are offered by both ministers and laymen. They appear to follow a pattern in which many of the attitudes toward God and the present world-order are recurrent.

> The Attitude Toward God:
> God is all powerful and ever present. He is very close to the individual, just as a friend or any living individual may be. He is also to be feared and appeased; and unlimited gratefulness belongs to Him for all good things.
>
> (1) Gracious Father, the father of us all and of our Lord and Savior, Jesus Christ, our elder brother. We thank Thee from the depths of our hearts that we are allowed to be present this morning within these consecrated walls. We thank Thee that this opportunity to worship Thee is denied no man but that every man and woman and child who believes can fall down and worship Thee. Lord, we come to Thee pleading no merits of our own. At best we are but poor feeble worms of dust, asking mercy that Thou abide with us. Sanctify our whole being. We know that we are short, Lord, but we are coming up to the throne of mercy pleading that Thou will make us the kind of servants that Thou would have us to be. Banish from our minds everything that destroys our faith in Thee.
>
> (2) Oh God, our Heavenly Father, we come to Thee this morning, so thankful that Thou hast allowed us the privilege of coming before Thee. Thankful, O Lord, that Thou hast called us the sons of God. Thankful, that Thou hast chosen us out of the world to be Thy followers and hast led us in the paths of truth and light.
>
> (3) Dear Lord, we are gathered here this blessed morning to sing praises to Thee and ask Thy forgiveness of our many sins since we gathered together on last Sunday morning. We want to thank Thee for all Thy blessings bestowed upon us. Help us always to be thankful of Thy kindness. Guide our footsteps toward right and righteousness always. Give us strength to go forward in life and do the world's work for Thee. Bless all that are gathered here this morning. Bless those that are afflicted.

God Dwells in the Church:

(1) We have come today, Father, into Thy Holy presence. We pray, Father, that as we gather here, we shall be conscious of Thy abiding presence, and that there shall be great rejoicing because Thou art with us. Abide with us. We thank Thee for this privilege.

(2) Lord, our Heavenly Father, we meet with you this morning to give Thee thanks for the past blessings Thou hast bestowed upon us. We pray Thee sincerely for help; get into our wondering minds and faltering steps. We earnestly pray your blessings upon this great congregation. We pray Thy blessings upon the choir, preaching the gospel through song. Help them wake up to the understanding of their duty. We ask Thy blessings upon the personnel of this church.

Dependence Upon God:

(1) Lord, Thou knowest we can do nothing tangible without Thy assistance. We beg Thee, O Gracious God, give of Thy supernatural strength and power from on high, that we may do better. We ask Thy blessing for the speaker this morning; that his message will thrill our humble souls; strengthen him; help his family that they will be able to accomplish in every way their undertakings. We pray a prayer for the poor and needy, the sick and afflicted; we ask Thee to help all of us that we may do better for Thy glory.

(2) But we ask Thee for Thy holy privilege. We know we can do nothing without Thy aid or assistance. Make us conscious of the fact that we are all Thy children in that vineyard, striving to work our souls' salvations. We ask Thee, give us the spirit of Christ and determination to press onward and upward. We ask Thee to give us, Father, grace, hope, patience, and keep our feet in the straight and narrow path and ever to be willing to do the task Thou hast assigned to us.

(3) Help us, O Blessed Savior, that we may surrender ourselves to Thee, that we may come with humbler hearts. We come to Thee because we feel that we need Thee, we feel that we have

need of Thee as never before. In these times when there is so much mistrust, in these times when sons and daughters are turning against their parents, and when there is so much suffering in this world, will Thou bless this pastor and give him courage this morning. Help us that we may give courage to some discouraged heart, help them so that they may not give up all hopes.

Biblical References in Prayers:

(1) When we consider Thy mercies, we say as David, what is man that Thou are mindful of him, and the son of man that Thou visited him? For Thou has made him a little lower than the angels and crowned him with glory and honor.

(2) We thank Thee that because of Thy wonderful blessings men no longer have to lay at the pool and wait for the troubling of the waters, but that men and women may come and be reclaimed and fall our of their sinful ways.

Anticipating Another World:
Other-worldly expressions occur in the closing sentences of some of the prayers.

(1) And when we are called from time to eternity, we will not go before the justice bar wanting, but having done the things commendable in Thy presence forever and ever. Amen.

(2) Bless Thy children, and when we come to press a dying pillow, may we hear the sweet voice of him, who taught us to say, (Lord's Prayer chanted by the choir). Amen.

(3) Bless all for whom we are duty bound to pray. Bless the unemployed, bless the suffering everywhere. Then, dear Father, when we have finished our work, when all our work is over here and when we can do no more for Thy Kingdom among the children of men, bring us into Thy presence where all the redeemed of God are blessed. Amen.

The Present World:

References to the present world order are more often general than special.

(1) We pray for the sick. Bless the low in spirit. Bless this city of ours, O Lord. Bless this country and the world over. Bless the conditions of this country, we ask Thee. Give us peace and love and charity towards all mankind. Give us power. Give us a greater desire to serve Thee. We ask in Thy name.

(2) Some have come this morning because of bereavement over the loss of a loved one, some have come because of the economic depression that is prevalent and they haven't the necessary comforts of life.

As one listens to these prayers, and as one reads them, they are impressive primarily because there is a deep ring of sincerity in each of them.

Announcements

In some services, the making of announcements or the reading of notices consumes quite a large part of the time. Many of the church announcements and notices given by the reading clerk are repeated and emphasized at other times during the same service by the pastor.

Bulletin boards or weekly church papers and printed bulletins are used by many churches to acquaint the members with the notices. Twenty-Two of the 609 urban churches studied have weekly or monthly papers.

Announcements in the churches that give them a place in the worship program include financial, social, business, church program, and other notices. The value of this practice has not been thoroughly tested; and not all of the churches equally emphasize it. The announcements usually precede the sermon, although reiterations may follow the sermon. The following from stenographic reports are typical.

(1) Summary of Announcements — The pastor announced a church conference meeting on ____. All the members were urgently requested to be present. He states the purpose of the conference was to discuss financial matters pertaining to the church, and to fill certain vacancies in the church offices.

The pastor also announced that a worthy individual, a member of the church, had been ill for some time but had not desired to request assistance. He, therefore, requested that a contribution be lifted to assist this member. This contribution was taken. Hymn—"Grace Enough for Me."

(2) Verbatim Announcements — It is very warm this morning, so we are going to rush through the announcements.

The ____ Club will please meet in the Gymnasium directly after the close of the services.

The ____ Club will hold their meeting Tuesday evening at 8 p.m. at the home of Mrs. ____.

The ____ Club will hold their weekly meeting, Wednesday evening at 8:30 p.m. They are urging all members to be present as there will be business of importance.

The Junior Church is extending a special invitation to you to be present at their musical to be given this afternoon at 3:00 p.m. We urge the parents to be there to encourage these children.

Miss ____ wishes to meet all those wishing to go to ____ after the services.

Mr. ____ died ____. He was the brother of ____. Funeral dates will be given later.

Will everyone please vacate as soon as possible after services so that the Sunday school will be able to meet.

Further remarks in regard to the announcements by pastor.

This little bunch of sunshine wants to make an announcement: (a little girl made an announcement in connection with the Junior Church Musical).

Announcement by chorister: Friends, do not forget tonight, we have our regular monthly musical and we want you all out. There will be much pleasure in store for you in spite of the weather.

Remarks by pastor:

If you do not get here on time tonight, you will have to stand and standing won't be very comfortable.

You ought not to miss the Junior Church service this afternoon. May I call your attention to the membership cards, they are now in the hands of the Bureau of Information. We will be very glad to have you get them there and leave your contribution.

Next Tuesday night we are expecting a very interesting night. I hear it is to be a double header. The choir will start singing at 7:30 p.m. If you want to hear the beginning, you had better be here on time. Following the meeting we will have the concert by the orchestra under the auspices of the _____ Club.

Next Sunday will be _____. In the morning we will have our regular morning services. In the afternoon we will have memorial services by the citizens. There will be many prominent men here. In the evening the young people will bring their tribute.

The _____ Department is having a fruit sale, and they are selling this fruit almost at cost price.

Since _____ called and said her brother was very sick, and would be very glad to have you visit him at home.

There will be a program here tomorrow given by _____. Admission 10 cents.

Mr. _____ left these fans here yesterday, and with it $1.00 for today's collection. He would like to you to patronize his place of business. There are several helpful hints on these fans, you will read them and at the end of the services you will please leave fans here. At times we all walk off with the fans by mistake, but let's try and remember to leave these here.

Listen friends, I want to tell you this very quietly. On _____ occurs the birthday of _____. It would be very nice if each one would send her a card.

Taking of collection.

Remarks by pastor:

Let each one of us go down in our pockets and get $1.00. This hot weather does not cut down our expenses very much. We want to send another payment on our financial obligations. We are behind in our obligations. While you are getting your contribution ready, Sister _____ has Church _____ which she would like you to relieve her of. You will find in them an account of the _____.

(Ushers take up collection. The choir sings "The Wonder of His Word.")

Prayer after collection by pastor:

> Our Heavenly Father we are thanking Thee for this collection and your many blessings to us in the past, and that in the future they may not be less. Bless those that helped to contribute to this cause. Help them in these times of strife. May we use this contribution in Thy name. Amen.

Remarks by pastor:

> You will recall that I asked you to patronize ____. During that month you are credited with $305.17. You also remember that the church was to receive 5 percent. I am turning over a check for $17.14.

Many people find the worship services lacking in effectiveness because the continuity of the service is broken by long, over-emphasized remarks and announcements. Churches might profit by more intelligent use of printed or posted bulletins.

Invitations to Church Membership

Usually at the close of the sermon, the minister or his assistant "opens the doors of the church" as an invitation to persons wishing to become members; or to those who are not "professed Christians" to accept Christianity and church membership. These invitations vary from brief and simple statements to long statements and the use of music, as the following samples reveal:

> I suppose there are those here who do not know Christ this morning. But my friends even though you have a historical knowledge of him, you need an experimental knowledge of him. If you know him both historically and experimentally but have no specific church home, won't you come this morning? What's the use of living if you can't make life better? You can't make it better unless you know Jesus Christ. If you do not wish to join this particular church, give us the name and address of the one you would like to join and we will send you there. Won't you please come today before it is too late? (Choir sings "Savior Lead Me"—baptism of a member—choir sings "In the Garden.")

I want to open the doors of the church this morning. I want to see if there is a man or woman who feels that his or her ways please God; that he will triumph over anything with which he comes in contact. We will now sing.

Hymn—"Bye and Bye." Two persons joined the church, one being baptized.

The pastor stated the object of his sermon to be "to strengthen the Christian faith." He then requested that as many of the congregation, both members of the church and visitors, who had acquiesced in his stand, to rise. The entire congregation stood up.

Is there anyone who wants to join the church this morning? Come right on now. Let us sing that song "He's the One." Won't somebody come right on now? Come on!

Hymn—"He's the One."

In conclusion, the worship activities may be summarized by pointing out that in the worship of the Sunday church school the interpretation of religion in terms of the experiences of children and youth is no doubt overshadowed by adult ideas and the appeal to adult satisfactions. Whereas in the public worship, although there is an apparent profound sense of the nearness of God, there is probably an under-emphasis upon the practical application of Christianity to life.

The organized teaching and worship activities by no means absorb the entire attention of the churches. They share the program with fellowship and community activities.

The Tradition of Worship

by William D. Watley
from *Singing the Lord's Song in a Strange Land:*
The African American Churches and Ecumenism, published in 1993

The Social Setting of Worship

In his famous "Letter from a Birmingham Jail," Dr. Martin Luther King, Jr., poignantly described the painfully dehumanizing conditions that caused African Americans to reject the philosophy of gradualism with respect to our rights. In words that have become immortal, King wrote:

> Perhaps it is easy for those who have never felt the stinging darts of segregation to say, "Wait." But when you have seen vicious mobs lynch your mothers and fathers at will and drown your sisters and brothers at whim; when you have seen hate-filled policemen curse, kick and even kill your Black brothers and sisters; when you see the vast majority of your twenty million Negro brothers smothering in an airtight cage of poverty in the midst of an affluent society; when you suddenly find your tongue twisted and your speech stammering as you seek to explain to your six-year-old daughter why she can't go to the public amusement park that has just been advertised on television, and see tears welling up in her eyes when she is told that Funtown is closed to Colored children, and see ominous clouds of inferiority beginning to form in her mental sky, and see her beginning to distort her personality by developing an unconscious bitterness toward White people; when you have to concoct an answer for a five-year-old son who is asking: "Daddy, why do White people treat Colored people so mean?"; when you take a cross-country drive and find it necessary to sleep night after night in the uncomfortable corners of your automobile because no motel will accept you; when you are humiliated day in and day out by nagging signs reading

"White" and "Colored"; when your first name becomes "nig-
ger," and your middle name becomes "boy" (however old you
are), and your last name becomes "John," and your wife and
mother are never given the respected title "Mrs."; when you are
harried by day and haunted by night by the fact that you are a
Negro, living constantly at tiptoe stance, never quite knowing
what to expect next, and are plagued with inner fears and outer
resentments; when you are forever fighting a degenerating
sense of "nobodiness"—then you will understand why we find
it difficult to wait.[1]

How has the condition of Black America changed since Dr. King penned
these words? Some would say that much has changed; others would say that
little has changed; while still others would insist that conditions for Blacks in
America have actually worsened.

Certainly there has been progress. Old patterns of legalized racial segregation that denied access to certain facilities of public accommodations no
longer exist. However, legalized patterns of segregation based upon race have
been replaced by denial of access based upon economics. The same people who
were historically excluded because of racism now find themselves shut out
because of the enduring economic repercussions of racial segregation.

Progress, to be sure, has been made. The door to opportunities has been
wedged open and a number of individuals have managed to slip into positions
that were previously closed to them. But such small openings are designed for
individual or token achievement rather than for liberation of the masses.
And more often than not, those who manage to slip through the small
opening encounter the same racism that has kept the masses out altogether.
The only difference is that the racism that has held the masses outside is less
sophisticated than the racism of the corporate boardroom or the ecclesiastical
structure. But whether in the executive dining room or the employees'
cafeteria, whether in the ghetto or the suburbs, whether in high society or in
the streets, racism is just as intentional in blocking minority aspirations. It still
tries to instill the lesson of minority inferiority.

During the period of slavery, there were house slaves and field slaves.
House work was generally not as physically back-breaking as field work.
House slaves sometimes had amenities not afforded field slaves.
(Condescending slave masters often used these amenities or perks in their
arguments to justify the status quo.) Sometimes tensions existed between
house slaves and field slaves as each eyed the other with suspicion. However,

the reality was that whether one was in the house or the field, one was still a slave and still subject to sexual exploitation and physical, emotional, and psychological abuse from one's socially imposed masters and mistresses.

Whether one works in the house or in the fields, a slave is still a slave. The reality of the slave system is that house slaves can become field slaves overnight. Whether the minorities of which a church is made up are middle- or lower-class, whether one is viewed as an exception or as part of the masses, the position is a very vulnerable one.

How much have things changed since Dr. King wrote his "Letter from a Birmingham Jail"? More African Americans are working in the house to be sure, but the vast majority are still "smothering in an airtight cage of poverty in the midst of an affluent society." When drugs are inserted into the cage, with all the problems they bring, the possibilities for spontaneous combustion are immeasurably increased. African Americans are still the last hired and the first fired.

African American children still receive demeaning messages about their self-worth from a culturally biased media. In many subtle ways African American children receive the message that Black means inferior or not as good, Black means working harder to get what others take for granted, Black means encountering certain doors closed in one's face for the simple reason that one's face is Black. African American parents still find themselves fumbling for words as they try to explain to their children the racial facts of life. Black parents must still explain to their children that despite the assaults on their personhood that they receive every day, they are just as good as anyone else.

How much have things changed since the days of Martin Luther King, Jr.? Racism is as bold and as brash, as brutal and as brazen, as cruel and as cunning, as vile and as violent as it was before the great period of Black social unrest in the 1960s. Recent political developments in the West have brought overt racism back in vogue and made race-baiting and stereotyping popular again. Visible change has taken place to be sure. But the visible change is minuscule when the plight of the masses of African Americans are taken into consideration.

Thus, African Americans who gather within the shelter of the Black church on Sunday mornings are still far from being free—but the fact that they come to church also means that they are not yet defeated. The average Black worshipper is still a person who has "kept on keeping on" in spite of the forces that have tried to stop him or her from going forward. Some of those who gather to worship are angry and continually struggle not to give in to bitterness. Some are despondent victims struggling to become victors. All come from their various states of oppression with one central question: "Is there any word from the Lord?" (Jeremiah 37:17). Is there a word that will make sense out of a senseless situation and provide a rationale for continuing to believe in the possibilities of bright tomorrows?

How does the African American Church minister to such a constituency within the worship context? What is the function, purpose, and intent of the songs, the sermons and shouts of Black worship? What is the meaning behind the music, the messages, and the moods of traditional African American worship? I would identify at least three functions of Black worship—praise, pastoring, and prophecy.

Praise and African American Worship

Praise should be inherent in worship. The faith perspective makes praise possible irrespective of immediate circumstances. Even a casual review of the history of hymnody reveals that many hymns were born out of trials and circumstances that would seem to give a person little reason to sing. Faith, however, insists that even in midnight sorrow one can offer praise in anticipation of the joy that is coming in the morning. African American worship is inherently praise-oriented because of its theology of thanksgiving honed on the peripheral jagged edges of life. I have often heard people pray: "Lord, we know that everything in life is not as we desire, but we're just grateful that things are as well with us as they are." Black people have learned to be thankful that things are "as well with us as they are."

People who have a memory of times when things were much worse can be grateful for the small rays of sunlight that are visible and be grateful that things are as well as they are. People who have enough social sensitivity and political acumen to know that things could be much worse, are grateful that things are as well as they are. Does such a sense of gratitude stifle social unrest or cause one to look at life through rose-colored glasses? Not necessarily, because there is the consciousness that "everything in life is not as we desire." However, thanksgiving does provide a balance to the self-defeating despair that refuses to see any star in a midnight sky or measure any gains that have been made. While recognizing that one has a long way to go, one also gives thanks for the "mighty long way" that has been traversed thus far. African American worship is praise-oriented because it is grounded in thanksgiving.

The lyrics of an old familiar spiritual of the African American experience are:

> Just one mo' time,
> Just one mo' time,
> I'm glad to be in the number
> One mo' time.

Another indigenous praise song says:

> Another day's journey and I'm so glad,
> Another day's journey and I'm so glad,
> Another day's journey and I'm so glad,
> That the world can't do me no harm.

African American worship is praise-oriented because it is celebratory of the reality that one has survived another week or even another day of stress and strain, racism and abuse, of living on the edge of life where one is always a step away from death. One never knows what one will face from Sunday to Sunday in the precarious life of urban Black America. Life in the ghettoes is so fraught with dangers "seen and unseen," and the struggle to survive from day to day and week to week is so intense, that to be able simply to get to church, to "be in the number," is cause enough for celebration.

In communities in which "drive-by" drug-related shootings of innocent bystanders are all too common; in communities that are denied justice more often than they receive it; in communities that are perceived by the majority culture as dumping grounds for the dregs of humanity rather than the seedbeds of great potential, one never knows the battles that will be waged from day to day and Sunday to Sunday. Consequently, to be able to come to church, to have the opportunity of setting foot "one mo' time" on holy ground, to make "another day's journey," in which the forces of evil have not been able to defeat one, are reasons in and of themselves for celebration and praise.

African Americans celebrate in worship also because we are "more than conquerors" (Rom. 8:37). Faith has not only given balance but has helped to forge strong, vibrant, well-adjusted, and normal personalities in spite of the craziness that surrounds us. African Americans celebrate in worship because faith has provided a firm foundation upon which to walk in spite of the shifting sands beneath. African Americans assemble in worship to celebrate survival, to praise God for eternal goodness that continually flows into our lives to counteract the evil influences that assault us and help us to emerge as sane and strong individuals. African Americans gather in worship to praise God that things are as well as they are.

The Pastoral Mission of African American Worship

The pastoral dimension of African American worship fulfills the vital functions of comfort and empowerment. Those who have been engaged in daily struggles for survival and battles for dignity and self-worth need at times to be comforted. When individuals and communities encounter setbacks and defeat, discouraging moments and bewildering experiences, a word of comfort is needed. When a mother or father or set of parents are worried sick that the pull of the streets on their child is greater than the power of prayer, a word of comfort is needed. When individuals and families see loved ones lose their lives in senseless killings because of the self-consuming violence of the ghetto, which is built, supported, and maintained by White racism as a no-exit cage, a word of comfort is needed. When beloved and respected leaders are eliminated, corrupted, or co-opted by the system, a word of comfort is needed. When infant deaths and high morbidity rates are not just statistics but the painful personal realities of everyday life, a word of comfort is needed. When the pressure of cramped living conditions produces domestic violence and the abuse of those closest at hand, leaving unseen psychological and emotional scars, a word of comfort is needed. When feelings of powerlessness become overwhelming as questions far exceed answers, a word of comfort is needed.

The African American Church understands the pastoral responsibility of worship and its ministry of comfort. It knows how to speak comfortingly and minister tenderly to the aching hearts, bruised spirits, and perplexed minds of those who wrestle daily with the anomalies of racism. Comfort comes from songs born of struggle that tell of a better day and a brighter tomorrow. Comfort comes from the testimonies, stories, and autobiographical accounts of those who "have come over a way that with tears has been watered," and are still holding on, fighting on, and going on. Comfort comes from a prayer tradition that reminds worshippers that the promises, presence, and power of God are available to all who labor to live and love in this "lowland of sorrow." Comfort comes from the messages of preachers who know how to speak to the hurts of their people. Comfort comes from repeated assurances that Jesus has promised "Blessed are those who mourn, for they will be comforted" (Matthew 5:4) and "I am with you always, to the end of the age" (Matthew 28:20).

It has been said that the purpose of worship is to help people get over whatever they have been through and to help get them ready for whatever is ahead. Worship that *only* comforts may function as an opiate providing a temporary emotional or mental escape or momentary utopian high. Worship that empowers as it comforts prepares the participant to continue grappling with real day-to-day issues and conflicts. Worship that empowers as it comforts has heaven as its source of power and inspiration and the earth as the area of application and interpretation. African American worship not only comforts in the context of past and present hurts, it also empowers for the continuing quest for meaning, self-worth, and dignity.

The very context of African American worship is empowering. When one has to function in a world whose determinative standards are White or Eurocentric, a Black or Afrocentric cultural context is empowering in and of itself. Even when one lives in the Black American environment, one is always aware of the influence of "The Man" who pulls the strings behind the scenes and whose tentacles reach deep into the Black community. Corporations and major business interests are run by "The Man." Government officials or bureaucrats whose faces are Black must often have the economic support of White business interests or the blessings of White political bosses—in other words, "The Man"—in order to exercise the semblance of power that they have. Organized crime, which pumps drugs into the African American community, is engineered and controlled from the outside by "The Man."

Thus, to be in a Black worship setting, which is free of "The Man's" domination and infiltration, is an immensely empowering experience. In the African American worship context, Blacks can relax and breathe freely in an environment governed by what the minority determines to be appropriate cultural norms. White hymns are sung not as they are written, but according to a Black sense of timing, syncopation, and rhythm. Hymns that have their origins in the Anglo evangelical and reformed traditions may convey different meanings to Black worshippers, even as African American slaves heard a different message from that which pro-slavery White preachers delivered. An oppressed minority community often reads and hears things differently from their counterparts in the oppressing majority. When an African American sings "I once was lost but now I'm found," the theme of existential lostness and aloneness may be much broader than and different from what the slaveholder John Newton meant when he wrote the words of the great hymn "Amazing Grace." Thus, the very sight of a Black preacher delivering the gospel with freedom in sonorous and soulful tones, or of a Black choir singing with freedom in the Black idiom, or of Black church officials freely leading worship as they are "led by the Spirit," in appropriate attire and uniforms, is in and of itself an empowering moment.

But not only is the context of traditional African American worship empowering; the experience of worship itself empowers. Black worship is a two-edged sword. The same songs, prayers, testimonies, and sermons that comfort also strengthen and encourage the participant to "keep on keeping on." African American worship is empowering in that it looks beyond the present moment and tries to prepare the worshipper for whatever is ahead. Consequently, acts of praise are not only expressions of thanksgiving but responses to the inspiration and encouragement one has received for the journey ahead. Blacks celebrate in worship not only because we are comforted but also because we are empowered, encouraged, and strengthened to continue fighting the good fight of faith—the fight of liberation, the fight of self-affirmation, the fight of endurance—until the victory that is proclaimed and conceived becomes a reality.

African Americans in worship understand that celebration empowers. Sorrow is draining, but praise is empowering. Through worship that speaks the language of faith in a truly indigenous cultural context, strength comes to face difficult domestic situations, the terror of mean streets, and oppressive employment settings. Through worship African Americans are not only empowered to face our tomorrows, but to keep trying to change the face of our tomorrows.

Prophetic Resistance and African American Worship

Intuitively, African Americans, like many other oppressed peoples, have looked at worship through bifocal lenses. Blacks have simultaneously focused upon the personal needs of the individual worshipper and the cultural, political, economic, and social milieus which determine the character of African American life. Worship cannot meet the needs of the individual worshipper without being cognizant of the environment in which he or she must function, which has determined his or her particular needs. Worship at its best is a bridge between the individual and the environment with the word of God speaking to both.

Sin is not only individual but aggregate. Evil is not only personal but systemic. People bring the needs that they do to worship not only because they are fallen creatures who stand in need of redeeming grace, but also because of the environment in which they live. If that environment is conceived in sin and shaped in iniquity, as is any system of racism, covert or overt, then the word of God must speak to it as well. The gospel must address not only issues of individual morality but also of social justice.

African American worship not only has a tradition of praise and pastoral comfort, but also of prophetic protest. Black music, preaching, and prayer have focused on damning social evils as well as damning individual sins. It is no accident that the freedom songs of the Civil Rights movement of the 1960s came out of the Black Church. The spirituals which were the indigenous religious music of the slaves had a political and social meaning and application as well as a religious dimension for a number of those who sang them.

The great nineteenth century African American abolitionist Frederick Douglass once wrote that when he sang the words

> O Canaan, sweet Canaan
> I am bound for the land of Canaan,

he was referring to the North. The region north of the Mason-Dixon line (the demarcation between southern slave-holding and northern free states) was Canaan in the mind of Frederick Douglass and many other slaves. Douglass also pointed to the "double meaning" in a song with the words:

> "I don't expect to stay much longer here"—probably a variant
> of "Steal Away." On the lips of some it meant the expectation
> of a speedy summons to a world of spirits, but on the lips of
> our company...it simply meant a speedy pilgrimage to a free
> state, and deliverance from all the evils and dangers of slavery.[2]

During the 1960s, a traditional Black church song such as:

> If you miss me from singing down here,
> and you can't find me nowhere,
> come on up to bright glory,
> I'll be singing up there....

could be changed to a freedom song using the same tune, but the words:

> If you miss me from the back of the bus,
> and you can't find me nowhere,
> come on up to the front of the bus,
> I'll be riding up there....

> If you miss me from the cotton field,
> and you can't find me nowhere,
> come on down to the courthouse,
> I'll be voting right there....

> If you miss me from the picket line,
> and you can't find me nowhere,
> come on down to the county jail,
> I'll be staying right there....

The words of the song:

> I woke up this morning with my mind stayed on Jesus...
> Hallelu, Hallelu, Hallelujah....

were changed to:

> I woke up this morning with my mind stayed on freedom...
> Hallelu, Hallelu, Hallelujah....

When African Americans sing "We shall overcome," we are talking about overcoming more than personal problems or bad habits. We are talking about overcoming decayed housing with exorbitant rents, rat-infested ghettoes, separate and unequal systems of education, those who would try to keep us down, self-defeating attitudes and behavior that would hold us back, the whole plethora of institutional supports of an inherently racist system.

It is no accident that a high percentage of African American leaders have been clergy. The African American preacher was once described by DuBois as

> ...the most unique personality developed by the Negro on American soil. A leader, a politician, an orator, a "boss," an intriguer, an idealist—all these he is, and ever, too, the center of a group of men, now twenty, now a thousand in number. The combination of a certain adroitness with deep-seated earnestness, of tact with consummate ability, gave him his pre-eminence, and helps him maintain it.[3]

Historically, the Black preacher has had to serve in the dual capacity of prophet and priest. Not only has he attempted to give direction to the Black community and acted as its spokesman to the White power structure, but as priest he has carried on the worship tradition of African American religion and has been the guiding force in the liturgical life of Black religious expression. He has been the chief figure in the basic activity of the Black religious experience, the worship experience.

The Black preacher has first and foremost been a preacher. The prophetic role grew out of the basic priestly office as the Black community started looking to the preacher for leadership in more and more areas other than worship life. The combination of roles of prophet and priest was inevitable if one considers how the Black religious experience developed as a source of both solace and agitation. In other words, the dual function of the Black preacher was necessary when the religious experience of which he was a significant part had the dual nature and role of relief and protest.

Like latter-day Samuels, Elijahs, Nathans, Amoses, and Jeremiahs, African American preachers such as Martin Luther King, Jr., Benjamin Hooks, Jesse Jackson, Andrew Young, Congressman Bill Gray, Congressman Walter Fauntroy, Congressman Floyd Flake, and innumerable others have been part of a long and continuing line of African American preachers whose ministries encompass political as well as ecclesiastical involvements and whose messages address issues of social justice as well as personal morality.

The Theological Foundations of African American Worship[4]

While African American worship is multi-dimensional, we have lifted up only three of its elements—praise, pastoral comfort, and prophetic resistance. It is also important to realize that African American worship rests on a sound theological foundation.

Within the U.S. ecumenical scene, Black Americans are known for the dynamism of their worship and their sensitivity to justice concerns, particularly racism. Long before we were taken seriously enough (or sufficient White guilt had been aroused) to be invited to the conference table to share our concerns for the ecumenical agenda, already on the plantations of the antebellum South, White people loved to hear Blacks sing—though they had no idea what was really being said in song or meant in "moan."

Even now Whites love to hear Black gospel music and respond to its rhythm without hearing its message. I have seen Whites snap their fingers and dance a jig to Black gospel song, as if it were another kind of popular secular music. They fail to understand that this musical genre is as sacred as any anthem and is designed not for entertainment but for praise.

Although Black preachers during slavery were admired for their charismatic gifts, they were also caricatured for their preaching style, known as "whooping." They were laughed at for their homespun theology and broken English, and feared because of their leadership and influence on Black people. Many Black preachers were not formally trained, and the worship they led seemed to be marked by a preponderance of heat and a dearth of light. The implicit conclusion of outside observers of Black worship was that any group who worshipped in such an emotionally charged fashion and chose such "witch doctors" to lead them could not be intellectually astute.

How then could anything be expected from them in terms of theology? Black worship was fascinating, if at times somewhat eerie to observe. Black music was enjoyable. The concept of Black sermonizing was surely interesting and different. But was there, is there, any intellectual substance to the Black worship tradition?

Two points may be made briefly in response. First, let the observer or phenomenologist beware: what you see is not necessarily what you are getting. Second, worship at its core is an intellectual enterprise because it rests on certain theological foundations.

The emotional outbursts that characterize part of the Black worship tradition have led some to the facile conclusion that Black people have little or no sense of liturgy and do not honor the admonition to do things decently and in order. What one sees, however, is not necessarily what one gets. From the beginning, Black worship has been apocalyptic. Its meaning has been veiled to those outside the community. Already on the plantations, Whites sent to observe the slaves' worship services to ensure that no seditious activity occurred received one message while the worshippers received another.

African American worship has been mysterious since its inception. "Mystery" here does not refer to some nefarious world of spooks, hobgoblins, and superstition; it is used as it was in the New Testament era, when meaning existed behind the apparently strange actions of the mystery cults but one had to be initiated into the community to perceive it. One can easily miss the nuances of a community's language and culture if one has not lived in that community. The conclusions of outsiders notwithstanding, Black worship *is* liturgical and has its own propriety.

Without apology, traditional Black worship appeals to the emotion as well as the intellect. Some people view emotional expression as a kind of opiate— a passive response to the condition of oppression. What they call emotional compensation, however, others recognize as celebration and affirmation. Black people rejoice in worship because we have not hung our harps upon the willows, even in a strange land; we have sung for those who required songs of us. They were amused by what we sang, but we were strengthened. We knew what our songs meant, and their meaning was not what our captors thought they were hearing.

We continue to sing. Our preachers continue to proclaim God's word in apocalyptic language. And thus we affirm ourselves, celebrate life and, in the midst of nightmarish realities, find comfort for broken hearts and receive political, social, and personal strength for the days and struggles ahead. When like Job we had enough reasons to curse God and die, we glorified God. We weep when we remember our Zions on the shores of Africa, but we also rejoice because we know that "trouble don't last always." This affirmation is not theological pie-in-the-sky but eschatological realism.

A God Who Brings Down Walls

Eschatology depends on certain assumptions about the nature of God and the meaning of the cosmos. The unique character of Black worship resides in its theological underpinnings. When a community or a people clearly understands God's identity, omnipotence and love for them, then despite their exile in Babylon they are empowered to fight the temptation to hang their harps upon the willows. Eschatology rests on the premise that the God who raised Jesus from the dead is able to order the events of life and history in accordance with heaven's will.

Black people, in other words, are theists for whom God is infinite. The God we believe in is a God who is not only good and just but all-powerful. Our God can make a way out of the wilderness, bring down the walls of Jericho, and lock the jaws of hungry lions. Despite the tenuousness of Black life, our worship affirms that life does have purpose because it is held by God who is able to bring victory out of defeat, even as Easter rose from Good Friday's tragedy. Our worship is not grounded in a condition of oppression but in God, who gives strength to endure oppression and the rationale for struggling against it.

If God is just, as Black people affirm, then God's children are commanded to struggle against injustice and are empowered by the Holy Spirit to do so. Black worship is not a self-forgetting, self-deluding experience but an empowering one. When worship is open to self-expression that leads to enablement and ennoblement, liturgy has truly become the work of the people.

The powerful tradition of worship in the Black community cannot be traced to some alleged innate predisposition to song, dance, and rhythm. Nor can it be explained by the great revivals and awakenings that brought scores of

293

Blacks into the fold, nor by a cultural heritage of praise that reaches back to Africa's shores. Black worship is rooted essentially in a message, a belief system, a theology that serves as the basis of worship.

Black worship is exciting because it has an exciting message. It tells Black people that, in spite of the shifting winds of politics and economics, "Your God reigns" (Isaiah 52:7). It tells Black people that we have a savior: "For a child has been born for us, a son given to us; authority rests upon his shoulders; and he is named Wonderful Counsellor, Mighty God, Everlasting Father, Prince of Peace. His authority shall grow continually, and there shall be endless peace....The zeal of the Lord of hosts will do this" (Isaiah 9:6–7).

The message of Black worship tells us that we are empowered by God's Spirit, for "those who wait for the Lord shall renew their strength, they shall mount up with wings like eagles, they shall run and not be weary, they shall walk and not faint" (Isaiah 40:31). When this kerygma is combined with a liturgical tradition of self-expression, then Pentecost occurs within the Black worship context.

Much Did We Know Before

The worship tradition in the Black community has emerged as we have wrestled with such heart-searching questions as "How shall we sing the Lord's song in a foreign land?" Before the rise of Barthian theology, we were applying the word of God to our existential situation. Before Paul Tillich, we understood God as the ground of our being and saw the necessity of the union of love, power, and justice for the kingdoms of this world to become the kingdoms of God and Christ.

Before Dietrich Bonhoeffer wrestled with the violent option in resisting Nazi oppression, the slave preacher Nat Turner in South Hampton, Virginia, faced the same dilemma. We knew about the schizophrenia produced by racism in the individual and corporate psyches of oppressors. Thus we understood the thesis of moral human beings and immoral societies before Reinhold Niebuhr.

Before we heard about Edgar Sheffield Brightman, we were praying to a God who in our belief regarded personality as sacrosanct; otherwise that God would not have answered so many of our prayers. Before Pierre Teilhard de Chardin, we understood God as point Omega, because that was the only point that could pull together the cruel disparities of our history. Certainly we appreciate the insights of Jürgen Moltmann, but we didn't need him to tell us about hope. After all, it is hope that prompts us to keep singing the Lord's song in a strange land.

"How shall we sing the Lord's song in a foreign land?" Only a people who have a strong theological foundation can do that.

---

1 *Why We Can't Wait,* p. 81f.

2 Quoted by Vincent Harding, in "Religion and Resistance Among Antebellum Negroes, 1800–1860," in *The Making of Black America,* ed. by August Meier and Elliot Ridwick (New York, 1969) I, p. 196.

3 DuBois, *The Souls of Black Folk,* p. 211.

4 This section is adapted from an essay first published in the *Journal of the Liturgical Conference*, VIII, no. 1, pp. 59–63. Used by permission.

Some Aspects of Black Worship

by Charles G. Adams
from *The Andover Newton Journal*
Vol. LXIII, No. 3, published in 1971

We shall not be able to avoid referring to the Black Church as an institution, even if such a concept might prove to be elusive at best and nebulous at worst. The term "Black religion" is preferable because rather than pointing to an institution, it indicates an experience. The institutional Black Church is difficult to capture, but the Black religious experience as expressed in the way that Black people worship is undeniably real. It is this experience that shall engage the attention of this article. But to substitute some other term for "Black Church" in every instance would be pedantic and awkward.

I have found no infinite qualitative distinction between the Black and White religious experience. They are not separated by sharp lines but by overlapping zones. The aspects of Black worship which shall herewith be enumerated are not absolutely unique. They simply appear in Black religion with greater frequencies and, therefore, typify Black worship. These aspects were not altogether absent from the White experience; however, they are atypical rather than frequent. The distinctions between Black and White religion will turn out to be matters of shades and colors. Thus, if shouting or ecstatic emotionalism enjoys a certain at-homeness in the Black experience, it is also to be found in certain spiritualistic forms of White religion. This does not contradict the conclusion that the phenomenon of shouting is predominantly an element characterizing Black religion rather than typifying White religion. Also this does not deny the fact that there are some Black churches where shouting is neither welcomed nor allowed. It has ever been thus.

There has always been in America a small sector of the Black population that managed somehow to identify itself completely with White society in repudiation of those aspects which typify the Black experience. Franklin

Frazier relates this perdurable Black sector in which the typical Black experience is unfamiliar to the free Negroes during slavery, many of them mulattos as well as unmixed Blacks, who attained an almost complete assimilation to White or European culture. These differences of cultural assimilation between the unassimilated slave and the well-assimilated free Black during slavery were reflected in the differing characters of religious worship in the two sectors.[1] Take the Black spiritual, for example. Miles Mark Fisher writes about Alexander Payne, a Bishop in the African Methodist Episcopal Church, "Alexander Payne during his ministry about 1846, might be said to have represented the type of educated Negro who opposes the singing of spirituals. Bishop Payne commonly wrote of them as 'rings,' songs of 'fist and heel worshipers,' 'cornfield ditties,' and 'voodoo dances.' He said: 'The time is at hand when the ministry of the A.M.E. Church must drive out this heathenish mode of worship or drive out all the intelligence, refinement, and practical Christians.'[2] Already in 1845 certain Blacks had identified intelligence and refinement with European culture and thereby became aliens to the peculiarity of Black experience. If Bishop Payne repudiated the singing of spirituals as reflecting ignorance and backwardness, what would be his estimation of the phenomenon of shouting or the moaning of the preacher? Surely he would be likely to disdain and discourage any conspicuous display of ecstasy or loud demonstrations or religious emotionalism.

Bishop Payne's type of cool and collected religious expression has endured to modern times within certain areas of Black experience. If the color red can be used to represent shouting, a symbolic diagram of Black religion would feature crimson in its largest sector, turning to pink on the periphery with small blotches of white here and there. The largest sector of the diagram of White religion would be White in main-center ebbing into an off-white and turning into pale pink around the edges with a spasmodic paucity of red dots here and there. The diagrams illustrate the fact that there are some few Black churches which are indistinguishable from White churches except for the skin color of the worshippers, and there are some White churches which feign the salient aspects of the Black religious experience. They will not be discussed in detail. Rather, we shall point up what might be recognized as the predominating elements of Black religion which distinguish it from White religion.

The Music of Black Worship

In discussing this first and succeeding element or aspect of Black worship, I shall draw heavily upon my experience in the Black independent Baptist church, which was first to emerge in the burgeoning independent Black Church movement of the late eighteenth century. Well over one-half of the Black churchgoing population is contained in various Baptist denominations. Also, the Black Baptist Church is the "feeder Church" or historic source for the other Black denominations with the exception perhaps of the Black Methodists who freed themselves from the White Methodists in the early nineteenth century. What goes in the Black Baptist Church is not unfamiliar to any worshipping person or group in the Black community.

Music is the term which, I believe, gathers up what's happening in Black worship more completely than any other single concept. The Black worship experience is poetic and musical throughout. Everything that occurs within Black worship either is or becomes poetry and music. Whether it be plain talking, praying, or proclaiming the Gospel, it eventually turns into singing. This, to me, is the most distinctive creative aspect of Black worship—its persistent musical character.

Music in Black worship is splendidly various as it runs the gamut from classical hymns and anthems to the sophisticated arranged spirituals to the raw, unadulterated spirituals, to the Black metered hymn to the jazzy, improvised gospels. All of these types of music are known, rendered, and appreciated in Black churches. There is no other church where such a wide variety of music is integrated, rendered, and sustained within a unified experience of worship. The Black churches which I know do not force the worshipper to choose between J. S. Bach and James Cleveland (a famous current Black Gospel writer and performer). The Black worshipper is free to move easily between all types of music produced out of the free Protestant spirit of religious expressions.

The anthem has a place in the worship service of most independent Black Methodist and Baptist congregations. The mastery of the anthem represents to the Black choir the same kind of achievement as the rendering of German Lieder represents to Roland Hayes and Marian Anderson. It is a sign of being progressive, liberated, and educated to be able to sing anthems, indicating a high level of technical musical attainment. The Christmas oratorio and the Easter cantata are annual events which along with the weekly rendering of a sacred anthem represent emancipation, education, and the freedom to understand and reflect the highest in White European and American musical

299

culture. The worshippers who listen tolerantly to the anthems take just as much pride in being able to listen to them as do the singers in being able to perform them. Their presence in the worship service is an indication of a liberated congregation that has "arrived." Sometimes the communal contemplation of a familiar biblical text of an anthem plus the pride and joy at having "arrived" intensifies into shouting on the anthem in certain churches known to be spiritually and emotionally uninhibited. Cornerstone Baptist Church in Brooklyn is known to shout aloud and demonstrate boisterously at the conclusion of a rousing anthem whose text is Psalm 150. I have heard the Concord Baptist Church in Boston and Concord Baptist Church of Brooklyn shout at the conclusion of Handel's "Hallelujah Chorus."

The standard Protestant hymn also finds its place in the Black worship experience. These hymns are not unfamiliar to White Protestants:

> Holy, Holy, Holy, Lord God Almighty
> The Church's One Foundation
> Faith of Our Fathers
> Rejoice, Ye Pure in Heart
> Glorious Things of Thee Are Spoken
> A Mighty Fortress Is Our God
> Lead On, O King Eternal
> Once to Every Man and Nation
> Love Divine All Loves Excelling
> O God, Our Help in Ages Past
> O Worship the King
> All Hail the Power of Jesus' Name
> Where Cross the Crowded Ways of Life
> O Love That Wilt Not Let Me Go
> Joyful, Joyful, We Adore Thee
> I Love Thy Kingdom, Lord
> In Christ There Is No East or West
> Christ the Lord Is Risen Today
> Beneath the Cross of Jesus
> Jesus, I My Cross Have Taken
> Be Thou My Vision

These hymns are usually sung by the choirs and congregation as they are written with very few or no embellishments. They do not lend themselves to improvisation, and they are not readily mutated beyond recognition. When they occur within the worship service with limited and controlled frequency, they represent the versatility of the Black worshipper in his ability to move freely between two worlds; but when they are sung almost exclusively with little of any other type of congregational song, they represent the fact that the given Black congregation has lost its flexibility in an overly anxious attempt to identify wholly with White culture as a sign of emancipation. Friendship Baptist Church of Atlanta and Tabernacle Baptist Church of Detroit represent this tendency as they seem to get stuck on the standard White Protestant hymn to the exclusion of other types of congregational music.

The next step in the counterpoint of the Black worship experience is the White revivalistic hymn learned from the White evangelical missionaries. These hymns are typified by the following samples:

A New Name in Glory
Are You Washed in the Blood
Yield Not to Temptation
God Will Take Care of You
Blessed Assurance
Blessed Quietness
Down at the Cross Where My Savior Died
Dwelling in Beulah Land
Faith Is the Victory
God Be With You
He Lives
He Lifted Me
Higher Ground
In the Garden
I Must Tell Jesus
Jesus Is All the World to Me
Love Lifted Me
Lead Me to Calvary
One Day
My Hope Is Built on Nothing Less
Nothing But the Blood of Jesus
Pass Me Not Oh Gentle Savior
The Old Rugged Cross
Saved!
Since Jesus Came into My Heart

When We All Get to Heaven
The Name of Jesus
'Tis So Sweet to Trust in Jesus
We're Marching to Zion
What a Friend

These songs are much more simply structured than the standard Protestant hymns. They are freer musically and are more emotional and personalistic theologically. They lend themselves easily to many improvisations and mutations. Placed in the spirited context of an enthusiastic Black congregation, they may be sung with syncopated or "stop time" rhythms and may be rendered at a much slower or faster pace than the composer intended depending upon the mood of the congregation. They are not always recognizable after undergoing improvisation.

The Black worshipper moves now from the White evangelical or revivalistic hymn to the Black hymn composed by trained Black clergymen and laymen. These hymns have not been published in White hymnbooks and are, therefore, unfamiliar to Whites. They are often unknown and disregarded. I have seen no written study of these and of their value to Protestant religion, but to the Black worshipper they represent a rich musical and theological heritage. I refer to such hymns as are published among other types in the *Baptist Standard Hymnal* (published in 1924 by the Sunday School Publishing Board of the National Baptist Convention, U.S.A.), *The Gospel Pearls* (published in 1921 by the same publisher), and *The African Methodist Episcopal Hymnal* (revised and published by the A.M.E. Sunday School Union in 1954). These Black hymns are:

Some Day
We'll Understand It Better By and By
Take Your Burden to the Lord and Leave It There
Hold to God's Unchanging Hand
I Will Trust in the Lord
I Feel Like Going On
I'll Live On
My Loved Ones Are Waiting for Me
Stand by Me
Precious Lord Take My Hand
Lift Him Up
Is Thy Heart Right with God

Never Alone
What Are They Doing in Heaven Today
Think of His Goodness to You
Nothing Between
I'm Going Through, Jesus
Life Is Like a Mountain Railroad

Black hymnology seemed to flourish in the late nineteenth and early twentieth centuries when the above were written. But in the mid-1940s, Dr. Gordon B. Hancock, late Professor at Virginia Union University and Pastor of Moore Street Baptist Church, Richmond, Virginia, wrote a common meter prayer hymn called "Contrition," the text of which I shall quote simply because it does not appear in any published anthology of hymns:

Contrition
O Lord, in Love, Thine ear bow down;
O hear thy people pray;
O may that love that knows no bound,
Upon us be today.

O Lord, that humble, contrite heart
In rev'rence deep we bring;
Hear Thou the prayer our hearts would pray,
The songs our hearts would sing.

O Lord, in love, our hearts incline
To rest upon Thy Word;
O Hear, O bless, O save we pray;
Have mercy on us Lord.

This prayer hymn is used in Black churches across the country. Its simple, plaintive, mournful melody pulls on the heart strings, moistens the eyes, and sets the mood for fervent prayer.

The Church gets higher spiritually as one moves from the Black hymn to the Black spiritual, which represents the bedrock of all Black music. Miles Mark Fisher acknowledges that Black spirituals have furnished the initial tune vocabulary for all kinds of Black songs.[3] Dr. Hancock, mentioned above, related in a private interview that the Black spiritual is distinguished by its fertility in that so much fine music has sprung from it. It is the "mother music" of all the other forms of Black musical creativity. These songs have the following salient characteristics:

303

1. They originated within the experience of slavery. They are, thus, "slave songs" and represent music conceived in pain, born of suffering, and characterized by pathos.

2. They have biblical and/or theological content. Like the Black sermon, they are built around biblical themes of:

   Creation
   Deliverance
   Miracles like Jacob wrestling with the angel or Joshua
     at the Battle of Jericho
   The Calling of the Prophets
   The Birth of Christ
   Baptism
   Communion
   The Experience of Salvation
   The Coming of Christ
   Life in the Upper Bright World

   Later some of these original spirituals were mutated into work songs and other secular types, but this does not contradict the contention that they were originally spirituals and, thus, religious in character, message, tune, and rhythm.

3. They are anonymous and represent the productivity of the group rather than the musical genius of an individual. This is, however, not an absolute distinction as the groups had to be inspired by a charismatic individual and that individual had to be emotionally and artistically influenced by the group. They are, thus, the spontaneous, outburst expression of the group and also the work of individual talented composers. The production of spirituals represents a symbiosis of the talented individual leader and the sensitive group.[4] An example of how the leader and the group cooperated in the singing and probably the production of the slave songs is illustrated below:

   Leader: Swing, low, sweet chariot,
   Group: Coming for to carry me home.
   Leader: Swing, low, sweet chariot,
   Group: Coming for to carry me home.
   Leader: I looked over Jordan, what did I see
   Group: Coming for to carry me home.

Leader: A band of angels coming after me.

Group: Coming for to carry me home.

Most students of the slave songs maintain that they are indeed anonymous. A notable exception to this theory is Miles Mark Fisher's contention that the internal "evidence" of the spiritual can be correlated with the external evidence of history in such a way as to specify the composer, place, time, and situation of the spirituals. For example, Fisher "demonstrates" that "Steal Away" was most assuredly written by Nat Turner in 1825 at Southhampton County, Virginia, on the occasion of his call to be a prophet.[5] I submit that this is a reconstruction based on pure conjecture. So far as we are able to prove, the spirituals must remain anonymous with no conclusive evidence identifying the composers, dates, places, or circumstances.

4. The spirituals are simplistic. The austere simplicity of the spirituals accounts for their astounding beauty. Musically, they represent the most amazing economy of tonal intervals. The intervals between notes are very short and the variety of tones is indeed scarce. Thus, the spirituals are easy to learn, remember, and transmit. This accounts for the fact that while most of them are yet unpublished, they still exist in the historical memory of the Black community and are being handed down to the present generation by octogenarians who learned them in their childhood. Below are listed some published and familiar spirituals:

Deep River
Go Down Moses
Joshua Fit the Battle of Jericho
We Are Climbing Jacob's Ladder
Swing Low
There's No Hiding Place Down Here
It's Me, O Lord
Roll, Jordan, Roll
Steal Away to Jesus
Every Time I Feel the Spirit
Were You There?
O, Freedom
O, What a Beautiful City
Down by the Riverside
Wade in the Water

Let Us Break Bread Together
Nobody Knows the Trouble I See
My Lord, What a Morning
Sit Down, Servant

Listed below are some unfamiliar and/or unpublished spirituals:

Let Jesus Lead You
Heaven Belongs to You
Pray, Somebody Pray
The Blood's Done Sign My Name
Lord, I Can't Stay Away
Press on, I'll Meet You There
See How They Done My Lord
Got to Go to Judgment
Ah, Lord
Crown Him Lord of All
When My Heart Is Burdened Down
Gonna Tell It
Mighty Rocky Road
Way in the Kingdom
In a Time Like This
One of These Days
Christ the Lord's Done Set Me Free
Away in Bethlehem
The Good Old Ship of Zion
Life's Day Closing
When My Heart Is Burdened Down
I'm Going to Stay on the Battlefield
Land on the Shore
Gonna Do All I Can for My Lord
Until My Changes Come

The Church gets still higher as the worshipper climbs from the Black spiritual to highly animated, rhythmically syncopated gospels which are modern jazz improvisations of spirituals and hymns. These songs represent religious adaptations of hard rock jazz. Gospels are characterized by the following features:

1. Folk vocal style rather than concert style;
2. Call-and-response patterns;
3. Polyrhythms or simultaneous rhythms;
4. Hard and pronounced syncopation;
5. Ostinato figures (repeated musical patterns);
6. Percussion, hand clapping, shouting, and stamping; and
7. Liberal improvisation and variation.

Gospel music has been popularized, secularized, and commercialized by such artists as Clara Ward, James Cleveland, Mahalia Jackson, Rosetta Thorpe, and Harold Smith. They have won wide acceptance and acclaim in the White world, and this has accelerated their value in the Black Church which gave them birth.

This brings us to a discussion of an unfortunate conflict now going on in the Black community between traditional music and the hard rock gospel jazz. There was a time when gospels were not allowed in sophisticated Black churches or on Black college campuses. If spirituals were sung in either the pretentious church or on the dignified campus, they were so designed and arranged as to have assumed classical European musical form. But as gospels became secularized and commercialized, they acquired status and acceptance in the White world and found their way into "silk stocking" Black churches and college campuses. Recently, a gospel choir was formed at Howard University and quickly became the most popular musical ensemble on campus. They are in great demand of every department of the university, and whenever they are scheduled to sing they draw capacity crowds. They are also called upon to sing frequently in the District of Columbia and across the United States. They do not sing tamed gospels with a simple, straight-time beat, but they are singing the accentuated and polyrhythmic patterns of hard rock jazzy unmitigated gospels. One cannot effectively sing gospels in a detached attitude of the cool manipulator of an alien musical or thematic form. One has to enter into the substance and guts of the rhythm and the message in order to sing gospels convincingly. It is not uncommon for those who sing them to go into a frenzy. The elements of gospel music are capable of producing a state of ecstasy. Men and women, screaming, fall to the floor and run, shouting, from the room. The emergence of the gospel movement on the Howard University campus has temporarily put the traditional University Choir out of business. This traditional ensemble is not presently functioning due to certain administrative complications. But this conflict which is occurring at Howard and in some few Black churches will be resolved as the younger Black, trained in both classical and gospels, develops a music organizational structure that will accommodate the skillful rendering of both types. The Black Church has demonstrated throughout the years that it can be done. The conflict at Howard is really unnecessary and will be of short duration because the students required to sing in the University Choir are quite willing to sing in the gospel choir also. The current student, living in the brave new world of the soul movement, has no difficulty singing either J. S. Bach or James Cleveland and can move easily from one to the other.

The Black Church with its musical versatility prepared and conditioned the Black student to such breadth and tolerance. The older authoritarian who fled from the Black Church because of its lack of sophistication is unable now to move from anthem to gospel because the latter seems to him to repudiate his training and his social goals. He allowed his schooling to alienate him from spontaneous musical forms and liberal improvisations. But the new Black awareness has produced a new professional Black musician who can perform the European classics admirably and just as skillfully produce the spontaneity and unpredictable improvisations of gospel music-making. They have given to gospel music certain embellishments that only a trained musician can afford: authentic harmonizations, clever chord progressions, creative cadenzas. In like manner, they have taken their "soul power" into classical musical forms and made them come alive spiritually. This is the genius of Paul Robeson, Marian Anderson, Roland Hayes, Leontyne Price, George Shirley, Shirley Verrett-Carter, Gracy Bumbry, etc. These Black musicians have infused "soul" into standard White musical forms and have sung them with a certain indescribable "something within" that makes them outstanding. A Howard University girl was singing opera in Lincoln Center. She hit a high "c" and held onto it with vocal skill intensified by "soul power." A Black sister singing in the operatic chorus felt a strange awakening within, walked out of the chorus, went to the apron of the stage, put her hands on her hips, shook her head from side to side, and said aloud, "My Lord!" This is the greatness of the Black musician. If he doesn't let himself get hung up on choosing between one or the other, he can perform well in a variety of musical mediums. This is what has been going on all the time in the mainline Black church, which didn't train itself away from spontaneity or improvise itself away from training.

When asked this year what he regarded as the greatest stroke of Black musical genius, Dr. Hancock at age eighty-six replied, "The peculiar gift of metrical singing is the Negro's greatest stroke of musical creativity. When

Negroes sat in the balconies of the churches of the old slave South, he hears Whites singing according to hymnic meters. Being unable or unwilling to follow according to the meters which the Whites sang, the Negroes invented their own meters which they learned how to harmonize in miraculous ways." The singing of these hymns in the worship service usually immediately precedes or succeeds the sermon and represents a high point in the worship experience. The Black meters, though equal in length to White meters, are artistically unique, unpublished, and unknown to Whites. These hymns are usually "lined out" by a leader and sung by the congregation. They are slow, mournful, and plaintive. They have a primitive, unsophisticated beauty that is difficult to describe to anyone who has not heard them. The words of these hymns are taken from eighteenth century English hymnologists like Isaac Watts, Charles Wesley, and John Newton. Their lyrics like "Amazing Grace," "Alas and Did My Savior Bleed," "My Soul Be on Thy Guard," or "Come Ye That Love the Lord" are placed in the musical forms of Black metrical tunes. Gordon Hancock remembered common meter in thirteen tunes unknown to Whites, long meter in five tunes unknown to Whites, and short meter in six distinct tunes which cannot be found in hymnals.

Let us now reconstruct the order of worship and illustrate how this wide variety of musical forms fits within the Black experience of worship.

ORDER OF WORSHIP

THE FORMAL PROCESSIONAL HYMN: "Holy, Holy, Holy" or "The Church's One Foundation"

SCRIPTURE

PRAYER

THE REVIVAL HYMN: "Blessed Assurance"

RESPONSIVE READING

THE ANTHEM: Classical, romantic, or modern anthem or highly sophisticated and arranged spiritual by William Dawson, Nathaniel Dett, or John Work

THE OFFERTORY: A traditional, unarranged spiritual: "Were You There"

THE MEDITATION PERIOD—A Black hymn: "Some Day"

THE PRE-SERMON PRAYER

A MODERN GOSPEL SONG: "I Know the Lord Will Make a Way, Yes He Will"

THE ANNOUNCEMENT OF THE TEXT

THE OLD, UNPUBLISHED BLACK METERED HYMN

THE GOSPEL SERMON

THE INVITATION TO CHURCH MEMBERSHIP with metered hymn, Black hymn, spiritual, or gospel

RECESSIONAL HYMN: Standard Protestant hymn, "Fight the Good Fight"

BENEDICTION

CHORAL AMEN

The lowest music spiritually is the highest music liturgically, and vice versa. One moves upward in the service from a liturgical high to a liturgical low, which represents movement from a spiritual low to a spiritual high. The higher the worship progresses spiritually, the more "soul" the worshipper invests in the service and the less formal and inhibited he becomes.

Preaching in the Black Church

The pulpit stands at the center of the undivided chancel. This very common arrangement indicates the centrality of preaching in the Black religious experience. It is the climax of the worship hour; it is the apex of the worship experience. It is regarded as veritable theophany through the spoken word.

The preacher in the Black church does not necessarily represent any predictable academic qualifications. He may range from a grammar school dropout to a Ph.D., and I have oftentimes discovered that the grammar school dropout is more gifted and more effective. Some of the best sermons that I have ever heard were preached by an unlearned and unlettered man from Mississippi who came to Detroit preaching the Gospel and thereby took a congregation of thirty and increased it to three thousand. I shall never forget how this "country preacher" impressed my grand-uncle, who himself was a Harvard graduate and a college professor.

The character of Black sermons reflects a persistent biblical orientation.

The preacher will almost invariably engage his congregation in the consideration of a biblical text. The sermons will move dramatically from a low-keyed announcement of the text to a crescendo and progressive development of the text until the sermon reaches a climax of dramatic and emotional appeal.

Black sermons are imaginative interpretations and interpolations of scripture. It seems that while the White man is demythologizing the Bible, the Black man is remythologizing and supermythologizing Scripture. He uses his imagination freely without violating the meaning of the text.

The most unique quality of Black preaching is its becoming artfully intensified into music and rhythm. As the discourse develops and the congregation enters into a rhythmic dialogue with the preacher, answering him with emotional fervor, the spoken discourse begins to boil into an opera-like musical dramatization of the Gospel. The language becomes rhythmically poetic, the tune becomes evident, and the speech fulfills itself in song. The most beautiful aspect of Black preaching is that it sets the Gospel to music in a dramatic and unusual way. It is my belief that the Black sermon preceded and became the source of the Black spritual.

Shouting in the Black Church

Without a doubt this is the strangest, most bizarre, and most systematically misunderstood aspect of Black religion. Most scholars who treat the subject, whether they be Black or White, have a tendency to refer to shouting as a negative manifestation of ignorance and frustration, which will disappear as more Blacks become educated.[6] According to this literature, shouting is compensatory because through it impoverished Blacks enjoy a certain satisfaction that is denied them in their physical circumstances. It is anticipatory in that it anticipates the glory and joy of a projected heaven. It is relieving in that it serves as a valve through which Blacks can let off the built-up steam of their accumulated misfortunes and frustrations. As one who has observed shouting across the years and has even himself shouted, allow me to take issue with the scholars who, having never shouted, attempted an objective analysis of it which I think is misleading.

Shouting as religious ecstasy is based in the origin and purpose of the Black independent church which emerged in the eighteenth century. Black Christians seceded from White churches and formed their own churches because they were denied full participation in White ecclesiastical structures. They had also become disenchanted with the White church as a possible instrument of emancipation as it became clear to them that according to the

White ecclesiastical leadership, membership in Christ was not to be confused with freedom in society. They had taken from Black Christians the right to hope for freedom based on membership in Christ by explaining conversion and baptism as an inner experience of the soul having no effect whatsoever upon one's external situation. The independent Black church was formed to combat this theory and to create for Blacks a religious context of love and acceptance. The Black slave encountered social solidarity and acceptance nowhere but in his church. His family was shattered on the auction block; his schools were disallowed; his businesses were crushed; his churches were persecuted but they endured. It gave Black people meaning and value, faith to persevere, courage to resist, and love to lift themselves and their children from bondage to liberty. This is still the function of Black religion. At a time when the gap between the races is widening and injustice falls with greater force on the Black side of the gap, and at a time when the repression and suppression of minorities has reached a new peak, the Black Church still makes "somebodies" out of the "nobodies" of an oppressive society. Everybody is loved in the free Black Church; the low and the high, the young and the old, the rich and the poor—the Church loves them all and accepts them all in a community of freedom and hope. That is why we "get happy" and shout in our churches. It is not a negative phenomenon but a positive, glorious expression of being overwhelmed by the presence of Absolute love in the midst of a loving community. The occasion of ecstatic shouting is the experience of loving and being loved. It means that God draws near, the Holy Spirit is poured out, love is felt all around, and we rejoice in the presence of the Glory of God. Shouting also indicates an intuitive confidence and the unshakable hope that the Love will yet prevail within and above the divisions and hostilities of a world at war.

1 E. Franklin Frazier, *The Negro Church in America* (New York: Shocken Books, 1964), pp. 30, 31.

2 Miles Mark Fisher, *Negro Slave Songs in the United States* (Ithaca: Cornell University Press, 1953), pp. 189-190.

3 Ibid., p. 189.

4 James Weldon Johnson and J. Rosamond Johnson, *The Book of American Negro Spirituals* (New York: Viking Press, 1925), p. 21.

5 Fisher, *op. cit.,* pp. 66, 67.

6 See Joseph R. Washington, Jr., Black Religion (Boston: Beacon Press, 1964); Gunnar Myrdal, *An American Dilemma: The Negro Problem and Modern Democracy* (New York: Harper and Row, Publishers, 1964), Vol. II; and Benjamin Elijah Mays and Joseph William Nicholson, *The Negro's Church* (New York: The Institute of Social and Religious Research, 1933).

The Liturgy of Zion:
The Soul of Black Worship

by William B. McClain
from *Come Sunday: The Liturgy of Zion*, published in 1990

Undoubtedly, for as long as African Americans or Black Americans have grappled with the problem of being both Christian and Black in a racist society, some form of Black Christian theology has existed in America. Somehow, the slaves found a relationship between the God whom they had met in Africa whose sigh was heard in the African wind and the God of Abraham, Isaac, Jacob, and Jesus. And even when White people said one thing about their God, the African heard something else. When the White preacher, as a tool of the slavemaster, stressed the demands of God for the Africans to be slaves, obedient to their masters, the African heard the clear call of a righteous God for justice, equality, and freedom.

Much of the Black theology is reflected in the religious tradition and worship experience of Black people. For it has been their understanding of God through their own Black experience that they searched for meaning, relevance, worth, assurance, reconciliation, and their proper response to the God revealed. This is what religion is all about; it's where the Black worship experience was born. And at any historic point the gathering of the community is central to what happens later and is the support of the souls of Black folks.

The Civil Rights movement of the 1960s was the most telling illustration of the importance of gathering. Hundreds and thousands of people, protesting segregation and discrimination in the South, were willing to face fire hoses, police dogs, cattle prods, inhumanly cruel sheriffs, police, and state troopers. Children and adults marched in Selma and St. Augustine, in Birmingham and Montgomery to decry second-class citizenship and segregation. But always before marching they *first* gathered in the church to engage in songs of praise and protest, to entreat the God of history to be their guide, and to hear sermons and testimonies that related the gospel to their unjust social situation, and challenged them to act. The gathering of Black folks in worship services reveals the rich culture and the ineffable beauty and creativity of the Black soul. Indeed, it intimates the uniqueness of the Black religious tradition.

Songs of the Soil and the Soul

The Negro spirituals, which speak of life and death, suffering and sorrow, love and judgment, grace and hope, justice and mercy, were born out of this tradition. They were the songs of a people weary at heart. The Negro spirituals were the songs of an unhappy people; and yet they are the most beautiful expressions of human experience. The music is more ancient than the words. These songs are the siftings of centuries, telling of exile and trouble, of strife and hiding; they grope toward some unseen power and sigh for rest in the end. "But through all the sorrow songs," as William E. B. DuBois pointed out, "there breathes a hope for a faith in the ultimate justice of things."

Gospel songs created in the North became the northern, urban counterparts of the Negro spirituals of the South. The gospel song combines the sheer joy of living with deep religious faith. It arose in the midst of the early exodus from the farms and hamlets of the South when Black folks arrived in Chicago, New York, Detroit, and other northern cities, and found themselves in a strange land. The simple lines of the gospel were written on their minds and hearts, and were translated into songs on their lips and praise in their mouths. Now there is little argument that *these* gospel songs and sounds have supplied the roots for much of contemporary music—from rock symphonies to detergent commercials.

Black Worship and White Fundamentalism

Some have argued that there is no difference between Black worship and White fundamentalist emotionalism. The answer can be found by experiencing authentic Black worship or attending a southern White fundamentalist meeting. Clearly, a people's religion and mode of worship derive from the experiences, the physical and psychological realities of their day-to-day existence. Nobody who knows anything about Black people and White fundamentalists would argue that their experiences are the same. The White experience in its critical essence is not the Black experience.

There is a basic and critical difference between Blacks and White fundamentalists as it relates to Scripture. One can search in vain through the official statements of faith, even among Black Pentecostals, to find references either to "verbal" or "plenary" inspirations of the Bible, which are code words among White fundamentalists. While many Blacks can easily be classified as neo-evangelicals who believe in inspiration, they do not generally make statements about inerrancy of Scripture.

This leads to a particular manifestation in preaching and the use of Scripture. Black preachers take much more liberty than do Whites with elaborating and the using of imagination in telling biblical stories for the benefit and enjoyment of their listeners. Neither do they make such a fine distinction between the Old and the New Testaments, as if the New superseded the Old. In fact, Black preachers tend to preach more often from the Old Testament. And even when they preach from the New Testament, the text is more often drawn from the gospels rather than the epistles.[1]

Toward a Definition of Black Worship: The Re-shaping of Worship

Worship, to be authentic, must be the celebration of that which is most real and which serves to sustain life. To be Christian worship, it must necessarily and inevitably relate to the eternal God revealed in Jesus Christ. It involves transcending and deciphering the existential dilemma, discovering the transcendence grounded in being.

Styles and theologies of worship are determined largely by the context in which a people's faith is experienced. Their mode of worship, religious practices, beliefs, rituals, attitudes, and symbols are inevitably and inextricably bound to the psychological and physical realities of their day-to-day existence. This is at least part of what William James called "varieties of religious experience." It is quite clear that when the Christian faith flowed through the contours of the souls of Black folk, a new interpretation, a new form, a new worship style emerged. Reflecting the cultural and historical background of transplanted Africans, it moved with the rhythms of a soulful people and rolled like a prancing river. The Black people responded to the Christian faith in their way, not in the way of their oppressor. They reshaped, refashioned, and recreated the Christian religion to meet their own particular needs.

Worship in the Black tradition is celebration of the power to survive and to affirm life, with all of its complex and contradictory realities. The secular and the sacred and Saturday night and Sunday morning come together to affirm God's wholeness, the unity of life, and God's lordship over all of life. Such a tradition encourages spontaneity and improvisation, and urges

317

worshippers to turn themselves loose into the hands of the existential here and now, where joy and travail mingle together as part of the reality of God's creation. In this context, Black people experience and participate in the life and community of faith.

Is Black Worship Distinctive?

"Is Black worship distinctive?" Dr. Larry Jones, formerly of Union Theological Seminary in New York, criticizes this question and is somewhat right but for the wrong reasons. In response to Gayraud Wilmore's question-naire for the National Committee of Black Churchmen on Black Theology, Dr. Jones makes the following observations:

> It is commonplace where Black clergy gather to hear long dissertations on the genius of Black worship, but the documentations for the dissertations are more often than not part poetry, part testimony, part exaggeration, part embroided memory, and part personal testimony.[2]

In the first place, there is ample documentation for Black worship being a product of the Black experience and having its own uniqueness and genius. Part of that documentation is in the widespread efforts of some White Christians to add a little "soul" to their styles of worship, creating congregational participation, dialogues, happenings, and celebrations with programmed spontaneity. However, the more dependable documentation is in the souls of Black folk who disappear from Black churches when services become too stilted, cold, and staid. European-oriented worship services are generally shorter, more rigid in worship form, less emotional. And the music is less spontaneous. Black people go in search of a church where there is some spirit and where exuberant ejaculations of "Thank you, Jesus," "Praise God!" "Preach!" and "Amen!" are not considered to be overreaction of superstitious simple folk or religious revelry. In fact, that is why many Black churches, including Union Church in Boston, were separated from White congregations.[3]

In the second place, any serious conversation about worship or anything else that relates to emotional experience is based on "part testimony, part memory, and part personal history." In fact, theology as a discipline would be enhanced by personal history and testimony. To say, "This is what happened to me," and to avoid the kind of pervasive gnosticism so current in many systematic theologies is effective and refreshing. Personal testimonies are not irrelevant. In fact, the farther away one is from it, the more imprecise memory's embroidery.

In the third place, every book on worship by White thinkers is based on their experience and understanding of worship in a White context. It reflects the persons' means of transcending and deciphering their existential dilemma. It represents what is most real and sustains life for them.

What are the distinctive elements of Black worship? What documentation can be offered for claiming that there is genius in Black worship? Is James A. Joseph's description of Black worship as "Sunday morning gatherings with group psychotherapy and soul music"[4] all that can be said? Is the essence of Black worship simply a dramatic ritualization of what Joseph Washington has called "Negro folk religion"?

To some extent, the genius of Black worship is the same as that which made Shakespeare a literary genius, the ability to create the new and fresh out of the old and stale, to lend a refulgence to the dark and somber, to create a *tertium quid* out of the coming together of two diverse influences so distinct and different as to be called unique.

This is not to suggest that worship in all Black churches has reflected that genius. God alone knows how many times and in how many places Black religious gatherings have engaged in "sound and fury signifying nothing." But as we have been willing to recognize the transcendent God in the turmoil of our existential dilemma and to see the "prophetic face of divine anger, undergirded by the Holy Spirit, to bring the sword in pursuit of the positive peace without which no person can experience salvation,"[5] we have participated in the spiritual celebration of life and witnessed the opening up of the "windows of heaven."

Let us look briefly at two aspects of Christian worship in the light of the Black experience of faith: ritual and music. The next chapter will focus on preaching.

Ritual: "What Meaneth These Stones?"

In an age when repetition leads to boredom, many see ritual as a bad thing. They equate ritual with formality and see it as something superficial, meaningless, empty, lacking in creativity, cold. A different point of view can be taken for our discussion. Contrary to the arguments of some, ritual is not a bad thing. It allows a people to make a metaphoric statement about the paradoxes and the contradictions of the human situation. Ritual provides an opportunity to connect with others who share the same experience, allowing a recollection of experiences. With rituals people can express their dependency on continuity for their identity and draw upon their memories and the faith of those around them. It is a way of responding to our children's question of, "What meaneth these stones?"

Ritual is not the exclusive property of any particular group. Ritual and ceremony have always been important to Black life and Black worship. From the ancient tribal rituals and ceremonies of the Fon-speaking people of Dahomy, the Yoruba of Nigeria, and the Akan of Ghana to the grand processionals and recessionals of the multicolored robed choirs, the white starched uniforms of usher boards, and to the grand marches of the Masonic and fraternal groups, Black people have engaged in ritual. It is an essential part of Black life and worship. But a ritual that is meaningful can't be created for all people at all times and places.

Either ritual is rooted in a common culture or it is nothing. And when it ceases to be relevant to the lives of the people, it is no longer useful. Genuine religious ritual has to be accessible to the unsophisticated and naive as well as the informed and liturgical. James Russell Lowell was right:

> New occasions teach new duties.
> Time makes ancient good uncouth.

Ritual must fit the time and the place. One can say about ritual what Merton said about church architecture:

> (People) build churches as if a church should not belong to our time. A church has to look as if it were left over from some other age. I think such an assumption is based on an implicit confession of atheism as if God did not belong to all ages.[6]

God does belong to all ages, and ritual used in Black worship ought to reflect the meaning of life in relation to God and what God is doing about the experience of living as Black people in this world. To be meaningful in Black worship, ritual must speak to the needs of Black folk and must reflect their problems, affirm their worth in the sight of God, and inspire them militantly to seek the solutions to their problems. Rites, ceremonies, and liturgies, like theology, cannot be developed in isolation from the crucial problems of a people's survival. Ritual ought to affirm the liberating presence of God in our human experience. As Major Jones has rightly put it, "God is not on our side: we are on His side if we are for liberation." And that ought to be reflected in liturgies and rituals.

Ritual loses its effectiveness when it alienates a people from their heritage, their society, and their family. Carlton W. Molette, author of *Afro-American Studies,* has pointed out that there are different purposes for African American ritual drama than the traditional purposes of modern Euro-American ritual drama. Using the African American church service as the model, since it is the most widely supported ritual drama in the Black community, Molette delineates the difference in purpose.

One of these purposes is *to celebrate the affirmation of a sense of community, a feeling of togetherness.* This is sometimes emphasized through ritual mass physical contact, such as joining hands or touching in some way, so that spiritual togetherness is reaffirmed and heightened by a ritual form of physical togetherness. The accent is on *community* rather than on the individual, *fellowship* rather than individual uniqueness.

A second purpose, according to Molette, is *to serve some functional, useful purpose.* The ritual drama is expected to have some future effect outside of the framework of the ritual itself. This can be illustrated by the funeral ritual in which the soul of the deceased is expected to be affected by the ritual itself.

A third purpose of the ritual drama is *to create a spiritual involvement (or emotional involvement) in the event.* This is designed to provide a purgation of the emotions. The church service is expected to allow all to be emotionally and spiritually involved.

When these purposes are met in the worship service, Black people are apt to say: "We *had* church today!" Molette's analysis is instructive. The ritual that does not take into account this cultural heritage and does not relate to the emotional, day-to-day existence of Black people is seen as meaningless. Liturgy ought to reflect and relate to everyday life as Black Christians struggle to make sense of life, and worship ought to reflect a captive and alienated people in a strange land, a people in pursuit of liberation, freedom, health, and wholeness. Part of this change may mean making use of poetry and other works developed in the First and Second Renaissance of Black Culture and the poetry and literary works being developed by young Black prophets today.

This is not to suggest change in ritual as a vogue. Fads come and go. And God knows that the Black community knows that well. But there is a difference between faddism and change. Change is the natural evolution, but faddism is artificial. Faddism seeks change simply for change's sake and may lack taste, judgment, and sensitivity. We want change for liberation's sake. We want change for God's sake; and we make the rituals we use relevant to the people's lives and to their struggle to survive, to be liberated, and to celebrate.

Let's find new and interesting ways to praise the Lord. Some will accuse us of having an aspect of entertainment about it, and worship in the Black tradition *is* art. It is *drama*, as Molette points out. The Black experience is one where a person dramatizes. Let our rituals reflect a people in pursuit of their liberation and what God means in that struggle and celebrate the wholeness found.

Music: Is There a Song?

Music in the Black worship tradition is as close to worship as breathing is to life. It has been the songs of Zion in this strange land that have often kept Black folks from "starting down the steep and slippery steps of death" in suicide. These songs have cut a path through the wilderness of despair.

There is no one more eminently qualified to comment on the spirituals than John Wesley Work, who was for many years professor of Latin and history at Fisk University and one of the pioneers in collecting, arranging, and presenting the Negro spirituals. He says in his book, *Folk Songs of the American Negro:*

> To our fathers who came out of bondage and who are still with us, these songs are prayers, praises, and sermons. They sang them at work; in leisure moments; they crooned them to their babies in the cradles; to their wayward children; they sang them to their sick, wracked with pain on beds of affliction; they sang them over their dead. Blessings, warnings, benedictions, and the very heartbeats of life were all expressed to our fathers by their song.

These songs of hope and promise have helped to bring a people through the torture chambers of the last two centuries.

The music of the Black religious tradition has said that just being alive is good and worth celebrating, singing, and shouting about. It is impossible to conceive of the Black religious tradition in any authentic sense without the songs of survival, liberation, hope, and celebration. That music has nourished the Black community, soothed its hurts, sustained its hopes, and bound its wounds. It has proclaimed that God whom we knew in the forests of Africa, the Lord whose voice was heard in the sighing of the night wind, the God whom we met in the cotton field of the Southland is the joy of our salvation. It is that God who makes us glad to come into the house of the Lord. The music of the Black religious tradition has enabled a people to keep on going, to keep on tramping. Black music lifts the heads, hearts, and spirits of the congregation in readiness to hear the gospel word of grace and liberation.

The role music plays in Black worship has its antecedents in Western Africa, where most Black slaves came from. Black worship in America recreates patterns which have been observed in East African religious practices. Music in ritual in both cultures is of dominant importance. Leroi Jones (Imamu Baraka) quotes in *Blues People* an old African dictum which says, "The spirit will not descend without song." In Africa, ritual dances and songs were integral parts of African religious observances. This heritage of emotional religion was one of the strongest contributions that the African culture made to the African American. The puritan Christian Church by and large saw dancing as an evil, worldly excess, but dancing as an integral part of the African's life could not be displaced by the still White notes of the Wesleyan hymnal.

From the earliest times when the Black slaves sang:

> Oh, freedom! Oh, freedom all over me! When I am free!
> An' befor' I'd be a slave, I'll be buried in my grave, an' go
> home to my Lord an' be free. (#102)

until the singing of

> Go down, Moses, way down in Egypt land,
> Tell ole Pharaoh, to let my people go. (#112)

Black people were not *simply* singing a song, they were expressing *a definite point of view*. That point of view was that the God of justice and the God of Jesus is on the side of the oppressed. This was and is at the heart of Black religion in America. And it must be reaffirmed in our worship experiences and taught to our children. We must not neglect our past, our roots. Our children must be made aware that "we have come over a way that with tears has been watered" (#32 and #210); that we have sung the songs of freedom and liberation and hope—even when "hope unborn had died."

Some have argued that the gospel songs that originated primarily in the North, and are popular throughout the states, border on the secular. The gospel songs are characterized by the beat, rhythm, and group vibrations. Some have maintained that the lyrics are banal. The truth is that the songs talk about the things that matter most to poor people. When you are well off, you can write songs about individual neuroses. But poor people struggling to survive—whether in rat-infested ghetto flats or on a sharecropper's farm in

Mississippi—are concerned about staying alive. They can sing and mean, "It's another day's journey and I'm glad about it!"

As to whether gospel songs are secular, a statement made by the late Duke Ellington at a 1965 Christmas program at Fifth Avenue Presbyterian Church in New York City is helpful. The Duke was speaking to the question of "What makes music sacred?" He said:

> Sacred music in all of its forms offers a universal point of meeting. But what makes music sacred is not a rigid category nor a fixed pattern of taste. The sole criterion is whether or not the hearts of the musician and the listener are offered in response and devotion to God.[7]

While the Duke was not a prince of the church, his statement is sufficiently sound for all of us. The Black religious tradition understands that the rational and the emotional go together. Life is emotional as well as rational. The late Howard Thurman, Dean of Marsh Chapel, Boston University for many years, used to say: "The mind is the latest addition to man's equipment, and when you minister to him on the assumption that he is mind only, you are a fool." The Black religious tradition in its authenticity is not that foolish; it erases the line between mind and body, intellect and emotion, and ministers to the rationality and emotionality of the whole person. It is this gift of faith that God has given us through the Black experience. We must boldly offer it on the altars of the church without fear and without shame.

If Luther's "A Mighty Fortress Is Our God" can raise the blood pressure of Lutherans, and if the sons and the daughters of the founders of the American Church can be stirred to tears in the singing of the Quaker hymn, "Dear Lord and Father of Mankind," and if James Russell Lowell's hymn can make thunder roll for the sons and daughters of the New England abolitionists and the vanguards of White liberals, then Thomas Dorsey's "Precious Lord, Take My Hand" ought to be able to make lightning flash in Black congregations—even those held in bourgeois captivity. And Charles Tindley's "We'll Understand It Better By and By" (#55) ought to raise spiritual tumult in any Black Methodist church.[8]

Even with the hymns of the church, and especially those about the unearned and the unmerited grace of God, Black folks are not always singing the same song the White folks are singing. A hymn like "Amazing Grace"— even though written by an ex-slave trader—becomes a song of survival and liberation in a different cadence and sound. It becomes a new song. For what

Black people sing about is the miracle of their survival. Imamu Baraka (Leroi Jones) has quite rightly observed:

> The God spoken about in Black songs is not the same one in White songs. Though the words might look the same. (They are not even pronounced alike.) But it is a different quality of energy they summon.[9]

---

1 William B. McClain, "What Is Authentic Black Worship?" *Christianity and Crisis* (October 1970); see James S. Finney, "Doctrinal Differences Between Black and White Pentecostalists," *Spirit*, Vol. 1, No. 1, (July 1977).

2 Marner R. Traynham, *Christian Faith in Black and White* (Boston: Parameter Press, 1973), p. 92.

3 Union United Methodist Church, Boston (then Fourth Methodist), separated from the Bromfield Methodist Church in 1819 in order that Blacks could practice a more emotional religion. They were urged by their fellow White Methodists to establish their own church.

4 James A. Joseph, "Has Black Religion Lost Its Soul?" *The Black Seventies*, Floyd Barbour, ed. (Boston: Beacon Press, 1970), p. 20.

5 Jefferson P. Rogors, "Black Worship: Black Church," *The Black Church*, Vol. 1 (Boston: Black Ecumenical Press, 1972). pp. 64–65.

6 James P. Shaughnessy, ed. *The Roots of Ritual* (Grand Rapids: William B. Eerdman Press, 1973), p. 86.

7 Program for Christmas Concept, Fifth Avenue Presbyterian Church, New York City, December 25, 1965.

8 Charles Albert Tindley was the Methodist pastor of what is now known as Tindley Temple United Methodist Church, Philadelphia, from 1902 until his death in 1933. Dr. Tindley is credited with writing the first gospel songs to be published. "Stand By Me" and "We'll Understand It Better By and By," both in 1905 (pp. 41 and 55 in *Songs of Zion*).

9 Leroi Jones (Imamu Baraka), *Blues People* (New York: Grove Press, 1975), p. 22.

Encountering Jesus in Worship

by Zan W. Holmes, Jr.
from *Encountering Jesus,* published in 1992

Show me a vital congregation and I will point you to a church that gives faithful attention to its worship. And there is no litmus test for the degree of liturgy. Many churches that experience vitality, faithfulness, and growth are churches that have a high degree of liturgy, and others have hardly any fixed liturgy at all. (And I don't mean by "growth" just number: I often make the distinction to my congregation between "growing" and "swelling." One is a sign of health, and one is a clear sign of illness.) Perhaps there are tests of the degree of congregational participation; the extent to which the Bible is used as source book, study book, and a book of enrichment; and the uses of music are, in fact, praise to God rather than a rehearsal for a concert hall performance.

My former colleague at Perkins, James F. White, probably one of the best in the business on worship, has observed in an article in *Pulpit Digest,* appropriately titled "Christian Worship in the 1990s," that...

> no one visiting these churches [so-called evangelical churches] can fail to be impressed by the importance of preaching in worship.... In some churches, the whole congregation participates vigorously in response to preaching so that it becomes almost dialogue. After visiting various Black and Pentecostal churches, I sometimes wonder if other churches know what *participation* really means.

Well, I'm not sure that they do. But one thing my experience has taught me is that you have to bring something to the sermon to get something out of it. The expression is familiar in the African American Church: "If you don't put anything in, you won't get anything out!" And sometimes it is a mere openness to the Spirit. For worship is neither something that the clergy does and the people sit back and watch nor something that is an optional activity for the people. Worship is work—hard, active, disciplined, and sometimes painful work that demands something from us as it gives something to us. That is literally what the word that the New Testament uses so often for worship, *leitourgia,* means—"the work of the people." This reminds me of the story of a young college student who returned home for the holidays and accompanied his mother to church one Sunday. After they returned home, the young man said, "The preacher was not too good today." His mother said, "Well, maybe not." He said, "I noticed that the choir was not too good today." His mother said, "Well, maybe not." Then she said to him, "Well, son, tell me, how good were *you* today?"

Father Clarence Rivers, a Black Roman Catholic priest and expert in liturgy, has made the observation: "I have never heard a Black church minister exhort his congregation to turn out for some particular religious celebration when he did not promise: 'We are going to have a good time!'"[1]

As a matter of fact, "having a good time" is so much characteristic of the authentic Black worship experience that the phrase "to have church" has become synonymous with "to have a good time."[2] It even carries over into the funeral service. I asked one of my members how the funeral service of her nephew had gone, since I was not able to attend the service. She replied: "It was a good funeral; we had a good time!" What she was saying was that the service was a celebration, that "they had church!"

This approach of celebration and festive worship does not deny the seriousness of worship. It is joy in the midst of sorrow. It is hope in the very depths of despair. It is a way of saying with Charles Albert Tindley: "I believe it. I believe it. Jesus died to set me free!" It is an affirmation of the words of Jesus: "In the world you face persecution. But take courage; I have conquered the world!" (John 16:33). And every pastor ought to know that every Sunday is a season of the gospel, and every occasion of gathering is an opportunity to say with the Church and the Christ of the Church: "Come to me, all of you who are heavy laden," all of you who desire purpose and meaning, all of you who have lost hope, all of you who need rest, all of you who seek, come!

I have been pleased to see the emphasis of congregational participation in the liturgical renewal movement in the United Methodist Church. The new Service of Death and Resurrection, officially adopted by the 1984 General Conference and now a part of the new *United Methodist Hymnal,* reflects this. It is a service of Christian worship suitable for funerals and memorial services in which the congregation actively participates. This is a great improvement over the clergy-dominated earlier service where, if you wanted any extensive congregational participation, a bulletin had to be printed. It is more than an improvement; it is recapturing what is so essential to vital worship that is faithful to the Church's beginnings.

But congregational participation alone does not make worship necessarily Christian worship. And not all worship done within the so-called "Christian community" is Christian, in spite of the celebrative spirit. It can sometimes be mere self-worship or ego trips or worship of something or somebody who is not the Holy One. As H. Grady Davis was so fond of saying: "The worship of the pagan is a *search,* but the worship of a Christian is *recognition.*" What, then, makes worship Christian?

First, it is Christian worship when it is our response to God's initiative in addressing us and inviting us through Jesus Christ. In other words, it is not something we do. It begins with something God has already done through Jesus Christ. Our worship is in response to a gracious invitation that has been extended through Jesus Christ.

At least part of what this means is that we don't come to worship to find God. We come to be found by God or to acknowledge we have already been found by God and to encounter Jesus. Really, we come because we have heard of or know of a God who is seeking us, as a shepherd who goes hunting for a sheep, as a woman who sweeps the floor of a candlelit room to find a lost coin, as a father who takes the initiative to greet a lost son who has returned home; even before he gets all the way to the porch, the father is saying, "That's my boy who I've been waiting for. Let's have a celebration." And that same God is our God or can be our God.

Second, it is Christian worship when it is an upward look, a recognition and adoration of God. In the classic passage in the sixth chapter of Isaiah, we note that, according to the prophet's own words, the service begins with an *overpowering awareness* of the presence and the majesty of God. He said:

> I saw the Lord sitting on a throne, high and lofty; and the hem of his robe filled the temple. Seraphs were in attendance above him; each had six wings: with two they covered their faces, and with two they covered their feet, and with two they flew. And one called to another and said: "Holy, Holy, Holy is the Lord of hosts; the whole earth is full of his glory."
>
> —Isaiah 6:1–3

Worship is, in a real sense, a response of praise. We gather and respond in acts of praise and adoration.

In the third place, Christian worship involves an inward look. The moment I look up to God I also recognize myself for what I am. After Isaiah saw the glory of the Lord, he realized how far short he had fallen from the glory of God. So after an inward look he cries out: "Woe is me! I am lost, for I am a man of unclean lips, and I live among a people of unclean lips" (Isaiah 6:5). Here it is important to note that he *recognized* and *confessed* his own uncleanliness before he acknowledged the uncleanliness of other people.

It is an act that corresponds to the teaching of Jesus in the Sermon on the Mount. Jesus said:

> Why do you see the speck in your neighbor's eye, but do not notice the log in your own eye? Or how can you say to your neighbor, "Let me take the speck out of your eye," while the log is in your own eye? You hypocrite, first take the log out of your own eye and then you will see clearly to take the speck out of your neighbor's eye.
>
> —Matthew 7:3–5; see also Luke 6:41–42

Isaiah's act of acknowledging the corporate nature of sin as well as personal sin also reminds us of the corporate nature of worship. A distinguishing characteristic of Christian worship is that it is never a solitary undertaking. Instead, it is thoroughly social and organic in character. Jesus said, "Where two or three are gathered in my name, I am there among them" (Matthew 18:20). This does not negate the fact that common worship ought to be supplemented with private devotion. But the distinction needs to be clear. Both need to take place—*common worship* where there is the physical presence of the rest of the Body of Christ and *personal devotion*, which usually occurs apart from the gathered community. There needs to be a balance of each.

After Isaiah confessed his sins and acknowledged the corporate nature of sin and worship, he experienced the forgiveness of God. He said: "Then one of the seraphs flew to me, holding a live coal that had been taken from the altar with a pair of tongs. The seraph touched my mouth with it and said: 'Now that this has touched your lips, your guilt has departed and your sin is blotted out'" (Isaiah 6:6–7). The uniqueness of this act in Christian worship is that it comes through Jesus Christ, our liberator, who is at the center of all that happens. Christian worship is encountering Jesus.

Christian worship must also have an outward look. After Isaiah's sins are forgiven, he said that he heard the voice saying to him: "Whom shall I send, and who will go for us?" Then Isaiah answers: "Here am I; send me!" (Isaiah 6:8). And God said: "Go!" Thus Christian worship is a come and go affair.

In worship Jesus extends a gracious invitation for us to come to him; he wants us to rest. He wants us to learn of him. But he also wants us to go for him. He not only wants us to be the *gathered church*, he also wants us to be the *church scattered*.

There is the classic occasion in the Gospel that illustrates the challenge of this truth. It is usually called "The Transformation." Jesus took Peter, James, and John, and went to the top of a mountain, where Jesus was transformed before them. Jesus talked with Moses and Elijah. Peter became so captivated by it all that he said: "Lord, we are having such a good time, let's stay here! Let's build three booths and stay here forever! Let's freeze time. Let's eternalize this moment." But Jesus said to Peter: "No, Peter, we didn't come up here to stay. This is a *come and go affair*. We have come up, but we must go down. There is a distraught father in the valley who needs help. A sick boy needs healing. There is a woman who has been hemorrhaging for twelve years and needs healing. There is an unbelieving, stumbling, and fumbling church that needs better organization. Let's go down."

In this regard, the Puritans had the right idea. They did not apply the word "service" to the gathering of worship. For them the *service* began at the church door when the church meeting was over. There they crossed the threshold of life to go back into the world, and there the service began as an outgrowth of the renewal that had come as they worshiped together. Worship loses its essential Christian nature when it becomes an end in itself and does not send its worshipers out into the world to engage in Christian service, to deal with the problems of the poor and the oppressed.

The Jesus who invites us to worship is the same Jesus who proclaimed in his first sermon, as recorded in Luke 4:18–19:

> The Spirit of the Lord is upon me,
> because he has anointed me to bring good news to the poor.
> He has sent me to proclaim release to the captives
> and recovery of sight to the blind,
> to let the oppressed go free,
> to proclaim the year of the Lord's favor.

James Cone has often made the point that in Black worship there is a sense of what he calls "the eschatological community." This is found in the belief of the people that the Spirit of Jesus is coming to visit with them in the worship or what I have continued to refer to in this chapter as "encountering Jesus in worship."

This presence of the Holy Spirit is a liberating experience from complete control of the ritual. Ritual is important, but it is not an end in itself. Ritual is interrupted freely when the Spirit moves. The clock is not worshiped. The preacher is told by the congregation, "Take your time!" And if he or she is saying something, the people will stay and listen, for part of what happens when the Spirit visits is a radical transformation in the people's identity. Those who were no people become God's people. Those who have thought of themselves as nobody become somebody. You can see it in their walk. You can hear it in their talk. And if you give them a chance, they will tell the story of how an encounter with Jesus enabled them to overcome their lack of identities!

Where worship is vital and faithful, and this is certainly not confined to Black and Pentecostal churches, several elements must be present. The first is celebration—that is, a sense that life and the gathering itself are pure gift. Praise to God and acknowledgement to God for God's gracious gifts and acts of grace are necessary. Surely Christians who "gather in his name" have even more to celebrate or at least ought to be aware of more for which to give thanksgiving and praise than those who gather at our weekly fall and winter secular celebration—the American football game. And yet one sees much more enthusiasm and joy expressed at these gatherings than most of our weekly worship services. Can it be that these secular gatherings tend to be simple, aggressive, direct? Frank C. Senn thinks so and writes in his book *Christian Worship and Its Cultural Setting* that "celebrations must make an impression on those who participate in them if what cult communicates is nothing less than reality itself—a world-view and lifestyle that is intended to be shared by all members of the society."[3]

A second element is inclusiveness. The makeup of the congregation ought to reflect the makeup of the community, and a hearty welcome should be extended to everyone. Historically, it was not unusual in the Black congregation to include both the poorest of the poor and the wealthiest African Americans in the community The educated and the uneducated sat side by side. Congregations were intergenerational; children and youth and young adults and middle-aged and the elderly were all present together. The very nature of such a diverse congregation demanded that the service have something for everyone, that all the sheep be fed. I suspect where there are vital and faithful churches that is still true. But one of the greatest threats to the integrity of worship in the African American Church is the rising classism among Black Christians. There is a widening social gap between upwardly mobile, middle-class Blacks and poor Blacks. This gap is reflected in the membership of many Black churches today. My heart aches as I see this develop. A common expression of the early Black churches was that the ground is level at the foot of the cross. Our challenge is to recover this notion in all our churches today. The invitation Jesus issued was to all. There are some invitations we do not receive because we do not necessarily meet the criteria or the standards or don't have the credentials or we would be out of place. But not so with the Church. The invitation goes out to all: "Whosoever will, let them come." The old Charles Wesley hymn captured Jesus' invitation well. It is worth looking at every word to remind us, and especially *all* Methodists, of our good beginnings:

> Come, sinners, to the gospel feast;
> Let every soul be Jesus' guest.
> Ye need not one be left behind,
> For God hath bid all humankind.
>
> Sent by my Lord, on you I call;
> The invitation is to all.
> Come, all the world! Come, sinner, thou!
> All things in Christ are ready now.
>
> Come, all ye souls by sin oppressed,
> Ye restless wanderers after rest;
> Ye poor, and maimed, and halt, and blind,
> In Christ a hearty welcome find.
>
> My message as from God receive;
> Ye all may come to Christ land live.
> O let his love your hearts constrain,
> Nor suffer him to die in vain.
>
> This is the time, no more delay!
> This is the Lord's accepted day;
> Come thou this moment, at his call,
> And live for him who died for all.[4]

A third element is an understanding of Scripture from the perspective of the underside. Both in preaching and teaching we must draw freely from the

Old and New Testaments. The Christian Church is a two-testament church. We cannot and shall not forget the Exodus theme: "Let my people go!" even as we hear the Resurrection story and live out a Resurrection faith. The Old Testament prophets denounced social injustices and called for "justice to roll down like waters and righteousness like an ever-flowing stream." In preaching, it means interpreting the scripture story of David by not identifying with David the king, but by helping the people to identify with David the shepherd boy who, though he was an underdog, overcame the giant, Goliath, with a sling shot and a few stones. It is preaching that identifies with the wounded, and not with the Levite and the priest in the story of the good Samaritan. It is preaching that identifies with a Christ who was born activity of Jesus as a clue for understanding our life and ministry. Not only do we understand the Resurrection event as victory over sin and death, but also as the power to overcome oppressive and unjust conditions. And the challenge to see both Good Friday and Easter Sunday must be present in our proclamation of the faith. There can be no Resurrection without the Crucifixion.

We have discussed earlier the role of the Bible in the Black Church. What also must be added here is that we are not merely talking about a fundamentalist, proof-texting, uncritical, and unthinking use of the Bible. We are talking about a reverence for the scriptures as authority, a confronting as well as comforting word, and a realization that the Book has been a real source of oral tradition that is inherently embedded in our lives and our culture. This understanding has given a certain freedom of interpretation that is perhaps absent in many other church circles. It is clearly present in the way the Black preacher can take an ancient text like that of the good Samaritan or the prodigal son or the story of the Hebrew men in the fiery furnace and make it live in twentieth century America.[5]

To be sure, one of the greatest challenges for the whole church in the twentieth century is to rediscover the Bible as our authority and guide for faithful discipleship. The challenge was underscored by pollster George Gallup, Jr., at a recent convention of the Evangelical Press Association. He noted that most Americans say they believe in God and Jesus and trust the Bible. "However, statistics show that Americans are ignorant of the doctrines and history of their chosen faiths, and half of the nation's Christians do not know who delivered the sermon on the mount," he said. "We revere the Bible, but don't read it," he continued. "We believe the Ten Commandments to be valid rules for living, although we can't name them."

A fourth element in worship is music. I have always felt that the music of the church ought to be diverse. That has not always been true of the congregations I have served. It was only after I was able to work on the advisory committee that produced *Songs of Zion*, a book containing spirituals and gospel songs as well as hymns and anthem arrangements, that I was able to convince my congregation that a variety of music in worship was acceptable. It is a treasured resource now in our worship. And I gladly welcomed the chance to sit on the national advisory committee to produce *Come Sunday* (the companion to *Songs of Zion*) by William B. McClain. It helps us integrate liturgy and music so that every service can reflect the inclusiveness and diversity I spoke of earlier.

But after all is said and done about worship, there is only one criterion for Christian worship: gathering in Jesus' name. It is recorded in the Gospel of Matthew 18:20: "For where two or three are gathered in my name, I am there among them." Whether the gathering together is in a rural clapboard building or in an urban Gothic cathedral; whether there are three thousand, three hundred, or just two or three, the criterion is the same: to gather in Jesus' name. Christians gather in worship around the Word and the Table to speak and touch in Christ's name, and the promise in the New Testament Gospel is that he will be present.

In an age when so many are lonely and seek companionship and friendly groups to be with or to join just to avoid boredom or merely being alone, the church must be clear that the purpose of its worship is to gather in Christ's name, to encounter Jesus, the Holy One, and to call his name, praise his name, and to be encountered by him in prayer and praise and preaching. So many congregations fail to experience genuine worship and spend much time in solemn assembly or in extra efforts to create the friendly atmosphere and "tingly feelings" because they forget the purpose for gathering.

Added to the problem is the unfortunate notion that if people look alike, think alike, talk alike, dress alike, and have about the same amounts in their bank accounts, they can huddle together and sing a few songs and read a few prayers and listen to a talk on a religious subject, and then they have worshiped. such gatherings are much more numerous than we at first want to admit. This is at least a part of our problem as we struggle to understand why so many congregations are neither vital nor faithful. There can be no vital congregation without people who intentionally gather to encounter Jesus— even in those old and familiar places where, in the past, perhaps perverted gatherings have replaced the authentic worship of the people of God.

Vital and faithful worship is necessary and sufficient condition for building vital and faithful congregations. While the forms and styles may be diverse, the musical genres varied, the degree of liturgy different in quantity and kind, the Word preached and read in different ways and languages, the questions become: Was there a rehearsal of the gracious acts of God in the past, the present, and the promise for the future? Was there an encounter with a Holy God? Was there a sense that we are the created and a people prone to dip into the social swine pen of life and stay to live as if we are not those who are called to be God's people? Was there a reminder that we owe thanks and praise to the one from whom all blessings have come? Did we say, "Much obliged!" Did we show gratitude for goodness and grace? Was there a reminder of our obligation to act and care about those people and things that the Grace-giver cares about? Did we encounter Jesus in his risen power?

Chapter Summary

- The purpose of worship is to gather in Christ's name, to encounter Jesus.
- Worship is hard work. It demands something from us as it gives something to us.
- Worship is a response to what God has already done for us in Jesus Christ. It is a response of praise.
- We come to worship not to seek God, but to be found by Him.
- Worship loses its value when it becomes an end in itself and does not send participants out into the world to engage in Christian service.

Discussion Questions

1. What did you learn about worship that you had not known before?
2. In what ways do we encounter Jesus in worship?
3. What is a common weakness in most worship services?
4. What do you personally get the most out of in worship?
5. How should a person feel at the conclusion of a worship service?
6. How does a person prepare for worship?
7. What are the causes of failure to encounter Jesus in a worship service?
8. What part should the Bible play in worship?
9. How could one person make a difference at a worship service?
10. What fuels worship?
11. How do we speak to God in worship?
12. How do we listen to God in worship?

Practical Applications/Activities

- Develop a list of worship criteria. (See the last paragraph of this chapter for examples.)
- As a group, discuss ways your congregation could be educated about worship.
- List three ways of worship at your church that could be improved.
- List what your church does well in worship.
- Brainstorm ways your church could be more welcoming and inclusive in worship.

Prayer: Jesus, we thank you for the privilege of encountering you in worship. Please help us to learn in worship to draw closer to you so we can go out into the world in Christian service. We praise you for your constant love and your many blessings, especially for this opportunity to explore how we can become a more vital and faithful church. Open our eyes to the needs of this church and grant us the wisdom to do your will. In Jesus' name. Amen.

---

1 Clarence Joseph Rivers, *The Spirit in Worship* (Cincinnati: Stimuli, Inc., 1978), p. 16.

2 [bk].

3 Frank C. Senn, *Christian Worship and Its Cultural Setting* (Philadelphia: Fortress Press, 1983). p. 4

4 Franz Hildebrandt and Oliver A. Beckerlegge, eds., *A Collection of Hymns for the Use of the People Called Methodist in the Works of John Wesley* (Nashville: Abingdon Press, 1988), p. 81.

5 See William B. McClain, *Come Sunday: The Liturgy of Zion* (Nashville: Abingdon Press, 1990), especially chapter 5, "Black Preaching and Its Message: Is There Any Word from the Lord?" pp. 59–71. See also William D. Watley, *Preaching on Special Occasions* (Valley Forge: Judson Press, 1989); and Henry Mitchell, *The Art of Black Preaching* (Nashville: Abingdon Press, 1990).

The Dynamics of Black Worship: A Psychosocial Exploration of the Impulses That Lie at the Roots of Black Worship

by Edward P. Wimberly[1]
from *The Black Christian Worship Experience: A Consultation*
Vol. XIV, published in 1986

Albert J. Raboteau in his work, *Slave Religion*, points out that our slave parents risked floggings to attend forbidden secret gatherings to worship God.[2] Sometimes these meetings lasted long into the night, and at these meetings the slaves poured out their pain, sufferings, and needs to each other and to God. Raboteau goes on to point out that these secret meetings were so important because they provided the slave community an opportunity to fashion its self-image as well as to help others as individuals to shape their self-image. The development of this self-image was contextual and evolved as they reflected on their own experiences, communal symbols, values, and stories picked up from their African past and the Bible. In short, they risked their lives in order that they could discover for themselves who they were, where they were going, and how they were going to get there. This task could not be undertaken under the direct supervision of the slave master, however. It had to take place in secret, unhindered by meddling interruptions calling for conformity to the slave master's specifications.

One impulse behind Black slave worship, then, was the need for a positive self-image. This self-image related to the sense of a positive self that had dignity and worth. Self-image was for the slave that personal and corporate definition of self that transcended the pejorative societal definitions of Black people. Not only did the self-image define personal and corporate worth and dignity, it also defined a personal and a communal sense of purpose and mission in life. In short, Black people came to worship during slavery to seek a personal and corporate sense of identity that could define for them their true place in the universe.

Closely related to the need to find a positive self-image was the need for wholeness that the slave brought to worship. They sought to be whole and to grow in mind, body, spirit, and in relationship to God and others. Self-definition, positive self-image, transcendence of negative societal images of slaves, and finding meaning and purpose in life are all dimensions of the need for wholeness. Yet the need for wholeness helps us to envisage how all these dimensions are contextual and relational. That is, self-image, self-definition, positive self-regard, self-transcendence, and the need for meaning and purpose in life all are enhanced when the person participates in community and grows in relationship to others and to God. A positive sense of self, then, is relational and developmental, and it grows as one participates in a community.

A sense of self grows as one participates in a community that affirms others and that has a worship that affirms. Quality of communal life and quality of worship through self-affirmation are inseparable. This affirmative communal and worship quality in the slave community is what brought the slave to worship. In worship and in community life, the slave found a place for wholeness and affirmation.

Seeking to define a self-image and to find wholeness as individuals and as a people are two impulses that led the slave to risk harsh and cruel punishment in order to worship. The self-image and wholeness impulses could only be expressed if there were viable options to meet this need. That is, expression of human need takes place more vigorously when there are opportunities to have that need met. There had to be those around in the slave community who knew that the risk of being caught was worth it if the end result was encountering within community the God who satisfied needs for wholeness and for positive self-images. Thus, seeking and finding the Divine Master in the midst of suffering was worth the risk of flogging.

The third impulse, then, behind Black worship was the need to respond through praise and thanksgiving to a God who sought them, loved and cared for them, responded to their needs, and bestowed salvation, deliverance, self-worth, meaning, and wholeness to them in the midst of degradation. The slaves risked worshipping because they knew that their salvation was in the hands of God and not in the hands of those who held the whips. They risked worshipping to praise a God whom they knew had responded to and would respond to their needs. Indeed, worship was their response to a God who joined them in their struggle. Worship, then, grew out of their encounter with God in their midst.

From this brief exploration of the slave worship context, three impulses have emerged that lie at the base of Black Christian worship historically. These impulses are 1) the need for a positive self-image; 2) the need for wholeness in the midst of degradation, oppression, and suffering; and 3) the need to respond to God's incarnational presence in their midst, who brought about hope, meaning, salvation, healing, wholeness, and a positive sense of self.

These three impulses are not just the impulses behind the slave motivation for worship. These impulses are still the primary impulses at the roots of Black Christian worship today. Black people will worship where they have an opportunity to gain a positive sense of self, meaning, healing, wholeness, and a sense of purpose to their existence. They will give up a lot if they expect that they will meet the divine Source of their self-worth and wholeness when they attend worship. Indeed, Black people will turn out in droves to give thanks and praise to a God who responded to and will respond to their needs for meaning, hope, a positive sense of self, and wholeness. Moreover, Black people will seek out a community and worship service where they are affirmed.

Today, worship cannot ignore these three impulses and still meet the needs of Black people. It is the task of Black worship to respond to the corporate and individual needs for positive self-image and wholeness as well as to respond to an incarnational God who responds to and fulfills our most important needs. Our task as Black Christians is to become aware of the depth of the needs related to these impulses and facilitate their satisfaction and expression in worship as well as in service within the church and outside the church.

A Concrete Problem and Its Solution

Black Christian worship today has, in many churches, sought to respond to the self-image/wholeness needs of Black people through ideological battles over cultural forms and expressions of Black worship. The goal should be rather to investigate how worship can assist people to discover their self-image and wholeness as children of God and how it can help people to praise God, who is the source of our self-image and wholeness. Ideological struggles become negative when they ignore or obscure a real understanding of the three impulses that people bring to worship.

Part of the ideological battle is a failure to link worship form and expression to the lived life of the community. Form and cultural expression are always related to communal experience, and our task today is to improve the quality of communal experience within the total life of the church. When this happens, worship form and expression become a natural outgrowth of lived life within community. More precisely, worship is an expression of the lived life of a particular community and its ongoing relationship with God. The problem in Black worship in my mind is that we have given too much attention to the form and expression of Black worship without giving the same attention to the quality of lived life within the total worshiping community. There is an imbalance in emphasis.

Several solutions to the imbalance of focus between worship form and expression and the quality of lived life are for the Black church to 1) understand the meaning of worship as it plans worship, 2) examine the historical communal ways that the slave community assisted its members to achieve a sense of wholeness and self-esteem, 3) improve the quality of communal life within the Black church, and 4) create worship form and expression that reflect the lived communal life within the worshipping community.

The Meaning of Worship

Worship is the response of praise, adoration, and reverence to God who enters the lives of Black people and brings meaning, healing, sustenance, and wholeness to them as individuals and as a group. Black worship grows out of what God has done, is doing, and will do on behalf of people of color. Because worship is a response of individuals and of a community, it is something that emerges out of lived life and relationships. The quality of lived life cannot be separated from what the people do to respond to God's activity in the past, present, and in the future.

The response of a community to God's activity requires work by the respondents. Worship in its inclusive sense involves the work of liturgy. William Williman in *Worship as Pastoral Care* points out that liturgy literally means the work of the people.[3] Praise, adoration, and reverence are work, and they are related to the quality of communal and relational life developed in response to God's presence in the midst of that life.

This understanding of worship that involves praise, adoration, and work that is related to the quality of communal life can be envisaged in historical Black worship. The quality of life within the Black Christian community combined work and worship and involved three dimensions that can be called work functions or liturgical functions. These dimensions are organizing, celebrating, and mediating.

Organizing relates to the Black church community centering its lived life around the values emerging out of its encounter with God. One important value has been the agape love ethic on which the self-image of Black people as children of God is based. These values are transmitted and reinforced continually through ongoing relationships, preaching, praying, singing, and scripture reading. They are part of the environmental worldview and provide the symbols and concepts for interpreting experiences within the community. In short, important values become the focal point around which the worship life and the entire life of the community is centered.

Celebrating refers to the joyful affirmation and praise of God. It is the celebration of God's past, present, and future activity of caring and healing on behalf of Black people. Celebrating is more than a catharsis of negative feelings that have built up over the week. While catharsis cleanses one's emotions so that an opportunity is created for God to enter a person's life, celebration grows out of actually being engaged by God and God's people at the level of one's frustration and having found God's activity sufficient for the circumstance. Healing and wholeness only result when catharsis is followed by encountering God at the depth of our need. Too often worship becomes a psychological release valve for pent-up negative emotions that are incomplete. To complete the healing process, the person must be open to God's ministra-tion during and after the catharsis. Celebration truly takes place when the healing process is completed in worship. That is to say, (1) there is catharsis; (2) there is openness to God's presence and God's ministration; and (3) finally, there is healing and wholeness.

Mediating refers to transmitting central values and their dynamic power and properties to those within and outside the worshiping community. The dynamic activity is God's activity, and it relates to caring, healing, affirming, and making people whole. This dynamic power is expressed through the values that organize the community's life, and these values are expressed in the quality of lived life taking place within the community and the quality of lived life of the church's members in the world. The quality of the lived life inside and outside of the church community gets communicated through the quality of relationships the church members are able to establish.

Mediating also relates to the work of creating an environment where people not only respond to God, but it is also creating an environment where people can encounter and be united and reunited with God continually. As they worship, Black people are also continually being renewed by God's presence in their midst. As people worship, wholeness and healing are mediated as they take part in the life of God in their midst. Hope, meaning, and new perspectives are mediated also by encountering God.

These three dimensions of the work functions of worship overlap. In organizing, there are aspects of celebration and mediating. This is also true in the case of the others. Each dimension cannot be fully understood without the help of the other two dimensions.

These three dimensions of the work of worship also help to set the proper stage for relating worship form and expression to the quality of lived life within the community. Indeed, worship form and expression must relate to the organizing, celebrating, and the mediating tasks of worship in the Black church. What we do in Sunday morning worship must be related to the total lived life of the worshiping community. If it is not, worship is sterile regardless of how emotional or unemotional it is.

The Slave Way to Wholeness

The link between worship and the quality of communal life can be envisaged by exploring the ways in which the slave community provided the context and the processes for each slave to experience himself/herself as an affirmed and accepted child of God. This meant that the slave community had within it a communal means of helping its members to experience a positive self-image and to achieve wholeness. The comments contained in this section come from an examination of the slave conversion tradition contained in a forthcoming book by my wife, Anne, and me called *Liberation and Human Wholeness: The Conversion Experiences of Slaves and Ex-Slaves*.[4]

The major question in this section is how did the slave Christian community help to affirm the worthwhileness and wholeness of each of its members? The answer relates to the community carrying out the organizing, celebrating, and mediating dimensions of its worship work.

The organizing task can be envisioned by looking at a youth who had been exposed to the secret meetings where the slaves "stole away to Jesus" in order to sing God's praises and to celebrate God's activity. This youth would join in with the singing and would listen to the grown-ups pray, testify, and preach. This listening activity would provide the youth some symbols, images, and stories on which he/she could organize his/her own experience. These stories, symbols, concepts, and images became the tools of interpreting and reinterpreting that person's life in relationship to the values held high by the community. In this sense, organizing in worship was a hermeneutical task in that worship helped the youth to bring a theological perspective to bear on his/her life.

There was another level at which the slave community enabled the organizing and hermeneutical task. At this level, organizing became closely related to the mediating task. For example, one day this same youth discovered a new and strange stirring in his/her soul. He/she was now not only an observer learning from what adults did, this person became aware of God's action on his/her behalf. At this point, the community became empathic to the youth and identified with him/her by listening to the story that the person shared with the congregation. The congregation mediated affirmation to the person by listening and encouraging the person to tell the story in the midst of the secret meeting. The community not only mediated affirmation, but the mediation facilitated the hermeneutical task. The community gave further interpretative handles to the youth where he/she could better understand and organize his/her life around what was going on. The stories, images, concepts, and communal values gave meaning and focus to the youth's life, and the community empathy facilitated this process.

In summary, the slave community provided a conceptual framework where each person could interpret his/her experiences. This affirmed the person as part of the community. It gave him/her a sense of having a link with the community. At a deeper level, it mediated a personal affirmation that was rooted in God's affirming love. This affirmative love communicated to the community's members that they had infinite worth as God's children. This affirmation was the foundation of the positive self-image and wholeness for each slave.

When this process of interpretation and affirmation was completed, worship moved into celebration. The youth was welcomed into the fold as a mature follower of Jesus Christ, and everyone celebrated what God had done within the person's life and within the community.

Indeed, there was a balance between worship and communal life in the slave community. We need to take a closer look at the mechanisms that facilitated communal affirmation and the content of interpretive world-view that helped the slave to interpret his or her experience.

The brush harbor was the name given to the place where the slaves went to worship. Most of the descriptions of the brush harbor in the literature lead me to conclude that a typical meeting was a small, face-to-face, intimate group. Not only was it small, but there were opportunities for each person to express himself/herself and to have the rest of the people respond affirmatively. Moreover, opportunities were provided for people to express deep emotions through shouting and body movement, although care had to be given so that the noise would not alert the slave master to what they were doing. There was a "pot tradition" where the emotionally excited slave would put his/her head into an iron pot as a way to limit the "noise of joy." There was also the mechanism of sharing called story-telling and listening by analogy that was used by the slave to convey meaning, caring, experiences, and interpretations of reality.[5] This mechanism will be described in further detail in the next section of this presentation.

Important also in the brush harbor secret meeting was the content of the world-view that undergirded the interpretations of reality and the total affirmative behavior of the community. By world-view is meant the undergirding idea framework that gave meaning to the activity taking place within the slave community. The idea framework was usually composed of values that the community cherished and held high. Many of these values operated at the subconscious level and can only be inferred for descriptive purposes from the actual testimonies found in the slave conversion tradition.

The typical slave conversion story was like a three-act play where a need or problem was introduced; then an agent of God, normally a little man, appeared with the solution to the problem; and finally, the solution to the problem was achieved. The story always followed a vision in a semi-dream state which the slave described as a revelation from God.

The conversion stories had themes that were consistent from story to story. Most of the major themes were themes of salvation, liberation from sin, death and rebirth, wholeness, assurance of salvation, encountering Jesus the deliverer, finding healing in the midst of sickness, finding assistance in a crisis situation, and deliverance from the hand of evil.

Repetitive images also accompanied the themes. The most frequent image of the conversion stories was the image of Jesus the liberator and deliverer.

Examination of the themes and images of the conversion stories revealed a world-view whose content was made up of both classical Christian doctrines and an African understanding of the universe. The classical Christian ideas were the sovereignty of God over all of life; the goodness of God; God incarnated in Jesus Christ; a proleptic hope that the eschatological future of peace, freedom, and justice could be experienced partially in this life; God's self-manifestation or revelation through visions and dreams; and the need for repentance and conversion.

The African influence related to a view of the universe as made up of two interpenetrating realities. One reality was the physical and material world, and the other reality was the spiritual world. Yet these two worlds were not mutually exclusive, but they formed a feedback response so that each was informed by the other. The spiritual world often impacted the material world and conversions, visions, healings, and wholeness were often the result. A great deal of sustenance was received by the slaves because they believed that the resources of the spiritual world were available to them through visions, small community life, worship, and many rites.

These Christian classical notions and the African cosmology formed the world-view that helped to inform how the slave interpreted reality. These ideas were organized, mediated, and celebrated through story-telling and listening within the context of small intimate face-to-face groups in worship in the brush harbor. Through the small group and its story-telling and listening, modality, self-affirmation, and wholeness took place.

Improving the Quality of Life within Community Today

The slave empathic environment and its religious world-view are instructive for the Black Church today. In a word, we must begin to improve the quality of care within small groups so that worship can be an expression of the quality of lived life. Moreover, the small groups must be a place where the Christian world-view provides the basic tools for helping people to find personal affirmation and wholeness. Church growth and renewal is taking place because people are finding their needs for affirmation and wholeness met through Bible study and prayer.[6] The small group has become a very vital vehicle for improving the quality of lived life. When more and more of the congregation is engaged in the small group life of the church, the quality of worship will reflect the quality of life.

As already mentioned, worship in the slave environment took place in small groups of people where the primary means of sharing intimately was through a model of analogy—story-telling—listening. That is, this model was used for the purposes of the liturgical functions organizing, celebrating, and mediating. Someone shared their story within the small group and the community listened empathetically. When the story struck an analogous chord similar to someone else's story within the small group, affirmation and celebration occurred. The story of the story-teller had to ring true with other similar stories to be authentic. When the story proved to be authentic, the person's experience and story were affirmed. Through this method, identities were affirmed, interpretations of stories were corrected in the light of the community's experience, and caring was demonstrated.

Like the slave method, many churches are finding that the small group is the primary means where the gospel can affirm selfhood and Christian character is formed. In fact, there would be no real church growth and quality of lived life without the small group today.

The major task of small groups today is to improve the quality of lived life within the church for as many people as possible. In this way, people can come to know personally the care and love of God operating through the power of the Holy Spirit in the midst of community.

Another task of the small group is to help people look at themselves through the eyes of God revealed through others and the scriptures. This is a very strong impulse today just as it was for the slaves. People need to examine their lives and their experiences in a supportive environment in light of the gospel message. This takes place best in small groups, and lends itself to growing in mind, body, spirit, and in relationship to God and others.

The model of small groups for Black churches to improve the quality of lived life is the small slave secret meeting.[7] These groups provided practical models of sustaining relationships of support, empathy, and group presence to persons in need, guidance for practical matters of life, and practical examples of opportunities for persons to care for others. These small groups provided examples of leadership, models for interpreting life in light of the gospel, spiritual guides, and symbols and stories that gave meaning to a theological perspective to life. In summary, the small group experience during slavery can point us to a vital renewal of the church and its worship experience. It is a natural means for developing positive self-images and mediating wholeness.

Creating Worship Expressions

A critical issue is how the small group experience relates to the gathered community celebration. The modern phenomenon is that the local Black church is on the whole not the small plantation group of people that slipped away for a secret worship service. The slave community small gathering combined worship as well as the other face-to-face functions in an intimate, small group. Today, however, connecting the experiences of the small group to the communal expressions of worship on Sunday morning becomes a real challenge because these two aspects are not as intimately related as in the days of slavery.

The slave Christian experience has provided an example that we can follow here. The slave narrative materials are full of examples of songs that emerged spontaneously out of the communal life in the small groups.

One example comes from the testimony of Anderson and Minerva Edwards, a Black Baptist preacher and his wife who were slaves in Texas.

> We didn't have no song books and the Lord done give us our songs and when we sang them at night it jus whispering so nobody hear us. One song went like this.
>
> > "My knee bones am aching,
> > my body's rachin with pain,
> > I lieve I'm a chile of God, and this ain't my home,
> > cause Heaven's my aim."[8]

Another example of a spontaneous song was "Swing Low, Sweet Chariot," but as one slave respondent said, "Us sing 'Sweet Chariot' but us didn't sing it like dese days."[9] This statement referred to slavery days, but the statement was made in the 1930s. The song they sang had the following words:

> Swing low, sweet chariot,
> Freely let me into rest,
> I don't want to stay here no longer,
> Swing low, sweet chariot,
> when Gabriel make las alarm,
> Cause I don't want to stay here no longer.

Most of these songs originated spontaneously out of the lived life experience of people in small groups. This same human occurrence is possible today.

Communal life and experience must find expression in worship on Sunday morning; it is the logical place for the essence of the communal life in the small group to come into full expression. Thus, worship as the work of the people through organizing, celebrating, and mediating the central values and dynamics of the faith can draw on the lived experience within the church.

Small group life consists of personal confessions, forgiving of sins, intercession in prayer on behalf of others and the community, Bible study, building up and encouraging others, and singing. Often emerging out of these experiences are prayer needs, stories of conversions and God's work, stories of growth, development and wholeness, poems, and inspirational words that can be set to music. These group creations, expressions, and stories can become part of the larger worship experience with the proper coordination, sensitivity to privacy, and planning. How this can be accomplished is the subject of this section. The goal is to relate the quality of life taking place in the lived life to renewal in worship.

Depending on the polity, tradition, doctrine of the Black Church and the denomination, the pastor and a worship committee need to have a vital link with the small groups. This can be accomplished by several means. The small group leaders could report the prayer needs and significant developments to the pastor and to a worship committee on a continuous basis, or the pastor could find ways of securing the necessary information through periodic visits and contacts with the small groups. Once such a liaison is established, the pastor and worship committee could pay attention to the unique work of God's Spirit within the small group and find creative ways to incorporate these Spirit-led developments in worship.

Some ideas that could be helpful are: 1) the use of brief testimonies by people from the small group; 2) special times in the service to pray for specific needs (taking care not to violate confidences); 3) coordinating sermons with Bible study and issues of the small group; and 4) special music could be selected that relates to themes and issues growing out of the small group experience. When special musical and lyric expertise exists, new songs can be developed for congregational use. Often new outreach and missionary concerns grow out of small groups. This could be a spark for special sermon series and worship emphasis.

The possibilities are endless for the worship of the small group to impact worship. Yet, this influence is not one way. The corporate worship influences the work and quality of group life also. It gives the overall theological and dynamic inspiration for the small group life. For example, five Texas conferences of the Eighth Episcopal District of the Christian Methodist Episcopal, under the leadership of Bishop C. D. Coleman, meet jointly for one week during the summer at Texas College for a Christian Workers School. Each day at noon, there is corporate worship for the over six hundred participants. In the morning there are large classes for the ministers, Christian workers, and the youth. In the afternoons, there are small, face-to-face classes where there is more group participation. By the middle of the week, the worship services begin to reflect the life taking place in the lived small group. This could be envisaged in the selection of participants, speakers, and liturgy. Great care and effort are taken to have the worship reflect the activity and themes of the small groups.

Not only did the worship receive input from the small group, the small group was the place where worship experiences and ideas could be discussed and integrated. For example, toward the end of the week in the summer of 1984, there was a play on the Book of Revelation. Following an invitation at the end of the play, 130 young people between the ages of twelve and eighteen gave their lives to Christ. That was quite an exciting time; there was great emotional upheaval taking place in each person.

Many of the young people did not understand fully all that was taking place in their lives. The small group and the noon worship service experiences on the next day were devoted to helping the young people to interpret and integrate what happened in their lives. Efforts were also developed for the pastor and church members to follow up on the newly converted when they returned home.

What took place with the youth in worship was linked to the small group experiences earlier in the week. Thus, worship and small group life were integrally related and mutually influenced each other. This example provides a brief glimpse of how worship and lived group life can take place in worship.

Conclusion

Three impulses are at the roots of Black worship today. There is the psychosocial need for a positive self-image as individuals and as a people in a negative environment of oppression. There is also the need to be whole and to grow in mind, body, and spirit, and relationship to others and God. The third need is a worship response to a God who affirmed Black people and bestowed identity on them as individuals and as a group in the midst of oppression. Our task as a Church today is to provide concrete opportunities for worship and for community to respond to these primary needs.

The challenge of meeting these three primary needs has been hindered by our tendency to separate the form and expression of worship from communally lived life in small groups. Yet, worship understood as the people's work of response to God's act through organizing, celebrating, and mediating God's life and activity can be revitalized by connecting lived communal life and worship in more intentional ways. Indeed, worship form and expression, and the quality of communal life are mutually related. Our efforts as leaders need to be two-fold: we need to improve the quality of lived life at the small group level while linking our worship form and structure to that life.

1 Dr. Wimberly is Associate Professor of Homiletics, Garrett Evangelical Theological Seminary.

2 Albert J. Raboteau, *Slave Religion: "The Invisible Institution" in the Antebellum South* (New York: Oxford University Press, 1980), pp. 213–214.

3 (Nashville: Abingdon Press, 1979), p. 48.

4 Edward P. Wimberly and Anne E. Wimberly, *Liberation and Human Wholeness: The Conversion Experiences of Slaves and Ex-Slaves* (Nashville: Abingdon Press, 1986).

5 The link between Bible study and renewal within the Black Church has been demonstrated by Doctor of Ministry graduates from the I.T.C. program. See Marion H. Arnold, "A Theoretical Analysis of a Bible Study Group of Elderly Persons Coping with Change" (D.Min. Project Dissertation, The I.T.C., 1983); Grady Butler, "An Evaluation of the Process of Developing an Openness to Change in a Bible Study Group of a Black Baptist Church" (D.Min. Project Dissertation, The I.T.C., 1979); Philemon S. MKhize, "Evaluation of the Impact of Bible Study Group Upon a Group's Openness to Mission" (D.Min. Project Dissertation, The I.T.C., 1979).

6 Wimberly and Wimberly, *Liberation and Wholeness,* p. 83.

7 Ibid., pp. 69–85.

8 George P. Rawick, ed., *The American Slave: A Composite Autobiography,* Vol. 4, Part II, of the Texas Narrative (Westport, CT: Greenwood Publishing Co., 1972), p. 5.

9 Ibid., p. 26.

Definitions of Praising and a Look at Black Worship

by Brenda Eatman Aghahowa
from *Praising in Black and White:*
Unity and Diversity in Christian Worship, published in 1996

I was glad when they said unto me, "Let us go into the house of the Lord!"
—Psalm 122:1, KJV

Despite the diversity of ways we flesh out worship in actual ritual performance from denomination to denomination, from church to church, and from culture to culture, there is some unity in the form of definitions and common purposes. In chapter 5, worshipers will share what *they* think worship should be and do. For the moment, however, we turn to theoretical discussion by scholars to gain expert insight into the art of praise.

The two congregations under consideration in this book are both predominantly Black in predominantly White denominational structures. One offers worship that is Afrocentric in flavor, the other has a more traditional Eurocentric liturgical style.

Without serious attention to Black worship as a category unto itself, much of the analysis in chapters 3 and 4 will not make sense to those unfamiliar with Black worship. Thus, alongside the rather generic discussion of worship here, we offer insights from Black intellectuals on "praising in Black" and how this differs from Eurocentric worship. We also offer a rationale for highlighting differences between the two styles in the midst of discussions of unity.

Toward a Definition of Worship

In discussing the various ways in which Christian thinkers speak about worship, James White, professor of Christian worship at Perkins School of

Theology, Southern Methodist University, shows affinity for Lutheran theologian Peter Brunner's term, *Gottesdienst*.[1] For White, the word "carries a fine ambiguity, reflecting both God's service to humans and humans' service to God. Brunner capitalizes on this ambiguity and speaks of the 'duality' of worship," says White.[2]

Discussion of the term by John Reumann further illuminates this duality:

> The German "Gottesdienst" means "service to God," but the tricky question is whether to take the genitive, "Gottes-," "God's service," as an objective or subjective genitive. The former would make God the object of the action in serving; Gottesdienst in this sense would be "serving God" and implies much of what "worship" does—honor, veneration, acts of homage, e.g., in cult. The subjective genitive, however, takes the "Gottes-" part of the compound as the subject of the action of serving, and so the sense is "God's serving us." Worship, on that reading, means when God ministers to [us] and brings the Good News and...grace into [our] lives.[3]

The latter definition of the term means, "God doing something for us which we cannot do for ourselves," Reumann continues. He suggests that German scholar Ferdinand Hahn understands the term in just that sense:

> The basis of worship is God's saving action; word and sacraments are God's service to the community. Coupled with it is, however, also a reciprocal aspect, the response side from [human beings], namely service by the community before God. But as Professor Hahn reads the New Testament—and again this is characteristic of Evangelical thought, in light of Romans 12—the church's service before God takes place in the world and especially takes the form of service to the [sister or] brother.[4]

Thus, it seems that the term, from Hahn's point of view, provides two dualities: (1) God's service to human beings and (2) human beings' service to God. The latter is seen not only as public religious ritual, but as social action as well.

This theme of worship as both religious ritual and social action in the world is also developed in Frank Senn's discussion of the Greek term *leitourgia,* from which the word *liturgy* is derived:

Leitourgia derives from *leiton,* "pertaining to the people," and *ergon,* meaning "work" or "service." The term is used variously in the New Testament to refer to the priestly service of Zechariah in the Temple (Luke 1:23), the sacrificial ministry of Christ (Heb. 8:6), the worship of the church (Acts 13:2), and the collecting of money for the poor and suffering saints (2 Cor. 9:12). In these New Testament uses of *leitourgia* the public and social dimensions of cult are exemplified. In its specific Christian use, liturgy is not only public worship but also social action.[5]

A look at the secular roots of our English word *worship* provides another definition or understanding of the word, an understanding that is perhaps implicit in the first two terms *(Gottesdienst* and *leitourgia).* White traces its origin to the Old English word *weorthscipe,* which signifies attributing worth, value, or respect to someone. He points out that it "was and still is used to address various lord mayors in England, and the Anglican wedding service since 1549 has contained that wonderful pledge: 'with my body I thee worship.'… The basic insight we gain is that worship means attributing value and esteem or ascribing worth to another being."[6]

Thus, worship is the duality of God's service to human beings and human beings' service to God, as the work of the people (both in terms of ritual and social action) and as adoration and reverential fear of God. This in no way exhausts the ways of thinking about worship.

White reminds us, for instance, of Paul W. Hoon's discussion (in *The Integrity of Worship)* of worship as "revelation" and "response," and of Evelyn Underhill's suggestion that, "worship, in all its grades and kinds, is the response of the creature to the eternal."[7] Further, White suggests that a survey of the enduring forms of Christian worship—of the seven classical liturgical families (St. Basil, Gallic, Byzantine, Roman Rite, Western Syrian, Eastern Syrian, and Alexandrian) and of the seven Protestant liturgical families (Lutheran, Reformed, Anglican, Free Church, Quaker, Methodist, and Pentecostal)—would provide additional food for thought and "help others clarify for themselves what they mean when speaking of 'Christian worship.'"[8]

Why Distinguish Black Worship from Other Forms?

It will not be possible to understand the description of worship in the two Black congregations without first seeking some understanding of the distinguishing characteristics common to much Black worship, and of its African origins. Some may ask, "Why talk about *Black* worship at all? Why raise barriers? We're all Christians, and we all worship. Worship is (or should be) generic." It might be instructive for any of that mindset to consider the remarks of Black Catholic scholar Cyprian Lamar Rowe, regarding declarations like "We're all human" or, in this case, "We're all Christians who worship":

> Whenever we hear someone say, "We are all human," as if it therefore is quite clear that we are all the same, we must be very careful. Humanity provides a potential. Culture actualizes the potential. I suggest that *there can be no really true and helpful discussion of the sameness of human beings until there is an understanding of our cultural differences....* Obvious truths can conceal very cunning, very destructive lies. So the statement, "We're all human," can be used to camouflage or sweep under the carpet real differences of culture, of identity, of gifts. It can become a lie. There is a psychic as well as an historical truth in Matthew's conviction that if Jesus is the one who is to come, he must come out of the progeny of Abraham. To forget who we are and where we come from is to invite death to ourselves and destruction to our people.[9]

Rowe asserts that for Blacks and Whites (or any other contrasting racial ethnic groups) to engage in dialogue about worship (or any other topic, for that matter), superficially glossing over significant cultural differences is to foster a false cooperation—to create a lie. Indeed, the beauty of true dialogue is that each party has something unique and special to contribute to the conversation, and is allowed to do so. Citing Psalm 137, "How could we sing a song of the Lord in a foreign land? If I forget you, Jerusalem, may my right hand be forgotten?" Rowe points out that the psalmist is saying, "I must not forget, because the Lord gives us our culture as a primary witness." Rowe concludes:

> *If I throw this aside in the interest of some vague commonness,* I am working against what God has clearly indicated I should do.... If I do not share myself and all that I am, then I share nothing. Some people appear to think that all the discussion about and attempts to experience ourselves as Blacks is a

negative reaction. They do not understand. They see it as fragmenting us, tearing us apart. They ask, "Why do you not talk about similarities, rather than our differences?" But *until there is an absolute respect for our differences and a cherishing of a variety in culture and in* gifts, *there can be no talk about similarities that is of genuine and true value.* [10]

In the interest of increased cooperation, then—not only between liberal mainline and Pentecostal Christians, but also between Christians of varying racial and ethnic backgrounds (either within the same faith group or in contrasting faith groups)—Rowe would argue that true cooperation requires us to cease regarding diversity as a hindrance to unity. Rather, we must begin to appreciate differences and to regard them as a mark of God's infinite creativity.

Liturgical Imperialism

Rowe suggests that for African Americans to affirm their own distinctiveness in no way constitutes a denial of others. Perhaps, on the contrary, for others to deny the uniqueness of Black worship (and to deny the *validity* of the existence of such uniqueness) constitutes a kind of *liturgical imperialism* that suggests, "They (African Americans) should worship like us."

Finally, commenting on such imperialism, Rowe describes a Ghanaian novel, *The Torrent*, which he recommends to anyone who desires a better understanding of the predicament of Blacks in a mostly White society. The novel describes a British-run secondary school in Ghana that endeavors to "turn bushboys from their 'savage' condition into 'civilized' people." In so doing, the students are taught to reject much of their own culture in favor of European norms, including the stricture that "one should worship God quietly and with physical restraint, not with emotional rejoicing and body movement." Rowe observes that:

> This kind of *psychic and cultural imperialism* can be stark and bold or it can be a very subtle process. In either case, it has devastating effects on the persons whose culture is not respected and understood. Such a person loses the ability to know where truth is and even to enter into the process of arriving at truth. The whole epistemological procedure which has been part of that person's inheritance is fouled up. What African Americans are asserting, with their growing freedom

to face these problems, is that they want to revive a manner of arriving at and perceiving truth that is congenial to their deep cultural traditions. What is involved in this is *not a denial* of what others do, but an affirmation of what the Lord has wrought in us, a different people and a people who are chosen, in the same way other peoples are chosen.[11]

Generally, then, *liturgical imperialism* has to do with the imposition of European American worship preferences on Christians of African or other descent. It is related to the notion of cultural Christianity, which links European American culture and Christianity, as if the two were one, and views European American worship styles as normative and superior.

This issue is very close to home for me, as my minister-husband is a Nigerian by birth who grew up under the influence of missionaries of an American fundamentalist denomination in the 1940s and 1950s. His love-hate relationship with that particular group eventually prompted him to choose the National Baptist Convention of the USA, an African American denomination, for his ordination rather than his original faith group. His ambivalence toward the denomination in which he was first spiritually nurtured stems from a great deal of rage over losing some of his own rich traditions, only to come to the United States for seminary and discover that African Americans are reclaiming a lot of what he has lost!

Some of the missionaries responsible for his very fine academic and religious education, as a youth and beyond, required those who took on Christianity to put aside many of their own worship styles and rich cultural traditions. They did this in the mistaken belief that these were connected in some instances with the worship of tribal idols. For example, Stephen was required to take on a "Christian" name at baptism. Apparently, his own very meaningful birth name, Iyalekhuosa (pronounced ee-yah-lay-HOE-sah, which means "God's pardon"), was not good enough.

Western suits and dresses often replace the more colorful, beautifully woven traditional garb at worship. Certainly, the style of worship, while spirited anyway, is still more formal and subdued than it would be without the influence of the missionaries.

Liturgical imperialism can be imposed by European Americans on African Americans and others, or even by others on themselves (e.g., by African Americans on other African Americans, by Hispanic Americans on other Hispanic Americans, by Korean Americans on other Korean Americans, etc.). For this to occur (for Blacks, for example, to victimize other Blacks by liturgical imperialism), usually indicates the presence of an identity crisis in the congregation. That is, some congregants wish to include more elements of African American heritage in the worship while others reject these traditions, perhaps previously having run away from Black denominations specifically to avoid them.

Insights from African American theologian Henry L. Mitchell address these matters of identity crisis and the value of maintaining one's own cultural practices in worship.[12] Mitchell describes the experiences of a group of Black ministers who spent a summer in West Africa participating in the Martin Luther King, Jr. Program in Black Church Studies (which he directed in Rochester, New York). The purpose of the trip was to enable these minister-scholars "to see, from a scholarly perspective, the usefulness and validity of Black-culture practices." Mitchell goes on to explain that this experience was necessary because "very often, in our thinking, our traditional practices of Black folk religion seemed to be an interim kind of thing: done for the time being, because that was what moved people and program." Viewing African patterns in Black American worship as an interim kind of state until Black church members become more educated, Mitchell explains, is unacceptable. Because these traditions have integrity and represent Blacks historically and psychically at deep levels, they are not be done away with. Nor are they to be merely tolerated until the masses folk come "up" to the level of the trained Black clergy. Rather they are to be celebrated, preserved, refined, and shared with the world. Mitchell states later in his article that African culture, as manifested in worship and in other aspects of Black American life "refuses to be obliterated" and "cannot be readily erased."[13]

Basically, what we are addressing here and encouraging readers to think about, is the need to distinguish—in worship and other areas of spiritual life—that which is universally Christian from that which is culture-specific. If we can begin to rid ourselves of various types of cultural-spiritual imperialism and try to view things through the broad lens of Christ's saving, inclusive love, then our perspectives on such issues as worship, women in positions of authority, and the Church's involvement in social action will tend more toward tolerance and unity than toward divisiveness, spiritual arrogance, and exclusion.

Black American Worship: Its African Roots

Mitchell also provides help in discerning some characteristics of African culture that are carried over into the worship and everyday life of African Americans. Among other issues, he talks about the Black African world-view, the notion of extended family, and the person in West African culture.

The world-view of African traditional religion does not allow for a separation of sacred culture from secular culture. "African culture is decidedly not dualistic. It has a holistic world view, which is only the tip of an iceberg of contrast between Western or European American culture and African culture," Mitchell comments.[14]

African scholars, including John S. Pobee, formerly of the University of Ghana, discuss the importance of ancestors to the living and how reverence for ancestors, who are a part of the spirit world, points to a meshing of sacred and secular cultures. Pobee notes for instance, the Ghanaian Akan tribal customs of putting down the first morsel of food for the ancestors and of pouring some drink on the ground for ancestors before eating or taking a drink.

> Behind all such acts, at both the individual and communal levels, stands the rationale that a person is surrounded by numerous hosts of spirit-beings, some good, some evil, which can and do influence the course of human life for good or for ill. Consequently, their goodwill is actively and constantly sought, thereby acknowledging the dependence of the living on the spirit world. In this connection, *Akan society hardly draws any distinction between the sacred and the secular.* This is not the same thing as saying that African religion is sacralist, i.e., so preoccupied with the sacred as to prejudice the material well-being of the community and to impede [human] control over [the] environment. Rather the sacred, described by Rudolph Otto as *mysterium tremendum et fascinosum* and representing integrity and order beyond [human] control and challenging [humankind] to the pursuit of development and perfection, on the one hand, and the secular, representing integrity and order such as are within the comprehensive control of [humanity], on the other hand, are not alternatives; rather, they are two complementary ways of looking on reality.[15]

Mitchell contends that the African world-view is based on the extended family. "People in African cultural traditions know no other way to relate to each other.... Every woman is mother, aunt, grandmother, sister, or daughter, and there is no title for a person whose respect and status is in any way to be disassociated from one's own family."[16]

His comments are born out and amplified by Africans themselves, who speak often of the importance of community with respect to the African world-view. Says Mercy Amba Oduyoye, lecturer at the University of Ibadan, Nigeria:

> Africans recognize life as *life-in-community*. We can truly know ourselves if we remain true to our community, past and present. The concept of individual success or failure is secondary. The ethnic group, the village, the locality, are crucial in one's estimation of oneself. Our nature as beings-in-relation is a two-way relation: with God and with our fellow human beings. Expand the communal ideology of clans and ethnic groups to nations and you have a societal system in which none is left in want of basic needs.[17]

United Methodist elder Gwinyal H. Muzorewa, of Zimbabwe, treats the same theme:

> So we find that African humanity is primarily defined by a sense of belonging, serving one's own folk, and kinship. For the African, it is not enough to be a human being; unless one shares a *sense of community*, one can easily turn out to be an enemy. African theology may derive the criteria for belonging to a community of believers from this traditional concept of humanity in community. Such a definition of the community of believers takes collective survival very seriously. Thus, two major concerns of African theology, solidarity and humanization, find clear expression in the context of the community.[18]

Yet the African concept of community is not stifling to the individual or to the development of individual gifts. As J. Deotis Roberts suggests in describing the work of Aylward Shorter on the content of African traditional religions, the "life-in-community" concept has to do with the nature of community, *freedom of the individual within community*, as well as responsibility of the individual for the community.[19]

Mitchell agrees, stating that, with respect to the *person*, African culture seems "more declarative of the uniqueness of each human being and of the fact that that uniqueness ought to be held in utter awe and reverence." This stands in sharp contrast to the culture of mainstream America:

> White people read music and are criticized when they do not follow what is on the paper. A Black person who is trying to be middle class and wants to be like White folks says, "She don't

know how to play what's on the paper. She play anything she feel like playing." Well, that is exactly what African art invites, because African art is done with the understanding that *everybody is artist*. Everybody fulfills himself/herself as he/she feels like being fulfilled, in whatever it is one happens to be doing…. *It is understood* that everybody fashions his [or her] own offering of praise to God in his [or her] own way…. One is supposed to know the theme well enough to use it in the fashion that befits one's spirit. You will hear folk in the congregation say, "Sing your song, child!" And when they say it, they themselves are, in a vicarious way, fulfilled. It is understood that it is "*your* song" and that Beethoven, or whoever, just sort of gave you the initial theme on which you thereafter improvised.[20]

As Roberts notes, "one cannot claim absolute continuity between African traditional religion and Black religious experience…. Too much time and too many circumstances divide Africans from African Americans."[21] Yet, he suggests, it is clear that many Africanisms did in fact survive slavery and continue to this day:

The divergence between E. Franklin Frazier and Melville Herskovits as to the extent to which Africanisms have survived slavery among Blacks in the United States has been much discussed. The slave system broke down the linguistic and cultural patterns of the Africans. Yet the influence of African music, rhythm, and dance is unmistakable in Black culture. It is quite obvious that slaves did not come to America without any religious traditions. In a word, since Africa is a historic reality for Blacks, the African background to the understanding of Black religious experience will always be important. Any enlightenment we can bring through studies made by Africans themselves is needed.[22]

Drawing on Roberts's remarks here as well as similar insights from other scholars and a lifetime of personal experience in the Black church, it seems safe to make the following assertion: As a result of African cultural heritage—combined with the culturally homogenizing effects of the American slavery experience, Jim Crowism, and continuing discrimination—there are some enduring characteristics of Black worship, and these are evident without regard to denomination or American geographical location. As we continue our discussion of the general characteristics of Black worship and then go on to describe worship in the two Black congregations, we will readily see the continuity of the holistic African world-view, the notions of extended family and community, and the view of the person as Mitchell and the others have described them.

Enduring Characteristics of Black Worship

James Cone, in "Sanctification, Liberation, and Black Worship,"[23] offers great help in speaking about characteristics of Black worship. He outlines six principal components of Black worship: preaching, singing, shouting, conversion, prayer, and testimony.[24]

For Cone, the Black preacher is primarily a prophet and the sermon "a prophetic oration wherein the preacher 'tells it like it is' according to the divine Spirit who speaks through the preacher."[25] Cone says the sermon in the Black church is not intended to be "an intellectual discourse on things divine or human."

> That would make the preached Word a human word and thus dependent upon the intellectual capacity of the preacher. In order to separate the preached Word from ordinary human discourse and thereby connect it with prophecy, the Black church *emphasizes the role of the Spirit in preaching.* No one is an authentic preacher in the Black tradition until called by the Spirit. No person, according to this tradition, should decide to enter the ministry on his or her own volition. Preaching is not a human choice; it is a divine choice.[26]

Cone further emphasizes the role of the Spirit in the sermon event by describing Black preaching as essentially "telling the story," and as "proclaiming with appropriate *rhythm* and passion the connection between the Bible and the history of Black people." Spirit-filled, Spirit-inspired presentation of the Word is then coupled with informal "call and response"[27] between preacher and hearers. "Amen," "Praise the Lord," "Hallelujah," and other affirmations voiced spontaneously by the people as they hear the sermon help the preacher know that he or she is on the right track, and that what he or she says "rings true to the Spirit's presence in their midst."[28]

For Cone, *song* in the Black worship experience opens the people's hearts for God's Spirit and intensifies the power of the Spirit's presence. Says Cone, It is possible to 'have church,' as the people would say, without outstanding preaching, but not without good singing. Good singing is indispensable for Black worship, for it can fill the vacuum of a poor sermon.[29] "Good singing" from the Black church vantage point is impassioned, intense, emotional, and spiritually powerful. This is because the soloists and choir members are full of *conviction* about whatever sermon they deliver in song—be it about God's grace, God's provision, God's salvation, whatever.

In the Black church, it is not enough for singing to be technically correct. The priority, to echo Mitchell's comments on improvisation, is to know the main melody well enough to offer musical praise in your own way, thus the common introduction of soloists, "Sister Sally will come to us in *her own way*, singing, 'I Must Tell Jesus,'" or whatever selection. Further, the singer is to offer musical praise in such a way as to bring home biblical truths in a compelling fashion for the hearers.

As the Spirit meets the Spirit, as Spirit-inspired soloist touches the hearts of Spirit-moved hearers, often "all holy hell breaks loose," in the words of Northwestern University professor Leon Forrest.[30] What results is the "shout" that, Cone says, refers not to sound but to bodily movement in response to the Spirit's presence in the worship.

> The Spirit is God's way of being with the people, enabling them to shout for joy when the people have no empirical evidence in their lives to warrant happiness. The Spirit sometimes makes you run and clap your hands; at other times, you want just to sit still and perhaps pat your feet, wave your hands, and hum the melody of a song: "Ain't no harm to praise the Lord."[31]

To this list of responses to the Spirit's movement in the worship service, one might add crying, dancing, and (particularly in Pentecostal churches, but not limited to these) speaking in tongues and other charismata.

Forrest, in a *Chicago* magazine article on worship in several Chicago Black Baptist churches, provides a colorful description of "the shout" or of "getting happy" in response to Spirit-filled singing. Observing worship at Christian Tabernacle on the South Side, Forrest writes:

> The choir here is professional and solemn in the beginning, and then all holy hell breaks loose. On this Sunday, tenor Melvin Smothers leads in a voice of power and fire heading

toward furor. The song is "He Walks with Me," and when Smothers disengages himself from the body of the choir— "Got a new walk...got a new talk" and begins to speak in a witness-bearing, singsong voice, I'm reminded that theater emerged from religion. It is the force of the music—the obsessive and repetitive rhythm—tied to lyrics suggesting a reordering out of chaos that leads one from a state of self-possession to the momentary state of blessed assurance, when you "take hold of your life through Jesus Christ." The singer—as caught-up spiritual performer—is in control and then loses control over his spirit. When he appears on the verge of losing control, he is actually opening himself up to be taken over by the Holy Spirit. And that is why Melvin Smothers and the others can "get happy." Just now two young men become so enraptured that they can't break the spell. Nurses move quickly to the rescue, but the lads are starting into a holy jumping, stomping dance to Jesus, and they are [speaking] in tongues.[32]

Cone has much to say about the phenomenon of "shouting" and how difficult it is for the uninitiated to grasp its meaning:

For White intellectuals, including theologians, Black folks' shouting is perhaps the most bizarre event in their worship services. White intellectuals often identify shouting in the Black church with similar events in White churches, trying to give a *common* sociological and psychological reason for the phenomenon. Such an approach is not only grossly misleading from my theological perspective but also from the premises and procedures that White scholars claim guided their examination. How is it possible to speak of a common sociological and psychological reason for religious ecstasy among Blacks and Whites when they have radically different social and political environments, thereby creating differing psychological and religious orientations? It is absurd on sociological, psychological, and theological grounds to contend that the Ku Klux Klansman and the Black person who escaped him are shouting for the same or similar reasons in their respective church services. Because Whites and Blacks have different historical and theological contexts out of which their worship services arise, they do not shout for the same reasons. The authentic dimension of Black people's shouting is found in the joy the people experience when God's spirit visits their worship and stamps a new identity upon their personhood in contrast to their oppressed status in White society. This and this alone is what the shouting is about.[33]

Cone speaks of shouting in terms of dying and rising again, as a conversion experience. Although conversion is a one-time event associated with baptism in one sense, he says, in another sense "one is continually converted anew to the power of the Spirit and this is usually connected with shouting."[34]

It is possible to take issue with Cone's linking of shouting and conversion simply because there is abuse of shouting in some Black churches. African Americans know what the phenomenon looks like. Thus, some shout whether or not they've been converted by baptism or whether or not they've been "converted" in the second sense Cone speaks of—that is, spiritually renewed by God's Spirit in worship. This is because spiritual enthusiasm is highly valued and prized in Black churches.

When some speak of "conversion," in typical evangelical-Pentecostal terms, the individual who is converted has received Christ as personal Savior, resulting in having a transformed heart and living a transformed life on a daily basis through the empowerment of the Holy Spirit. Some have had this experience of conversion; some have not but shout anyway. They shout artificially, and the seeming spirituality exhibited in worship somehow does not carry over into personal behavior and relationships after worship is over.

The spiritual "glow" derived from shouting in authentic Black worship lasts longer than the duration of the shout itself, and longer than the length of the worship service, for those who are truly converted (converted in either of the two senses Cone suggests or in the evangelical-Pentecostal sense). For the truly converted, the glow of authentic Black worship often lasts until it is time to spiritually "recharge" at the next scheduled worship service.

But Cone is correct in identifying conversion as a significant emphasis in Black worship. Nearly all Black services include an "altar call" near the end of worship. The call is for the unchurched, who are invited to come forward to join the church ("The doors of the church are open") and/or to receive Christ as personal Savior. As Cone points out, the altar is also for the churched who care to renew their commitment to the faith. It might be added that the altar is also the place where the churched and unchurched symbolically can leave their burdens. "Take your burdens to the Lord and leave them there," as the song goes.

In terms of renewing one's commitment to the faith, Cone notes that such renewal is often expressed in testimony:

> To testify is to stand before the congregation and bear witness to one's determination to keep on the "gospel shoes." "I don't know about you," a sister might say, "but I intend to make it to the end of my journey. I started this journey twenty-five years ago, and I can't turn back now. I know the way is difficult and the road is rocky. I've been in the valley, and I have a few more mountains to climb. But I want you to know this morning that I ain't going to let a little trouble get in the way of me seeing my Jesus."[35]

The last element of Black worship Cone highlights is prayer. African Americans believe they have a direct line to God in prayer; that, as is often sung in the Black church, "Jesus is on the main line." Prayer is as impassioned as singing and preaching. "Black prayer should be heard and not read, because the rhythm of the language is as crucial to its meaning as is the content of the petition," Cone remarks.[36] In other words, style and content are inextricably linked.

> The *style* of Black worship is constituent of its *content,* and both elements point to the theme of liberation. *Unlike Whites who often drive a wedge between content and style in worship (as in their secular-sacred distinction), Blacks believe that a sermon's content is inseparable from the way in which it is proclaimed.* Blacks are deeply concerned about how things are said in prayer and testimony and their effect upon those who hear it. The way I say "I love the Lord, he heard my cry" cannot be separated from my intended meaning as derived from my existential and historical setting. For example, if I am one who has just escaped from slavery and my affirmation is motivated by that event, I will express my faith-claim with the *passion* and *ecstasy* of one who was once lost and now found. There will be *no detachment* in my proclamation of freedom. Only those who do not know bondage existentially can speak of liberation "objectively." *Only those who have not been in the "valley of death" can sing the songs of Zion as if they are uninvolved.*[37]

In summation of Cone's points, the "presence of the divine Spirit...accounts for the *intensity* in which Black people engage in worship. There is no understanding of Black worship apart from the rhythm of song and sermon, the passion of prayer and testimony, the ecstasy of the shout and conversion as the people project their humanity in the togetherness of the Spirit."[38]

Cone's discussion of Black worship centers around things like ecstasy, passion, intensity, and liberation (as in freedom of body movement, freedom of verbal affirmation and response, freedom to improvise musically, freedom to respond to the Spirit's movement in the service in any number of ways). Some of the same ideas are echoed and augmented by at least one other African American scholar, the late Dr. Nathan Jones, formerly a Catholic consultant of Black church education and pastoral ministry in Chicago.

In his book *Sharing the Old, Old Story*,[39] Jones develops a schema of the religious expectations of African Americans using phrases and terms that describe nine different aspects of Black religious experience. He touches on issues like the charismatic nature of Black worship (recall Cone on passion in preaching, prayers, and singing, which stems from conversion by the Spirit), its immediacy (which can be likened to Cone's intensity), and its general affective nature (related to Cone's comments on detachment in much European American worship). Jones's discussion of the nine descriptive phrases, and their relationship to Cone's concepts, are summarized in the sections that follow.

1. "I Have Come to Feel God's Presence Near"

Black worship and religious experience emphasize the *subjective* and *intuitive* (feeling), rather than objective, abstract, or rational thinking, Jones says.[40] Jones does not suggest that Black worship is strictly subjective or emotional, that it is mindless. On the contrary, a great deal of thought is necessary to link Black struggles for equality and justice in a mostly White society to the gospel message.

Yet, the most renowned and powerful Black preachers (like the Rev. Dr. Martin Luther King, Jr., the Rev. Mr. Jesse Jackson, the Rev. Dr. James Forbes, and others) consistently package sophisticated theological and political concerns in a charismatic, colorful fashion so that their audiences not only *learn* something important intellectually that relates to their faith but also *feel* God's Spirit active in their midst. Dry, abstract discourses linking the gospel and liberation issues do not go over well with most Black religious audiences, no matter how brilliant in content.

It is probably fair, then, to say that African Americans are often an affective people in worship, which is Jones's point. But to push the point too far and assume that African Americans don't think at all in worship would be an inexcusable denial of their history as a religiously activist people. It need not be recounted in detail here, but it is commonly known that African Americans historically have organized and mobilized for social action in the Black church since other options in the wider society have not always been open to them. The current rash of Black church fires around the United States set by racial bigots is a powerful testimony of the sociopolitical significance of these institutions. These churches pose a real threat to those who still erroneously believe that Blacks are inferior and are to be kept "in their place" in the societal order.

Historically, the Black church has been the only organization African Americans could truly call their own. They have derived (and continue to derive) not only the intellectual, cognitive information, but the spiritual vision, energy, and creativity needed to launch and carry out crucial political and social movements *from* their affective worship and vibrant spirituality. Further, as Clarence Rivers poignantly states, the Western/European American worship tendency toward puritanism (i.e., detachment and suspicion of involving emotion and enjoyment) "has no exclusive claim to religiousness, nor has discursiveness an exclusive claim to intellectuality. *Emotion is also a way of knowing and relating to the world.*"[41]

2. "Make It Plain, [Rev]!"

The learning in Black religious experience is largely *inductive*, rather than *deductive*, with emphasis on the concrete. In spelling out the implications of this for catechesis in Black churches, Jones observes a "serious concern for lively presentations, story-telling, drama, and arts in catechesis in Black churches with a special attention given to the relationship of message to life."[42]

3. "Reach Out and Touch Your Neighbor"

Frequent visitors to Black worship will know of its relational character. Worshipers might be instructed to ask the names of those sitting next to them, to shake hands with people around them, or to turn to their neighbors and say, "God bless you" or "I don't know what *you* came to do, but I came to praise the Lord." Or they might be instructed to leave their seats for a brief period of time and go around the sanctuary to hug and greet as many people as they can. Often, for the benediction, worshipers may be asked to join hands, even across aisles, for the final doxology. All will sway together rhythmically in time to the music as they sing a gospel version of "Praise God from Whom All Blessings Flow." The clasped hands are lifted to the ceiling as the final Amen of a three-fold "Amen" concludes the doxology.

Jones further observes that Black religious experience *relates* to theology, and vice versa. "Theology as well as catechesis uninformed by daily life is virtually meaningless."[43] Thus, the implications for catechesis and worship are "emphasis on *participatory learning* where everybody has a role. Relationships in the learning community are taken seriously, enriching the quality of the session. We are all lifelong learners in the school of faith. *Testifying* gives persons confidence in community, removes barriers between self, God, and others, while it *edifies* the hearers."[44]

Black worship is *participative*, Jones says, as indicated, for example, by the informal "call and response" between minister and worshipers. But also, through testifying (another term encountered in Cone's work), people relate to one another and relate the faith to life, thus edifying (or spiritually building up) all present.

In many Black churches, it is clear from the testimonies and other elements of worship that the *members have a heavy emotional investment in one another.* They are not simply smiling politely and superficially on Sunday and having no relationship during the rest of the week. They are involved in one another's lives—sharing struggles and convictions in testimony, and carrying one another's burdens in prayer. Black worship is relational.

4. "Let Go and Let God"

Black religious experience is *circular* rather than linear in approach to communication. Jones notes an "openness to spontaneity and God's movement, especially in celebration and prayer." He observes "less emphasis on printed materials and greater emphasis on creating a prayerful mood, calling forth the learner's deepest needs, and bringing these to prayer. *No one is hurried. The order of the worship service or liturgy is not the overriding concern.*"[45]

Evidence for the spontaneous and unhurried worship, Jones observes, is to be found in the practice of some Black Pentecostal churches that dispense with any printed order of worship at all. But even in most Black churches, where a printed order of worship is used, the unspoken understanding of the congregation is that the printed order is not set in concrete and is subject to change. This freedom exists in the spirit of "letting go and letting God."

Depending on how the Spirit moves, the choir *might* sing the selections listed in the program, or it might not. At the pastor's or choir leader's direction, choir members might sing something else that seems more appropriate for the needs of the congregation on that particular day.

The pastor *might* preach from the notes or manuscript prepared for that day, or s/he might be led a different direction entirely by the Spirit. Commonly, a Black pastor might say to a congregation something like, "Church, I was planning to preach from Isaiah 6:8 today, but the Lord is directing me to deal with 2 Peter 3:10 instead. So just bear with me." The informal affirmations always come immediately, heartily, and in great quantity: "Help yourself, Rev!" "Well, that's all right!" "Amen!" "Fix it up real good now!" "Take your time!"

And the pastor *will* take his or her time, as will the choir, and other participants in the service, resulting in worship length anywhere from two hours each Sunday at some churches to three hours (or more) at others. For the most part, members do not complain about the length of their worship service or suggest that it should be scaled down to, say, an hour. Every portion of the service "ministers" or provides spiritual uplift and edification. Whether it is the prayer time (when everyone is encouraged to go forward to the altar), the praise time (or the time of "shouting" and rejoicing), testifying, congregational singing, the sermon, the call to Christian discipleship, or even the offertory period—no element or moment in the service is considered dull, a waste of time, unimportant, or uninspiring.

Often, too, highly joyful worship is a very positive alternative to what is waiting at home. It is a pleasure for many African Americans intentionally to leave behind the stresses and strains of home life. These pressures are either intensified and/or caused at least in part by larger societal problems and factors related to the continued second-class citizenship of Blacks in America.

African Americans continue to face discrimination in the job market and in the search for housing. They encounter far higher rates of race-related police brutality in their communities than in others. They confront these and other problems in *addition* to the spiraling inflation and other concerns that all Americans face. This added stress takes its toll on African Americans' health and personal relationships, as evidenced by higher rates among Blacks of divorce and single parenthood; of cancer, hypertension, infant mortality, and the like.

So the church is a welcome refuge. For a few hours on Sunday (and perhaps on selected evenings during the week), there is shelter from the storm. There joy, relief, solace, affirmation, and escape can be found in a warm, intimate, ecstatic worship environment, which ultimately points the Black

Christian back to the world and equips him or her for living, social action, and evangelism in the world.

Certainly, socioeconomic factors also partly determine how much time people spend at church and why. Of nearly 2.5 million Black families in the United States, about 31 percent (almost one-third) live below the poverty level (according to 1993 U.S. Census Bureau statistics). This compares with 12.3 percent for the general population.[46]

Given these economic realities, there often is little money for expensive diversions. Thus, the church serves as a social meeting place as well. Sometimes there are also theological prohibitions against many of the available social entertainments in the wider society, particularly in the more conservative denominations.

But, again, even the African Americans who enjoy a certain measure of educational, professional, and financial success endure a profound sense of alienation and precariousness of position in a mostly White society. Since African Americans have not "arrived" in terms of equality and full acceptance in the larger society, feeling "at home" in worship with others who share one's culture, struggles, and experiences is a high point of the week for many.

The Black church, therefore, serves an important social as well as spiritual/religious role. For large numbers of African Americans (particularly those in the Pentecostal-Holiness tradition who worship several times a week), it would be safe to guess that worship is practically "the only game in town" in terms of social outlets. Furthermore, the best Black worship is always highly enjoyable and never boring. It provides a "good time in the Lord" because of its spontaneity and other joyous elements.

5. "We Want Some of the Action"

Black religious experience is communal rather than hierarchical, Jones stresses, elaborating on his third point about the relational nature of Black worship and religious experience. The implication for catechesis is that it is planned in such a way as to maximize participation by the total community. "No 'Lone Ranger' shows here," he says.[47] Again, the informal "call and response" between minister and congregation during the sermon makes for a colorful dialogue in community rather than a lecture or one-way communication. The sermon is, thus, a communal event.

Similarly, choral selections are also communal events that "maximize participation by the total community." Choral selections, like sermons, are punctuated throughout with the informal affirmations of worshipers: "Amen!"

"Sing your song, girl!," "Yes!," "Thank you, Jesus!," "Well! Well!," and the like. In this way, choral music is shaped by the total community and, as such, is the property of the total community. A musical selection is not simply performance by the choir. It is a communal happening.

6. "Everybody Talkin' 'bout Heaven Ain't Goin' There"

Black religious experience is praxis-oriented. Religious instruction and preaching lead a congregation into action for justice. "Action/reflection is the Church's model. Christian education must be informed and transformed by action. Action must not be hasty but rather shaped by careful reflection in community," Jones says.[48]

Jones seems to reiterate an earlier point—that charismatic worship/ religious experience and thoughtfulness with respect to the larger social questions often go hand in hand. To present the choice of *either* thought-provoking, sedate worship or charismatic, mindless worship, as some do, is to present false alternatives. Charisma and thought-provoking, action-oriented content often go together in Black churches, and indeed they must.

It is critical that the two (lively worship that is personally nurturing and thought-provoking worship that leads to social action) go together, not only in Black churches but in all churches. Some might suggest, for instance, that the liberal mainline churches' dramatic decline in membership over the last thirty years or so (in contrast to a corresponding dramatic increase in membership in the conservative, Pentecostal, and evangelical churches) has much to do with the sterile intellectual worship of these churches—worship that is unappealing to the youth they fail to attract and hold.

7. "God's Not Finished with Us Yet"

Black worship/religious experience is process-oriented rather than static. Says Jones, "No form of catechesis is absolute. Christian life by its very nature is movement, change, pilgrimage for such is God's action among [the] people."[49]

8. "God's Grace Will Run Ahead of You"

Black worship is charismatic, "drawing forth the gifts of the Holy Spirit present in the community of believers." Jones remarks in this regard, "Community gathers around the charisma of a minister of the Word, the catechist. However, it is imperative that the minister have personally experienced the overwhelming power of God's mystery and that he/she is free and willing to share this relationship with others."[50] Jones emphasizes here (as does Cone) both the charisma of the African American preacher and the necessity of this person having a *personal experience of conversion*, an experience about which he or she is willing to testify to others.

9. "My Soul's So Happy I Can't Sit Down"

Jones wants to emphasize the immediacy of God's presence in the life of the believer. He refers to this as "realized eschatology," a concept Cone emphasizes as well in the following passage:

> The Black church congregation is an eschatological communi-
> ty that lives as if the end of time is already at hand. The
> difference between the earliest Christian community as an
> eschatological congregation and the Black church community
> is this: The post-Easter community expected a complete
> cosmic transformation in Jesus' immediate return because the
> end was at hand; the eschatological significance of the Black
> community is found in the people's believing that the Spirit of
> Jesus is coming to visit them in the worship service each time
> two or three are gathered in [God's] name, and to bestow upon
> them a new vision of their future humanity. This eschatologi-
> cal revolution is not so much a cosmic change as it is a change
> in the people's identity, wherein they are no longer named by
> the world but named by the Spirit of Jesus.[51]

What comes through from both Jones's and Cone's comments on the eschatological nature of Black worship is the emphasis on the *immanence* or immediate closeness of God in worship, as opposed to *transcendence* or removedness of a God who is high and lifted up—up and above this earthly realm and earthly affairs.

Jones talks about experiencing the immediacy of God's presence in Black worship in terms of "feeling the presence of the Spirit moving across the altar of your heart in real ways and not vicariously."[52] God's presence is given expression in outward manifestations of "shouting" (recall Cone). Once again, shouting is not just verbal exclamation but also body movement: running the aisles, foot tapping, dancing, clapping, and hand waving.

In a 1985 series of lectures on Black worship at Chicago's McCormick Theological Seminary, Jones also spoke of "silent shouting" or "glowing." He noted that the faces of the quieter "saints," who are not as demonstrative in praise during Black worship, seem to exhibit a supernatural glow of joy and contentment in response to the Spirit's immediate presence in worship. To be sure, this is not all that can be said either on worship as a general category or on Black worship in particular. Obviously, the distinctive features of Black worship that Cone, Jones, and others lift up reflect Black worship at its best— when it is most successful. All Black churches do not attain the worship heights described here, nor does any one Black church perfectly exhibit the best combination of these features all the time. But it is hoped that against this backdrop of information readers can judge for themselves the success of Black worship in the two study churches as the next chapters unfold.

1. Explain the dual meanings of the terms *Gottesdienst* and *leitourgia*. What are the implications for lay participation in worship and the church's involvement in social action?

2. Why is it important to distinguish Black worship from other worship? What are its enduring features?

3. What does liturgical imperialism mean? Can you think of examples of this, either in your denomination currently or in world church history?

---

1 James F. White, *Introduction to Christian Worship* (Nashville: Abingdon Press, 1982).

2 Ibid., pp. 17–18.

3 Ibid., p. xvi.

4 Ibid., pp. xvi–xvii.

5 Frank Senn, *Christian Worship and Its Cultural Setting* (Philadelphia: Fortress Press, 1983), p. 6.

6 White, *Introduction to Worship*, p. 17.

7 Ibid., p. 18. White refers here to Evelyn Underhill's classic study, *Worship* (New York: Harper, 1936).

8 Ibid., pp. 16, 38–43.

9 Cyprian Lamar Rowe, "The Case for a Distinctive Black Culture," in *This Far by Faith: American Black Worship and Its African Roots*, Robert W. Hovda ed. (Washington, DC: National Office for Black Catholics and the Liturgical Conference, 1977), p. 21.

10 Ibid., p. 24.

11 Ibid., p. 26. [Emphasis mine.]

12 Henry L. Mitchell, "The Continuity of African Culture," in *This Far by Faith*, Robert W. Hovda, ed., p. 9.

13 Ibid., p. 13.

14 Ibid., p. 10.

15 John S. Pobee, *Toward and African Theology* (Nashville: Abingdon Press, 1979), pp. 45–46. [Emphasis mine.]

16 Mitchell, "The Continuity of African Culture," p. 9.

17 Mercy Amba Oduyoye, "The Value of African Religious Beliefs and Practices for Christian Theology," in *African Theology en Route*, Kofi Appiah Kubi and Sergio Torres, eds. (Maryknoll, NY: Orbis Books, 1979), pp. 110–111. [Emphasis mine.]

18 Gwinyai H. Muzorewa, *The Origins and Development of African Theology* (Maryknoll, NY: Orbis Books, 1985), p. 17. [Emphasis mine.]

19 J. Deotis Roberts, *Black Theology in Dialogue* (Philadelphia: Westminster Press, 1987), pp. 23–24.

20 Mitchell, "The Continuity of African Culture," p. 12.

21 Roberts, *Black Theology in Dialogue*, pp. 22–23.

22 Ibid., p. 23.

23 James H. Cone, "Sanctification, Liberation, and Black Worship," *Theology Today* (July 1978), pp. 139–152.

24 Ibid., p. 143.

25 Ibid.

26 Ibid.

27 Ibid., p. 139.

28 Ibid., p. 144.

29 Ibid., p. 145.

30 Leon Forrest, "Souls in Motion: Spirited Sundays in Black Churches," *Chicago* (July 1985), pp. 128–35, 148.

31 Cone, "Sanctification, Liberation, and Black Worship," p. 142.

32 Forrest, "Souls in Motion," pp. 134–135.

33 Cone, "Sanctification, Liberation, and Black Worship," pp. 145–146.

34 Ibid., p. 146.

35 Ibid.

36 Ibid., pp. 146–147.

37 Ibid., pp. 142–43. [Emphasis mine.]

38 Ibid., p. 140. [Emphasis mine.]

39 Nathan Jones, *Sharing the Old, Old Story* (Winona, MN.: St. Mary's Press, 1982).

40 Ibid., p. 35.

41 Clarence Joseph Rivers, "The Oral African Tradition versus the Ocular Western Tradition," in *This Far by Faith*, pp. 39–41.

42 Jones, *Sharing the Old, Old Story*, p. 35.

43 Ibid.

44 Ibid. [Emphasis mine.]

45 Ibid., pp. 35–36.

46 U.S. Bureau of the Census, *Statistical Abstract of the United States:* 1995, 115th ed. (Washington, DC: Bureau of the Census 1995), Table no. 752, p. 484.

47 Jones, *Sharing the Old, Old Story*, p. 36.

48 Ibid.

49 Ibid.

50 Ibid.

51 Cone, "Sanctification, Liberation, and Black Worship," p. 140. [Emphasis mine.]

52 Jones, *Sharing the Old, Old Story*, p. 36.

INDICTED

by V. Michael McKay
from *Gospel Industry Today*
published in March 2001

The choir loft has been transformed into a stage. The choir members are now the performers. Choreographed routines are periodically rehearsed to accompany the vocal calisthenics expected of the choir. The staff of church musicians is now called the band. They no longer play with the choir, but for the choir. The band is positioned on the stage, but away from the choir (highly suggestive of a disjointed body). They need not know God to get hired for the 'gig.' As long as they play well, 'they're on.' Their resume is impressive when it reflects whom they have previously played for, or shall I say performed with. They are not required to know much about the church, the Bible, or church music literature. As a matter of fact, they are highly revered when the public knows that their prior involvement has been with a high profile, non–Christian artist. The God–gifted vocalist is now the featured artist, who wouldn't dare sing with the church choir. They just wait for an opportunity to 'get their praise on' as a soloist, with hopes of someday getting discovered. The Minister of Music is no longer called into the ministry and placed in the church by God, but rather recruited by a music search committee, hired by the Director of Human Resources, and managed by the church's attorney. The responsibilities associated with this position are easily understood once one becomes familiar with the culture of the church, always remembering the hiring procedure, instead of the calling principle. This role of the choir director has changed from serving God's people and leading believers into the presence of God, to producing nationally recognized, award–winning recording choirs. Our once hidden agendas are now blatant, especially within the music ministry. Isn't it interesting how we sometimes miss the real moments in life? God, the intended object of our praise, has already made the discovery. We were discovered when He gave us a gift. He simply wants us to seize every opportunity to use it as we praise Him, while He increases our borders.

The sanctuary or building is filled. Congregations or audiences religiously attend worship, holding invisible stubs to tickets purchased for the performance. Once worship officially begins, there is obviously an absence of spontaneity in the experience. The new-testament church experienced spontaneous, unplanned, unpredicted outbursts of praise from saints as they reflected on the good things that God had done for them prior to their arrival into the sanctuary. However, in many of our twenty-first century churches, that does not exist. The Holy Spirit is invited, yet held accountable to the ticking of our clocks. We have made it very clear to Him when to come…and leave. He is scheduled to visit only at specified periods of worship. He is no longer privileged to break–in, but is there by invitation only, sometimes with an RSVP request. Once the visitation privileges are violated, church leaders are quick to pencil Him out, just as we penciled Him in. In the past, we sought the will of God through the leadership of the Holy Spirit. Now we seemingly know God better than He knows Himself, and have overall knowledge far greater than His. We no longer obey His permissive will, but expect Him to obey ours. We no longer honor His presence, but expect Him to honor ours. Church parishioners, impersonating liturgical bodyguards (obviously guarding the wrong body), have been sighted standing on the sideline of our sanctuaries making gestures to worshippers to cease worshipping, when they feel, or have been told to feel, that the spiritual climate for worship is too hot. They bring invisible water hoses with extended footage and high-pressure gauges, ready to shower down those who really desire to worship God and put out fires lit by the Holy Spirit. I must admit, they do their jobs well and know their scripts. When questioned about their actions, they are proud to acknowledge from whom they have been deputized. In my thirty years in church music ministry, I do not recall hearing any of them say that God, Jesus Christ, or the Holy Spirit gave such instructions.

Now, concerning mystical methods for this mammoth madness: Despite all that we have done to create havoc in our worship, I concur with songwriter Bill Gaither…*the church triumphant is alive and well.* It is those of us who have been given charge over God's business who are dead to some of the truths about His plan and purpose for worship. We show symptoms of a severe spiritual illness that only God can cure. Let us explore God's Word and see if we can digest enough spiritual food to heal us. Signs of our healing will be reflected in our worship!

Jesus Christ refers to His house as "the house of prayer" (Matthew 21:13). The church house is His house. I agree with you. It is only wood, brick, and mortar. Nevertheless, it is still His house. What is your house made of? Consider your feelings about my unsolicited actions and activities in your house without your approval, permission, or participation. Would I be *indicted* for invasion of your space, disrespect of your property, and trespassing? How do you really think God feels about our activities in His house? Instead of transforming the choir loft into a stage, let us acknowledge the stage that God sets for each of our visits. That stage is set with possibilities for the broken to be mended, the sick to be healed, those drowning to be rescued, and the lost to be saved. Where do we position ourselves on that stage? While we are performing our 'hot songs,' receiving our accolades, flaunting our skills, doing our dance, navigating our paths to make an artist appearance, reciting our resumes, believing our own press, trying to get discovered, who is living out God's will on His stage? God is depending on us. He depends on us to be good caretakers of gifts, His house, and His people. Who will sit with His children? Who will teach them and give them instructions? Our lack of preparedness as musicians, singers, choir directors, and music leaders is critical. Though this generation's musicians and singers are exceptionally skillful, that alone is just not good enough. The descriptions of David in I Samuel 16:17-18 are essential tools for preparation for the church musician and singer. Here they are. Like David: 1) be a skillful musician, 2) be a brave warrior, 3) be prudent or wise in matters, 4) let your countenance reflect the Christ that lives in you, and 5) keep Christ as the center of your being. We must know God, be good students of His Word, and be good stewards of His gifts. We must love Him, love ourselves, and love one another. Imagine the awesome power of such a triune.

Let us continue with more remarkable remedies for this mammoth madness. The Holy Spirit is a very intelligent being, and the Spirit-filled Christian has the ability to access qualities likened to Him. He, the Paraclete, walks alongside us. He, the Comforter, protects us from all harm, hurt, and danger. When the sanctuary is filled with the Glory of God, that same Comforter and Paraclete is present to perform duties that only He can perform. I must warn that He calls all the shots, operating without our permission. He alone guides us through worship. He sets the climate, and controls the hands on the spiritual clock of which He alone can see. He lights a fire that consumes us, and is much too intelligent to put out His own fire! That powerful fire really never stops burning, but is shut up within the bones and souls of God's people indefinitely. It is He, the Holy Spirit, who warms us, transforms us, renews us, restores us, and keeps us safe along this Christian walk.

Maybe we are intimidated by the Holy Spirit, or afraid to allow Him to take control in our worship services. Are we afraid that if we simply praise God, He will perform all and leave nothing for us to do? In II Chronicles 20:21-22a, God models the power in obedience and of praise: "After consulting the people, Jehoshaphat appointed men to sing to the Lord and to praise Him for the splendor of His holiness as they went out at the front of the army saying: 'Give thanks to the Lord, for His love endures forever.' As they began to sing and praise, the Lord set ambushes against the men of Ammon and Moab and Mount Seir who were invading Judah, and they were defeated." Look at God work! Their praise pleased God and confused the enemy, causing the enemy to turn against each other and destroy themselves. Isn't that what God intends for us today? I believe so. I believe that we should be emphatically empowered by the Holy Spirit so that our praise, our offerings, our testimonies, and our songs will do two things: 1) bring pleasure to God, and 2) confuse the devil and his imps who show up in our sanctuaries, causing all yokes of bondage to be destroyed and broken. I furthermore believe that we should avail ourselves to the power of the Holy Spirit in our attempt to relive II Chronicles 5:13-14: "Accompanied by trumpets, cymbals and other instruments, they raised their voices in praise to the Lord and sang: 'He is good; His love endures forever.' Then the temple of Lord was filled with a cloud, and the priests could not perform their service because of the cloud, for the glory of the Lord filled the temple of God."

I encourage you, my fellow laborers in the faith, to give back to God the house, the gifts, and the control. Completely surrender to Him. Let us seek God's forgiveness for the indictment. We are already forgiven. I look forward to hearing of your victories in worship, and I will tell you of mine!

V.
Composers

Church Music by Black Composers: A Bibliography of Choral Music

by William Burres Garcia
from *The Black Perspective in Music*
Vol. 2, No. 2, published in 1974

This bibliography is a compilation of selected choral compositions by Black composers which are suitable for performance in both Protestant and Catholic worship. In regard to both the compositions and the composers included, the list is not to be considered in any way complete or exhaustive. Rather, my objective has been to provide a listing that is representative of the broad spectrum of church choir literature currently available by these composers. With the exceptions of West Indian Edward Henry Margetson, British Samuel Coleridge-Taylor, and Nigerian Fela Sowande, the composers included were born in the United States.

For the most part, Black Protestant churches traditionally have long incorporated into their worship services the diverse musical styles that constitute the church music revolution now current in White Protestant and both Black and White Catholic worship. The Black church has always had a senior choir to perform anthems and spiritual arrangements and a gospel choir to sing the emotion-filled, folksy gospel music. Today, the music heard in both Black and White churches ranges from unaccompanied singing of Gregorian chant to folk music accompanied by guitars, electric piano, electric organ, percussion, and wind instruments.

Now the church choir conductor is faced with the tremendous challenge of keeping abreast with the trends in today's church music. More than ever before, he is looking to the Black composer for both the so-called revolutionary and the traditional in church choir literature. And rightly so, for the Black composer's output includes some of both. Demand for the choral music of Black composers has made it necessary for someone to make available a listing of their contribution to this body of literature. This is the purpose of the present essay.

Since early 1970, an investigation into the choral music of Black composers has been an ongoing research project of mine. During this time, I have collected an extensive library of the published and unpublished music by these composers. In May 1972, I developed a short bibliography for the Blackhawk Chapter (Northeastern Iowa) of the American Guild of Organists entitled "Church Music by Black Composers: A Selective Bibliography." It included a listing of choral and organ works and a list of ten books on Black music recommended for the church library. This present bibliography is an expansion and revision of the earlier one but with the omission of the organ compositions. A good bibliography of organ works is Herndon Spillman's "A Preliminary Listing of Organ Music by Black Composers," which is available from the Black Music Center, Indiana University, Bloomington, Indiana 47401.

The music was selected with the average church choir in mind. I consider the average church choir to be one whose members have varying levels of musicianship, one with a rather consistent membership stability, and one which abounds with eagerness and commitment. No attempt has been made to grade these compositions in regard to difficulty, as that is a rather elusive thing to measure. Critical examination of sample or reference copies of the literature obviously is the best means of determining usability, suitability, and difficulty.

The majority of the works are for mixed chorus (SATB). The exceptions include Robert Nathaniel Dett's *The Lamb* and *Now Rest Beneath Night's Shadows* for women's voices; Eugene W. Hancock's collection *Thirteen Spirituals* for equal voices in unison and two parts; Undine Smith Moore's *The Lamb* for two parts; and numerous compositions by Father Clarence Joseph Rivers which incorporate unison and/or congregational singing as alternate versions.

One of the greatest innovations in Catholic church music has been the recent practice of including spirituals, gospels, jazz, and other folk music in the church's liturgy. The impact of this revolutionary practice has been felt in many of the Protestant churches as well. Probably the most influential pioneer in this revolution is Father Rivers, a Black priest of the Archdiocese of Cincinnati and an accomplished musician. Father Rivers has incorporated both the Black spiritual and gospel idioms into his compositions. They are ecumenical in nature, being suitable for Protestant worship as well as Catholic. He provides clearly defined performance suggestions for each of his more than twenty compositions included in this listing.

The categories of literature represented in this listing are Black spiritual arrangements, gospel anthems, original church anthems (that is, in the traditional sense of the term), and multi-movement works. Black composers have been especially prolific in the choral medium, particularly with regard to compositions based on religious texts. One significant reason is that a large number of Black composers, like their literary counterparts, utilize Black folk themes in their works, which results in a large output of choral compositions based on Black spirituals. By using the spiritual in this way, these composers have, in a sense, fulfilled a prophecy given by many of the early Black spokesmen and writers—among them, John Wesley Work II in *Folk Song of the American Negro* (1915), James Weldon Johnson in that important Preface to his *Book of American Negro Poetry* (1922), and Alain Locke in *The Negro and His Music* (1936). They predicted that there would yet come great composers who would take the "sorrow songs" and develop them into great art compositions, throbbing with the race's own heartbeat and worthy to be bound in gold.

More than two generations of such composers are represented in the listing of Black spiritual arrangements. Among them are Edward Boatner, Harry T. Burleigh, Salone Clary, Elmer L. Davis, William L. Dawson, Dett, Jester Hairston, Frederick D. Hall, Eugene W. Hancock, Willis Laurence James, Hall Johnson, Lena Johnson McLin, Herbert F. Mells, Moore, Noah Francis Ryder, William Henry Smith, and John Wesley Work III.

Like the spirituals, gospel songs belong to the people, but there are noticeable differences between the two types. The spirituals grew out of an anonymous group effort and were passed down orally. The gospel song, a product of the twentieth century, is the creation of a composer who is responsible for both the words and music and who preserves the composition either by setting it in notation or by recording it. Gospel music is quite similar to the Black secular folk music forms—especially blues and jazz—in that it is improvisational, spontaneous, rhythmic, and emotional. Unlike the unaccompanied folk spiritual, the gospel song is almost always performed with instruments.

Through the years the gospel song has evolved from a solo song with relatively simple accompaniment to an intricate composition which may be performed by a huge chorus to the accompaniment of many instruments and led by a conductor. Most frequently the published gospel composition provides only a small hint to the typical or expected performance style of the music. Composers of gospel music, and especially those of recorded gospel music, tend to set simplified versions. The performers are expected to draw clues to the performance style of a particular gospel by listening to the recorded composition, or similar recorded ones if it has not been recorded, and by listening to the performances of respected local and nationally known gospel artists. Some of the gospel anthems by Robert J. Fryson and James Furman represent exceptions in that these two composers are successful in their attempt to capture the contrapuntal, improvisatory gospel flavor in the printed score. Also successful in this regard are some original compositions by Davis, Arthur Cunningham, McLin (niece of the distinguished gospel composer Thomas Dorsey), and Father Rivers. My list includes some of their pieces which convey a gospel character, though the pieces are not designated as gospels. These include Davis's *You Gotta Cross the River When You Die*, Cunningham's *Lord, Look Down* and *We Gonna Make It*, McLin's *If They Ask You Why He Came*, and Rivers's *Spirit of Life*.

My listing also includes original anthems by Dett, Cunningham, McLin, Moore, Work, Edward Henry Margetson, Samuel Coleridge-Taylor, Ulysses S. Kay, Mark Fax, and Thomas Kerr. Under the general heading of multi-movement compositions, there are Robert Banks's Negro folk gospel cantata *The Praise Chorale*, Margaret Bonds's cantata *Ballad of the Brown King*, Dett's oratorio *Ordering of Moses*, Hall's oratorio *Deliverance*, McLin's *Eucharist of the Soul*, Father Rivers's *Mass Dedicated to the Brotherhood of Man*, William Grant Still's *Las Pascuas*, and Work's cycle *Isaac Watts Contemplates the Cross*.

Finally, there is a list of ten books on Black music at the conclusion of the choral bibliography, which is strongly recommended for inclusion in the church library. Though some of them reach back to the late nineteenth and early twentieth centuries, the majority of the books represent recent scholarship in the area.

Banks, Robert (b. 1930).
> *The Praise Chorale*, A Negro Folk-Gospel Cantata: I. *Oh, Praise His Holy Name*, II. *The Rivers of Babylon*, III. *Strong Deliverer*, IV. *Land of Peace*, V. *The Amen Song*. SATB, solo, piano. Melville, NY: Belwin-Mills, 1972. #S.B. 893. 47 pp.

Billups, Kenneth Brown (b. 1918).

Cain and Abel! (In the Beginning). SATB, piano. New York: Choral Art, 1968. #S-166. 6 pp.

Stand the Storm, spiritual. SATB, piano. New York: Choral Art, 1968. #R210. 8 pp.

Boatner, Edward (b. 1898).

The Angel Rolled the Stone Away, Easter spiritual. SATB. New York: Ricordi, 1954. #N.Y. 1657. 11 pp.

I Want Jesus to Walk with Me, spiritual. SATB. New York: Galaxy, 1949. #GMC 1735. 7 pp.

Spirituals Triumphant Old and New, edited and arranged by Boatner and assisted by Willa A. Townsend, spiritual collection. Nashville, TN: Sunday School Publishing Board, National Baptist Convention, USA, 1927. 98 pp.

The Star, Christmas spiritual. SATB. Melville, NY: Belwin-Mills, 1964. #F.C. 2379. 9 pp.

Trampin', spiritual. SATBB. New York: Galaxy, 1954. #2019. 8 pp.

Bonds, Margaret (1913–1972).

The Ballad of the Brown King, Christmas cantata with text by Langston Hughes. SATB, SATB solos, piano or organ. New York: Sam Fox, 1961. 56 pp.

Hold On, spiritual. SATB, piano. New York: Mercury, 1962. #MC427. 11 pp.

Mary Had A Little Baby, from *Ballad of the Brown King*, with text by Langston Hughes. Version for SSA, piano. New York: Sam Fox, 1963. 9 pp.

Burleigh, Harry T. (1866–1949).

Deep River and Dig My Grave, spirituals. SATTBB. New York: G. Schirmer, 1913. #5815. 8 pp.

Hold On, spiritual. SATB. New York: Ricordi, 1938. #N.Y. 1113. 13 pp.

My Lord, What A Mornin', spiritual. SATTBB. Melville, NY: Franco Colombo, 1924 (Belwin-Mills, 1969). #FCC412. 7 pp.

Nobody Knows de Trouble I've Seen, spiritual. SATB. New York: Ricordi, 1924. #N.Y. 406. 7 pp.

Were You There?, Easter spiritual. SSAATTBB. New York: Ricordi, 1924. #N.Y. 423. 7 pp.

Were You There?, Easter spiritual, simplified version. SATB. New York: Ricordi, 1925. #N.Y. 592. 7 pp.

Clark, Edgar Rogie (b. 1817).

Go Down, Moses, spiritual. SATB. New York: Bourne, 1953. #731. 9 pp.

Six Afro-American Carols for Christmas: *Christ Is Born, Creole Christmas Carol, Rise Up, Shepherd, The New-Born King, Go Tell It on the Mountain, Mary Had a Baby*. SATB, piano or organ. New York: Piedmont, 1971. 7 pp.

Six Afro-American Carols for Easter: Were You There?, One Sunday Morning, Calvary, They Led My Lord Away, The Crucifixion, He Arose from the Dead. SATB, organ or piano. New York: Piedmont, 1972. 7 pp.

Six More Afro-American Carols for Christmas: *Sister Mary, O, Mary, Sing Christ Is Born, Song of Judea* (words and music by the composer), *Go Where I Send Thee, Angels, Ring Them Bells*. SATB, piano or organ. New York: Piedmont, 1973. #MC 4600. 7 pp.

Clary, Salone (b. 1939).

The Blind Man Stood on the Road and Cried, spiritual. SATB. New York: Warner Bros., 1970. #WB118. 8 pp.

I Want to Live with God, words and music by the composer. SATB. New York: Warner Bros., 1967. #R3490. 8 pp.

When You Hear Those Bells, words and music by the composer. SSAAT-TBB. New York: Warner Bros., 1970. #WB 117. 4 pp.

Where Shall I Go?, words and music by the composer. SATB. New York: Warner Bros., 1969. #W7-1030. 5 pp.

Coleridge-Taylor, Samuel (1875–1912).

By the Waters of Babylon, text from Psalm 137. SATB, SATB solos, organ. London: Novello, 1899. #Anth. 644. 8 pp.

Lift Up Your Heads, text from Psalm 24. SATB, SATB solos, organ. New York: Church Music Review. #1460. 5 pp.

O Ye That Love the Lord, text from Psalms 97. SATB, organ. New York: H. W. Gray. #1623. 4 pp.

Cunningham, Arthur (b. 1928).

Two Prayers: Lord, Look Down, We Gonna Make It, words and music by the composer. SATB, solo. Bryn Mawr, PA: Theodore Presser, 1972. #312-40966. 8 pp.

Timber, words and music by the composer. SATB. Bryn Mawr, PA: Theodore Presser, 1972. #312-40970. 5 pp.

Davis, Elmer L. (b. 1926).

Mary's Little Baby, words and music by the composer. SATB, ST solos. New York: G. Schirmer, 1963. #11076. 8 pp.

You Gotta Cross the River When You Die, words and music by the composer. SATBB, ST solos. New York: G. Schirmer, 1958. #10601. 11 pp.

Dawson, William L. (b. 1898).

Behold the Star, Christmas spiritual. SATB, S T solos, echo chorus. Tuskegee Institute, AL: Music Press, 1946. #T111. 10 pp.

Feed-a My Sheep, text by G. Lake Imes. SATB, piano. Tuskegee Institute, AL: Music Press, 1971. #T134. 11 pp.

Jesus Walked This Lonesome Valley, spiritual. SATB, piano. New York: Warner Bros., 1927. #G821. 6 pp.

Mary Had a Baby, Christmas spiritual. SATB, S solo. Tuskegee Institute, AL: Music Press, 1947. #T118. 6 pp.

Out in the Fields, text by Louise Imogen Guiney. SATB, piano. Chicago: Gamble-Hinged, 1929 (Neil A. Kjos, 1957). #T130. 10 pp.

Soon Ah Will Be Done, spiritual. SATB. Tuskegee Institute, AL: Music Press, 1934, 1947, 1962. #T102-A. 11 pp.

There Is a Balm in Gilead, spiritual. SATB, solo. Tuskegee Institute, AL: Music Press, 1939. #T107. 8 pp.

Dett, Robert Nathaniel (1882–1943).

City of God, text by Samuel Johnson. SATB, Bar or T solo, organ. Glen Rock, NJ: J. Fischer & Bro., 1941. #7736. 12 pp.

The Dett Collection of Negro Spirituals, four volumes. SATB, accompaniment. Minneapolis: Schmitt, Hall & McCreary, 1936, 1964.

I'll Never Turn Back, No More, theme traditional after singing of Mr. Dola Miller; additional texts from *Church Hymns and Tunes.* SATB, S solo. Glen Rock, NJ: J. Fischer & Bro., 1918. #4435. 8 pp.

The Lamb, text by William Blake. Idyll for SSA. Glen Rock, NJ: J. Fischer & Bro., 1938. #7401. 7 pp.

Let Us Cheer the Weary Traveler, spiritual motet. SATB. Bryn Mawr, PA: John Church, 1926. #322-35044. 11 pp.

Listen to the Lambs, a religious characteristic in the form of an anthem. SATB, S solo. New York: G. Schirmer, 1914, 1936, 1941. #8010. 11 pp.

Now Rest Beneath Night's Shadows, hymn anthem, with text by Paul Gerhardt, 1656. SSAA. Glen Rock, NJ: J. Fischer & Bro., 1938. #7399. 8 pp.

O Holy Lord, from the *Story of the Jubilee Singers.* SSAATTBB. New York: G. Schirmer, 1916, 1944. #6579. 8 pp.

The Ordering of Moses, A Biblical Folk Scene, oratorio with text based on scripture and folklore. SSAATTBB, SATB solos, piano or organ, with orchestral parts available on rental. Glen Rock, NJ: J. Fischer & Bro., 1939, 1965. #7230. 123 pp.

Rise Up Shepherd and Follow, Christmas spiritual. SATB, solo, organ. Glen Rock, NJ: J. Fischer & Bro., 1936, 1964. #7218. 7 pp.

Weeping Mary, spiritual. SATB. Glen Rock, NJ: J. Fischer & Bro., 1918. 8 pp.

Fax, Mark (1911–1974).

In Christ There Is No East or West, hymn anthem, hymn by Reinagle. SATB, organ. Manuscript, 1969. Contact: School of Music, Howard University, Washington, DC 20001.

O Holy Night and Silent Night, hymn anthem. SATB, organ. Manuscript, 1963. Contact Howard University, School of Music.

Out of the Depths. SATB. Manuscript, n.d. Contact Howard University, School of Music.

God Be Merciful Unto Us, from Psalm 67. SATB. Manuscript, n.d. Contact Howard University, School of Music.

Rise Up, O Men of God, hymn anthem. SATB, organ. Manuscript, 1969. Contact Howard University, School of Music.

Rise Up Shepherd and Follow, Christmas spiritual. SATB. Manuscript, 1963. Contact Howard University, School of Music.

'Round the Glory Manger, Christmas spiritual. SATB. Manuscript, 1963. Contact Howard University, School of Music.

This Little Light of Mine, spiritual. SATB. Manuscript, 1969. Contact Howard University, School of Music.

Whatsoever a Man Soweth, text from Galatians 6:7–9. SATB, organ. Minneapolis: Augsburg, 1958. #1229. 7 pp.

Fryson, Robert (b. 1944).

Give Your Life to Jesus, gospel anthem, words and music by the composer. SATB, piano. New York: Warner Bros., 1972. #WB 275. 8 pp.

Furman, James (b. 1937).

Go Tell It on the Mountain, gospel anthem, spiritual. SATB, solos I, II, brass ensemble, percussion, piano, organ, and electric bass. New York: Sam Fox, 1972. #PS-183. 14 pp.

Some Glorious Day, gospel anthem. SATB, solo, piano, and electric organ. New York: Sam Fox, 1972. #PS-185. 8 pp.

Hairston, Jester (1901–2000).

Don't Be Weary, Traveler, spiritual. SSATB. New York: Schumann, 1955. #S-1019. 5 pp.

Mary, Mary, Where Is Your Baby?, Christmas spiritual. SSATB. New York: Schumann, 1950. #S-1003. 5 pp.

Oh, Holy Lord, spiritual. SATTBB. New York: Bourne, 1950. #S-1005. 4 pp.

Who'll Be a Witness for My Lord?, spiritual. SATB. New York: Schumann, 1957. #S-1029. 11 pp.

Hall, Frederick Douglass (b. 1898).

Deliverance, an oratorio. SATB, S T Bar solos, piano, with orchestral parts available on rental. Winona Lake, IN: Rodeheaver Hall-Mack, 1963. 76 pp.

Sing...Songs of the Southland, spiritual collection Number III: *Rise-Shine, Great Day, Wait Till I Put on My Crown, Somebody's Knockin' at Yo' Do', Ain't Dat Good News, Hallelujah, I Want to be Ready, Trampin', Stan' the Storm, New Born, Live a Humble, I Can Tell the World*. SATB. Winona Lake, IN: Rodeheaver Hall-Mack, 1955. 31 pp.

Swing Low, Sweet Chariot, spiritual. SATB. Winona Lake, IN: Rodeheaver Hall-Mack, 1925. #1949. 7 pp.

Yonder Come Day, spiritual. SSAATTBB. Evanston, IL: Summy-Birchard, 1955. #B-973. 6 pp.

Hancock, Eugene W. (b. 1929).

Come Here, Lord, spiritual. SATB, solo. Melville, NY: J. Fischer & Bro., 1973. #F.E.C. 10078. 11 pp.

A Palm Sunday Anthem, text from St. Matthew 21:8–9, St. Mark 11:8–10. SATB, youth choir, organ. Melville, NY: Belwin-Mills, 1971. #C.M.R. 3125. 7 pp.

Thirteen Spirituals, collection: *Calvary, Go, Tell It on the Mountain, I'm Troubled in Mind, Let Us Break Bread Together, Lord, I Want to Be a Christian, My Soul's Been Anchored in the Lord, O Redeemed, Swing Low, Sweet Chariot, There's a Star in the East, This Little Light of Mine, Wade in the Water, Walk Together, Children, Were You There?* Equal voices in unison and two parts, with organ and unaccompanied. Melville, NY: H. W. Gray, 1973. #GB 626. 48 pp.

Handy, William C. (1873–1958).

Give Me Jesus, spiritual. SATB, organ. New York: Handy Brothers, 1927, 1954. 5 pp.

James, Willis Laurence (1909–1966).

Negro Bell Carol, text adapted by the composer from folk sources, Christmas. SSAATTBB. New York: Carl Fischer, 1952. #CM 6683. 7 pp.

Oh, Po' Little Jesus, Christmas spiritual. SATB, solo. New York: G. Schirmer, 1937. #8170. 4 pp.

Roun' de Glory Manger, Christmas spiritual. SATTBB. New York: G. Schirmer, 1937. #8169. 8 pp.

Johnson, Hall (1888–1970).

Ain't Got Time to Die, words and music by the composer. SSAATTBB, T solo. New York: G. Schirmer, 1955. #10301. 16 pp.

Cert'ny Lord, spiritual. SSSSATTBB, TB solos. New York: Carl Fischer, 1930, 1952. #CM 6641. 11 pp.

City Called Heaven, spiritual. SATB. New York: Robbins, 1930, 1947. #R3303. 7 pp.

Crucifixion, Easter spiritual. SATB, T solo. New York: Carl Fischer, 1953. #CM 6703. 9 pp.

Fix Me, Jesus, spiritual. SATTBB, S solo. New York: G. Schirmer, 1955. #10278. 7 pp.

Go Down, Moses, spiritual. SATB, Bar solo. New York: Carl Fischer, 1930, 1954. #CM 6739. 7 pp.

Hold On!, spiritual. SATB, T solo. New York: Robbins, 1930, 1958. #3299. 9 pp.

Honor, Honor!, spiritual. SATTBB, T solo. New York: Carl Fischer, 1935. #CM 4579. 4 pp.

I'll Never Turn Back No Mo', spiritual. SATB, Bar solo. New York: Robbins, 1949. #3452. 7 pp.

I've Been 'Buked, spiritual. SATB. New York: G. Schirmer, 1946. #9560. 7 pp.

Jesus, Lay Your Head in de Winder, spiritual. SATB, T solo. New York: Robbins, 1930, 1958. #R3301. 8 pp.

Lord, I Don't Feel No-Ways Tired, spiritual from *The Green Pastures*. SATBB, T solo. New York: Carl Fischer, 1930, 1950. #CM 6502. 9 pp.

Mary Had a Baby, Christmas spiritual. SATTBB. New York: G. Schirmer, 1955. #10359. 8 pp.

Oh Lord, Have Mercy on Me, spiritual. SSSAATTBB. New York: G. Schirmer, 1946. #9558. 8 pp.

Ride on, Jesus!, spiritual. SATTBB. New York: G. Schirmer, 1957. #10483. 11 pp.

Walk Together, Chillun!, spiritual. SATTBB, T B solos. New York: E. B. Marks, 1956. #4006. 15 pp.

When I Was Sinkin' Down, Old American Hymn. SATB. New York: G. Schirmer, 1946. #9559. 9 pp.

Johnson, J. Rosamond (1873–1954).

Lift Ev'ry Voice and Sing, text by James Weldon Johnson. SATB, piano. New York: Jos. W. Stern, 1900 (E. B. Marks, 1928). #831. 4 pp.

Kay, Ulysses S. (b. 1917).

Grace to You, And Peace, text adapted from the Epistle of St. Paul to the Ephesians by Theodore Melnechuk. SATB, organ. New York: H. W. Gray, 1957. #2467. 12 pp.

Lo, the Earth, hymn anthem on "Monkland," text by Samuel Longfellow, melody by John B. Wilkes. SATB, organ. New York: MCA Music, 1966. #12614-062. 4 pp.

Love Divine, hymn anthem on "Beecher," text by Charles Wesley, melody by John Zundel. SATB, organ. New York: MCA Music, 1964. #12615-062. 7 pp.

A New Song, three Psalms for chorus.

    I. *Sing unto the Lord*, text from Psalm 149:1–2. SATB. New York: C. F. Peters, 1961. #6136. 8 pp.

II. *Like as a Father,* text from Psalm 103:13–16. SATB. New York: C. F. Peters, 1961. #6222a. 4 pp.

III. *O Praise the Lord,* text from Psalm 117. SATB. New York: C. F. Peters, 1961. #6229a. 7 pp.

O Worship the King, hymn anthem on "Hanover," text by Sir Robert Grant, 1833. SATB, organ. New York: C. F. Peters, 1960. #6223. 7 pp.

Kerr, Thomas Jr. (b. 1915).

Antiphonal Silent Night. SATB. Manuscript, 1968. Contact the composer: c/o School of Music, Howard University, Washington, DC 20001.

I Will Extol Thee, text from Psalm 145. SSAATTBB. Manuscript, 1942. Contact the composer: c/o School of Music, Howard University, Washington, DC 20001.

Joyous Fanfares for the Nativity. SATB, organ. Manuscript, 1970. Contact the composer: c/o School of Music, Howard University, Washington, DC 20001.

Poor Wayfaring Stranger, folk hymn. SSAATTBB. Manuscript, 1945. Contact the composer: c/o School of Music, Howard University, Washington, DC 20001.

Lindsley, Phil V. S., and K. D. Reddick, editors.

National Jubilee Melodies, collection of spirituals. Nashville, TN: National Baptist Publishing Board, n.d. 158 pp.

McLin, Lena Johnson.

All the Earth Sing Unto the Lord, text from Psalm 96. SATB. Park Ridge, IL: Neil A. Kjos, 1967. #5459. 4 pp.

Cert'nly Lord, Cert'nly, Lord, spiritual. SATB, S or T solo. Park Ridge, IL: Neil A. Kjos, 1967. #5458. 12 pp.

The Earth Is the Lord's, text from Psalm 24. SATB, S solo, organ. Westbury, NY: Pro Art, 1969. #2531. 8 pp.

Eucharist of the Soul, a liturgical Mass in English: *Gloria in Excelsis (Glory to God), Kyrie Eleison (Lord, Have Mercy), Trisagion Holy God, Credimus (We Believe), Sanctus and Benedictus (Holy, Holy, Holy), Pater Noster (Our Father), Pascha Nostrum (Christ, Our Passover), Agnus Dei (Lamb of God).* SATB, organ or piano. Park Ridge, IL: General Words and Music, 1972. #Ed. GC 41. 24 pp.

Glory, Glory, Hallelujah, spiritual. SATB, organ or piano. Park Ridge, IL: Neil A. Kjos, 1966. #Ed. 5430. 8 pp.

If They Ask You Why He Came, words and music by the composer. SATB, piano. Park Ridge, IL: General Words and Music, 1971, #Ed. GC 35. 8 pp.

Is There Anybody Here?, spiritual. SATB, optional piano. Westbury, NY: Pro Art, 1969. #2532. 7 pp.

I Want Jesus to Walk With Me, spiritual. SATB, piano. Westbury, NY: Pro Art, 1969. #2533. 8 pp.

Let the People Sing Praise Unto the Lord. SATB, piano or organ, B-flat trumpet. Park Ridge, IL: General Words and Music, 1973. #Ed. GC 48. 11 pp.

Lit'le Lamb, Lit'le Lamb, spiritual. SATB, S solo. Park Ridge, IL: Neil A. Kjos, 1969. #Ed. 5457. 8 pp.

My God Is So High, spiritual. SATB. Park Ridge, IL: Neil A. Kjos, 1972. #Ed. 5881. 7 pp.

Psalm 117, Praise the Lord, All Ye Nations. SATB, piano or organ. Westbury, NY: Pro Art, 1971. #2604. 7 pp.

Sanctus and Benedictus, with English text. SATB. Park Ridge, IL: General Words and Music, 1971. #Ed. GC 34. 4 pp.

Margetson, Edward Henry (1891–1962).

Far From My Heavenly Home, text by Rev. H. F. Lyte. New York: J. Fischer & Bro., 1932. #6607. 8 pp.

Hark, Hark, My Soul, text by Frederick W. Faber. SATB, children's unison choir. Boston: Boston Music, 1949. #2556. 15 pp.

He Stooped to Bless, text anonymous. SATB. Glen Rock, NJ: J. Fischer & Bro., 1936, 1964. #7198. 4 pp.

Hosanna, Blessed Is He that Comes, hymn anthem, hymn by C. Gregor, 1765. SSAATTBB. Boston: The Boston Music, 1945. #10707. 4 pp.

I Think When I Read That Sweet Story, old Christmas song, text from Jemima Luke, 1841, and freely adapted from the old melody "Salamis." SATB, S B solos, organ. Boston: Boston Music, 1949. #2713. 15 pp.

Jesus Lives! Alleluia!, text by Frances E. Cox and Charles Wesley. SATB, organ. Boston: Boston Music, 1943. #2376. 11 pp.

Lord, What Am I?, text by Lope de Vega, translation by H. W. Longfellow. SATTBB, S T solos. New York: H. W. Gray, 1936. #1374. 7 pp.

Morning Hymn of Praise, text by Benjamin Schmolck, translation by Catherine Winkworth. SATB, organ. Boston: Boston Music, 1945. #2476. 12 pp.

Search Me, O Lord, text from Psalm 139:23–24, Psalm 140:1–4, 8, 10. SATB. New York: J. Fischer & Bro., 1935. #6969. 16 pp.

Sing Me a Joyous Measure, Christmas carol-anthem, text compiled by the composer. SATB. New York: H. W. Gray, 1936. #1409. 8 pp.

Sing Unto the Lord, O Ye Saints, festival anthem text from Psalm 30:4, 5, 7, 10–12. SATB, T solo, organ. Boston: Boston Music, 1954. #2891. 17 pp.

Soft Shines the Starlight, words and music by the composer. SATB. Boston: Boston Music, 1945. #2551. 10 pp.

Still, Still with Thee, text by Harriet Beecher Stowe. SATB. Boston: Boston Music, 1950. #2746. 11 pp.

Strong Son of God, Immortal Love, text by Alfred Tennyson. SATB, S solo, organ. Boston: Boston Music, 1946. #2554. 12 pp.

Whoso Dwelleth under the Defense of the Most High, text from Book of Common Prayer, Psalm 91:1–5, 10–12. SATB, S A Bar solos, organ. Boston: Boston Music, 1942. #2365. 15 pp.

Mells, Herbert F. (1909-1956?).

I Heard the Preaching of the Elders, spiritual. SSAATBB. Boston: C. C. Birchard, 1951. #1576. 7 pp.

Oh When I Get to Heaven, spiritual. SATB, piano. New York: Chas. H. Hansen, 1951. #520. 7 pp.

Merrifield, Norman L. (b. 1906).

Remember, O Lord, text from Psalm 25:6, 7. SATB, organ. Boston: Boston Music, 1964. #13205. 7 pp.

Show Me Thy Way, O Lord, text from Psalm 25. SATB, S or T solo, organ. Boston: Boston Music, 1962. #12733. 7 pp.

Moore, Undine Smith (b. 1904).

Bound for Canaan's Land, spiritual. SATB, T solo. New York: M. Witmark & Sons, 1940. #W3653. 7 pp.

Fare You Well, spiritual. SATB, S T solos. New York: M. Witmark & Sons, 1951. #5-W3419. 7 pp.

Hail Warrior, spiritual. SATB. New York: M. Witmark & Sons, 1958. #W3544. 8 pp.

The Lamb, text by William Blake. SS, organ. New York: H. W. Gray, 1958. #2531. 5 pp.

Let Us Make Man in Our Image, text from *Paradise Lost* by John Milton. SSAATTBB. New York: M. Witmark, 1960. #W3652. 7 pp.

Lord, We Give Thanks to Thee, text from Leviticus 25:9. SATB. New York: Warner Bros., 1973. #WB299. 15 pp.

Perry, Julia (b. 1924).

Our Thanks to Thee, words and music by the composer. SATB, A solo, organ. New York: Galaxy, 1951. #1860. 8 pp.

Song of Our Savior, words and music by the composer. SATB. New York: Galaxy, 1953. #1946. 8 pp.

Ye Who Seek the Truth, words and music by the composer. SATB, T solo, organ. New York: Galaxy, 1952. #1901. 7 pp.

Pittman, Evelyn LaRue.

Anyhow, spiritual. SATB. New York: Carl Fischer, 1952. #CM6692. 3 pp.

Reece, Cortez D. (b. 1910).

Mary Had a Baby, Christmas spiritual. SATB, S solo. Evanston, IL: Summy-Birchard, 1959. #5316. 7 pp.

Rivers, Clarence Joseph (b. 1931).

Amen, five different Amens, plus nine alternate settings. SATB, congregation, and organ. By Rivers, with William Foster McDaniel, Mark Trotta, and Edward Stanton Cottle. Cincinnati: Stimuli, 1970, 1972. 9 pp.

The Anamnesis, with Edward Stanton Cottle and William Foster McDaniel. Settings for congregation and SATB, piano. Cincinnati; Stimuli, 1970, 1972. 4 pp.

Bless the Lord, with Henry Papale and Mark Trotta. Three settings for congregation, SATB, piano. Cincinnati: Stimuli, 1964, 1968, 1972. 7 pp.

Freedom, song by James DeWitt Johnson, new verses by Rivers, arrangement by William Foster McDaniel. SATB, solo, piano. Cincinnati: Stimuli, 1973. 8 pp.

God Is Love, with Henry Papale. Cantor, congregation, SATB, piano or organ (optional guitar). Cincinnati: Stimuli, 1964, 1968, 1970, 1972. 11 pp.

Hail Mary, with Henry Papale. SATB, solo, descant, piano. Cincinnati: Stimuli, 1971. 4 pp.

Like a Dry Land, with Henry Papale and Edward Stanton Cottle. SATB, leader, congregation, piano. Cincinnati: Stimuli, 1970, 1972. 9 pp.

Mass dedicated to the Brotherhood of Man, unison settings by Rivers, and two different choral settings by William Foster McDaniel and Henry Papale: *Lord Have Mercy, Glory to God, Apostles' Creed, Holy, Holy, Lamb of God.* SATB, unison, piano, orchestral parts available on rental. Cincinnati: Stimuli, 1972. 59 pp.; choir books; congregation books; accompaniment score.

A Messianic Psalm, with Edward Stanton Cottle and Henry Papale. SATB, gospel solo, congregation, piano. Cincinnati: Stimuli, 1970, 1972. 9 pp.

My God Is So High, with Edward Stanton Cottle and Mark Trotta. SATB, solo or unison, piano. Cincinnati: Stimuli, 1970, 1972. 5 pp.

Our Father, with Henry Papale and Mark Trotta. SATB, solo, piano. Cincinnati: Stimuli, 1964, 1968, 1972. 7 pp.

Prayer of St. Francis, with Edward Stanton Cottle. SATB, solo or unison, piano. Cincinnati: Stimuli, 1970, 1972. 13 pp.

Resurrection, with Edward Stanton Cottle and William Foster McDaniel. Settings for unison and SATB, piano. Cincinnati: Stimuli, 1970, 1972. 27 pp.

Ride On, King Jesus!!!, spiritual with new verses and adaptation by Rivers, with Edward Stanton Cottle, William Foster McDaniel, and Mark Trotta. Unison, SATB, congregation, piano. Cincinnati: Stimuli, 1970, 1972. 7 pp.

Sing a Song Unto the Lord, with William Foster McDaniel, Edward Stanton Cottle, and Mark Trotta. SATB, cantor, piano. Cincinnati: Stimuli, 1970, 1972. 9 pp.

Soul, words by Rivers, music by William Foster McDaniel. Unison, piano, bass. Cincinnati: Stimuli, 1971. 8 pp.

Soul-Brothers, based on the spiritual "Walk Together, Children," with Edward Cottle. Unison, piano. Cincinnati: Stimuli, 1971. 4 pp.

Spirit of Life, based on the hymn "Come Holy Ghost," with James DeWitt Johnson and Edward Cottle. Unison, piano. Cincinnati: Stimuli, 1971. 5 pp.

Take Away Our Hearts of Stone, text from Ezekiel 11:19; 36:26. with Edward Stanton Cottle and Mark Trotta. SATB, unison, piano. Cincinnati: Stimuli, 1970, 1972. 5 pp.

That We May Live, with Edward Stanton Cottle and William Foster McDaniel. SATB, cantor, congregation, piano. Cincinnati: Stimuli, 1970, 1972. 5 pp.

There Is None Like Him, with Edward Stanton Cottle and Henry Papale. SATB, cantor, congregation, piano. Cincinnati: Stimuli, 1964, 1968, 1972. 5 pp.

Toward One Goal, with Henry Papale and Edward Stanton Cottle. SATB, cantor, congregation, reader, piano. Cincinnati: Stimuli, 1970, 1972. 7 pp.

Trisagion, with William Foster McDaniel and Edward Stanton Cottle. SATB, unison, congregation, piano. Cincinnati: Stimuli, 1970, 1972. 4 pp.

Witness of Christ, text by Paul F. Leibold, music by Rivers, with William Foster McDaniel. SATB, solo, piano and/or organ, guitar, bass, percussion. Cincinnati: Stimuli, 1972. 15 pp.

Ryder, Noah Francis (1914–1964).

An' I Cry, based on a traditional Black theme. SATB. New York: Handy Brothers, 1939. 8 pp.

By and By, spiritual. SATB, S solo. New York: Handy Brothers, 1938. 6 pp.

Gonna Journey Away, words and music by the composer. SATB, A solo. New York: Handy Brothers, 1938. 5 pp.

Let Us Break Bread Together, spiritual. SATB, Glen Rock, NJ: J. Fischer & Bro., 1945. #8117. 4 pp.

My Soul Doth Magnify the Lord, text from St. Luke. SATB, organ. Glen Rock, NJ: J. Fischer & Bro., 1958. 6 pp.

Smith, William Henry (ca. 1908–1944).

Children, Don't Get Weary, spiritual. SATB. Park Ridge, IL: Neil A. Kjos, 1937. #Ed 1007. 4 pp.

Good News, spiritual. SATB. Park Ridge, IL: Neil A. Kjos, 1937. #1005. 4 pp.

Plenty Good Room, spiritual. SSATTBB. Park Ridge, IL: Neil A. Kjos, 1937. #1003. 6 pp.

Ride the Chariot, spiritual. SATB, S solo. Park Ridge, IL: Neil A. Kjos, 1939. #1015. 8 pp.

Southall, Mitchell B. (b. 1922).

The Blind Man Stood on the Road and Cried, spiritual. SATB. Cincinnati: Ralph Jusko, 1960. #J-205. 8 pp.

In Silent Night, A Christmas Vignette in Pastel, with text adapted by composer. SATB. Cincinnati: Ralph Jusko, 1957. #J-106. 5 pp.

I Want Jesus to Walk with Me, spiritual. SATB, S or T solo. Cincinnati: Ralph Jusko, 1960. #J-208. 10 pp.

Steal Away, spiritual. SATB. Cincinnati: Ralph Jusko, 1959. #J-212. 7 pp.

There's No Hiding Place Down There, spiritual. SATB. Cincinnati: Ralph Jusko, 1959. #J-213. 11 pp.

Sowande, Fela (b. 1905).

Heav'n Bells Are Ringin', spiritual. SATB, solo. New York: Ricordi, 1961. #N.Y. 2095. 12 pp.

Still, William Grant (b. 1895).

Christmas in the Western World ("Las Pascuas"), text adapted by Verna Arvey: *A Maiden Was Adoring God, the Lord* (Argentina), *Ven, Nino Divino* (Nicaragua), *Aguinaldo* (Venezuela), *Jesous, Ahatonhia* (Canadian Indian), *Tell Me, Shepherdess* (French Canadian), *De Virgin Mary Had a Baby Boy* (Trinidad), *Los Reyes Magos* (Puerto Rico), *La Pinata* (Mexico), *Glad Christmas Bells* (Brazil), *Sing! Shout! Tell the Story!* (American Negro). SATB, piano or with string orchestra and piano, or with string quartet and piano. New York: Southern, 1967. 44 pp. (chorus and piano).

A Psalm for the Living, text by Verna Arvey. SATB, piano (orchestra parts available on rental). New York: Bourne, 1965. #825. 20 pp. (piano reduction).

White, Clarence Cameron (1880–1960).

Search My Heart, spiritual. SATB. New York: Choral Art, 1952. 4 pp.

Work, John Wesley (1901–1967).

All I Want, spiritual. SATB, S or T solo, organ. Dayton, OH: Lorenz, 1962. #9980. 8 pp.

Do Not I Love Thee, O My Lord?, text by Philip Doddridge. SATB, S solo, organ. Bryn Mawr, PA: Theodore Presser, 1950. #312-40041. 8 pp.

For All the Saints, text by William Walsham How. SATB. New York: H. W. Gray, 1949. #2107. 8 pp.

Give Me Jesus spiritual. SATB, T or S solo, organ. Dayton, OH: Cathedral, 1991. #9901. 7 pp.

Going Home to Live with God, spiritual. SATB, S T solos. Glen Rock, NJ: J. Fischer & Bro., 1934, 1962. #6794, 8 pp.

Golgotha Is a Mountain, from the cantata *Golgotha Is a Mountain*, text by Arna Bontemps. SATB, organ. New York: Galaxy, 1959. 9 pp.

Go Tell It on the Mountain, Christmas spiritual, text adapted by John Wesley Work II. SATB, S T solos. New York: Galaxy, 1945. #GMC 1532. 11 pp.

How Beautiful Upon the Mountains, text from Isaiah 52. SAATB. New York: Galaxy, 1934, 1953. #633. 8 pp.

Isaac Watts Contemplates the Cross, a choral cycle.

    I. *When I Survey the Wondrous Cross* (includes a Prelude to be used only when the entire cycle is performed as a whole). SATB, organ. #485-37033. 13 pp.

    II. *Alas, And Did My Savior Bleed.* SATB, T solo, organ. #485-37034. 10 pp.

    III. *'Twas on that Dark, That Doleful Night.* SATB, B solo, organ. #485-37035. 8 pp.

    IV. *How Condescending and How Kind.* SATB, S solo, organ. #485-37036. 7 pp.

    V. *Now for a Tune of Lofty Praise.* SATB, organ. #485-37037. 10 pp.

    VI. *Hosanna to the Prince of Light.* SATB, S A T B solos, organ. #485-37038. 9 pp.

    Nashville, TN: Broadman, 1962.

I've Been Listening, spiritual. SATB, solo, organ. Dayton, OH: Temple, 1965. #C259. 7 pp.

Jesus, Thou Joy of Loving Hearts, text by Bernard of Clairvaux. SATB, organ. Philadelphia: Elkan-Vogel, 1967. #1247. 9 pp.

Jubilee, spiritual collection: *Were You There When They Crucified My Lord?; Keep Me from Sinking Down; Walk Together, Children; Oh Peter, Go Ring Dem Bells; Let Us Cheer the Weary Traveller; Run, Mourner, Run;*

Let Us Break Bread Together on Our Knees; We'll Die in the Field; Tell All the World, John; Go Down, Moses. SATB. New York: Holt, Rinehart and Winston, 1962. 62 pp.

The Light of God, text by R. Confer. SATB, piano or organ. New York: Remick, 1962. #R3424. 6 pp.

The Singers, text by Henry Wadsworth Longfellow. SATB, Bar solo, piano or organ. New York: Mills, 1949. 23 pp.

Sinner, Please Don't Let This Harvest Pass, spiritual. SATTBB, S solo. Bryn Mawr, PA: John Church, 1952. #322-40020. 11 pp.

The Sun Himself Shall Fade, text from Gallagher. SATB, A solo, organ. New York: Galaxy, 1951. #1848. 8 pp.

This Little Light O' Mine, spiritual. SATB, S solo. New York: Galaxy, 1943. #1384. 7 pp.

Wasn't That a Mighty Day?, adapted from a Christmas spiritual. SATB. Glen Rock, NJ: J. Fischer & Bro., 1934, 1962. #6835. 7 pp.

Way Over in Egypt Land, spiritual. SATB. New York: Galaxy, 1947. #1574. 11 pp.

You Hear the Lambs A-Crying, spiritual. SATB, S T solos, organ. Dayton, OH: Cathedral, 1965. #9934. 7 pp.

You May Bury Me in the East, spiritual. SATB, S or A solo. Boston: E. C. Schirmer, 1958. #2413. 10 pp.

Recommended Books on Black Music for the Church Library

Cone, James H. *The Spirituals and the Blues: An Interpretation.* (New York: Seabury Press, 1972).

de Lerma, Dominique-René, ed. *The Black-American Musical Heritage* (Kent, OH: Kent State University Press, 1970).

Ibid. *Reflections on Afro-American Music* (Kent, OH: Kent State University Press, 1973).

Lovell, John, Jr. *Black Song: The Forge and the Flame* (New York: Macmillan, 1972).

Roach, Hildred. *Black American Music: Past and Present* (Boston: Crescendo, 1973).

Southern, Eileen. *The Music of Black Americans: A History* (New York: W. W. Norton, 1971).

Ibid. *Readings in Black American Music* (New York: W. W. Norton, 1971).

Trotter, James Monroe. *Music and Some Highly Musical People* (Chicago: Afro-American Press, 1969). (Reprint of Boston, 1878).

Work, John Wesley III, ed. *American Negro Songs and Spirituals* (New York: Crown, 1940).

Work, John Wesley II. *Folk Song of the American Negro* (New York: Negro Universities Press, 1969). (Reprint of Nashville, TN, 1915).

Publishers of Choral Music

Augsburg Publishing House, 100 South Fifth St., Minneapolis, MN 55415.

C. C. Birchard, Summy-Birchard Inc./Warner Bros., 265 Secaucus Rd., Secaucus, NJ 07096.

Boston Music Co., Frank Distributing Corp., 116 Boylston St., Boston, MA 02116.

Bourne, Inc., 5 West 37th St., New York, NY 10018.

Broadman Press, 127 Ninth Avenue, N., Nashville, TN 37234.

Cathedral Press, Lorenz Publishers, 501 East Third St., Dayton, OH 45401.

Choral Art Publications, Sam Fox Publishing Co., Plymouth Music Co., 170 NE 33rd St., Ft. Lauderdale, FL 33334.

Church Music Review, Belwin Mills Publishing Corp., Warner Bros. Music, 10585 Santa Monica Blvd., Los Angeles, CA 90025.

John Church Company, Theodore Presser Co., Presser Place, Bryn Mawr, PA 19010.

Franco Colombo, Belwin-Mills Publishing Corp., Warner Bros. Music, 10585 Santa Monica Blvd., Los Angeles, CA 90025.

Elkan-Vogel Co., Theodore Presser Co., Presser Place, Bryn Mawr, PA 19010.

Carl Fischer, Inc., 65 Bleecker St., New York, NY 10012.

J. Fischer & Bro., Belwin-Mills Publishing Corp.,Warner Bros. Music, 10585 Santa Monica Blvd., Los Angeles, CA 90025.

Sam Fox Publishing Corp., Plymouth Music Co., 170 NE 33rd St., Ft. Lauderdale, FL 33334.

GIA Publications, Inc., 7404 S. Mason Ave., Chicago, IL 60638.

Galaxy Music Corp., 2121 Broadway, New York, NY 10023.

General Words and Music Co., Neil A. Kjos Music Co., 4380 Jutland Dr., San Diego, CA 92117.

H. W. Gray Music, Belwin-Mills Publishing Corp., Warner Bros. Music, 10585 Santa Monica Blvd., Los Angeles, CA 90025.

Handy Brothers Music Company, 200 West 72 St., New York, NY 10023.

Hansen Publications, Inc., 1842 West Avenue, Miami, FL 33139.

Holt, Rinehart and Winston Publishers, 383 Madison Avenue, New York, NY 10017.

Hope Publishing Co., 380 Main Place, Carol Stream, IL 60188.

Ralph Jusko Publishing Co., The Willis Music Co., 7380 Industrial Rd., Florence, KY 41042.

Neil A. Kjos Music Co., 4380 Jutland Dr., San Diego, CA 92117.

Lorenz Publishing Co., 501 East Third St., Dayton, OH 45401.

MCA Music, 445 Park Ave., New York, NY 10022.

E. B. Marks Music Corp., Hal Leonard Publishing Corp., 7777 W. Bluemound Rd., Milwaukee, WI 53213.

Mercury Music Corp., Theodore Presser Co., Presser Place, Bryn Mawr, PA 19010.

Mills Music, Belwin-Mills Publishing Corp., Warner Bros. Music, 10585 Santa Monica Blvd., Los Angeles, CA 90025.

National Baptist Publishing Board, 523 Second Ave., N., Nashville, TN 37201.

Novello and Co., Belwin-Mills Publishing Corp., Warner Bros. Music, 10585 Santa Monica Blvd., Los Angeles, CA 90025.

C. F. Peters Corp., 373 Park Avenue South, New York, NY 10016.

Piedmont Music Co., E. B. Marks Music Corp., Hal Leonard Publishing Corp., 7777 W. Bluemound Rd., Milwaukee, WI 53213.

Theodore Presser Co., Presser Place, Bryn Mawr, PA 19010.

Pro Art Publications, Inc., Warner/Belwin, 15800 NW 48th Ave., Miami, FL 33014.

Remick Music, Warner Bros. Publishing Co., 10585 Santa Monica Blvd., Los Angeles, CA 90025.

G. Ricordi, Belwin-Mills Publishing Corp., Warner Bros. Music, 10585 Santa Monica Blvd., Los Angeles, CA 90025.

Robbins Music Corp., Big Three, 1350 Sixth Avenue, New York, NY 10019.

10019.

Rodeheaver Hall-Mack Co., Word Inc., Waco, TX 76703.

E. C. Schirmer, 138 Epswich St., Boston, MA 02215.

G. Schirmer, 257 Park Ave. South, New York, NY 10010.

Schmitt, Hall and McCreary Co., Warner/Belwin, 15800 NW 48th
Ave., Miami, FL 33014.

Schumann Music, Bourne, Inc., 5 West 37th St., New York, NY 10018.

Southern Music Co., 1619 Broadway, New York, NY 10019.

Stimuli, Inc., Box 20066, Cincinnati, OH 45220.

Summy-Birchard Co., Warner Bros., 265 Secaucus Rd., Secaucus, NJ
07096.

Sunday School Publishing Board, National Baptist Convention, USA,
330 Charlotte, Nashville, TN 37201.

Temple Press, Lorenz Publishing Co., 501 East Third St., Dayton, OH
45401.

Tuskegee Music Press, Neil A. Kjos Music Co., 4380 Jutland Dr., San
Diego, CA 92117.

Warner Bros. Music, 10585 Santa Monica Blvd., Los Angeles, CA
90025.

M. Witmark & Sons, Warner Bros. Music Publishing Co., 10585 Santa
Monica Blvd., Los Angeles, CA 90025.

"Introduction" from Choral Music by African American Composers: A Selected, Annotated Bibliography

by Evelyn Davidson White
published in 1996

Black composers have made substantial, noteworthy contributions to both the repertory of choral literature and the cultural heritage of America. Unfortunately, much of this literature, which represents all styles from simple four-part settings to avant-garde pieces, has not been performed because of the difficulty of locating many of these works and also because of a lack of interest. Conductors of singing ensembles should program with much greater frequency choral works representative of the styles of African American composers so that the public will become better educated as to the quality, quantity, and rich variety of compositions and arrangements by Black composers. Throughout the country, we have witnessed an unprecedented increase in choral activities on the part of public schools, colleges, churches, and communities.

> Of all the forms of musical expressions, choral singing is the most accessible to the amateur.... Because extensive and serious musical study is not an essential prerequisite for a satisfying choral experience, many children, teenagers, and adults throughout the world find delight and fulfillment as regular participants in this form of musical endeavor. It is the one art form that can provide for the nonprofessional a glimpse of

transcendental beauty and musical self-fulfillment usually reserved for those who have devoted years of practice and study to their instruments.[1]

Opportunities for public performance of choral music are greater now than ever. Conductors should become more actively involved in helping the public to develop appreciation for choral music by African American composers as well as for choral music representing a broad spectrum of styles and nationalities.

Special mention at this point should be made of choral conductors, now active, who have encouraged and promoted Black composers by regularly programming their art music as well as arrangements of spirituals. These conductors diligently search for music and attract the attention of Black composers, who frequently dedicate compositions to them and their chairs. Such a list would include the names of Kenneth Billups (St. Louis), Wendell Whalum (Morehouse College, Atlanta), Nathan Carter (Morgan State University, Baltimore), William Garcia (Talladega College, Talladega, Alabama), Carl G. Harris (Virginia State University, Petersburg), Noel Da Costa. (New York City and Rutgers University), and Brazeal Dennard (Detroit). The author, who conducts the Evelyn White Chorale, regularly performs music by Black composers and has presented many programs devoted entirely to art music and spirituals of these composers, including a major performance at the National Gallery of Art in Washington, DC, in December 1976.

My experience as conductor and clinician and my involvement as teacher of choral conducting for many years have made me acutely aware of the urgent need for properly annotated bibliographical materials that might serve as a useful tool for busy conductors who wish to perform music by Black composers. Because of the numerous requests I have received for information about these composers, and because of my deep conviction that their representative choral music must be heard and accepted as standard program literature, I have made a comprehensive survey of this music with the fervent hope that such a compilation will serve as an incentive to choral conductors to program little-known composers as well as familiar and unfamiliar works by established Black musicians. Especially does the Black choral conductor have an obligation to introduce to the public music of the highest quality as well as reasonably competent music representing the total spectrum of styles and compositional techniques of Black composers. To fail to do so would be an abrogation of responsibility. The conductor is the critical link between the listener and composer, bringing to life the printed page of music. The conductor's role is significant in the process of weaving music of quality and uniqueness by African American composers into the total fabric of our music culture, where it quite properly belongs.

> Although the classical music of Black composers has received an increasing amount of attention in recent years…it still remains largely an unknown quantity to the public. When references are made to the music of Black composers by the press and the media, it is generally assumed that such references are to blues, spirituals, gospel, or jazz…. Only when this music is provided the opportunity to be heard can a valid judgment be made as to its worth and whether it should have a place in the concert repertory and in music history.[2]

Choral conductors frequently complain about the lack of source material and the limited samples of choral music by Black composers found in most retail music stores. The purpose of this compilation is to supplement inadequate source materials about choral music of these composers and thereby encourage the performance of their music. One has little difficulty locating works by composers who have made significant contributions to choral literature—among them such well-known names as William Dawson, R. Nathaniel Dett, Hall Johnson, Ulysses Kay, Undine Smith Moore, George Walker, and John Work III. A more comprehensive list might well include the names of other highly gifted men and women: Leslie Adams, Noel Da Costa, Mark Fax, James Furman, Adolphus Hailstork, Robert Harris, Thomas H. Kerr, John Price, and Dorothy Rudd Moore, to mention only a few.

Most composers find it difficult to get their works published by major companies, and with the exception of a very small group that would include Ulysses Kay and Hale Smith, this is especially true of Black composers. Several musicians were questioned about problems encountered in getting their works performed, published, and recorded.[3] Some of their responses were as follows:

Thomas Jefferson Anderson
> "I am personally convinced that the availability of records, performances, commissions, and publishers has little to do with musical worth."

David N. Baker

"It is extremely difficult to get your works published or recorded."

Undine Smith Moore

"The role of the Black artist in the culture is not fully recognized. It is as though he does not officially exist…only a small percentage of what I have written has been published or recorded."

Howard Swanson

"I feel that the Black creative artist has, to a great extent, been excluded from American history and the American cultural scene."

The author examined several recommended lists of choral music and found dramatic illustrations of the extent to which the music of African American composers has been neglected. Two widely publicized books on choral conducting include lists of choral music. In one book (1975), approximately 500 compositions are cited; 2 percent of the composers are Black. Only the arrangements of spirituals by these composers are included; no art music is listed. In the second book examined (1974), approximately 300 compositions are listed; only one was written by a Black composer. The glaring omission of works by African American composers is even more notable in the case of another popular list that includes approximately 1,200 titles of choral music. The list of sacred and secular music includes one composition by a Black composer. Approximately 90 spirituals are cited, and even in this category, only 15 are arranged by Black composers.

The quoted comments of recognized composers about the difficulty of publication and the instances of omission of names on popular lists of recommended choral music are incontrovertible examples of the neglect of African American composers. Unfortunately, there is a yawning chasm between our desire to be accepted into the mainstream of the music culture of America and the actual accomplishment of this fact. These circumstances pose a steadily sharpening dilemma for Black composers and for Black America.

(Brief reference should be made here to compositions in manuscript that are included in this compilation. These works represent a rich treasury of choral music and in most cases are available upon request to the composer or surviving family member. The search for works of genuine quality among manuscripts can indeed be an exciting and rewarding venture. In many instances, the best works of a composer are in manuscript because of the difficulty of publication.)

In a bibliography of choral works by Black composers, it is not unexpected that a high percentage of compositions and arrangements would be based on thematic material from African American spirituals and folk songs. Many of these arrangements are extended, elaborated forms—for example, "Way Over in Beulah Lan'" and "Cert'n'ly Lord," by Hall Johnson; "Soon-Ah Will Be Done" and "There Is a Balm in Gilead," by William L. Dawson; "Po' Wayfaring Stranger" and "Talk About a Child," by Thomas H. Kerr, Jr. In these arrangements and many others included in this compilation, the authenticity and uniqueness of the spirituals and folk songs are retained in the extended forms. Nathaniel Dett (1882–1943) was the first composer to use the theme of a spiritual as the "musical" idea on which an anthem ("Listen to the Lambs") is based. In discussing the anthem, Dett stated:

> I recall that I wrote "Listen to the Lambs" out of a feeling that Negro people, especially the students of Hampton Institute, where I was then teaching, should have something musically which would be peculiarly their own and yet which would bear comparison with the nationalistic utterances of other peoples' work in art forms.[4]

Other composers have followed the example of Dett and have fused the elements of the spiritual with elements of the European style in settings and extended choral works.

Nevertheless, because of the policy of some publishers, Black composers have often complained that many of their works that are based on African American folk song literature are not published. Hale Smith, a Black composer and music editor, has observed:

> More esoteric music might be published at times, but the odds are overwhelming that these works will sit on the shelves for years and make no money for anyone. Yet there is recognition that throughout the country there is rising pressure, especially in the school systems, for music relating to the Black experience.[5]

As to the purpose and scope of this bibliography, no attempt has been made to present an all-inclusive list of choral music by African American composers, or to make judgments as to the quality of compositions included; the latter decision must be made by the conductor. While annotated sources are useful, they cannot substitute for the painstaking, time-consuming task of carefully examining, analyzing, and evaluating each choral work. Appropriateness and suitability of program selections must always be determined by the conductor with the capability and resources of a particular choir in mind.

Important sources used for this research project were the Moreland-Spingarn Collection at Howard University, Washington, DC; the Library of Congress; and the Azalia-Hackley Collection in Detroit. The extensive collection of the author and collections of other persons acknowledged earlier were also valuable sources of information. Catalogs of music publishing companies were examined as well as music in local stores.

Probably the most difficult phase of this project was that of locating unpublished music and music published by small companies. In this area of investigation, composers were the chief sources of information.

The entries included in this bibliography are arranged by composer in alphabetical order, and right items of information, as follows, are given for each:

a. Copyright date (first copyright date only)
b. Number of pages
c. Voicing and solo requirements
d. Vocal ranges
e. Range of difficulty
f. A cappella; type of accompaniment
g. Publisher
h. Catalog number (if available)

The category "range of difficulty" may be open to criticism because it is the only subjective evaluation made for each entry and needs to be explained in some detail. This evaluation is made with the "average choir" in mind. The following characteristics have been used to define what may be assumed to be the average choir:

1. A few sight-readers who quickly grasp new music, comprising at least 10 percent of the membership.

2. A high percentage of members who learn notes quickly even though they remain somewhat dependent on the sight-readers.

3. Capabilities for hearing and listening to intervals, rhythmic patterns, harmony parts, and accompaniment.

4. Sufficient capability to handle reasonable ranges with ease.

5. Chorus sections that are strong enough to cope with their own musical assignments while help is being given to other parts.

6. An accompanist who is technically capable.

As Charles Burnsworth has noted,

> No choir, of course, can rise above the technical capabilities and musical sensitivity of its conductor. The old adage that there are no bad choirs, only bad conductors is probably more true than is generally admitted. The standard of the average choir can be met or exceeded only to the extent of the conductor's musical endowments.[6]

The following elements were considered by the author in order to make a determination as to the range of difficulty for each entry:

a. Horizontal movement of each voice part
b. Intervallic relationships
c. Harmonic texture
d. Chromaticism
e. Vocal range
f. Dynamic range
g. Rhythmic complexity
h. Tempo
i. Frequency of modulations
j. Frequency of changing meters
k. Polytonality, atonality
l. Textual complexity
m. Type of accompaniment

The biographical sketches of African American composers and arrangers included in this compilation reveal that approximately 50 percent at some point in their careers conducted college, high school, church, or community choirs.

Black college choirs and their directors have made significant contributions to our musical future by presenting to audiences, most especially the

African American audiences, programs representing a broad spectrum of styles and generally including music by African American composers and singers. Composers have often turned to college choirs for premiere performances of their work. Annual tours and concerts performed on college campuses have probably been the most important means of publicizing the contributions of African American culture until recent years. Some of the best-known touring college groups, many of which still follow a tradition of excellence, have been Cotton Blossom Singers (Piney Woods, Mississippi), Jubilee Singers (Fisk University, Nashville, Tennessee), Hampton Choir (Hampton, Virginia), Howard University Choir (Washington, DC), Morehouse Choir (Atlanta), Talladega Choir (Talladega, Alabama), Tuskegee Institute Choir (Tuskegee, Alabama), and the Utica Jubilee Singers (Utica, Mississippi).

Eileen Southern points out that the "new" generation of composers including Ulysses Kay, Thomas J. Anderson, Arthur Cunningham, George Walker, and Hale Smith won their reputations as composers before becoming college professors.... There has been no pressure on them to write music specifically for performance by Black artists and groups."[7]

Carl G. Harris, Jr., has categorized the chief composers of choral music as follows:

> Black Trailblazers: Harry Burleigh, John Wesley Work, Frederick J. Work, Robert Nathaniel Dett, Clarence White, James Weldon Johnson, J. Rosamond Johnson
>
> Black Nationalists: Hall Johnson, William Levi Dawson, John Wesley Work III, Frederick Douglass Hall, and William Grant Still
>
> Black Innovators: Margaret Bonds, Ulysses Kay, Hale Smith, and Undine Smith Moore[8]

Turner Lawson referred to the early group of composers and the "Afro-American Five":

> If the "Russian Five" achieved success and recognition for their work in the folk idiom of their country, then five Negro composers, born after 1866, deserve the title of "Afro-American Five." These five include Henry Thackery Burleigh (1866–1949); Clarence Cameron White (1880–1960);

R. Nathaniel Dett (1882–1943); William Grant Still (1895–1978), and William Levi Dawson (b. 1899). Covering a total span of ninety-seven years, they bridge successfully the gap between raw folk music and concert music…. In large measure, the creative contribution of the "Afro-American Five" is as nationalistic as is the work of the "Russian Five." If their creative significance falls short of the Russians' achievement from a world point of view, this is understandable when one realizes the racial obstacles which yet, at that time, had to be overcome.[9]

Eileen Southern refers to most of the "post-slavery Black composers—i.e., those born before 1900" as nationalists in the sense that they turned to the folk music of their people.[10]

The young Black composers who emerged during the mid-century years were eclectic…. The one quality they shared in common was that each believed it important to chart his own course…. Some exploited more thoroughly the African tradition with its emphasis on functionalism, communication, and purpose; others made the effort to combine African and European traditions into an integrated whole; a few ignored the problems and wrote wholly in the European tradition.[11]

With this generation of composers, and younger gifted composers including James Furman, Adolphus Hailstork, John Price, Robert Harris, Dorothy Rudd Moore, and many others, the creative activity of African American composers has come to a notable peak, representing a growing diversity of styles and variety in the use of musical forces.

---

1 Ray Robinson, *The Choral Experience* (New York: Harper and Row, 1976), p. 3.

2 Dorothy Maxine Sims, "An Analysis and Comparison of Piano Sonatas by George Walker and Howard Swanson," *The Black Perspective in Music*, 4, 1 (Spring 1976), p. 70.

3 David N. Baker, Lida M. Belt, and Herman C. Hudson, eds., *The Black Composer Speaks* (Metuchen, NJ: Scarecrow, 1978).

4 Vivian Flagg McBrier, R. *Nathaniel Dett: His Life and Works* (Washington, DC: Associated Publishers, 1977), p. 36.

5 Dominique-Rene de Lerma, *Black Music in Our Culture* (Kent, OH: Kent State University Press, 1970), p. 116.

417

6 Charles C. Burnsworth, *Choral Music for Women's Voices* (Metuchen, NJ: Scarecrow, 1968), pp. 55–56.

7 Eileen Southern, "America's Black Composers of Classical Music," *The Music Educator's Journal*, 62, 3 (November 1975), pp. 46–59.

8 Carl G. Harris. "A Study of Characteristic Trends Found in Choral Works of a Selected Group of Afro-American Composers and Arrangers" (D.M.A. dissertation, University of Missouri, Kansas City, 1972), pp. 9–32.

9 Warner Lawson, "American Negro Music and the American Negro Composer—1862–1962," (unpublished).

10 Eileen Southern. *The Music of Black Americans* (New York: Norton, 1971), p. 283.

11 Ibid., p. 462.

Black Composers and Religious Music[1]

by Geneva Southall
from *The Black Perspective in Music*
Vol. 2, No. 1, published in 1974

When James Weldon Johnson published his poem, "O Black and Unknown Bards," in the *Century Magazine* in 1908, he paid homage to the slaves as the creators of America's only true folk music, a priceless legacy of historical Americana. In 1899, the famed Bohemian composer Antonin Dvorák, writing for the same magazine, had lauded the so-called plantation songs as "the most striking and appealing melodies found on this side of the water" and had urged composers to "turn to them as a foundation for a serious nationalistic school of American music." The Negro spirituals are genuine folk songs, for no one individual composer or poet was involved in their creation, and as a group expression they reveal the emotions and experiences of the slaves in America. Removed as we are from the times and conditions which brought them about, it is almost impossible to sense the mood expressed in their melodies and natural harmonies or to grasp the form and content of their texts without becoming familiar with the circumstances of their evolving.

The Roots of Black Religious Music

An examination of slave-song texts provides evidence of how the slaves were able to fashion a lifestyle and set of values which combined Africanisms and New World elements, making it possible for them to endure and maintain their essential humanity despite the process of dehumanization that slavery necessarily forced upon them. The spiritual, then, holds a key to the slave's description and criticism of his environment and, more important, to his positive folk group's answer to life. These songs represent the unconscious efforts of the slave to make sense of a shattering life situation. In the songs, the slave expresses in words, nuances, and melody his weariness, loneliness, sorrow, hope, determination, and assurance.

For the most part, the themes of the spirituals were lifted directly from the Hebrew-Christian Bible. The poetic material was reshaped, however, to apply to the slave's own immediate concerns, the religious concepts being interpreted in the light of the slave's everyday experiences. It is of interest to note that the satirical parody came into being side by side with the spiritual, both song types providing a storehouse of images for the folk composers. These songs, which contained many Africanisms, served as a second language for the slaves and functioned as the prime emotional safety valve during the antebellum and post-emancipation eras.

As the genuine expression of the slave's deepest thought and yearnings, the spiritual speaks with convincing finality against the legend of the docile, happy, contented slave! As W. E. B. DuBois has said, they are truly "sorrow songs" in which the Black man speaks and testifies to his faith in the ultimate gesture of things. In numerous ways the songs are the voice—sometimes strident, sometimes muted and weary—of a people for whom the burden of suffering too often became overwhelming. The frustrations were expressed in the piercing sound of "I've been buked and I've been scorned" and in the entreating prayers of "Lord, keep me from sinking down" for "Nobody knows de trouble I've seed." Despite the brutalities and tortures of slavery, there is a marvelous absence of expressions of hate in the religious folk music of Black Americans. Even in the midst of the greatest inhuman experience endured by man they could sing, "Lord, I want to be a Christian," "I want to be like Jesus," and seek solace in their togetherness, singing "Walk together children, don't get weary" for "Children, we shall be free." In these songs one hears the loud cry for deliverance and freedom; the songs are laments, expressing their aspirations for physical as well as spiritual release. The majestic, old spiritual "Go down, Moses" reminded the slave that the struggle for freedom was age-old, but in "Lord, how much longer" he reveals his weariness and indicates that he would welcome even death to remove him from his misery. At other times his longing for death takes on more optimistic tones; "Deep river, my home is over Jordan, I want to cross over into camp ground" he sings as he pictures himself standing on the bank of the mighty symbolic river. The slave had to be his own analyst. He realized that in his helplessness he was as a child, and he sang "Sometimes I feel like a motherless child" who is "Troubled in mind" and "If Jesus don't help me, I surely will die."

Yes, these simple slave songs reflect the experiences and feelings of a people who suffered tremendously, and the listener must try to understand the real message of the songs if he would really appreciate them. They are not songs of entertainment, and there is little of humor in the sentiments they express—even in the dialect or the rhythms of the music. Frederick Douglass, the famed abolitionist and a runaway slave himself, put the matter quite clearly:

> They were tones, loud, long, and deep, breathing the prayer and complaint of souls boiling over with the bitterest anguish. Every tone was a testimony against slavery, and a prayer to God for deliverance from chains. The hearing of those wild notes always depressed my spirits, and filled my heart with ineffable sadness.... The songs of the slaves represent the sorrows, rather than the joys, of his heart; and he is relieved by them, only as an aching heart is relieved by its tears.[2]

Composers and the Spirituals

Large numbers of Black composers have identified with and understood the songs of their forefathers. This heritage has been used as a source of musical inspiration for their vocal and instrumental composition. Their aims have been to remain true to the spirit of the music, to use the tools of music theory and composition to knit the characteristic idioms of the race music into an ordered expression, but remembering at all times those circumstances which brought about the creation of the folk song models. Most frequently, the choral spiritual arrangements are intended to be performed a cappella, hums and moans being assimilated into the music to heighten the emotion and retain the pathos.

It was the Fisk Jubilee troupe of singers who first introduced the Negro spirituals to the world in 1871 when they embarked on concert tours to "sing money" from audiences in order to ensure that the newly established Fisk Institute would not have to close its doors for lack of money. Their first European tour in 1873 was conducted under noble patronage; they received praise from royalty, musicians, music critics, and music lovers, subsequently appearing in a command performance for King George. The young ex-slaves' rendition of the slave songs brought tears to the eyes of audiences everywhere, and they accomplished several things at the same time: they raised an initial sum of $150,000, which saved Fisk and provided money for the erection of the famed Jubilee Hall; they won an international reputation for themselves; and they made it possible for the world to hear the orally transmitted slave songs for the first time. The song collections derived from the repertory of the

Jubilee Singers may be regarded as the prototypes for the various settings and arrangements produced later by both Black and White composers.

The celebrated African English composer Samuel Coleridge-Taylor (1875–1912) heard spirituals for the first time in 1899 at a Fisk Jubilee concert in London. Although only twenty-four years old, Coleridge-Taylor had already won a reputation as one of the leading composers of his country. His best-known oratorio, *Hiawatha*, had been performed by leading choral societies in Europe and America, and many of his instrumental and vocal works had appeared on the concerts of world-renowned artists. He was fascinated by the slave melodies and determined to make arrangements of them suitable for concert performance. He completed a collection of piano arrangements, entitled *Twenty-Four Negro Melodies*, by December 1904, only a month after his return from a triumphant tour of the United States, and published the set in 1905. In his introduction, Coleridge-Taylor explained his purpose in writing the pieces:

> The Negro melodies in this volume are not merely *arranged*— on the contrary they have been amplified, harmonized, and altered in other respects to suit the purpose of the book. I do not think any apology for the system adopted is necessary. However beautiful the actual melodies are in themselves, there can be no doubt that much of their value is lost on account of their extreme brevity and unsuitability for the ordinary amateur. What Brahms has done for the Hungarian folk music, Dvořák for the Bohemian, and Grieg for the Norwegian, I have tried to do for these Negro melodies. The plan adopted has been almost without exception that of the *Tema con Variazioni*. The actual melody has in every case been inserted at the head of each piece as a motto. The music which follows is nothing more nor less than a series of variations built on the said motto. Therefore my share in the matter can be clearly traced, and must not be confounded with any idea of "improving" the original material any more than Brahms's Variations on the Haydn theme "improved" that.[3]

Harry T. Burleigh (1866–1949) was the second pioneering composer to establish a tradition in Black religious music. He was the first to arrange spirituals for solo voice with piano accompaniment in the style of art songs, thus making them available to singers for use on the concert stage. Even before the publication of his famous "Deep River" in 1916, however, Burleigh had written a piano piece, "Jubilee," which reflects the more spirited expressions of the ex-slaves and points to the growing influence of the then-popular ragtime on religious music. Another composer of a later time, John Wesley Work, Jr. (1901–1967), who won acclaim for his vocal and choral arrangements of spirituals, also wrote a piano piece using Negro idioms. His "At a Certain Church" reflects the influence of the nineteenth century revival songs and camp meeting hymns. And the late Margaret Bonds (1913–1972) made a significant contribution to the repertory of keyboard spirituals with her "Troubled Water" (based on "Wade in the Water"), which shows the influence of the impressionistic style and traces of jazz and blues while retaining at the same time the quiet simplicity of the spiritual.

The tradition of making vocal and choral arrangements of spirituals begun by Burleigh was destined to be long-lived. Hardly without exception, most Black composers have contributed to the ever-enlarging repertory of the "art-song" spirituals. Hall Johnson (1888–1970) provided a new dimension to the tradition with his arrangements, which included not only original texts and tunes but also those of his own invention. Possessing strong opinions about how Negro folk songs should be sung, he organized a professional chorus in 1925 for the express purpose of preserving the genuine performance style of the spiritual. The Hall Johnson Choir performed in concert halls, in motion pictures, and on Broadway. Johnson's aim was to recreate with his professional group the original folk style of singing before the world would have forgotten what a glorious sound Blacks produce when they sing in a truly spontaneous and uninhibited manner.[4]

The Gospel Tradition

Students of Black history know that the old-time Black preacher is not yet dead. He has survived not only in Black literature, but also in the flesh. James Weldon Johnson's *God's Trombones* provides a vivid picture of the early Black preacher and his highly imaginative approach to the gospel. The effectiveness of the Black sermon lay in the preacher's tone of voice, dynamic and rhythmic nuances, and emotionally charged oratory rather than in his vocabulary and intellectual message. Because this style has been passed down from generation to generation, the Black sermon belongs to the oral tradition in the same manner as folk music and is to be distinguished from sermons belonging to the historical tradition in which ideas are circumscribed and closed in by the written word. Martin Luther King, for example, knew this oral tradition intimately. Although he was university trained, his sermons were infused with and enlightened by the interpretation of the gospel message as be heard it in the pulpits of the southern Baptist churches. He was a part of the growing body of young university-trained Black preachers who combine the intellectual approach with the manner and style of their elders, melding the traditions of the scholar and the folk preacher.

Early Black preachers were, first of all, interpreters of the Bible, and their sermons were designed to meet the needs of Blacks in a hostile world. The chief concern of the Black preacher was to lead his congregation in a way not spelled out for them in the White religious traditions of the nation. Interaction between the preacher and his followers resulted from their shared experiences, and the congregation felt free to respond vocally as the preacher shaped the issues at hand with scriptural references and skilled allegory. Thus, the Black worship service became one in which the congregation participated as fully as the choir and the preacher, the whole resulting in a total communal intimacy.

The roots of Black gospel music probably lie in the African-style ring shout of the nineteenth century church with its lively shouting spirituals which allowed for a kind of "hot rhythm" and communal participation in the offbeat hand clapping, foot patting, and shuffling around in a circle. Daniel Payne describes these "praying bands" beautifully in his *Recollections of Seventy Years* (Nashville, 1888). The *composed* gospel song, however, owes its origin to Thomas A. Dorsey, who enjoyed in the late 1920s a wide reputation among house-party crowds and theater audiences as a jazz pianist called "Georgia Tom." Dorsey accompanied such celebrated figures of the show world as Ma Rainey and Tampa Red. It was after a miraculous recovery from a serious illness that Dorsey decided to dedicate his talents to the service of God; thereafter, he would perform and compose only religious songs. The success of his songs was due not only to his ability to capture the spirit of "soul singing," but also to the fact that he published both words and music on a single sheet, thus making his songs available to large numbers of persons who could not afford to buy song books. He promoted his music tirelessly in churches all over the nation and gradually gained acceptance for his songs as suitable for performance in the home as well as the church. Later he received the endorsement of the National Baptist Convention. This Black religious music, containing more direct African carry-overs than the extant spirituals, was confined at first in non-orthodox storefront churches but eventually found its way into the large urban churches and into the lives of Black people everywhere. The style of the music bears little similarity to religious music in the European tradition. Its most prominent features are its blues-like quality, highly embellished melodic lines, use of special vocal effects, heavily syncopated rhythms, and great emphasis on a special accompaniment style (most frequently, piano or organ).

The fact that these "Dorsey songs," as they were called, were composed by individuals and disseminated through publication does not deny them a place in the tradition of Black religious music. While there is obviously a close kinship between the blues and gospel, Mr. Dorsey also brought to the songs an intense religious devotion—and this is reflected in the gospel music.

The Black man's religion sustained him throughout the period of slavery and has continued to do so up to the present. It served as the organizing force around which his life was structured. The church was his school, his forum, his political arena, his social club, his art gallery, and his conservatory of music. It was lyceum, gymnasium, and inner sanctum—all at the same time. The Black man's religion was his fellowship with his fellow man and his audience with God, giving him the strength to endure when endurance gave no promise. This religion gave birth to unique forms of religious musical expression, the spiritual and the gospel song, which have left an indelible impression upon the music of the world.

---

1 This paper is a revision of a lecture presented in conjunction with the Zion Baptist Church Choir at the Zion Baptist Church on February 13, 1972, in Minneapolis, Minnesota.

2 Quoted from Frederick Douglass, *My Bondage and My Freedom in Readings in Black American Music*, Eileen Southern, ed. (New York, 1971), p. 84.

3 Samuel Coleridge-Taylor, Foreword to *Twenty-Four Negro Melodies transcribed for the piano* (Bryn Mawr: Oliver Ditson Company, 1905).

4 See further in Hall Johnson, "Notes on the Negro Spiritual" in *Readings in Black American Music*, Eileen Southern, ed. (New York, 1971), pp. 268–275.

VI.
The Organ

A History of the Pipe Organ in the Black Church

by Wayne A. Barr
From *The History of the Pipe Organ in Black Churches
in the United States of America*, Dissertation, published in 1999

It is almost impossible to pinpoint when the first pipe organ was acquired by a Black church. Few churches have well-maintained archives which may shed light on the topic. St. Philip's Episcopal Church, New York, may have purchased an organ as early as 1826.[1] St. Thomas' Episcopal, Philadelphia, purchased one two years later.[2] Quinn Chapel A.M.E. of Louisville, Kentucky, received its first pipe organ around 1854, perhaps the first Black church in that city to do so.[3] Even so, in many churches the introduction of instruments did not come without a fight. W. H. Gibson, Sr., explains that when he introduced a violin into the service in 1847, "the old sisters and brothers declared that the officers had admitted the devil into the church, but they became used to it and seemed to admire the change."[4] After the pipe organ was purchased for Quinn Chapel, "...the sisters threatened to throw it into the street," so they "abandoned the instrument for a while."[5] By 1900, only thirty-seven years following emancipation, pipe organs were common. Gibson, who wrote his *History* in 1897, commented that "at this writing there are but few churches that have not pipe organs and splendid choirs."[6]

Unfortunately, the addition of the pipe organ meant in too many cases the discarding of the rich musical heritage of African American culture. African American culture was considered by the larger society to be primitive and backward. This sentiment prevailed upon the Black churches the idea that distancing oneself from such labels was the way to elevate the race. So, on the one hand, the Black church gained a rich musical tradition with the addition of the pipe organ, but it also lost a part of itself which is essential to its own identity.

The entrance of the pipe organ into the Black church is based on both musical and sociological reasons. Many Blacks enjoyed the music they heard in the slave master's churches. In many cases, this music was best rendered at churches with pipe organs; these churches could usually afford the best-quality music. The pipe organ, therefore, became associated with the best music programs. Naturally, when the free Blacks began to found churches, they wanted the best music programs.

The entrance of the pipe organ also had sociological implications. In order to survive in a hostile society, many Blacks tried to take on the attributes of White society. Assimilation, they may have thought, was the quickest way toward social acceptance and equality. Wyatt Tee Walker reasons that Blacks tended to imitate or look up to any symbol of freedom which, of course, was to be found in the White culture—indeed the dominant White culture itself represented freedom.[7] The same gravity toward perceived symbols of freedom led Blacks away from perceived symbols of primitivism and social unacceptability. Many shunned anything reminiscent of slavery: spirituals, the ringshout, even the method of singing, such as the lining-out of hymns. Daniel Alexander Payne, a prominent bishop of the African Methodist Episcopal Church, frequently spoke against the ringshout as heathen. He once described it in this way:

> After the sermon, they formed a ring, and with coats off sung, clapped their hands, and stamped their feet in a most ridiculous and heathenish way. I requested the pastor to go and stop their dancing. At his request they stopped their dancing and clapping of hands, but remained singing and rocking their bodies to and fro.[8]

C. Eric Lincoln and Lawrence H. Mamiya elaborate that the spirituals of the "invisible" slave church were "antistructural," while worship in the institutional church was very structured.[9] Indeed, this very "antistructure" was once a part of the White church. The lining-out of hymns was at one time the sole means of ensuring full congregational participation.[10] This kind of singing, however, was thrown off with the introduction of instruments and choral singing into the service.[11] So-called "antistructure," then, came to represent everything that was unacceptable to the larger White society and, therefore, needed to be cast off.

Since structure was necessary, why not adopt everything associated with structure? This is precisely what many Black churches did. The pipe organ was an emphatic statement against antistructure. What better counter could one find to the antistructure that the spiritual seemed to represent than the pipe organ, with its grandeur and sense of permanence and stability? One thing is certain—no more lined-out hymns!

The pipe organ, to be sure, represented much more than "good music." It was the embodiment of the struggle for equality and acceptance. With the pipe organ came a change in the structure of the worship service, in the literature that was sung, and in the manner or style of singing. It may even be said that the pipe organ was quietly at the center of the free Blacks' search for identity in an unfamiliar and hostile society.

---

1 *Reaching Out: An Epic of the People of St. Philip's Church* (Tappan, NY: Custombook, 1986), p. 20.

2 "Journal of the Proceedings of the Forty-Sixth Convention of the Protestant Episcopal Church in the State of Pennsylvania," held in St. Peter's and St. James' Churches, in the city of Philadelphia, on Tuesday, May 20th—Wednesday, May 21st—Thursday, May 22nd—and Friday, May 23rd, 1828 (Philadelphia: Jesper Harding, 1828), p. 56.

3 W. H. Gibson, Sr., *History of the United Brothers of Friendship and Sisters of the Mysterious Ten* (Louisville: Bradley and Gilbert Company, 1879), p. 56.

4 Ibid.

5 Ibid.

6 Ibid.

7 Wyatt Tee Walker, *"Somebody's Calling My Name": Black Sacred Music and Social Change* (Valley Forge, PA: Judson Press, 1979), p. 84.

8 Daniel Payne, *Recollections of Seventy Years* (Nashville, TN: A.M.E. Sunday School Union, 1888), p. 69.

9 C. Eric Lincoln and Lawrence H. Mamiya, *The Black Church in the African American Experience* (Durham, NC: Duke University Press, 1990), p. 356.

10 Gilbert Chase, *America's Music,* 2nd rev. ed. (New York: McGraw Hill, 1966), p. 31, as quoted in Eileen Southern, *The Music of Black Americans: A History,* 2nd ed. (New York: W. W. Norton & Company, 1971), p. 30. The Reverend John Cotton states in a treatise of 1647: "…it will be necessary help, that the lines of the Psalm, be openly read beforehand, line after line, or two lines together, that so they who want either books or skill to read, may know what is to be sung, and join with the rest in the duty of singing."

11 Southern, *Readings,* p. 26, states that the first permanent church organ, the "Brattle organ," was installed in 1714 in Boston's King's Chapel. Boston was the first center for music in the colonies, giving rise to the first singing school in 1722.

The Church Organist, African American Organ Music, and the Worship Service: A Useful Guide

By Mickey Thomas Terry, previously unpublished

There are many questions that one might ask concerning African American organ music: how much music is there; where is it found; and how might it fit the needs of my worship service? All of these questions and more are addressed during the course of this essay. The old aphorism "Good things come to those who wait" certainly applies in this instance because it has taken many decades to bring much of this music into print, thereby making it commercially available to the public.

The reason that it has taken so long is because most music publishers, performers, and much of the general public had no interest in classical music produced by anyone other than White males. Women composers were often disregarded because many White male musicians who dominated the field considered music composition as a masculine pursuit. Due to the time-honored practice of Black racial stereotyping by American society, many chose to believe that African Americans possessed a talent only for simple, mundane music, and were otherwise devoid of the skill and intellect to compose the more complex forms of Western classical music. Even Thomas Jefferson advances this notion in his 1784 treatise entitled *Notes on Virginia*.[1]

Fortunately, this negativity did not stop Black men and women composers from writing classical music in all forms. The result is hundreds of organ compositions written by dozens of individuals. Among them are George

Walker, Mark Fax, Thomas Kerr, Betty Jackson King, Adolphus Hailstork, Evelyn Simpson Curenton, Noel Da Costa, Ruth Norman, Eugene W. Hancock, William B. Cooper, David Hurd, and several others that comprise a list too extensive to cite here.

For a long time, one of the central problems encountered in performing African American organ music concerned the matter of obtaining access to it. Even today, the problem persists. Much of this music existed, and currently appears, only in manuscript form. Compounding the problem is the fact that it is necessary to contact either the composers themselves or other individuals to gain access to the music. This task is much easier said than done. When the composer is deceased, it is oftentimes necessary to contact the surviving spouse, who is generally the copyright holder. If the spouse is also deceased, then it becomes a matter of discerning and locating the copyright holder of the particular composition in question. In the latter instance, it is usually, but not always, a family member. In some instances, and depending upon the temperament of the copyright holder, this individual could prove to be quite helpful and sympathetic to your cause. Unfortunately, for whatever reasons, this is not always found to be the case.

In my own research, I discovered early that word-of-mouth is a very significant factor in discovering the existence of either a composer or a body of music. It is necessary to follow leads and to speak not only with the composers, but also with their students, relatives, and colleagues to obtain information. Sometimes the music may be found in church libraries, private and public libraries, and even in academic theses and dissertations.

During the early 1970s, when I was studying organ in college, there was little or no African American organ music that was commercially available; therefore, students, music professors, and performers, regardless of race, were oftentimes unfamiliar with this musical literature. There were no published books or articles on the topic whatsoever. Moreover, at that time, the few pieces that had once had the good fortune to be published were, in some instances, no longer commercially available in print. Thomas Kerr's prize-winning composition, "Arietta," constitutes a prime example of this situation.

Thomas Kerr (1915–1988) was a native of Baltimore, who served as Professor of Piano in the Howard University School of Music from 1943–1976. He was the recipient of a Rosenwald Fellowship in Composition (1942) and won First Prize in the Composers and Authors of America Competition (1944). Although primarily a pianist, he wrote most effectively for the organ. Kerr submitted this work in a national organ composition competition that was sponsored by the American Guild of Organists. Of the 150 entries that were submitted, "Arietta" was one of 15 compositions selected for publication. Kerr's work appeared in the 1957 edition of *American Organ Music*, Volume II, edited by Leslie P. Spellman. This volume is now long out of print; however, in the summer of 2000, "Arietta" was published once again as a part of the *African-American Organ Music Anthology* that I am currently editing for MorningStar Music Publishers. This composition has also been recorded by the writer and appears on the Minnesota Public Radio compact disc *Pipedreams Premieres*, Volume II, released in summer 2000.

"Arietta" is truly one of the most beautiful organ compositions that I have ever had the pleasure either to hear or play. Every time that I perform this work, it never fails to move me. Because it is based on the Christmas/Epiphany Negro spiritual "Rise Up, Shepherds, and Follow," "Arietta" would be an excellent choice either for church or recital use. It is a work of some difficulty to play well, but well worth the effort to learn.

Not until I had received a copy of this very work many years ago had I ever been exposed to organ music written by Blacks. Upon my first reading of "Arietta," I was so taken with the sounds that I was hearing that I actually stopped playing and asked the question aloud, "Who was this man?" (i.e., Kerr). From that point on, I began to seek more of his organ works and to make inquiries concerning those of other Black composers. From there, I ventured into the realm of Black chamber, symphonic, choral, and piano works. The result is that I discovered a rich treasury of compositions, some of which I consider to be masterpieces of musical form and creative inspiration. During the course of this essay, I will focus my attention on what I consider to be some of the finer, more recently published compositions that are appropriate for the worship service.

Firstly, I would like to mention the initial volumes of the *African-American Organ Music Anthology* that I am editing for MorningStar Music. Currently, there are plans for four volumes with each volume containing five compositions. I have already addressed Kerr's "Arietta," which is contained in Volume I. However, there are two other works published in Volume I that are quite accessible for the average church organist. The first work is Betty Jackson King's "Nuptial Song"; the other is Mark Fax's "Prelude on St. Martin's."

Betty Jackson King (1928–1994) taught on the faculties of several institutions including Dillard University in New Orleans. Composed in 1969, King's "Nuptial Song" comprises the middle of a three-movement organ work entitled *Nuptial Suite*. It is her only work for organ solo. King wrote this work for the wedding of some friends. "Nuptial Song" is a lyrical, quiet, and reflective work that uses various combinations of stop colors as well as the chimes. This piece may be used for the worship service as well as the wedding ceremony. For the purposes of the church bulletin, the composer suggested that the title be changed to "Meditation" or "Andante." At first sight, this piece appears to be somewhat simple; however, if one utilizes a solid legato technique in its execution, it can prove to be rather a rewarding challenge.

Mark Fax (1911–1974), a distinguished colleague of Kerr and fellow Baltimore native, was the former Director of the Howard University School of Music. He also taught music composition. In addition to his duties as a professor and administrator, Fax served for approximately thirty years as organist and music director of Asbury United Methodist Church in Washington, DC. During the course of his tenure there, Fax composed several organ pieces for use during the worship service. The following piece is, no doubt, one of them. "Prelude on St. Martin's" is based on a William Tans'ur [sic] hymntune that is found in the 1964 Methodist hymnal. Fax created a rather clever and lovely setting of this hymntune. The solo melody appears (in augmentation) in the left hand, but does not make its initial appearance until the second page of the piece. The work is quiet, of moderate difficulty, and would be an excellent choice for the worship service.

The two concert works represented in Volume I are William B. Cooper's "Toccatina,"[2] and Eugene W. Hancock's "Fantasy."[3] Because this essay features music for the worship service, these pieces will only be given a passing mention. However, other works by Cooper and Hancock that fit the worship context will be discussed at a later point.

Volume II of the *Anthology of African-American Organ Music* was published in fall 2000. One of the composers represented is Undine Smith Moore (1905–1989), who served on the music faculty of Virginia State University in Petersburg from 1927–1972. Moore is primarily known for her fine choral compositions. "Variations on the Hymntune *Nettleton*," better known in most hymnals by the title "Come, Thou Fount of Every Blessing," constitutes the only existing organ work of this well-esteemed composer and educator. It consists of the hymntune theme and four variations. It is of moderate difficulty and is an excellent selection for the church service.

Cooper has another piece that appears in Volume II entitled "Pastorale" that would be delightful in the context of worship. William B. Cooper (1920–1993) was a native of Philadelphia; however, he spent much of his professional career as an organist-choirmaster and composer in New York

City. In addition to holding teaching posts at Hampton University, Bennett College, and the New York City school system, Cooper served for many years as organist-choirmaster of historic St. Philip's Episcopal Church in Harlem and subsequently at St. Martin's Episcopal Church in Harlem.

Based on a tune from William Walker's nineteenth century hymn compilation *The Southern Harmony and Musical Companion,* Cooper's "Pastorale" is a lovely set of variations of moderate difficulty. At the beginning of the work, Cooper places the melody on a four-foot pedal reed and alternates it, at various points, with the soprano and tenor voices. Like the Moore work, this piece is in the form of symphonic variations that provide the organist with ample opportunity to be creative with registrations.

Robert A. Harris (b. 1938) is represented by his only work for organ solo. It is hoped that this will be the first of many organ works yet to come. A highly distinguished choral conductor and composer, Harris currently serves as Professor of Conducting and Director of Choral Organizations at the School of Music at Northwestern University in Evanston, Illinois. "Solemn Processional" is a voluntary that may be used for a service prelude, processional, or postlude. It would also make a fine recital piece. Originally written for the wedding of two friends, it is very majestic in nature and would be appropriate for any solemn or festival occasion. This work is one of great beauty and effect. Thomas H. Kerr is represented in this volume by two concert works from his *Suite Sebastienne*[4]: "Miniature Antiphonal on a Pedal Point" and "Procession of the Gargoyles."

Volume III of the *African-American Organ Music Anthology* is tentatively scheduled to appear in summer 2001. The composers represented are Ulysses Kay, Adolphus Hailstork, Noel Da Costa, Eugene W. Hancock, and Evelyn Simpson Curenton.

Ulysses Kay's "Finale" from his *Suite for Organ* and Adolphus Hailstork's "Prelude" from his *Suite for Organ* are exciting pieces that are more of a concert or recital idiom. However, the remaining three pieces are particularly appropriate for the worship service. The first composition that I would like to mention is by Noel Da Costa.

Currently, Noel Da Costa (b. 1929) is Professor of Music Emeritus at the Mason Gross School of the Arts at Rutgers University in Brunswick. He has written a brief set of four variations on the hymntune *Maryton* (better known as "O Master, Let Me Walk With Thee"). This work dates from 1955 and is written in a somewhat modern twentieth century idiom. It is of moderate difficulty.

437

Hancock's "Go, Tell It on the Mountain" is another composition that will be featured in this volume. Eugene W. Hancock (1929–1994) served as assistant organist-choirmaster at the Cathedral of St. John the Divine in New York during the early 1960s. In addition to other academic and church posts, he succeeded William B. Cooper as organist-choirmaster at St. Philip's in Harlem. Hancock's "Go, Tell It On the Mountain" is extracted from his *Book of Spirituals*,[5] which is currently out of print. It is an easy and delightful piece for manuals only. Hancock's book contains several other short, relatively easy, and effective compositions that are conceived for manuals only.

Evelyn Simpson Curenton's lovely "Meditation on *Were You There*" is a newly composed work that adorns Volume III. Based in the Washington, DC area, Evelyn Simpson Curenton (b. 1953) has distinguished herself as a composer, arranger, choral director, lecturer, and accompanist. Her compositions have been performed by Washington's National Symphony, the Philadelphia Orchestra, and the Minneapolis Symphony. Unlike the Hancock piece previously mentioned, Curenton's "Meditation" is quiet, somber, and reflective in nature. It uses dense harmonies and requires the use of a singing legato for best effect. It would make a particularly fine prelude to a Good Friday or Holy Week service.

These pieces are well suited to electronic instruments as well as pipe organs. For those with Hammond organs, there are pieces that will fit well on these types of instruments. This anthology is the first of its kind to feature African American organ music.

There is another collection that is worth mentioning. In 1996, the American Guild of Organists (AGO) collaborated with E.C. Schirmer Music Company of Boston (ECS) to produce a series of organ compositions by African American composers. I was one of five individuals who were invited to serve on an advisory panel for the series. However, to date, there are only six works that have been published. I am not aware of any plans for expansion.

The first of these pieces that I would like to mention is William B. Cooper's "Spiritual Lullaby." This serene work is based on the Negro spiritual "Baby Bethlehem." In addition to it being a lovely piece of music, I have a particular affinity for it because Cooper dedicated it to me. Cooper's "Meditation on *Steal Away*" is full of dense chromatic harmonic textures and is very reflective, even somber in mood. It features the foundations and string stops of the organ. During the better part of the work, the theme appears on a pedal solo stop.

Adolphus Hailstork (b. 1941), of whom we spoke earlier, is represented in this series by his fiery "Toccata on *Veni Emmanuel.*" Currently, he serves as Professor of Music at Old Dominion University in Norfolk, Virginia. The recipient of several composition awards, Hailstork has written for chorus, voice, various chamber ensembles, and band. Composed in 1983, "Toccata on *Veni Emmanuel*" is a brilliant showpiece that is based on the advent plainchant (also known in English as "O Come, O Come, Emmanuel"). It would make an excellent postlude to the church service as well as a fine recital work. Although the pedal part is not particularly demanding, the manuals require a solid, if not brilliant, keyboard technique to carry it off effectively. Despite the difficulties inherent in the work, it is a joyous work that is well worth the effort to learn.

Mark Fax's *Three Pieces for Organ* are also a part of the AGO-ECS series. The first movement does not actually have a title per se. In the original manuscript, its title is implied by the mood/tempo indication "Freely, Hauntingly." This work is based on the Negro spiritual "Sinner, Don't Let This Harvest Pass." It is rather slow, quiet, and pensive in nature. Of the three movements, the first is perhaps the most appropriate for the worship service. The second movement which follows is entitled "Allegretto." This movement is a brief, delightful work that is very tuneful. Although no registrations are offered by the composer for the piece, the writer finds that 8´ and 4´ flute stops are quite in keeping with the mood of this piece. "Allegretto" could also be used for a prelude or an offertory. The final movement, "Toccata," is a rather brilliant work that is perhaps more appropriate for recital than for worship, although one could perhaps use it as a postlude to a festival or holy day service. Fax's organ music is heavily influenced stylistically by twentieth century neo-classicism. One of the more salient features of neo-classicism apparent in this work are the sparse harmonic textures and simplicity of registration. These features are pervasive in Fax's organ music.

Another composer represented in this series is Roger Dickerson (b. 1934), who is Professor of Music and choir director at Southern University in New Orleans. In addition to his music composition training from Indiana University, Dickerson studied on a Fulbright Fellowship at the Akademie fur Musik und Darstellende Kunst (Academy for Music and the [Dramatic] Performing Arts) in Vienna. Dickerson's *Das Neugegborne Kindelein* (The Newborn Little Child) utilizes a twentieth century neo-classical idiom. It is a contrapuntal chorale prelude in which the theme (cantus firmus) is placed in the pedal, with which one could use a 4´ reed. This piece is quiet, brief, and lovely. The remaining composer in the E.C. Schirmer/AGO series yet to be mentioned is J. Roland Braithwaite.

Braithwaite (b. 1927) taught for many years on the music faculty of Talladega College where he also served as college organist and Dean. His "Prelude on *O Fix Me*" is a chromatic setting of the spiritual. It is of moderate difficulty.

In addition to the *African-American Organ Music Anthology*, MorningStar Music has recently published other organ works by Black composers such as Adolphus Hailstork whose *Four Spirituals for Organ*[6] and *Adagio and Fugue in F Minor* are available in print. Both sets of works would be suitable for the worship service, particularly in the capacity of prelude or postlude material. Hailstork also has a set of *Five Spirituals for Organ* that is tentatively scheduled for publication by Concordia Music.

Ralph Simpson (b. 1932) also has two works published by MorningStar Music that are worth mentioning: *Roll, Jordan, Roll* and *Two Spirituals for Organ*.[7] The first work is of moderate difficulty. The *Two Spirituals for Organ* are relatively easy. Simpson is currently on the music faculty of Tennessee State University in Nashville.

Another set of works worth special mention are by Pulitzer Prize-winning composer George Walker (b. 1922) who has, to date, written six works for solo organ. A native of Washington, DC, Walker studied piano with Rudolf Serkin at the Curtis Institute of Music where he was the first Black to receive the Artist Diploma (1945). He subsequently became the first Black to receive the Doctorate of Musical Arts from the Eastman School of Music. In April 1996, Walker added to a series of many "firsts" by becoming the first Black ever to be awarded the Pulitzer Prize for Music. In retirement from Rutgers University, he now spends much of his time composing, performing, and lecturing.

Four of Walker's works are particularly suitable for the worship service. Three of these works comprise Walker's *Three Pieces for Organ*[8], published by MMB Music of St. Louis. Of the three, two are particularly accessible to the average organist and listener. These are "Chorale Prelude on *Wir sind hier*" (also known as "Liebster Jesu" or "Dearest Jesus, We Are Here") and "Elevation." Both are slow, quiet, reflective pieces of exquisite beauty. The chorale prelude is a particular favorite of this writer. Although it is brief and slow, it requires many subtleties, thereby making it much more difficult to play than it would at first appear. Once again, it is well worth the effort of learning. Both pieces are well suited for use during the prelude or offertory. The last movement, "Invocation," is considerably more demanding from a technical standpoint. It is somewhat fast, full of changing meter and difficult rhythms. It would make an effective postlude. Written during the early 1960s, Walker had intended these pieces to be part of a Protestant organ Mass; however, he never completed all of the movements.

The other Walker piece previously mentioned is entitled "Prayer." Comprising the first movement of Walker's *Two Pieces for Organ*,[9] "Prayer" was written for the 1997 American Guild of Organists Region III Convention in Washington, DC. The mood of this work is suggested by its title. All of Walker's works are published by MMB Music.

It may surprise some of the readers to discover that among this "classical" literature, there are some transcriptions of live Gospel improvisations by Henry Sexton (b. 1940) performed when Sexton was Director of Music at Concord Baptist Church in Brooklyn. These transcriptions are cleverly arranged by Raymond S. Henry (b. 1931) and are now published by Augsburg Fortress Press. Currently residing in New Jersey, Sexton is retired from the New York City school system. Among his published transcriptions are "I'll Fly Away," "The Lord Will Make a Way," and "He Knows Just How Much We Can Bear." Sexton also has a setting of "I Want Jesus to Walk with Me" that is published in the same volume. The latter is a rather easy, but effective arrangement that I have personally used for both church and recital. In both instances, the audience has been most receptive.

Epilogue

The works that have been mentioned do not by any means represent the totality of the Black organ literature that is appropriate for the worship service, much less the totality of that which exists in general. The number of works that exist in print is relatively small compared to the huge number of unpublished manuscripts that exist. In view of this fact, the intent of this essay has been to focus on some of the most recent publications of this music.

Because it is not feasible during the course of an essay to be all inclusive, it has been necessary to be somewhat selective about the compositions discussed; however, it is hoped that the content of this essay will prompt the reader to acquire and perform these works as well as to quest for others that might fit their needs, both within and outside the context of worship. It is also hoped that the intrepid reader will not be bound by the limitations of the printed page, but might also venture into the vast arena of unpublished musical manuscripts. There are incredible treasures to be found therein, a few of which are just now coming to public attention because of their recent publication.

Because many African American composers were trained in western European musical techniques and choose to utilize them in their musical creations, some Blacks have turned their backs on them and their music. This is quite tragic, because this is music written by Black men and women who have lived the life. They have written in response to their cultural milieu (i.e., being Black in America). Despite the techniques utilized, this makes the music Black. It is necessary to remember that it is well documented that Debussy, Stravinsky, Dvořák, Gershwin, and several other celebrated White American and European composers were influenced by and utilized techniques found in Black music; nonetheless, this did not make their music "Black music." Our African American classical music is important because it constitutes a significant part of our rich cultural heritage just as does jazz, rhythm and blues, and gospel music. It should be celebrated, studied, performed, recorded, and regarded with unrelenting pride. The appearance of African American organ music in print marks the beginning of a whole new day. With this thought before us, let us reflect, give thanks, and shout: *"This is the day the Lord has made; let us rejoice and be glad in it."*

---

1 Terry, Mickey Thomas, "Cultural Perspectives of African-American Organ Literature," *Essays in American Music,* James R. Heintze, ed. (Garland Publishing Co., 1999); pp. 225–241. For other articles pertaining to African American organ literature, please consult: Terry, "African-American Classical Organ Music—A Case of Neglect," *The American Organist* (March 1997); Terry, "African-American Organ Literature: A Selective Overview," *The Diapason* (April 1996); Terry, "A Second Glance: African-American Organ Literature," *The Diapason* (May 1998); Terry, "African-American Neglect," *Choir and Organ* (Nov./Dec. 1998).

2 Cooper's "Toccatina" dates from 1977 and is dedicated to his friend and colleague Dr. Eugene W. Hancock. It is a playful scherzando movement that is as clever as it is cute. "Toccatina" is a short chromatic work that is of great substance, both musically and technically.

3 Hancock's "Fantasy" is a virtuoso work that was written for Dr. Herman D. Taylor, and premiered at the 1985 Black American Music Symposium in Ann Arbor, Michigan. This work features the pedals in a virtuosic manner that is somewhat reminiscent of the pyrotechnics found in Leo Sowerby's "Pageant."

4 With the exception of the last system, "Miniature Antiphonal on a Pedal Point" has alternating F-sharps in the pedal that are consistent throughout the duration of the piece. "Procession of the Gargoyles" is a rather playful march in 5/8 time. If played on a large organ in a very reverberant room, the effect is breathtaking. *Suite Sebastienne* is a multi-movement cyclic work based on an original composer theme.

5 Hancock's *Book of Spirituals* (now out-of-print) was originally published by Lorenz Publishing Company in 1966. It includes eight other spirituals in addition to "Go, Tell It on the Mountain."

6 The contents of this volume are: "Prelude on *We Shall Overcome*," "Postlude on *We Shall Overcome*," "Prelude on *Deep River*," and "Toccata on *Great Day*."

7 These settings by Simpson are based on the spirituals "Swing Low, Sweet Chariot" and "We Are Climbing Jacob's Ladder."

8 Mickey Thomas Terry has recorded Walker's *Three Pieces for Organ* on a 1994 compact disc release produced by Albany Records [*George Walker—A Portrait* (Troy-136)].

9 The other composition in this set is entitled "Improvisation on *All Glory, Laud, and Honor*." Although this work is based on a popular hymntune, this is a concert setting conceived in a modern idiom. It is a work of great difficulty both rhythmically and technically.

Service Playing for Organists

compiled and edited by James Abbington, previously unpublished

I was invited to present a workshop for the 1999 Hampton University Choir Directors' and Organists' Guild Conference entitled, "Service Playing for the Church Organist: The Essentials." It was a rather difficult topic considering that so many of the church organists gathered had little or no formal study or training in organ. Most African American churches have Hammond organs or Allen or Rodgers electronic instruments and, nowadays, synthesizers. While the purpose and objective of the workshop was to neither demonstrate the use of the Rodgers, Allen, or Hammond organ nor to show how they were all related, its primary focus was to discuss the preparation, duties, responsibilities, and function of the church organist in worship.

In preparation for the presentation, I consulted and drew heavily from the most unparalleled, scholarly, well-written, and most frequently used sources: *The Organists' Manual: Technical Studies and Selected Compositions for the Organ* by Roger E. Davis (W. W. Norton and Company: New York); *Method of Organ Playing*, 8th edition, by Harold Gleason, edited by Catharine Croizer Gleason (Prentice Hall: Upper Saddle River, NJ); *Church Service Playing* by Joyce Jones (Bradley Publications: New York); and *The Organist and Hymn Playing* by Austin C. Lovelace (Agape: Carol Stream, IL).

These sources provided much of the information contained within the handout. The presentation was divided into ten sections: (1) Hymn Playing, (2) Introductions, (3) Phrasing, (4) Tempo, (5) Repeated Notes, (6) Amens, (7) Registration, (8) Free Accompaniments, Descants, and Interludes, (9) Adapting Piano Accompaniments, and (10) Suggested Repertoire for the Church Organist.

[In the sacred service] the organist should keep the congregation in tune, and through his playing help to encourage devotion and inspiration, or seek to heighten, in the hymn, the significant meaning.

—Daniel Gottlob Turk
Von den wichtigsten Pflichten, 1787

[The organist's] participation in the worship of God is no less important than that of the preacher. He, also, should persuade the hearts and minds of those present, not through words but through musical sounds.

—Johann Christian Kittel,
Der angehende praktische Organist, 1801

When the organist incessantly aspires to the goal which he wants to reach through his music, when he earnestly, properly, heartily devotes himself to tasteful performance and spares no trouble to obtain, within his power, the lofty expression of his way of thinking and feeling, so he may hope that his playing will always come nearer to the quality of church style in the most complete, dignified, and noble expression.

—Johann Christian Kittel,
Der angehende praktische Organist, 1801

The organ music, hymns, accompaniments for vocal solos, anthems, oratorios, [cantatas], and liturgical music should be prepared with utmost care. All the service should be of high quality and related to the season of the church year or the mood of the service.

—Harold Gleason,
Method of Organ Playing, Eighth Edition

The church organist should be prepared, loyal, prompt, alert, cooperative, flexible, musical, sincere, and committed to the highest ideals of his (or her) religion. Next to the minister, the organist can have the greatest impact in the worship service, in the smooth running of the service, and in its effectiveness on the congregation.

—Joyce Jones,
Church Service Playing

Proficiency in hymn playing is probably the most important requirement of the church organist. A congregation is inspired to sing with confidence and enthusiasm when the organist plays the hymns with clarity, rhythmic vitality, and accuracy. Organists must study and practice hymns as they would any polyphonic organ composition; attention must be given to phrasing, fingering, pedaling and, in particular, to the rhythmic execution of repeated notes.

—Roger Davis,
The Organists' Manual

Playing for a church service has always been one of the organists' most important functions. It can be as rewarding as any part of the organist's profession and demands the utmost musical and technical competence. However, a facile technique and mastery of the organ literature do not prepare one completely for the art of service playing, which requires special techniques in the preparation of hymns, accompaniments, and liturgical music. Since many organists are also choirmasters, a knowledge of the techniques of singing and the ability to conduct the choir from the console are indispensable. Modulation, improvisation, transposition, accurate sight-reading, and the ability to read a vocal score are also important parts of the church musician's equipment and should be cultivated from the beginning of the student's study.

—Harold Gleason,
Method of Organ Playing, Eighth Edition

Lose no opportunity of practicing on the organ; there is no other instrument which takes a swifter revenge on anything unclear or sloppy in composition or playing.

—Robert Schumann

Playing hymns is a craft, not a bore. I regard hymns as vehicles of the Gospel. I regard the organist's task as a ministry, not a profession...

Never play a hymn for a congregation without reading it first.

Be able to play the hymn as it is written.

Know that the first necessity, after accuracy and before inventiveness, is rhythm.

In playing a hymn, play expressively, but do not anticipate your climaxes.

Present the ancient truth as a present truth. You are taking those words and notes out of the printed book and presenting them to the congregation as

447

a new, fresh, contemporary thing. They are not only words written in 1740 by Charles Wesley or written in 1701 by Jeremiah Clarke. They are a present experience, a new gift.

—Erik Routley,
The Organist's Guide to Congregational Praise

It is an unfortunate but true statement that many organists graduate who are able to play brilliant preludes and postludes but cannot play a single hymntune. Hymn playing should be the foundation of any organist's education, for it is the most important part of one's ministry.... Try out every principle and suggestion and master them so they can be applied to other material. Remember that your most awesome responsibility is that of leading a congregation in worship through the playing of hymns.

—Austin C. Lovelace,
The Organist and Hymn Playing

A musician may have the best imagination in the world, but in the end that which he truly expresses will be what he has first impressed on his own mind and character. The organist cannot put on artistry with his gown on Sunday morning and throw it off at night. His kingdom of music is within him. His expression is the reflection first of what he is, and next of what he would be.

—Willan Swainson

It is in the area of taste and emotion...that the organist makes his chief contribution to hymn singing. He can by means of registration and tempo so clarify the meaning of the hymn and uncover its emotional drive that the congregation is, as it were, lifted beyond itself. This is an art which defies description and which cannot be achieved simply by following a set of directions, but it is an authentic and necessary part of service playing and one of the great values of hymnody.

—Carl Halter

It is your duty, your contribution to the service, to interpret as well as to play.... You are taking those words and notes out of the printed book and presenting them to the congregation as a *new*, fresh, contemporary thing.... Do nothing mechanically, by habit, or lightly, or casually. Do all by decision.

Do all after thought and prayer. And may the beauty of the Lord our God be upon us, and may He prosper our handiwork.

—Erik Routley,
The Organist's Guide to Congregational Praise

I. Hymn Playing

"A strong feeling for rhythm, clarity, the right tempo, and the mood of the words is of first importance in inspiring the congregation to sing."

—Harold Gleason

• Study the words of the hymn; sing them during practice and playing in the church service. The words, the music, and the season of the church year will determine the mood, phrasing, tempo, touch, registration, and rhythmic pulse.

• Mark the pedaling and learn the pedal part before practicing the manual parts. *Play the pedal part in the octave in which it is written.*

• The tenor part will be played with the left hand and the bass with the pedal. Also practice the hymn without the pedal, playing the tenor and bass with the left hand.

• Legato should be the principal touch in hymn playing. A non-legato touch will often be needed in reverberant churches, and detached chords at certain points will be effective when the words suggest strong accents.

• Study the form, harmonic rhythm, type of melody, note values, and phrase lengths of the music. Play the hymns with understanding and vitality.

II. Introductions

As an introduction to the singing of a hymn, the organist should play through the entire hymn in the exact tempo intended for congregational singing.

An abbreviated introduction may be used for a familiar hymn or for a special one sung regularly as part of the service. Sometimes the first and last phrases of a hymn will be suitable as an introduction. Other possibilities include the last phrase only, the first phrase only, or the last two phrases. Whatever is chosen should be rehearsed beforehand to make sure the melodic and harmonic features of the phrases are compatible.

In general, a good hymn introduction should begin with the opening notes of the hymn (so that the congregation has an opportunity to recognize the hymn) and should end on the tonic chord, not on a half cadence.

In introducing an unfamiliar hymn, it is helpful to play the hymntune in octaves, adding harmony only for the last two or three notes of each line.

Another way to emphasize the melody of an unfamiliar hymn is to play the melody only in the right hand on a solo combination (or solo reed, such as a trumpet), play the alto and tenor on the other manual with the left hand, and play the bass in the pedals.

The hymn introductions can be true introductions, not merely the playing of a portion of the hymn as written in the hymnal. When well done, this can be very effective in the service. The more elaborate introductions should be used with familiar hymns.

There are many books of hymn introductions and free harmonizations which should be of help to the church organist. Later, it is good to make up one's own, first writing them out and practicing carefully before using them in the service.

III. Phrasing

"...one who renders only notes, keys, scales, and intervals, without comprehending the meaning of phrases—even if he is precise otherwise—is nothing but a 'note-gobbler'!"

from Rousseau's *Dictionnaire de musique*, 1775

Hymns are phrased at the end of each line either by lifting all the parts to create a rest or by lifting only the soprano part.

When playing a hymn, all parts should be lifted for a rest at the bold bar lines. The first line of text within a score is usually phrased by lifting only the soprano part.

Phrases within a line of text may by acknowledged when the meaning of the words and music is thereby enhanced; but not every comma in the text calls for a break in the music. When the musical phrase does not agree with the punctuation of the text, it is preferable to phrase according to the text.

At the end of each stanza hold the last chord a full measure or a half measure, and make a rest in the same rhythmic pulse before beginning the next stanza. The rhythmic pulse is based on the word accents of the hymn.

It is of utmost importance that the length of rest between stanzas is always the same. Do not ritard at the end of any stanza, except the last, when a slight ritard may be made.

IV. Tempo

Each hymn will have its own particular tempo, which will grow out of the study of the words and music.

Long phrases require a somewhat faster tempo than short phrases.

Do not play hymns metronomically, but with a strong rhythmic pulse.

Hymns with many short notes should not be played too quickly or those with long notes too slowly.

Consider the acoustical environment in the church.

An appropriate tempo for a particular hymn can best be determined by singing it through while taking note of the meaning and phrasing of the text.

If the congregation is lagging behind the organ, there are several solutions:

1. Perhaps the organist is playing too fast. The obvious solution to this is to play slower.
2. The registration may be too soft or too dull.
3. The organist may be playing too legato. Often, playing all the bass notes in the pedal, in a pizzicato manner, will provide more feeling of a beat.
4. As an alternative, play the bass line smoothly, with the manuals detached.

V. Repeated Notes

To maintain clarity and a strong rhythmic pulse, there should be little, if any, tying of repeated notes.

Never tie the soprano part.

A series of repeated notes may sometimes be tied in the alto and bass parts from strong to weak beats of the measure.

VI. Amens

An Amen is sung when the phrase "So be it" is appropriate.

Hold the final chord of the hymn the same length and rhythmic pulse as between stanzas. Tie the common note between the final chord and the Amen, and release the other notes of the chord on the rest.

Play the Amen in a positive manner and in the tempo of the hymn.

Do not reduce the volume of the organ for the Amen.

VI. Registration

"An organist must endeavor thoroughly to understand the organ which he is about to play, in order that he may achieve the best possible results. One has often heard an organ, treated by two equally good organists, that sounded better in the hands of one than in those of the other in combination of registers."

—Dom Bedos be Celles' *L'art du facteur d'orgues*

"For one thing is certain; not every registrational approach works with all stops. Therefore, discerning musical judgment and a good ear are the best means."

—Andreas Werckmeister, *Orgelprobe*, 1698

The art of registration is one aspect of organ playing that can occupy a great deal of time and effort. After pedal technique, it is possibly the single most fascinating aspects of being an organist. There are two extremes to this: the organist who uses the same registrations year after year with no thought to changing and the organist who is constantly 'fiddling' with the stops, changing on every phrase, with or without reason. The first type will lead to stagnation and sameness of sounds, which can become quite deadly. The second leads to a restlessness, a constant feeling of uneasiness, on the part of the listener.

The best way to get to know a new organ is to try each stop separately, playing a chord and then a simple five-note passage (such as C-D-E-F-G) on each stop. Note the relative volume and tone quality of each stop.

Although it is possible to overdo changes of registration, the reverse can be dull and uninspiring. Avoid playing every hymn in the same manner.

The general character of the words, the size of the congregation and church, and the acoustics should be taken into consideration in selecting a suitable registration. Make sure that the registration is strong enough to lead the singing.

Hymns of praise and brilliant martial hymns are played on clear, full registration—the great principal chorus. The words, however, may suggest slight reduction in registration while other stanzas may call for greater brilliance, even to the inclusion of chorus reed stops.

Sudden and extreme changes of registration within a stanza serve no purpose and should be avoided.

Prayer and meditative hymns may be played on principals 8' and 4'. For variety, some stanzas may be played with all, or if easier, they may be played in the usual manner without the 16' stops in the pedal.

Registration for the introduction to a hymn should be similar to that planned for the first stanza.

Reeds may be added for the more brilliant hymns, or for one or two climatic stanzas when the words and music are appropriate. The occasional omission of the pedal part, playing all four parts on the manuals, will provide relief and variety, especially in the longer and quieter hymns.

The hymntune may be played as a solo with a powerful reed or combination. The alto and tenor parts will be played by the left hand on another manual.

One stanza may be sometimes be sung without the organ. The choir should be well rehearsed and the congregation informed by a note in the worship bulletin or worship leader.

Avoid the use of muddy 16' stops on the manuals.

VIII. Free Accompaniments, Descants, and Interludes

The occasional use of free accompaniments and descants will provide variety and stimulate congregational singing.

Free accompaniments and descants are most effective in well-known hymns but should not be used on more than one or two stanzas of a hymn. The climactic stanzas, frequently the last or next-to-last stanza, are usually most suitable for free accompaniments and descants.

Descants may be sung by all or part of the soprano section, or played by the organist as a part of a free accompaniment.

During long processionals, interludes between stanzas of the hymn are often used. The interludes should be played strictly in time, in the style of the hymn, and consist of at least eight measures. When an interlude is used, do not make a break at the end of the stanza without a pause. Lead back unmistakably to the beginning of the next stanza. The ideal way to conclude the interlude is to repeat part or all of the last phrase of the hymn. It is also effective to end on the dominant chord, preceded by a slight *ritardando*.

Do not play interludes between stanzas that express one thought.

Avoid modulations and interludes without a proper justification of the hymntext. Too many modulations and interludes in a hymn become unmusical, theatrical, and expose bad musical taste.

IX. Adapting Piano Accompaniments

The arrangement of piano scores must be idiomatically effective on the organ.

Widely separated notes, octaves, and chords should be brought into the middle range of the keyboard. Avoid thick chords in low registers.

Observe the musical values of the piano score. These include rhythm, phrasing, characteristic figurations, accents, and written instructions.

Preserve the motion of the music, and do not reduce all pianistic devices to chords.

Rapid bass passages may be played on the manuals with the 16' pedal playing only the accented beats.

Passages with a clearly defined bass line may be played with 16' pedal and even 32' when appropriate.

When playing a bass line written in octaves, it is usually better to play the upper note. This will preserve the integrity of the bass line and will prevent the monotony of all notes sounding in the lower octave.

Conclusion

There is certainly so much more to being an organist than just simply playing the organ on Sunday mornings or at funerals, weddings, and revivals. Being gifted and talented and/or well-trained are the non-negotiable essentials needed to fulfill the musical requirements and responsibilities of the organist. In addition to being a leader in hymn playing, a skilled musician at modulating, transposing, and improvising, an excellent accompanist of anthems, other choral selections, and solos, and having the ability to choose effective and tasteful registrations, the church organist must be skilled at working with people—the director, the choir, the clergy, and the congregation. The organist must be dependable, prompt, and faithful at rehearsals and services, flexible, and cooperative; the organist must view himself or herself as an essential contributor to the total worship experience. The expertise of the organist to make sudden changes and adjustments in the service is quintessential.

The ability of the organist to effectively compliment the worship experience without calling attention to himself or herself as concert virtuoso is imperative and necessitous. The temptation to use the organ as a concert instrument in worship or a display bench of the organist's talents is distracting, disruptive, self-exalting, and self-aggrandizing.

If the organist is to "play skillfully" as the Bible teaches, the organist must practice the instrument! This is absolutely, positively non-negotiable. Church services should never become a weekly sight-reading session or unofficial practice and warm-up exercise. A full-time church organist should practice two to four hours a day as part of the workload.

Personal growth and development are indispensable and necessary. Church music conferences, workshops, and seminars keep the organist alert to new repertoire and materials and fresh approaches, and would provide the necessary stimulation, motivation, and inspiration for personal growth and achievement. The church organist should have active membership with the American Guild of Organists (AGO) and receive magazines and journals such as *The American Organist*, *Journal of Church Music*, *The Diapason*, and *Clavier*. These provide listings of activities, resources, job announcements, and other pertinent information for the organist.

References Used

Davis, Roger E., *The Organists' Manual: Technical Studies and Selected Compositions for the Organ* (New York: W. W. Norton & Company, 1985).

Gleason, Harold, Catharine Crozier Gleason, ed. *Method of Organ Playing*, 8th edition (Upper Saddle River, NJ: Prentice Hall, 1996).

Jones, Joyce, *Church Service Playing* (New York: Bradley Publications, 1981).

Lovelace, Austin C., *The Organist and Hymn Playing* (Carol Stream, IL: Agape, 1981).

Suggested Repertoire for Church Organists

Johann S. Bach:
>*The Liturgical Year* (Orgelbuchlein)
>*The Neumeister Chorales*
>Miscellaneous chorales

Johannes Brahms, *Eleven Chorale Preludes*, Op. 122

Marcel Dupre, *Seventy-Nine Chorales*, Op. 28

William Farley Smith, *Songs of Deliverance: Organ Arrangements and Congregational Acts of Worship for the Church Year Based on African American Spirituals*

The Parish Organist, Heinrich Fleischer, ed.

Flor Peeters, *Hymn Preludes for the Liturgical Year* (24 volumes)

Louis Vierne, *Twenty-four Pieces in Free Style* (2 volumes)

VII.
Contemporary Perspectives

What Lies Ahead?

by Wyatt Tee Walker
from *Somebody's Calling My Name*, published in 1979

The preceding chapters have set forth in some detail the story of the development of Black sacred music. The ground and root of all music indigenous to America is the music art form commonly known as the Negro spiritual. (See the "Music Tree" on the frontispiece.) Its antecedents were the first slave utterances, moans, and chants for deliverance that can be traced to the early slave experience. The spiritual evolved from the rhythm forms of the West African oral tradition as a folk response to and index of the social dynamics and culture of the slave community. The oral tradition was the primary means of the spiritual's survival and dissemination throughout the slave and folk community. In the course of the accommodation necessary in the New World, in the areas of religion, language, and mores, music revealed what was going on in the life of the antebellum slave community and registered the varied responses to servitude. Out of that response preserved chiefly in the spiritual, there grew an identifiable Black musical tradition. This book has focused on the religious segment of the music of the Black experience and followed the sacred-secular distinctions of the West in order to present in bold relief the distinct tradition.

There is, then, a Black sacred music tradition that is identifiable and distinguishable from the sacred music tradition of the dominant (or White) society. It is obvious that the forms of celebration in the worship of the folk churches of the Black community and the European American-influenced worship of the White community are vastly different. To be sure, as has been indicated earlier in this book, much of the language and trappings are similar, if not identical, but the style of the worship is markedly different. It does not require much analysis to discover that the chief influence and distinguishing ingredient is the music. The Black musical tradition, by its very character, induces a style of worship that lends itself to great freedom of expression. The music of the dominant society in worship is performed within the print-oriented structures of the melodic and harmonic discipline common to the

West. Improvisation is rare in White worship, and neither is there as wide-spread use of choirs and congregational singing.

Music is one of the key ingredients that influences the style of worship in Protestant church life in America. As stated in chapter 1, there are some Black congregations whose worship style is imitative of the dominant society and a key ingredient is, again, *the music.* In the worship services of the Black masses, music plays very nearly as central a role as preaching. The reader may recall that the style of preaching and praying in the Black religious tradition was influenced by the music of the Black religious experience.

Similarities do exist between what might be called Black-style worship and White-style worship. The principal similarity is in language. While there is a great store of Black-rooted musical repertoire used, better than half of the printed music adapted for us in contemporary Black church life is European American in origin. The first similarity, then, is in language. The second similarity is in the words. A traditional favorite and standard of any Black folk congregation is "Amazing Grace,"[1] authored by John Newton, an English slave trader turned Anglican priest.[2] However, the similarity is principally in the words, with only slight reference to the melodic line, when one compares the use and performance of this hymn in historic Black church life with the use and performance in White church life.

The form and style of Black sacred music generally followed the folk religion, that is, the religion of the masses who are generally low income and rural in origin. Again, the folk religion of the Black community had naturally and inevitably felt some influence of the dominant society. But the folk-style religion has remained intact because the persistent thread of the oral tradition has preserved a musical idiom unique to the Black religious experience.

There are, of course, exceptions to the rule on both sides of this religious coin: some all-Black congregations sing like White folks, and a few White worship services are filled with the fervor of traditional Black religion, *but the music is not the same!* It might be argued that this is evidence of cross-cultural influence, to which this writer would hastily agree. Cross-culture feeds and alters; it does not devour and destroy.

One additional observation might be added in this regard. The corollary to the fact of the existence of an observable Black sacred music tradition is that the dominance of that tradition *musically* is in direct proportion to the influence of the religious folk tradition. That is to say, the folk religion lives where the folk music is sung, and vice versa. A converse truth prevails. As the influence of Euro-American music increases, the folk-style religion decreases.

The Black Sacred Music Tradition

The existence of a Black sacred music tradition is made evident by the several types of music, still extant, that are utilized in varying degrees in the folk religion of the masses. In summary, let us retrace the bloodline of this body of musical literature.

The spiritual is the name given to that body of music that developed from 1760 to the Emancipation (1863). It embraces the Sorrow Songs, Field Songs, Praise Songs, Shouts, Hollers, Work Songs, and the like. This musical art form was sufficiently developed by the beginning of the nineteenth century to color and transform the meter music tradition that had its roots in Europe. The spiritual form had its impact on the use made of the European American hymns that were introduced on a broad scale to the Black community following the Civil War. It was not long before the rhythm, mode, style, and ad-lib character of performance stamped Black America's imprint upon the music in question. The Hymns of Improvisation, as they have been named in this book, dominated the worship of historic Black churches until the hard times of the Great Depression, when the vogue of authentic Gospel music first appeared. The experience of placing their imprint on "borrowed" hymns created sufficient confidence internally for Blacks to produce their own Black hymnody—gospel!

The advent of the Martin Luther King era of radical social change ushered in a period of broad acceptability of the gospel idiom, which had not been altogether welcome in all-Black church circles prior to that time.[3] The nonviolent movement in the South, at its inception, "updated" many of the historic Negro spirituals and transformed them through slight word changes into freedom songs.[4] As the movement gained momentum, with the broad popularity of freedom songs and the close similarity to their musical parents, the spirituals, the door was opened for the most recent development in Black hymnody—modern gospel. Modern gospel is a composite of the Black sacred music tradition. Its musical idiom is very often "bluesy" and/or jazzy. Its lyrics are traditional, either from the European American tradition or variations on the faith language long existent in the Black religious experience. It is not uncommon in the worship service of a church of the Black masses to hear under the gospel umbrella a selection that has elements of several of the types reviewed here. For example, the formula might take shape as follows: meter music + gospel + spiritual (text or verse) = contemporary gospel.

Lord, Don't Move the Mountain[5]

I love the Lord: he heard my cries,
And pitied every groan:
Long as I live, when troubles rise,
I'll hasten to his throne.[6]

(Refrain)
Lord, don't move the mountain;
Just give me the strength to climb.
Lord, don't take away my stumbling block;
Just lead me all around.[7]

Stanza (typical)
Lord, I don't bother nobody,
I try to treat everybody the same;
But every time I turn my back,
They scandalize my name.[8]

The spirituals, the Hymns of Improvisation, the Black meter music tradition, and historic and modern gospel are the major forms of musical literature that comprise the Black sacred music tradition. Wherever the tradition has lived, measurable growth in personal and collective wholeness has proceeded.

The internal development of the Black community has centered in the Black Church institution, and the cohesive influence to a large degree has been the music of the Black religious tradition. The examples cited earlier in this regard are evidence of the long- and short-range positive influences and results that were made possible through the oral tradition that has permeated the development of Black sacred music. The music of the Black Church was crucial in the institution's development as the dominant influence in the life of the Black community, past and present.

Black Sacred Music and Social Change

Black sacred music is the primary link to the African past of the Black people in the Americas. It has survived against tremendous odds. Black sacred music could not and would not have survived without the instrumentality of the oral tradition. The illiteracy of the Black community (by Western standards) made the oral tradition essential. As the Black community became more Westernized, the historic past of the New World African became more distant and obscured. The Western value system (color, economics, intellectualism) discourages a sense of "Negro" identity, but an irreducible minimum remains.

The Black community developed as an appendage to American society. Sociologists use the term "subculture." It was in Black religious life earlier on, and later in the church and the entertainment world, that Black expression was given vent without having to absorb the neutralizing effect of White non-acceptance.

Slavery and its successor, segregation, produced a psychological and emotional disorientation in Blacks that remains observable today. In their collective consciousness, the Black people have not been absolutely sure who they are. They are not thoroughly American; they are not thoroughly African. They move in an ambivalent world of being *African American.*

The most positive neutralizing effect on this disorientation of identity came as a result of the nonviolent movement in the South and the intense but brief "Black Power" movement. Whatever happened, the primary and most significant result was the psychic impact these events had on Black consciousness. Both periods fed the gnawing need for identity and self-image that White America had sought to destroy through historical and cultural genocide. White America had made Blackness taboo; Martin Luther King, Jr., Malcolm X, and Stokely Carmichael made it fashionable.

In the treatment of Jews and Blacks by White Americans, there are sufficient similarities for instructive comparison. It is obvious that Jews have fared somewhat better for a couple of reasons. One reason is, of course, their "Whiteness," which serves as a camouflage to their Jewishness in many circumstances. The other reason is their Jewishness—the mystique of the heirs of Moses who are remaining, generally, unapologetic for being Jews. This is buttressed by their separateness (religion) and their sense of exclusivity (chosen people). The Old Testament and the tradition of the Torah have done much to fortify and insulate the Jewish community from persecution and discrimination that might have demoralized a lesser people.

Sterling Plumpp in his book *Black Rituals* is more explicit as to how this Jewish mystique functions:

> The reason that Jews are so functional in mobilizing their strength all over the world when their survival is endangered is that Jews are unified. There are no Black men heading Jewish organizations, there are no Black critics telling Jews how to sing, what to write, and how smart they are—only Jews define what a Jew is and how a Jew should and shouldn't act. Jewish

463

culture is rooted in centuries of Jewish history.... What is very essential to any correct understanding of the "success" of the Jews in any country is the fact that they learn to play roles, wear many different masks, in order to make it, advance in technological and industrialized jungles. This means they learn how to act like Americans...but in their familiar religious institutions they also learn how to live as Jews must live if they are to survive; they learn this from the cradle.[9]

The irony of the Black people's sojourn on the North American continent is that as they have become more and more Westernized—literate and elevated in economics and social status—they have become more removed from their real past. The continuing dilemma of African Americans in the U.S. is to discover ways to resist complete Westernization which obliterates ethnic pride and identity. On the basis of the American experience, the Westernization mentioned above invariably induces the subject (victim) to join with the dominant (oppressive) community in its mores, lifestyle, and value system. This is notwithstanding the fact that Western culture, historically, has been anti-Black.

There is no indication of a mass exodus from America. Thus, it is safe to presume that Black people will stay. If they remain, how can they keep their sanity? Imitate the Jewish experience? Well, at least learn from it.

The parallels of the Jewish and Black experiences are profoundly similar. In the Black ancestral home, family life and religious life were central. The slave period disrupted that tradition, but not totally. The historical umbilical cord needs to be rejoined. Plumpp has already underscored the importance of this influence in the survival technique of the Jewish community. The centrality of the family, synagogue, and tradition has served them well. Blacks must acquire the skills and expertise of the dominant society and at the same time preserve and strengthen ethnicity—Blackness. The basis of that preservation is grounded in a *sense of history*. The Jewish model is well worth considering as an option—an example of bicultural competence.

Black Americans who dismiss the slave experience are foolish and short-sighted. This is not a brief for masochism. However, once the slave experience has been faced, more important questions arise: "What were we before we were slaves?" "What set of circumstances led to our enslavement?" "How did we survive and by what means?" The cloak of historic invisibility must be lifted from the collective and individual consciousness of American Blacks in order to cope with the reality of systemic White racism.

It has been set forth earlier in this book that the dominant institutional influence in the lives of African American is the Black Church. The Black people's sense of personhood—being—has been nurtured and fed by the Black religious experience. The "invisible church" was the chief resistance movement against slavery. The "visible church" is uniquely equipped to serve as the instrument to awaken and reawaken the sense of history so sorely needed. The music of the Black religious experience has been and remains a reservoir of the Black community's response to enforced servitude and oppression. The music which developed from the basic idiom that survived the Middle Passage was fashioned into a cry for deliverance. Transmitted via the oral tradition of West Africa and adapted to the experience of the New World, this faith music provided the cement that held the fragile "invisible church" together until the organization of the "visible church" became possible.

The inhumanity of pre-Civil War existence was made bearable by the presence and function of the "invisible church." The religious beliefs, captured and preserved in song, transformed the property of the slave owners into the children of God.

The music of the Black religious experience in the folk tradition induces and reinforces a clearer sense of heritage. The quality of performance, style, beat, and emotion of Black worship assists Blacks in discovering and remembering who they really are.

The spiritual form, in the antebellum style or post-Civil War style, in Black consciousness has always been associated with the slave experience. On at least four occasions since the act of Emancipation, the spiritual form has experienced a pronounced renaissance, both in interest and in use. Shortly after the executive order for Emancipation was signed by Lincoln, the spirituals lapsed into gradual neglect, only to be resurrected by the domestic and international tours of the Fisk Jubilee Singers. Then, at the beginning of the twentieth century, with the increased use of hymntexts, the use of spirituals declined again until the John Work years (1914–1930). The period of the Great Depression saw still another decline in the popularity of spirituals while the new "gospel" music of the Black church began to take root. World War II, a time of national crisis, marked another renaissance led by the internationally famous Wings Over Jordan Radio Choir,[10] based in Cleveland, Ohio. As America wound down from World War II prosperity, interest in the spiritual waned again, in deference to the gospel era, which now held full sway. The fifties could be accurately called the era of the quartet phenomenon, so strong was this phase of the gospel movement.

The meteoric rise of Martin Luther King, Jr., and the stirring movement against the racist forces in the South created still another renaissance. The heightening of the collective Black consciousness and the marching feet needed music to bolster the morale of Blacks and give them courage. Martin King was a Baptist preacher; the movement that he led was church-based; the most suitable music for this moral struggle was the music of the antebellum slave who one hundred years earlier intoned:

> Go down, Moses,
> Way down in Egypt land.
> Tell ole Pharaoh,
> Let my people go.[11]

God had sent another Moses to lift the affliction of slavery from the oppressed. Their song in a strange land was the Lord's song coined generations earlier by their slave forebears. The spirituals were in business again!

As detailed earlier in this book, the freedom songs (contemporized spirituals) gave the spiritual art form its broadest acceptance. The impact of television and instantaneous news reporting was of no small importance in this regard. The entire nonviolent movement was religious in tone, and the music did much to reflect and reinforce the religious base on which it stood. In the course of its development, the movement drew into its wake many people who were nonreligious, irreligious, and antireligious, but singing freedom songs for them and for others of diverse persuasions was a means of comfortable participation. It was this development that contributed most to minimizing the distinction between sacred and secular within the Black music tradition. The evolution of freedom songs and the impact of rhythm and blues prepared most of the ground in which modern gospel grew.

All of this review only serves to illustrate again the relationship between music and crisis in the Black community. Since the chief repository of authentic Black religious music remains in the church, and the church collectively attracts the largest segment of the Black community, it follows, then, that the music of the Black religious tradition can be a vital instrument for a ministry of social change. The Black Church has the troops and the inspiring music. The music of the Black religious tradition operates on two levels: first, psychologically and emotionally—it locates the people's sense of heritage, their roots, where they are and where they want to go; and secondly, it mobilizes and strengthens the resolve for struggle. A people's sense of destiny is rooted in their sense of history. Black sacred music is the primary reservoir of the Black people's historical context and an important factor in the process of social change.

The preceding paragraph might seem "visionary" or at least presumptuous. However, when one considers the hostile context and arduous route of development of Black sacred music, deference must be accorded its track record.

The enslavement of Black people in this republic and the cruelties that have accompanied it approach the unspeakable. Yet the Black community, for the most part, emerged with its humanity intact. Eugene Genovese, a Marxist, spent eleven years studying the slave system; and his recent monumental work, *Roll, Jordan, Roll,* concludes that Black people's religion was the means of their survival.[12] Aside from Genovese's corroborating conclusion, which church-oriented Blacks have always known, it is interesting that he titled his important work with a spiritual.[13] Part and parcel of that survival documented in his book is the crucial role of the faith music in preserving the personhood of the New World African. The spirituals, root of the Black sacred music tradition, kept the small flames burning on the heart altars of an oppressed people. The several facets of the spirituals' instrumentality in this regard have been delineated. The specific uses, over and above the general importance of spirituals to the slave community, are illustrated by their use as a signal for Nat Turner's rebellion, the jailing of Blacks in Georgetown, South Carolina, for singing of freedom,[14] and the frequent use of spirituals made in the days of the underground railroad.[15]

Without the body of music that was born and transmitted orally across the South from plantation to plantation and town to town, the "invisible church" that followed the Emancipation Proclamation would not have survived. The musical phenomenon of Black religion was the primary support system of the developmental period of historic Black churches. These same churches and the denominations they have produced (African Methodist Episcopal, African Methodist Episcopal Zion, National Baptist Convention, Inc., National Baptist Convention of U.S.A., Christian Methodist Episcopal, Progressive National Baptist Convention) have all benefited in their growth and development from the cohesive influence of Black sacred music. Very little serious argument can be found to deny the maxim "As goes Black music, so goes the Black Church."

In more recent days, the central role of music of the Black religious experience has been more clearly demonstrated. Who can deny that the nonviolent movement of the sixties did more for raising the consciousness level of the Black and White communities in America on the issue of justice than any other set of events since Emancipation? An integral part of the whole process of radical social change, primarily in the South, was the music of the Black religious experience.

> It is safe to say that the Freedom Movement in the South is a "singing movement." This is somewhat to be expected when one considers that music has strange power to evoke various emotional responses in the human animal. It has, historically, been of special value to the oppressed in every age. Somehow, the literature and idiom of music makes possible the restoration of lost hopes, it binds up the wounds of the broken-hearted, and by its character welds together the cohesive sentiment of a group of people of common experience.[16]

In point of specific reference:

> It is perfectly clear that the recent nonviolent thrust of the Negro community might not have had the vitality and dynamism that it has were it not for the impact of the Negro spiritual. The natural response to music, coupled with the deep meaning of the Negro spiritual, has produced a unique effect on the Freedom Movement in the South. It must always be remembered that religious orientation of the Freedom Movement intensifies the effect produced. Perhaps it should be said that the Freedom Movement's natural character of being religiously oriented is inseparable from the effect of...the Negro spiritual. They are each a supplement of the other.[17]

As a participant for nearly a decade in the nonviolent movement in the South, most of the time in the front lines, this writer is thoroughly convinced that there would have been very little "movement" without the music of the Black religious tradition. The author crisscrossed the South from Virginia to Texas, winter and summer, spring and fall, and there was no *movement* that did not sing the music of the Black religious tradition.[18]

One other excerpt documents this commonality:

> How has the Negro spiritual served the Freedom Movement in the South?...it is no mystery that with the Negro community's social life focused in the church and his protest movements religiously oriented, it would follow that the music

of the movement similarly would be that which is most informal and expressive of the deep yearnings of the ethnic group from which it has sprung.[19]

Most knowledgeable chroniclers of the Martin Luther King era consider Birmingham as one of the chief watersheds of the nonviolent movement in the South. In January of 1963, the late John F. Kennedy met with the heads of the major civil rights groups and indicated that he felt there was sufficient legislation on the issue of civil rights. In June of the same year, in a network radio and television address, he pleaded with America to face this "moral crisis," as he introduced what was to become the Civil Rights Act of 1964 (Public Accommodations Bill).[20] This radical change in presidential posture is directly attributable to the historic confrontation in Birmingham in the spring of the same year. Of course, there were several necessary ingredients that made the Birmingham movement the huge success that it was, and chief among these was the fact that the Birmingham movement was a great singing movement.

Most of the key figures were handsomely skilled song leaders. Andrew Young, Dorothy Cotton, James Bevel, Fred Shuttlesworth, and Bernard Lee were accomplished song leaders, and none was better than Ralph Abernathy.[21]

A standard technique of the movement was to move the mass meetings from community to community in order to encourage, support, and provide accurate information. It is important to note that on the very day that demonstrations were launched in Birmingham, after three postponements (stretching from November 1962 to April 3, 1963), the city bus system went on strike. Without public transportation, it was thought that the infant movement was doomed. Yet for thirty-nine nights, without interruption, the rallies were held in support of one of the most significant struggles in the South. A great deal of the stimulus for the sustained rallies was the quality of the music that made the mass meetings attractive in spite of the transportation dilemma.

Birmingham was not the only outstanding "singing movement." Equally distinctive in quality and fervor were the two Albany, Georgia campaigns (1961), Nashville, Tennessee (1960), Petersburg, Virginia (1960) and, of course, the "granddaddy of them all," the Montgomery, Alabama bus protest, 1955–1956.[22]

The strength of the movement was mobilized and programmed through the instrumentality of Black sacred music. The great churches, both in influence and in size, came to their positions of prominence with the heavy influence of the music of the Black religious tradition. The large numbers of people gravitated toward the music that was familiar to their experience and spoke to their hearts and souls.

The Continuing Importance of Black Sacred Music

The present moment in Black church life is one of severe crisis. The high-speed events of the last fifteen years in social change (much of it church-sponsored and/or church-led) have raised measurably the expectations of the Black and oppressed community. As the backlash sets in as a response to the identifiable gains made in recent years, the combination of events has placed an awesome challenge on the doorstep of the Black Church, which it is hard pressed to answer. The virtue of having been the dominant influence in the life of the oppressed community has seemingly been distorted into cardinal sin. Many strident voices, outside and inside the church, are asking, "What have you done for me lately?" Pointing to the record of yesteryear is insufficient to slough the persistent criticism leveled at the Black Church. It is undeniably true that the humanity of Black people could never have survived without their Africanized Christianity. The record speaks for itself. Nonetheless, James Russell Lowell said in poetic verse, "Time makes ancient good uncouth."[23]

It's a new age so far as the expectancy of the oppressed community is concerned, and it looks, properly so, to that institution which has been the chief liberating influence in its history. There are about fourteen million people of African descent in the various denominations across the United States, and the onus is upon the Black Church to give an account of its impact on Black life commensurate with its resources and the age in which it purports to serve. The very survival of the Black community can be directly attributed to the role that the Black Church has played in the lives of the people it served, but this can be no excuse to rest on its laurels of past performance.

Given the Black condition in America, the Black Church has a greater potential for a ministry of social change than does any other quarter of Black life. The cruel irony of this moment in history is that at the very instant the oppressed community's expectancy is highest, the climate in the republic is such that the likelihood of realization is lowest. The harsh reality of American life for the Black people is that as far as the delivery of services, employment, quality education, income dollars, housing, and such are concerned, they are worse off now than they were prior to the Supreme Court decision of 1954. This is no denial of gains made during what has been termed the King era, but for the most part the gains have been symbolic and not substantive. The great masses of Black people have been untouched by the societal changes that have been so visible. It follows, then, that calculated efforts must be made to maximize the liberating influence of the Black Church enterprise in the lives of the people it serves.

How shall the Black Church proceed? It is an oversimplification to say that the Black Church must serve this dilemma-ridden generation just as the "invisible church" served its generation. The enemy is the same; only his methods have changed. What can the Black Church do? It can remain as the citadel of hope and faith to a people too long oppressed, and in this generation it can try to create a model that delivers twentieth century answers to twentieth century problems. The injunction of the Galilean Prince is timeless and timely: "Feed the hungry, clothe the naked, heal the sick, give shelter to the homeless, bind up the wounds of the broken-hearted, set at liberty the captives, and preach the good news to the poor." (See Matthew 25:35–38; Luke 4:18)

The Black Church cannot do it all, but it can *begin!* Much of the criticism against the present-day Black Church is unwarranted, but some of it has legitimate grounds. The energy of the Black Church is too precious to be spent making defenses; it must address itself to correcting and strengthening the areas of its responsibility which are under legitimate attack. There is no way, generally or specifically, that the Black Church can function in the real world of the American nightmare without the instruments of the struggle: *a theology grounded in liberation, a contemporary sense of historical context, a God-ordained sense of destiny in this land, and the determination to endure.* Each of the above could require an inquiry in the context of the Black experience in America. They are listed here as ingredients which are contained in the music of the Black religious tradition. It is a very short step to conclude that maximizing the potential of the Black Church enterprise can be facilitated best through the use of its primary culture vehicle—Black sacred music!

It is obvious, then, the first step for any congregation that is genuinely interested in a ministry of social change is to preserve the integrity of the Black sacred music tradition. That is to say, churches peopled by the oppressed community must be diligent in resisting the temptation to "improve" so much that the musical idiom which helped them to survive is lost or diluted beyond recognition.

Music is central in Black worship and this is the real index of where a people are religiously and culturally. If Black churches lose their unique and distinctive musical idiom, then those same Black churches will be culturally and religiously out of context. The temptation to sing "good" music within the aura of urban churches with robed clergy and choirs, printed orders of worship, and the like is real. Stringent measures must be taken to preserve the integrity of the cultural vehicle, Black sacred music in this instance, so that the sense of history so crucial to an oppressed people is not destroyed. In many ways, it is not an overstatement to say that Black music is the Black experience, whether it is secular or sacred.

The foregoing is not a brief for a total Black experience worship style. This is neither necessary nor desirable. Black people in America are not altogether American *culturally* or altogether African *culturally*. As they are biracial in most instances, they are also bicultural. They speak the language of the realm; they are acculturated to the mores via religion and custom; they have adopted, to a large degree (unfortunately), the value system of the dominant society. Black people are probably more American than they are African. But the African influence is present, and its presence has been an important ingredient for Black people culturally and, more especially, musically. Through their music, Black people have made a singular contribution to Americana. It is very likely that if the integrity of Black music is maintained, they may, as well, make a singular contribution religiously by restoring to America its humanity. The religion of America is far removed from the substantive ethic of the Lord Jesus Christ. Reinhold Niebuhr states that Christianity in America has been corrupted into the manifest destiny of the nation. Things have become more important than people. When one reviews the agenda of the White and Black churches in America, the Black Church has been generally much closer to the concerns of the Galilean Prince than its White counterpart.

There is no need or desire to exclude the Western influence from the Black people's lifestyle but, rather, to make use of the most positive of those influences to give clearer expression in the American context to their own particular cultural genius. Black people are American like all other ethnic groups—Irish, German, Italian, or Polish—and like all others, they are no less American because they preserve the ethnicity of culture and ancestry. In the religious arena, this translates directly to developing the Black Church into an up-to-date institution that meets the challenges of the era with equanimity, without any loss of its cultural or ethnic identity. This means a Church with the very best equipment and resources that it can acquire, without any abridgment of its commitment to maintain the integrity of the Black community's unique and peculiar odyssey on these shores.

It is not enough to accept intellectually the concept of developing a bicultural stance in the central communal act of worship. The concept must take on a consciousness that gives flesh and sinew to programmatic development aimed at *maintaining the integrity of the cultural vehicle* (including the music of the Black religious tradition) and at the same time produce a bicultural stance reflective of the real world in which the Black Church exists.

The first step is a clear understanding and definition of what this cultural vehicle is and whence it has come. It is hoped that this book and other related materials would serve as a base for this first step. The maximum use of Black sacred music cannot be even approximated without an understanding and appreciation of what the instrument is. Secondly, at the individual church level at least and, one would hope, at denominational and educational levels as well, a conscious decision must be made to preserve the musical idiom of the Black religious experience. It will not suffice for any such program to move on the charisma of the pastor, who may be gone next week. An unsympathetic successor can undo in five months what a predecessor has labored five years to develop. The conscious decision might well take the form of a church resolution of policy, acted upon by the entire body that says in substance, "We will be true to our heritage and preserve the musical idiom of our forefathers, whose faith has brought us as far as we have come." This step is buttressed by conveying to musicians employed by the congregation that the use of Black sacred music in all of its traditional forms (in conjunction with European American music) is a matter of *church policy*.

The next step may be troublesome. Good musicians cost money. The effective development of a musical program with a pronounced bicultural stance will not proceed with a church policy statement alone. It must have the parallel *budget* commitment. Church musicians generally have received short shrift for any number of reasons too varied to list here. The primary reason is low-budget priority. It will become the responsibility of church leadership to see to it that the companion budget commitment is made attendant to the policy commitment.

All of the above helps to put the train on the track. The task is still far from complete. One must not underestimate the strong and persistent pull of western influences that threaten to dilute or supplant that which has given "staying power" to the Black Church community. A conscious and deliberate program such as that outlined above will need buttressing of several sorts. In the historic Black churches, there is no substitute for "pulpit stress." Many worthwhile and well-conceived programs in church life fail and drift into the sunset solely because "Rev." didn't provide adequate pulpit support. Silence from the pulpit has killed many a project aborning.

In that same vein, announcements are helpful and supportive, but preaching maintains a high priority. There is an inexhaustible mine for serious and creative preaching in Black sacred music. The intense, personal identification with Black hymnody is such that it cannot help giving fresh meaning to the everyday experiences of the worshipers. Sermon series can be effective and productive. The spiritual insights of the spirituals and other types of Black hymnody are so profound that those insights lend themselves to contemporary preaching. The possibilities are enormous with the choir(s) tied in directly to the theme of the minister's preaching.

Add to the sermonic efforts music workshops aimed at and focused on Black hymnody, gospel festivals, and Black culture series, with dramatic presentations that tell the story of the music of the Black religious experience. In urban centers, especially though not exclusively, the tradition of fellowship or exchange services might be used for joint programs built around the theme of the music of the Black religious experience. Some communities sponsor such festivals on a citywide bases. Those congregations that have adequate resources and competent choirs often record. Thus, in an informal and sometimes commercial way, they continue the musical idiom that so far has been preserved chiefly through the oral tradition that has tenaciously persisted in Black church life.

"Rise Up and Walk," an original music-narrative, written and directed by Clinton Utterbach, depicts the struggle for freedom in word and song. A sample of Harlem church life came alive on Broadway and provided an evening of culture and entertainment to an appreciative "standing room only" audience. (See Figure 15)

There is one other touchstone that is directly related to the matter of keeping the integrity of Black sacred music. It has to do with the impact of Black hymnody and the European American use of hymnody. It is observable in the level of participation. White congregations tend to be more spectator-oriented, while Black congregations tend to be more participant-oriented. The contrast is between a "proper" worship stance and the verbal free expression in Black churches. Depending upon the roots of the music, this distinguishing feature is true of secular music as well. There is a direct connection between this distinguishing feature of Black and White hymnody and the experiential versus rational character of Black and White worship. Churches that are heavily European American in their worship style tend to celebrate the rational; the worship in non-European churches tends to celebrate the experiential as well as the rational.

Figure 15

Town Hall, Friday Evening, November 15, 1974 at 8:00 p.m.

CANAAN BAPTIST CHURCH OF CHRIST
The Rev. Dr. Wyatt Tee Walker, Minister
presents

CLINTON H. UTTERBACH
AND
THE RECORDING CHOIR

in

"RISE UP AND WALK"
A MUSICAL TRIBUTE TO ALL THE HEROES OF
THE BLACK STRUGGLE FOR FREEDOM

EUGENE COOPER, Organist CLARENCE STROMAN, Drums
ROBERT HARGROVE, Organist EARL WALKER, Bass Guitar
NAOMI THOMAS, Pianist WILLIAM ALLEN, Bass Guitar
CLINTON UTTERBACH, Writer/Conductor

Creation
 HE DOTH ALL THINGS WELL . . . . .Carolyn Byrd Allen
 GREAT AND MARVELOUS . . . . .Choir (Henry Farmer)

Of Bondage
 SOMETIMES I FEEL LIKE
  A MOTHERLESS CHILD .Rubena Parker
 SOON WILL BE DONE . . . . . . .Clint Utterbach & Carolyn Byrd Allen

Of Hope
 TROUBLE IN DE LAND . . . . .Choir
 DIDN'T MY LORD DELIVER DANIEL . . . . .Beaulah Johnson
                 & Vivian Ross

WASN'T THAT A WIDE RIVER

Thus, the flavor of the worship celebration is determined largely by which mode obtains. White-style services are shorter, more rigid in worship form, and less emotional, and the music is conformity-oriented. On the other hand, Black-style worship is of longer duration, less formal and less rigid, emotion-filled, and expression-oriented. Authentic Black-style worship does not proceed without frequent exhortations of "Amen," "Tell the truth," "Say it," "Preach, brother," "Sing your song," and the like. Without signal, an entire congregation will join with a soloist at a peak moment in the rendition. Black-style worship, if it is anything, is a spontaneous communal celebration affirming God's presence and activity in the individual and collective lives of the worshipers.

Beyond the worship experience, the deeper concern is the impact observable in the everyday life of the oppressed community. Of what value is the music of the Black religious experience in the personal and collective lives of the people themselves?

The significance of the impact of the music of the Black religious tradition is broad. Given the dilemma of Black people in America, it is a marvel of religion that great numbers actively pursue a faith in God. The abundance and variety of religious experiences within the Black Protestant Christian tradition context is demonstrative of the vitality of that faith. There are a few, if any, Black churches on the American scene closing, or merging, in order to survive. Whatever the genius of the Black Church that keeps its members' hopes alive, Black sacred music plays a central role.

The devices of the music are many. Black people have always lived in a state of emergency. They are a crisis people. Their history is punctuated with trials and tribulations of every color and hue. Yet Blacks have survived. The music of faith, especially the spirituals, mirrors the social context of the Black people's travail in this land. Consequently, Black sacred music in the worship celebration calls forth recollections personally and collectively of past hardships and victories over trouble. The message of the music reminds the burdened of today that just as "God delivered Daniel in the lions' den," so would they be delivered from the afflictions of this life.

The music of the Black Church often verbalized poetically that which the individual has difficulty articulating. It is not uncommon to hear, in the everyday speech of the faithful, the idiomatic use of snatches of lines of hymns and spirituals. The religion of Black Christians is so largely encouched in their musical tradition that the verbiage is familiar to all, young and old. A common response to the courtesy greeting, "How are you?" is very often, "I'm holding on," a shortening of the Gospel hymn title, "I'm Just Holding On." When some occurrence takes place that smacks of good fortune, a frequent response in explanation is, "It pays to serve Jesus *every day*." Much of this idiomatic usage of the music language is a spin-off from the heavy use of hymn lyrics in preaching. One practice reinforces the other, and the singing of the music strengthens both.

The music of the Black religious experience was born and developed and shaped in a specific social context of suffering and oppression. Thus, the recollection of past trials through which God sustained and/or delivered his children strengthens the faith of the believer. Harlem is a very difficult place to keep one's faith in God. The widespread church life among Blacks and the concomitant activity that goes on is evidence that the people who comprise the congregations of the Harlems of this land are continually renewing their faith.

Much of the morale building necessary to faith renewal is traceable to the impact and influence of Black hymnody in the life of the individual worshiper. Church members who frequent night services in the inner city or weeknight activities are adamant about the inherent dangers of the crime-ridden streets. They earnestly believe that "God will take care of you."[24] In spite of muggings and burgled apartments, choir members and officers and lay members keep Black church life alive by their tenacious resolve. Much of the fear quotient is drained away in the Sunday worship celebrations and weekday meetings that strengthen their resolve. Central in both is the broad use of the music of the Black religious experience. One other important aspect of Black hymnody's impact on the life of the congregation is its unifying influence. People are diverse by nature; yet the Black Church enterprise is the *prima facie* example of the Black people's cooperative effort in the face of adversity. There is no need to set forth again the crucial importance of music in the development of the Black Church, but it is important to suggest the psychological basis for that success story. It is grounded in both the medium (singing) and the circumstance (oppression). Within the faith-worship context, the physical act of singing collectively in response to problems that are *collective* and *individual* expresses a commonality of circumstance that induces a sense of unity. It is very possible and probable that the input of the music at this level contributed significantly to the growth and development of the Black Church enterprise. All of the available evidence argues strongly that the music of the Black religious experience is inseparably intertwined with the origin, growth, and development of the Black Church as we know it today.

The Black Church of the future must seriously and systematically preserve, develop, and utilize this rich resource if it is to engage in service commensurate with both its past history and its future challenges. And when the oppression is over and the experiences have leveled off, Black sacred music *will* be one of the gifts of Black people to the Church universal, both here and hereafter.

---

1 Mrs. A. M. Townsend, *The Baptist Standard Hymnal* (Nashville: Sunday School Publishing Board, National Baptist Convention, USA, 1924), #500, p. 427.

2 George A. Buttrick, ed., *The Interpreter's Bible* (Nashville: Abingdon Press, 1952), vol. 8, p. 408.

3 Alfred A. Duckett, "An Interview with Thomas A. Dorsey," *Black World*, vol. 23, no. 9 (July 1974), pp. 5–6.

4 Wyatt Tee Walker, "The Soulful Journey of the Negro Spiritual: Freedom's Song," *Negro Digest* (July 1963), pp. 93–94.

5 Doris Akers.

6 Townsend, *op. cit.,* #700, p. 590.

7 Refrain of Doris Akers's tune.

8 Traditional stanza paraphrased from spiritual; used interchangeably with different songs.

9 Sterling Plumpp, *Black Rituals* (Chicago: Third World Press, 1972), p. 88.

10 Tony Heilbut, *The Gospel Sound* (New York: Simon and Schuster, Inc., 1971), p. 28.

11 *Southland Spirituals* (Chicago: The Rodeheaver Hall-Mack Co., 1936), p. 17.

12 Eugene Genovese, *Roll, Jordan, Roll* (New York: Pantheon Books, div. of Random House, 1974), p. 280.

13 Ibid., title page.

14 Ortiz Walton, *Music: Black, White and Blue* (New York: William A Morrow and Company, Inc., 1972), p. 27.

15 Philip Sterling and Rayford Logan, *Four Took Freedom* (Garden City, NY: Zenith Books, imprint of Doubleday and Company, Inc., 1967), pp. 9, 10, 30.

16 Walker, *op. cit.,* pp. 84–85.

17 Ibid., p. 86.

18 The author served as executive director of the Southern Christian Leadership Conference, 1960–1964.

19 Walker, *op. cit.,* p. 92.

20 Lerone Bennett, Jr., *Before the Mayflower: A History of the Negro in America, 1619–1964,* rev. ed. (Baltimore: Penguin Books, 1966), p. 345.

21 Administrative staff, SCLC: in order, program director; director, Citizenship Education Program; direct action specialist; national secretary of SCLC; administrative assistant to Wyatt Tee Walker; and treasurer, SCLC.

22 The Albany Movement, Dr. W. G. Anderson, president; Nashville (TN) Christian Leadership Council, Rev. Kelly Miller Smith, president; Petersburg (VA) Improvement Association, Rev. Wyatt Tee Walker, president; and the Montgomery Improvement Association, Dr. Martin Luther King, Jr., president.

23 From *The Service Hymnal* (Chicago: Hope Publishing Company, 1935), p. 373.

24 Townsend, *op. cit.*, #488, p. 415.

Conflict and Controversy in Black Religious Music

by Mellonee V. Burnim
from *African American Religion:*
Research Problems and Resources for the 1990s, published in 1992

Two indigenous genres of music have historically dominated and distinguished the worship of Black Christians—Negro spirituals and gospel music. Negro spirituals were the products of slaves; in comparison, gospel songs emerged during the first quarter of the twentieth century among members of a free urban working class population. Though the advent of these two forms was separated by a span of over 150 years, contemporary research has shown that Negro spirituals and gospel music function similarly in religion and culture for Black Americans.[1] Black composer John Work III has even argued that early gospel songs were "composed *by* [emphasis mine] the identical people who formerly created the spiritual, and is composed *for* [emphasis mine] the same people who used to worship by the spiritual—the Negro folk."[2]

In contrast to interpretations that cast gospel music and Negro spirituals as strongly linked cultural symbols, there are those analysts who emphasize the structural and textual distinctiveness of the two genres, casting a view of the Negro spiritual as fundamentally superior to gospel music. Some bemoan the fact that gospel songs now sometimes replace spirituals as the genre of choice to end Black college choir concerts.[3] Still others contend, however questionably, that spirituals have been "abandoned" altogether in the religious repertory.[4] It is not uncommon to encounter arguments that gospel as music and as message is undeserving of its position of prominence in the worship of Black churches of today.

Those commentaries that unfavorably juxtapose these two genres typically indict gospel for its "poor theology" and performance practices closely identified with secular music expressions.[5] What such arguments consistently lack is the historical perspective that reveals how perceptions of the Negro spiritual in its *original* form were conceptually identical to prevalent views of gospel music at its comparable stage of development.

This investigation will explore the historical tension that has existed between the "folk" or "core Black culture,"[6] which created both spirituals *and* gospel music, and those White and Black educated elite whose valuative predispositions and judgments were tempered, however unwittingly, by standards of excellence defined by Euro-America. It will be shown that valuative judgments that hierarchically rank Negro spirituals and gospel music are based on the type of spiritual created on Black college campuses following the aftermath of the Civil War, some one hundred years after the original folk version had emerged.

The intent of this discussion is to (1) illustrate the inherent relatedness of folk spirituals and gospel music and (2) show how the failure to view these genres through the appropriate cultural lens has negatively influenced both the content and the quantity of research devoted to these musical forms. It will be argued that an accurate sociocultural analysis of Black religious music can only be achieved through an intimate, historical grasp of the total Black religious music spectrum.

The Folk Spiritual

The earliest form of the Negro spiritual emerged during slavery, probably during the latter half of the eighteenth century. It was a uniquely African response to an institution that waged a systematic, though unsuccessful, onslaught onto the cultural legacy of the Black people in America. When introduced to Christianity, African slaves reinterpreted their religious instruction through an African cultural lens. From a sociocultural perspective, the development of the spiritual can actually be considered an overt act of resistance to the subjugation imposed by the Europeans. Consequently, the Negro folk spiritual symbolized Black cultural identity and Black religious expression as it evolved on North American soil.[7]

The spiritual developed in both the North and South as a genre distinctively different from music that characterized European American musical practice of the period. In both geographical contexts, the critical factor that allowed Blacks to articulate and advance a unique musical identity was autonomy. In the South, the invisible church was the spawning ground. Whether in the ravine, gully, field, or living quarters, African American slaves fiercely guarded their privacy, not merely out of fear of reprisal, but out of their collective desire to express themselves in a way that was uniquely meaningful to them. The following testimony from ex-slave Charles Grandy of Norfolk, Virginia, shows how Blacks often merely tolerated White religious leadership, preferring instead to conduct worship in their own time in their own way.

> Whites in our section used to have a service fo' us slaves ev'y fo'th Sunday, but dat wasn't 'nuf fo' dem who wanted to talk wid Jesus. Used to go 'cross de fields nights to a old tobacco barn on de side of a hill…. Had a old pot hid dere to catch de sound. Sometimes would stick yo' haid down in de pot if you got to shout awful loud. 'Member ole Sister Millie Jeffries. Would stick her haid inh de pot an' shout an' pray all night whilst de others was bustin' to take dere turn.[8]

Ecstatic worship, in which participants expressed themselves through shouting, was commonplace in the invisible church. The slaves offered extemporaneous prayers, compelling personal testimonies, and fiery sermons. When spirits were particularly high, services sometimes lasted far into the night, the duration being determined only by the collective energy that fueled the group.[9]

The establishment of the independent African Methodist Episcopal congregation under the leadership of Richard Allen set the stage for the same kind of autonomy that fostered the growth of the spiritual in the South. After splitting from the White Methodist parent church in Philadelphia in 1787, Allen made a conscious choice to reject Methodist control and domination, while simultaneously embracing its doctrines. Allen was quite satisfied with the "plain and simple gospel" of the Methodist Church, which in his view well suited his congregation because it was a gospel that "the unlearned can understand and the learned are sure to understand."[10] Allen's selective identification with Methodism was further evident in his decision to reject the standard Methodist hymnal, choosing instead to compile his own, which included songs he felt had greater appeal for Black people.

The research of Portia Maultsby and Eileen Southern details the innovations that characterized the songs in Allen's hymnal. Texts were simplified, and refrain lines and choruses were added routinely. Southern suggests that Allen wrote some of the texts for his 1801 hymnal (the book contained no music); for tunes, he probably composed some himself and utilized popular songs of the day, as well.[11] Allen's goal was to generate congregational participation and assure freedom of worship for his members.[12]

The results were undoubtedly pleasing to both Allen and his congregation, for non-Black observers were frequently struck by the high level of congregational participation in spirited singing in Allen's church. Not surprisingly, such early commentaries did not hesitate to register displeasure at the AME song style. The following reference is from an 1819 publication by John Watson entitled *Methodist Error or Friendly Christian Advice to Those Methodists Who Indulge in Extravagant Religious Emotions and Bodily Exercises:*

> We have too a growing evil, in the practice of singing in our places of worship, *merry* airs, adapted from old *songs*, to hymns of our composing, often miserable as poetry and senseless as matter, and most frequently composed and sung by the illiterate *Blacks* of the society.[13]

Southern speculates that Watson, a leading figure in the Methodist Church in Philadelphia, was actually referring to Bethel, the "dominant Black Methodists in the Philadelphia conference at the time."[14] Watson poses further that Mr. Wesley, Methodist Church founder, was equally displeased with those who chose to reject his hymnal for questionable substitutes. Watson notes that Wesley actually went as far as expelling three ministers "for singing '*poor, bald, flat, disjointed hymns,* and…singing the same verse over and over again with all their might 30 or 40 times,' to the utter discredit of all sober christianity [sic]."[15]

In his book, *Negro Slave Songs in the United States,* Miles Mark Fisher documents that, "Often Negroes were not permitted to enter Methodist church buildings at all since they disturbed quiet and dignified worship by beating out the rhythm of songs with feet patting and hands clapping in place of African instruments." "Moreover," he continues, "Negroes shouted in religious services, exercising their bodies until their odors were quite repulsive."[16]

Both the song texts and the aesthetic principles that embraced musical and textual repetition, hand clapping, foot stomps, and body movement clearly met with great disapproval from the White Methodist establishment. It was especially disconcerting that Blacks were known to utilize secular melodies in composing sacred songs. Watson was even more annoyed with the Blacks in the church who incorporated elements of dance in their songs. In his view, the aggregate of these behaviors completely nullified the religious dimension of the ritual.

> Here ought to be considered too a most exceptionable error, which has the tolerance at least of the rulers of our camp

meetings. In the *Blacks'* quarter, the Colored people get together, and sing for hours together, short scraps of disjointed affirmations, pledges, or prayers, lengthened out with long repetition *choruses*. These are all sung in the merry chorus-manner of the southern harvest field, or husking-frolic method of the slave Blacks.... With every word so sung, they have a sinking of one or other leg of the body alternately; producing an audible sound of the feet at every step, and as manifest as the steps of actual Negro dancing in Virginia, etc. If some, in the meantime sit, they strike the sounds alternately on each thigh. What, in the name of religion, can countenance or tolerate such gross perversions of true religion![17]

Watson's attitude toward the folk spiritual[18] was echoed by Daniel Alexander Payne, nineteenth century minister, historian, and bishop of the A.M.E. Church. People in the local churches viewed the shout as the essence of religion; rings were considered necessary for conversion. In contrast, Bishop Payne likened the ring shout ritual to a "bush meeting"; the songs he referred to as "cornfield ditties," and the participants he referred to as "ignorant but well meaning." His efforts to make the bands "disgusting" and to teach the "right, fit, and proper way of serving God" were, for all practical purposes, an abysmal failure among the masses of his congregants.[19] The following account of one of Payne's confrontations with the ring shout is an illustration:

> After the sermon they formed a ring, and with coats off sung, clapped their hands, and stamped their feet in a most ridiculous and heathenish way. I requested the pastor to go and stop their dancing. At his request, they stopped their dancing and clapping of hands, but remained singing and rocking their bodies to and fro. This they did for about fifteen minutes. I then went, and taking their leader by the arm requested him to desist and to sit down and sing in a rational manner. I told him also that it was a heathenish way to worship and disgraceful to themselves, the race, and the Christian name. In that instance they broke up their ring, but would not sit down, and walked sullenly away. After the sermon in the afternoon, having another opportunity of speaking alone to this young leader of the singing and clapping ring, he said: "Sinners won't get

converted unless there is a ring." Said I, "You might sing till you fell down dead, and you would fail to convert a single sinner, because nothing but the Spirit of God and the word of God can convert sinners." He replied: "The Spirit of God works upon people in different ways. At camp meeting there must be a ring here, a ring there, a ring over yonder, or sinners will not get converted." This was his idea, and it is also that of many others.[20]

Payne's view of appropriate music and behavior in worship was clearly aligned with those of Watson and other White Methodists. Those Blacks most likely to agree with his perspective were, in his view, ones with some degree of education. Unquestionably a perceptual rift between "the folk" and the educated elite was emerging.

The first collection of Negro spirituals was published by three White Northerners in 1867, almost one hundred years after spirituals had become an identifiable entity. Dena Epstein documents the response of the White press to this publication, noting that "Review after review stressed the *curious* aspect of the collection, as if even the most sympathetic critic could not quite conceive of these ungrammatical, strange songs as art worthy of appreciation on its own terms."[21] The *Lippincott Magazine* review was the most devastating, lambasting both the melodies and the song texts as worthless, reminiscent of Watson's evaluation forty-eight years earlier.

> As regards the collection of tunes and words in the book under notice, we have played many of them on the piano, but have failed to discover melody in any of them, except where the *idea* of the tune was clearly traceable to some old hymn tune, to the composition of which no Negro could lay claim. As to the words of the (so-called) hymns, they are generally so absurd and unmeaning, and often so absolutely profane (though, not so intended) that it would be well for the teachers in the schools and meeting houses where they are sung to commence, as speedily as possible, the destruction of the entire lot, in the interest, temporal and spiritual, of the wards in their care....
>
> It was hardly worthwhile to perpetuate this trash, vulgarity, and profanity by putting it in print.[22]

The Negro spiritual had now been written down and, in a sense, publicly sanctioned with this landmark collection. Yet not even this achievement was sufficient to eradicate grave assaults on its creative worth. Both the musical and poetic worth of the folk spiritual were lambasted and labeled as inappropriate repertoire for any young Black children who might be exposed to them.

The Arranged-Spiritual Tradition

It is common knowledge to students of African American music that prior to the efforts of the Fisk Jubilee Singers in the early 1870s, the Negro spiritual was known and respected almost exclusively by Blacks.[23] With the formation of this group, however, the spiritual assumed a character and purpose that differed radically from its folk antecedent. The small band of singers, mainly ex-slaves, was established under the leadership of George White, the White treasurer of Fisk University, who viewed musical concerts as a viable way of raising much-needed funds for the fledgling institution. Guided by his own cultural and musical heritage, and cognizant of the musical dispositions of the White audiences to whom this group would direct its efforts, George White molded the character of the music itself and the manner in which it was sung. According to John Work:

> Mr. White decided on a style of singing the spiritual which eliminated every element that detracted from the pure emotion of the song.... Finish, precision, and sincerity were demanded by this leader. While the program featured spirituals, variety was given it by the use of numbers of classical standard. Mr. White strove for an art presentation....[24]

Music in the African American Religious Tradition

The folk spiritual, created as an expression of African American culture and religion, was now transferred to the concert stage. This change in function was accompanied by a change in performance practices. Hand clapping, foot stomping, and individual expression were eliminated; predictability, control, and the absence of overt emotionalism became the aesthetic norm. The values that characterized George White's own musical culture were superimposed onto the Negro spiritual. As Louis Silveri put it, "Singing spirituals in the field was one thing, singing them to sophisticated audiences [read *White*] was something else."[25]

The Fisk campaign was an overwhelming financial success, prompting the formation of similar groups at other Black colleges. Following White's initiative, generations of Black composers established careers as arrangers of folk melodies for performance on the concert stage. The acclaim achieved by these performers and composers was international in scope and, in the minds of many, continues to symbolize the best in the Black college choir tradition to the present day.

George White's motives in recasting the Negro spiritual were both clear, from the standpoint of Fisk's financial state, and understandable, in view of his own cultural background and those of his audiences. White audiences were charmed by the unfamiliar, yet quaint melodies. At the same time, by stripping away the aesthetic fiber that most strongly contrasted with European American musical values, White created a comprehensive performance concept that was not only palatable, but pleasing to White listeners. But the rise to prominence of the concert version of the Negro spiritual was not without detractors.

The transformation of the spiritual resulted in a product far removed from the musical value system and the communal religious context of those who had spawned its growth. One outspoken critic of virtually all concert performances of spirituals was Zora Neale Hurston, who asserts:

> There never has been a presentation of genuine Negro spiritu-als to any audience anywhere. What is being sung by the concert artists and glee clubs are the works of Negro composers or adaptors *based* on the spirituals. Under this head come the works of Harry T. Burleigh, Rosamond Johnson, Lawrence Brown, Nathaniel Dett, Hall Johnson, and Work. All good work and beautiful, but *not* the spirituals.[26]

Unmoved by arguments that these "adaptations" represented an improve-ment over the original, Hurston contends instead that the transformation of the spiritual destroyed its essence—sapped it of its spontaneity. Her assessment is far from mere romanticism, for she acknowledges the right of the folk spiritual and its offspring, which she labels "neospirituals," to coexist. She cautions: "This is no condemnation of neospiritual. They are a valuable contribution to the music and literature of the world." Her clinching sentence clearly defines her stance—"But let no one imagine they are the songs of the people, as sung by them."[27]

In the following account, John Work indicates that folk spiritual tradition bearers shared the Hurston point of view. The commentary of the seasoned practitioner reveals that the aesthetic character of the folk spiritual resulted from conscious choices.

> The folk do not like these arrangements themselves. Once when I performed an arrangement of a spiritual for a folk singer from whom I had learned the spiritual in question, he told me that he did not like my arrangement because it was too "pretty." This was the first time that it had occurred to me that in their original performances, spirituals were not "pretty." Grand, majestic, moving perhaps, but never "pretty."[28]

Although the arranged spiritual was unquestionably an outgrowth of the folk spiritual, the two forms differed radically in function, in mode of transmission, and in performance style. As a genre developed in the Black college context, the arranged spiritual continues to be transmitted largely through the Black college choir. Those who most strongly support this tradition are most likely to be products of the Black college environment. But the arranged spiritual has never served as the core of religious repertoire among the Black masses. Performance of the folk spiritual, which functioned to nurture and sustain during slavery, was not directed outward to an audience, as was the arranged version, but inward as a means of sharing with one another and with God. The self-conscious dimension that caused the respondent to label the concert arrangement as "too pretty" was not a part of the folk concept.

It is this musical, cultural, and religious ideal that was translated into the twentieth century expression called gospel music. The continuum between the folk spiritual and gospel music, which bypasses the arranged spiritual altogether, will be discussed in the treatment of gospel music that follows. It is my contention that a lack of understanding of this connection generates those negative appraisals of gospel music that surface so often in the written literature and verbal lore of Black communities.

The Legacy of Gospel Music

By the 1920s, when gospel music started its slow but steady climb to respectability and widespread popularity among Black people in the United States, the folk spiritual had been in existence for over 150 years. The advent of gospel music was precipitated by the Great Migration of Blacks from rural to urban contexts during the years surrounding World Wars I and II.[29] The natural predisposition of the migrants to continue familiar patterns of behavior was evident in virtually every aspect of their new life in the city— ranging from patterns of dress and foodways to musical performance and worship styles.[30] Gospel pioneer Mahalia Jackson recalls:

> Gospel music in those days of the early 1930s was really tak-
> ing wing. It was the kind of music Colored people had left
> behind them down South and they liked it because it was just
> like a letter from home.[31]

The one-room folk church of the rural South became the storefront church of the urban North—a key setting for the emergence of gospel music. As I have written elsewhere:

> Black urban religious music, particularly in the newly formed
> Pentecostal denomination, differed little from the folk spiritu-
> al of the rural South, except for instrumental accompaniment.
> Both song types were based on the call-response structure;
> both required a demonstrative style of delivery, complete with
> hand clapping and dancing in the spirit; and both were sung in
> heterophony.[32]

Documenting the actual process of musical transformation that took place in southern urban churches, Work indicates:

> A visitor to southern Negro folk churches will hear much
> interesting music. Some of the music will be from the tradi-
> tional hymnody. Occasionally, traditional spirituals will be
> heard.... But he will hear also some exciting new music, which
> possibly will disturb him....
>
> Most notable of course are the instruments which are
> being added to the singing today. The accompaniments are
> just as integral a part of the performance as is the singing and,
> in a like manner, equally an expression of the folk.[33]

The continuation of Work's field account is especially valuable for its revealing distinction between this "new," potentially "disturbing" music and the arranged spiritual. He cautions that the accompaniments in arranged spirituals "must not be confused" with those of the urban folk church. The former, he contends, "is stiff and formal and bears little relation to the style and feeling of the song itself."[34]

Although the musical texture of the folk spiritual was altered with the addition of musical instruments, the expressive character—the "style and feeling"—remained unchanged. The following excerpt from a 1930 sermon by

Sanctified preacher Elder Curry in Jackson, Mississippi, transcribed with explanatory commentary by Paul Oliver, is a classic illustration.

> "People try to condemn us everywhere; they all say we are wrong. We dance you know in service, we can talk in service. We praise God on string inst'ments in service, now it's got to be proven tonight." He drew his proof from "'the 149th Division of the Psalms' and Mark, chapter 16, verse 16, 'Make a joyful noise unto the Lord'—now some people they don't like that noise"—but his vociferous congregation responded with the gospel song "when the Bible's right, somebody's wrong."[35]

As is clear from Elder Curry's defense, this emergent musical style was not universally sanctioned by Black churches. Like the folk spiritual, gospel music in its formative years faced staunch opposition and criticism. When gospel pioneer Thomas Dorsey began to systematically promote his own brand of gospel music, he too faced rejection. He recounts how initially most Black preachers and congregations of mainline Baptist and Methodist churches viewed the music with derision.

> ...gospel music was new and most people didn't understand. Some of the preachers used to call gospel music "sin" music. They related it to what they called worldly things—like jazz and blues and show business. Gospel music was different from approved hymns and spirituals. It had a beat.[36]

The religious sanctity of gospel music was so severely questioned that Dorsey was confronted with serious resistance when seeking acceptance for his new music. It was not until the 1930s that the gospel music support base was broadened to include significant numbers of Blacks in mainstream denominations. The achievement resulted in large part from the efforts of trailblazers like Thomas Dorsey, Mahalia Jackson, Mother Willie Mae Ford Smith, and Sallie Martin. Mahalia Jackson's experiences illustrate:

> Most of the criticism of my songs in the early days came from the high-up society Negroes. There were many who were wealthy, but they did nothing to help me....
>
> In those days the big Colored churches didn't want me and they didn't let me in. I had to make it my business to pack the

little basement-hall congregations and storefront churches and get their respect that way. When they began to see the crowds I drew, the big churches began to sit up and take notice....[37]

Mahalia Jackson initiated her own "audience development" strategy, one that bypassed the Black religious and musical establishment altogether. At one point, Mahalia developed a partnership with Thomas Dorsey, through which they countered resistance to gospel music by taking it "to the streets."[38] Dorsey recalls:

> There were many days and nights when Mahalia and I would be out there on the street corners.... Mahalia would sing songs I'd composed, and I'd sell sheet music to folks for five and ten cents.... We took gospel music all around the country too.[39]

As a direct result of the determination and perseverance of these and other pioneering spirits, gospel music has risen to its current position of prominence in the Black Church. Originally a music of the Sanctified Church, gospel music is now a pervasive force among Black worshippers of virtually every denomination. It is by no means a "fad," as some have labeled it,[40] for not unlike the folk spiritual, it was generated by a desire of the Black majority to worship in a culturally relevant way.

In one sense, gospel music is akin to the arranged spiritual; both are genres in which specific compositions or arrangements are the product of individual composers. Unlike the arranged spiritual, however, the actual score for a given gospel composition merely serves as a point of departure; performers are not expected to rigidly adhere to the printed page, but to freely interpret this basic guide according to the parameters of the Black gospel music aesthetic.[41] In a 1956 interview, gospel publisher-composer Kenneth Morris explains:

> We don't write it too difficult by including all of the harmony. The people who play it are not interested in harmony. There is no attempt to include perfect cadences and the like. It's not written for trained musicians.... A musician is a slave to notes. It's not written for that kind of person. It's written for a person who can get the melody and words and interpret the song for himself. We give only the basic idea and the person suits his own concept. If it were written correctly, we would go out of business. They wouldn't buy it...too complicated.[42]

Because of the marginal importance of the score in gospel music, it is perhaps more accurate to refer to it as essentially an oral tradition, like the folk spiritual, rather than a written one. As Thomas Dorsey once indicated, "Negroes don't buy much music. A White chorus of one hundred voices will buy one hundred copies of a song. A Negro chorus of the same size will buy two: one for the director and one for the pianist."[43]

The Western European-trained musician may well be chagrined at this apparent breach of musical ethics. But Kenneth Morris's quote reminds us that the patterns for teaching, disseminating, and performing gospel music are not representative of cultural deficiencies, but of cultural choices. Gospel composers are aware of the predispositions of their constituencies and *choose* therefore to meet them at the point of their needs and desires, just as Richard Allen did in making modifications in standard hymns for his congregation.

On this basis, the conceptual link between the folk spiritual and gospel music becomes even more evident. In fact, other writers[44] have argued as I do that

> the aesthetic values and practices intrinsic to the gospel music tradition do not represent a break with the traditional past. Instead the gospel tradition is concrete evidence of the existence of a continuum in Black music, and a "continuity of consciousness" flowing through various aspects of Black culture.[45]

Conclusions

The dynamic role that music plays in the worship of Black Americans has been well documented. From the vivid descriptions of songs shouted out in the invisible church of the Black slave, to the musical innovations standardized in the newly independent A.M.E. congregation founded by Richard Allen, we learn of the repertoire, performance practices, and function of the eighteenth century genre called the folk spiritual. From studies of migration patterns and storefront churches in the early decades of the twentieth century, we learn of the transference of these musical concepts into the modern Black religious context, resulting in the development of gospel music.

At the same time that folk spirituals and gospel music functioned to nourish, support, and sustain Black Americans, responses to the music by cultural outsiders and by members of the educated Black elite were often highly critical. Those spirituals that are held in esteem today by this educated, musically literate body are those that demonstrate the greatest affinity to Western European musical practice.

The Negro spiritual in its original form is not the outgrowth of the post-Civil War college tradition. In its infancy, it was not a source of pride for many Black religious leaders, but an evil to be eradicated, just like gospel music. Its texts and performance were much maligned by Whites and members of the Black elite, just like gospel. Even more revealing, and indeed culturally enlightening, is the knowledge that the musical chasm so widely construed as demarcating spirituals from gospel is more myth than reality. Though the two forms differ in their outward manifestations, they are indeed conceptually, functionally, and culturally synonymous.[46]

Implications

Research in gospel music has been the victim of benign neglect since its beginning. In my view, this neglect results, at least in part, from an evaluation of gospel music as unworthy of serious study. The first dissertation devoted to gospel music was completed in 1960. In the two decades following, a total of six dissertations were completed on this topic[47] Although the output virtually doubled in the 1980s, there is tremendous need for research on this subject.

To date, published biographies exist for only one Black gospel performer—Mahalia Jackson. The recent publication on Thomas Dorsey by Michael Harris[48] promises to be a major contribution in this area. Yet, there are still no in-depth analyses of the Gospel Music Workshop of America, the National Convention of Gospel Choirs and Choruses founded by Thomas Dorsey, or the annual Black College Gospel Choir Workshop. The membership of each of these interdenominational bodies comes primarily from the ranks of the local church choir. The personal narratives of choir members who hold such dual memberships can provide revealing insights into the manner and extent of influence these national bodies have on church music programs at the local level.

Perhaps the greatest need in gospel music research is to establish an accurate historical record that documents the creativity, imagination, and genius of musical performance in the Black church. Clearly all aspects of material culture are of value—recordings, photographs, and programs, not only of the traditional morning worship service, but also of rehearsals and special events such as choir, pastor and church anniversaries, musicals, and holiday celebrations.

Interviews of those involved in church music programs should include ministers of music, choir directors, accompanists, and vocalists. The interview process should seek to answer questions regarding the actual content and character of performance as well as evaluations of its function and quality. Such data will contribute greatly to the development of a more accurate and balanced cultural portrayal of music in the Black Church.

---

1 George Robinson Ricks, "Some Aspects of the Religious Music of the United States Negro: An Ethnomusicological Study with Special Emphasis on the Gospel Tradition" Dissertation, Northwestern University, 1960; Lawrence Levine, *Black Culture and Black Consciousness* (New York: Oxford University Press, 1977), pp. 174–189; Mellonee Burnim, "Functional Dimensions of Gospel Music Performance," *Western Journal of Black Studies* 12/2 (Summer 1988), pp. 113–114.

2 John Work, "Changing Patterns in Negro Folk Songs," *Journal of American Folklore* 62 (1949), p. 141.

3 Romeo Phillips, "Some Perceptions of Gospel Music," *The Black Perspective in Music* 10/2 (Fall 1982): p. 166; Roland Carter, Comments during Morgan State University Choir Concert, Black Composer's Symposium, Smithsonian Institution, Washington, DC, February 3–4, 1984.

4 Jesse Wendell Mapson, *The Ministry of Music in the Black Church* (Valley Forge, PA: Judson Press, 1984).

5 Phillips, "Perceptions"; Mapson, *Ministry of Music;* Marion Joseph Franklin, "The Relationship of Black Preaching to Black Gospel Music," Dissertation, Drew University, 1982, DAI 43/04A, p. 1188; George W. Crawford, "Jazzin' God," *The Crisis* 36/2 (February 1929), 45; Tony Heilbut, *The Gospel Sound,* 2d ed. (Garden City, NY: Anchor Press, 1975), p. xxi.

6 John Gwaltney, *Drylongso: A Self-Portrait of Black America* (New York: Random House, 1980).

7 Gilbert Chase, *America's Music,* rev. 3d ed. (Urbana and Chicago: University of Illinois Press, 1987), p. 214; Albert Raboteau, *Slave Religion: "The Invisible Institution" in the Antebellum South* (New York: Oxford University Press, 1978; paperback, 1980), pp. 72–74; Richard Waterman, "On Flogging a Dead Horse: Lessons Learned from the Africanism Controversy," *Ethnomusicology* 7 (1963).

8 Charles Perdue, et al., ed., *Weevils in the Wheat: Interviews with Ex-Virginia Slaves* (Bloomington, IN: Indiana University Press, 1980), p. 119.

9 Raboteau, *Slave Religion,* pp. 220–222.

10 Charles Wesley, *Richard Allen: Apostle of Freedom* (Washington, DC: Associated Publishers, 1935), p. 72.

11 Eileen Southern, *The Music of Black Americans: A History*, 2d ed. (New York: W. W. Norton, 1983), p. 77.

12 Portia Maultsby, "Music of Northern Independent Black Churches during the Antebellum Period," *Ethnomusicology* 19/3 (1975), 413; Southern, p. 75.

13 John F. Watson, *Methodist Error* (1819); excerpts reprinted in *Readings in Black American Music*, 2d ed., Eileen Southern, ed. (New York: W. W. Norton, 1983), pp. 62–63.

14 Southern, *Music of Black Americans*, p. 62.

15 Watson, *Methodist Error*, p. 63.

16 Miles Mark Fisher, *Negro Slave Songs in the United States*, 2d ed. (New York: Citadel Press, paperbound, 1969), p. 35.

17 Watson, *Methodist Error*, p. 63.

18 The folk spiritual has been variously referred to as the shout, ring shout, or "runnin spirchil." For a more detailed discussion of this genre, see preface to William Francis Allen, Charles Pickard Ware, and Lucy McKim Garrison, *Slave Songs of the United States* (1867; reprint New York: Oak Publications, 1965).

19 Daniel Alexander Payne, *Recollections of Seventy Years* (1888); excerpts reprinted in Southern, *Readings in Black American Music*, p. 69.

20 Ibid., pp. 68–69.

21 Dena Epstein, *Sinful Tunes and Spirituals* (Chicago: University of Illinois Press, 1977), p. 338.

22 Ibid., p. 339.

23 Southern, *Music of Black Americans*, p. 225; Robert Nathaniel Dett, "The Emancipation of Negro Music," *Southern Workman* 47 (April 1918), p. 173.

24 John Work, *American Negro Songs and Spirituals* (New York: Bonanza Books, 1940), p. 15.

25 Louis Silveri, "The Singing Tours of the Fisk Jubilee Singers: 1871–1874," in *Feel the Spirit: Studies in Nineteenth Century Afro-American Music*, George R. Keck and Sherrill V. Martin, eds. (Westport, CT: Greenwood Press, 1988), p. 107.

26 Zora Neale Hurston, "Spirituals and Neo-Spirituals," in *Negro Anthology 1931–1933*, Maud Cunard, ed. (London: Wishart & Co., 1934), p. 360.

27 Ibid.

28 Work, "Negro Folk Songs," pp. 136–137.

29 Ricks, "Religious Music," pp. 10–13; Pearl Williams-Jones, "Afro-American Gospel Music: A Brief Historical and Analytical Survey (1930–1970)," in *Development Materials for a One-Year Course in African Music for the General Undergraduate Student*, Vada E. Butcher, ed., project of Fine Arts Department, Howard University (Washington, DC: U.S. Department of Health, Education and Welfare, 1970), p. 205.

30 For a detailed discussion of the transfer of cultural patterns from rural southern communities to the city of Chicago, see Arna Bontemps and Jack Conroy, *Anyplace But Here* (New York: Hill and Wang, 1966; originally published as *They Seek a City,* 1945).

31 Mahalia Jackson (with Evan Wylie), *Movin' On Up* (New York: Hawthorne, 1966), p. 60.

32 Mellonee Burnim and Portia Maultsby, "From Backwoods to City Streets: The Afro-American Musical Journey," in *Expressively Black,* Geneva Gaye and Willie Baber, eds. (New York: Praeger, 1987), p. 121.

33 Work, "Negro Folk Songs," p. 136.

34 Ibid.

35 Paul Oliver, *Songsters and Saints: Vocal Traditions on Race Records* (New York: Cambridge University Press, 1984), p. 174.

36 Alfred Duckett, "An Interview with Thomas Dorsey," *Black World* (July 1974), p. 5.

37 Jackson, *Movin' On Up,* p. 66.

38 Duckett, "Thomas Dorsey," p. 6; see also Lorraine Goreau, *Just Mahalia Baby* (Waco, TX: Word, 1975), p. 56.

39 Duckett, p. 6.

40 Phillips, "Gospel Music," p. 173.

41 For a detailed discussion of the gospel music aesthetic, see Burnim, "Gospel Music Performance"; Pearl Williams-Jones, "Afro-American Music: A Crystallization of the Black Aesthetic," *Ethnomusicology* 19/3 (September 1975); and Horace Boyer, "Contemporary Gospel Music," *The Black Perspective in Music* 7/1 (Spring 1979): Part II.

42 Ricks, "Religious Music," p. 143.

43 Ibid., p. 144.

44 See Work, "Negro Folk Songs," p. 141; Williams-Jones, "Afro-American Gospel Music," pp. 205–206; Levine, *Black Culture,* p. 189; Ricks, "Religious Music," pp. 10–13.

45 Burnim, "Gospel Music Performance," p. 114.

46 See Burnim, "Gospel Music Performance" and Burnim and Maultsby, "From Backwoods to City Streets."

47 See Mellonee Burnim, "Gospel Music Research," *Black Music Research Journal 1/1* (1981).

48 Michael W. Harris, *Thomas A. Dorsey and the Rise of Gospel Music* (New York: Oxford University Press, 1991).

Church Music:
A Position Paper
(with special consideration
of music in the Black Church)

by Wendell Phillips Whalum
Morehouse College
Atlanta, Georgia, published in 1975

In her essay, "The Dilemma of Church Music Today,"[1] Helen E. Pfatteicher makes an important point on which to begin:

> Church music has many different meanings. What it means to an individual depends to a large degree on what he hears from his childhood on, and in his adult life his willingness to concentrate upon and think about what he hears. The subconscious mind tucks away sounds from our early life which we were scarcely conscious of hearing. These influence our taste and surprise us by coming to the surface many years later.[1]

The first sentence of this quotation is the most important for what I am about in considering where we are today. We are in the midst of what may become the greatest period of church music experimentation of all times. Not all of this is good.

With the current scene of jazz masses, rock hymns, sacred jazz services, gospel-blues, plus all the other musics of the past, it is not difficult to agree that it "has many different meanings." Most of the churches that make use of the various innovative types mentioned have wrangled theological justification for their kind of music. Such arguments are difficult to combat especially if we remember that above all, the music should have meaning for the people and its message fully endorsed by them.

The subject of church music has often been examined by scholars. Some of these have been general in approach and some have been very specific. The specific ones cover the topics of chant, hymn, the choir and its function, the organ, instruments in worship, and the like. And these, of course, are most often slanted in the direction of the church responsible for the publication or study.

The result is that the historical church organizations that have education as one of their chief concerns have theirs well established as to what good music is, and this always includes a solid idea of what a standard choir program contains. Since there are usually schools, colleges, and universities under their general control, they have no problem keeping the level of quality performance high and producing good musical offerings for their services. One does not need to be reminded that these churches are, primarily, those whose roots are European and reach far back in history.

In America we have not held a genuine concern for the welfare of music in the churches that are real products of American soil. Perhaps they should not have been allowed to flourish and should have been nipped in the bud. With religious freedom and some regrets imposed by the American way, we must accept the fact that we do have religious bodies that have developed a concept of music that often reflects bad musical form and weak religious texts and which, in the service, often bears no resemblance to continuity in worship. This is especially true of those churches at the far end of the non-liturgical groups, Black and White. Some of these, even though they use familiar denominational names, really have little resemblance to what that denomination holds as its philosophy and concern.

Consequently, we have allowed for "hymns" of this group to be created that tell strange stories of, usually, a personal testimony and do not speak well for the group. In some settings, we have allowed for a religious song to be developed that was endorsed more for its rhythms than its texts. We have allowed for a music to be developed that is called a hymn but, by definition, is no hymn at all.

The polarity that has developed is one that holds on the one hand a guarded music, strict, unbending, and appointed for a specific function, against one that is free, bending, and not always with a specific understanding in mind. The result at present is that any innovation coming after the widespread strict music concept is viewed with much criticism. It tends to make the lesser bodies react adamantly and causes them to work even harder for the unconventional, though they might not call it such.

Certain rationalizing arguments using scriptural injunctions for this different music come to mind that allow for the freedoms that are now exercised by these various groups. They argue that "the Lord said:" "Sing unto the Lord"; "Make a joyful noise"; "Let everything that hath breath" all join to allow for these differences. But what of quality and preparation level? It seems to me that these are the most important lines in judging the music offerings of our religious services. It appears that this is what is often forgotten. Further, it remains that what we offer unto God should bear the mark of being our best. Therefore, I am not here as concerned with the form of musical offering as I am with the quality which, in the end, might take care of the question of the form.

There is a kind of cheapness in much religious music today that chisels away at its sincerity, its directness, and its ability to support our intentions in worship. Since worship stands very well by itself without the addition of music or, for that matter, without any outward sound, it certainly seems that any disturbance of this silence should never embarrass it, but always exalt to the highest the praise of the Almighty. When there is sound from the congregation, less it be otherwise noise, it should be fully understood by all who make it or by all for whom it is made. Otherwise, why the sound at all? Now, in order for it to be understood, pondered, and used by the congregation, the process of education is all-important.

This process leads to an examination of the history of church music and to view its development and successful musical practices as it moves toward our time. It is in this study that we will find, for example, the accounts of the uses of hymns, the chief congregational music, and how hymns support the art of praise for corporate worship. Carl F. Price, in his paper, "What is a Hymn"[2] reprints Saint Augustine's definition of a Christian hymn:

> Do you know what a hymn is? It is singing to the praise of
> God. If you praise God and do not sing, you utter no hymn. If
> you sing and praise not God, you utter no hymn. If you praise
> anything which does not pertain to the praise of God, though
> in singing you praise, you utter no hymn.

The serious question of the quality of hymn singing today comes to mind. Too, the quality of the hymnbooks in many churches also comes to mind. Both result in rather disturbing thoughts. And this, I am afraid, to borrow a phrase from Erik Routley, is because there seem to be few today who can "bring to the study of church music a sense of theology." Routley goes on to say that in order "to do it adequately will be to return to the Middle Ages, in music's nonage when gifted theologians were not above turning their attention to the relations between theology and music, and proceed from there to a position which takes account of music's 'coming of age,' but does not involve that failure of theological nerve which I hold to be at the root of our present disorders, and to imply a much greater threat to future church music than most of us are at present aware of."[3]

Nancy White Thomas[4] states her concern for the church universal as follows:

> The greatest single need in church music today is precisely what it was in Paul's day, namely, that the people understand what they are singing and that they sing from their hearts.
>
> In making this pronouncement I am saying four fundamental things: (1) all is not well with church music; (2) hymn singing is the most important part of church music; (3) the meaning of the words is central in hymn singing; (4) the meaning should be clear and vital to the congregation.

The paucity of books and articles that deal directly with the music of the Black Church is unfortunate. The student must rely heavily on general writings of John W. Work III, Miles Mark Fisher, Eileen Southern, James Weldon Johnson, R. Nathaniel Dett, Benjamin E. Mays, E. Franklin Frazier, Carter G. Woodson, Daniel Payne, Wesley Gaines, and Benjamin G. Brawley. But most of these do not specifically speak of the music, per se. The student must be willing to piece together the musical contributions of Dr. and Mrs. A. M. Townsend, E. W. D. Isaac, Lucie E. Campbell, and several other Black men and women who worked through the National Baptist Publishing Board and the African Methodist Episcopal Church. He must be able to tie together the middle ground held by this group that really linked a Black sacred music growing out of the spiritual to what would later become the Black concept of gospel music. The middle ground contains the gems known now only through vanishing Baptist books as *The Awakening Echoes, Carols of Glory, The Baptist Standard Hymnal,* and *Gospel Pearls.* It is also the group that wrote gospel hymns and then moved on to create a new gospel.

The neglect of Black church music by most scholars leaves me without choice. I must state my position, my sincere considerations, and my conclusions, and then offer a guide for improving what I criticize. I must not allow my mind, not for a moment, to engage in the thought that what is now happening in music in the Black Church is here to stay and that the music program cannot be redeemed. I feel that it can, but certain truths must first come to light. I trust my feelings are clear.

Music in the Black Church[5]

There is probably no area of Black church life more perplexing and pathetic than music and what we have let happen to it. Not only have a conglomerate of styles and functions crept into our church music, but there seems to be little knowledge of the "why music in worship" concept in the minds of those whose responsibility it is to govern the church and its music. The pathetic aspect is that the music, often enjoyed by worshippers, offers little by way of Christian education or kingdom building, and the effect lasts only a few minutes after its "embers" fade away.

A pragmatic approach to correcting the problems is offered here in hope that through citing specific problems an immediate attempt toward correction will begin. It is also hoped that these criticisms will be accepted as being wholly constructive since this is the sole reason for offering them. I must underscore that my remarks are directed to the church in general and not to any specific denomination. My feeling is that careful explanation of what I consider offensive will serve to identify the problem where it exists.

As I see it, the clergy and musicians are both to be blamed for what has occurred, and logically, it is their responsibility to correct it. Of the blame, too, will inevitably point to many of us who, in addition to being practicing church musicians, also have, little by little, abdicated our responsibility of instructing those who have not had good solid training but who, for various reasons, assume the task. We are, therefore, guilty of standing by through the years watching music in the Black Church, to a large degree, deteriorate and, to some extent, decay.

The following categories represent the levels of music personnel found serving in many churches today:

1. *The talented, but untrained musicians.* These musicians often cannot read music, have no knowledge of choir organization or directing, and no knowledge of a study of hymns, liturgy, or religion in history.
2. *The untrained and untalented, but willing musicians.* This group, larger in number than one would suspect, is made up of those who usually have had one or two years of piano, not music, and are willing because no one in the church will (or can) assume the music responsibility.

3. *Those musicians with basic music training who take church music duties without understanding what the program should be about and how it should be conducted.* The result here is that much that is offered is out of focus with the needs and understanding of the congregation.

4. *Those with good training and excellent exposition who shut their eyes to what the level of their congregation actually is and, instead of educating them, operate on a plane always too sophisticated.* It is this group that will frequently impose oratorios, cantatas, and pageants on a people not yet fully educated in hymns and anthems and who are, therefore, not ready for extended works.

5. *Those with excellent training who, unfortunately, take an attitude of superiority and make no attempt to lift the level of musical awareness upward except by chance.* This kind of musician is usually organist-director and is so "important" until he will only officiate at Sunday morning services, funerals, and weddings of families of prominent citizens in the community.

Members of the clergy have sometimes been or are guilty of misusing the music portions of the church program. Usually without even good layman's ability to appreciate music, they have imposed inferior standards, for various reasons, on their congregations. Hymnbooks of good, solid reference are lacking and choirs are formed as fund-raising organizations rather than for the purpose that they should serve. Afraid of costs, many ministers have selected instruments for their church houses, organs, and pianos without any knowledge of quality models. Too, as a money-saving gimmick, the minister will often hire a musician who will accept a nominal fee, but who also knows nothing of standard literature or instruments or choir training, and all too frequently knows not enough about the history of the Black Church.

The early Black church, mid-nineteenth century, had no choir and because of the nature of things, the entire congregation did all the singing, and much there was, without aid of instruments. It was led, not conducted, by one in the congregation who had the ability to lead, remember the songs, and who could line-out the hymns. This practice of lining-out in itself is not originally Black, but comes from England in the eighteenth century to the new singing schools of White America. Black Christians once introduced to the technique, adopted it, blackened it and made, what I consider, some of the most beautiful music of the Black religious experience. This type of hymn singing is in danger of vanishing.

As denominations developed, the Baptist Church becomes the pervasive group for continuing this singing. Indeed it has not been abandoned in a precious few churches, especially the Primitive Baptist and a few of the National and Progressive Baptist. Methodist, especially African Methodist, used this music less frequently in favor of a more conservative Methodist hymnody. Often, even now, a minister, presiding elder, or bishop who has known the technique will use it when preparing to preach. This, though, unlike the Baptist, is not consistent in use as in prayer services before the Sunday worship service begins.

As the denominations are developing alongside developing educational institutions, through increased literacy, music via organs, choir and hymnbooks, and aspiring clergy comes to the fore. The result is an immediate cessation of the use of these grand old hymns. In time the choirs usually being patterned by the new college choirs, that were more often directed by White directors than not, embarked on fat nineteenth century anthems and advanced to the level where they could perform in church choir festivals. Wonderful![6] As the main two denominations moved toward conventions, music by the best choirs would be performed for delegates and the model worked, at least for a while.

Political and social upheaval closing the last century and continuing through the first thirty-five years or so of the twentieth century, gradual at first and then with speed, brought all manner of religious groups into focus. The educated were isolated either by themselves or by the abandonment of those who felt inferior. This left the former with their pipe organs, choirs and hymnbooks, and usually handsome structures. The "new" churches sought men who could preach, not necessarily pastor, and who could lead them in a different religious experience, and men who would, above all else, let the people, irrespective of ability, have much input into what would occur in their services.

The music in these new groups took various twists. One group used the music of the great White revivalists movement—shape notes. Others outlawed the use of music instruments in services, while others brought in any and all instruments that would aid in heightening the emotional aspect of worship.

By the time of the depression, 1929, a still newer concept in music, half borrowed from the White gospel hymn movement and half adapted from secular sources, takes hold. The new music, gospel music, becomes the favored of the less educated and during the economic crisis grew by leaps and bounds.

It concentrated in varying degrees through the 1960s when it seemed to have made its greatest strides. Little by little, trained musicians, unwilling and often unable to play and sing gospel music, left the choir, organs, pianos and, in many instances, the church. Today we are suffering from this exodus of musicians.

What would our church music be like if we had, instead of cutting away, built upon the spiritual, added the lined-out hymns, anthems, gospel (with serious concern for its composition, structure, and performance), and made music education an essential part of Christian education? I have the idea that we would have fabricated a church music truly representative of the people and, in quality, a token par excellence to God! Instead, we are heirs to attitudes often resentful of any musical ideas different from those with which we find satisfaction, and we are often unwilling to bend our preferences.

Gospel choirs today, though very talented and entertaining, often turn the act of worship, which is at best well-planned drama, into a religious circus in which the profane often exceeds the religious. But the choirs themselves are not to blame here. Blame is directed at the ministers who have allowed a musical hodge-podge to develop. I underscore *there is nothing wrong with the concept of gospel music; the wrongness comes with what we have done with it (or shall we say, what we have not done).* Much beautiful and appropriate gospel music has been written that contains pertinent religious texts. Excellent renditions have been given by many Gospel choirs. When the best of these are used, there can be no complaint.

Black people have been called a musical people. I hasten to add, what have we done, by and large, with the talent? In my judgment, we have, to the extent of writing it down, reading notes, and singing under direction, "hid it under a bushel." The present day finds us in increasing numbers unable to converse about spirituals as well as to sing them, unable to sing lined hymns, unable to recognize Black gospel hymns as opposed to gospel music, and unable to learn gospel music unless it is first recorded by some popular group. One thing is sure. Gospel music today is following the route of popular music. Unlike the spirituals that have withstood almost two centuries, one seldom finds a gospel song being sung today that was sung in the 1930s, or 1940s, 1950 and now the 1960s. It is ever-changing.

The mandate for the Black church musician is that he recall through comprehensive study the historical root of music of the slave experience, which music, more than any other single lyric, provides dignified commentary on the journey to "freedom." He must then use it in its natural unarranged form and, with advancing maturity of Western musical forms, tie it to all other pertinent musics of the Church. He must critically examine the efficacy of all subsequent musics of Black people and shape it well for his use, knowing as he does it that all music cannot be salvaged even though it be well liked and popular. If it does not meet the test of an offering of praise to God from a grateful and responsible people, it must be discarded. This will ensure a quality representative for posterity.

The clergy and musician must always bear in mind that "music is the handmaiden of theology" and, as such, serves as an aid in the need for a critical explanation of the Word. The hymn must be studied and carefully chosen. It must never allow sentimentalism to prevail over logic in the text, and it should always support corporate worship so that unity in singing it will bespeak our commitment and our determination to follow Christ until the desired goal is attained.

I conclude this with a paragraph from the pens of three persons well known in American Church history: Rev. Paul Austin Wolfe, D.D.; Helen A. Dickinson, Ph.D.; Clarence Dickinson, Mus. Doc.; Litt. D. The paragraph appeared in a booklet, *The Choir Loft and the Pulpit*, published by H. W. Gray Co. in 1943:

> ...the question of need is a difficult one. What does the Church of God need for worship? Surely the Church is not dependent upon a choir. There have been periods in church history during which there was not only no choir but no organ, no formal music of any kind. But then, the Church is not dependent upon a minister. There have been periods when the head of every household was his own priest. And the worship of God is not dependent upon a sanctuary. There have been times in which the Christian Church worshipped in the homes of its members. Need depends upon the standard, the quality of service, one wishes to maintain. Lear said something like this to his eldest daughter who told him that he needed neither fifty, nor twenty-five, nor ten, nor even five attending knights:
>
> > "Allow not nature more than nature needs.
> > Man's life's as cheap as beast's."

There is the word: "cheap." The question is, how cheap do we wish to make the service of the Church? It can be made very cheap; it can be made tawdry. But let us not imagine that we will glorify God in so doing. A service without a good choir will be much more inadequate, much less moving, much less thrilling than a service with it.

And before the time comes to meet the laymen, ministers ought to clarify their minds on the importance of this ministry [of music]. What is the ministry of music? What does it do? Well, of course, there is the routine contribution. The choir and the organ lead the congregation in worship and the singing of the hymns; they provide the responses, the anthems. But the service is much greater than this. Every minister who has shared the ministry of a good choir is aware of it. He knows, how often, when a service began to lag, an anthem by the choir has picked it up, sat it on a high plane again, carried it forward. He has read the Scripture and preached the sermon the better because of that anthem. And he knows that many times it was an anthem or a response that redeemed the entire service. The congregation went home remembering a prayer that had been sung more than one that had been spoken....

No, one cannot speak of this ministry lightly. It is an integral part of the worship of the Church. It must be retained and improved if the Church is to render its fullest service.

I am determined to do all that I can to improve the role of music in divine worship. Are you?

Bibliography

Allen, William Francis, et al. *Slave Songs of the United States.* (New York: A. Simpson & Co., 1867).

Anderson, Marian. *My Lord What a Morning.* (New York: The Viking Press, 1966).

Awakening Echoes. (Nashville: The National B.Y.P.U. Board, 1931).

Ball, Charles. *Fifty Years in Chains.* (New York: Dover Publications, Inc., 1978).

Ballanta-Taylor, C. J. S. *St. Helena Island Spirituals.* (New York: Scribners, 1923).

Baptist Hymnal, The. (Philadelphia: The American Baptist Publication Society, 1953).

Barton, William E. *Old Plantation Hymns: A Collection of Hitherto Unpublished Melodies of the Slave and the Freedman, with Historical and Critical Notes.* (Boston: Wolfe & Co., 1893).

Black-American Musical Heritage, The. A Preliminary Bibliography by Dominique-Rene de Lerma. (Black Music Center, Indiana University, May 1969).

Boatner, Edward and Willa Townsend. *Spirituals Triumphant.* (Nashville: Sunday School Publishing Board, National Baptist Convention, 1927).

Bontemp, Arna, ed. *Great Slave Narratives.* (Boston: Beacon Press, 1969).

Botkin, B. A., ed. *Lay My Burden Down.* (Chicago: University of Chicago Press).

Brawley, Benjamin. *Women of Achievement.* (Women's American Baptist Home Mission Society, 1919).

Brawley, Benjamin. *Negro Builders and Heroes.* (Chapel Hill: The University of North Carolina Press, 1937).

Brown, William Wells. *The Anti-Slavery Harp,* 2nd ed. (Boston: 1849).

Brown, Sterling; Arthur P. Davis, and Ulysses Lee, eds. *The Negro Caravan.*

Burlin, Natalie Curtis. *Negro Folk Songs.* Hampton Series, Book I, II Spirituals; Book III, IV Work and Play Songs, Nos. 6716, 6726, 6756, 6766.

Carawan, Guy, and Candie (Recorders). *Ain't You Got a Right to the Tree of Life?* (New York: Simon and Schuster, 1966).

Chase, Gilbert. *America's Music.* (New York: McGraw-Hill Company, Inc., 1955).

Christy, E. P. *Plantation Melodies.* (1851).

Clark, George. *The Liberty Minstrel.* (New York: 1844).

Coleridge-Taylor, Samuel. *Twenty-Four Negro Melodies.* (Transcribed for Piano). (Boston: Oliver Ditson Company, 1905).

Cook, Mercer, and Stephan C. Henderson. *The Militant Black Writer in Africa and the United States.* (Madison: The University of Wisconsin Press, 1969).

Couch, Jr. William, ed. *New Black Playrights: An Anthology.* (Baton Rouge: Louisiana State University Press, 1968).

Countee. *The Imperial Jubilee Sacred Song Book.* (1919).

Courlander, Harold. ed. *Negro Songs from Alabama.* (New York: Oak Publications, 1967).

Curry, W. Lawrence, ed. *Service Music for the Adult Choir.* (Philadelphia: Westminster Press, 1956).

Curtis-Burlin, Natalie, ed. *Negro Folk Songs, Book I.* (New York: G. Schirmer, Inc., 1918).

Daly, John Jay. *A Song in His Heart.* (Philadelphia: The John C. Winston Company, 1951).

Dett, R. Nathaniel, ed. *Religious Folk-Songs of the Negro as Sung at Hampton Institute.* (Hampton: 1924).

Dietz, Betty Warner, and Michael Babatunde Olantunji. *Musical Instruments of Africa.* (New York: The John Day Co., 1965).

Dorson, Richard M. *American Negro Folktales.* (Greenwich: Fawcett Publications, Inc., 1967).

Douglass, Winfred, and Leonard Ellinwood. *Church Music in History and Practice.* (New York: Scribners, 1937).

DuBois, W. E. B. *Dusk of Dawn.* (New York: Harcourt, Brace and World, Inc., 1940).

DuBois, W. E. B., and Booker T. Washington. *The Negro in the South.* (New York: Citadel Press, Inc., 1970).

Fagg, John Edwin. *Cuba, Haiti, and the Dominican Republic.* (Englewood Cliffs, NJ: Prentice-Hall, Inc., 1965).

Fisher, Miles Mark. *Negro Slave Songs.* (New York: Cornell University Press, 1952).

Fisher, Williams Arno. *Seventy Negro Spirituals.* (Boston: Ditson Company, 1926).

Franklin, John Hope. *Reconstruction: After the Civil War.* (Chicago: The University of Chicago Press, 1961).

Frazier, E. Franklin. *The Negro Church in America.* (New York: Schocken Books, 1963).

Gatell, Frank Otto, and Allen Weinstein, eds. *American Negro Slavery.* (New York: Oxford University Press, 1968).

Gospel Pearls. (Nashville: Sunday School Publishing Board, 1921).

Guzman, Jessie Parkhurst, ed. *Negro Year Book.* (Tuskegee Institute: The Department of Records and Research, 1947).

Halter, Carl. *The Practice of Sacred Music*. (St. Louis, Concordia, 1955).

Hare, Maud Cuney. *Negro Musicians and their Music*. (Washington: The Associated Publishers, Inc., 1936).

Handy, W. C., and Abbe Miles. *Blues: An Anthology*. (New York: Albert and Charles Boni, 1926).

Hayes, Roland. *My Songs*. (Boston: Little, Brown, and Co., 1942).

Heilbut, Tony. *The Gospel Sound*. (New York: Simon and Schuster, 1971).

Higginson, Thomas Wentworth. *Army Life in a Black Regiment*. (Boston: Atlantic Monthly, 1867).

Hill, Herbert, and Arthur Ross, eds. *Employment, Race and Poverty*. (New York, Harcourt, Brace and World, Inc., 1967).

Howard, John Tasker. *Our American Music*, 3rd. ed. (New York: Thomas Y. Cromwell, Co., 1994).

Hughes, Langston. *Famous Negro Music Makers*. (New York: Dodd, Mead & Company, 1955).

Hughes, Langston. *I Wonder As I Wander*. (New York: Hill and Wang, 1969).

Hughes, Langston. *Twenty-Eight Negro Spirituals*. (Dodd, Mead & Co., 1940).

Jackson, George Pullen. *Down-East Spirituals and Others*. (New York: 1943).

Jackson, George Pullen. *Spirituals, Folk Songs of Early America*. (New York: 1937).

Jackson, George Pullen. *White and Negro Spirituals. Their Life Span and Kinship*. (New York: 1943).

Jackson, George Pullen. *White Spirituals in the Southern Uplands*. (Chapel Hill, NC: The University of North Carolina Press: 1933).

Jackson, Marylou I. *Negro Spirituals and Hymns*. (New York: J. Fisher and Brothers, 1935).

Jahn, Janheinz. *Muntu: The New African Culture*. (New York: Grove Press, Inc., 1961).

Jahn, Janheinz. *Neo-African Literature: A History of Black Writing*. (New York: Grove Press, Inc., 1968).

Jessye, Eva. *My Spirituals*. (New York: Robbins-Engle, 1927).

Johnson, Guy B. *John Henry*. (Chapel Hill, NC: The University of North Carolina Press, 1929).

Johnson, J. Rosamond, and J. Weldon Johnson. *The Book of American Negro Spirituals*. (New York: The Viking Press, 1925).

Johnson, James Weldon. *Along This Way.* (New York: The Viking Press, 1933).

Johnson, James Weldon. *God's Trombones.* (New York: The Viking Press, 1927).

Jones, Le Roi. *Black Music.* (New York: William Morrow & Co., 1967).

Joplin, Scott. *Treemonisha.* (New York: Scott Joplin, 1911).

Katz, Bernard, ed. *The Social Implications of Early Negro Music in the United States.* (New York: Arno Press and the New York Times, 1969).

Keil, Charles. *Urban Blues.* (Chicago: University of Chicago Press, 1966).

Kemble, Frances A. *Journal of a Residence on a Georgia Plantation in 1838.* (New York: Harper and Brothers, 1963).

Kennedy, Louise Venable. *The Negro Peasants Turn Cityward.* (New York: Arno Press, Inc., 1969).

Kennedy, R. Emmett. *Mellows.* (New York: Albert and Charles Boni, 1925).

King, Edward. *Negro Songs and Singers—The Great South.* (Hartford: The American Publishing Co., 1975).

Krehbiel, Henry E. *Afro-American Folksongs.* (New York: G. Schirmer, 1914).

Lee, George W. *Beale Street: Where the Blues Began.* (College Park: McGrath Publishing Co., 1994). (Reprint).

Locke, Alain LeRoy. *The Negro and His Music.* (Washington: The Associates in Negro Folk Education, 1936).

Logan, William. *Road to Heaven.* (University of Alabama Press, 1925).

Love, E. K. *History of the First African Baptist Church.* The Morning News.

Marine, Gene. *The Black Panthers.* (New York: The New American Library, 1969).

Marrocco, W. Thomas, and Harold Gleason. *Music in America.* (New York: W. W. Norton and Co., 1964).

Marsh, J. B. T. *The Story of the Jubilee Singers: With Their Songs.* (Boston: Houghton, Mifflin and Co., 1975).

Mays, Benjamin E. *The Negro's God.* (Kingsport: Kingsport Press, Inc. 1938).

Mead, Frank S. *Handbook of Denominations in the United States,* 4th ed. (New York: Abingdon Press, 1965).

Meier, August, and Elliott M. Rudwick. *From Plantation to Ghetto.* (New York: Hill and Wang, 1966).

Meier, August, and Elliott M. Rudwick, eds. *The Making of Black America,* Vol. I. (New York: Atheneum, 1969).

Meltzer, Milton, ed. *In Their Own Words: A History of the American Negro.* (New York: Thomas Y. Cromwell Co., 1967).

Metfessel, Milton. *Phonophotography of Folk Music.* (Chapel Hill: University of North Carolina Press, 1928).

Murphy, Jeanette Robinson. *Southern Thoughts for Northern Thinkers and African Music in America.* (New York: 1904).

National Jubilee Melodies, 25th ed. (Nashville: National Baptist Publishing Board).

Nketia, J. H. Kwabena. *Music in African Cultures.* (Institute of African Studies. University of Ghana, 1966).

Odum, Howard, and Guy B. Johnson. *The Negro and His Songs.* (Chapel Hill: University of North Carolina Press, 1923).

Oliver, Paul. *Blues Fell This Morning.* (London: Cassell, 1960).

Oliver, Paul. *Savannah Syncopations.* (England: November Books Limited, 1970).

Parrish, Lydia. *Slave Songs of the Georgia Sea Islands.* (New York: Creative Age Press, Inc., 1942).

Pike, G. D. *The Jubilee Singers.* (Boston: Lee and Shepard, 1973).

Pollard, Edward A. *Black Diamonds Gathered in the Darkey Homes of the South.* (New York: 1859).

Riedel, Johannes, ed. *Cantors at the Crossroads.* (St. Louis: Concordia, 1967).

Rose, Arnold. *The Negro in America.* (Harper Brothers, 1948).

Routley, Erik. *Church Music and Theology.* (Philadelphia: Muhlenberg Press, 1959).

Ryder, C. J. *The Theology of Plantation Songs.* (New York: American Missionary Association Bible House, 1891).

Seward, Theodore. *Jubilee Songs: As Sung by the Jubilee Singers of Fisk University.* (New York: Biglow and Main, 1872).

Smith, Ralph A., ed. *The Journal of Aesthetic Education.* Vol. 3, No. 2. (Urbana: The University of Illinois Press, 1969).

Southern, Eileen. *The Music of Black Americans: A History.* (New York: W. W. Norton & Co., 1971).

Sperry, William L. ed., *Religion and Our Racial Tensions.* (College Park: McGrath Publishing Company, 1969). (Reprint).

St. Clair, David. (trans.) Carolina de Marie St. Jesus. *Child of the Dark*. (New York: E. I. Patton & Co., Inc. 1962).

Stearn, Marshall. *The Story of Jazz*. (New York: Oxford University Press, Inc., 1958).

Stevenson, Robert. *Protestant Church Music in America*. (New York: W. W. Norton & Co., 1966).

Talley, Thomas. *Negro Folk Rhymes*. (New York: The Macmillan Co., 1922).

Thomas, Kurt. *The Choral Conductor*. (New York: Associated Music Publishers, 1971).

Thurman, Howard. *Deep River: An Interpretation of Negro Spirituals*. (California: Mills College Press, 1945).

Trotter, James M. *Music and Some Highly Musical People*. (Boston: Lee and Shepard, 1879).

Walker, David, and Henry Highland Garnet. *Walker's Appeal and an Address to the Slaves of the United States*. (New York: Arno Press and the New York Times, 1969).

Wallascheck, Richard. *Primitive Music: An Inquiry into the Origin and Development of Music, Song, Instruments, Dances and Pantomines of Slave Races*. (London: 1893).

Walter, Samuel. *Basic Principles of Service Playing*. (Nashville: Abingdon Press, 1963).

Washington, Booker T., William E. B. DuBois, and James Weldon Johnson. *Three Negro Classics: Up from Slavery, The Souls of Black Folk, and The Autobiography of an Ex-Colored Man*. (New York: Avon Book Division, 1965).

Washington, Jr., Joseph R. *Black Religion*. (Boston: Beacon Press, 1964).

Washington, Jr., Joseph R. *Black Sects and Cults*. (Garden City: Anchor Press, 1972).

Weatherford, W. D. *American Churches and the Negro*. (Boston: The Christopher Publishing House, 1967).

Westley, Charles H., and Carter G. Woodson. *The Story of the Negro Retold*. (Washington: The Associated Publishers, Inc., 1959).

Wharton, Vernon Lane. *The Negro in Mississippi, 1865–1890*. (New York: Harper and Row, 1965).

White, Clarence C. *Forty Negro Spirituals*. (Philadelphia: Theodore Presser Co., 1927).

White, Newman I. *American Negro Folk Songs*. (Folklore Associates, 1965).

White, Newman I. *American Negro Folk Songs*. (Cambridge: The University Press, 1928).

Wolfe, Paul Austin, Helen Dickinson, and Clarence Dickinson. *The Choir Loft and The Pulpit*. (New York: H. W. Gray Co., Inc., 1943).

Woodson, Carter G. *The History of the Negro Church*. (Washington: The Associated Publishers, 1945).

Woodson, Carter G. (Founder). *The Journal of Negro History*, Vol. 39. (New York: United Publishing Corp. 1969).

Work, John W. *American Negro Songs: A Comprehensive Collection of 230 Folk Songs, Religious and Secular*. (New York: Crown Press, 1940).

Work, John W. *The Folk Songs of the American Negro*. (Nashville: Fisk University Press, 1915).

Work, John W., and Fredrich, J. Work. *New Jubilee Songs*. (Nashville, TN: Work Brothers, 1901).

Yetman, Norman R. *Life Under the "Peculiar Institution."* (New York: Holt, Rinehart and Winstons, Inc., 1970).

Articles

Allen, Cleveland G. "The Negro's and His Songs." *Musical Courier*, CIII (October 3, 1931).

Allen, Cleveland G. "The Negro's Contribution to American Music." *Current History*, XXVI (May 1927).

Ballanta, Nicholas. "The Blight of Jazz and the Spirituals." *Literary Digest*, CV (April 10, 1930).

Ballanta, Nicholas George Julius. "Gathering Folk Tunes in the African Country." *Musical America* (September 25, 1916).

Barton, William E. "Hymns of the Slave and the Freedman." *New England Magazine* (1899).

Brown, John Mason. "Songs of the Slave." *Lippincott's Monthly Magazine* (December 1868).

Burlin, Natalie Curtis. "Negro Music at Birth." *The Music Quarterly* (1919).

Burlin, Natalie Curtis. The Negro's Contribution to the Music of America." *The Craftsman* (1925).

Butcher, Veda E. Final Report: U.S. Department of Health, Education, and Welfare. Development of Materials for a One-Year Course in African Music for the General Undergraduate Student (Project in African Music). (Washington, September 1970).

Calverson, V. F. "The Negro and American Culture." *Saturday Review of Literature,* XXII (September 21, 1949).

Cleveland, James the Rev. Gospel Music Workshop of America, Association. Organized 1969. Headquarters: 3908 Warren Street, Detroit, MI.

Conrad, Earl. "General Tubman, Composer of Spirituals." *Etude Music Magazine,* LX (May 1947).

Crisis, The. James Weldon Johnson Centennial Issue. (New York: Crisis Publishing Co., Inc., 1971).

Dorsey, Thomas A. National Convention of Gospel Choirs and Choruses, Inc. Organized 1939. Headquarters: Chicago, IL.

Hall, Johnson Choir, The. Notes on the Program of this Organization (1928).

Hare, Maud Cuney. "Africa in Song." *Metronome,* XXXVIII (December 1922).

Hornbostel, Von E. M. "African Negro Music." *Africa,* Vol. I, No. 1 (1928).

Hymn, The, Vol. 15, No. 3 (July 1964). Published by the Hymn Society of America.

Hymn, The, Vol. 26, No. 1 (January 1975). Published by the Hymn Society of America.

Hymn Society, The Papers of, XIII (1947). Published by the Hymn Society of America.

Hymn Society, The Papers of, XVI (1951). Published by the Hymn Society of America.

Hymn Society, The Papers of, XIII (1962). Published by the Hymn Society of America.

Hymn Society, The Papers of, XIII (1964). Published by the Hymn Society of America.

James, Willis Laurence. "The Romance of the Negro Folk Cry in America." *Phylon,* Vol XVI, No. 1.

Johnson, Charles S. "Jazz Poetry and Blues." *Caroling Magazine* (1928).

Journal of the Ecumenical Institute, Vol. I, No. 2.

Lomax, John A. "Sinful Songs of the Southern Negro." *The Music Quarterly*, Vol. XX (1934).

Murphy, Jeanette Robinson. "The Survival of African Music in America." *Popular Science Monthly*, LV (September 1899).

Murray, Charlotte V. "The Story of Harry T. Burleigh." *The Papers of the Hymn Society*, Vol. 17, No. 4 (October 1966).

"Negro Music: A Contribution to the National Music of America." *Musical Observer*, XIX (March 1920).

"Negro Music and Minstrelsy." *The American History and Encyclopedia of Music* (1910).

"Negro Songs." *Dwight's Journal of Music*, XXI (August 9, 1862).

Niles, John J. "White Pioneers and Black." *The Musical Quarterly* (1932).

Odum, Howard W. "Folk-song and Folk Poetry As Found in the Secular Songs of the Southern Negroes." *Journal of American Folklore*, XXIV (July–October 1911).

Parrish, Lydia. "The Plantation Songs of Our Old Lord Slaves." *Country Life*, LXIX (December 1935).

Pierce, Edwin H. "Gospel Hymns and Their Tunes." *The Musical Quarterly*, Vol. 26 (1940).

"Religious Life of the Negro Slave, The." *Harper's New Monthly Magazine*, Vol. XXVII (June–November 1863).

Seeger, Charles. "Contrapuntal Style in the Three-Voice Shape Note Hymns." *The Musical Quarterly*, Vol. 26 (1940).

Smith, Reed. "Gullah." *Bulletin of the University of South Carolina*, No. 190 (November 1, 1926).

Speight, W. L. "Notes on South African Native Music." *The Musical Quarterly*, Vol. XX (1934).

"Spirituals Are Preserved." *The New York Sun* (October 24, 1929).

Turner, Lucille P. "Negro Spirituals in the Making." *The Musical Quarterly* (1931).

Whalum, Wendell P. "Black Hymnody." *Review and Expositer* (Summer 1973).

Whalum, Wendell P. "James Weldon Johnson's Theories of Performance Practices of Afro-American Folksongs." *Phylon* (Special J. W. Johnson Centennial Issue) (December 1971).

Whalum, Wendell P. "The Spiritual As Mature Choral Composition." *Black World* (July 1974).

White, Clarence Cameron. "The Musical Genius of the American Negro." *Etude Musical Magazine,* XLII (May 1924).

Williams, Alberta. "A Race History Told in Song." *World Review,* IV (February 14, 1927).

Work, John W. "Changing Patterns in Negro Folk Songs." *Journal of American Folklore,* Menasah, (April–June 1949). (Reprint of a paper delivered at the nineteenth annual Fisk Festival of Music and Arts, Nashville, TN, April 29–May 1, 1948).

Work, John W. "The Negro Spiritual." *The Papers of the Hymn Society,* XXIV (September 1961).

Work, John W. "Plantation Meistersinger." *Musical Quarterly,* Vol. 27 (1941).

---

1 Helen E. Pfatteicher, "The Dilemma of Church Music Today," *Cantors at the Crossroads* (St. Louis, 1967), p. 157.

2 Carl F. Price, "What Is a Hymn," *The Papers of the Hymn Society* (New York, 1937), p. 3.

3 Erik Routley, *Church Music and Theology* (Philadelphia, 1959), pp. 11, 12.

4 Nancy White Thomas, "A Guide to Hymn Study," *The Hymn* (Hymn Society of America, Vol. 15, No. 3, New York, 1964), p. 69.

5 See my article, "Black Hymnody," in the Black Experience and the Church. Review and Expositor. Vol. LXX, No. 3, Summer 1973 (The Southern Baptist Theological Seminary, Louisville, Kentucky), pp. 341355.

6 See the discussion of festivals in Eileen Southern's *Music of Black Americans* (W. W. Norton, New York, 1971).

Music and Worship in the Black Church

by J. Wendell Mapson, Jr., published in 1986

The Bible is full of music and song, giving testimony to the fact that music is inseparably tied to worship. Martin Luther called music the "handmaiden of theology." Think of the Old Testament without the Song of Moses, or the New Testament without the Song of the Lamb. How stale and flat worship would be without a song.

This is especially true in the Black church, where music is more than just a component of worship. The whole of worship is a song sung to God by the people of God. In Black worship music is in prayer and sermon. Miles Mark Fisher in his book, *Negro Slave Songs in the United States,* suggests that in African culture music was woven into the very fabric of life.[1] No human activity was allowed to go without accompaniment of a song.

Many are under the false notion that music in the Bible is confined to the Old Testament collection called the Psalms. It is true that the Psalms were songs sung in temple and synagogue worship. This collection might be labeled the hymnbook of the Hebrew faith. For example, Psalms 120–135, labeled Pilgrim Psalms or Songs of Ascent, were sung by pilgrims as they journeyed to Jerusalem for the holy feast days. Traveling the dangerous highways leading to the holy city, they sang,

> "I lift up my eyes to the hills. From where will my help come?
> My help comes from the Lord, who made heaven and earth."
> Psalm 121:1–2

We are told by scholars such as Arthur Weiser that Psalm 24 has really three sections, although arising out of the same cultic situation.[2] Perhaps it was sung for some occasion celebrating the enthronement of God as king. Scholars note that it is a processional hymn. Verses 7 through 10 form an antiphonal song sung as the procession moves toward the gates of Jerusalem.

Such responsorial psalms can be used effectively in worship. Worshippers in one section of the sanctuary can respond to worshippers in another section. Males can respond to females, children to adults, choir to minister, minister to congregation, etc.

Other psalms call for instrumental accompaniment. The word "Selah," which is used in several of the psalms, is thought to have been a musical notation signaling the instruments to begin accompanying the voices.

There are psalms that cover the full range of human emotions. This is why the Psalms give resounding testimony to the importance of music in the worship of God.

However, we must keep in mind that not even the Psalms can contain biblical song, for it bursts forth and spreads from Genesis to Revelation. Songs and hymn fragments can be identified by style, vocabulary, theology, and contextual location.

One of the easiest to spot is found in the fifteenth chapter of Exodus. Notice that the first great song in the Bible was given birth because of something God had done for His people. Before the act of deliverance, there was no song of the people.

This particular song, called the Song of Moses though sung by Miriam, was sung in response to God's mighty acts. The Israelites stood helplessly at the edge of the Red Sea. Behind them was pharaoh's army, their swords and shields shining in the sun, their mighty horses prancing, chariot wheels rumbling. In front of them was the Red Sea, a liquid barrier behind whose wall was death and destruction.

They couldn't fight, and swimming would be fruitless. Yet God opened up the waters, and they crossed on dry ground. When they got to the other side, they looked back over their shoulders and saw pharaoh's army being swallowed up by the mighty waters. They watched as the enemy sank in a liquid grave.

They certainly couldn't go any further without "having church." They sang a song:

> I will sing to the Lord, for he has triumphed gloriously; horse and his rider he has thrown into the sea. The Lord is my strength and my might, and he has become my salvation; this is my God, and I will praise him, and my father's God, and I will exalt him.
>
> —Exodus 15:1–2

Notice that the subject of the song is God. The reason for the song is God. The theme of the song is the mighty acts of God.

Notice also the beautiful language and imagery, which are key aspects of music. Here we get spiritual snapshots of what God is like and who God is. We stand in awe of His power. Yet he is merciful enough to save. Verse 8 tells us, "At the blast of your nostrils the waters piled up, the floods stood up in a heap, the deeps congealed in the heart of the sea." What word power.

Now, we know full well that God doesn't really have nostrils. God, of course, is Spirit. Yet Black worshippers have never been ashamed to describe the divine in anthropomorphic terms. So the writer of Genesis can say that Adam and Eve "heard the sound of the Lord God, walking in the garden in the cool of the day...." The writer of 2 Kings can say that the Lord spoke to Elijah in a "still, small voice." And Miriam can sing, "...the floods stood up in a heap...."

In the New Testament, the Lord sent an angel to the backside of Palestine, to a place called Nazareth, and recruited a peasant girl with no royal blood in her veins to bear in her womb God's only Son. Mary could not contain her joy. She sang a song. "...My soul magnifies the Lord, and my spirit rejoices in God my Savior...." (Luke 1:46–55)

Again, the subject of the song is God, His mighty acts. Time and time again the songs in the Bible glorify God, not us. And there are other examples of songs, hymns, doxologies, and worship responses (1 Timothy 3:16; Hebrews 1:3; Revelation 4:11, 5:9–10, 12–13).

Against this backdrop of the biblical witness, the Black church seems to be in danger of losing its song. There are several reasons for this.

First, ministers and worship leaders have not provided leadership and guidance in the worship of God, and the role of music in worship. Many pastors assume that not being a musician disqualifies them from speaking an authoritative word on the subject. This should not be the case. The pastor is also worship leader, and he or she has the responsibility of guiding and directing worship. The pastor is over the music and the worship. This calls for more pastors and ministers recognizing the need to be informed and trained in music and worship. It is the pastor who directs the program of the church, and this includes music. It is he or she who must step forward, set the tone, and articulate the purposes of worship to the entire congregation.

Second, many musicians, though competent in their field, have no idea what worship is all about. A musician who plays for a church is one thing. A church musician is something else. The difference is that a church musician has a feel for worship and understands the relationship between music and worship. He or she has been claimed by the God who inspires the music in the first place.

Third, many choir members do not understand their function in worship. Choir is also congregation. Choir members are in church to worship, as well as lead in the song of worship. Their purpose is not to entertain, or perform. Sunday morning worship is no time for a concert. The truth of the matter is that the people of God really don't need a choir in order to worship God. In fact, the church has not always had a choir. The Black church has not always had a choir.

We have allowed musical instruments to intrude too far in the worship of God. Certainly the organ and even the piano add a dimension to worship that is both rich and majestic. Who cannot be lifted by the lofty tones of a pipe organ? Yet, many organists "over-play" during the service of worship. The role of instruments is to supplement, complement, and accompany the song of the congregation. Organists need not feel the need to "doodle" all the way through the worship service. Many organists play too loud during prayer, as if God won't hear the prayer unless he also hears the organ. There are times when the appropriate response of the organ is silence. Sometimes during the singing of hymns, the organist might choose to allow the congregation to sing a verse or two without accompaniment.

This brings us to a fourth observation, which is that congregational singing in the Black church is at an all-time low. Music in the church has become so specialized and commercialized until very often the congregation becomes the spectator. The singing of hymns allows the congregation to participate in a more meaningful way.

Fifth, we no longer seem to be offering a balanced musical diet in the worship of God. By limiting our musical offerings, we are robbing the worshipper and God of the rich variety of sacred music within the Black church tradition. In worship we ought to hear hymns, anthems, spirituals, as well as gospel songs. Hymns should be sung with power and enthusiasm, for a church is known by the hymns it sings and how those hymns are sung.

Finally, we fail to take a critical look at the songs we sing. Often, form and feeling take precedent over theological substance. We ought to ask ourselves whether or not the song has any "God content." By this we mean more than just a casual reference to deity. A parenthetical insertion of God's name does not give a song theological integrity.

Many secular songs refer to the name of God. That alone does not make them theologically sound. Does the song glorify God, or our own accomplishments? Is the song biblically accurate? Does the song reflect the pilgrimage of the congregation where the song is sung? Religious songs sung on the radio for commercial gain are not necessarily appropriate for the worship of God. An "old personal favorite" may not in fact speak to the need of the congregation as a whole.

Music in the Black church will improve when we remember the context in which it was born: the quest of a people to find meaning by seeking God. Pastors, worship leaders, choir members, and musicians must come together to give the Lord a better song, and modulate to a new key.

Isn't it fitting that as the biblical drama of deliverance opens with the Song of Moses, it closes with the Song of the Lamb—on the first page a garden, and on the last page a city. On the first page Old Adam, and on the last page New Adam. On the first page a tree whose fruit was an excuse for rebellion. On the last page a tree with fruit good for the healing of the nations. On the first page alienation. On the last page restoration and communion. On the first page Adam, who died. On the last page Christ, who said, "I was dead, but behold, I am alive forevermore."

> Great and amazing are thy deeds,
> Lord God Almighty;
> Just and true are thy ways,
> King of the nations!
> Lord, who will not fear and glorify your name?
> For you alone are holy.
> All nations will come and worship before you,
> for your judgments have been revealed.
> —Revelations 15:3–4

---

1 Miles Mark Fisher, *Negro Slave Songs in the United States* (New York: The Citadel Press, 1953), p. 65.

2 Arthur Weiser, *The Psalms* (Philadelphia: The Westminster Press, 1962), p. 232.

Black Sacred Music: Problems and Possibilities

by Rev. Jeremiah A. Wright, Jr., previously unpublished

Abstract

Since its inception, the African American Church has experienced tension, disagreement, debate, and misunderstanding over the issue of sacred music. Many Africans sought to use music from the African idiom in their services of worship. Other assimilated and acculturated Africans saw only European music as "legitimate" or sacred enough for use in the sanctuary.

This project illustrates how Trinity UCC incorporated the full spectrum of Black sacred music into its worship experiences; and it provides a replicable model for other churches who desire similar programs. Results show that this program is both healing and educational Other churches using its findings will benefit greatly.

Introduction

Since the inception of the African American Church as an independent institution, there has been tension, disagreement, debate, and much misunderstanding over the issue of sacred music, or what is and what is not allowed musically in a service of worship. In many ways, as it pertains to this issue, I feel like a person who has walked in on a play midway through its last act. Instead of enjoying that portion of the play I have been privileged to see, I have been spending all my time trying to piece together the plot ever since I got here. Let me explain what I mean.

I was born in the Black Church, and although I did not know it at the time, I was born right at the height of one of those periods of furious debate within the urban Black church tradition over what constituted "proper" music for educated or upwardly mobile Black Baptists in Philadelphia, and what did not. Growing up midway through the debate gave me that "middle-of-a-play" feeling.

I was born to a pastor and an educator—both of whom had graduated (prior to 1940) from Virginia Union University, a southern Black, church-related college, and both of whom had earned graduate degrees from universities and professional schools in the North prior to 1950. Having relocated from two rural areas of Virginia—Caroline County (my dad) and Surry County (my mom)—my parents settled in Philadelphia, and my sister and I were born there and raised there.

Each summer and most holidays, however, we were on the road, traveling south to my parents' home, and though a "native" Philadelphian, having relatives in rural Virginia gave me some exposure to another side of the African American church experience that I did not get to see in Philadelphia. It also made more confusing for me the "fight" I was witnessing within our churches and religious communities over the issue of Black sacred music; or the issues raised by the question as to where the boundary lines were to be drawn when it came to what was or what was not sacred music.

In the South, I heard the songs and felt the rhythms[1] of our African past that were not a part of my Philadelphia church experience—at least not on a Sunday morning when the "senior"[2] choir was singing and our pipe organ was playing. I could hear (if not feel)[3] the northern first cousin to those songs and those rhythms during a midweek prayer service when there was neither an organ nor a choir in the service, but somehow it was just not the same. The way we sang in Virginia—out in the country in Gravel Hill Baptist Church or St. John's Baptist Church—was not the way we sang in Philadelphia, either at Grace Baptist Church or Mt. Zion Baptist in Germantown or in any of the other "silk stocking" Baptist churches whose members were (and whose pastors tended to be) middle income and "educated."[4] One could tell that those two styles of singing were related (the midweek prayer service style and the "down-home" country style, but somehow they were just not the same.

In the North, I heard hymns (as printed!), arranged spirituals, and European anthems on a Sunday morning three Sundays out of the month. On the fourth Sunday morning, however, I heard the Wright's Gospel Chorus sing hymns, arranged spirituals, and the "tamer" version of what was then called "Dorsey music."[5] Every Christmas I heard Handel's Messiah and every Easter I heard Dubose's "The Seven Last Words," plus Handel's "Hallelujah Chorus." Those were primarily Sunday morning services, however, where we heard the "high brow" music in our "high" church services. On Sunday afternoons and evenings at teas and the organization's annual services, I got to hear quartets and quintets like the Dixie Hummingbirds, the Swan

Silvertones, and the Highway Q.C.'s.

On the "Black"[6] radio stations, I got to hear Clara Ward, the Davis Sisters, Roberta Martin and the Martin Singers, Professor Alex Bradford, and Mahalia Jackson. Plus, those stations would also play choral selections by the Wings Over Jordan Choir and the Utterbach Ensemble. All those songs (from the quintets to the choirs) were appealing to me and sounded even more like what I heard, felt, and experienced down in Virginia than did the songs from our midweek prayer service; but those songs, and that kind of singing, were not allowed in my church on a Sunday morning!

In addition to the different songs and the different styles that I heard in the North and in the South, during the first nineteen years of my life I heard countless debates and heated arguments over what was sacred music and what was not, or what was "fitting" for a Sunday morning worship service and what was not. The "battle lines" were drawn even more sharply for me when I entered Virginia Union University and joined the University Concert Choir. Now I already knew that there was a drastic difference between the music in the rural churches of Virginia and those in the urban centers because of my relatives who pastored both kinds of churches, and my having attended their worship services.

My maternal grandfather, Rev. Hamilton Martin Henderson, pastored two rural churches during my lifetime—one in Surry County, Virginia, and one in Temperanceville, Virginia, which is on the "Eastern Shore"[7] of the state. My mother's brother, Dr. John B. Henderson, pastored the Bank Street Baptist Church of Norfolk, Virginia, and the music in those two settings was as different as night from day. Even knowing that there was a difference between rural and urban Black churches, however, did not prepare me for the cultural shock and the "battle lines" that I ran into at Virginia Union University in the concert choir.

First of all, the spiritual tone of the chapel services (and our concerts across the country) were different from anything I had ever experienced. We did all the European anthems and we also did the arranged spirituals, but I got to hear them, sing them, and experience them as never before! Professor William Goodwin required excellence in his choir and with breath control, staggered breathing, diction, interpretation, and rehearsal five days a week, the sound that he got from his choir was far different from any sounds that I had ever heard from any "senior" choir anywhere. I got to experience European music as it was meant to be performed, and the result was a deep spiritual experience that produced a pensive, meditative, and "inspired" mood. That was new to me.

But then, in addition to the new mood I experienced, there was also this outright hatred and disdain for Black gospel music that "Prof." Goodwin had that made absolutely no sense to me. He would not teach us any of those songs nor allow any of that *genre* anywhere near his choir's repertoire. He was also adamant about our not singing it *anywhere*—even among ourselves, behind his back, or on the bus away from his earshot when we were on choir tour! Gospel music was considered (by him) to be uncultured, unworthy of "serious" study, and undesirable for anyone who was aspiring to be educated.

That attitude set up some tensions within me that were not satisfactorily resolved until I began pastoring my own church and was able to put together a music program that took down the walls of hostility and combined the "best of both worlds" within one music department of one congregation. This project is a description of that music program which has incorporated the full spectrum of Black sacred music into each of the Sunday morning worship services. It is offered also as a replicable model for other churches who desire to implement similar programs. The results have shown that this program (a resolution of those tensions I have known all my life) is both healing and educational, and other churches which use its findings will benefit greatly.

---

1 The issue of rhythm is a major issue in the debate over "sacred vs. secular" and will be developed further in this study. Suffice it to say here that the rhythms we experienced in the South were primarily from the hand clapping and the foot patting on wooden floors of the country churches where we worshipped. Sometimes the songs would become so lively that you could feel the whole floor bouncing to the beat of the song being sung.

2 The use of the word "senior" *with* the quotation marks is to point out the arrogance and the cultural assumptions being made by the very use of the term. The word "senior," which denotes older or priority (having been here first and, therefore, being primary), also has several subtle connotations, e.g., more serious, less frivolous, more settled, to be taken more seriously and more important. The "senior" choirs in the Black church in this century were to become the choirs which did the "serious" music such as cantatas, anthems, and arranged (or "concertized") spirituals, and were at all costs to be distinguished from the gospel choruses which did not do the "serious" or *important* music. Thus, gospel music is by definition and the very terminology used relegated to an inferior position in the minds of those who set the cultural standards, the norms, and the curricula in the educational institutions!

3 We couldn't "feel" the rhythms in Philadelphia as we did in Virginia first of all because the floors of the churches in Philly were concrete or tile. Most importantly, however, was the fact that we could not feel the beat in Philadelphia because the hand clapping and foot stomping

that went on in the country churches of the South was for some reason, stifled in the "high Baptist" churches of the North *and* South.

4 The four years of college in a Eurocentric educational system, which tended to degrade or negate anything African, tended to produce a person (prior to 1968) who had been taught to emulate, imitate, and idolize all European cultural forms and—more devastatingly—to equate European culture with Christianity.

5 "Dorsey music" was the music named after the "Father of Gospel Music," Professor Thomas A. Dorsey. His "tamer" songs were the songs like "Precious Lord" and "The Lord Will Make a Way Somehow"—songs which, if they had a beat, had a "tame" or soft beat. What was most preferred, however, was music with *no* beat, because it was the beat that caused worshippers to want to move their bodies, clap their hands and pat their feet.

6 The term "Black radio stations" is used advisedly. There were no Black-owned or -operated Black radio stations in the 1940s, 1950s, 1960s, or 1970s in Philadelphia, Pennsylvania, or in most of the other metropolitan areas of North America. The stations were "Black-oriented" in that they played rhythm and blues, rock and roll, jazz, and gospel music on Sunday mornings. They also allowed Black churches to air their services on Sundays, but they were (please make no mistake!) totally owned by White people.

7 The "Eastern Shore" of Virginia has a different cultural milieu from the rest of Virginia and deserves a separate study at the hands of some skilled cultural anthropologist like Margaret Creel, whose work among the Gullah people has enriched our understandings immeasurably about this sea coast island culture, its religion, and its African retentions in language, music, belief systems, and concepts of community. The Eastern Shore itself is a sea coast culture with islands like Chincoteague that cry out to be studied and interpreted. The language, the culture, and the religion of the people in Eastern Shore, for instance, were different from that which this observer noted in both Caroline County and Surry County, Virginia.

Christ Against Culture: Anticulturalism in the Gospel of Gospel

by Jon Michael Spencer
from *Protest and Praise: Sacred Music of Black Religion,*
published in 1990

The Meaning of Gospel Music

Gospel music derives its name and theology from the gospel of Jesus Christ. Among the composers and practitioners of the genre, it is generally agreed that the "gospel of gospel" is "good news" amidst "bad times." "Black music is called gospel," defines Louis-Charles Harvey, "because it attempts to relate the 'good news' of Jesus Christ primarily to the existence of Black folk in this country."[1] For Blacks who encountered oppression and desolation upon migrating to southern and northern cities following Reconstruction, this jubilant music has been, according to Wyatt Tee Walker's assessment, "a song of faith which rallies the hope and aspiration of the faithful in the face of devastating social conditions."[2] Irene Jackson concurs that gospel songs "deal with the immediate problems affecting Blacks and are specifically designed to help Black people to surmount immediate circumstances of their lives."[3]

While Jackson further defines "gospel" as reflecting the same "existential tension" found in the spirituals,[4] Lawrence Levine points out that the "tension" in gospel is not quite as unyielding. The reason is that while the Jesus of the spirituals is a "warrior," the Jesus of the gospel songs is "a benevolent spirit" who promises a restful, peaceful, and just afterlife.[5] Therefore, if there is any "tension," it is not so much in the existential aspect of gospel as in the paradox that Jackson and Levine, in their opposing views, are both correct.

Some theological thinkers are not as sympathetic to gospel as Harvey, Walker, Jackson, and Levine. Calling gospel "the most degenerate form of Negro religion," Joseph Washington sharply criticizes the weakening of the theology of the spirituals. "Gospel music is the creation of a disengaged people," he says. "Shorn from the roots of the folk religion, gospel music has turned the freedom theme in Negro spirituals into licentiousness. It is...sheer entertainment by commercial opportunists."[6] Washington wrote this in 1964, and eight years later there was no change in his opinion: "Blacks created a whole new religious music in gospel songs which revolutionized music in the Black congregations through the leadership of jackleg preachers and evangelists who went from rags to riches by means of bringing the secular world of blues and jazz into worship."[7]

The intention here is not to measure the theology of gospel music against that of the spirituals and certainly not against the best theories of Christian ethics. (Such comparisons probably led to Washington's disgruntlement.) Rather, the aim is to take gospel as it is and determine just where it stands theologically. It will be helpful to review the studies of Charles Copher and Mary Tyler in order to be informed as to the characters, events, places, images, and means used to propagate the theology of gospel.

Charles Copher's investigation of characters, events, places, and images in three hundred gospel songs defines the distinctiveness of the genre. Copher found relatively few references to biblical characters and events in the fifty songs of Tindley and his counterparts (1895–1935). In these songs God is simply addressed as Father, occasionally as God Most High and Rock of Ages, whereas references to Jesus are far more numerous and varied. Not only is Jesus addressed as King and Savior (seven times each) and Lamb, Lily of the Valley, Son of God, Truth Divine, and Word of Life (once each), but the few references to events almost always deal with his life: his teaching (three times), his trial before Pilate and crucifixion (two times each), and his walking on water, last supper, prayer in Gethsemane, and declaration of the great commission (once each). The places catalogued by Copher include heaven (six references), the Jordan River and Calvary (two references each), the Red Sea, wilderness, Sea of Galilee, and New Jerusalem (one reference each).[8]

In the 250 gospel songs covering the period 1930 to the present, Copher found that references to characters predominate over events. Naturally Jesus is the principal personage with ninety-eight of the 250 songs being about him. Fourteen of those ninety-eight deal with his second coming. In comparison with the spirituals, twice the number of gospel songs address the crucifixion, resurrection, and final triumph of the Lord. While God is addressed simply as Father or God (twenty references), Jesus is referred to by a variety of interesting names: Bread of Heaven, Cornerstone, Fortress, King, King of

Kings, Lamb, Lily of the Valley, Lion of Judah, Lord of All, Master, Rock of Ages, Solid Rock, Rose of Sharon, Savior, Shepherd, Shield, Son of God, Bright and Morning Star, Sword, Way, and Wonderful. The places of reference catalogued are twenty-five accounts of heaven (one-tenth of the 250 songs examined), eight accounts of Calvary, four each of the Jordan River and Beulah Land, three of Zion, two each of Canaanland and New Jerusalem, and one each of Bethany, Galilee, Promised Land, and Bethlehem.[9]

In Mary Tyler's study of the 104 gospel songs of Charles Henry Pace, five categories are used to characterize the variety of Pace songs: (1) personal testimonies, (2) questioning belief and introspection, (3) scriptural messages, (4) dialogue with God, (5) personal counsel to listeners.[10] Adjacent to the reflections of Harvey, Walker, Jackson, and Levine, the studies of Copher and Tyler copiously complete a general definition of gospel.

Theological Typologies for Anatomizing Gospel

The reason for citing the following studies of William T. Dargan, Louis-Charles Harvey, and Henry H. Mitchell (and Nicholas Cooper-Lewter) is that each gives additional information about the inner theological meaning of gospel music. These particular studies will help prepare for the adaptation of H. Richard Niebuhr's typology in his book, *Christ and Culture* (1951), which will address the finer issue of where gospel stands theologically amidst Christian pluralism.

Dargan's examination of 104 gospel songs sung at a single Holiness church in Washington, DC, concludes that the four most prevalent theological themes in gospel music are *power, praise, salvation,* and *struggle.* The aspect of *power,* he says, includes the three subcategories of "cross-bearing," "crown-wearing," and "crown-wearing" in the course of "cross-bearing" (sometimes referred to by believers as "joy in the midst of sorrow" or "victory in the valley"). The primary *power* symbols that authorize and enable believers to carry out the will of God are the "name" and the "blood" of Jesus (the latter being invoked in moments of crisis). The theme of *praise,* continues Dargan, includes the aspects of celebration and thanksgiving, means by which believers encounter and attest to the *power.* The theme of *salvation* is comprised of three subcategories—witness to the unsaved, the saving deeds of the Savior, and the believer's quest for or response to her or his own salvation. The theme of *struggle* includes such aspects as trouble, battle, danger, fear, judgment, desperation, determination, and steadfastness. Dargan concludes that the common threads running through all of these concepts are human frailty and dependence and the severity of the eschatological teachings of Jesus.[11]

In Henry H. Mitchell and Nicholas Cooper-Lewter's book, *Soul Theology* (1986), an extensive typology is constructed in which gospel songs and other Black musical genres are categorized theologically. The first six of the ten types deal with attributes of God, the remaining four with humanity: (1) the Providence of God, (2) the Justice of God, (3) the Majesty and omnipotence of God, (4) The Omniscience of God, (5) the Goodness of God and Creation, (6) the Grace of God, (7) the Equality of Persons, (8) the Uniqueness of Persons: Identity, (9) the Family of God and Humanity, and (10) the Perseverance of Persons. The authors' thesis is that Black people intuitively select songs that provide them with the nourishment and therapeutic affirmation they need to endure.[12]

Louis-Charles Harvey's study, "Black Gospel and Black Theology," based on an assessment of 1,700 gospel songs, found that nearly a third of the number (452) are centered around the person of Jesus Christ. The remaining include 393 references to the Christian life, 354 to heaven, 237 to God, 154 to humanity, 32 to Satan, and 29 to the Holy Spirit. This Christocentrism led Harvey to derive as his thesis that "The most fundamental statement made about Jesus Christ is that he is Everything. He is Everything because he is *Friend, Protector,* and *Liberator.*" It is in these ways that Jesus is regarded as the answer to the problems of Black life.[13]

Of the theological typologies of Dargan, Mitchell, and Harvey, it is Harvey's that seems most useful for the present study. Part of the reason is that it distills and translates into the jargon of gospel music Jesus Christ is "Everything"—Friend, Protector, and Liberator. If Harvey's typology is sufficiently comprehensive, then the more numerous categories in Dargan's and Mitchell's typologies ought to reduce to the three categories in Harvey's typology; and they do. In Dargan's typology, songs of *power* and *salvation* coincide with Jesus as Liberator, songs of *struggle* with Jesus as Protector and Friend, and songs of *praise* with Jesus who is all three concurrently— "Everything." In Mitchell's typology, *The Goodness of God and Creation* coincides with Jesus as Friend, *The Justice of God* with Jesus as Protector, *The Grace of God* with Jesus as Liberator, and *The Providence of God, The Majesty and Omnipotence of God,* and *The Omniscience of God* with Jesus as "Everything."[14] Having checked Harvey's typology, and imbuing it with the implicit meaning of the other two typologies, it will become a point of reference as the theological history of the gospel music movement is examined.

The Christ-Culture Dilemma in Gospel

Gospel music is the creation of a people who exist amid the absurdity of American race conventions and, thus, is a music that constantly raises questions about the relationship of faith and culture or society. Therefore, H. Richard Niebuhr's historically derived typology seems to be a useful context for theological analysis. In *Christ and Culture*, Niebhur delineates five principal ways Christians have attempted to address the water and oil of Jesus Christ and human culture. He terms these five types: (1) Christ against Culture, (2) Christ of Culture, (3) Christ above Culture, (4) Christ and Culture in Paradox, and (5) Christ the Transformer of Culture. While theological types such as Dargan's, Mitchell's, and Harvey's examined gospel music itself, what is presently attempted is an analysis of gospel music in the context of an extraneous matrix. The objective critique Niebuhr's typology promises to yield makes its application even more provocative. A brief word shall be said about the theological implications each of the five types has for gospel music in general.

1. That gospel music is basically of the "Christ against Culture," or radical anticultural, type is implied in Mitchell and Cooper-Lewter's study, in that all their categories reference gospel songs except "The Equality of Persons," "The Uniqueness of Persons," and "The Family of God and Humanity." Gospel music does not encourage individuals to be truly *unique* (or equal in their uniqueness) in order to apply their particular vocations to converting the world for the good of the family of God and humanity; rather, individuals are taught to lose their identities in Christ's. "Do not love the world or the things in the world" is obviously a scriptural tenet to which they ascribe. *"If any one loves the world, love for the Father is not in him."* (1 John 2:15). Levine agrees that in regard to long-term solutions for the problems of human beings, the space between the here and the hereafter has widened. "There [are]…few songs portraying victory in the world," he says. "Ultimate change when it [comes takes] place in the future in an otherworldly context."[15] It is actually through gospel's denial of the world that it makes the "news"—friendship, protection, and liberation—seem unequivocally "good" and a convincing alternative, not only to the world, but to one's friends, family, and neighbors.

2. By interpreting culture through Christ, the "Christ of Culture" advocates regard those aspects of the world that are in accord with Christ as the

most essential; and by interpreting Christ through culture, they distill from Christianity those teachings that seem most congruent with the best culture the world has to offer.[16] In such a cultural Christology, human martyrs are often regarded as the apostles of Christ insofar as they prophetically aid human beings into bringing the gospel to bear in he world;[17] whereas in gospel music Christ who is far-removed from culture is "Everything," so that everyone else of culture is nothing. A charge against these Christians is that their love of culture has so qualified devotion to Christ that the Lord has been displaced by an idol called by his name.[18] However, inasmuch as gospel music predicates the antithesis of cultural Christology—irreconciliation between church and the world, the gospel and social law, grace and human effort—it cannot be accused of the idolatry of serving two masters.

3. The *synthesists* of the "Christ above Culture" type hold that both Christ and culture are to be affirmed in that the Lord is holistically human and divine, concurrently of the here and the hereafter.[19] On the other hand, advocates of gospel almost entirely neglect the human aspect of Jesus Christ, including his ascription to Jewish culture[20] and his careful distinction between the culture of the oppressors and that of the oppressed. Furthermore, whereas for the synthesists salvation does not presuppose the destruction of God's creation,[21] in gospel God's creation is perceived as coalescent with human culture and subject to destruction upon the apocalypse. While the synthesists believe in having all this world and heaven too,[22] gospel advocates can be accused of nothing but faith in "Jesus only."

4. The *dualists* of the "Christ and Culture in Paradox" type are also anticulturalists but contend that human laws prevent humanity from worsening its perpetually fallen condition.[23] In gospel music, the paradox of "the lesser evil" is the consequential synthesis of several theses and antitheses. First, gospel condones human denial of the world insofar as it is a social commentary revealing what it means to be Black and oppressed[24]—*thesis*. Yet it is an evangelical music that makes no direct claim on the need for human liberation and social reconciliation—*antithesis*. Second, amidst socioeconomic oppression, Blacks have made a decision to be themselves in a way that gospel is a means of "identity awakening" and "identity nourishing"[25]—*thesis*. Yet gospel music enjoins Christians to lose their individual identities in Christ's—*antithesis*. The *synthesis* of these theses and antitheses, the paradox, is that that which is cultural or

"worldly"—human oppugnancy toward oppression and identity nourishing—is being utilized as a "lesser evil" to lead the worldly to the Ultimate
Alternative, Christ. That is to say that the entire gospel music movement
is a dualistic statement that it is better to sing gospel than to burn.

5. The *conversionists* of the "Christ the Transformer of Culture" type are also
anticulturalists. However, in believing that the world is perverted rather
than inherently evil, they maintain that creation (which includes human
culture) can be transformed to its original good. This notion, suggested
at several points in the Gospel of John,[26] is misconstrued when interpreted by gospel songwriters. According to "the gospel of gospel," it is not so
much that *"God so loved the world that he gave his only begotten son,"* as it is
that which follows—that *"whosoever believes in him should not perish but
have eternal life."* (John 3:16). In gospel music the individual, not the
world or the vocations of the worldly, are evangelized and transformed by
love. Moreover, Christ may be Friend, Protector, and Liberator in gospel
music, but the one thing the Lord essentially is not portrayed as is
Reconciler. Customarily gospel does not command individuals to love
those who despitefully use them but rather to turn away from them. This
turning away from the world heavenward to the Ultimate Alternative is
an end in itself rather than serving as a means of turning back toward
friend, kindred, and neighbor in reconciliation. If Jesus as "Everything" is
the "ideal symbol of wholeness in gospel music,"[27] it is more the wholeness of each individual's spiritual self than of the family of God and
humanity.

In summary, the Niebuhrian "Christ and Culture" typology has illustrated
that the entire history of gospel music is an anticultural *movement*. Of the
three historical epochs in gospel—the Transitional Period (1900–1930),
Traditional Period (1930–1969), and the Contemporary Period (1969–
present)—all but a few gospel songwriters of the modern era are of the "Christ
against Culture" type. The few conversionists of the "Christ the Transformer
of Culture" type are also anticulturalists, but less radical. With this overview,
the next step is to closely examine each of the three periods of the gospel music
movement in order to determine the specific ways in which anticulturalism is
manifested.

Anticulturalism in Transitional Gospel

The Transitional Period, or Pre-Gospel Era (1900–1930), commenced
with the gospel hymns of Charles Price Jones, the founding bishop of the

Church of Christ (Holiness) USA, and Charles Albert Tindley, a Methodist minister of Philadelphia. While Tindley, author of some thirty gospel hymns, has been credited as the first Black to publish an original collection in 1901, Jones, the more prolific poet and musician and composer of over one thousand songs, was actually the first with his *Jesus Only No. 1* (1899), which was followed by his *Jesus Only Nos. 1 and 2* (1901).[28]

The songs of Jones consider the "traditions of men" to be "unworthy of authority,"[29] and they depict the world as an evil realm wherein "ev'ry trusted friend forsake[s]," "kindred drive thee from their door," "thou art despised and lone," and "none will speak a word of cheer." Life, he lyricizes, is an "open sea" swept over by "raging storms of sore affliction," and those who ascribe to its ways are woefully wicked:

> From the malice of the wicked I will hide,
> From their tongues deceitful slander, from their pride;
> From the evil that they do, From their worldly pomp and show—
> In Thy presence I will happily abide.

In another song, Jones speaks not only of being hidden from the lives of malice and slander, but also from the temptations thereof: "Hide me from the world's alluring," he implores.[30]

To Jones, the "world of sin" is nontransformable. He almost sounds like a conversionist in one of his songs when he says, "Yes, there's a fountain deep and wide to cleanse the world from sin." But in another he explains that all is not lost, not because human beings can change things, but because it is "abundant grace" that "God bestows upon a sinful race." Moreover, the nations are "perishing in sin," implying that sin in the world will remain untransformed to the destructive end. When the "King of glory" comes, "the nations, long so sinful, shall approach their awful doom." Simply seeking to endure in what Jones often refers to as "a lost world" and "a land of woe," Christian believers typically assume a passive role in their human destiny. Their principal vocation is not itself transformative of the world, but spiritual warfare against the "foe," the world, under the spiritual protection of Jesus. Only once does Jones speak more trenchantly, albeit figuratively, of helping level the carnal land of licentiousness:

> There are cities great and high, Hallelujah!
> Strong and wall'd up t'ward the sky, Praise the Lord!
> But by faith we'll bring them low, Hallelujah!
> And Jehovah's pow'r we'll show, Praise the Lord![31]

For the most part, believers are not Samsons or Joshuas. They are, in Jones's words, "weary pilgrims toiling through a world of woe." The only means of liberation from this toilsome pilgrimage is for them to "keep on looking away to Jesus" so that the Holy Ghost will "a citizen of heaven make [them] while on earth below." This turning away from the world heavenward to Jesus is what Jones denotes the "heavenly calling":

> I am so glad of the heavenly calling,
> Calling away from the world and its charms;
> I am so glad I have fled for a refuge,
> Into the Savior's strong arms.[32]

It was Jones's lifelong intention to convince his people of the value and beauty of holiness, for he was sure that worldly gain would only promote robbery, engender pride, breed strife, and cause fatality. The appropriate response to the "heavenly calling" is surrender to Jesus by subverting man-made tradition and exalting the Lord:[33]

> I have surrendered to Jesus,
> Conquered by weapons of love;
> I have forsaken earth's treasures
> Seeking a treasure above.

In order to withdraw from the world of lust and pleasure, which Jones calls the world of the flesh of Satan, one has to "surrender all." Probably drawing from Luke 14:26, he implies that surrendering all not only means denying one's father, mother, wife, children, brothers, and sisters, but also one's own life. Only if the Christian disciple has denied self can she or he sing, "I am wholly sanctified."[34]

Another song predicating the idea of surrendering all to Jesus is "I'm Happy with Jesus Alone." Jones writes about this piece: "I would know nothing but Jesus. No name but His. No master but Him. No law but His word. No creed but Jesus. I [have] to be 'happy with Jesus alone.' All else [is] trash to me."[35] While the worldly are "the enemies of holiness" and the very "trash" of humanity, the holy "citizens of heaven" are in a sense the enemies of "the world." In his probing song, "Are You a Christian," Jones exhorts, "The noblest men the earth has known, and the noblest women too…forsook the world and served the Lord." Reflecting the radical eschatological ethic of Jesus, Jones writes in another song that "Friends and kindred, earthly honor, wealth and ease I all would flee." Except for Jesus, he claims, "I would count all else but loss." The title song of Jones's first and second collections of gospel hymns, *Jesus Only*, is a further explanation of what it means to surrender oneself to the Lord:

> Jesus only is my motto,
> Jesus only is my song,
> Jesus only is my heart-thought,
> Jesus only all day long.
> Then away with ev'ry idol,
> Let my Lord be all to me;
> Jesus only is my Master,
> Jesus only let me see.[36]

Three important theological threads (all related to *surrender*), which have woven through the history of the gospel music movement, clearly coalesce in the above piece. The first is the espousal of the nontrinitarian formula for evoking spiritual authority and power—the "name" of Jesus, stated here as "Jesus only." The second is that Jesus is "Everything," stated by Jones as the Lord being "all to me." And the third is the desire to see Jesus face to face: "Jesus only let me see."

Although most of Jones's songs are eschatological in calling for converts of holiness to renounce their kindred, some of the gospel songs of his era contain an empirical element by reflecting the tragedies of urban life during the first quarter of the twentieth century. For instance, the following song may be referring not just figuratively to a daughter or son spiritually forsaken by worldly relatives but actually physically abandoned by abusive parents:

> Should father and mother forsake me below,
> My bed upon the earth be a stone,
> I'll cling to my Savior, He loves me I know,
> I'm happy with Jesus alone.

Not only will Jesus speak a word of cheer to make the spiritually forsaken and physically abandoned happy, he will also give individuals rest from their daily concerns of subsistence:

> Have you cares of business, cares of pressing debt?
> Cares of social life or cares of hopes unmet?
> Are you by remorse or sense of guilt depressed?
> Come right to Jesus, He will give you rest.

Notwithstanding the empiricism, ultimate rest is rewarded in heaven, which is the Christian's principal endeavor in life. The world is unjust and unhappy, but heaven is a place of justice and joy:

> There's a happy time a-coming,
> There's a happy time a-coming,
> When oppressors shall no longer sit on high,
> When the proud shall be as stubble,
> For their sins receiving double;
> There's a happy time a-coming by and by.[37]

The gospel hymns of C. A. Tindley are also the "Christ against Culture" type. Anyone familiar with Tindley's sermons, particularly his sermon "The World's Conqueror," is probably already convinced that the theology of this Methodist minister is the type "Christ the Transformer of Culture." In this great sermon, Tindley contends that love is the principal force God uses to conquer evil and lead human beings, their vocations, and all of their possessions back to God, their primal source. Alluding to the conversionist theme in 1 John 3:16, Tindley says that it was only after Jesus Christ came into the world that love was "harnessed and adjusted to the lifting of the old world from hell to heaven."[38] Tindley, as the pastor of socially active East Calvary Methodist Church in Philadelphia, also carried out a strong social advocacy and welfare ministry.

In spite of the conversionist motif in this sermon, there is little that distinguishes the Tindley gospel hymns from those of C. P. Jones. Tindley does not espouse the tenets of holiness or sanctification, but like Jones he complains in his songs that the human domain is a "world of sin" and a "world of tears," a "wilderness" from which, he writes, "I shall be free some day." Whereas Jones tends to generalize about the spiritual transgression of the world, Tindley typically specifies social aspects of its decadence, as the following verse illustrates:

> Our boasted land and nation, Are plunging in disgrace;
> With pictures of starvation, Almost in every place;
> While loads of needed money, Remains in hoarded piles;
> But God will rule this country, After a while.

Tindley also grimaces about modernism: "The world of forms and changes is just now so confused, that there is found some danger in ev'rything you use." In one of his most celebrated songs, "We'll Understand It Better By and By,"

Tindley further specifies the dilemma of impoverishment as one that makes the nation so repressive to his people:

> We are often destitute of things that life demands,
> Want of food and want of shelter, thirsty hills and barren lands.
> We are trusting in the Lord, and according to his word,
> We will understand it better by and by.[39]

The life Tindley depicts in song is not only one of worldly destitution for Christian disciples but also one of sheer loneliness. There are no decent persons to be found in the world, and even Christians' friends misunderstand them and are never around when they are needed. In Tindley's response to these "trials dark on ev'ry hand" and to being "tossed and driv'n on the restless sea of time," he most resembles the radical anticulturalism of Jones's millenarianism. Tindley's reaction is to divest himself of the world and seek a better "home" in heaven:

> By and by when the morning comes,
> When the saints of God are gathered home,
> We'll tell the story how we've overcome:
> For we'll understand it better by and by.

Because the world is no friend to Christians, Tindley looks away to heaven in his song "I'm Going There":

> Although a pilgrim here below,
> Where dangers are and sorrow grow,
> I have a home in heaven above,
> I'm going there, I'm going there.[40]

Spiritualizing the kingdom of God idea in the Sermon on the Mount, Tindley claims that those who are already in heaven are the little ones who "lived and suffered in the world," whose "hearts [were] burdened with cares," and whose "bodies were full of disease" because "Medicine nor doctor could give them much ease." They were the "poor and often despised," he says, who "looked to heaven through tear-blinded eyes." However, until the "morning" comes ushered in by Christ Liberator Jesus, those who suffer in this world are exhorted to endure, a charge attainable only if Christ Friend and Protector Jesus is standing by:

When the storms of life are raging, Stand by me (2x)
When the world is tossing me, like a ship upon the sea,
Thou who rulest wind and water, Stand by me.[41]

Anticulturalism in Traditional Gospel

The Traditional Period, or Golden Age of Gospel (1930–1969), dominated by the Baptists, gained momentum under Thomas A. Dorsey, a Baptist songwriter influenced by the gospel hymns of Tindley. Other gospel composers and arrangers of the era are Doris Akers, J. Herbert Brewster, Lucie Campbell, James Cleveland, Theodore Frye, Dorothy Love, Roberta Martin, Sallie Martin, and Kenneth Morris. Together, these musicians transformed the congregational *gospel hymn* of the Transitional Period into the solo, quartet, and choral *gospel song* of the Traditional Period.

Akin to Jones's and Tindley's hymns, Dorsey's songs also disparage the "world of sin" and "worldliness" and complain adamantly about life being full of despair and heavy burdens, sorrow and troubles, earthly trials, and battles with foes pressing in on every side. Dorsey, in portraying the friendship of Jesus as an ultimate alternative, reveals further distrust of and detachment from the world. When you cannot share personal secrets with your mother, father, friend, or neighbor, he says, you can always tell Jesus in confidence. And when friends and kindred "forsake you and cast you aside," he advises, "There's a Savior who's a friend all the way." Thus it is that gospel's portrayal of friends and families, which is the very best of culture, is one full of shade and shadow and no light.[42]

Dorsey's "good news" about Christ Liberator, Friend, and Protector Jesus is that "When Satan oppresses me, His grace will caress me" and that "When troubles depress me, He won't fail to bless me." And because Jesus is present, figures Dorsey, "God is not dead":

> The times may get hard/Your way may be drear
> The road may be dark/The storm is severe
> But don't forget the name of Jesus.
> Your way may be lost/You grope in despair
> God is not dead/And Jesus is there
> Now don't forget the name of the Lord.

That "God is not dead" is sublimely lyricized in the image of God taking one's hand in Dorsey's time-honored masterpiece, "Precious Lord, Take My Hand":

> Precious Lord, take my hand,
> Lead me on, let me stand
> I am tired, I am weak, I am worn,
> Through the storm, through the night,
> Lead me on to the light,
> Take my hand precious Lord,
> Lead me on.[43]

Dorsey portrays the Christian's principal vocation as one of mere "watching and waiting" for the Savior's return because he finds that life is "uncertain" and "full of confusion." It is then that one's "tired and weary work" will yield to the "real life"—an existence of comfort and rest in a heavenly home:

> Watching and waiting singing my song,
> Darkness all fading shadows most gone
> Jesus will greet me it won't be long
> Real life awaits me when I get home.

According to other Dorsey songs, the "real life" is not only an entity of peace and joy with "riches to share" in "a city so fair" far away from "burdens and cares," but a reality in which real justice rules:

> By and by, by and by,
> When we reach that home beyond the sky,
> There the wicked will cease from troubling
> And the weary will be at rest
> And ev'ry day will be Sunday by and by.[44]

When Dorsey expresses the desire to "do some good thing every day" in order to "help the fallen by the way" and to "bring back those who've gone astray," it implies that "life" in the world is also "real" and that its transformation into the kingdom of God is perhaps a motif hidden behind the front of his apparent radical anticulturalism. However, any hint to conversionism is obliterated when Dorsey implies that good deeds for the victimized of the world are but for the sake of earning salvation and the congratulations "Well done." In this regard, human life is not really "real," it is a mere "race" on a "highway" to "the glory land," in which "when the last mile is finished" the saved "shall receive a crown."[45]

The gospel songs of Rev. W. Herbert Brewster are theologically indistinguishable from Dorsey's. Brewster's songs also portray the earthly realm as "a world of sin." In living amidst this "mean and sinful" world, Brewster murmurs that one's life is incessantly gloomy and burdensome. Until those who are saved by grace ascend into an eternity of sorrowfree, painfree, and carefree existence, Jesus makes life's toilsome pilgrimage more bearable. Brewster's "good news" is that the troubled, discouraged, oppressed, wounded, sick, and sore who have broken and bleeding hearts, weary souls, longings, trials, aches, and conflicts should come unto Jesus. "Weeping may endure for a night," he solaces, "but joy will come in the morning":

> Take up your cross and follow Him,
> Through failing and through great sorrow,
> Through stormy night and valley dim,
> And joy will come tomorrow.[46]

Jesus can make this futile life more bearable because while the world wears a frown the Lord wears a smile.[47]

The songs of James Cleveland are also homologous with the theology of radical anticulturalism. They are distinct from the songs of Dorsey and Brewster only because they highlight the aspects of "cross-bearing" and Christ-dependence. Cleveland attempts to console the distressed by admonishing that "cross-bearing" is a prerequisite to salvation—believers must weather the storms and rains of life if heaven is to be their final resting place. "If you can't stand it when your so-called friends put you down," he taunts, "Just remember no cross...no crown!" The second prominent theme in Cleveland's music is the contention that Christian disciples must completely depend on Friend, Protector, and Liberator Jesus. Joining his counterparts in declaring that Jesus Christ is "Everything," Cleveland carries the idea further in decreeing that the Lord is also to *do* "everything" for the believer. In a song appropriately titled "Take Them and Leave Them There," he exhorts that you must carry your burdens to Jesus, for "You know you cannot solve your own problems." In another song, Cleveland subjects his audience to examination: "Who will make all my decisions for me?" he questions; the choir answers, "Jesus will."[48]

Anticulturalism in Contemporary Gospel

The Contemporary Period, or Modern Gospel Era (1969–present), is dominated by Pentecostal artists of the Church of God in Christ, particularly Edwin Hawkins, Walter Hawkins, Andrae Crouch, Sandra Crouch, and the Clark Sisters. The era commenced with the Edwin Hawkins Singers' recorded arrangement of the old Baptist hymn "O Happy Day" in 1969.

In the music of Edwin Hawkins, the last quarter of the twentieth century remains replete with toils, snares, burdens, cares, and friends that forsake friends. As the Ultimate Alternative, Jesus is of course Friend, Protector, and Liberator of those who walk "with" or "in" him. The distinction is that Hawkins is far more optimistic about the world than his predecessors, resulting in a music with less heavenward polarity. Moreover, not only is Jesus savior of those who choose to follow him, but also "of this world He is Savior," affirms Hawkins. For the first time in the history of the musical movement, the "gospel of gospel" is more than merely a petition for the oppressed to turn away from the world heavenward. Under Hawkins's ministry the songs exhort Christ's followers to apply their love-transformed vocations toward the conversion of the world to its coming good:

> If you want the world to be a better place to live in (3x)
> Try real love, Try real peace,
> Don't put it off, Try the Real Thing today.[49]

The importance of this solicitation to "Try the Real Thing" is that practicing "real love" in order to make the world "a better place to live in" is for the sake of love itself, rather than for the singular end of seeing Jesus' face. "It's not by works that I'm saved today, through many good deeds that I've done," confesses Hawkins. Hence, to the conversionist Jesus is "Everything" when he is Friend, Protector, and Liberator, plus Reconciler:

> Where there's hatred, try a little love in its place.
> where there's sadness, try a little happiness.
> Where there's madness, try a little kindness.
> Where there's confusion, try a little peace.
> Give your brother a smile as you're passing by.
> Try to do, try to do something good.[50]

No longer are Christians enjoined to turn heavenward from hatred, sadness, madness, and confusion, but rather to be reconciliatory, to "do something good" by applying "real love." And no longer is Jesus the Ultimate Alternative—a smile—to a world that perpetually wears a frown, but rather the Lord is active in the world reconciling it unto himself. In Hawkins's music, Jesus' love shines through the world as neighbor gives neighbor a smile when passing by. Rather than being the Ultimate Alternative to the world, the Lord is the Ultimate Source of its transformation.

With Blacks making substantial gains in their quality of life during the final quarter of the twentieth century, it fits that the music of Edwin Hawkins has responded with a more positive world-view—the conversionist or "Christ the Transformer of Culture" type. However, there remain those, such as Hawkins's brother Walter Hawkins, for whom Jesus Christ is still the Ultimate Alternative. In terms of its anticulturalism, the music of Walter Hawkins is not quite as radical as that of transitional or traditional gospel. Yet it still depicts human beings as cross–bearing hoboes rambling through a destitute land engaging in whatever charity they can muster up in order to at long last hear the Lord say, "Well done." So-called friends are still not friends at all: "Just when you need a friend," Hawkins lyricizes, "they're not around at all, they just watch you fall."[51] The "good news" Hawkins has for his audiences is not to simply "be grateful" because "a little pain makes [one] appreciate the good times, but to be grateful because a little friendlessness helps one to appreciate the Ultimate Alternative:

> If you ever need a friend that sticks closer than a brother,
> I recommend Jesus because He's that kind of friend.
> He'll walk right in front of you to always protect you
> So the devil can't do you no harm.
> He is faithful ev'ry day to help you along the way,
> He's that kind of friend.[52]

The music of Andrae Crouch occasionally characterizes life as full of sleepless nights, burdens, and wickedness. Crouch also applies the customary means of consoling the disconsolate by heralding the virtues of cross-bearing:

> I thank God for the mountains
> And I thank Him for the valleys.
> I thank Him for the storms he brought me through,
> For if I'd never had a problem
> I wouldn't know that He could solve them,
> I'd never know what faith in God could do.

Nonetheless, in highlighting the entity of power in the Holy Ghost and in the "name" and the "blood" of Jesus, Crouch places far greater emphasis on the joy of "crown-wearing" than on the sorrow of "cross-bearing." This substantially depletes the radical edge of anticulturalism in Crouch's music. There are no definite conversionist motifs, like the songs of Edwin Hawkins, but Crouch depicts God's created humanity in a much more positive light. For instance, in

"Somebody Somewhere Is Praying Just for You," he characterizes human beings as capable of something other than deceit—as capable of caring ("the real thing"). In another song, he confidently exclaims, "I've got a whole lot of friends and I'm thankful." Crouch's hope is that heaven will be his "final home," and he urges believers to be ready for Christ's return—to "walk right" and "talk right" in preparation for the "great celebration." But again, there is neither a sense of anticulturalism being radical in his music nor of urgency to get to heaven at the earliest opportunity.[53]

Similar to the music of her brother Andrae, a large number of the compositions of Sandra Crouch are songs of praise. Pieces like "Magnify the Lord with Me," "He's Worthy," "My Soul Loves Only You," "Glorify the Lord," and "My God How Excellent Is Your Name" are of a "crown-wearing" rather than "cross-bearing" type. In spite of her joyous praise for the Creator, Sandra Crouch nevertheless recognizes the reality of a world that is destructive. In her song "We Need to Hear from You," she beckons God for his "perfect way." "There is no other way that we can live," she pleads:

> Destruction is now in view,
> Seems the world has forgotten all about You,
> And children are crying,
> People are dying.
> They're lost without You,
> So lost without You.

In Sandra Crouch's music, the world is not characterized as inherently evil, but as "a world that needs the Lord." However, unlike true conversionism, the reason the world needs God is not for it to be transformed presently, but so it might be prepared for the transformation to occur in the hereafter. In songs like "Souls for the Kingdom" and "We're Waiting," there is a strong sense of expectancy in terms of Christ's early return and a sense of urgency for believers to be ready. Yet Crouch's repeated beckoning, "Come, Lord Jesus," never implies that the urgency is due to this world being so irreparably destitute and devoid of inherent reconciliation.[54]

Christ-Everything the Ultimate Alternative

The single stream of thought that issues through the history of the gospel music movement is the notion that Jesus Christ is "Everything." For instance, Jones says, "Christ is all," or further, "all and all." Tindley also claims Jesus as his "all," adding that his allness is such that "there's nothing between." Morris sings, "Christ is all, all and all this world to me." The Lord is "all and all" to Brewster because he is friend to the friendless, mother to the motherless, and father to the fatherless. Dorsey lyricizes, "He's ev'rything to me cause he saved me." To Cleveland, Christ is also "Everything," in fact, *everything* that anyone will ever need. And Sandra Crouch prayerfully proclaims, "You are my ev'rything, dear Lord. You are the source that I draw from; My joy, my strength, Oh Lord, is in You."[55]

In gospel music, Jesus Christ is Everything—Friend, Protector, and Liberator—because he is portrayed as the Ultimate Alternative to a world that is essentially nothing, that is, no friend, offering no protection, and conditioned by captivity. It becomes acutely evident that nothingness, the condition of human nonbeing, is the oppressive aspect of culture causing Black people to look away heavenward to Everything through gospel music. Everythingness is the light at the end of the human tunnel which is just bright enough to allow human beings to see the alternative to the light—the irreconcilable darkness of nothingness. What highlights the depiction of Jesus Christ as the Ultimate Alternative is the fact that the Lord is not customarily characterized as Reconciler. The fact that in gospel music Jesus Christ is Everything but Reconciler is basically what makes him stand over against culture, which to the conversionists is nothing but creation in need of reconciliation.

Each gospel song and each gospel composer captures only a minute part of a Lord who is Everything, but the entire gospel music movement draws a more composite picture of the Savior. Of course these characterizations are mere interpretations that generally seem to satisfy millennialists who customarily subscribe to radical anticulturalism. But for other Christians who have experienced the Lord as "Christ of Culture," "Christ above Culture," "Christ in Paradox with Culture," or as "Christ the Transformer of Culture," the picture gospel music paints is quite partial. If gospel music is theologically problematic, it is not because it captures the "hard times" God's little ones have faced in the twentieth century and that it offers alternative "good news," which is to look away heavenward from nothing to Everything. If the "gospel of gospel" is problematic, it is because the individuals who are its preachers and its audience may be irreproachably convinced that Jesus Christ is no more and no less than the Everything gospel music pictures him as. Not even Roberta Martin escapes this critique in denoting the Lord "more than all,"[56] for insofar as Jesus Christ is not generally characterized as Reconciler in gospel, he is not "more than all" because he is not *all* at all.

In the final analysis, Jesus Christ is more than the Everything gospel music casts him as. The Lord is Everything beyond the world's wildest imaginations. Nevertheless, the power and potency of the gospel music movement in history is the unanimity of its anticulturalism as a profound critical measure for balancing the other more positive views of culture amid Christian pluralism.

---

1 Louis-Charles Harvey, "Black Gospel Music and Black Theology," *The Journal of Religious Thought* 43, no. 2 (Fall–Winter, 1986–1987), p. 26.

2 Wyatt Tee Walker, "Somebody's Calling My Name," *Black Sacred Music and Social Change* (Valley Forge, PA: Judson Press, 1979), p. 127.

3 Irene V. Jackson, ed., *Afro-American Religious Music: A Bibliography and a Catalogue of Gospel Music* (Westport, CT: Greenwood Press, 1979), p. 74.

4 Ibid., p. 73.

5 Lawrence W. Levine, *Black Culture and Black Consciousness: Afro-American Folk Thought from Slavery to Freedom* (New York: Oxford University Press, 1977), p. 175.

6 Joseph R. Washington, Jr., *Black Religion: The Negro and Christianity in the United States* (Boston: Beacon Press, 1964), p. 51.

7 Joseph R. Washington, Jr., *Black Sects and Cults: The Power Praxis in an Ethnic Ethic* (Garden City, NY: Anchor/Doubleday, 1972), p. 78.

8 Charles B. Copher, "Biblical Characters, Events, Places and Images Remembered and Celebrated in Black Worship," *Journal of the Interdenominational Theological Center* 14, nos. 1–2 (Fall 1986–Spring 1987), pp. 75, 85, 78.

9 Ibid., pp. 78, 85.

10 Mary A. L. Tyler, "The Music of Charles Henry Pace and Its Relationship to the Afro-American Church Experience," Ph.D. dissertation, University of Pittsburgh, 1980, p. 101.

11 William T. Dargan, "Congregational Gospel Songs in a Black Holiness Church: A Musical and Textual Analysis," Ph.D. dissertation, Wesleyan University, 1983, pp. 112, 115, 122, 127, 128, 131.

12 Henry H. Mitchell and Nicholas Cooper-Lewter, *Soul Theology: The Heart of American Black Culture* (San Francisco: Harper & Row, 1986), pp. 95, 4.

13 Harvey, p. 27.

14 The remaining aspects of *The Equality of Persons, The Uniqueness of Persons,* and *The Family of God and Humanity* (which in Mitchell's book have no gospel song references) coincide with Jesus as Reconciler—an atypical attribute for the Lord in almost all of gospel music.

15 Levine, p. 176.

16 H. Richard Niebuhr, *Christ and Culture* (San Francisco: Harper & Row, 1951), p. 83.

17 Ibid., pp. 102–103.

18 Ibid., p. 110.

19 Ibid., pp. 120–121.

20 See Matthew 5:17–19; 22:21; Romans 12:1, 6.

21 Niebuhr, p. 143.

22 Ibid., p. 144.

23 Ibid., pp. 165–166.

24 Harvey, p. 26.

25 Walker, p. 144.

26 See John 1:29; 12:32, 47.

27 Harvey, p. 27.

28 In 1906, Jones published a third songbook titled *His Fullness.*

29 Cited in Otho B. Cobbins, ed., *History of Church of Christ (Holiness) U.S.A.* (New York: Vantage Press, 1966), p. 407.

30 See Jones, "The Time Will Not Be Long," "None But Christ," "I Will Hide," "Precious Savior."

31 See Jones, "Go, Wash, and Be Clean," "Hear, O Hear the Savior Calling," "O Tarry for the Power," "O Sinner, Where Will You Stand?" "There's a Happy Day at Hand."

32 See Jones, "The Fount Is Flowing," "The Time Will Not Be Long," "Praise Ye the Lord in Faith and Hope," "Saving Me Wholly by Grace."

33 Cited in Cobbins, pp. 24, 28.

34 See Jones, "I Have Surrendered to Jesus," "I Am Wholly Sanctified."

35 Cited in Cobbins, p. 409.

36 See Jones, "Can You Stand?" "God Forbid That I Should Glory," "Jesus Only."

37 See Jones, "I Am Happy with Jesus Alone," "Come unto Me," "There's a Happy Time a-Coming."

38 Cited in Ralph H. Jones, *Charles Albert Tindley: Prince of Preachers* (Nashville: Abingdon Press, 1982), pp. 157–158, 161–162.

39 See Tindley, "Some Day," "After a While."

40 See Tindley, "We'll Understand It Better By and By," "I'm Going There."

41 See Tindley, "What Are They Doing in Heaven," "Stand By Me."

42 See Dorsey, "Tell Jesus Everything," "Someday, Somewhere."

43 See Dorsey, "I'll Tell It Wherever I Go," "Don't Forget the Name of the Lord," "Precious Lord, Take My Hand."

44 See Dorsey, "Watching and Waiting," "Someday, Somewhere," "Every Day Will Be Sunday By and By."

45 See Dorsey, "My Desire," "When the Last Mile Is Finished." See also "That's All That I Can Do."

46 Brewster, "Weeping May Endure for a Night."

47 See Brewster, "Just Over the Hill," "Make Room for Jesus in Your Life," "Weeping May Endure for a Night," "I Want the World to Smile on Me."

48 See Cleveland, "I'll Do His Will," "No Cross, No Crown," "Take Them and Leave Them There," "Jesus Will." To elaborate on the theology in the songs of Lucie Campbell, Dorothy Love, Roberta Martin, Sallie Martin, Kenneth Morris, and others of this period is basically to rehearse all that is typical in the music of Dorsey, Brewster, and Cleveland.

49 See Hawkins, "Jesus," "Have Mercy," "Try the Real Thing."

50 Hawkins, "Have Mercy."

51 Walter Hawkins, "Love Is God." See also "Try Christ."

52 See Walter Hawkins, "Goin' to a Place," "I'm a Pilgrim," "Love Is God," "Try Christ," "Be Grateful," "He's That Kind of Friend."

53 See Crouch, "Through It All," "Living This Kind of Life," "No Time to Lose (I Wanna Be Ready)."

54 See Sandra Crouch, "Souls for the Kingdom," "Come, Lord Jesus."

55 See Jones, "All I Need," "Is Thy Life Too Good for Jesus?" "Jesus My All in All"; Tindley, "Nothing Between"; Dorsey, "I'll Tell It Wherever I Go," "I Know Jesus"; Morris, "Christ Is All"; Brewster, "Surely God Is Able"; Cleveland, "I Can't Stop Loving God," "He's Everything You Need," "He's Got Everything You Need"; Crouch, "I'll Always Love You."

56 Martin, "More than All."

"I Am the Holy Dope Dealer": The Problem with Gospel Music Today

by Obery M. Hendricks, Jr., written in 2000

> People need to get high off something spiritual, and I'm the holy dope dealer. I got this drug, I got this Jesus rock. And you can have a type of high that you've never experienced.
>
> —Kirk Franklin[1]

Introduction

Ecstatic, euphoric, celebratory worship has always been an important part of the Black religious experience. It both pre-dates and lives on in the African American sojourn, as numerous scholars have attested.[2] Those of us that have grown up in the Black Church not only know Jesus for ourselves, as the old saints said that we must, but also know for ourselves the centrality of ecstatic worship. We know for ourselves what it means to "make a joyful noise unto the Lord, all ye lands!" We know for ourselves what it means to lift up holy hands in tearful supplication and joyful thanksgiving. We know for ourselves what it means for arms and legs to be carried away by some other spirit, for old and calloused feet to dance unctioned dances of praise, for fire-kissed tongues to speak languages unknown, yet uplifting. Yes, the euphoric, the celebratory, the praise-filled runs in our people as deeply as marrow. Yet, it has never been the only blood coursing our veins; praise and celebration for deliverance, without a concomitant critique of the events and conditions that our people looked to the Lord to deliver us from, is never what has characterized the heart of African American religious expression.

That is, until today. Today we are witnesses to a phenomenon that must turn Nat Turner[3] and Fannie Lou Hamer[4] in their miry graves. Today the prophetic consciousness that, with head and heart, once told Black people to resist the White supremacist oppression that bedeviled their every step, no longer informs the music that once inspired us to action. Although White skin color preference remains the creed of this nation,[5] today the prophet's call to "let justice roll down like waters, and righteousness like a mighty stream" is seldom voiced in Black sacred songs, songs that once moved the Fightin' 54th of Massachusetts to brave death for Glory;[6] songs that emboldened Fannie Lou to proclaim to the forces of J. Edgar KKK that she was sick and tired of being sick and tired; songs that helped us to brave Bull Connor's vicious beatings with our eyes stayed on freedom, even as our daughters lie bombed in our churches and our sons lie lynched in our yards.

Black sacred music had this power because it took pains to remind us that "Pharaoh's army got drowned-ed"; to remind us that "Didn't my Lord deliver Daniel, so why not everyone?"; to remind us that against all odds, Joshua and his poor band of Hebrew outcasts "fit the battle of Jericho and the walls came tumblin' down." It gave us songs of the comforting Jesus, yes, but also songs of the warrior Jesus; songs that helped us to stand boldly and unbowed before the most efficient engine of oppression and de-humanization ever conceived to declare, "Ride on, King Jesus! No man[7] can-a hinder me!" Songs of hope and love and resistance and change. Songs that reminded us, long before Einstein drew breath, that the arc of the universe is long, but it bends toward justice—on earth, as in heaven.

However, despite the empowering nature of the Black sacred music of the past, in the dominant mode of Black religious music today—contemporary Gospel music—this prophetic voice, this resistance voice, this biblical logic of justice, is all but stilled. Gospel music is heard everywhere today, yet, unlike the spirituals, it does not press our suit for freedom; it does not call, like the spirituals did, for "Moses, way down in Egypt land, tell ole Pharaoh to let my people go."

Once the Black songs of Zion were heard only in the hush arbors and sequestered hearth-warmed quarters of clandestine slavery times; then in the soft, spare safety of those humming houses of refuge we called "church"; then in the rented halls and auditoriums where the studiedly sweet and mournful voices of church-dressed women and shiny-suited men brought to ultimate rejection the all-American notion that Black folk ain't nobody; then as the fruit of paternalistic bemusement, occasionally emerging in the curiously commercial eyeball venues of Dinah Shore, Arthur Godfrey, Jack Paar, and Ted Mack, where many White folks thought our music enjoyably interesting, but too exotic, too raw, and much too jungle-fied for anyone but the downwardly mobile and Aunt Hagar's children to claim as their own.

But the day of limited venues for Black religious music is now past. Today, gospel music is featured daily by the most popular entertainment media in the land. The market for gospel in recent years has grown at a seemingly exponential rate. Several gospel artists are even numbered among the pantheon of international entertainment superstars! Yet, despite the ubiquity of gospel music today, barely a prophet's voice doth grace the chorus; indeed, the prophet's call for justice is nowhere to be found. Today Kirk Franklin, arguably the most commercially successful artist in the history of gospel music, can even utter the probably well-intentioned, yet deeply problematic description of his role as a gospel artist that is the epigraph of this essay, and cause no uproar or even audible dissent among his gospel compatriots. Sadly, in gospel music today seldom is proclaimed the God of liberation—just the God of escape. Seldom is heralded the God that will deliver the world from evil, just a God who delivers us from reality. Seldom is Moses invoked, or Joshua, or dauntless Hebrew judges and freedom fighters. And no longer is proclaimed the Exodus, that great event of liberation, that paradigmatic event of our faith, that event that empowered our people through the horrors of slavery and the unrelenting pain of Jim Crow to keep on keeping on, to keep on struggling; that event that assured us, by example and analogy, that Pharaoh in the big house is accursed of God and doomed to fail, while we, the tortured heirs of the chosen Hebrew children, are blessed by heaven and bound to be free. Gospel music has gained the world, but it has lost the prophetic heart of Black sacred music—the Exodus and its divine mandate of freedom, the same divine imperative of liberation echoed by Jesus as he proclaimed the purpose of his earthly ministry: "The Spirit of the Lord is upon me, because he has anointed me to bring good news to the poor...to proclaim release to the captives...to let the oppressed go free" (Luke 4:18).

Statement of Thesis and Terms

It is the central thesis of this essay that the social orientation of gospel music today, at best, is unmindful of and uninvolved with the ongoing freedom struggle of Black people in America; at worst, it unwittingly undermines that struggle. To elucidate this thesis, in this paper I examine the reasons for the absence of a liberation imperative in gospel. My point of debarkation is the radical departure of gospel music from the sociopolitical emphases of the spirituals. I begin my study of this departure through analysis of the shift from the eschatological employment of Old Testament liberation motifs and prophetic sensibilities that permeate the spirituals, to the celebratory, "other-worldly Jesus"-centered proclamations of gospel music today that offer virtually no reference to the harsh social realities that bedevil Africans in America. In addition, I examine the factors underlying the socioaesthetic shift from the sensibilities of the spirituals to the origins of gospel music. In turn, I also examine the relationship of this shift in genres to the change in the predominant mode of Black production from rural agrarian to urban industrial, an evolution that was, itself, the result of the great urban migration of African Americans in the early part of this century. Finally, I identify the ways the particular emphases of the contemporary gospel music scene are too often anathema to the sociopolitical interests of African Americans. I conclude by offering a proposal to address the aesthetic excesses of gospel that keep it from reaching its potential as a force for holistic Black liberation.

Just a word on my use of terms. As I use it here, the term "spirituals" refers to the body of Black sacred songs that evolved as the collective cultural expression of enslaved and, to a lesser extent, the later experience of Jim Crow-ed Africans in America, representing a period spanning from the early seventeenth century to about the third quarter of the nineteenth century. This is a straightforward and, I believe, traditional definition of the term. My use of the term "early" or "historic" gospel is self-evident, referring as it does to the first several decades of that genre, roughly form the 1920s to the 1950s and early 1960s. My use of the term "contemporary gospel music" is less straightforward, however. The roots of contemporary gospel can be traced to the pioneering works of Andrae Crouch and Edwin Hawkins in the late 1960s and early 1970s. The compositions and performances of these gospel innovators combined pop riffs and rhythm and blues instrumentation and production techniques with traditional gospel music, to create the genre called "contemporary gospel." Although my use of "contemporary gospel" includes Crouch and Hawkins in its purview, because of the cultural currency of the gospel phenomenon today, in this essay the term should be understood as primarily referring to the most contemporary of African American religious music, that is, to the gospel music produced in the present decade.

It is clear that the gospel music scene today is not homogenous. Yet in terms of popular exposure and acceptance, as well as measured by commercial success, it is dominated by those artists, songs, performances, and sensibilities that focus almost exclusively on "praise-singing," that is, on the ecstatic and the celebratory, to the virtual exclusion of the prophetic, thus excluding not only the explicitly socially referential but, for that matter, excluding even the encoded references to social and political conditions that characterized the spirituals. This sector of the gospel music scene has become so dominant, in fact, as to virtually define the gospel genre today. Artists that can be understood as typifying the contemporary gospel music scene by virtue of their commercial success and wide popular acceptance are located along a broad, stylistic continuum. They include Franklin, Richard Smallwood, Fred Hammond, Hezekiah Walker, Take 6, and BeBe and CeCe Winans, among others. It is to this stratum of the gospel music genre that my use of the term "contemporary gospel music" in this paper will refer.

I write this essay as a lover of gospel music. My fondest and earliest memories are tied to gospel music. My grandmother, Laura Banks, singing "Precious Lord" (she pronounced it "pry-shush") and "Glory to His Name," back home in Charlotte Court House, Virginia, as she snapped fresh beans for our supper. My extended family, with joyful familial anticipation, following my uncle Leon Banks and his "quartet" as they traveled to myriad tiny venues in rural Virginia to place their musical gifts at the service of the Lord before handfuls of joyous believers. Our later home in East Orange, New Jersey, warmed every Sunday morning by Brother Jonathan Joe Crane and his Gospel Caravan on WNJR ("1400 on your radio"), as my father read his Bible, contentedly drinking his daily Sanka, and my mother readied my sister and I for Sunday School. As a child of six, my father and me going to a "Battle of the Quartets," headlined by the Five Blind Boys, at Newark's Greater Abyssinian Baptist Church. Even today, among the hundreds of recordings in my personal collection, the works of the Soul Stirrers, Mahalia Jackson, the Five Blind Boys, Helen Baylor, and Richard Smallwood hold pride of place with Miles Davis, Thelonius Monk, John and Alice Coltrane, Gerri Allen, and Wynton Marsalis.

As much as I love gospel music, however, I love the freedom of my people more. African American children continue to die, on average, eight to ten years younger than their European American counterparts. Black folks suffer disproportionately higher rates of cancer, strokes, heart disease, diabetes, and infant and maternal mortality than the national average, while our access to adequate and timely healthcare is shamefully limited; we receive far less justice from the criminal justice system; we pay significantly higher interest rates for mortgages and auto loans than other groups; and have far less access to higher education and high-wage employment. By every significant measure, the systematic suffering of Black people continues. Yet, as the praise songs of gospel music thunder across the land, one listens in vain for lyrics of protest or even explicit acknowledgement of our plight. Therefore, because I love both gospel music and my people, I must engage gospel as one would a dear, beloved friend: honestly, candidly, unflinchingly. Thus, in this essay I offer gospel music the supreme compliment of taking it seriously by submitting it not to uncritical hagiography, but to the same level of analytical rigor with which thoughtful scholars should engage all subjects they respect. In this I humbly, but sincerely, follow those who have so boldly treaded this ground before me, including W. E. B. DuBois, James Weldon and J. Rosamond Johnson, Amiri Baraka, Wyatt Tee Walker, James H. Cone, Bernice Johnson Reagon, and countless others.[8]

The Spirituals: The Prism of the African American Social Experience

Wyatt Tee Walker has asserted, "The political and social significance of the spiritual will be obscured if one loses sight of the fact that the spirituals were born in slavery."[9] The importance of this point cannot be overstated, for it underscores the social setting in which the spirituals were formed, and the social conditions and social relations with which they were invariably in dialogue. The spirituals' tone of ceaseless hope in the inevitability of deliverance to justice empowered Black people to resist White supremacy's devaluation of our humanity and its definition of our lot as without hope. In this sense, the spirituals are part of what can be called a discursive formation of resistance. A discursive formation is a set of rules determined by the collective needs and aspirations of a particular social group; it arises out of the social and political conditions of that group's particular setting in life. It is the discursive formation that determines "what can and must be said" by the members of that group, and what the terms that are used within that discourse ultimately mean, particularly with regard to their sociopolitical plight.[10] The discursive formation that gave meaning to the terms and images of the spirituals was the ongoing African American discourse of resistance to systematic *de jure* White supremacy in America. The term "resistance discourse" denotes terms, phrases, figures of speech, concepts, poetry, and songs that are common to a particular grouping of subjugated persons and that are widely understood by them as exhortative in nature, calling their hearers to resist in some way the oppression to which they are subjected.[11] The modes that these discursive forms of resistance may take range from the relatively benign, like feigning inability to understand a command or directive, to the outright use of violence.[12]

The great freedom fighter Frederick Douglass contended that the resistance sensibilities of the spirituals were so pronounced that "Every tone was a testimony against slavery, and a prayer to God for deliverance from chains."[13] However, to say that spirituals fit within the spectrum of African American resistance discourse is to recognize that while not every individual song of the spiritual genre explicitly refers to freedom from bondage and the eschatological institution of justice, still all spirituals do in some way hope, counsel, or proclaim resistance to the negation of our forebears' humanity, the negation of their right to have life and that, more abundantly, the negation demanded by the very tenets of the system of oppression that weighed upon them. Because of the omnipresence of the oppressive gaze during the period of African American enslavement, often this resistance was expressed in coded language, what Mikhail Bahktin has called "double-voiced" discourse, in which "the word in language is half someone else's. It becomes 'one's own' only when the speaker populates it with his own intention, his own accent, when he appropriates the word, adapting it to his own semantic and expressive intention."[14] Music scholar Gwendolin Warren observes of the double-voiced nature of the spirituals that, "without understanding...double meanings it is impossible to get a complete sense of the significance of the [s]piritual as a way African Americans resisted enslavement."[15]

The "double-voiced" resistance nature of spirituals took a number of forms. Some songs explicitly bemoaned the slaves' suffering beneath the White supremacist heel without naming the specifics of their subjugation:

> Sometimes I feel like a motherless child,
> A long, long ways from home.

Some were songs of perseverance in the struggle for personhood and liberation:

> I ain't got weary yet,
> I ain't got weary yet,
> I been in the wilderness a mighty long time,
> And I ain't got weary yet.

Others were outright proclamations of resistance, such as "Marching Up the Heavenly Road," whose lyrics are possessed of such powerful resistance sensibilities that one could well imagine it being sung by Nat Turner's army, or by soldiers in the hundreds of other slave revolts as they marched to battle:

> Marching up the heavenly road,
> I'm bound to fight until I die.
> O fare you well friends, fare you well foes,
> Marching up the heavenly road,
> I leave you all my eyes to close,
> Marching up the heavenly road.

Also consider "Great Day! Great Day!":

> This is the day of jubilee...
> The Lord has set his people free,
> God's going to build up Zion's walls!
> We want no cowards in our band,
> We call for valiant-hearted men,
> God's going to build up Zion's walls!

And, of course:

> Oh, freedom!
> Oh, freedom!
> Oh, freedom over me!
> And before I'd be a slave,
> I'll be buried in my grave,
> And go home to my Lord and be free!

Spirituals have played a pivotal role in the articulation of African American resistance discourse in general because their public assertions of personhood, by definition, resist the oppressive definitions and importunities of the White supremacist social order, as well as because they occur in a collective medium of expression in which all can participate. In fact, the collective, communal nature of the spiritual genre is important for two primary reasons.

First, the very act of collective song, whether in sequestered sites outside the oppressive gaze or in postures of unobtrusive, feigned guilelessness squarely in the oppressors' presence, nonetheless helped to develop and to eventually normalize the significance of resistance themes, terms, and figures into a collective cultural product. James C. Scott calls this process "making space for a dissident subculture,"[16] with "dissidence," or rejection of the world-view and definitions promulgated by the dominant class, being the operative word. After the process of cultural dissidence has repeatedly and systematically discredited those claims, in order for the process to be meaningful to the oppressed, the claims, notions, and definitions that undergird oppression must be redefined, given constructive new meanings, or replaced by terms, concepts, and figures that serve the liberative interests of the oppressed. What cultural dissidence ultimately seeks is to counter the ideological claims, or "hegemony," of the oppressive power. Hegemony is the process by which the lines between the interests of an oppressed group and those of the class that dominates it become blurred by the systematic obfuscatory efforts of the oppressor, with the result that the oppressed unwittingly come to give assent to social definitions, even social policies, that are anathema to their own interests thus, in effect, becoming complicit in their own oppression.[17] In this sense, the cultural dissidence task of countering the effects of the hegemonic process can be called "counter-hegemony."

Citing the ethnohistorical work of Werner Sollors,[18] Theophus Smith refers to the particular counter-hegemonic process by which the African American slaves effectively redefined biblical events and characters by the term "typological ethnogenesis." He defines this process as "the formation of peoplehood through the hermeneutic of biblical typology" in which enslaved African America "envisioned and revised its existence in terms of characters and events found in the Exodus story."[19] Albert Raboteau observes:

> Slaves prayed for the future day of deliverance to come, and they kept hope alive by incorporating as part of *their* mythic past the Old Testament exodus of Israel out of slavery.... The Christian slaves applied the Exodus story, whose end they knew, to their own experience of slavery, which had not ended.... Exodus functioned as an archetypal event for the slaves. The sacred history of God's liberation of his people would be or was being repeated in the American South [emphasis by the author].[20]

Because of the affinity the enslaved Africans felt with the enslaved Hebrews, the Old Testament figures of Moses, Joshua, Daniel, and the Pharaoh of Egypt became typologies through which the slaves expressed their hope, their approbation, their derision and, most importantly, their definitions of justice and injustice. What is significant in this process is that the primary biblical figures used typologically in the spirituals were resistance figures who struggled with and triumphed over *worldly* oppression. They were not mystical, ethereal, or pacific characters, but freedom fighters, servants of God who expressed their faith by struggling for the liberation of their people. Likewise, the litany of biblical liberation events, particularly those of t he Exodus, the vanquishing of the Hebrews' enemies at Jericho, Daniel's deliverance from annihilation at the hands of his oppressors, and the Hebrews' possession of the land beyond the chilly Jordan, together constituted the most significant and widely invoked motifs of the entire spiritual genre, with the Exodus being the primary subject of typological ethnogenesis among them. In this sense, Wendel Whalum's assertion that freedom was the constant theme of the spirituals is wholly accurate.[21]

Another significance of the spirituals as collective cultural products is that they reflect the communal, cooperative mode of production in which they were produced, i.e., the agrarian or farming mode of production which, because it was fully dependent upon cooperative labor, extolled the virtue of, accorded normative status to, and eventually sacralized the ethos of cooperative, communal production as part of its underlying moral economy.[22] Because spirituals are products of this agrarian-based culture of reciprocity and cooperative action, they are not individual efforts; rather, they are collective expressions of the collective ethos, hopes, dreams, fears, aspirations, angst, and anger of the African American communities that collectively produced them. Nor were spirituals produced as commodities, that is, for commercial transfer or exchange; they were produced for their producing communities' own collective edification and consumption. Spirituals were not crafted by their producers as personal appeals to the emotions of others but, rather, to express the collective sentiments of the communities that produced them. In other words, in the settings that produced them, the spirituals were not performance vehicles, but products of collective expression and edification. This is an important point of difference between spirituals and gospel songs, as we shall discuss in greater depth later in this essay.

The agrarian or farming mode of production had a further significance with regard to the formation of the spirituals. Although the enslaved Africans labored for others under the severest compulsion, still the agrarian nature of most slaves' labor and the setting of that labor in rural expanses conspired to offer them a certain sense of empowerment or, at least, possibility. It is important to note that the slaves' agrarian labor was not fully alienated in the Marxist sense, that is, it was not fully devoid of a sense of the satisfaction of creation or achievement,[23] for often the slaves literally saw the fruit of their labor grow to fruition. They raised crops they themselves planted and nurtured, and sometimes lived off of the fruits of their own toil. As a result, despite the compulsory nature of their labor, the slaves could still experience some measure of the fulfillment that came from shepherding the span of cultivation to production, planting to harvest. Therefore, although their labor was forced and often pain-filled, it was not without meaning. Moreover, the rural expanses of most slaves' settings in life offered the omnipresent hope and possibility of escape to new, more humane surroundings in which they would know a greater measure of justice in their lives. If nothing else, there always loomed for them the Promised Land of the North and its ideal of freedom. And in the immediate post-emancipation era in which the later spirituals were produced, agrarian labor would have been of even greater meaning to freedmen and freedwomen who had become smallholders working their own soil. Some sense of the meaning labor gave to the lives of Black agrarian workers, whether enslaved or experiencing the circumscribed "freedom" of sharecropping or rural proletariat "day work," can be culled from the blues singer B. B. King's recollection of his own boyhood as an agrarian day worker:

> In the Mississippi Delta of my childhood, cotton was a force
> of nature.... It's how I beat back the wolf. Cotton turned me
> from a boy to a man, testing my energy and giving me what I
> needed—a means to survive. But I did more than cope with
> the crop. I actually loved it. It was beautiful to live through the
> seasons, to break the ground in the chill of winter, plant the
> seeds against the winds of spring, and pick the blossoms in the
> heat of summer.[24]

Although the pain that accompanied these factors must not be underestimated, nonetheless they must be counted as contributing to the abiding sense of hope in the face of inhumane oppression that is expressed in the spirituals. In turn, that hope reflected a sense of relative power on the part of oppressed African Americans, albeit small, that they might in some way effect changes in their worldly circumstances.

This measure of control offered by the agrarian mode of production, as well as the perceived possibility of effecting change in their own circumstances, is reflected in the eschatological nature of the slaves' hope. Eschatology generally refers to one's belief or understanding of how the present world order will end. From a perusal of the spiritual genre, it is clear that the slaves harbored eschatological hopes for the comfort of heaven, but it is also clear that they expected justice in this world as well or, as W. E. B. DuBois put it, they held "a faith in the ultimate justice of things."[25] This eschatological expectation for justice in this world is richly expressed by David Walker's 1829 polemical *Appeal:*

> Remember [White] Americans, that we must and shall be free, and enlightened as you are, will you wait until we shall, under God, obtain our liberty by the crushing arm of power?... We must and shall be free, I say, in spite of you. You may do your best to keep us in wretchedness and misery, to enrich you and your children, but God will deliver us from under you.[26]

Walker uses "shall" and "must," terms that brook no uncertainty. The eschatology of justice that he expresses knew neither the day nor the hour, but it held no doubt of the outcome. This is the same eschatological certainty of deliverance that is expressed by the spiritual when it proclaims:

> I ain't got long to stay here.

The Normative Elements of Black Sacred Music

The spirituals grew out of the collective root experience of the exclusion and oppression that has always pervaded African American reality and, as a genre, was at every step informed by the contours of that experience. Because the awareness and expression of that root reality is an intrinsic constituent of the spiritual genre and, as well, because the spiritual is the earliest form of African American music, it is compelling cultural logic that the sensibilities of the spirituals be considered to constitute the normative elements of Black sacred music. These sensibilities include the prophetic functions of naming the oppressive reality and exhorting resistance to it, and the eschatological expectation of justice *in this world.* Moreover, because an important characteristic of spirituals is that they also offer empathy and comfort for suffering even as they counsel resistance, the empathic nature of the genre should also be included among the normative elements of Black sacred song.

Because they constitute the well out of which Black sacred music sprang, these normative characteristics must be considered to collectively constitute the primary evaluative criteria by which the cultural relevance of Black sacred music to the ongoing struggle of African Americans for equity and justice may be determined. To summarize, these criteria include: (1) collective acknowledgement of oppression, (2) prophetic critique of the race-based system and sensibilities that produce and perpetuate that oppression,

(3) exhortation to resist the importunities of that systematic oppression, (4) while simultaneously offering comfort and empathy in its midst. It is a thesis of this essay that with the exception of its stress on the empathic, contemporary gospel music fails to fulfill these criteria which, ultimately, are so crucial to the quest of African Americans to have life with the same abundance in American society as citizens of European descent. Below we will explore this claim.

Gospel Music: Hear No, See No, Speak No (Political) Evil

In many of today's churches, gospel music has virtually replaced spirituals, yet gospel music represents a real shift in consciousness and world view from the spirituals. Despite the very real differences, however, there are significant points of continuity between the two.

Commonalities with Spirituals:
Hope, Immanence, and Deliverance from Burdens

First, both spirituals and gospel songs are primarily expressions of hope and affirmation. Thomas A. Dorsey (1899–1993) who, along with Charles A. Tindley (1851–1933), was a seminal figure in gospel music, said of his role in the origins of the genre during the Great Depression, "I wrote to give [the people] something to lift them out of that depression."[27] He went on to explain, "We intended [g]ospel to strike a happy medium for the downtrodden. This music lifted people out of the muck and mire of poverty and loneliness, of being broke, and gave them some kind of hope anyway."[28] Gospel great Mahalia Jackson epitomized the overall significance of hope to gospel music in this way: "[G]ospel songs are songs of hope. When you sing them you are delivered of your burden."[29]

The unrelenting hopefulness of gospel songs is seen, for instance, in "I've Got a Feeling (Everything's Gonna Be Alright)" and Dorsey's "The Lord Will Make a Way Somehow," which reflects the certainty of God's mercy and deliverance from suffering. The spirituals hold a similar certainty that despite the pain of the present moment, "There Is a Balm in Gilead." In addition to the certainty of eventual comfort and rest, the spirituals also held the eschatological certainty of justice, as seen in "Jacob's Ladder":

> We are climbing Jacob's ladder...
> Every round goes higher and higher...
> We are climbing higher and higher,
> Soldiers of the cross.

In addition, both spirituals and gospel music attest to the immanence and omnipresence of God as central to their proclamations. While the spiritual testifies, "God Don't Ever Change," "He's Got the Whole World in His Hands" and "My God Is So High You Can't Get Over Him," gospel music sings "He Has Never Left Me Alone," "His Eye Is on the Sparrow and I Know He Watches Me," and "Hold to God's Unchanging Hand."

Moreover, even as gospel evolved its own distinctive markings, forms, and accompanying musical culture, in some quarters the early gospel music retained from its spiritual roots something of the character of a collective cultural product, at least in the sense that performance of it was not specialized or individualized. This is attested by no less than Sallie Martin, an important associate of Dorsey and a pioneer of gospel music in her own right, who recalls of those early years, "We didn't have no soloists. We would all sing together."[30]

Differences: Meek Jesus, Absent Moses, Individuation, and the Timetable of Justice

Despite the similarities between the two genres, however, their differences are profound, with world-views that differ radically. Whereas typologies of Old Testament liberation themes and motifs were central for spirituals, not so with gospel music. It is not the Hebrew children struggling for freedom that dominate gospel songs, but Jesus. And not just any Jesus, but specifically the pacific, meek, mild, otherworldly Jesus. As Lawrence Levine observes, the figure of Jesus that predominates in the gospel songs "is not the warrior Jesus of the [s]pirituals but a benevolent spirit who promised His children rest and peace and justice in the hereafter."[31] This is attested today by gospel titles such as "Christ Is All," "I'd Rather Have Jesus," "Jesus Knows and Will Supply My Every Need," "Jesus, Lover of My Soul," and "Jesus Is the Answer to Every Problem," to name just a few.

Moreover, spirituals generally were the product of anonymous collective authorship and, therefore, knew nothing like identification with a particular individual member of the community. Conversely, although the thoughts and emotions expressed in gospel songs are often universal in scope and emphasis, the songs themselves have, from the beginning, been written, copyrighted, and often widely identified with individuals. Thus, unlike the communal nature of spirituals, gospel songs are the stuff of individual authorship and ownership. One commentator observes, "The creation and development of that African American art called [g]ospel music and its wide acceptance by 1950 can be attributed to fewer than one dozen composers."[32]

Furthermore, whereas the eschatology of the spirituals ultimately foresees the establishment of God's justice in this world, the eschatology of gospel songs is apocalyptic and other-worldly in orientation. Apocalyptic as a worldview is an expression of a sense of powerlessness to effect meaningful positive change in an unjust social order, a sense that because the odds against victory and vindication in this world are so overwhelming and so insurmountable that there is nothing one can do but "wait on the Lord" for a new day.[33] Thus, although both genres hold hope in common, the gospel hope is not for justice in this world, as is the hope of the spiritual, but for deliverance *from* this world. The locus of the hope of gospel songs is "over yonder," as seen in "I'll Fly Away":

> Just a few more weary days and then,
> I'll fly away.
> To a land where joys will never end,
> I'll fly away.

Apocalyptic is seen in even bolder relief in the evocation of 1 Thessalonians 4:16–18, one of the foremost examples of New Testament apocalyptic, in "I'll Be Caught Up in the Air to Meet Him":

> I'll be caught up to meet him,
> I'll be caught up to greet him.
> Joy and happiness will be mine...

Also, unlike the spirituals' general tone of response to and expression of collective, communal woes as they were experienced within the community, gospel songs generally have a personal, individual tone. Indeed, they are generally written out of specific personal experiences and personal realizations. For instance, "Take My Hand, Precious Lord," the world's best-known gospel song (it has been translated into some fifty languages), was written by Thomas Dorsey after the death of his young wife and unborn child. Similarly, Lucie Campbell wrote "He Understands; He'll Say Well Done" after her fellow congregants rescinded her beloved local church membership after a bitter church controversy.[34]

Another area of difference between the two genres lies in their respective moral foci. The primary moral focus of spirituals is largely horizontal, i.e., upon group morality, in that it is concerned with effecting right relations with humankind; the practical measure of its ethics and morality is how one functions in community. It is important to note that the spirituals' focus on collective ethics or morality does not imply that the communities that produced them valued personal moral behavior less highly than collective morality. However, because of the baldness of the systematic White supremacy under which they lived, it was crucial to the survival of the subjugated African Americans that they also adjudge moral behavior by one's role in the plight of the Black community, i.e., as either oppressor (this included collaborators, such as loyal "house Negroes," and Black overseers)[35] or as resistor to oppression, the latter being defined by one's relative contribution to the edification and survival of the Black community.

Instead of the collective morality of the spirituals, however, the primary moral focus of gospel music stresses vertical moral behavior, i.e., piety whose main concern has to do with one's individual relationship to God, with secondary emphasis upon actively striving to serve one's neighbor (although the only real evidence of such a relationship with God is right treatment of those God created). This difference in moral focus can be seen by considering Jesus' summation of "the greatest Law" in Mt. 22:37–39. While the spirituals can be understood to stress the horizontal, communal facet of the pronouncement, "Love your neighbor as yourself" (Mt. 22:39), gospel music stresses its vertical, personal aspect, i.e., "Love Your Lord Your God with All Your Heart" (Mt. 22:37). Even gospel songs with seeming resistance sensibilities, such as "I Am on the Battlefield for My Lord," ultimately have reference to struggles with personal morality, rather than to struggles against the oppressive forces of the world. This difference in emphasis is rooted in changes in both the social and material conditions of African Americans, as we shall explore below.

This emphasis on individual morality was an important emphasis of early gospel music and is reflected in admirable ways in the lives of its early pioneers who, for the most part, were apparently men and women of great conviction and dramatic personal moral rectitude. This moral emphasis is expressed in songs such as Thomas Dorsey's "Live the Song I Sing About" and his "Highway to Heaven":

> It's a highway to heaven
> None can go up there but the pure in heart.

In her inimitable way, Sallie Martin reflects the emphasis on personal morality in the early gospel culture: "There isn't but one thing that I say will keep us back and that is singing one thing and then doing…different when you get out of your service…. If we can't live right, then why did Jesus leave it here with us?"[36]

As the result of this emphasis on individual feelings and experiences and personal morality, at its core gospel music evolved a deeply empathic tone. The empathy of gospel music, however, differed from the spirituals' acknowledgement of common suffering under an oppressive social order. Instead, the empathy of gospel inhered in its acknowledgement of personal angst and suffering, personal doubt, and feelings of unworthiness. Its personal, emphatic nature fuels the emotionalism of gospel music today which, in turn, informs the highly emotion-charged performance orientation that today underpins the genre.

Eschewing Prophetic Critique

Cited above was the explanation by Thomas Dorsey, who is universally hailed as the father of gospel music, that hope lay at the heart of gospel music. Dorsey's concluding comment in that explanation illustrates the difference between the hope of the spirituals and the hope of gospel songs: "Make it anything [other] than good news," he says, and "it ceases to be [g]ospel."[37] In addition to highlighting the contrasting emphases on hope in the two genres, Professor Dorsey's remark reveals that in its quest to soothe the suffering of the Black masses, gospel music consciously eschews both prophetic critique and activist engagement of the social order that underlies much of the suffering gospel music seeks to assuage. It is understandable that Dorsey sought to lighten the load of a people already inundated daily by more bad news at the hands of White supremacy than any people should be asked to endure. Indeed, lightening their load was necessary for African Americans' pyscho-emotional health. In addition to the great source of comfort gospel music came to constitute for the beleaguered Black community, however, the general unwillingness of gospel artists to cite bad news, to critique or even acknowledge the systemic causes of Black folks' pain, resulted in an extremely unfortunate consequence: the tone of gospel music became studiously and conscientiously non-prophetic.

Prophetic Critique and Painful Memory

Prophetic critique can be defined as principled public criticism of and opposition to systemic injustice, based upon the biblical logic of justice that is reflected, for instance, in Psalm 72:

> Endow the king with your justice, O God, the royal son with
> your righteousness. He will judge your people in righteous-
> ness, your afflicted ones with justice.... He will defend the

afflicted among the people and save the children of the needy;
he will crush the oppressors (Ps. 72:1–2, 4).

Prophetic engagement of social and political issues is grounded in the enduring example of biblical prophets such as Isaiah, Jeremiah, and Amos, who all spoke "thus saith the Lord" against the oppressors in their own socio-historical settings. In fact, one of the most powerful and memorable phrases of the great freedom fighter Martin Luther King, Jr., is from Amos: "Let justice roll down like waters, and righteousness like a mighty stream" (Amos 5:24). Close examination of the spirituals reveals that many of them embodied the concern for social justice that is goal of prophetic critique. Examples from the spirituals include "You Shall Reap (what you sow)," "You Got a Right (to the tree of life)," and "Some of These Days (I'm gonna tell God how you treat me)."

To be sure, similar prophetic critique of the foremost institutional evil of the present age, i.e., systematic White skin color privilege in America, is indispensable to the struggle to alleviate the ongoing marginalization and oppression of African Americans. Despite its importance, however, prophetic critique is yet another reminder for the victims of oppression of the omnipresence of their suffering; it simply is not good news in the sense in which Professor Dorsey speaks. It certainly would not have been good news for Dorsey to have reminded his hearers that, for instance, just a few years before he wrote, President Woodrow Wilson had refused to sign an anti-lynching law, or that Wilson had tearfully praised the preposterously racist movie "Birth of a Nation" for its "truth," or that one Black man, woman, or child was then being lynched every thirty-six hours. The humanity of people of African descent was so devalued that Africans were exhibited as subhuman curiosities in American zoos little more than a decade before Dorsey began his gospel career. In one of the most infamous of these instances, in 1906 Ota Benga, a Pygmy from southern Africa, was imprisoned and displayed in a monkey cage at New York City's Bronx Zoo.[38] That Black folks could once again legally be detained as animals could only have heightened their ongoing sense of insecurity living in the overarching context of White supremacy in America; for most, particularly Black children, it must have been traumatic and frightening beyond words.

It is understandable, then, that according to Dorsey's stated logic, discussion of or even allusion to the painful social reality of African Americans would have to be off limits if gospel music was to "strike a happy medium for the downtrodden,"[39] as Dorsey stated as his goal. Unfortunately, the sad result

570

of this unwillingness to explicitly address the bad news of African American oppression is that from its inception, generally the gospel music genre has self-consciously avoided prophetic critique of the ravages wrought upon Black people by White supremacy. In the final analysis, the political quietism of gospel music, that is, its unwillingness to critique the bad news of the injustice and exploitation suffered by Black folks, has contributed to the maintenance of the oppressive American social order by domesticating the outrage that would otherwise have fueled political resistance and activism bent on establishing a more just American society.

Residues of the Prophetic

To acknowledge the generally non-prophetic character of gospel music, however, is not to claim that the genre has been totally devoid of songs exhibiting sociopolitical sensibilities. To be sure, some of the early gospel songs seem to stray from Dorsey's definition of the genre. In fact, a number of the early gospel songs do explicitly acknowledge sociopolitical and socioeconomic realities. Significant examples include "No Segregation in Heaven" and "Stalin Wasn't Stallin'," both recorded in 1942 by the Golden Gates Quartet, and C. A. Tindley's early (Tindley died in 1933), yet still popular composition "Leave It There," which begins:

> If this world from you withhold,
> All its silver and its gold
> And you have to get along on meager fare....

Indeed, some of Tindley's songs were exhortations specifically addressed to the poor and downtrodden, as in "I'll Overcome":

> If in my life I do not yield
> I'll overcome some day.

Sociopolitical sensibilities are also seen in early gospel pageants that stressed racial pride. The remarkable Lucie Campbell (1885–1963) who, incidentally, was the first African American woman to publish a gospel song, was hailed for presenting a number of such events, including "Ethiopia at the Bar of Justice" and "Ethiopia, Stretch Forth Your Hands unto God."[40] And who can listen to Mahalia Jackson's renditions of "How I Got Over" and "My Soul Looks Back and Wonders" without hearing the sting of Jim Crow, the hurt of exclusion, the gnawing pain of unjust, enforced impoverishment? Or the Soul Stirrers' "Any Day Now," in which the plaintive tones of the group's lead singer, Sam Cooke, as Michael Dyson observes,

> "evokes a world teeming with cultural nuances hidden from White society.... Though Cook is singing about going to heaven, he masks a complaint about earthly restrictions on Black life by pining for a day when there's "no sorrow or sadness/ Just only complete gladness...." It's the way Cook bends the notes, shaping his desire for freedom...."[41]

Rev. W. Herbert Brewster is probably the most noteworthy example of a gospel songwriter whose works reflect sociopolitical sensibilities. A political radical for his time, Brewster wrote numerous tracts urging Black liberation. He coined the motto "Out of the amen corner onto the street corner," by which he both indicted the lack of social action of his ministerial colleagues and attempted to cajole them to act. Among his musical compositions was a pageant play with pronounced political resonances entitled "From Auction Block to Glory," as well as "Deep Dark Waters," a social commentary about drugs.[42] In a clear act of racial pride, Brewster even renamed a young choir singer "Q. C. Anderson" in honor of Queen Candace of Ethiopia.[43]

Brewster's lyrics seemed always to have as a subtext the sociopolitical/economic realities facing African Americans. Songs like "How I Got Over" and "Move on up a Little Higher" (both later popularized by Mahalia Jackson), while extolling the "good news" of triumphant deliverance, in good prophetic fashion also evoked the injustice that the singer—and the hearer—seeks to triumph over. "The fight for rights here in Memphis was pretty rough on the Black Church," explains Brewster. "The lily White, the Black, and the tan were locking horns; and the idea struck me and I wrote that song, "Move on up a Little Higher".... That was a protest idea and inspiration."[44] For instance, consider "These Are They," Brewster's rich evocation of images found in the Book of Revelation:

> These are they from every nation
> Who have washed their garments White,
> Coming up, coming up through great tribulation
> To a land of pure delight.

The line "coming up..." evokes the image of "they" as the downtrodden who, in the context of Brewster and his African American audience, would certainly be identified as Black folks struggling against oppression. A student of New Testament Greek, Brewster was probably aware that *thlibo,* the Greek term from which "tribulation" is typically translated in the New Testament, does not simply signify bad luck or random trying circumstances, but literally means "to press down"—signifying "oppression," which is political and systemic in nature.

Other songs exhibiting sociopolitical sensibilities featured applications of biblical passages that exhorted deliverance from subjugation, such as "If I Had My Way":

> Well they tell me God almighty
> Rode on the wings of the wind
> And he saw old Samson and he called to him
> Said he whispered low into Samson's mind
> Said "Deliver my children from the Philistines."

Thus, it is clear that some of the early Gospel songs do acknowledge exploitation and social injustice; nonetheless, the consistent solution they prescribe is not the kind of prophetic engagement that is prescribed by the spirituals; they do not critique the social order that withholds wealth from Black folks and relegates them to subsisting on meager fare, to use Tindley's lyrical social description. Rather than prescribing action against the systemic causes of poverty, the gospel songs can instead be understood to counsel *inaction*. An instructive example is seen in Tindley's "Leave It There." Although the song laments the effect of the exploitative American social order, it concludes by advising, in effect, "Don't bother to try to change things, simply..."

> Take your burdens to the Lord and leave them there.

Despite the existence of a sociopolitically conscious stratum in the genre, most early gospel songs eschewed explicit reference to the ongoing bad news of the sociopolitical plight of African Americans. Still, because oppression, marginalization, and exploitation represented a large part of the lived experience of African Americans, some early gospel songs did implicitly reflect that social reality nonetheless, sometimes consciously so, if in the most subtle terms. Unlike early gospel, however, the gospel music of today not only seldom reflects recognition of African Americans' plight, but often seems to gloss it over. This can, of course, reflect the lower level of politicization of African Americans today that apparently is the result of the dismantling of systematic *de jure* White skin color privilege, and the lowering of the most blatant barriers to Black advancement. But it probably also reflects an alarming lack of popular awareness of the continuing legacy of *de facto* White skin color privilege in

America that, in turn, is the result of successful hegemonic obfuscation of the racist underpinnings of much of United States domestic and foreign policy. Of contemporary gospel's lack of recognition of sociopolitical realities, gospel pioneer Miss Sallie Martin observes, albeit a bit exaggeratedly, "I think the old songs were written out of some kind of burden.... Nowadays nobody has no worry or struggles."[45]

The Evolution of Gospel Music

If the spirituals are normative Black sacred music, as we have argued, then why did gospel music evolve sensibilities that diverged from it? Indeed, how do we account for the development of the gospel music genre?

As we saw above, the fundamental theological shifts and perspectival differences between the spiritual and gospel musical genres are pronounced and, in some ways, profound. It is my belief that these differences are largely the result of the shift in the mode of production of the masses of African Americans from rural agrarian to urban industrial.

If the rural agrarian setting of the spirituals in some ways empowered Black folks, the urban industrial settings to which they migrated in the first decades of this century in other ways disempowered them. Whereas the rural settings of the spirituals afforded some measure of expanse and possibility, the tone of the stifling, overcrowded urban ghettoes was one of constriction and severely limited horizons. And whereas many enslaved Africans and, later, Black sharecroppers and smallholders had known the sometimes small, yet often meaningful affirmation that comes from agricultural production, most urban Blacks knew only alienated labor which, as we saw above, is labor that afforded them little sense of the satisfaction of creation and accomplishment.[46]

The majority of Black laborers in urban industry, particularly males, worked in factories, most as assembly line workers of some sort. What is significant about this fact is that assembly line labor, by definition, is mind-numbing and disempowering. Indeed, Frederick Taylor, the father of assembly line production, or "Taylorism," as it first was called, declared, "In our scheme, we do not ask the initiative of our men. We do not want any initiative. All we want of them is to obey orders we give them, do what we say, and do it quick."[47] To assembly workers in general he remarked, "[We] have you for your strength and mechanical ability, and we have other men for thinking."[48] Being confronted by a mode of labor that so discounted their basic humanity could only have compounded the migrants' sense of disempowerment and further dashed their sinking hopes for life abundant.

The Apocalyptic Origins of Gospel Music

Although the *de facto* chattel status that Black migrants found in northern urban industrial settings was in many ways no worse than they were accustomed to in the rural South, because of the stifling working conditions and the alienated nature of the labor they performed, ultimately their chattel status in the North was not offset by the psychic satisfaction of being producers and cultivators as it had been offset, to some extent, in the South. The Black workers were now simply cogs in a wheel who produced neither crop, craft, nor the fruit of personal ingenuity; as assembly workers they performed tasks that, by themselves, were meaningless and abstract. Under both the slavocracy and Reconstruction, the hope of would-be immigrants to the northern cities was on freedom, on leaving behind the White-hot heat of southern oppression. But having followed the drinking gourd to the northern Promised Land that was proclaimed by the spirituals and still finding themselves counted as chattel, the Black migrants' hopes of justice were sorely disappointed. Urban life subjected them to new indignities that were compounded by their alienation from the agrarian lands to which their lives and livelihoods had been tied. Instead of fertile soil and the ubiquitous greenery of nature, they now pondered concrete and asphalt. In the rural South, there at least had been the possibility that they might one day own a plot of land free and clear, but in the urban landscape property ownership was a grudgingly, if not bitterly, accepted impossibility for most. Further, limited and grossly inadequate urban living facilities often resulted in the separation of the extended families that had been a mainstay of their lives in the rural South. In short, the world of the Black urban migrants offered few of the social support mechanisms they had known in the South. As one commentator put it, "There was no Promised Land to own in the North, just landlords threatening eviction of those who fell behind in their rent. A better name would have been the 'Promises Land.'"[49]

When the harsh realities of their new setting in life became inexorably clear, it must have seemed to the weary migrants that if neither Lincoln's emancipation nor urban migration had brought them relief from oppression, then maybe there simply was no relief to be had in this world. So, like the oppressed and beleaguered first century Christians who, as the result of their accumulated traumas, became unable to envision justice under the Roman Empire, and looked instead to "a new heaven and a new earth" (cf. Rev. 21:1) so, too, the Black urban migrants also succumbed to apocalypticism and began to direct their fading hopes from the here and now, which was the locus of defeat and disappointment for them, and which did not offer the prospect of justice, to the apocalyptic "new heaven and new earth," a locus that did offer the possibility of justice and victory. Indeed, having left the South for the idealized freedom of the North, where else could these Black migrants now hope to run except to a "new heaven and new earth"? In this sense, the hope of gospel music is a hope born of disappointment, of powerlessness, of conceding the dominion of life on earth to the principalities and powers of earthly domination. It is a hope that says, in effect, "It is clear that there will be no justice for me in this world. Nothing I can do will make a difference, so I'll just wait on the Lord. I'll just leave it all to Jesus." At its core, then, gospel music embodies the classic apocalyptic feeling of powerlessness to forestall the oppressive forces of this world which, in turn, is accompanied by a sense of resignation to ongoing social misery at the hands of oppressors until the apocalyptic "day of the Lord" (cf. 1 Thess. 5:2).

Mode of Production, Mode of Presentation: Assembly Lines and Trickeration

The influence upon the evolution of gospel music by both urban industrialism and the assembly line mode of production that emerged in the first quarter of the twentieth century is not only seen in the apocalyticism of the genre, but also in the way gospel music itself is produced, i.e., in its own mode of production. Just as the restrictive housing patterns and living conditions that were the result of industrialism fractured the extended family form that had characterized the agrarian mode of production, causing discrete, separate nuclear families and fragmented families to eventually predominate; and just as the demands of Taylorism divided manual labor into firmly regimented sets of separate and specialized tasks, gospel music was also influenced by and succumbed to the specialization demands of the new urban industrial culture in which the new migrants found themselves. Notwithstanding Sally Martin's testimony that the early gospel she witnessed and participated in retained some of the sense of the collective production of the spirituals,[50] the production of most gospel music, almost from its beginnings, was caught in the wake of the larger productive forces of the American political economy, itself becoming widely specialized and individualized. The roots of this process lie with none other than Thomas Dorsey, who in 1926 published his first gospel tune, "If You See My Savior, Tell Him That You Saw Me." This began the process of gospel songs being sold as commodities, first as sheet music, then as recordings. Individuals owned copyrights to the songs, which were not identified with locales or the conditions and plights that spawned them, as was the case with the spirituals, but with particular individual performers, thus effectively removing them from their respective contextualizing sociopolitical referents.

The specialization spawned by the urban industrial mode of production is also reflected in gospel's mode of presentation, with soloists for the first time becoming the norm in Black sacred song. There had often been a leader in the spirituals' tradition of call-and-response, which was the descendent of the traditional African ringshout, but the role of the solo in gospel music is much more pronounced. In gospel music, there are two basic types of soloists: individual soloists singing alone and solo leads of quartets. The earliest "quartet"[51] soloists, or lead singers, generally were not emphasized; the accepted practice was that they were given no special position with respect to other group members, but simply sang their solos and blended back into the group harmony. This practice changed as the result of the innovations of several gospel groups, particularly the Soul Stirrers, who not only brought the lead singer physically out in front of the other singers, but who also incorporated a second "lead" singer to replace the first lead's role in the quartet harmony. This innovation effectively freed the first lead to take much longer solos without concern for disrupting the group's harmonic flow. This innovation also yielded another development that has become a mainstay in gospel music: the technique of ad-libbing, or "hard gospel" style, which was given its first wide exposure, again by the Soul Stirrers and their original lead, Robert H. Harris, on the recording "Shine on Me, Featuring R. H. Harris," which was produced in the mid-1940s.

The Advent of "Clowning"

Initially, for all its ecstatic, emotional quality, the limits of the performance orientation of gospel music were, for the most part, circumscribed by the emphasis on dignified comportment that most gospel singers were known to maintain even at the height of ecstatic celebration, or "getting happy," in keeping with gospel's emphasis on emotional comfort and personal moral and spiritual uplift. For instance, the decorum and dignified bearing of singer/songwriter Miss Lucie E. Campbell was said to be so inspiring that folks came from miles around just to see her walk across stage.[52] However, the freedom to perform and ad-lib that evolved in gospel music eventually led to a startling new development that transformed gospel's emphasis on dignified bearing. That development, with its apparent beginnings in the 1940s, was the practice of "clowning," so-called by early gospel aficionados to denote actions or phrasings undertaken primarily for their entertainment value. In a startlingly candid recognition of the emphasis of this practice on manipulation of the audiences' emotions to maximize the impact of gospel performances, Ira Tucker, the veteran leader of the Dixie Hummingbirds, called it "trickeration."[53]

Rev. Julius Cheeks of the Sensational Nightingales, a highly popular group in the 1940s and 1950s, claims to have begun the practice of clowning: "I was the first to cut the fool...[to] do what the people wanted."[54] Ira Tucker made the same claim, asserting that all gospel singers before him sang "flat-footed." "I started this hip-slapping all the quartets do," Tucker claimed. "I jumped off my first stage in Suffolk, Virginia [in 1944].... Shoot, what James Brown does, I've been doing."[55]

Despite the claims of Cheeks and Tucker, the "clowning" performance orientation in gospel music was also in evidence as early as the 1940s in the Virginia-based Golden Gate Quartet's performances with swing bands, and in the appearances of the guitar-playing Sister Rosetta Tharpe at New York's Cotton Club and Cafe Society Downtown night spots.[56] Although the emphasis on performance orientation does seem to have been heightened, if not originated, by the antics of Ira Tucker, it became much more marked in the 1950s and 1960s with the Clara Ward Singers, who regularly performed their highly stylized and flamboyant act in night clubs, often sporting huge identical wigs and fancy outfits sometimes bordering on the outlandish. It can be argued that it was the Ward Singers who set the stage for the intense commercialism and widespread acceptance of the heightened performance orientation that now characterizes contemporary gospel music. In this sense, Ward can be seen as the precursor of such developments in gospel as Kirk Franklin's appearance on the long-running R&B, funk, rap television show "Soul Train," as well as of similar appearances by gospel artists in other pop music venues.

Like many gospel performers today, Clara Ward defended her group's behavior by paraphrasing Luke 14:23, the biblical verse often used to justify gospel performances in secular commercial entertainment venues: "The Lord told us to go into the highways and hedges as well." On one such occasion, an angry young man is said to have replied to Ward," You know folks don't come to clubs to get saved. They want to see Negroes make damn fools of themselves."[57]

The exaggerated "clowning" performance orientation of gospel music was taken to new heights in the 1960s and 1970s by a number of artists, including the flamboyant Alex Bradford, whom gospel music scholar Anthony Heilbut calls "gospel's Little Richard."[58] By this time, "wrecking the house," i.e., moving an audience to the heights of emotional pandemonium, had long been the widely accepted goal of gospel performances, and remains so today. In the contemporary era, this performance orientation is seen not only in the vocal gymnastics and the purposefully repetitive arrangements by which gospel artists routinely attempt to eke every bit of emotion out of songs, but also in the choreography of artists such as Hezekiah Walker and Ricky Dillard, the latter of whom "cut up" as a featured performer in "Leap of Faith," Steve Martin's motion picture critique of the excesses of the performance-based strain of contemporary evangelical religion.

In response to the pervasive emphasis on the "clowning" and performance orientation of the genre, one of the key figures in early gospel, Rev. Claude Jeter, who sang with the Swan Silvertones from the 1940s to the 1950s, acknowledges, "We've had too much form and fashion on stage."[59] The venerable Thomas Dorsey was a primary architect of the apolitical apocalyptic perspective that came to permeate gospel, and his business acumen was an important factor in its commercialization. Still, Dorsey professed to be no advocate of "clowning" and excessive performance orientation:

> I find some...who have too many embellishments that may be mistaken for spirit. Variations on the piano or organ or swing-ing a song beyond its beauty is not spirit. Loud vociferous singing, uninspired gesticulations, or self-incurred spasms of the body is not spirit. I believe in shouting, running, and crying out if the Holy Spirit comes upon one, but I don't believe in going to get the Spirit before it comes.[60]

The politically astute Rev. Herbert Brewster goes further, characterizing the performance orientation of gospel music as "all heat and no light."[61] Brewster observed of the early days of gospel," We didn't have none of this modern clowning."[62] No less than Aretha Franklin argues passionately that "when it makes you want to dance and pop your fingers, believe me, it isn't [g]ospel....gospel is a higher calling; [g]ospel is about God."[63] In the final analysis, however, although "clowning" initially caused Cheeks and other practitioners of it to be ejected from churches rejecting what they felt to be the trivialization of Black sacred music, the practice eventually became an accepted phenomenon, its entertainment value and appeals to emotion apparently winning the day. The triumph of entertainment sensibilities can be witnessed weekly in every broadcast medium. One of the most popular of these venues is "Bobby Jones Gospel," a syndicated television program seen weekly by five million viewers. "Bobby Jones Gospel" presents gospel performers in a variety show entertainment format in which each seems intent not only on praising the Lord, but on "wrecking the house" as well. "Bobby Jones Gospel" is the epitome of the performance orientation that has pervaded gospel. Unfortunately, "Bobby Jones" and programs like it regularly showcase this orientation to America as being normative for Black sacred music, thus effectively mitigating popular critical engagement of the excesses of gospel.

Commodification and the Evolution of "Audience"

With the development of the specialization and the heightened performance aspects of gospel, members of the believing community for the first time became auditors of the music; that is, they became "audience" to performances by gospel soloists or quartets, rather than the full participants in collective community expression they had been in the production and performance of the spirituals. It is the advent of this performer/audience dichotomy that underlies gospel music's presentation orientation. It apparently is also with the advent of this dichotomy that audience acceptance became a driving force of the genre, causing it to become even more entertainment-oriented and geared even more toward engendering responses that elicited audience approval, having jettisoned the spirituals' apparently less performance-friendly prophetic proclamation of justice on earth as in heaven. This separation of the production of the music into writer/performer + audience was of crucial significance because it signaled the production of gospel songs for *exchange*, i.e., in return for popular acceptance resulting in some form of remuneration, rather than being primarily produced for the psycho-emotional and sociopolitical edification of the communities that spawned them. The forms this remuneration can take range from public acclaim and deference to financial compensation, although the latter is usually a function of the former. In this sense, the production of gospel music has become overwhelmingly market-driven. By this measure, gospel songs are *commodities*, that is, goods produced for sale. Anthony Heilbut observes of this development in the genre, "Instead of looking to the hills [i.e., to God; cf. Ps. 121:1–2], it looks to the charts."[64] However, this does not mean that gospel music does not have the edification of its consumers as its goal. Rather, it means that the forms that edification takes are strongly influenced, if not driven, by market forces. Therefore, the problem with the commodification of gospel music today is not that it is profitable; if financial compensation is to be realized at all, it should be realized by the creators and performers of gospel music. No, the problem with the commodification of gospel music is not that it is profitable, but that it is profit-*driven*.

Thus, it is the commodification of Black sacred music that was begun in earnest by the gospel genre that accounts for its mode of performance; in response to the demands of the market, it has become firmly and patently performance-oriented. This is particularly the case with regard to the genre's "clowning" aspects. Replete with highly stylized dress and sometimes dazzlingly choreographed movements, well-staged crescendos of "spontaneous" emotion, and music purposefully arranged to showcase vocal gymnastics and pyrotechnics, gospel music today appears to be almost totally performance-driven into a species of the cathartic vehicle of emotional release Karl Marx apparently had in mind when he bitingly rejected religion and its expressions as "the opiate of the masses."[65] In a recent Associated Press news article about the growing phenomenon of churches utilizing professional musicians and song stylists as a way to "lure" new members, the president of the Nashville-based Gospel Music Association willingly underscored the importance of the performance, entertainment orientation to gospel music: "[Churches] recognize this is one of the ways they not only minister to their flock spiritually but *also to their entertainment needs*" [emphasis in the original].[66]

Summary

The commodification of gospel music and the performance orientation it fuels, its reduction of the collective havoc wrought upon African Americans by systematic White skin color privilege into individual problems and needs, along with its apocalyptic apoliticality, have combined to make gospel music today a force of little consequence in the ongoing struggle of Black folks to enjoy the full measure of comfort and security of American society. As a genre, gospel lacks most of the normative elements of gospel music that evolved through Blacks' sojourn in America. Rather than collective acknowledgement of oppression, gospel offers individualized expressions of hope and praise. Instead of prophetic critique, it offers political quietism. Gospel songs do not exhort resistance to injustice; it counsels resignation instead. Thus, other than its empathic dimension, gospel music today does not embody the normative features of Black sacred music as this study has understood them.

Conclusion: No More Clowning, No More Dope

Kirk Franklin is the most commercially successful figure on the gospel scene today. His music reveals him to be sincere in his effort to bring the Gospel of Jesus Christ to the world. He is clearly a young man of great faith and purpose. In his touchingly revealing autobiography, Franklin writes, "I want to reach nonbelievers in nontraditional ways. I want to see revival come back to this land."[67] And in some of his songs, Franklin does reveal strong social sensibilities. Consider his song "Lean on Me":

> There's a man standing on the corner with no home
> He has no food and his blue skies are gone.
> Can't you hear him crying out?

Consider, as well, his hip hop-influenced "Revolution":

> Do you want a revolution?
> Sick and tired of my brothers
> Killing each other...
> No more racism...
> No pollution.
> The solution: a revolution.

It is important to note that although he speaks of "revolution," the social vision of Kirk Franklin excludes real revolutionary engagement of the systemic causes of the social ills he decries. As with most of his gospel contemporaries, Franklin's solutions to sociopolitical problems are exclusively in the realm of individualized conceptions of salvation. Moreover, in the startling statement to *Vibe* magazine that began this essay, Franklin inadvertently reveals his estimation of his own music to be consonant with Marx's assessment of religion and its modes of expression as "the opiate of the masses": "People need to get high off something spiritual, and I'm the holy dope dealer. I got this drug, I got this Jesus rock. And you can have a type of high that you've never experienced."[68] To be fair, Franklin probably spoke in such shocking terms to capture the attention of *Vibe*'s youthful, hip hop-oriented readership. Still, with his use of the term "Jesus rock"—clearly a metaphor for crack cocaine—Franklin himself characterizes his music as an opiate, a palliative, a drug—a description whose evocation of political quietism could apply as well to most contemporary gospel music.

In a nutshell, that is the basic problem with gospel music today. As the result of the "clowning" that has become normative for it; as the result of its pervasive performance orientation, its emphasis on "wrecking the house," and its shameless appeals to emotion, the contemporary gospel music genre *has* come to function as an opiate for the masses of African American people. Like a drug, sensations and emotions have come to be its focus. Like a drug, its goal is not to empower its users to change reality, but simply to change the way they feel. Like a drug, it temporarily lifts the people's despair yet, in direct contradistinction to the prophetic mandate of the spirituals, leaves the causes of that despair unaddressed, unscathed, even unmentioned. Gospel music doesn't attempt to free the people, but simply seeks to make them feel good. It doesn't exhort them to political liberation; instead, it lights their emotional fires. Rather than calling for resistance, it rocks the house. And in place of the prophetic mandate, today's gospel music offers "praise." In fact, "praise," which focuses on extolling God's mercy, grace, and magnificence, has become an important part of the gospel music equation. Certainly God is worthy of all praise. But unfortunately, the definition of "praise" offered by gospel music is an attenuated one that begins and ends with singing, clapping hands, speaking in sometimes suspiciously well-timed "unknown" tongues, and "holy" dances that, amazingly, seem never to miss a beat. Sadly, the genre never goes so far as to praise God as a God of justice or to advocate praising God by dismantling the systems of oppression that afflict God's beloved human creation of all colors and creeds. Gospel music hears not, sees not, and speaks not of the evil of the oppression of the very people that love it so. The sad reality is that if we follow the lead of gospel music today, not only will systemic evils never be addressed, they will never even be mentioned! The "holy" dope will continue to tell us to just "leave it to Jesus" while we sing, dance, shout, and overdose on the musical opiates we so gladly consume and purvey. Indeed, if African Americans did everything that gospel music asks, where would we be? Would we be moved to address the social system that continues to devalue our humanity and our intelligence, that demonizes our children, that seems poised to try to turn back the clock on the social progress that we have made? If Black folks followed the social vision of gospel music, would we be free?

Put simply, for all its popularity, gospel music today no longer embodies the best of the Black sacred music tradition. Indeed, as basic a constituent of that tradition as the empowering logic of the Exodus liberation typology is almost nowhere to be found in today's gospel. This absence of liberation sensibilities is reflected in the observation of Cheryl James of the popular rap group Salt-N-Pepa, who also shared her views on gospel music with *Vibe*. Ms. James, who appears on Franklin's hip hop-influenced platinum recording

"Stomp," explains that the appeal of the gospel music that Franklin and his contemporaries exemplify is precisely that it does *not* evoke liberation motifs or resistance sensibilities. "It's not about slavery and the old ways," she remarks.[69] This posture of refusing to inform the relative freedom of the present with awareness of the freedom struggles of the past is a basic constituent of the apoliticality of contemporary gospel music. What is overlooked by Ms. James and those that believe as she does is that the "old ways" they discount are, in reality, the resistance sensibilities that have brought Black people this far. However, in actuality it is not simply old-fashioned ways that are discounted by contemporary gospel music, but the historical logic of freedom that is still much needed by African Americans if we are to throw off the importunities of systematic White skin color privilege that afflict us even now. That it is resistance sensibilities and not simply old-fashioned ways that are rejected by contemporary gospel artists is evidenced by the unwillingness of those artists to evolve new resistance paradigms that fit their own sensibilities. The importance of this is seen in the example of the enslaved African Americans who produced the spirituals. Not only did they live under the most intense form of systematic domination and dehumanization ever enacted, but also under the most intense campaign of obfuscation and sacralization of oppression ever waged. Yet, through the prophetic critique and prophetic consciousness of the spirituals, they were ever reminded that although chattel was their status, it was not their identity. Indeed, it was the slaves' clear-headed understanding of their plight that gave the spirituals their power and the slaves their perseverance. The clear understanding of African Americans' situation today that can result from prophetic proclamation and prophetic critique can afford us that same power—not only to persevere, but to change the world.

Epilogue: From Spirited Singing to Spirit-led Action

I personally do not want to live in a world without gospel music. It has produced songs possessed of great power and unspeakable beauty. It can move its listeners to emotional and spiritual peaks as no other musical genre can. Who can hear Richard Smallwood's "Total Praise" or "My Tribute" by Andrae Crouch or Kirk Franklin's "Silver and Gold" without being moved to the heights of reverence? The beauty and power of gospel must ever be maintained. Yet, it cannot be left unchanged, not as long as its energies are spent on entertainment and emotion rather than on exhorting freedom, justice, and equality for and by its listeners. Let those of us that love gospel build upon its strengths, and together strengthen its weaknesses. Therefore, I call upon gospel music today to reject the "clowning," the trickeration, the entertainment orientation, the dealing of dope—"holy" or not. It must stop acquiescing to the popular sensibilities that seductively equate entertainment with evangelism. It must end its refusal to engage in prophetic critique of systemic evil. It must stop reducing the causes of human suffering to weak faith or poor morality on the part of the victim, or to ethereal, disembodied sources for which no one has responsibility, for the sad consequence of this trivializing of the oppression of Black people is that systematic White skin color privilege not only is ignored, but ultimately is exculpated from responsibility for the everyday horrors it continues to wreak upon Black people of all ages and all social strata.

Half a century ago, the great gospel songwriter and prophetic social critic Herbert Brewster offered the prescient observation that gospel must be a marriage of "sentiment and doctrine,"[70] that is, a coupling of inspired emotion and informed sociopolitical sensibilities. I propose that we who both love gospel music and are dedicated to freedom for all God's children labor together to marry the emotionality of gospel music with the prophetic consciousness and resistance sensibilities of the spirituals to produce a new generation of resistance music, music that moves Black people, indeed, all people, not just to emotional frenzy but to that divinely inspired *action* we know as the struggle to establish God's kingdom of justice—on earth, as in heaven. Gospel music must move beyond preaching Jesus, to preaching what Jesus preached; it must move beyond spirited singing to Spirit-led song that proclaims to all, "The Spirit of the Lord is upon me, because he has anointed me to bring good news to the poor...to proclaim release to the captives...to let the oppressed go free." Amen.

1 Quoted in Alan Light, "Say Amen, Somebody," *Vibe* (Oct. 1997): p. 92. Franklin's statement is discussed in the "Conclusions" section of this essay.

2 Among them are Albert J. Raboteau, *Slave Religion* (Oxford: University Press, 1978), pp. 56–74; Lawrence W. Levine, *Black Culture and Black Consciousness* (Oxford: University Press, 1977), pp. 19–29; Wyatt Tee Walker, *Somebody's Calling My Name* (Valley Forge: Judson, 1979), pp. 15–36; and Jon Michael Spencer, "The Rhythms of Black Folks", *Ain't Gonna Lay My 'Ligion Down,* Alonzo Johnson and Paul Jersild, eds. (Columbia, SC: University of South Carolina Press, 1996), pp. 39–51.

3 It is believed that "Steal Away to Jesus" was among the spirituals used by Nat Turner to signal his compatriots for battle. See Arthur C. Jones, *Wade in the Water: The Wisdom of the Spirituals* (Maryknoll: Orbis, 1993), pp. 44–45.

4 Fannie Lou Hamer was known for rousing her compatriots in the Civil Rights movement with her passionate, spontaneous eruptions into spiritual song. See Kay Mills, *This Little Light of Mine: The Life of Fannie Lou Hamer* (New York: Dutton, 1993).

5 Cornel West, *The Cornel West Reader* (New York: Basic *Civitas,* 1999), pp. 29, 31, reminds us that America is "a civilization that is shaped by 244 years of chattel slavery, enslavement of African people, and 81 years of Jim Crow…. White supremacy cuts through, saturates, and permeates every institutional nook and cranny…." Reflective of this reality is the well-orchestrated current offensive by numerous political, legal, social, philanthropic, corporate, and religious organizations against affirmative action, and the numerous other current legislative and juridicial attempts to counterbalance systematic *de facto* White skin color privilege. The *de facto* system of color privilege that pervades America today is heir to the *de jure* White supremacy that endured in one form or another from the earliest beginnings of the American republic until the Civil Rights Bill of 1965. For instructive summaries of the scope of this assault see George E. Curry and Trevor W. Coleman, "Hijacking Justice", *Emerge* (Oct. 1999): pp. 42–49; and Vern E. Smith, "Showdown in Atlanta", *Emerge* (Nov. 1999): pp. 49–56, n.b. 54–55. W. E. B. DuBois offers an extremely insightful analysis of the psychosocial dynamics of White supremacy that remains instructive today. See "The Ways of White Folks," in *Darkwater: Voices From Within the Veil* (New York: Harcourt, Brace and Howe, 1920), pp. 19–52.

6 This is dramatically portrayed in the acclaimed motion picture "Glory."

7 The language of the spirituals is patriarchal, as is that of the entire gospel genre, for that matter. In this sense both reflect the systematic patriarchy that has always been part of the American social order. Although I am a staunch advocate of inclusive language and recognize its necessity in the struggle to dismantle the ravages of patriarchy, in this essay I cite all lyrics using their original wordings for the sake of historical accuracy and authenticity.

8 W. E. B. DuBois, *The Souls of Black Folk* (New York: Vintage Books, 1990; originally published in 1903), pp. 180–190; James Weldon Johnson and J. Rosamond Johnson, *The Books of American Negro Spirituals* (New York: Da Capo Press, 1973; originally published as two separate volumes in 1925 and 1926); LeRoi Jones (Amiri Baraka), *Blues People: Negro Music in White America* (New York: Morrow, 1963); Walker, *Somebody's Calling My Name;* James H. Cone, *The Spirituals and the Blues* (Maryknoll, NY: Orbis Books, 1991); "Bernice Johnson Reagon, ed., *We'll Understand It Better By and By: Pioneering African American Gospel Composers* (Washington: Smithsonian, 1992). Also see the important essays in Bernard Katz, ed., *The Social Implications of Early Negro Music in the United States* (New York: Arno Press, 1969).

9 Walker, *Somebody's Calling My Name,* p. 43.

10 See Terry Eagleton, *Ideology* (London: Verso, 1991), pp. 19–196. Also see Michel Foucault, *Power/Knowledge,* ed. Colin Gordon (New York: Pantheon, 1980), p. 195.

11 See Margaret Wetherell and Jonathan Potter, Mapping the Language of Racism: Discourse and the Legitimation of Exploitation (New York: Columbia University Press, 1992), p. 85; and Fredric Jameson, The Political Unconscious: Narrative as a Socially Symbolic Act (Ithaca: Cornell University Press, 1981), p. 84.

12 See James C. Scott, *Domination and the Arts of Resistance* (Yale: University Press, 1990), pp. ix–16.

13 Frederick Douglass, *The Life and Times of Frederick Douglass,* [1885] (New York: Collier, 1962), p. 99.

14 Mikhail Bahktin, *The Dialogic Imagination: Four Essays,* ed. Michael Holquist (Austin: University of Texas, 1981), p. 352.

15 Gwendolin Sims Warren, *Ev'ry Time I Feel the Spirit* (New York: Henry Holt, 1997), p. 16.

16 See Scott, *Domination,* pp. 108–153.

17 See Antonio Gramsci, *Selections from the Prison Notebooks* (New York: International, 1971), 5–23; and Joseph Femia, *Gramsci's Political Thought: Hegemony, Consciousness, and the Revolutionary Process* (Oxford: Clarendon, 1987), pp. 44–45.

18 Werner Sollors, *Beyond Ethnicity: Consent and Descent in American Culture* (New York: Oxford University Press, 1986).

19 Theophus Smith, *Conjuring Culture: Biblical Formations of Black America* (Oxford: University Press, 1994), p. 7.

20 Raboteau, *Slave Religion,* p. 311.

21 Wendel Phillips Whalum, "Black Hymnody", *Review and Expositor* 70/3: 342.

22 A moral economy is a constellation of ethics and values that guide and drive social relations in a particular social group. See James C. Scott, *The Moral Economy of the Peasant: Rebellion and Subsistence in Southeast Asia* (New Haven: Yale University Press, 1976).

23 See Karl Marx, *Economic and Philosophic Manuscripts of 1844* (Buffalo: Prometheus Books, 1988), pp. 69–84. For a succinct treatment, see Tom Bottomore, ed., *A Dictionary of Marxist Thought*, 2d ed. (Cambridge: Basil Blackwell, 1991), pp. 11–17.

24 B. B. King, *Blues All Around Me: The Autobiography of B. B. King* (New York: Avon, 1996).

25 DuBois, Souls of Black Folk, pp. 188.

26 David Walker, *Appeal in Four Articles* (Salem, NH: Ayer, 1989; originally published in 1829), p. 80.

27 Quoted in Anthony Heilbut, *The Gospel Sound*, revised ed. (New York: Limelight, 1997), p. 27. This has proven to be an important resource, particularly for the study of the culture of gospel music.

28 Ibid, p. 35.

29 Mahalia Jackson, *Movin' On Up* (New York: Hawthorne, 1966), p. 72.

30 Heilbut, *Gospel Sound*, p. 7.

31 Levine, *Black Culture*, p. 175.

32 Horace Clarence Boyer, "Charles Albert Tindley: Progenitor of African American Gospel Music", Reagon, *We'll Understand It Better*, p. 53.

33 See John J. Collins, *The Apocalyptic Imagination* (New York: Crossroad, 1989).

34 Reverend Charles Walker, "Lucie E. Campbell Williams: A Cultural Biography," *Understand It Better*, pp. 129–130.

35 This kind of moral judgment is reflected, for instance, in the unyielding refusal of the insurrectionist Denmark Vesey to include "house N[egroes]" among his co-conspirators. See David Robertson, *Denmark Vesey* (New York: Knopf, 1999), p. 70.

36 Quoted in Heilbut, *Gospel Sound*, p. 17.

37 Quoted in Ibid, p. 35.

38 See Phillips Verner Bradford and Harvey Blume, *Ota Benga: The Pygmy in the Zoo* (New York: St. Martin's Press, 1992).

39 Heilbut, *Gospel Sound*, p. 35.

40 Luvenia A. George, "Lucie E. Campbell: Her Nurturing and Expansion of Gospel Music in the National Baptist Convention, U.S.A., Inc.," *Understand It Better*, Reagon, ed., pp. 116–117.

41 Michael Eric Dyson, *Between God and Gangsta Rap* (New York: Oxford, 1996), pp. 60–61. Here Dyson uses "Cook," the original spelling of the singer's name before it was changed for show business purposes.

42 Kip Lornell, Happy in the Service of the Lord: African American Sacred Vocal Harmony Quartets in Memphis, 2nd ed. (Knoxville: University of Tennessee, 1995), p. 141.

43 Ibid., 143.

44 Reagon, "Herbert Brewster: Rememberings," *Understand It Better*, p. 201.

45 Heilbut, *Gospel Sound*, p. 17.

46 See note 23.

47 Quoted in George F. Will, review of *The One Best Way: Frederick Winslow Taylor and the Enigma of Efficiency*, by Robert Kanigel, in the *New York Times Sunday Book Review*, June 15, 1997, p. 8.

48 Ibid.

49 Karl Evanzz, *The Messenger: The Rise and Fall of Elijah Muhammad* (New York: Pantheon, 1999), p. 55.

50 Heilbut, *Gospel Sound*, p. 17, *op. cit.*

51 In Gospel parlance, the term "quartet" refers generally to a small group of indeterminate number singing in harmony, rather than specifically denoting a group of four members. Thus, the term can designate a quintet or even a sextet. The term's emphasis is on function rather than form. See Lornell, *Happy in the Service*, p. 49.

52 George, "Campbell," in Reagon, ed., *Understand It Better*, p. 126.

53 Quoted in Heilbut, *Gospel Sound*, p. 49.

54 Ibid., p. 121.

55 Ibid., p. 48.

56 In some of her recordings, Tharpe sounds eerily reminiscent of the seminal depression-era Delta bluesman Robert Johnson, particularly in her classically bluesy "Nobody's Fault But Mine." Interestingly, this song mentions neither God nor Jesus, although it does mention prayer. For comparison, consider "Robert Johnson: The Complete Recordings" (Columbia/Legacy C2K 64916). For further information on Johnson, an important figure in Black music in his own right, see, in addition to the accompanying liner notes, Robert Guralnick, *Searching for Robert Johnson* (New York: Plume/Penguin, 1989).

57 Heilbut, *Gospel Sound*, p. 105.

58 Ibid., p. 145.

59 Heilbut, *Gospel Sound*, p. 116.

60 Thomas A. Dorsey, "Ministry of Music in the Church", Kenneth Morris, ed., *Improving the Music in the Church* (Chicago: Martin and Morris, 1949), p. 42.

61 Heilbut, *Gospel Sound*, p. 104.

62 Ibid., p. 117.

63 Aretha Franklin, *Aretha: From These Roots* (New York: Villard, 1999), p. 220.

64 Quoted in Warren, *Ev'ry Time*, p. 270.

65 Karl Marx and Friedrich Engels, *On Religion* (New York: Schocken Books, 1964), p. 42.

66 Frank Breeden quoted in Janelle Carter, "Rocking the Flock: More Churches Using Professional Musicians," *Dayton Daily News*, September 4, 1999.

67 Kirk Franklin, *Church Boy: My Music and My Life* (Nashville: Word Publishing, 1998), p. 21.

68 See Light, "Amen", *op. cit.*

69 Ibid.

70 Heilbut, *Gospel Sound*, p. 98.

Contributors

James Abbington
Associate Professor of Music, Shaw University, Raleigh, NC, and Executive Editor of the *African American Church Music Series* published by GIA Publications, Inc., Chicago, IL.

Charles G. Adams
Pastor, Hartford Memorial Baptist Church, Detroit, MI.

Brenda Eatman-Aghahowa
Professor of English, Chicago State University, Chicago, IL.

Wayne A. Barr
Assistant Professor of Music and Director of Choral Activities, Tuskegee University, Tuskegee, AL.

Sister Thea Bowman, F.S.P.A. (1937–1990)
Franciscan Sister of Perpetual Adoration, singer, dancer, liturgist, educator, evangelist, and consultant for intercultural awareness, Jackson, MS.

Horace Clarence Boyer
Professor Emeritus of Music, University of Massachusetts at Amherst.

Mellonee V. Burnim
Associate Professor of Folklore and Ethnomusicology, Indiana University, Bloomington.

Melva Wilson Costen
Helmar Nielsen Professor of Worship and Music, Interdenominational Theological Center, Atlanta, GA.

Joseph A. Donnella, II
Chaplain, Gettysburg College, Gettysburg, PA.

William Edward Burghardt DuBois (1863–1963)
Writer, social scientist, critic, and public intellectual; cofounder of the Niagara Movement, the National Association for the Advancement of Colored People (NAACP), and the Pan-African Congress; editor of the NAACP magazine *Crisis.*

William Burres Garcia
Professor of Music, Fort Valley State University, Fort Valley, GA.

Carl Haywood
Professor of Music, Norfolk State University, Norfolk, VA.

Obery M. Hendricks, Jr.
President, Payne Theological Seminary, Wilberforce, OH.

Zan W. Holmes, Jr.
Pastor, St. Luke Community United Methodist Church, Adjunct Professor of Preaching, Perkins School of Theology, Dallas, TX.

Harold T. Lewis
Rector, Calvary Episcopal Church, Adjunct Professor of Preaching, Pittsburgh Theological Seminary, Pittsburgh, PA.

C. Eric Lincoln (1924–2000)
Sociologist, author, and Professor of Religion, Duke University, Durham, NC.

William B. McCain
Pastor, Tindley Temple United Methodist Church, Philadelphia, PA, and Professor of Preaching and Worship, Wesley Theological Seminary, Washington, DC.

V. Michael McKay
Lyricist, composer, and conductor, Houston, TX.

Lawrence H. Mamiya
Professor of Religion, Vassar College, Poughkeepsie, NY

J. Wendell Mapson, Jr.
Pastor, Monumental Baptist Church, Adjunct Professor, Eastern Theological Seminary, and Chairman of the Music Department, National Baptist Convention USA, Inc., Philadelphia, PA.

Portia K. Maulstby
Professor of Folklore and Ethnomusicology and Director of the Archives of African American Music and Culture, Indiana University, Bloomington.

Benjamin Elijah Mays (1894–1984)
Educator, author, President of Morehouse College from 1940-1967, and Baptist Minister.

J-Glenn Murray, S.J.
Director of the Office for Pastoral Liturgy, the Diocese of Cleveland, OH.

John Nunes
Senior Pastor, St. Paul Lutheran Church, Dallas, TX, Editorial Consultant, Concordia Publishing House, St. Louis, MO.

Cheryl J. Sanders
Pastor, Third Street Church of God and Associate Professor of Christian Ethics, Howard University School of Divinity, Washington, DC.

Geneva Southall
Professor Emerita of Music, The University of Minnesota at Minneapolis.

Eileen Southern
Professor Emerita of Music and Afro-American American Studies, Harvard University; founded and edited the journal *The Black Perspective in Music* (1973-1990).

Jon Michael Spenccer
Professor of Religion, University of South Carolina at Columbia.

Mickey Thomas Terry

Editor of the *African American Organ Music Anthology* published by Morning Star Music Publishers, Fenton, MO, and concert organist, Washington, DC.

Wyatt Tee Walker

Pastor, Canaan Baptist Church of Christ, Harlem, NY, and chief strategist for the Southern Christian Leadership Conference during the Civil Rights Movement.

Karen M. Ward

Associate Director for Worship, Evangelical Lutheran Church in America, Member of the Lutheran World Federation Worship and Culture Study Team.

William D. Watley

Pastor, St. James African Methodist Episcopal Church, Newark, NJ.

Wendell P. Whalum (1932–1987)

Fuller E. Callaway Professor of Music, Morehouse College, Atlanta, GA.

Don Lee White

Retired Professor of Music, California State University, Los Angeles.

Evelyn Davidson White

Professor Emerita of Music, Howard University, Washington, DC.

Edward P. Wimberly

Executive Vice President and Academic Dean, Interdenominational Theological Center, Atlanta, GA.

John W. Work, III (1901–1967)

Composer, educator, choral director, ethnomusicologist, and chairman of the Fisk University Department of Music, Nashville, TN.

Jeremiah A. Wright, Jr.

Pastor, Trinity United Church of Christ, Chicago, IL.